ARE 5 Practice Exam

for the Architect Registration Exam

David Kent Ballast, FAIA, NCARB, CSI
Holly Williams Leppo, AIA
Rima Taher, PhD, PE

Professional Publications, Inc. • Belmont, California

Benefit by Registering This Book with PPI

- Get book updates and corrections.
- Hear the latest exam news.
- Obtain exclusive exam tips and strategies.
- Receive special discounts.

Register your book at **ppi2pass.com/register.**

Report Errors and View Corrections for This Book

PPI is grateful to every reader who notifies us of a possible error. Your feedback allows us to improve the quality and accuracy of our products. You can report errata and view corrections at **ppi2pass.com/errata.**

ARE 5 PRACTICE EXAM FOR THE ARCHITECT REGISTRATION EXAM
First Edition

Current release of this edition: 1

Release History

date	edition number	revision number	description
Sept. 2016	1	1	New book.

Printed in the United States of America.

PPI
1250 Fifth Avenue, Belmont, CA 94002
(650) 593-9119
ppi2pass.com

ISBN: 978-1-59126-517-7

Library of Congress Control Number: 2016946615

F E D C B A

TABLE OF CONTENTS

PREFACE AND ACKNOWLEDGMENTS

ARE 5 Practice Exam for the Architect Registration Exam is written to give you realistic practice to help you prepare for the Architect Registration Exam 5 (ARE 5). This book is a companion to the *ARE 5 Review Manual*, which gives a comprehensive review for those preparing for the ARE 5.

This practice exam is organized to match the structure of ARE 5. The problems reflect the most recent editions of a number of codes and standards, including

- 2007 AIA Contract Documents
- 2009 SectionFormat
- 2010 *Americans with Disabilities Act (ADA) Standards for Accessible Design*
- 2011 AISC *Steel Construction Manual*, 14th edition
- 2013 LEED Rating Systems
- 2014 ACI 318, *Building Code Requirements for Structural Concrete*
- 2014 *National Electrical Code* (NFPA 70)
- 2015 *International Building Code*
- 2015 *International Energy Conservation Code*
- 2015 *International Green Construction Code*
- 2015 *International Mechanical Code*

- 2015 *International Plumbing Code*
- 2015 *Life Safety Code* (NFPA 101)
- 2016 CSI MasterFormat

ARE 5 Practice Exam covers subject areas that are new to the ARE with version 5. Recent developments in architecture and construction in a number of areas are covered on the exam and in this book, including

- building commissioning
- business development and operations
- concrete reinforcement
- conformance with sustainability requirements
- construction manager as adviser or constructor
- contract documents for sustainable projects
- contractor selection
- cost control
- curtain walls
- design-build project delivery
- elevator design
- environmental context
- ethical standards
- financial management
- human resources
- integrated project delivery
- integrating building systems
- mechanical rooms
- office organization
- paving
- planning construction documentation
- plenum requirements
- post-occupancy evaluation
- practice methodologies
- project delivery methods, execution, follow-up, planning, and management
- quality control
- supplemental contract documentation
- sustainable materials
- value engineering
- weather barriers
- wood framing

The ARE contains a variety of problem types, including multiple-choice problems, check-all-that-apply problems, and fill-in-the-blank problems. ARE 5 has introduced three more types: hot spot problems, drag-and-place problems, and case study problems. We wrote this book to mimic the exam's problem types so that you will become familiar with them as you use *ARE 5 Practice Exam.*

Many people have helped in the production of this book. We would like to thank Gary E. Demele, FAIA, NCARB, and Bradley E. Saeger, AIA, who reviewed the book for technical accuracy and offered many good suggestions for additions and improvements. We would also like to thank all the fine people at PPI including Steve Buehler, associate director of acquisitions; Nicole Evans, acquisitions editor; Thomas Bliss, Sierra Cirimelli-Low, and Tracy Katz, associate project managers; Scott Marley, senior copy editor; Robert Genevro, Tyler Hayes, Richard Iriye, Ellen Nordman, Ceridwen Quattrin, and Ian A. Walker, copy editors and typesetters; Tom Bergstrom, cover designer and technical illustrator; Sam Webster, publishing systems manager; Cathy Schrott, production services manager; and Grace Wong, director of publishing services.

Although we had much help in preparing this new edition, the responsibility for any errors is our own. A list of known errata for this book is maintained at **ppi2pass.com/errata**, and you can let us know of any errors you find at the same place. We greatly appreciate the time you take to help us keep this book accurate and up to date.

David Kent Ballast, FAIA, NCARB, CSI
Holly Williams Leppo, AIA
Rima Taher, PhD, PE

INTRODUCTION

ABOUT THIS BOOK

ARE 5 Practice Exam for the Architect Registration Exam contains over 600 problems organized into six divisions that follow the structure of version 5 of the Architect Registration Exam (ARE 5). Each division includes the same number and types of problems and covers the same subject areas in its corresponding division of the ARE.

- Division 1: Practice Management, 80 problems
- Division 2: Project Management, 95 problems
- Division 3: Programming & Analysis, 95 problems
- Division 4: Project Planning & Design, 120 problems
- Division 5: Project Development & Documentation, 120 problems
- Division 6: Construction & Evaluation, 95 problems

This book is designed to be used in conjunction with PPI's *ARE 5 Review Manual* and *ARE 5 Practice Problems*. Like this book, each companion book covers all six divisions in a single volume.

THE ARCHITECT REGISTRATION EXAM 5

Version 5 of the Architect Registration Exam (ARE 5) consists of six divisions, each of which is a separate, standalone test taking between 3.5 hours and 5 hours. You may take the divisions in any order, but you must complete all six divisions within a five-year period.

The topics covered on each division and the approximate distribution of problems are as follows.

Division 1: Practice Management

Business operations (20–26%)

- assessing resources within the practice
- applying regulations and requirements that govern work environment
- applying ethical standards to comply with accepted principles in given situations
- applying appropriate standard of care for given situations

Finances, risk, and development of practice (29–35%)

- evaluating practice's financial well-being
- identifying practice policies and methodologies for risk, legal exposures, and resolutions
- selecting and applying practice strategies for given situations

Practice-wide delivery of services (22–28%)

- analyzing and determining response for client services requests
- analyzing the applicability of contract types and delivery methods
- determining project's potential risk and/or reward and its impact on practice

Practice methodologies (17–23%)

- analyzing impact of practice methodologies in relation to structure and organization of practice
- evaluating design, coordination, and documentation methodologies

Division 2: Project Management

Resource management (7–13%)

- determining criteria required for assembling project team
- assessing criteria required for allocating and managing project resources

Project work planning (17–23%)

- developing and maintaining project work plan
- determining criteria required for developing and maintaining project schedule
- determining appropriate communication to project team—owner, contractor, consultants, and internal staff

Contracts (25–31%)

- evaluating and verifying adherence to owner/architect agreement
- interpreting key elements of and verifying adherence to architect/consultant agreement
- interpreting key elements of owner/contractor agreement

- interpreting key elements of owner/consultant agreement to integrate consultant's work into project

Project execution (17–23%)

- evaluating compliance with construction budget
- evaluating and address changes in scope of work and scope creep
- evaluating project documentation to ensure it supports specified delivery method
- identifying and conforming with the requirements set forth by authorities having jurisdiction in order to obtain approvals for the project

Project quality control (19–25%)

- applying procedures required for adherence to laws and regulations relating to project
- identifying steps in maintaining project quality control and reducing risks and liabilities
- performing quality control reviews of project documentation throughout life of project
- evaluating management of design process to maintain integrity of design objectives

Division 3: Programming & Analysis

Environmental and contextual conditions (14–21%)

- evaluating site-specific environmental and socio-cultural opportunities
- evaluating site-specific environmental constraints
- determining optimal use of onsite resources by incorporating sustainability principles

Codes and regulations (16–22%)

- identifying relevant code requirements for building and site types
- identifying relevant zoning and land use requirements
- identifying relevant local and site-specific requirements

Site analysis and programming (21–27%)

- evaluating relevant qualitative and quantitative attributes of site as they relate to program
- synthesizing site reports with other documentation and analysis
- analyzing graphical representations regarding site analysis and site programming

Building analysis and programming (37–43%)

- evaluating relevant qualitative and quantitative attributes of new or existing building as they relate to program
- evaluating documentation, reports, assessments, and analyses to inform building program
- identifying and prioritizing components of building program
- assessing spatial and functional relationships for building program
- recommending a preliminary project budget and schedule
- identifying alternatives for building and structural systems for programmatic requirements, preliminary budget, and schedule
- analyzing graphical representations regarding building analysis and building programming

Division 4: Project Planning & Design

Environmental conditions and context (10–16%)

- determining location of building and site improvements based on site analysis
- determining sustainable principles to apply to design
- determining impact of neighborhood context on project design

Codes and regulations (16–22%)

- applying zoning and environmental regulations to site and building design
- applying building codes to building design
- integrating multiple codes to a project design

Building systems, materials, and assemblies (19–25%)

- determining mechanical, electrical, and plumbing systems
- determining structural systems
- determining special systems such as acoustics, communications, lighting, security, conveying, and fire suppression
- determining materials and assemblies to meet programmatic, budgetary, and regulatory requirements

Project integration of program and systems (32–38%)

- determining building configuration
- integrating building systems into project design
- integrating program requirements into project design
- integrating environmental and contextual conditions into project design

Project costs and budgeting (8–14%)

- evaluating design alternatives based on program
- performing cost evaluation
- evaluating cost considerations during design process

Division 5: Project Development & Documentation

Integration of building materials and systems (31–37%)

- analyzing integration of architectural systems and technologies to meet project goals
- determining size of mechanical, electrical, plumbing systems and components to meet project goals
- determining size of structural systems to meet project goals
- integrating specialty systems such as acoustics, lighting, fire suppression, conveying, security, and communications to meet project goals
- detailing the integration of multiple building systems and technologies
- coordinating mechanical, electrical, plumbing, structural, and specialty systems and technologies

Construction documentation (32–38%)

- determining appropriate documentation of building design

- determining appropriate documentation of site features
- determining appropriate documentation of detailed building drawings within individual architectural systems
- applying required standards to assemble a set of clear and coordinated construction documentation
- determining impact of project changes on documentation requirements and method to communicate those changes to owner and design team

Project manual and specifications (12–18%)

- identifying and prioritizing components needed to write, maintain, and refine project manual
- identifying and prioritizing components needed to write, maintain and refine project specifications
- coordinating specifications with construction documentation

Codes and regulations (8–14%)

- determining adherence to building regulatory requirements at detail level
- determining adherence with specialty regulatory requirements at detail level

Construction cost estimates (2–8%)

- analyzing construction cost estimates to confirm alignment with project design

Division 6: Construction & Evaluation

Preconstruction activities (17–23%)

- interpreting architect's roles and responsibilities during preconstruction, based on delivery method
- analyzing criteria for selecting contractors
- analyzing aspects of contract or design to adjust project costs

Construction observation (32–38%)

- evaluating architect's role during construction activities
- evaluating construction conformance with contract documents, codes, regulations, and sustainability requirements
- determining construction progress

Administrative procedures and protocols (32–38%)

- determining appropriate additional information to supplement contract documents
- evaluating submittals including shop drawings, samples, mock-ups, product data, and test results
- evaluating contractor's application for payment
- evaluating responses to nonconformance with contract documents

Project closeout and evaluation (7–13%)

- applying procedural concepts to complete closeout activities
- evaluating building design and performance

EXAM PROBLEM TYPES

There are several types of problems on ARE 5 and in this book.

- multiple-choice problems
- check-all-that-apply problems
- fill-in-the-blank problems
- hot spot problems
- drag-and-place problems
- case study problems

Multiple-Choice Problems

Multiple-choice problems have two types. One type of multiple-choice problem is based on written, graphic, or photographic information. You will need to examine the information and select the correct answer from four given options. Some problems may require calculations. A second type of multiple-choice problem describes a situation that could be encountered in actual practice. Drawings, diagrams, photographs, forms, tables, or other data may also be given. The problem requires you to select the best answer from four options.

Multiple-choice problems often require you to do more than just select an answer based on memory. At times it will be necessary to combine several facts, analyze data, perform a calculation, or review a drawing.

Check-All-That-Apply Problems

Check-all-that-apply problems are a variation of a multiple-choice problem, where six options are given, and you must choose all the correct options. The problem tells how many of the options are correct, from two to four. You must choose all the correct options to receive credit; partial credit is not given.

Fill-in-the-Blank Problems

Fill-in-the-blank problems require you to fill in a blank with a value that you have derived from a table or a calculation.

Hot Spot Problems

Hot spot problems are used to assess visual judgment, evaluation, or prediction. Hot spot problems include the information needed to make a determination, along with an image (e.g., diagram, floor plan) and instructions on how to interact with the image. The problems will indicate that you should place a single target, also known as a hot spot icon, on the base image in the correct location or general area. On the exam, you will place the target on the image by moving the computer cursor to the correct location on the image and clicking on it. You will see crosshairs to help you position the point of click. You will be able to click on an alternate spot if you think your first choice is not correct. Your choice is not registered until you exit the problem. You can click anywhere within an acceptable area range and still be scored as correct.

Drag-and-Place Problems

Drag-and-place problems are similar to hot spot problems, but whereas hot spot problems involve placing just one target on the base image, drag-and-place problems involve placing two to six design elements on the base image. Drag-and-place problems are used to assess visual judgment or evaluation with multiple pieces of information. The problem statement describes what information is to be used to make the determination, and provides instructions on how to interact with the image or graphic item.

A drag-and-place problem, for example, may require you to drag and place design elements such as walls or beams onto the base image. On the exam, you will use the computer cursor to place the elements on the image by clicking and holding elements and dragging and releasing the elements on the correct location on the image. Depending on the question, you may use an element more than once or not at all. This type of question also provides an acceptable area range for placing the elements. The range may be small for questions about a detail or large for something like a site plan.

Case Study Problems

Each division's exam includes one to two case studies. Case studies are performance problem types comprising a scenario, a set of related resource documents (for example, code resources, drawings, and specifications), and a set of case study-specific problems. During the exam, you will be able to click on browser-like tabs at the top of the computer screen and flip back and forth between the case study scenario and resource documents. The case studies will test your ability to examine and use multiple pieces of information to make decisions about scenarios that could be encountered in the practice of architecture.

Case study problems may be multiple-choice, check-all-that-apply, fill-in-the-blank, hot spot, or drag-and-place.

For more information and tips on how to prepare for ARE 5, consult the *ARE 5 Review Manual* or visit PPI's website, **ppi2pass.com/arefaq**.

HOW TO USE THIS BOOK

This book is a practice exam, and the main issue is not how you use it but when you use it. You could take the practice exam at the beginning of your studies to help you decide what subject areas you need to review most, but you will not get the most benefit from using it this way.

The value in this book is in giving you an opportunity to practice your test-taking skills. The best time to take the practice exam is near the end of your studies. This is the only time you will be able to focus on your time management skills without the distraction of trying to recall dimly remembered subjects.

A week or two before you are scheduled to take a division, when you feel you are nearly ready for the exam, do a "dry run" by taking the practice division in this book. The experience will be most valuable to you if you treat each division as though it were an actual exam. Do not read the problems ahead of time and do not look at the solutions until after you have finished. Try to simulate the exam experience as closely as possible. This means locking yourself away in a quiet space, setting an alarm for the exam's testing time, and working through the entire practice exam with no coffee, television, or telephone—only your calculator, a pencil, and a few sheets of scratch paper. (On the actual exam, an on-screen calculator will be provided.) This will help you prepare to budget your time, give you an idea of what the actual exam experience will be, and develop a test-taking strategy that works for you.

The target times for the divisions are as follows.

- Division 1: Practice Management, 3.5 hours
- Division 2: Project Management, 4 hours

- Division 3: Programming & Analysis, 4 hours
- Division 4: Project Planning & Design, 5 hours
- Division 5: Project Development & Documentation, 5 hours
- Division 6: Construction & Evaluation, 4 hours

Within the time allotted for each division, you may work on the problems in any order and spend any amount of time on each one. Record your answers for the multiple-choice sections using the "bubble" answer sheet at the front of each division.

Here are some tips for taking the exam.

- Go through the entire exam in one somewhat swift pass, answering the problems that you are sure about and marking the others so you can return to them later. If a problem requires calculations, skip it for now unless it is very simple. Then, go back to the beginning and work your way through the exam again, taking a little more time to read each problem and think through the answer. (Another benefit of initially going through the entire exam is that occasionally there is information in one problem that may help you answer another problem somewhere else.)
- If you are unsure of a problem, pick your best guess, mark it, and move on. You will probably have time at the end of the exam to go back and recheck these guessed answers. But, remember, your first response is usually the best.
- Always answer all the problems. An unanswered problem is counted wrong, so even if you are just guessing, it is better to choose an answer and have a chance of being correct than to skip the problem and be certain of getting it wrong. When faced with four options, use the strategy of eliminating the options that are definitely wrong and then making your best guess among the two or three that remain.
- Some problems may seem too simple. Although ARE 5 includes a few very easy and obvious problems, more often the simplicity should serve as a red flag to warn you to reevaluate the problem. Look for an exception to a rule or for special circumstances that make the obvious, easy response incorrect.
- Watch out for absolute words in a problem, such as "always," "never," and "completely." These are often a clue that some little exception exists, turning what reads like a true statement into a false one or vice versa.

When you are finished with a division exam in this book, you can check your answers quickly against the filled-in answer key at the back of the corresponding Solutions section. Then turn to the solutions and read the explanations of the answers, especially those you answered incorrectly. The explanation will give you a better understanding of the intent of the problem and why individual options are correct or incorrect.

Evaluate your strengths and weaknesses, both in regard to your test-taking skills and your knowledge of subject areas. Look at where your time management worked well and where it can be improved on the actual exam. Plan some extra study in the areas that you have found to be your weakest.

CODES AND STANDARDS USED IN THIS BOOK

ACI 318: *Building Code Requirements for Structural Concrete*, 2014. American Concrete Institute, Farmington Hills, MI.

ADA Standards: *2010 Americans with Disabilities Act (ADA) Standards for Accessible Design*, U.S. Department of Justice, Washington, DC.

AIA: Contract Documents, 2007. American Institute of Architects, Washington, DC.

AISC: *Steel Construction Manual*, 14th ed, 2011. American Institute of Steel Construction, Chicago, IL.

ANSI/ASHRAE 62.1: *Ventilation for Acceptable Indoor Air Quality*, 2016. American Society of Heating, Refrigerating and Air-Conditioning Engineers, Atlanta, GA.

ANSI/ASHRAE 62.2: *Ventilation and Acceptable Indoor Air Quality in Low-Rise Residential Buildings*, 2016. American Society of Heating, Refrigerating and Air-Conditioning Engineers, Atlanta, GA.

ANSI/ASHRAE/IESNA 90.1: *Energy Standard for Buildings Except Low-Rise Residential Buildings*, 2013. American Society of Heating, Refrigerating and Air-Conditioning Engineers, Atlanta, GA.

ANSI/BOMA Z65.1: *Office Buildings: Standard Methods of Measurement*, 2010. Building Owners and Managers Association, Washington, DC.

ASCE/SEI7: *Minimum Design Loads for Buildings and Other Structures*, 2010. American Society of Civil Engineers, Reston, VA.

CSI: MasterFormat, 2016. Construction Specifications Institute, Alexandria, VA.

CSI: SectionFormat, 2009. Construction Specifications Institute, Alexandria, VA.

IBC: *International Building Code*, 2015. International Code Council, Washington, DC.

ICC/ANSI A117.1: *Accessible and Usable Buildings and Facilities*, 2009. International Code Council. Washington, DC.

IECC: *International Energy Conservation Code*, 2015. International Code Council, Washington, DC.

IgCC: *International Green Construction Code*, 2015. International Code Council, Washington, DC.

IMC: *International Mechanical Code*, 2015. International Code Council, Washington, DC.

IPC: *International Plumbing Code*, 2015. International Code Council, Washington, DC.

IRC: *International Residential Code*, 2015. International Code Council, Washington, DC.

LEED: Leadership in Energy and Environmental Design (LEED) 2013 Green Building Rating System for New Construction. U.S. Green Building Council, Washington, DC.

NDS: *National Design Specification (NDS) for Wood Construction*, 15th ed., 2015. American Wood Council, Leesburg, VA.

NEC (NFPA 70): *National Electrical Code*, 2014. National Fire Protection Association, Quincy, MA.

NFPA 101: *Life Safety Code*, 2015. National Fire Protection Association, Quincy, MA.

The Secretary of the Interior's Standards for Rehabilitation, 2010. *Code of Federal Regulations*, Title 36, Part 67.

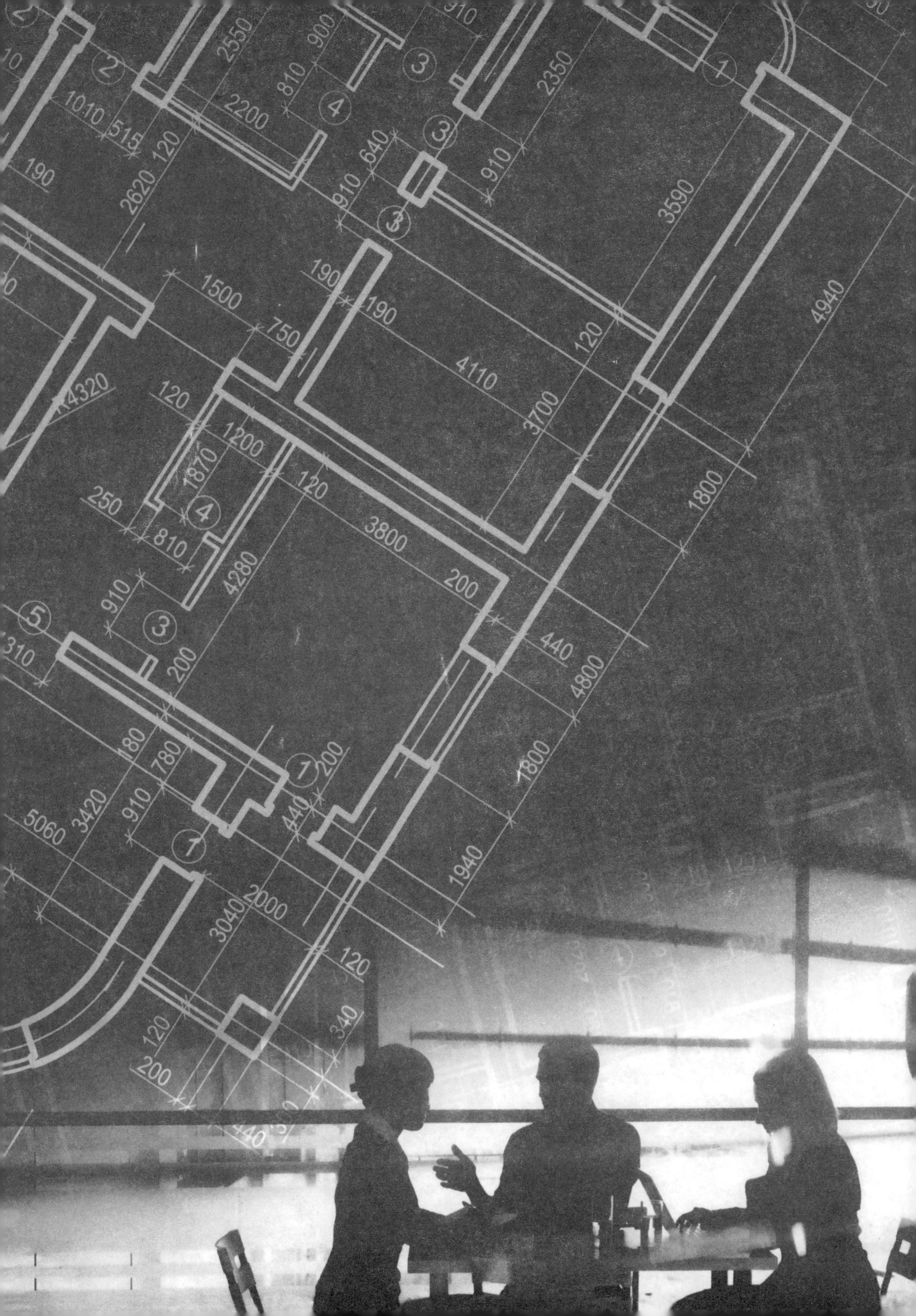

DIVISION 1: PRACTICE MANAGEMENT

Multiple Choice

1. (A) (B) (C) (D)
2. (A)(B)(C)(D)(E)(F)
3. (A)(B)(C)(D)(E)(F)
4. (A) (B) (C) (D)
5. (A) (B) (C) (D)
6. (A) (B) (C) (D)
7. (A) (B) (C) (D)
8. (A) (B) (C) (D)
9. (A) (B) (C) (D)
10. (A) (B) (C) (D)
11. (A) (B) (C) (D)
12. (A)(B)(C)(D)(E)(F)
13. (A) (B) (C) (D)
14. (A) (B) (C) (D)
15. (A) (B) (C) (D)
16. (A)(B)(C)(D)(E)(F)
17. (A) (B) (C) (D)
18. (A) (B) (C) (D)
19. (A)(B)(C)(D)(E)(F)
20. (A) (B) (C) (D)
21. (A)(B)(C)(D)(E)(F)
22. (A) (B) (C) (D)
23. (A)(B)(C)(D)(E)(F)
24. (A) (B) (C) (D)
25. (A) (B) (C) (D)
26. (A) (B) (C) (D)
27. (A) (B) (C) (D)
28. (A)(B)(C)(D)(E)(F)
29. (A) (B) (C) (D)
30. (A) (B) (C) (D)
31. (A) (B) (C) (D)
32. (A) (B) (C) (D)
33. (A) (B) (C) (D)
34. (A)(B)(C)(D)(E)(F)
35. (A) (B) (C) (D)
36. (A) (B) (C) (D)
37. (A) (B) (C) (D)
38. (A) (B) (C) (D)
39. (A)(B)(C)(D)(E)(F)
40. (A) (B) (C) (D)
41. (A) (B) (C) (D)
42. (A) (B) (C) (D)
43. (A) (B) (C) (D)
44. (A) (B) (C) (D)
45. (A) (B) (C) (D)
46. (A)(B)(C)(D)(E)(F)
47. (A) (B) (C) (D)
48. (A) (B) (C) (D)
49. (A) (B) (C) (D)
50. (A) (B) (C) (D)
51. (A) (B) (C) (D)
52. (A) (B) (C) (D)
53. (A) (B) (C) (D)
54. (A) (B) (C) (D)
55. (A) (B) (C) (D)
56. (A) (B) (C) (D)
57. (A) (B) (C) (D)
58. (A) (B) (C) (D)
59. (A)(B)(C)(D)(E)(F)
60. (A) (B) (C) (D)
61. (A) (B) (C) (D)
62. (A) (B) (C) (D)
63. (A)(B)(C)(D)(E)(F)
64. (A) (B) (C) (D)
65. (A) (B) (C) (D)

Case Study 1

66. (A) (B) (C) (D)
67. (A) (B) (C) (D)
68. (A) (B) (C) (D)
69. (A) (B) (C) (D)
70. (A) (B) (C) (D)
71. (A) (B) (C) (D)
72. (A) (B) (C) (D)
73. (A) (B) (C) (D)
74. (A)(B)(C)(D)(E)(F)
75. (A)(B)(C)(D)(E)(F)

Case Study 2

76. (A) (B) (C) (D)
77. (A) (B) (C) (D)
78. (A) (B) (C) (D)
79. (A) (B) (C) (D)
80. (A) (B) (C) (D)

1. An architecture firm is facing a deadline on a large library project and decides to hire a freelance computer-aided design (CAD) drafter who works from home to assist the firm in completing the construction documents on time. According to the National Council of Architectural Registration Boards (NCARB) *Rules of Conduct*, what must the architect of record do to sign and seal the final drawings?

(A) The architect must redline the drawings and have the drafter make the appropriate corrections.

(B) The architect must review and correct the work after it is prepared by the drafter and incorporate it into the construction documents.

(C) The architect must thoroughly examine the drawings prepared by the drafter and incorporate the work into the construction documents. The firm must also retain documentation of communications with the drafter throughout the drafter's involvement with the project and must keep records of the architect's coordination of the work for five years.

(D) The architect may be subject to disciplinary action from the state registration board if the architect signs and seals the drawings, as this is not permissible.

2. Which types of business organizations limit an individual's liability to the amount that an individual has invested in the company? (Choose the three that apply.)

(A) partnership

(B) corporation

(C) joint venture

(D) limited liability company

(E) limited liability partnership

(F) disadvantaged business enterprise

3. Which of the following are required to prove negligence? (Choose the three that apply.)

(A) agency

(B) breach

(C) cause

(D) commission

(E) damage

(F) duty

4. An architect writes a specification for floor tile for a public restroom, which states that the tile is to be "American Tile Company 12 × 12 porcelain floor tile, Pattern 463 Oceania, Color 42 Sandstorm or approved equal." The contractor contacts a local tile supplier and discovers that this product has a 12-week lead time, but it will be necessary to have the tile on site earlier to stay within the project schedule. If the contractor wishes to propose a different tile, when must that request to the architect be submitted?

(A) during preparation of submittals

(B) prior to submitting a bid

(C) after the contract is awarded and an agreement with the tiling subcontractor is signed

(D) during the project kick-off meeting

5. According to the National Council of Architectural Registration Boards (NCARB) *Rules of Conduct*, an architect's license or registration could be revoked if

(A) in talking with a potential client, the architect fails to disclose ownership of stock in the client's chief competitor and that personal financial interest may influence the architect's judgment

(B) in a television interview about a controversial casino project, the architect discloses that he or she is employed by the resort developer

(C) the architect pays for overnight accommodation and a dinner for a potential client so that the client may visit the architect's firm for a second interview about a large project

(D) the architect takes out a half-page advertisement in a local newspaper stating the firm's credentials and why the firm should be considered for a large development project in the city

6. What must architects do to protect their interest in the copyright on the instruments of service produced for a project and the design of a building?

(A) Register the drawings and photographs of the completed building with the U.S. Copyright Office.

(B) File a copy of the instruments of service in the Library of Congress.

(C) Put the copyright symbol © and the date on the drawings.

(D) Neither option (A), option (B), nor option (C) are required to protect the architect's copyright.

7. "Vinyl composition tile shall be maintained at a minimum of 65°F for 48 hours prior to installation, during installation, and for 48 hours after completion." In what part of the project specifications does the contractor find these instructions?

(A) Part I, General

(B) Part II, Products

(C) Part III, Execution

(D) Division 01, General Requirements

8. Which of the following is the best way to modify a standard American Institute of Architects (AIA) document?

(A) Retype the document, incorporating all of the changes.

(B) Attach supplementary conditions or amendments.

(C) Strike out portions of the contract by hand or insert handwritten additions.

(D) Have an attorney draft a new contract using portions of the language in the AIA documents applicable to the project.

9. "Claims-made" professional liability insurance policies

(A) base the cost of the insurance policy on the number of claims made against it

(B) require the policy to be in effect at the time a claim is made, as well as at the time services were rendered

(C) claims made against a retired partner if the policy was in effect at the time the incident that caused the claim occurred, but is no longer held by the firm

(D) are canceled if more than one claim is made against it in a specified period of time

10. Which type of construction compensation structure encourages a contractor to be most efficient?

(A) cost-plus with a fixed, lump-sum fee for overhead and profit

(B) cost-plus with the fee for overhead and profit based upon a percentage of construction cost

(C) stipulated sum

(D) unit price

11. Indirect liability imposed on a party resulting from the acts or omissions of another person for whom the party is responsible is known as

(A) transferred liability

(B) vicarious liability

(C) consultant liability

(D) limited liability

12. Which of the following are common inclusions of an all-risk insurance policy? (Choose the four that apply.)

(A) act of war

(B) boiler explosion

(C) employee theft

(D) fire damage

(E) theft

(F) vandalism

13. A potential client calls a small architecture firm and describes a set of house plans purchased from a shelter magazine. The client submitted the drawings to the local township for a building permit but was denied because the drawings did not include sufficient information, such as a foundation plan, and did not comply with local guidelines for insulation requirements. The client asks if the firm can use the computer-aided design (CAD) files that were purchased along with the prints to produce drawings that can be submitted for a building permit. How should the architect respond?

(A) Accept the job but with the condition that the architect can only supply the missing information, such as using the plan to develop a foundation plan.

(B) Accept the job but require the potential client pay for developing a completely new set of drawings and specifications, just using the magazines design as a starting point.

(C) Politely decline the job, explaining that it is a violation of the National Council of Architectural Registration Boards (NCARB) *Rules of Conduct* and of copyright to modify another designer's work.

(D) Politely decline the job, telling the client that the current workload makes it impossible to take on but suggesting that one of the intern architects in the office could do the job on a moonlighting basis.

14. An architect and the developer of a small office complex are preparing the project manual for a new project. The architect asks the owner for information regarding insurance requirements for this project. The owner, in turn, asks the architect what types of coverage and how much coverage is needed for the project. What is the most appropriate way for the architect to respond?

(A) Consult a copy of American Institute of Architects (AIA) Document G612, *Owner's Instructions to the Architect*.

(B) Give the owner some ballpark numbers based on previous projects.

(C) Advise the owner to consult with an insurance agent.

(D) Help the owner to determine reasonable amounts.

15. An architectural firm should retain project records

(A) for five years after substantial completion

(B) until the statute of repose period has ended

(C) until the statute of limitations period has ended

(D) indefinitely

16. Which of the following are characteristics of the design-build approach to project delivery, as compared to the design-award-build model? (Choose the four that apply.)

(A) The owner has more control over the quality of the materials and the types of construction methods used to build the project.

(B) The owner has more information about the cost of the project available at an earlier phase in the project.

(C) The combined design and construction time is generally less.

(D) The owner must approach the project with a clearly defined program or set of performance requirements.

(E) Constructability advice can be obtained early in the process.

(F) A bridging agreement is required for the greatest success.

17. Addenda are issued

(A) prior to receipt of bids

(B) after receipt of bids but before work commences

(C) after the award of the contract

(D) during construction

18. The owner of a large manufacturing plant needs to expand to a new facility quickly and without interruption in production. The owner has arranged for a flexible line of credit to finance construction and wants to minimize project costs. The new facility will be very similar to the previous one, but sized for greater production capacity. Which type of construction delivery method should be recommended?

(A) design-build

(B) fast-track

(C) multiple prime contract

(D) design-award-build

19. Which of the following are characteristics of partnering? (Choose the three that apply.)

(A) A partnering agreement applies only to the project at hand.

(B) Partnering places the architect in the prime decision making role with partners as advisers.

(C) Partnering is often used in conjunction with mediation and arbitration to prevent lawsuits.

(D) Partnering can include project participants other than the owner, contractor, and architect.

(E) Partnering requires a limited liability form of office organization.

(F) A partnering agreement becomes a part of the contract between the architect and owner and the owner and contractor.

20. A method of construction delivery that obtains an early fixed price for a project based on a set of design documents and then gives the contractor responsibility for determining the details of construction is called

(A) design-build

(B) bridging

(C) fast-track

(D) integration

21. Which of the following are characteristics of the construction management at risk (CMc) project delivery method? (Choose the four that apply.)

(A) The standard American Institute of Architects (AIA) Document A201, *General Conditions of the Contract for Construction*, is used during construction.

(B) The guaranteed maximum price is developed after documents are completed.

(C) The delivery method has two separate contracts.

(D) The delivery method has three prime players.

(E) The complete package of construction documents must be provided prior to the start of construction.

(F) The selection based on factors other than cost must be provided.

22. A local hospital is planning a new cardiac center. An architect and the hospital's project manager have been working for a year and a half to define the design requirements, and the project is approaching the end of the design development phase. The project manager learns that the hospital has recently received a gift of $10 million to build the cardiac center, and the hospital board of directors authorizes the project manager to do whatever it takes to open the new cardiac center in one year. Which project delivery method is a good choice in this situation?

(A) design-build

(B) design-bid-build

(C) fast-track

(D) negotiated contract with a guaranteed maximum price

23. Which of the following are true regarding joint ventures? (Choose the four that apply.)

(A) A joint venture is limited to a specific project.

(B) A joint venture pays no income taxes and earns no profits.

(C) A joint venture details that liability insurance held by one of the parties will cover both parties.

(D) A joint venture can be formed using American Institute of Architects (AIA) Document C101, *Joint Venture Agreement for Professional Services.*

(E) A joint venture is often used when one firm cannot complete a project due to lack of personnel.

(F) A joint venture increases risk to both parties.

24. A client has requested that the time for design and construction document production be shortened. The architect's best course of action will be to

(A) hire additional employees

(B) have the design team work overtime

(C) assign more existing employees to the design team

(D) ask the client to reduce the scope of the project

25. Which of the following statements is true?

(A) An owner has an exclusive license to reproduce drawings for the contractor's use in building the project.

(B) An owner may assign the license to the instruments of service to a lender if it is a condition of financing.

(C) If an architect is found to have defaulted on the owner-architect agreement, the owner receives a nonexclusive license to reproduce the instruments of service and may authorize another architect to complete the project.

(D) An owner may use the instruments of service from a project for an addition or renovation to that project.

26. An architect has proposed using an integrated project delivery (IPD) method for a large project. Resource allocation will follow best practices per the MacLeamy curve.

Using the MacLeamy curve as a guideline, during what phase of the project should the architect allocate the most resources?

(A) criteria design

(B) detailed design

(C) implementation documents

(D) agency coordination

27. Two architecture firms are considering collaborating on a large project. Before they bid on the work, what form of agreement should they establish?

(A) joint venture agreement

(B) letter of agreement

(C) prime consultant agreement

(D) teaming agreement

28. The National Council of Architectural Registration Boards (NCARB) requires aspiring architects in the Architectural Experience Program (AXP) to meet which four requirements? (Choose the four that apply.)

(A) have an architect supervisor

(B) possess an NCARB record

(C) obtain experience in specific categories

(D) complete interactive online activities

(E) submit online reporting

(F) work with state coordinators

29. The principals of a firm are considering adopting employment contracts instead of using the firm's current policy of at-will employment. Which possible outcome will have the largest impact on the firm?

(A) Recordkeeping requirements will increase substantially.

(B) Terminated employees will be required to receive a reason for their termination.

(C) Moonlighting on independent projects or for other firms will be prohibited.

(D) A specific job description for each employee will be required.

30. An architect designs an exterior wall assembly to meet the local code requirements for insulation and air barrier protection. A year later when the building is under construction, the state energy office increases the required *R*-value for walls. The building owner claims that the architect neglected to address the code requirements and demands that the architect pay to upgrade the construction of the wall assembly to meet the current local code. The architect should respond to the client by

(A) pointing out that the design met the requirements of the building code

(B) claiming that the state energy office arbitrarily changed insulation requirements

(C) stating that the actions taken were justifiable and in accordance with what any prudent architect would have done at the time

(D) arguing that the local code runs counter to the *International Energy Conservation Code* (IECC)

31. When developing the finish plans for an assisted living center, an architect fails to indicate that the wall finish in three rooms is vinyl wall fabric, as originally approved by the client. Instead, the architect shows a painted finish in the plan. The finish contractor notices the problem because of previous informal discussions with the architect, and the general contractor subsequently requires a change order. The client expects the architect to pay the cost resulting from the change order. What is the architect's best defense to minimize exposure if the issue is taken to mediation?

(A) the standard of care

(B) client approval of the plans

(C) errors and omissions insurance

(D) the concept of betterment

32. What type of accounting method should a 13-person architectural firm use?

(A) accrual-basis method

(B) double-entry method

(C) cash-basis accounting method

(D) modified accrual-basis method

33. A client embarking on a first building project has hired an architect to develop a modestly sized coworking facility. The client is concerned about the architect's fee. The architect is also concerned about being paid fairly for the job. Which pricing method meets the needs of both the client and the architect?

(A) cost-plus-fee method

(B) hourly not-to-exceed fee

(C) percentage of construction cost

(D) square-foot cost

34. While reviewing project reports, the head of an architectural firm notices that the overhead rate is too high at 1.8. What three significant actions should the architect take to reduce the overhead? (Choose the three that apply.)

(A) Monitor non-billable time more closely.

(B) Require administrative personnel to check direct expenses.

(C) Be more diligent with fee collection.

(D) Review telecommunication charges.

(E) Consider moving to a less expensive office space.

(F) Try to increase revenue per technical staff.

35. An architectural firm is evaluating its financial performance during the previous month. What report should be used?

(A) balance sheet

(B) net profit before tax

(C) office earnings report

(D) profit and loss statement

36. According to an architecture firm's office earnings report, two design projects are behind schedule. What should the office manager do first to get the projects on track?

(A) Determine if the appropriate personnel are assigned to the projects.

(B) Tell the project managers to increase productivity.

(C) Review the billed and unbilled expenses for the projects.

(D) Set up an overtime plan to align with the original schedule.

37. During construction on a townhouse, a fire on the job site destroys the wood framing of the structure. Which party's insurance covers the damage?

(A) architect

(B) contractor

(C) owner

(D) subcontractor

38. An architectural firm wants to shift the focus of its practice from general services to historic preservation. To expand its reach to potential clients, consultants, and contractors in the historic preservation market, what should the firm do first?

(A) Hire a professional who has experience in the desired market.

(B) Develop a new page on the firm's website targeted to the market.

(C) Begin social media networking.

(D) Research the market and identify possible contacts.

39. Which four actions will optimize the quality control of construction document production? (Choose the four that apply.)

(A) Employ an outside firm to check the final set of construction drawings.

(B) Maintain a regular exchange of progress drawings with consultants.

(C) Purchase and use appropriate drawings checklists from the Construction Specifications Institute (CSI).

(D) Use CSI's Uniform Drawing System (UDS) of the National CAD Standard (NCS).

(E) Apply standard details developed by the office when appropriate.

(F) Assign one person on a project to provide single source responsibility.

40. What legal concept protects an architect against claims made by a subcontractor?

(A) agency

(B) duty

(C) indemnification

(D) lack of privity

41. What is the best action an architectural firm can take to improve its level of expertise in sustainable design?

(A) Design all projects to meet the requirements of the *International Green Construction Code* (IgCC).

(B) Use the American Institute of Architects (AIA) standard documents written for sustainable design projects.

(C) Require that all architects in the office become Leadership in Energy and Environmental Design (LEED) Accredited Professionals.

(D) Adopt the Greenguard Certification Program for all office projects.

42. An architect has been approached by the board of a small church to help initiate the construction of a new building. The board has raised about 60% of the funds needed and is continuing its fund-raising efforts. In order to save money on the design, the board tells the architect that it has a floor plan already worked out and wants to propose ideas about the outside design. How should the architect respond?

(A) Decline the offer because an architect's value is in designing to the client's needs rather than being used as a drafting service, and suggest that the client should wait until more money is raised.

(B) Decline the offer, suggesting that the board wait until all the funds have been raised and the design can be reviewed.

(C) Accept a reduced fee because of the available design but require a 15% retainer due to uncertainty regarding funds.

(D) Accept the offer with the condition that the board's design must be reviewed and modified if necessary.

43. A restaurateur contacts an architect for services to build a new restaurant with an attached specialty food store. Shortly after the potential client discusses building plans with the architect, he mentions that he wants to use a design-build method of construction to minimize costs and have single-source responsibility, so he will not need the architect's services after all. What can the architect do to remain involved in the project?

(A) Ask the client to select a contractor who will hire the architect as a design consultant.

(B) Tell the client that design-build is not the preferred method to use on this project.

(C) Request that the architect be hired to provide bridging for the design-build approach.

(D) Assist the client in finding a suitable design-build company and solicit the company for the design work.

44. A client with extensive experience planning boutique hotel projects contacts an architect. The client wants to use specific consultants but wants the architect to hire them and coordinate as required. How should the architect respond to this request?

(A) Agree, but require an additional fee for extra coordination.

(B) Research the consultants before responding to the request.

(C) Decline to accept the job because the risks of using unknown consultants are too great.

(D) Agree to use the consultants but ask the client to hire and pay them directly.

45. What is a major risk in using a joint venture agreement to complete a project that uses a construction manager as constructor (CMc) delivery method?

(A) Each joint venture partner is responsible for his or her own actions as well as the actions of the other partners.

(B) It is difficult to allocate the expenses and profits of each joint venture partner fairly.

(C) The American Institute of Architects (AIA) architect-consultant agreements cannot adequately define the roles and responsibilities of the partners.

(D) The CMc method cannot be used with a joint venture.

46. An architectural firm with a reputation for excellence in sustainable design has been approached by a speculative developer to design a small office building. Although the firm has done many projects in the past four years, its lack of work is putting a strain on finances and the firm's ability to retain staff. The developer specifically tells the architect that it does not matter if any sustainable measures are incorporated into the building other that what is minimally required by the building code. What three issues should the firm analyze before deciding whether or not to accept the job? (Choose the three that apply.)

(A) the likelihood that the firm could persuade the client to use sustainable design

(B) the type of project delivery method and contract that the developer wants to use

(C) the cash flow of current and expected work for the next year

(D) how strongly the firm feels about its commitment to sustainable design

(E) the financial stability of the developer and of the project itself

(F) how to set fees and the fee amount that the developer will accept

47. If a firm takes on a financially risky commission even though there is already sufficient work in the office, what effect will that have on staff morale?

(A) The staff members will be relieved that they still have jobs.

(B) Morale will probably stay about the same.

(C) Some employees may leave the firm to find more secure work.

(D) Performance will suffer, since staff members will be unsure of their efforts.

48. What are the potential monetary rewards for an architect using an integrated project delivery (IPD) method with a multi-party agreement?

(A) The architect receives profits if the target cost and project-related goals are both met.

(B) The architect and contractor share bonuses as stated in the agreement.

(C) If the final cost is below the target cost, the architect receives part of the difference.

(D) The client pays an agreed upon percentage of actual costs to the architect as profit.

49. In lieu of a fee, a developer offers an architect ownership participation in a project if the architect will provide complete architectural services for the project. How should the architect first consider this proposal?

(A) Complete a thorough pro forma for the project and compare potential income and appreciation with an estimated professional services fee.

(B) Analyze the potential market for the project and the developer's history with such projects.

(C) Decline the offer and insist that the developer pay the architect using a cost-plus-fee professional services agreement.

(D) Investigate whether or not the architectural firm will be able to borrow enough money to cover the cost of services until income is realized by the project.

50. Three architects who went to college together have decided to go into business. Each has a different skill: marketing, design, and construction technology, which they think will form the basis of a successful architectural practice. They want the business to be easy to set up and manage, and they want there to be potential for financial growth. What type of business organization is best?

(A) general partnership

(B) limited partnership

(C) limited liability partnership (LLP)

(D) corporation

51. A 22-person architecture firm wants to specialize in only three building types: multi-family residential, religious, and small retail. What type of office organization is the most efficient for the firm to use?

(A) a single studio

(B) departmental

(C) three specialist studios

(D) departmental with three design specialists

52. For a small residential firm with a single architect or a few people, what type of business structure is the most appropriate?

(A) sole proprietorship

(B) sole proprietorship using freelancers as required

(C) limited liability company (LLC)

(D) professional corporation

53. A growing architectural firm has made a commitment to hiring and nurturing aspiring architects while still retaining core competencies. In addition to meeting the requirements of the National Council of Architectural Registration Boards (NCARB) Architectural Experience Program (AXP), what practice methodology should the firm adopt?

(A) Use a studio organization with aspiring architects assigned to an experienced mentor in each studio.

(B) Use a departmental organization and rotate aspiring architects through various departments.

(C) Maintain an "aspiring architects class" in the office with aspiring architects assigned to one or two supervisors.

(D) Assign one member of the firm as a mentor to each experience category.

54. In preliminary meetings between a client and an architect hired to design a new headquarters building for a local water district, the architect outlines the consultants that will be required on the project. The person responsible for retaining the geotechnical engineer is the

(A) client

(B) architect

(C) client with input from the architect

(D) architect with input from the structural engineer

55. A client for an industrial building insists on directly retaining the structural, mechanical, and electrical engineers with whom the client has previously worked. The architect wants to hire engineers directly, but the client prevails. What coordination methodology should the architect use with the engineers?

(A) Insist that the consultants sign a separate agreement with the architect for work procedures.

(B) Establish clear lines of communication with each engineer before beginning work.

(C) Require the engineers to attend design charrettes during schematic design and design development.

(D) Supply the engineers with progress drawings and design decisions on a weekly basis.

56. After a series of problems with construction documents on several projects, an architectural firm is reviewing its methods of document production. The firm already has an acceptable system of standard details, uses industry standards, and has a competent staff to complete the drawings. What additional action might be beneficial to the firm?

(A) Have one of the firm principals review all drawings before they are issued.

(B) Require that the project manager of each job be more responsible for checking.

(C) Hire an outside firm to review the final construction drawings thoroughly prior to issue.

(D) Develop a construction document checklist tailored to the needs of the firm.

57. Employee performance evaluations are required by the

(A) Wages and Fair Labor Standards Act

(B) National Labor Relations Act

(C) National Council of Architectural Registration Boards (NCARB) Architectural Experience Program (AXP) guidelines

(D) architectural office's policy

58. For an American Institute of Architects (AIA) member, which action is a clear violation of the AIA document *Code of Ethics & Professional Conduct*?

(A) accepting a commission to continue work for a project another architect relinquished

(B) advertising the capabilities of the firm on television and in local newspapers

(C) agreeing with a client not to design a sustainable building to save money

(D) acting as both the architect and the contractor on a project

59. For the past year, an architectural firm has not been getting paid on time. The firm principal has reviewed and evaluated how the firm develops, submits, and collects bills. To correct the situation and maintain the firm's financial success, what are the most important actions the firm should perform? (Choose the four that apply.)

(A) Threaten legal action if bills are not paid within 45 days after receiving an overdue notice.

(B) Ensure payment procedures are clearly stated in the agreement.

(C) Have the firm principal make personal contact with the client for overdue invoices.

(D) Send invoices promptly at a minimum interval of one month.

(E) Insist on having a retainer cover 25% of the anticipated fee, before design work begins.

(F) Itemize all work that the invoice covers and relate it to the agreement.

60. An architect is researching how to maintain the firm's financial solvency. To remain financially solvent over the next fiscal year, the firm must earn a certain amount of income. What value should an architect use to help estimate what income the firm will need in the next fiscal year in order to remain financially solvent?

(A) current ratio

(B) quick ratio

(C) net profit before tax

(D) revenue per technical staff

61. Based on past problems with on-site observations, a small committee in an architectural firm is revising its office manual to help staff conduct themselves correctly while on job sites. What important legal issue should be included along with examples of what to do and what not to do?

(A) agency

(B) implied duty

(C) negligence

(D) privity

62. A well-known and respected architectural firm experienced in evidence-based design has been approached to design the corporate headquarters building for a large company. To maximize profits, the firm is considering a unique fee structure likely to yield a greater profit than standard fee structures. The firm has proposed to charge the client a cost-based fee but with no built-in profit. Instead, additional fees are based on the company's increase in productivity, with fees increasing as the productivity value increases. The company and the architectural firm will measure productivity after six months on a mutually agreed basis. What is the greatest risk to the architectural firm?

(A) The architect and the company cannot agree on a method to measure productivity.

(B) There is no standard American Institute of Architects (AIA) contract document that covers this type of compensation method.

(C) At the time productivity is measured, there is little increase and little profit.

(D) The company disputes that any increase in productivity is a result of the design.

63. When an architectural firm works on an hourly basis, what actions can the firm take to minimize risk? (Choose the four that apply.)

(A) Use project management software that tracks time and fee progress weekly.

(B) Assign experienced staff to the project with less experienced staff in support roles.

(C) Monitor technical staff progress on a daily basis to compare with the project schedule.

(D) Increase the net multiplier slightly to account for inefficiencies, when negotiating fees.

(E) Include a not-to-exceed maximum fee in the agreement along with the hourly rates.

(F) Include a detailed description of services in the owner-architect agreement.

64. An architectural firm's principals want to improve the firm's design quality, efficiency, and profitability while reducing risks. The principals analyze the MacLeamy curve, which illustrates the differences between the integrated project delivery (IPD) method and the traditional design-bid-build approach. What organizational change should the firm make?

(A) Adopt the IPD method.

(B) Hire more designers and outsource document production.

(C) Encourage clients to use design-build construction.

(D) Change to a departmental organization for all projects.

65. A large architectural firm deploys a departmental organization with a separate design department and lead designer. If the firm reorganizes into a studio system, what are the positive effects?

(A) shorter project delivery times and more focused attention on problems

(B) improved communication and the ability to train aspiring architects in a specialty

(C) improved problem solving and diverse design approaches

(D) better use of specialists and flexibility in forming or dissolving studios

Case Study 1

Problem 66 through Prob. 75 refer to the following case study.

An architectural firm is a general services practice organized in a studio system with one principal, one project manager, six architects, a materials specialist/specifications writer, a contract/field administrator, a part-time marketing manager, and an administrative assistant/receptionist. The architects serve as project managers when required. Four of the architects are proficient with standard computer-aided design (CAD) software, but the office has not yet converted to building information modeling (BIM). The firm, however, expects to expand and use BIM for most of its projects in the future.

The firm has secured two commissions, one for an 80,000 ft^2 city recreation center in a nearby suburb and one for the space planning and interior design of a 15,500 ft^2 corporate office in a high-rise building. The architect is finalizing the agreements for services for both clients. The client of the recreation center has expressed interest in using BIM for design and ongoing maintenance but is unsure of its effectiveness.

66. After being notified that it has been awarded the projects, the firm reviews its workload and realizes that it does not have the staff to complete the two new projects in the required time. What is a reasonable course of action?

(A) Form a joint venture with another firm that has the experience needed.

(B) Hire freelance consultants on an as-needed basis.

(C) Establish a teaming agreement with a local office.

(D) Form a prime consultant agreement with another firm.

67. In deciding how to allocate work assignments with the existing staff, the firm principal decides to hire a computer-aided design (CAD) operator on an independent contractor basis to assist with one of the existing jobs in the office. To avoid potential problems with the Internal Revenue Service (IRS), the firm should be especially careful to

(A) require the contractor to work the same hours as the other staff

(B) establish a work schedule and milestone completion dates

(C) pay the contractor as agreed at the start of work, with no benefits

(D) give the contractor a bonus at the end of the project

68. During contract negotiations in which American Institute of Architects (AIA) standard forms are used, the recreation center client tells the architect to include a provision that there will be no cost overruns on the project. Since the architect plans on recommending a construction contract with a guaranteed maximum price (GMP), the architect agrees to include the provision. In doing so, the architect has

(A) raised the level of the standard of care

(B) violated an AIA ethical canon

(C) invalidated a standard insurance provision

(D) negated a provision of the owner-contractor agreement

69. While developing fee proposals for the two new projects, the principal of the firm also reviews the financial reports for the office. The principal finds that the utilization rate for technical staff is 71%. What should the principal do to make the two new projects profitable?

(A) Raise the office profit margin figured into the fees.

(B) Direct project managers to track chargeable time more closely.

(C) Increase the net multiplier for these two jobs.

(D) Carefully track the project progress report for the two jobs.

70. Shortly after the firm is awarded the recreation center project, the client initiates a meeting to discuss the possibility of using building information modeling (BIM). What is the most appropriate strategy for the office to adopt?

(A) Tell the client that BIM is not necessary for a project of this size and that it will require that the client make decisions earlier in the process.

(B) Agree to use BIM, and hire an experienced BIM operator to manage the process and train others in the office, recognizing that associated costs will have to be absorbed.

(C) Advise the client that although using BIM will be beneficial to the city, the client will have to cover the cost of new software and training for both the firm and the city.

(D) Suggest that the firm associate with another firm with BIM experience and cover startup costs by adjusting the amount specified in the fee proposal.

71. During negotiations to finalize the owner-architect agreement, the client for the corporate office tells the architect that for public relations purposes, a Leadership in Energy and Environmental Design (LEED) certification is desired. How should the architect respond?

(A) Agree that it is a good idea to be LEED-certified, but the client will have to pay fees for registration, certification, research, and documentation.

(B) Discourage the client from seeking LEED certification but express that sustainable measures may be incorporated in the project without the cost of LEED.

(C) Express that although it is a good idea, the office will have to hire a LEED-credentialed employee to manage the process.

(D) Inform the client that a LEED-credentialed consultant will need to be retained to administer the documentation and application process.

72. Which type of project delivery method should be used for the recreation center project?

(A) design-build (contractor-led)

(B) fast-track

(C) design-award-build

(D) integrated project delivery (IPD)

73. For one or both of the projects, a potential risk is

(A) the inability to complete the projects with current staffing

(B) the lack of leadership with only one principal to direct the projects

(C) financial stress caused by the migration to building information modeling (BIM)

(D) nonexistent—there is no significant risk

74. The architectural firm possesses talent and experience, even if the office is understaffed. If the principal of the firm is willing to direct the two jobs, what four professionals and responsibilities should each project team include? (Choose the four that apply.)

(A) a project manager for client contact and coordination

(B) architects for design only

(C) independent consultants for document production

(D) an associated firm for all document production

(E) an outsourcing firm for document production

(F) a specifications writer as needed

75. What three types of consultants should be retained to complete the corporate office project? (Choose the three that apply.)

(A) structural

(B) mechanical

(C) electrical

(D) security

(E) signage

(F) interior designer

Case Study 2

Problem 76 through Prob. 80 refer to the following case study.

An architectural firm is in the construction administration phase for a 75,000 ft^2, single-story, retail-development addition to an existing 15,000 ft^2 strip mall that was completed in 1970. The project is in the same city as the architect's office. Part of the existing building is being demolished down to the column and roof structure, the floor slab, and a few concrete masonry unit (CMU) walls that will remain. The project is four weeks ahead of schedule. The architect visits the site once a week.

The firm includes 3 principals, 4 project managers, 14 architects and technical staff, and other support staff. The office is organized under a studio system and uses a standard computer-aided design (CAD) software package but is considering using building information modeling (BIM). The retail project is being completed under standard American Institute of Architects (AIA) Document B141, *Standard Form of Agreement Between Owner and Architect with Standard Form of Architect's Services*, AIA Document A101, *Standard Form of Agreement Between Owner and Architect*, and AIA Document A201, *General Conditions of the Contract for Construction.*

The foundation, structure, roof framing, and some masonry exterior walls were finished when the project was about 40% complete. At that time, about 5000 ft^2 next to the existing structure collapsed, causing damage to some columns, the roof, part of the exterior, and a wall between the old and new portion of work. The cause of the collapse was found to be an inadequate structure in the original building built in 1970, which was weakened during the partial demolition.

76. During the repair of the collapsed portion of the building, several coordination problems arise with the general contractor and with many of the subcontractors and consultants. In addition to minimizing costs, what personnel resources should the architect dedicate to solve the problems?

(A) Increase the architect's job site visits from once per week to twice per week.

(B) Have the project architect visit the job site once per day and be on call for other problems.

(C) Assign an experienced architect to work full time on the job site until the problems are resolved.

(D) Have one of the principals take over site observation and problem resolution until the collapsed area is rebuilt.

77. Shortly after the collapse, the contractor investigates the cause of the collapse and the extent of repair work needed. The contractor discovers what is believed to be asbestos. The contractor is suspicious and immediately calls the architect. What should the architect do first?

(A) Tell the contractor to stop work until an asbestos abatement contractor can be called.

(B) Inform the owner of the situation and suggest asbestos abatement laboratories.

(C) Tell the contractor to write a letter about the situation to the owner.

(D) Instruct the contractor to retain an asbestos abatement laboratory to test the material.

78. The partial building collapse requires the architect to increase site visits and make minor modifications to the plans and details. Who is responsible for paying the architect's extra fees?

(A) bonding agency

(B) contractor

(C) insurance company

(D) owner

79. After the collapse, the owner decides to redesign the collapsed portion, adding a second story over part of the building. A company wants to lease the second story space for a restaurant. The owner notifies and instructs the architect to design and produce the necessary construction documents while they negotiate extra fees. How should the architect respond to this request?

(A) Determine the extra fee required, and have the owner agree to it in writing before beginning work.

(B) Start work on design and documentation, and advise the owner of the probable extra fee and time that will be required.

(C) Tell the owner that this work is not included in the agreement and will increase the time and cost above the client's budget.

(D) Confer with the architect's consultants and contractor to determine probable additional construction costs and fees.

80. The architect must document the planned repairs to the collapsed portion of the building and the addition of the second-story restaurant space. Given the other goals and schedule of the project and practice, which approach is best?

(A) Use hand-drafted sketches to produce the necessary drawings quickly.

(B) Use the architect's standard computer-aided design (CAD) software to develop a new set of drawings.

(C) Take the opportunity to start using building information modeling (BIM) for this small project.

(D) Outsource the production of new construction drawings with the project manager's oversight.

Solutions

Multiple Choice

1. A B ● D
2. A ● C ● ● F
3. A ● C D ● ●
4. A ● C D
5. ● B C D
6. A B C ●
7. A B ● D
8. A ● C D
9. A ● C D
10. ● B C D
11. A ● C D
12. A ● C ● ● ●
13. A B ● D
14. A B ● D
15. A ● C D
16. A ● ● ● ● F
17. ● B C D
18. A ● C D
19. ● B ● ● E F
20. A ● C D
21. ● B ● ● E ●
22. A B ● D
23. ● ● C ● ● F
24. A B ● D
25. A B ● D
26. A ● C D
27. A B C ●
28. ● ● ● D ● F
29. A ● C D
30. A B ● D
31. A B C ●
32. A B C ●
33. ● B C D
34. ● ● C D ● F
35. A B C ●
36. ● B C D
37. A B ● D
38. A B C ●
39. A ● C ● ● ●
40. A B C ●
41. A B ● D
42. ● B C D
43. A B ● D
44. A B C ●
45. ● B C D
46. A B ● ● ● F
47. A ● C D
48. A B ● D
49. ● B C D
50. A B ● D
51. A B C ●
52. A B ● D
53. ● B C D
54. A B ● D
55. A ● C D
56. A B C ●
57. A B C ●
58. A B ● D
59. A ● ● ● E ●
60. A B C ●
61. A ● C D
62. A B ● D
63. ● ● ● D E ●
64. ● B C D
65. A B ● D

Case Study 1

66. A B C ●
67. A B ● D
68. ● B C D
69. A ● C D
70. A ● C D
71. ● B C D
72. A B ● D
73. A B C ●
74. ● ● C ● E ●
75. A ● ● D E ●

Case Study 2

76. A ● C D
77. A B ● D
78. A B C ●
79. ● B C D
80. A ● C D

1. According to the NCARB *Rules of Conduct*, an architect may sign and seal technical submissions if they are

- prepared by the architect
- prepared by persons under the architect's "responsible control," which means that the architect has as much professional knowledge of the work done by the employee as if he or she had completed it personally
- prepared by another registered architect in that jurisdiction if the architect has reviewed the submission and incorporated the other architect's work into his or her own submission or coordinated its preparation
- prepared by another NCARB-certified architect who is registered in the United States, if the technical submissions have been reviewed by the architect and incorporated into his work or if they are prototypical building documents

Documents and work not required by law to be prepared by an architect may be signed and sealed by another architect if they are thoroughly reviewed and integrated with the architect's submission.

Special provisions exist when work is done by a person who is under the architect's responsible control but is not regularly employed in the architect's office. Such a case is described in this problem. The temporary employee is working under the direction and supervision of the architect to provide drafting services necessary to prepare drawings. The drafter is presumably working from sketches and design information prepared by the architect, and the drafter's work will be thoroughly reviewed and incorporated into the construction documents by the architect of record. The architect remains responsible for the design and the accuracy of the technical submission. This is permissible according to the NCARB *Rules of Conduct*; however, it is necessary for the architect of record or the firm to retain documentation of the drafter's involvement with the project and the architect's supervision of that work for five years.

The NCARB *Rules of Conduct* were developed to serve as recommendations for state licensing boards, but each state is responsible for developing its own standards of professional conduct. These requirements may differ from state to state or from NCARB's *Rules of Conduct*. However, for the Architect Registration Exam (ARE), candidates should be familiar with NCARB's standards. A copy of these standards may be downloaded from NCARB's website at ncarb.org.

The answer is (C).

2. Both corporations and limited liability companies limit individual liability to the amount invested. A limited liability partnership, like a limited liability company, also limits liability to a person's investment.

A traditional partnership exposes each partner to liability for the actions of the other partners. The partners' personal assets can be seized to pay judgments against the firm.

Disadvantaged business enterprises, like minority- or women-owned business enterprises, are small businesses certified by some states in order to encourage more participation from these groups in government-funded projects.

A joint venture is a temporary arrangement between two firms for the purpose of a specific project. The parties each retain their own organizational structures and the investors' liability is not changed.

The answer is (B), (D), and (E).

3. To prove negligence, three elements must be present.

- *duty:* One entity is legally obligated to another to provide something as a result of a written or oral agreement.
- *breach:* One entity did not provide what they were legally obligated to provide.
- *damage:* There must be actual harm caused as a result of the breach.

Negligence claims can be brought about from errors of omission on the part of the architect.

The answer is (B), (E), and (F).

4. The architect's specification defines the product desired, but the inclusion of the phrase "or approved equal" allows the contractor to propose a different type of tile that may be less expensive or easier to obtain within the project time frame. The contractor must submit any requests for substitutions prior to the bid. The responsibility for researching alternative products falls to the contractor, who must submit technical data with the request. Enough time must be allowed prior to the bid for the architect to review the substitution and issue an addendum notifying all potential bidders of the change.

The answer is (B).

5. A conflict of interest that is not properly disclosed to a client or employer is considered by the NCARB *Rules of Conduct* to be a violation that may bring about disciplinary action or revocation of an architect's license by a state licensing board. Each state's board has the responsibility of determining professional standards of conduct for architects, and these standards may differ from state to state or from NCARB's recommendations.

Option (B), option (C), and option (D) are not violations of the NCARB *Rules of Conduct*. In fact, Rule 3 states: "Full

Disclosure requires architects who make public statements about projects or issues to reveal if they are working for one of the interested parties or if they have a financial stake in the issue." In option (B), the architect properly disclosed his or her affiliation with the project developer. Option (C) falls under NCARB Rule 5: Professional Conduct. Rule 5.3 prohibits improper gifts to clients or potential clients; however, gifts of nominal value, such as reasonable entertainment and hospitality, are excluded. In option (D), advertising is not prohibited under the *Rules of Conduct* as long as the architect does not make false or misleading statements.

The answer is (A).

6. The architect automatically has a copyright on the work as soon as it is produced in a tangible form. U.S. Copyright Office Circular 41: *Copyright Claims in Architectural Works* explains that the work "includes the overall form as well as the arrangement and composition of spaces and elements in the design but does not include individual standard features or design elements that are functionally required."

The copyright for the architectural work itself (the building design) is separate from the copyright on the technical drawings.

To enforce the copyright to the fullest extent, it is recommended, but not required, that the © symbol and date be placed on the drawings and a claim to copyright be registered with the U.S. Copyright Office.

For more information on copyright and architectural works, refer to Circular 41, available from the U.S. Copyright Office's website at copyright.gov.

The answer is (D).

7. Instructions for installation are found in Part III, Execution, of the project specifications. This section describes how materials are to be prepared prior to installation, how substrates are to be prepared to accept the material, the methods for quality control, and requirements for cleaning and protecting the product after it is installed.

Part I, General, describes the submittals and warranties required for that product, project conditions, delivery, storage and handling requirements, and quality assurance requirements.

Part II, Products, includes information on the product, acceptable manufacturers, applicable standards and test methods, and technical requirements.

Division 01, General Requirements, includes requirements that apply to all specification sections. It explains the administrative procedures that will be used throughout the course of the project and gives the contractor instructions regarding issues such as temporary facilities and controls, submittals, items furnished by the owner, quality control, and final cleaning and protection of the work.

The answer is (C).

8. The most appropriate way to modify an AIA document is to attach supplementary conditions. AIA Document A503, *Guide for Supplementary Conditions*, suggests standard language for changes to the general conditions. The owner's attorney, not the architect, should write these conditions or any modifications if the document is an agreement between the owner and the contractor.

It is acceptable to strike out portions of the standard form of agreement or to add handwritten text, but only if all handwritten changes are initialed by the party to be bound. If handwritten modifications are made to the contract, the modifications may not render the original text illegible.

Retyping standard documents is a violation of copyright. In addition, one of the strengths of the AIA documents is that contractors are already familiar with the standard forms, and by reading the modifications they can understand quickly the unique requirements of a particular project. If the format and language of the document is revised, the contractor may determine it necessary to add fees to its bid to cover perceived risk.

Owners are not required to use AIA documents for construction contracts, and they have the right to have an attorney draft a new contract. However, an attorney who doesn't specialize in construction law may not understand conventional practices of the industry. Bids may be higher because contractors cannot rely on the "ground rules" they have come to expect. Architects should be extremely careful with contracts that are not based on the AIA documents because they may require the architect to fulfill a role or accept responsibility that is not traditionally required, and for which the architect may not be insured. The architect's insurance carrier and/or attorney should always review owner-drafted contracts.

The answer is (B).

9. Claims-made professional liability insurance policies require the policy to be in effect both at the time that the incident occurs and at the time that the claim is actually made. If a claim is made on a project that was completed a number of years earlier, the claim will only be covered if the architect is still insured under the same policy he or she held at the time services were rendered. This means that the architect cannot allow the policy to lapse, or past projects may not be covered. If a firm wishes to change insurance carriers and previously held a claims-made policy, the firm should investigate the purchase of prior acts policies to ensure that their previous work is adequately covered.

Accident- or occurrence-type policies will cover claims that are made for incidents that occurred when the policy was in effect, regardless of whether the policy is in effect at the time that the claim is made.

The answer is (B).

10. Most construction projects are bid as stipulated sum agreements; the contractor agrees to provide the work illustrated in the contract documents for a certain amount of money in a certain period of time, and the owner agrees to pay the contractor the specified amount. If it actually costs more to build the project, the contractor has to absorb the loss. If it costs less, the contractor gets to keep the extra money. The benefit to this type of contract is that all of the participants in the project know what the cost will be from the beginning.

However, owners may elect to use a cost-plus-fee contract for a number of reasons: If they have a hard and fast deadline that they must meet, if the scope of the work is unknown at the start of construction, or if the highest quality of construction is of critical importance, than cost-plus-fee structures are often to the owner's benefit.

A cost-plus agreement with a fee for overhead and profit based upon a percentage of construction cost does little to motivate the contractor to be efficient. As the contractor sees it, the more time and money it takes to build the project, the greater the contractor's payment for overhead and profit. If the contractor builds a project quickly and realizes savings for the owner, the contractor does not get a cut of those savings.

However, a cost-plus agreement with a fixed fee for overhead and profit can encourage a contractor to be more efficient. It is particularly motivating if the owner offers a bonus for expeditious completion of the work. If the contractor can reduce costs to the owner and build the project quickly, the contractor still receives the fixed amount of overhead and profit. The contractor may incur fewer administrative costs and, therefore, a larger share of the amount allocated for overhead becomes profit.

Unit prices are often a part of a contract when the exact amount of work cannot be determined at the time of contract negotiations. The contractor agrees to provide a given quantity of material for a certain price; that unit price is then multiplied by the actual amount incorporated into the project.

The answer is (A).

11. Vicarious liability is indirect liability imposed on a party resulting from the acts or omissions of another person for whom the party is responsible. Architects can encounter this situation when they hire consultants; the architect is liable for any errors or omissions on the consultant's documents. A firm may be held liable for the actions of its employees while performing tasks related to their employment, whether it be an error in a specification or drawing, or a traffic accident caused by the employee talking on a cell phone while en route to a job site.

In addition, a firm could be held liable for the actions of a moonlighting employee if that employee gives the client the impression that the firm is involved with the work (such as if the employee uses a firm title block on a drawing or sends a fax with a company cover sheet). To protect themselves from claims against their liability insurance policies, many firms have instituted "no moonlighting" policies or require prior approval from a supervisor.

The answer is (B).

12. American Institute of Architects (AIA) Document A201, *General Conditions of the Contract for Construction*, Sec. 11.3, requires the owner to purchase and maintain builder's all-risk or equivalent insurance.

Unlike insurance policies that cover only losses and damages due to causes specifically named in the policy, an all-risk insurance policy covers all losses and damages except those specifically excluded in the policy. Though all-risk policies are not all the same, most of them do not exclude losses due to

- fire
- vandalism, malicious mischief, or riot
- explosions from all causes
- water damage
- testing and start-up
- mechanical or electrical breakdown
- theft
- collapse
- earthquakes, floods, or windstorms
- falsework
- temporary buildings
- debris removal, including demolition occasioned by enforcement of any applicable legal requirements

Some common exclusions are

- acts of war
- terrorism (although acts of terrorism that meet certain criteria are not excluded based upon the Terrorism Risk Insurance Act of 2002)
- nuclear hazards
- fraud by the insured

- employee theft
- inventory shortage or mysterious disappearance
- mold
- asbestos

The answer is (B), (D), (E), and (F).

13. Simply supplying the missing information is risky without coordinating the information from the original plans of the magazine. It also may be seen as a violation of copyright law. Developing a completely new set of drawings also violates copyright law as a design itself is protected by the Architectural Works Copyright Protection Act. Suggesting that an unlicensed intern complete the job is in violation of the NCARB *Rules of Conduct*. An architect must comply with the registration laws and regulations governing the architect's professional practice, which, in this case, require a licensed architect.

The requirements of the NCARB *Rules of Conduct* are explicit regarding the need to obtain proper permissions and honor copyright, and both may be difficult to do in a situation such as this. The cost of the time and legwork it will take to "cover all the bases" and the potential risk and liability that this project may bring with it may be enough for the architect to decide to reject it.

The answer is (C).

14. An architect is not qualified to give a client advice regarding bonds and insurance. However, since architects often have more experience with construction than owners, clients often ask architects for assistance with these requirements. Architects can consult AIA Document G612 and provide a worksheet for defining the owner's requirements; however, the final advice regarding insurance should come from the agent, and it should be based on the agent's professional knowledge, not the architect's.

The answer is (C).

15. Project records should be kept until the end of the statute of repose period. The American Institute of Architects (AIA) *Best Practices* advise keeping them for one year past the longest applicable date and then destroying them. Exceptions to the guideline include projects with design or financial problems or projects in which new types of construction were employed. Some firms choose to archive these projects indefinitely to permit easy access to the records necessary to construct a defense in a potential lawsuit.

Archived project records should include

- contracts, correspondence related to those contracts, and any modifications, such as addenda, change orders, and construction change directives
- design criteria as approved by the owner
- research findings, calculations, and other evidence of due diligence on the part of the architect and consultants
- records of telephone conversations, meeting minutes, and other project correspondence
- copies of the drawings and specifications
- submittal logs, site visit reports, and correspondence with the contractor, such as requests for information
- closeout documentation

The answer is (B).

16. The design-build approach to project delivery allows an owner to contract with one entity who agrees to provide both design and construction services. This entity can be a construction company with in-house designers, an architect and a contractor approaching the project as a team, or a construction manager who subcontracts both design and construction. As a result of skipping the bidding phase, the overall time required for the project is shortened. With only one entity to deal with, contract administration is simplified. The owner also has more accurate cost information available early in the process.

In exchange for speed and simplicity, however, the owner often sacrifices control over the design and the materials and methods of construction. This approach requires that the owner have a well-defined program or list of criteria that the project must fulfill, as well as great confidence that the designer/builder will give a fair deal because eliminating bidding eliminates the opportunity for the owner to compare prices. An extended type of owner-supplied performance requirements uses the bridging approach, but bridging is not a characteristic of the design-build approach.

The design-build approach tends to work best for owners with previous construction project experience and very clearly defined needs.

The answer is (B), (C), (D), and (E).

17. An addendum is a written or graphic document issued by the architect prior to submission of contractors' bids that modifies or interprets the bidding documents. Addenda may be issued in response to errors discovered in the bidding documents, changes the client wants to make, questions from bidders, or additions or deletions needed. Addenda must be sent to all bidders at least four days prior to the bid date. Most bid forms ask bidders to acknowledge receipt of any addenda to help ensure that all bids are based on the same information.

The answer is (A).

18. The fast-track method helps keep costs down and is appropriate for a client who must move to a new facility as soon as possible. In this situation, it is likely that the owner is familiar with the construction process, knows what is needed in this particular building, and is comfortable with allowing some construction to proceed before the design is finalized. A disadvantage to the fast-track method of construction delivery is that the final cost of the work is often undetermined at the start of construction. However, with a flexible line of credit, a fixed price up front is not as important as with some other methods of financing.

The answer is (B).

19. Project relationships between owners, architects, and contractors may be based on the idea of partnering. Partnering is not a contractual relationship, but is an agreement between the parties to work together toward the common goal of constructing a building. The concept is based on eliminating the adversarial relationship that may develop between project participants. The partnering agreement is a commitment to one another to work together and respect the knowledge each party brings to the project. Potentially, it can result in a lower cost to the owner, a shorter construction period, and less paperwork for everyone, and it may reduce the number of project disputes.

A partnering agreement may or may not be a written document. American Institute of Architects (AIA) *Best Practices* recommends using a partnering charter, developed during a workshop facilitated by someone not involved with the project in which all team members participate, that outlines the responsibilities and goals of the team. Or, the agreement can be as simple as a discussion over lunch or a handshake on the golf course between companies with a long history of working together.

The American Arbitration Association established a task force to study partnering in 1995. The conclusions reached by the committee provide a good explanation of partnering. A link to these conclusions may be found at **ppi2pass.com/AREresources.**

The answer is (A), (C), and (D).

20. Bridging is a specific approach to the design-build model of project delivery that allows an owner to secure an early fixed price and take advantage of the contractor's knowledge of construction methods and materials and relationships with suppliers. Bridging allows an owner to establish which things he or she wants to control, gives responsibility for details of construction to the contractor, and permits the owner to obtain the advice and participation of an architect.

The primary advantages of bridging are that

- a contract price can be obtained more quickly and with a lower up-front cost than with a design-bid-build approach
- the contractor bears sole responsibility for the product of construction with the benefit of an architect's involvement
- it is more cost effective

The project is defined by an architect and/or project manager, sometimes called the "criteria architect" or "bridging consultant," who prepares drawings similar to the traditional product of the design development phase. These are referred to as the contract documents. The consultant obtains bids from prequalified design-build contractors, and the contract is awarded to the low bidder. Then, the design-build contractor develops the construction documents and is the architect of record for the project. The owner's architect/project manager reviews the construction documents to determine conformance with the original contract documents.

The contractor then builds the facility. The architect/project manager administers the contract for construction. The construction documents are used for construction and permitting, but the contract between the owner and contractor is based on the contract documents.

A link to an essay explaining bridging may be found at **ppi2pass.com/AREresources.**

The answer is (B).

21. CMc is a project delivery approach that employs a construction manager to oversee the project; this method is often used for fast-track construction, where the design and construction phases may overlap.

The architect is hired by the owner and begins the project. The construction manager is hired by the owner during the design phase and advises the owner on issues of scheduling, constructability, and cost. At some point, the construction manager usually offers the owner a guaranteed maximum price and, if the price is accepted, becomes the general contractor. The construction manager takes on the risk of performance. The construction manager may then subcontract the work to other contractors to complete construction.

A link to an essay on the CMc method of project delivery can be found at **ppi2pass.com/AREresources.**

The answer is (A), (C), (D), and (F).

22. The primary advantage to the fast-track method of project delivery is the ability to overlap the design and construction phases to complete a project more quickly. This method can be used in cases where an owner must occupy a new facility within a certain period of time or when other costs are rising rapidly, such as labor rates, material costs, or interest rates. Fast-tracking a project usually involves hiring a design-build firm or breaking the project into several prime contracts and awarding them sequentially as construction progresses.

The American Institute of Architects (AIA)/American General Contractors Association publication *Primer on Project Delivery* addresses methods of providing design and construction services. Links to it and an essay on project delivery strategy can be found at **ppi2pass.com/AREresources**.

The answer is (C).

23. Joint ventures are agreements between two firms collaborating on a specific project. For example, a national firm that specializes in stadium design may enter into a joint venture with a local firm for a project on a college campus. Two small firms may form a joint venture to pursue a project that is larger than either firm could handle alone.

A joint venture is a partnership and, as a business entity, functions like any other type of partnership. Any profits are passed along to the partners, as are the tax liabilities. The parties involved in the joint venture must determine how to handle insurance; each firm may be covered by their respective liability insurance policy, or they may purchase a project-specific policy for this venture.

AIA Document C101 may be used to establish the terms of the relationship.

The answer is (A), (B), (D), and (E).

24. Of the options given, trying to utilize existing employees will make the most sense from the standpoint of personnel and office management.

Hiring new employees is shortsighted unless their long-term need is assured. Having people work overtime is generally not an efficient or productive approach in the long run and should not be used to complete an entire project. The client should not have to reduce the scope of the project just to accommodate the lack of staffing in the architect's office. The architect may be justified in asking for a change to the owner-architect agreement if the original project parameters are changed by the client.

The answer is (C).

25. American Institute of Architects (AIA) Document B101, *Standard Owner and Architect Agreement*, Article 7, addresses issues related to the instruments of service. The instruments of service include sketches, drawings, models, specifications, CAD files, and any other deliverables that help move a project from an idea to a real building.

Section 7.3 grants the owner a nonexclusive license to the instruments of service for the purposes of constructing the project, which means that the owner may reproduce the documents as necessary to facilitate construction. If the agreement is terminated, the license is terminated and the architect retains ownership of the documents. If the architect is judged to be in default by a court or arbitration board, the owner is given a new, nonexclusive right to copy the documents and may use them to complete the project with the assistance of another architect.

Section 7.4 states that the owner may not assign his or her license to any other party without the architect's consent.

The answer is (C).

26. The MacLeamy curve compares project effort (staff time) versus influence (impact) and cost for two delivery methods: IPD and design-bid-build. From the curve, the IPD method front-loads the effort into the project's early phases. The greatest effort occurs during the design development phase. The architect should schedule more resources for the detailed design phase than for other phases.

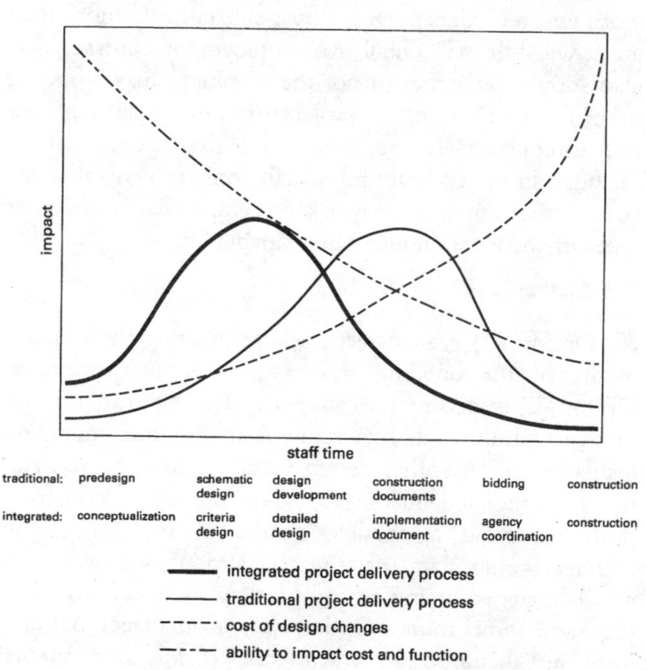

The answer is (B).

27. A teaming agreement (i.e., a memorandum of understanding) is an agreement between two or more firms that, prior to bidding on work, sets forth the roles, responsibilities, costs, and any other terms of agreement that the firms will accept. It forms the basis for a joint venture agreement or a prime consultant agreement, which will be put into place after the project is awarded. A teaming agreement does not indicate a formal business partnership or organization, only the terms that the firms agree on, should the job move forward.

The answer is (D).

28. Each aspiring architect is required to have a supervisor who is a licensed professional architect, possess an NCARB record, work in required experience categories and areas, and submit reporting online to NCARB. Interactive online activities are types of supplemental experience. State coordinators are volunteers who provide emerging professionals with information about AXP and about the licensing process, among other activities. While state coordinators serve an important function, they are not a required part of an aspiring architect's journey to licensure.

The answer is (A), (B), (C), and (E).

29. Employment at will means that there is no written contract and employees can be terminated at any time without explanation. An employment contract documents the terms of employment and may include valid reasons for termination. While developing contracts entails paperwork and recordkeeping, it is not substantially more than an at-will hire will entail. An employment contract may also stipulate whether or not the employee may work for other firms or on outside projects (i.e., moonlighting), but not all contracts restrict this. A job description may be included in the contract but usually only in general terms so that the employer may ask the employee to do other types of work within his or her capabilities.

The answer is (B).

30. Option (A) is incorrect because meeting the requirements of the building code is not enough evidence. Option (B) is incorrect because although the local jurisdiction can modify code requirements at any time, upgrading insulation or any other design feature cannot be retroactive to completed buildings or buildings under construction. To avoid a possible charge of negligence, the architect could state that the standard of care was met, which included acting as any prudent architect would in the same time frame. Option (D) is incorrect because local jurisdictions can amend the codes that modify requirements of any of the International series of codes.

The architect should justify that at the time of drafting, the design met the firm's standard detailing practices.

The answer is (C).

31. The concept of the standard of care does not apply in this situation because a prudent architect working under the same circumstances would not have made the mistake, so option (A) is incorrect. Although the client should approve the plans, the client is not responsible for a thorough and complete check of every detail, so option (B) is incorrect. Errors and omissions insurance covers only the cost to correct the mistake, so option (C) is incorrect.

The architect clearly made a mistake of omission, failing to include an important detail on the drawings. However, the architect can claim the concept of betterment in order to minimize the consequence of having to pay the full amount of the change order. The architect can claim that the vinyl wall fabric is a betterment to the project and the owner will have to pay for it anyway. Therefore, the architect should have to pay for only the additional charges caused by the change order and the charges that are above the original cost of labor and materials (e.g., charges related to the removal of paint to prepare the surface for the wall covering, and charges associated with calling back the workers to redo the three rooms).

The answer is (D).

32. Of the options listed, only three are accounting methods used by architectural firms. Accrual-basis accounting is required for corporations and other types of business organizations. An accrual method keeps track of revenue and expenses at the time they are incurred, not necessarily when money comes in or when a bill is paid. It offers a superior way to manage the finances of a firm and develop the various financial reports used by management. Double-entry accounting, or double-entry bookkeeping, keeps track of transactions with the accrual method.

The cash-basis accounting method is used by sole proprietors or very small businesses, but not with architectural firms. With the cash-basis accounting method, revenue and expenses are recognized at the time the transaction is made (e.g., revenue and expenses may be tracked with a basic checking account).

Typically used by architectural firms, the modified accrual-basis method combines accrual-basis accounting with cash-basis accounting. It includes consultant fees and expenses, plus all other direct and indirect expenses incurred, so that accurate profit and loss statements and balance sheets can be generated (as with accrual-basis accounting). Furthermore, revenues are recognized when they become available, and expenses are recognized when liabilities are incurred (as with cash-basis accounting).

The answer is (D).

33. An hourly not-to-exceed fee is not appropriate because an inexperienced client's indecisions and changes may cause the architect to go beyond the not-to-exceed amount. If the architect has built in a sufficient contingency, the maximum amount may exceed the client's comfort level. A percentage of construction cost is incorrect because the client may think the architect is increasing the construction cost to increase the fee, and the architect may not get paid an appropriate rate (i.e., the time and effort required for a project with a low construction cost may be as much as the effort required for a facility with a higher construction cost). A square-foot cost is risky for the architect because to arrive at fair compensation it requires accurate historical pricing information for facilities of this type, and it does not account for work resulting from changes that the client may require during the design process.

With a cost-plus-fee method, the architect's compensation includes actual work expenses (i.e., cost) plus a reasonable fee for profit (i.e., fee). Using this method, the actual costs will be covered regardless of what the inexperienced client wants and any inefficiency that might occur during design. The fee for profit is set in the fee proposal to match the perceived value of the service, helping the architect to know what kind of profit to expect. A cost-plus-fee method provides a fair compromise between the client and the architect.

The answer is (A).

34. The overhead rate should be in the range of 1.3–1.5. Overhead can be reduced most by decreasing non-billable time. Every hour that can be legitimately charged to a project should be, and the number of non-billable employees should be kept to a minimum. Beyond this, all related expenses should be charged to a job so that administrative personnel, project managers, or whoever is responsible can monitor these costs as well. Fee collection is important for cash flow but does not reduce overhead. A review of telecommunication charges can be made, but any decrease will be fairly insignificant compared to other actions. Since the cost of office space is an ongoing overhead burden, the architect should consider the feasibility of moving to a less expensive office space or one with a lower lease rate, or both. An increase in revenue per technical staff is useful for profitability but does nothing to reduce overhead.

The answer is (A), (B), and (E).

35. A balance sheet summarizes the assets and liabilities of the firm, along with its net worth. A net profit before tax report shows the percentage of profit based on net revenue, not counting consulting fees and reimbursable expenses. An office earnings report focuses more on individual jobs, not on the office's overall financial performance. The profit and loss statement shows all the income and expenses for a period of time, typically monthly or yearly, and gives an overall view of the profit made or the loss sustained.

The answer is (D).

36. An office earnings report shows, among other things, the percentage complete on a project at any given time and how many fees have been expended compared with the original schedule and fee projection. The office manager should first analyze whether the appropriate people are assigned to the projects. It may be that less experienced staff members are taking longer to do the work than the staff members with more experience. It is necessary to do this type of analysis prior to telling the project managers to increase productivity. The billed and unbilled expenses have nothing to do with the lagging schedule. Overtime may be required to bring the project up to schedule, but it only makes sense after the appropriate personnel are assigned to the jobs.

The answer is (A).

37. Neither the architect nor the subcontractor is required to carry insurance for fire loss. The contractor is required to carry insurance that is related to worker injury and damages, not to the work itself. The owner is required to carry insurance that covers loss due to fire, theft, vandalism, collapse, floods, and the like. This insurance should be of the "all risk" type. Neither the architect nor the subcontractors are required to carry insurance for fire loss.

The answer is (C).

38. It is premature to hire an experienced professional in the historic preservation market until some solid leads are developed or an actual commission obtained. It is also too early to develop a website page devoted to services related to the historic preservation market (i.e., architectural history, restoration, or historic interior design.) because the firm has no experience in it. Social media networking is an important ongoing task that should be initiated only after the firm has researched the desired market.

The firm should first learn as much about the market as it can by researching the size and scope of the market, the trade organizations associated with it, the key people in the organizations, local affiliates, the construction and design needs, and similar information. Then, the principal manager or marketing manager can begin to gain personal contacts, including connections made through social media networking, and add to the firm's list of potential clients, consultants, and contractors.

The answer is (D).

39. Although an outside firm can be used to check drawings, an architectural firm should try to do all checking in-house. Many larger firms have an experienced architect who has not worked on the project check the drawings with a fresh eye. Any questions can then be directed to the project team. The CSI does not have drawings checklists. Exchanging drawings, whether in paper or digital form, with consultants is a good way to encourage communication and coordination. UDS is an industry standard that is used in support of acting as any prudent architect does as part of the standard of care. Applying standard details is an excellent way to maintain quality while saving time in document production. Finally, if a single competent person is responsible for managing production, coordination, and checking among the project team, there is less of a chance for errors and omissions.

The answer is (B), (D), (E), and (F).

40. Agency is the concept that one person acts on behalf of another, as the architect does for the client. Duty is a concept in law whereby one person "owes" something to another. Duty can be established by a contract, by legislative enactment, and by conduct. Because there is no contract between the architect and subcontractors, the architect is theoretically protected from claims by the subcontractor. This concept is expressed in American Institute of Architects (AIA) Document A201, *General Conditions of the Contract for Construction*, in an indemnification clause that holds harmless either the owner or architect from claims made by anyone with whom the architect has no contractual relationship. Privity is a legal concept that means that two parties to a contract or other transaction have a connection or mutual interest. A lack of privity protects an architect against claims made by a subcontractor.

The answer is (D).

41. Although all the options are reasonable actions that a firm could take to design sustainable projects, the best way to improve expertise is to have all architects become LEED Accredited Professionals. Doing so will not only improve the architects' knowledge but will also lend credibility to the office in the eyes of potential clients. Using IgCC is a good way to design projects but does not necessarily increase expertise. Moreover, depending on the jurisdiction, the use of the code may be required anyway. The AIA documents for sustainable design projects require a process for design but they do not, in themselves, improve the expertise of the office. The Greenguard Certification Program is a part of the Underwriters Laboratories' (UL) program, UL Environment, and is mainly used for chemical emissions of products.

The answer is (C).

42. In this scenario, there are two "red flag" indications that the project could pose problems for the architect and should not be accepted. The first red flag is the funding. Although the funding is nearly complete, it is often difficult for small, nonprofit organizations to raise the money necessary for a building project. Second, a client may mean well by having a preconceived idea about design, but this usually indicates that the client may be difficult to work with if the architect finds obvious problems with the client's ideas.

The answer is (A).

43. Option (A) is not an ideal choice because the client's selected contractor may already work with one or more preferred architects, or have an in-house architectural staff. Option (B) is incorrect because the design-build method is probably ideal for this project and suggesting otherwise is in the architect's self-interest only. Option (D) is incorrect because the architect has not been hired to do any work and helping with the selection of a design-build firm does not guarantee being hired, as the design-build firm may already have its own architect.

A variation of the design-build method of project delivery is bridging, whereby an architect assists the client to prepare project requirements that the design-build firm uses to prepare a cost document and detailed construction document. The project requirements can be used for bidding by design-build firms or for a negotiated selection of a design-build firm. In a standard design-build project, the client is solely responsible for preparing the owner's criteria along with other responsibilities that many clients are not qualified to do. By serving as the client's consultant, the architect retains design involvement with the project and fee income, even though fees that are normally realized with construction documentation and contract administration are not earned.

The answer is (C).

44. There should not be any extra fee when the architect normally charges for coordination with consultants or when the architect builds it into the base fee. The consultants are probably competent or the client will not want to use them again. The architect should not give up the chance for this commission. If the client has used the consultants before, the consultants are unlikely to pose a risk.

Because the architect may not be familiar with or has not worked with the consultants before, there are potential difficulties with the forced working relationship. The architect might be more comfortable if the owner is responsible for payment. If the client has worked with the consultants before, they probably have a good relationship and the client should be comfortable with entering into agreements with them and paying them directly.

The answer is (D).

45. The expenses and profits can be assigned in the joint venture agreement, whether it is a standard AIA document or one drawn up by the partners. AIA Document

C101, *Joint Venture Agreement for Professional Services,* is specifically intended to be used by two or more parties to provide mutual rights and responsibilities in a joint venture. In this document, there are two choices concerning the joint venture operation: the division of compensation method and the division of profit and loss method. A joint venture can work with the construction manager as constructor method of project delivery.

Legally, each joint venture partner is responsible for the actions of the other partner or partners. Because of this risk, each partner must have an outstanding relationship with the others.

The answer is (A).

46. There are two major issues that the architectural firm needs to analyze, along with a third that will affect the decision. The first two are values and finances. The firm may not want to accept a job in which it cannot apply its skills and expertise along with its own values of sustainability. All other factors being equal, the firm should probably turn down the job. However, if the firm needs the work, this should certainly be reviewed with hard numbers from a cash flow analysis. It may be that the firm has enough cash on hand and expected income to maintain the office until other work is obtained, in which case the firm can also refuse the job. If the firm really needs the work, it can accept the project and view it as a stopgap measure until better projects arise. The third factor to consider is the financial situation of both the developer and the project. If this is a speculative office building, the market may not be strong enough to support it. Likewise, the developer may have a history of poor payments to architects and be financially unstable. These issues should certainly be researched. If the project is financially unfeasible, the first two issues become moot.

It is unlikely that the architect will persuade the developer to invest any more money than necessary for sustainable design in a speculative building. The project delivery method and contract type are of secondary importance until the primary decision is made about accepting the job. Likewise, the question of fees is discussed after the primary decision is made.

The answer is (C), (D), and (E).

47. If there is sufficient work, everyone will remain employed even if the risky project fails. Likewise, this is only one project and unless there are other mitigating circumstances, the staff will remain. Architects are professionals and should make their best efforts on any project.

Morale will probably stay about the same. Employees may feel that the office is taking the risk, not the employees themselves.

The answer is (B).

48. Option (A) is incorrect because the architect may receive profit if either the actual cost is below the target cost or if the project goals are met. Option (B) is incorrect because there are no bonuses as such in the agreement. Option (D) is incorrect because monetary rewards are not based on an agreed upon percentage of actual costs.

When the IPD method is used with a multi-party agreement—as with a single purpose entity agreement—the target cost is the estimate of all costs that the architect and contractor may incur while planning, designing, constructing, and commissioning the project. The target cost is established at the conclusion of the criteria design phase. If the final cost, which is called the actual cost in the agreement, as delivered by the architect and contractor is below the target cost, any savings is shared in accordance with the terms of the agreement (i.e., American Institute of Architects (AIA) Document C191, *Standard Form Multi-Party Agreement for Integrated Project Delivery*). Similarly, if the actual cost is above the target cost, the architect and contractor receive only the basic cost to provide their services with no profit. In addition to profit being tied to the target cost, if the architect and contractor meet specific project goals, the parties agree that when the target cost is established, they are entitled to receive additional compensation as set forth in the agreement.

The answer is (C).

49. Ownership participation will be potentially lucrative for the architect, both in monthly income from rent and from real estate appreciation. However, any development project must be approached with caution, including completing a pro forma and studying the market. A pro forma, a financial projection for a development project that includes the cost of developing the project and expected income, is used to determine if a project is feasible. The architect should complete the pro forma first to see how potential income and profit will compare to a standard architectural fee, and then the architect should research the market and the developer. If the architect is a cautious person, the architect should decline the offer immediately; however, doing so will forego any potential reward of ownership participation. Though the architect will need to investigate how much cash is on hand or if the firm will be able to borrow money to sustain the firm until income is realized, this is a secondary step after analyzing the project's feasibility.

The answer is (A).

50. With a general partnership, each of the three partners is liable for the actions of the others. With a limited partnership, the architects probably will be general partners and will be financially responsible. They are able to have limited partners who invest in the company but those partners have no say in its management. A corporation is more difficult to set up and manage, and it is taxed at two levels: the corporation itself and individual shareholders.

Although any of the four types of business organizations can be used, the limited liability partnership is easier to set up and manage than a corporation, and it limits the members' liability to just their investment. In a limited liability partnership, the partners have no personal liability.

The answer is (C).

51. A straightforward studio organization requires studios with experienced staff capable of working on any project and completing all the phases required. A studio organization is not the most cost-effective or efficient type of organization given the objectives. A strict departmental organization is more appropriate for larger firms and requires specialists in all departments to make it efficient. There may not be enough work related to any of the three building types to keep any one studio busy, let alone three. The studios have to be generalist studios in order to allow staff to move from one building type to another.

To be the most efficient in a limited number of building types, an office should employ a few experienced architects with specialized knowledge of the building types. These specialists can design the projects in response to the unique requirements of the program and then have the work move through departments such as drawing production, specifications, and contract administration. This type of project design suggests a departmental organization with design specialists. The firm can market these specialties and develop efficient methods for completing the projects using less experienced staff.

The answer is (D).

52. Although a sole proprietorship is easy to set up and maintain, its main disadvantage is that the owner is personally responsible for all debts and losses of the company, which is risky for an architectural firm. A limited partnership is probably not appropriate for a very small firm and is not an option if the firm consists of one person only. A professional corporation is not an appropriate choice because it takes more effort to set up and maintain and taxes are levied on both the corporation and the individuals within it.

An LLC can comprise one or more members who are protected from personal liability for business decisions or actions of the LLC. An LLC is easier to establish and maintain than a corporation, and taxes are passed on to the members just as with a sole proprietorship or a partnership. These features make an LLC ideal for a small firm with a single architect or a few people.

The answer is (C).

53. Unlike a studio structure, a departmental organization does not give the aspiring architects a comprehensive view of the process of taking a project from inception to completion. A class is unreasonable, because the whole point of work experience is to gain a range of active experiences rather than sit passively in a class. In addition, a class does not meet the requirements of NCARB. Assigning one member of the firm to each experience category breaks up the continuity of having a single mentor for each aspiring architect.

A studio organization exposes each aspiring architect to different tasks, such as design, programming, construction documentation, and on-site administration. A studio organization satisfies the experience hours in different categories required by NCARB. The mentors also serve as the AXP supervisors.

The answer is (A).

54. Under American Institute of Architects (AIA) Document B101, *Standard Form of Agreement Between Owner and Architect*, the owner is responsible for providing both land surveys and the services of a geotechnical engineer. The architect may assist the owner with procuring these services, which is usually necessary to explain what type of information is needed. For example, AIA Document G601, *Request for Proposal—Land Survey*, and AIA Document G602, *Request for Proposal—Geotechnical Services*, can be used.

The answer is (C).

55. Option (A) is not necessary and will most likely be opposed by both the consultants and the owner, who will have a separate agreement with the consultants. Option (C) and option (D) are just two of many ways to facilitate communication.

Communication is all-important when working with consultants, especially when working with unfamiliar consultants.

The answer is (B).

56. Unless the office is very small, the firm principals should not be responsible for checking drawings; this duty should be passed on to others in the firm. Even though the project manager plays an important role in quality control, the project manager's job should focus more on coordination and ensuring that all information is passed between those on the design and production team, including consultants. Although hiring an outside firm to check the final drawings can be useful, it adds expense to the job and takes more time. The firm should try to solve quality control problems in-house first because only the firm understands the nature of its projects.

In addition to using standard details, using a construction document checklist is one of the best ways to record the "corporate memory" of the firm and ensure that past mistakes are not repeated. Checklists are valuable for both experienced staff members and those new to the firm.

The answer is (D).

57. The Wages and Fair Labor Standards Act establishes minimum wage, overtime, pay, recordkeeping, and child labor standards. The National Labor Relations Act allows private sector employees to organize into trade unions and protects union employees from unfair labor practices. NCARB's AXP guidelines require that supervisors certify experience reports, act as a mentor, and discuss the aspiring architect's progress. The AXP does not require performance evaluations, which are for all members of a firm's staff, not just aspiring architects. Only a company's internal policies may require a performance evaluation.

The answer is (D).

58. Members may supplant or replace another architect on a project if the previous architect is not under contract with the client. Advertising is allowed as long as the architect does not make misleading or false statements. Architects may be involved with construction, such as with a design-build firm. One provision of the *Code of Ethics & Professional Conduct* Canon VI, Obligations to the Environment, states that members should advocate the design, construction, and operation of sustainable buildings.

The answer is (C).

59. Although legal action is sometimes necessary, it should be a last resort and, generally, the client should be given more than 45 days to make payment. Retainers may be requested of a client but an amount of 25% is excessive. The other actions are correct procedures for managing accounts receivable.

The answer is (B), (C), (D), and (F).

60. The current ratio is a measure of the firm's ability to meet current obligations. It is found by dividing total assets by total current liabilities. The quick ratio is a refinement of the current ratio. It is the sum of cash, accounts receivable, and revenue earned but not billed, divided by total current liabilities. Net profit before tax is the percentage of profit based on total annual revenue, minus reimbursable expenses and consultants' fees. New profit before tax cannot be used to estimate needed future income for solvency, but it may be used as a target goal for profitability. If the prior years' revenue per technical staff is available, that number can be multiplied by the planned number of technical staff members. The product approximately determines how much net operating revenue is required.

The answer is (D).

61. Agency is not necessary for on-site conduct. Negligence arises from a duty being established and that duty being breached and causing damage or injury. Privity refers to a connection between two parties to a contract. Although privity can insulate the architect from actions by the contractor, privity does not need to be included in an office manual. Architects operate under various kinds of the legal concept of duty. While on the job site, architects need to conduct themselves so as not to create less or more duty than reasonably established. Duty can be established in three ways: by contract, by legislative enactment, and by conduct. The first two are legally defined, but the architect's conduct on the job site can establish an implied duty, which needs to be included in an office manual. For example, the architect has an implied duty to cooperate with the contractor and share with the contractor any relevant information that could affect the project. A manual defines what is expected of the architect and what conduct to avoid, such as suggesting to the contractor how to build something.

The answer is (B).

62. The company does not accept the contract if the parties cannot agree on the method of measured productivity. Either the compensation article of a standard AIA agreement can be modified as necessary or an attorney can draft a new contract. The problem states the basis for productivity measurement will be mutually agreed, and the agreement will tie the compensation to a productivity increase regardless of where it might result.

The architect is risking any profit on productivity increases that may or may not happen, regardless of how confident the architect is in the effects of evidence-based design.

The answer is (C).

63. When setting the fees, if an accurate time estimate is made, the office multiplier is sufficient to complete the project with a profit, so option (D) is incorrect. Including a not-to-exceed amount in the agreement increases the risk because it sets an absolute limit on what the architect can charge, so option (E) is incorrect. The owner tries to limit costs. The architect wants to limit losses as much as possible, especially if problems arise during the project. The other options minimize risk.

The answer is (A), (B), (C), and (F).

64. The MacLeamy curve does not show or imply that a firm should hire more designers or outsource document production. It does not show how clients can use design-build construction. It does not favor a particular project organization. The MacLeamy curve shows how spending more time on schematic design and design development early in the process by all members of the project team (i.e., architects, owner, consultants, contractors, and others) can provide a greater ability to affect costs and the functional aspects of the building and actually shorten total project delivery time. The other options have nothing to do with the concept of the MacLeamy curve.

The answer is (A).

65. Reorganizing to a studio system does not necessarily result in shorter delivery times and may even lengthen delivery time. Problems are often given more holistic attention by a studio team than by several departments. Although communication usually improves, aspiring architects can still gain a variety of experience with a studio system by simply moving between studios and engaging in different types of work. A departmental organization is usually better at utilizing the talents and experiences of specialists in various phases of practice. Departments can be formed, rearranged, or dissolved as required to meet the changing needs of the office.

Within a studio organization, each project is completed with the staff in the studio, including design, production, and construction administration. Because everyone on the team is working nearby, ideas are introduced by people with different points of view, resulting in improved problem solving. When a firm organizes using a single lead designer, the result is often one style, influencing what can become known as a firm style. In a studio organization, because each studio has a different designer, the styles and approaches to projects vary, resulting in diverse designs.

The answer is (C).

66. In this case, the firm has been awarded the contract on the basis of being capable of doing the job. Joint ventures, while possible for most situations, are often proposed during marketing to potential clients if either partner does not have the ability to do the job alone. In this situation, the firm has many of the types of staff members to complete the projects, just not enough of them.

Hiring freelance consultants is also a possibility, though the firm will have to weigh the advantages and disadvantages of doing so. The freelancers may not be as committed as an employee or another consulting firm, and they may have conflicts with other jobs. There may be potential legal and tax issues in classifying the freelancers as independent contractors or employees.

A teaming agreement is a collaboration between two or more firms to market themselves for a project; it is not a formal business organization. After the contract is awarded, the firms then form a joint venture or a prime consultant agreement.

For this particular situation, the wisest course of action is to find another firm to serve as a consultant. The consultant firm will provide the necessary staff and skills to assist with the project, and the prime firm will be the architect of record and the main contact with the client. The two firms will agree to the roles and responsibilities of each, the methods of compensation, and all the other aspects of any consultant agreement. Using this approach will allow the firm to get the help needed from a known group of professionals with no commitment beyond the completion of the job.

The answer is (D).

67. The IRS uses three broad areas to determine if a worker is an employee or an independent contractor (i.e., a freelancer): behavioral control, financial control, and the relationship between the worker and employer. A person is an independent contractor if he or she is hired for a specific project, controls where and how work is performed after receiving the initial assignment, provides his or her own supplies and equipment, receives no benefits from the firm other than payment for services, and is free to work for other firms at the same time. In addition, the contractor should establish the amount of payment as a set fee or on an hourly basis but should not be otherwise financially tied to the firm.

Following these guidelines and before beginning any work, an agreement for the employer to pay the contractor only a set amount and not give the CAD operator sick leave or other benefits should be established. The firm should not require the freelancer to work the same hours as other employees (though he or she could, if desired) or establish a strict work schedule. Furthermore, there should not be any additional financial rewards other than the payment initially agreed upon by the contractor and employer.

The answer is (C).

68. As outlined in AIA Document B101, *Standard Form of Agreement Between Owner and Architect*, Article 2, the standard of care requires an architect to do as other architects will when practicing in the same locale, the same or similar set of circumstances, and the same time frame. AIA Document B101 states that cost estimates prepared by the architect represent the best professional judgment. It also states that the architect does not guarantee that costs will not exceed the budget or previous cost estimates; such a statement can appear in the owner-contractor agreement only. By agreeing to the client's demand, the architect has raised the level of the standard of care. There is no AIA ethical canon regarding guaranteeing costs. A guaranteed cost provision is not in the architect's insurance policy.

Including a promise of no cost overruns does not negate the GMP.

The answer is (A).

69. The utilization rate (i.e., the chargeable ratio) is the percentage of time or dollars spent on direct labor, which is chargeable to projects, divided by the total time or dollars spent on chargeable and nonchargeable labor, including paid nonworking time such as sick leave, vacations, and holidays. Because a 71% utilization rate is considered low, the office needs to have more chargeable hours. This is especially true for an office where very few employees do nonchargeable work. The project managers should monitor how the technical staff is spending and tracking time to make sure all time spent working on a project is recorded.

The answer is (B).

70. Option (A) is incorrect because both the client and the architect want to make the transition to BIM and this project is a suitable way to do so. Option (C) is incorrect because it is unreasonable to ask the client to purchase software and training. Option (D) is incorrect because if the firm wants to make the transition, the firm should probably keep the effort in-house to use on future projects.

The transition from standard CAD to BIM requires careful consideration of a variety of issues, including initial hardware and software costs, training, continuing ownership costs, and learning a different approach to project design and production. However, the benefits of using BIM are numerous, even for small firms. In this instance, the firm should consider this project as a way to get started with BIM, because the firm will eventually need to make the transition. The city should also consider using BIM, which is ideal for the design of and ongoing maintenance of its municipal facilities.

The difficult decision hinges on whether this project represents the right time to start the transition. One way to begin the transition is to hire an experienced BIM operator who can manage the process and train others in the firm; the cost of hiring, which is the largest cost, can be built into the fee proposal. The cost of software and additional training will have to be covered by the office, but that will have to be done at some point in any event. The cost of BIM software can be justified by the fact that the office's standard CAD software will also have to be upgraded at a future time even if the firm does not make the transition.

The answer is (B).

71. Option (B) is incorrect because the client has stated that he or she wants to proceed for a specific reason, while option (C) is incorrect because a LEED-credentialed person is not required. Having one on the design team, however, will improve the ease and accuracy of the process as well as earn the project a point toward certification. Option (D) is incorrect because, although a LEED consultant may be retained, it is not necessary.

In this case, the architect should ask what the client knows about LEED certification and its associated costs and if such a certification is critical. If the client still wants to proceed, the architect should provide an estimate of the extra costs that may be involved, which the client will have to pay.

The answer is (A).

72. Because this is a municipal project, the city will most likely require the project to be put out to bid in order to get the lowest cost. Most governmental agencies require this approach.

A contractor-led design-build method requires the architect to be a consultant to the contractor. In this instance, the architect has already been retained by the city. The design-build approach also requires the city to provide a detailed set of owner's requirements, which the city may not be in a position to do unless it has used a bridging method. There is no mention of scheduling or completion problems in the case study, so a fast-track method will not be required. An IPD method, even if allowed by the city rules, will probably not be required for a project of this size and scope.

The answer is (C).

73. Given the information provided, there is no significant risk that the firm can not mitigate. There are several ways to improve staffing: hire more people, take on independent contractors, or associate with another firm. For an office of this size, even with the two new projects, one principal can direct the projects with the help of the project manager and the other architects. Although there might be questions about the cost of using BIM, such financial uncertainty may be partially or wholly built into the fee structure.

The answer is (D).

74. The talents of the existing office staff should be used as much as possible and additional assistance should be provided by temporary help only. The office should use its existing project manager for client contact and coordination, its architects for the design, and a specifications writer. If a professional is needed for document production, the firm will have to decide which type of additional assistance is best. It is probably not best to hire independent consultants (i.e., freelancers) or an outsourcing firm. It will be difficult to coordinate freelancers and if they work in the office, there may be questions regarding whether or not they are employees or independent consultants.

Outsourcing often creates coordination problems. The firm will be better served by associating with another firm with the necessary experience and staff to complete the work unique to these two projects.

The answer is (A), (B), (D), and (F).

75. For an interior design project of this size, both a mechanical and electrical engineer will be required. An interior designer will also be needed, since the case study does not specify whether or not any of the architects have any interior design experience or specialized skills. There will be no structural requirements on the project as described. Security can be handled by a security vendor and the electrical engineer as required. A signage system can also be developed by the architect with the assistance of a signage vendor.

The answer is (B), (C), and (F).

76. Two job site visits per week is likely not enough, whereas having someone on site full time is too much. Having a principal visit the site wastes the principal's time. It is more appropriate for a project team member to visit the site instead. In this situation, one site visit per day is likely necessary until the problems caused by the collapse are resolved. After resolving the problems, the schedule returns to the original frequency.

The answer is (B).

77. After the owner has been notified of the issue, the owner—not the architect or contractor—must obtain the services of a licensed laboratory to verify the presence or absence of the asbestos. The owner must furnish to the contractor the names and qualifications of the persons or entities who will test, remove, or contain the material. After the asbestos is removed, work will resume, and the contract time and contract amount will be appropriately increased. According to provisions of AIA Document A201, *General Conditions of the Contract for Construction*, if the contractor finds asbestos, the contractor must immediately stop work and report the condition to both the architect and the owner in writing.

The answer is (C).

78. Neither the bonding company nor the contractor is responsible for paying the architect's extra fees. The insurance company may or may not reimburse the owner for the extra expenses resulting from the collapse. The insurance company itself is not directly responsible to the contractor or architect. According to provisions in AIA Document B141, *Standard Form of Agreement Between Owner and Architect with Standard Form of Architect's Services*, Article 1.3.3, if circumstances occur beyond the architect's control that require a change in services, the owner must adjust compensation to the architect. The article on compensation describes the method of calculating adjustments to services. If not specified, the compensation must be made in an equitable manner.

The answer is (D).

79. If the architect's services are increased by significant changes in the project, the architect is entitled to an adjustment in compensation according to AIA Document B141, *Standard Form of Agreement Between Owner and Architect with Standard Form of Architect's Services*, Article 1.3.3. In this case, the architect should not start work as the owner requested. The architect should accept the request only after an agreement is in place for the additional compensation. Determining additional costs is part of determining the extra fee required. The owner and architect, however, must mutually agree in writing before the architect provides any additional services.

The answer is (A).

80. Adding a second story with the necessary design features for a restaurant is a significant addition to the existing building structure. Hand-drafted sketches are not professional. The production of new construction documents needs to be immediately resolved, so it is not the right time to start using BIM. The restoration of the damaged portion of the building and the addition of the new restaurant space is too complex to outsource because it requires additional supervision. The required documentation to describe the revised construction necessitates extensive, competent drawings, including those provided by the consultants. Using the firm's standard CAD software takes the least time and ensures the best quality.

The answer is (B).

DIVISION 2: PROJECT MANAGEMENT

Multiple Choice

81. Ⓐ Ⓑ Ⓒ Ⓓ
82. Ⓐ Ⓑ Ⓒ Ⓓ
83. ⒶⒷⒸⒹⒺⒻ
84. Ⓐ Ⓑ Ⓒ Ⓓ
85. Ⓐ Ⓑ Ⓒ Ⓓ
86. ⒶⒷⒸⒹⒺⒻ
87. Ⓐ Ⓑ Ⓒ Ⓓ
88. Ⓐ Ⓑ Ⓒ Ⓓ
89. Ⓐ Ⓑ Ⓒ Ⓓ
90. Ⓐ Ⓑ Ⓒ Ⓓ
91. ⒶⒷⒸⒹⒺⒻ
92. ⒶⒷⒸⒹⒺⒻ
93. Ⓐ Ⓑ Ⓒ Ⓓ
94. Ⓐ Ⓑ Ⓒ Ⓓ
95. Ⓐ Ⓑ Ⓒ Ⓓ
96. Ⓐ Ⓑ Ⓒ Ⓓ
97. Ⓐ Ⓑ Ⓒ Ⓓ
98. Ⓐ Ⓑ Ⓒ Ⓓ
99. ____________________
100. Ⓐ Ⓑ Ⓒ Ⓓ
101. Ⓐ Ⓑ Ⓒ Ⓓ
102. Ⓐ Ⓑ Ⓒ Ⓓ
103. Ⓐ Ⓑ Ⓒ Ⓓ
104. Ⓐ Ⓑ Ⓒ Ⓓ
105. Ⓐ Ⓑ Ⓒ Ⓓ
106. ⒶⒷⒸⒹⒺⒻ
107. Ⓐ Ⓑ Ⓒ Ⓓ
108. Ⓐ Ⓑ Ⓒ Ⓓ
109. Ⓐ Ⓑ Ⓒ Ⓓ
110. Ⓐ Ⓑ Ⓒ Ⓓ
111. Ⓐ Ⓑ Ⓒ Ⓓ
112. Ⓐ Ⓑ Ⓒ Ⓓ
113. Ⓐ Ⓑ Ⓒ Ⓓ
114. Ⓐ Ⓑ Ⓒ Ⓓ
115. Ⓐ Ⓑ Ⓒ Ⓓ
116. Ⓐ Ⓑ Ⓒ Ⓓ
117. Ⓐ Ⓑ Ⓒ Ⓓ
118. ⒶⒷⒸⒹⒺⒻ
119. Ⓐ Ⓑ Ⓒ Ⓓ
120. Ⓐ Ⓑ Ⓒ Ⓓ
121. ____________________
122. Ⓐ Ⓑ Ⓒ Ⓓ
123. Ⓐ Ⓑ Ⓒ Ⓓ
124. Ⓐ Ⓑ Ⓒ Ⓓ
125. Ⓐ Ⓑ Ⓒ Ⓓ
126. Ⓐ Ⓑ Ⓒ Ⓓ
127. Ⓐ Ⓑ Ⓒ Ⓓ
128. Ⓐ Ⓑ Ⓒ Ⓓ
129. Ⓐ Ⓑ Ⓒ Ⓓ
130. ____________________
131. Ⓐ Ⓑ Ⓒ Ⓓ
132. Ⓐ Ⓑ Ⓒ Ⓓ
133. Ⓐ Ⓑ Ⓒ Ⓓ
134. Ⓐ Ⓑ Ⓒ Ⓓ
135. Ⓐ Ⓑ Ⓒ Ⓓ
136. Ⓐ Ⓑ Ⓒ Ⓓ
137. Ⓐ Ⓑ Ⓒ Ⓓ
138. Ⓐ Ⓑ Ⓒ Ⓓ
139. Ⓐ Ⓑ Ⓒ Ⓓ
140. ⒶⒷⒸⒹⒺⒻ
141. Ⓐ Ⓑ Ⓒ Ⓓ
142. Ⓐ Ⓑ Ⓒ Ⓓ
143. Ⓐ Ⓑ Ⓒ Ⓓ
144. Ⓐ Ⓑ Ⓒ Ⓓ
145. Ⓐ Ⓑ Ⓒ Ⓓ
146. ⒶⒷⒸⒹⒺⒻ
147. Ⓐ Ⓑ Ⓒ Ⓓ
148. Ⓐ Ⓑ Ⓒ Ⓓ
149. ⒶⒷⒸⒹⒺⒻ
150. Ⓐ Ⓑ Ⓒ Ⓓ
151. Ⓐ Ⓑ Ⓒ Ⓓ
152. Ⓐ Ⓑ Ⓒ Ⓓ
153. Ⓐ Ⓑ Ⓒ Ⓓ
154. Ⓐ Ⓑ Ⓒ Ⓓ
155. ⒶⒷⒸⒹⒺⒻ
156. Ⓐ Ⓑ Ⓒ Ⓓ

Case Study 1

157. ⒶⒷⒸⒹⒺⒻ
158. Ⓐ Ⓑ Ⓒ Ⓓ
159. Ⓐ Ⓑ Ⓒ Ⓓ
160. Ⓐ Ⓑ Ⓒ Ⓓ
161. Ⓐ Ⓑ Ⓒ Ⓓ
162. ⒶⒷⒸⒹⒺⒻ
163. Ⓐ Ⓑ Ⓒ Ⓓ
164. ____________________
165. Ⓐ Ⓑ Ⓒ Ⓓ

Case Study 2

166. ____________________
167. ____________________
168. ____________________
169. ⒶⒷⒸⒹⒺⒻ
170. ⒶⒷⒸⒹⒺⒻ
171. ⒶⒷⒸⒹⒺⒻ
172. ____________________
173. Ⓐ Ⓑ Ⓒ Ⓓ
174. Ⓐ Ⓑ Ⓒ Ⓓ
175. Ⓐ Ⓑ Ⓒ Ⓓ

81. According to the *International Building Code* (IBC), in which of the following applications would elements made of wood be categorized as Class A or Class B, based on the product's performance in flame spread and smoke developed tests?

(A) exposed heavy timber structural members

(B) cornice and base molding

(C) solid oak flooring

(D) paneled wainscoting

82. An architect is surveying an existing building to determine if the facility complies with *International Building Code* (IBC) requirements for accessibility. Which of the following elements must be modified to satisfy the code requirements?

(A) fire extinguisher cabinet with a "bubble" door that protrudes 5 in from the wall

(B) $1/4$ in beveled threshold at the main entrance doors

(C) clear floor area 24 in wide on the pull side of the door to the men's restroom from the hallway, which is approached from the front

(D) ramp from the original building to a later addition that rises 6 in over 8 ft

83. Which of the following hazardous materials may be found in insulation products? (Choose the two that apply.)

(A) asbestos

(B) lead

(C) polychlorinated biphenyls (PCBs)

(D) radon

(E) crystalline silica

(F) glass fiber

84. American Institute of Architects (AIA) Document A201, *General Conditions of the Contract for Construction*, requires the owner to

(A) purchase and maintain all-risk property insurance

(B) include the architect and contractor as additional insureds on all insurance policies

(C) purchase and maintain loss of use insurance

(D) carry professional liability insurance with limits of liability exceeding the total project cost

85. The contract documents, which are comprised of the agreement, conditions of the contract, drawings, specifications, addenda, and any other documents listed in the agreement, form the basis of the legal relationship between the

(A) owner and architect

(B) contractor and subcontractor

(C) architect and contractor

(D) owner and contractor

86. An architect is working on a restaurant project for a brilliant but eccentric world-famous chef. The architect and his client have an agreement based upon American Institute of Architects (AIA) Document B101, *Standard Form of Agreement Between Owner and Architect.* In which of the following situations would the architect be entitled to an adjustment to the agreed-upon project schedule and fees? (Choose the four that apply.)

(A) The architect is required to defend the owner's choice of sculpture and neon signage at several hearings of the city's architectural review board.

(B) The owner decides to negotiate with a contractor instead of bidding the project.

(C) The chef traveled to his villa in Italy during the design development phase and could not be reached for questions and project decisions.

(D) The mechanical and electrical engineers, consultants to the architect, fail to coordinate the power and ventilation requirements for the walk-in cooler.

(E) A new health code regulation was approved during construction, and the architect must revise portions of the kitchen layout to satisfy the requirements.

(F) The architect is asked to select the finishes and furniture for the restaurant because the interior decorator (the chef's sister) moved to Paris and abandoned the project.

87. According to American Institute of Architects (AIA) Document A201, *General Conditions of the Contract for Construction*, which of the following statements is true?

(A) The contractor is not required to name the owner as an additional insured on the contractor's commercial liability insurance policy.

(B) If the owner chooses not to purchase property insurance and does not notify the contractor of this decision, the owner becomes responsible for all losses that the property insurance would have covered.

(C) The owner may choose to carry either all-risk or named peril property insurance coverage.

(D) The contractor is responsible for paying property insurance deductibles.

88. A university is planning to build a new science center to house its chemistry and biology departments. The school wishes to encourage competitive bidding but also wants to ensure that the materials used meet a minimum standard of quality. Which type of specification should be used?

(A) proprietary

(B) base bid with "approved equal" language

(C) descriptive

(D) base bid with alternates

89. If a penalty clause is included in the owner-contractor agreement, what else must be included?

(A) liquidated damages

(B) guaranteed maximum price

(C) a bonus provision

(D) an incentive clause

90. Many American Institute of Architects (AIA) documents require parties to the agreements to submit their disputes to arbitration. Which of the following statements regarding arbitration is true?

(A) Arbitration is generally more expensive than litigation.

(B) If the agreement states that arbitration is binding, either party may appeal the findings.

(C) The initial decision maker (IDM) serves as one of the members of the arbitration board.

(D) Both parties are given an opportunity to object to potential arbitrators.

91. Which of the following are considered reimbursable expenses that can be charged to the owner by the architect, assuming that their agreement is based upon American Institute of Architects (AIA) Document B101, *Standard Form of Agreement Between Owner and Architect*? (Choose the four that apply.)

(A) plan review fees paid to the local code enforcement office

(B) overtime work

(C) a $1 million increase to the architect's normal limits of professional liability coverage, requested by the owner

(D) upgrading from an earlier version of computer-aided design (CAD) software to the most current release

(E) expenses incurred by the architect to prepare a response to the owner's original request for proposal

(F) state or local taxes on professional services

92. Which of the following pieces of information does American Institute of Architects (AIA) Document B101, *Standard Form of Agreement Between Owner and Architect*, require the owner to provide? (Choose the four that apply.)

(A) survey of the proposed site

(B) certification from the owner's lender or financiers that adequate funds are available to pay for design and construction of the proposed project

(C) proposed project schedule, including any special requirements such as "fast-tracking"

(D) information on the owner's preferred procurement and delivery method, such as a negotiated contract, competitive bidding, or employment of a construction manager

(E) project budget

(F) copies of applicable zoning ordinances, building codes, and other regulations in effect at the project site

93. In American Institute of Architects (AIA) Document A101, *Standard Form of Agreement Between Owner and Contractor,* Article 3, the date of commencement for a small remodeling project is March 15. The contractor is required to achieve substantial completion in 60 days. When is the target date for substantial completion?

(A) May 13

(B) May 15

(C) June 6

(D) June 8

94. What does the phrase "time is of the essence" mean in a contract?

(A) The project must be completed as quickly as possible.

(B) All work must be completed by the dates specified in the contract or the contractor has breached the agreement.

(C) The contractor must mobilize its forces and begin working on the project as soon as the contract is signed.

(D) The owner is responsible for setting the construction schedule.

95. Which of the following statements is true according to American Institute of Architects (AIA) Document B101, *Standard Form of Agreement Between Owner and Architect?*

(A) If the architect must carry more insurance coverage than usual to meet the owner's requirements, the architect is responsible for the additional cost without reimbursement.

(B) The architect must consider sustainable design technologies and materials where such approaches are within the project scope and budget.

(C) The architect is responsible for obtaining the building permit.

(D) The architect is required to prepare a punch list upon project completion.

96. For aesthetic reasons, the architect's specifications on a building project call for a specific method of constructing a concrete wall and slab that is not in accordance with normal construction practices. The contractor tells the architect that the contractor believes the specified method will create unsafe conditions. According to AIA Document A201, *General Conditions of the Contract for Construction,* what action must the contractor take?

(A) Proceed with construction following the instructions in the specifications.

(B) Notify the architect in writing, and propose alternate methods of construction.

(C) Give written notice to both the owner and architect of the safety concerns, and wait for instruction from the architect.

(D) Modify the method to make it safe, and proceed with construction.

97. American Institute of Architects (AIA) Document G612, *Owner's Instructions to the Architect Regarding the Construction Contract,* is a checklist that owners can use to define project requirements. Which of the following statements is correct?

(A) The architect will use the information provided in this questionnaire to write the supplementary conditions.

(B) The form is divided into three parts: programming, contracts, and insurance and bonds.

(C) The architect should request this information from the owner at the beginning of the design phase.

(D) The architect will use the information provided on the form to revise the general conditions for this specific project.

98. Which of the following statements about property rights is correct?

(A) Riparian rights give a property owner whose property abuts a river the right to construct means to access the water, such as a boat dock.

(B) Air rights give the owner of a property the right to prohibit aircraft from entering that space, such as the protective area around Washington, DC.

(C) Riparian rights apply equally to natural and man-made bodies of water.

(D) A property owner has the right to use the surface of the land and profit from minerals found underground.

99. The critical path time for the following critical path method (CPM) diagram is ______ days. (Fill in the blank.)

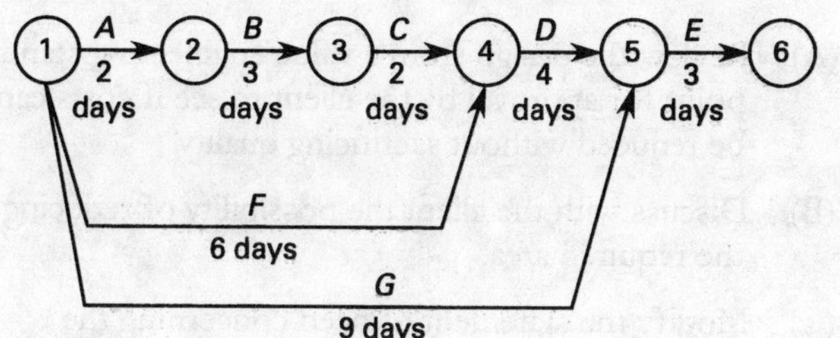

100. The primary purpose of a contract between an architect and a consultant is to

(A) pass through the rights and responsibilities of the architect to the owner detailed in the owner-architect agreement to the relationship between the architect and the consultant, and share risks and rewards

(B) require the consultant to carry liability insurance to protect the architecture firm in the event of errors or omissions on the part of the consultant

(C) establish terms of payment and affirm that if the architect is not paid by the owner, the consultant will not be paid

(D) define the consultant's responsibilities during the construction administration phase

101. An architecture firm is assigning staff to work on a small addition to a library. The principal architect has chosen a project manager and has decided to assign two interns to the job to assist with production. The project manager is developing a schedule for the project based on the available work hours and the client's deadlines. Which type of schedule is appropriate for this project?

(A) a milestone chart

(B) a bar chart

(C) a Gantt chart

(D) a critical path method (CPM)

102. Construction of a hospital in the design phase this summer is expected to begin next fall and be completed two years after notice to proceed is given. As the development budget is prepared, the costs should be escalated to reflect the projected price in

(A) during design

(B) at the start of construction

(C) in the middle of the project

(D) when construction is scheduled to be completed

103. According to American Institute of Architects (AIA) Document B101, *Standard Form of Agreement Between Owner and Architect*, who is responsible for developing the program?

(A) owner

(B) owner's attorney

(C) architect

(D) construction manager

104. The height of a proposed building will be most influenced by the decision to use

(A) daylighting

(B) indirect lighting

(C) underfloor ventilation systems

(D) interstitial spaces

105. In order to finance public improvements with the goal of encouraging private development, a city's redevelopment agency will most likely use

(A) general obligation bonds

(B) developer impact fees

(C) business improvement districts

(D) tax increment financing

106. Which of the following are considered additional services according to American Institute of Architects (AIA) Document B101, *Standard Form of Agreement Between Owner and Architect*? (Choose the three that apply.)

(A) preparation of the project manual

(B) programming

(C) construction administration duties

(D) existing facilities surveys

(E) commissioning

(F) structural engineering design

107. During the renovation of an office complex, a fire causes damage to a tenant space. Investigation determines that the fire was caused by a panel box that was not installed according to the manufacturer's instructions. The owner's insurance company compensates the building owner for the cost of the repairs. The insurance company then sues the general contractor and the electrical

Project Management

contractor. The insurance company gains the right to make a claim against the installer in this situation through

(A) limited liability

(B) subrogation

(C) indemnification

(D) negligence

108. A building project has just been completed in city A at a cost of $3,000,000. An identical building is planned for city B. A published cost index indicates an index of 1250 for construction in city A and an index of 1350 for construction in city B. The same index suggests that inflation will increase 2% by the time construction of the building in city B is completed. Approximately how much should be budgeted for construction of the building in city B?

(A) $3,180,000

(B) $3,300,000

(C) $3,305,000

(D) $3,366,000

109. A published cost index gives a figure of 1440 to construction in city A and 1517 to construction in city B. The same index suggests that inflation will increase by 5% by the midpoint of a project's construction. The project is now budgeted to cost $1,500,000 in city A. Approximately how much should be budgeted for an identical project in city B?

(A) $1,430,000

(B) $1,500,000

(C) $1,660,000

(D) $1,720,000

110. A school district is planning a new elementary school to replace an outdated facility and has prepared a budget and program for the architect's review. At the beginning of the schematic design phase, the architect prepares a plan that satisfies the owner's programmatic requirements and calculates that the cost of the building will exceed the available funds by 8%. What should the architect do first?

(A) Review the design from a value engineering standpoint for approval by the client to see if costs can be reduced without sacrificing quality.

(B) Discuss with the client the possibility of reducing the required area.

(C) Modify the statement of need concerning the desired level of finish and construction quality on noncritical portions of the facility after consultation with the client.

(D) Propose that building be postponed for a school term until more money can be allocated.

111. Which of the following has the greatest impact on labor costs?

(A) requirement to use union labor

(B) prime interest rate

(C) geographic location of the project

(D) overhead

112. Which of the following is a characteristic of a partnering agreement?

(A) The partnering agreement supersedes the contracts between the owner and the architect and the owner and the contractor.

(B) The partnering agreement makes the architect a party to the owner-contractor agreement.

(C) Participants in projects using partnering agree on dispute resolution methods at the beginning of the project.

(D) If a project using partnering loses money, all of the parties to the partnering agreement must absorb the loss; conversely, if a profit is realized, all parties will benefit.

113. An architect and owner decide to use design-assist contracting for a project that involves restoring and casting replacement parts for an intricately detailed cast-iron facade. Which statement about design-assist contracting is correct?

(A) Design-assist contracting allows the architect to seek guidance from a manufacturer or a specialty craftsman for a unique or innovative design.

(B) Design-assist contracting is most appropriately used with the design-bid-build method of project delivery.

(C) The design-assist contracting process has four phases.

(D) The vendor working with the architect in design-assist contracting arrangement provides design services with no compensation for design-phase efforts. In exchange, that vendor will be awarded the construction contract for the work.

114. Which act requires federal agencies to use qualifications-based selection processes to award design and engineering contracts for public works projects?

(A) Davis-Bacon Act

(B) Clinger-Cohen Act

(C) Brooks Act

(D) Miller Act

115. A project program is a type of _____ plan. (Fill in the blank.)

(A) operational

(B) tactical

(C) contingency

(D) strategic

116. Architectural fees can be estimated in a variety of ways. Which statement is true?

(A) Estimating design fees based on a project's square footage is an example of a bottom-up approach.

(B) The contingency amount included in a design fee budget increases as the project progresses.

(C) The percentage of fees allocated for each of the design phases (i.e., schematic design, design development, construction documents, and construction administration) is the same whether a project is a design-bid-build project or a design-build project.

(D) Preparing estimates using a bottom-up approach is more accurate than preparing estimates using a top-down approach.

117. A project's construction budget is \$3,125,000. The owner establishes a \$312,500 architectural design fee for a project based on 10% of the project construction budget. The architecture firm calculates that engineering consultants' fees, indirect labor expenses, allowance for profit, and other nonreimbursable expenses total \$162,500. The remaining money will be the architecture firm's compensation for work on the project.

The architect decides that 20% of the architecture firm's compensation should be allocated for work in the design development phase. The hourly billing rate for each of the five employees working on the project is \$125, and the firm uses a multiplier of 2.5 times the direct labor expense to determine the employee billing rates. These five employees work 40 hours per week and are assigned solely to this project. The utilization rate for each employee is 75%. Based on the information given, what is the minimum number of weeks that should be included in the schedule for the design development phase?

(A) 3 weeks

(B) 4 weeks

(C) 10 weeks

(D) 12 weeks

118. Which of the following elements would be included in a project work plan for the design of a large office building? (Choose the four that apply.)

(A) statement of work as defined in the owner-architect agreement

(B) project schedule

(C) series of weekly meetings to check on progress and discuss upcoming milestones

(D) task assignments for specific individuals

(E) list of deliverables

(F) architectural fee schedule

119. In a typical design-bid-build project, the project architect must complete and share detailed code data—including information on the structural systems, evolution of the building layout, and construction of the building envelope—with the mechanical engineer. In which phase should the architect share that data?

(A) programming

(B) schematic design

(C) design development

(D) construction documents

Project Management

Project Management

120. A document assigning tasks to project team members and outlining required deliverables is called a(n)

(A) responsibility matrix

(B) utilization ratio

(C) employee timesheet

(D) work breakdown structure

121. For a design-bid-build project, the owner has chosen to contract separately with the interior designer and architect. The electrical engineer does not have a lighting designer in-house, so an outside consultant is used to provide this service. Building systems engineering services will be provided as a subcontract to the architect's agreement with the owner.

The organizational chart shown establishes the contractual relationships between team members in a design-bid-build project. When complete, two positions will remain empty. Using the list of positions given, assign the appropriate staff member to each position.

- owner
- architect
- mechanical contractor
- electrical contractor
- interior designer
- general contractor
- commissioning agent
- electrical engineer
- mechanical engineer
- civil engineer
- lighting designer
- structural engineer

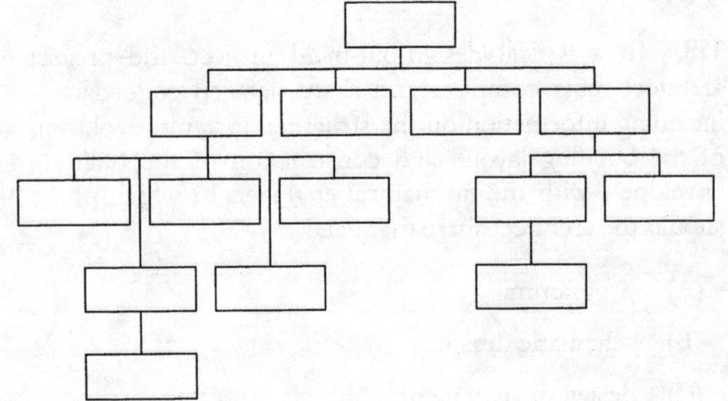

122. An architecture firm is designing a university's safety and security headquarters. The firm teams with a security consultant to design the emergency response center and prepare specifications for specialty equipment such as dispatch communications, closed-circuit cameras and monitors, and campus emergency telephones. The architect determines that this consultant's services will be necessary in the design phase only and that the consultant firm will not be involved with construction administration. The AIA publishes multiple sample agreements that an architect can use to team with a consultant. Which American Institute of Architects (AIA) document is most appropriate for use in this case?

(A) AIA Document C727, *Standard Form of Agreement Between Architect and Consultant for Special Services*

(B) AIA Document C401, *Standard Form of Agreement Between Architect and Consultant*

(C) AIA Document B142, *Standard Form of Agreement Between Owner and Consultant where the Owner contemplates using the design-build method of project delivery*

(D) AIA Document B206, *Standard Form of Architect's Services: Security Evaluation and Planning*

123. Which statement is true regarding American Institute of Architects (AIA) Document C401, *Standard Form of Agreement Between Architect and Consultant?*

(A) The architect is responsible for errors or omissions caused by the consultant, because the architect holds the prime contract with the owner.

(B) If the architect must modify the design because the cost of the work exceeds the owner's budget, the consultant must also modify the design with no additional compensation.

(C) The architect is required to carry the same amount of professional liability insurance as the consultant.

(D) The architect is required to pay the consultant for the consultant's services even if the owner does not pay the architect.

124. An architect designs a public works project and employs subconsultants for the design of the building systems. The owner has awarded multiple prime construction contracts. Communication between the mechanical engineer and the mechanical contractor should be facilitated through the

(A) general contractor

(B) architect

(C) architect and owner

(D) owner

125. According to the terms of American Institute of Architects (AIA) Document B101, *Standard Form of Agreement Between Owner and Architect*, the owner is responsible for providing which consultant service?

(A) electrical engineer

(B) code compliance reviewer

(C) specifications writer

(D) geotechnical engineer

126. The American Institute of Architects (AIA) design-build documents define a design-builder as a design-build entity, an architect, a construction contractor, a real estate developer, or any person or entity legally permitted to do business as a design-builder in the jurisdiction where the project is located. According to the AIA design-build documents, which statement is true?

(A) If the design-build entity is a construction company that contracts with an architecture firm to provide design services, the engineering consultants' contracts will be with the construction company.

(B) The architect is required to certify substantial completion of the project.

(C) The owner does not need to hire an owner's representative in a design-build project because the design-build firm will provide these services.

(D) The architect is not required to assume construction administration responsibilities.

127. Which statement about American Institute of Architects (AIA) Document C103, *Standard Form of Agreement Between Owner and Consultant without a Predefined Scope of Consultant's Services* is correct? AIA Document C103

(A) makes the architect a party to the agreement between the owner and the consultant

(B) includes the scope of work that the consultant is responsible for providing

(C) is used to contract for geotechnical and land surveying services

(D) is used to form the agreement between the owner and the architect instead of AIA Document B101, *Standard Form of Agreement Between Owner and Architect*

128. The owner of an out-of-state grocery chain contracts with a local architect to provide design services for a new store. The grocery chain insists that the architect use the mechanical engineering consultant that the grocery chain has employed for its other projects because that firm understands the refrigeration systems that have been used at other facilities. The architect is not familiar with this firm's work because the engineering firm practices near the grocery chain's headquarters. Through internet research, the architect discovers that a client has filed a claim against the engineering firm for an issue on another project. To minimize the architecture firm's exposure to risk, how should the architect respond?

(A) Agree to accept the project and hire the mechanical engineering consultant required by the owner.

(B) Agree to accept the project but require that the owner directly hire the mechanical engineering firm.

(C) Agree to accept the project if the owner will allow the architect to hire a mechanical engineering firm with whom the architect has previously worked.

(D) Decline the project.

129. Which statement about building codes is true?

(A) The *International Building Code* (IBC) is a performance code.

(B) The use of new technologies is allowed by a prescriptive code if the designer can prove that the design meets the intent of the code.

(C) The only way to fulfill code requirements, if a jurisdiction has adopted the *International Energy Conservation Code* (IECC), is to comply with ANSI/ASHRAE/IESNA 90.1, *Energy Standard for Buildings Except Low-Rise Residential Buildings.*

(D) The architect is entitled to additional fees for revisions if a new version of the building code is adopted after the building permit is acquired and the jurisdiction requires modifications to the design to comply with the new requirements.

130. An architect is asked to design a classroom building on a college campus. A sketch of the proposed floor plan, along with a list of the group occupancy categories, is shown. In the box shown in each room, write the group occupancy category. Then, designate the walls that are required to have a fire rating if the building does not have an automatic sprinkler system with a thick line.

Group A-3 Assembly

Group B Business

Group E Educational

Group H High Hazard

Group S Storage

131. Which statement about building codes is true?

(A) A code requirement represents the best practices of the construction industry.

(B) Only a certified code official can propose a change to the *International Building Code* (IBC).

(C) The most current versions of the International Code Council (ICC) codes are automatically adopted in every jurisdiction.

(D) States have the ability to adopt only parts of a model building code.

132. What is the difference between the statute of limitations and the statute of repose?

(A) The statute of repose begins when a design or construction defect is discovered. The statute of limitations begins when design or construction of the project is complete.

(B) The statute of repose is longer than the statute of limitations.

(C) The statute of limitations begins when a design or construction defect is discovered. The statute of repose begins when design or construction of the project is complete.

(D) The statute of limitations is longer than the statute of repose.

133. Which statement about project scheduling is correct?

(A) Phasing a project is usually less expensive overall because it allows the costs of the project to be spread out over time.

(B) The AIA documents consider fast-track design services to be basic services.

(C) Phased construction requires the contractor to perform more complex coordination than that required for a traditional project.

(D) Construction documents must be complete before construction of a fast-track project can begin.

134. An owner and an attorney are reviewing a request from the contractor for an extension to the contract due to adverse weather conditions. The agreement is based on American Institute of Architects (AIA) Document A101, *Standard Form of Agreement Between Owner and Contractor, where the basis of payment is a Stipulated Sum*, and AIA Document A201, *General Conditions of the Contract for*

Construction, with no supplementary conditions. Which statement is accurate?

(A) The contractor is entitled to an extension of time for any days when severe weather prevents the contractor's forces from working on the site.

(B) The contractor interprets conditions that qualify as adverse weather, such as a minimum amount of precipitation, or a temperature above or below which work must be suspended.

(C) The contractor's initial construction schedule must allow for the number of inclement weather days for which the contractor is submitting the claim.

(D) The contractor must submit data substantiating that weather conditions were abnormal for the period of time, the weather could not have been reasonably anticipated, and the weather had an adverse effect on the scheduled construction.

135. In the design development phase, a commonly used estimating method allows the designer to compare the cost implications of various building systems or components. This estimating method is the

(A) parameter method

(B) matrix costing method

(C) cost plus overhead and profit method

(D) unit cost method

136. According to American Institute of Architects (AIA) Document A101, *Standard Form of Agreement Between Owner and Contractor, where the basis of payment is a Stipulated Sum*, and AIA Document A201, *General Conditions of the Contract for Construction*, which statement is correct?

(A) The architect may delegate responsibility for the design of a building system or an element to the contractor.

(B) The owner may require the contractor to certify that the contract documents are in accordance with applicable code requirements.

(C) The contractor assumes responsibility for the work if the contractor is aware that there is an error in the drawings and constructs it as shown, without notifying the architect or owner of the problem.

(D) The architect is the initial decision maker on contractual matters.

137. An architect is expected to perform duties in accordance with the standard of care of the profession. Which business practice can minimize an architecture firm's exposure to errors and omissions claims?

(A) Establish a verbal agreement with the owner.

(B) Assign two or more staff members to oversee the production and coordination of a set of construction documents.

(C) Prepare drawings and details in accordance with industry standards.

(D) Develop a fee budget at the beginning of the job.

138. A firm decides to organize its staff into studios. In such an arrangement, a cross section of employees who have different levels of authority and experience are grouped into a team for a project. Grouping staff members into studios is an example of what type of firm organizational structure?

(A) horizontal

(B) vertical

(C) matrix

(D) combination

139. An architecture firm is designing an office building in the state capital complex that will house the transportation department. The project requires the designer to present a 20-year life-cycle cost analysis as a part of the deliverables in the schematic design phase. Which statement is true?

(A) A life-cycle cost analysis is only useful for public projects funded through a bond issue.

(B) A life-cycle cost analysis does not consider how the design of the building will affect employee productivity.

(C) Initial construction costs are generally greater than the cost of operating and maintaining the building over the life of the structure.

(D) A life-cycle cost analysis must compare more than one building scheme or alternative design in order to be an effective planning tool.

Project Management

140. Which of the following approaches will fulfill sustainable design objectives and contribute to meeting a building's safety and security objectives? (Choose the four that apply.)

(A) parking areas under the building

(B) constructed wetlands

(C) integrated building automation and control systems

(D) full-height glass walls around the building lobby

(E) Trombe walls

(F) natural landscaping and rainwater retention ponds

141. Which of these statements regarding scheduling is correct?

(A) Each item listed on the schedule must be completed by the target date or the project completion date will be affected.

(B) From the contractor's perspective, it is best if the duration of each activity is greater than the period between progress payments.

(C) Sequencing is generally depicted on a bar chart.

(D) Float is a property of activities that can be started or finished within a prescribed time range and does not affect the project completion date.

142. If cracking occurred along the joints of a brick wall in a generally diagonal direction from a window corner up to the top of the wall, which of the following would most likely be the cause?

(A) lack of vertical control joints

(B) horizontal reinforcement placed too far apart

(C) poor grouting of the cavity

(D) inadequate mortar

143. Which project best demonstrates the influence of the architect's structural engineering consultants on the overall design?

(A) Chrysler Building, William Van Alen, New York, 1930

(B) Sears Tower, Bruce Graham (Skidmore, Owings & Merrill), Chicago, 1973

(C) AT&T Building, Philip Johnson & John Burgee, New York, 1978

(D) Guggenheim Museum, Frank Gehry, Bilbao, Spain, 1997

144. According to AIA Document A201, *General Conditions of the Contract for Construction*, the party responsible for determining the time limits for construction is the

(A) owner

(B) contractor

(C) architect

(D) contractor and subcontractors

145. Division 1 specification sections

(A) establish duties of the owner and contractor

(B) define legal rights of the parties

(C) establish duties of the architect

(D) establish administrative procedures for the project

146. The indemnification provision in American Institute of Architects (AIA) Document A201, *General Conditions of the Contract for Construction*, indemnifies which of the following? (Choose the four that apply.)

(A) contractor

(B) owner

(C) architect

(D) subcontractor

(E) architect's consultants

(F) owner's construction manager

147. According to AIA Document A201, *General Conditions of the Contract for Construction*, who is required to file a certificate of insurance prior to commencement of work?

(A) owner

(B) contractor

(C) architect

(D) subcontractor

148. American Institute of Architects (AIA) Document C401, *Standard Form of Agreement Between Architect and Consultant* requires a mechanical engineering consultant to

(A) perform a code compliance review of the architect's work

(B) share responsibility for acts or omissions of the architect

(C) coordinate communications with the contractor regarding all mechanical work

(D) coordinate the mechanical system design with the design of the electrical and plumbing systems

149. A local volunteer fire company is planning construction of a new fire station. A limited amount of funding is available for the project, and the owner wishes to set a fixed limit of construction cost at $1.5 million. The architect agrees, and the parties sign American Institute of Architects (AIA) Document B101, *Standard Form of Agreement Between Owner and Architect.* The architect exercises his authority over the scope of the project and the materials specified to meet the budget, and his final cost projection for the project is just under the maximum price. When the bids are received, however, the lowest base bid is $10,000 over the fixed limit of construction cost. What are the owner's possible options? (Choose the four that apply.)

(A) Abandon the project and terminate the architect's contract.

(B) Rebid the project.

(C) Negotiate with the lowest bidder.

(D) Require the architect to revise the drawings, with no additional compensation, to comply with the budget.

(E) Require the architect to pay the difference between the cost projection and the low bid.

(F) Require the architect to negotiate with the contractor to achieve a lower price.

150. An analysis of the financial feasibility of a potential project is called a

(A) project budget

(B) feasibility study

(C) program

(D) pro forma

151. According to American Institute of Architects (AIA) Document B101, *Standard Form of Agreement Between Owner and Architect*, the architect must revise the construction cost estimate if bidding does not commence within

(A) 90 days after the start of the project

(B) 90 days after completion of the preliminary cost estimate

(C) 90 days after the architect submits the construction documents to the owner

(D) any number of days; bidding dates have no effect on the construction cost estimate

152. Radon testing is conducted in the basement of an elementary school that is under study for a renovation and addition project. The results show a concentration of 3 pCi/L. What is an appropriate course of action?

(A) Demolish the existing slab and install a new 4 in slab on a vapor barrier placed on top of a 4 in base course of gravel.

(B) Seal any cracks in the foundation walls and floor slab and ventilate the basement to the exterior.

(C) Install a membrane on the floor and ventilate beneath it.

(D) Do nothing; no action is required at this time, but the site should be monitored.

153. A grocer purchases a corner market in the middle of a historic residential neighborhood. The property includes a small garden and a seating area located beside the store. A clause in the deed requires the grocer to maintain the garden and keep it open to the public. This is an example of a(n)

(A) prescriptive covenant

(B) affirmative covenant

(C) conditional covenant

(D) conditional use permit

Project Management

154. Which of the following statements regarding eminent domain is true?

(A) A condemnor may initiate eminent domain proceedings without offering to purchase the property from the owner.

(B) Fair market value of a property is always based on the market data analysis method of valuation.

(C) The power of eminent domain may be delegated to a private, for-profit company.

(D) The right to eminent domain is granted to the government by the Tenth Amendment to the U.S. Constitution.

155. Which of the following are included in an architect's cost option for a project? (Choose the three that apply).

(A) professional fees

(B) hard costs

(C) contractor's overhead and profit

(D) contingency allowances

(E) insurance and legal expenses

(F) furniture, fixtures, and equipment purchased by the owner

156. Which of these items establishes unit prices?

(A) AIA Document A101, *Standard Form of Agreement Between Owner and Contractor, where the basis of payment is a Stipulated Sum*

(B) AIA Document A201, *General Conditions of the Contract for Construction*

(C) supplementary conditions

(D) special conditions

Case Study 1

Problem 157 through Prob. 165 refer to the following case study. Refer to Resource 2.1 and Resource 2.2 to assist in solving the problems.

Kelly is an entrepreneur who owns a successful franchise of a national ice cream chain. Her ice cream shop is located in a shopping center on the edge of town, but she is considering moving to a new space in a historic downtown area. A three-story building in a mixed-use zoning district appears to be perfect for her business—formerly a single-family home, the building is located in the middle of a popular block filled with restaurants, small retail shops, and a few service-oriented businesses. Because the property has a historic designation, all exterior modifications must be approved by the local architectural review board. Kelly can run her business on the first floor, live on the second floor, and rent the third floor as an apartment.

To determine whether the building can be used as such, Kelly has hired a local architecture firm to conduct a feasibility study. The firm is the same one that designed her existing shop location. If it is determined that the historic building is suitable, the architect will prepare documents for the proposed interior construction to be done in compliance with the ice cream company's layout and branding requirements. The documents can be submitted to obtain a building permit and to negotiate a construction price.

The company in which Kelly is invested offers franchisees assistance with designing the shop interior to comply with the company's standards, selecting and purchasing equipment through the company's vendor relationships, and interviewing and hiring a general contractor for the building fit-out. These services are provided through a construction manager who advises franchise owners in the design phase and sends a representative to the site during the construction phase to serve as a liaison between the owner and the general contractor. Kelly went through this process when she constructed her existing location, so she is familiar with the steps that need to be taken to open a shop.

The franchisor prescribes space requirements for storage, freezers, serving counters, cash register areas, and seating. Moreover, the franchisor has standard kitchen equipment and finishes packages that all locations are required to use to maintain brand consistency. Kelly already owns the majority of the equipment and furniture required for a shop. It can be reused and reconfigured at a new location.

The franchisor provides a general program for a typical retail location, upon which Kelly's shop must be based. The architect must comply with local code and health department requirements. Because these vary by location, they are not included in the program prepared by the franchisor.

Resource 2.1 Mixed-Use Zoning District Requirements (CX, neighborhood commercial, mixed use)

zoning code	usage	comments
101	purpose	This district is designed to accommodate mixed-use buildings with retail or service uses on the ground floor and residential units above the nonresidential space.
102	allowed uses	These uses are permitted on the ground floor: artist live/work space, animal services (i.e., boarding, grooming, veterinary), pharmacy, restaurant, tavern, retail, office, financial services (i.e., bank, tax advisor, accounting).
103	size limits	The gross floor area of commercial establishments must not exceed 50% of the gross floor area of the entire building.
104	floor area	Commercial floor area on ground floor must be at least 1000 ft^2 or 25% of the lot area where the street frontage is less than 50 ft, or at least 20% of the lot area where the street frontage is 50 ft or greater.
105	floor area ratio (FAR)	The maximum FAR must be 2.0 for mixed-use buildings and 1.0 for all other buildings.
106	setbacks	Building facades must be located within 10 ft of the front property line. The minimum rear setback is 20% of the lot depth. Existing construction is exempt from setback requirements.
107	building height	Maximum building height must be 4 stories for mixed-use buildings and 3 stories for all other buildings.
108	off-street parking	No off-street parking is required for nonresidential uses in CX districts under 2000 ft^2.
109	transparency	A minimum of 60% of the street-facing building facade between 2 ft and 8 ft in height must comprise clear windows allowing views of indoor space or product displays.
110	entrances	Buildings must have a primary entrance facing a public sidewalk.
111	driveway access	No curb cuts are permitted for lots that are adjacent to alleys. Delivery areas must be accessible from alleys.
112	operations	All permitted uses in this district must be conducted within completely enclosed buildings. Exceptions are off-street parking or loading areas, automated teller machines (ATMs), or outdoor seating areas.

Resource 2.2 Property Plan

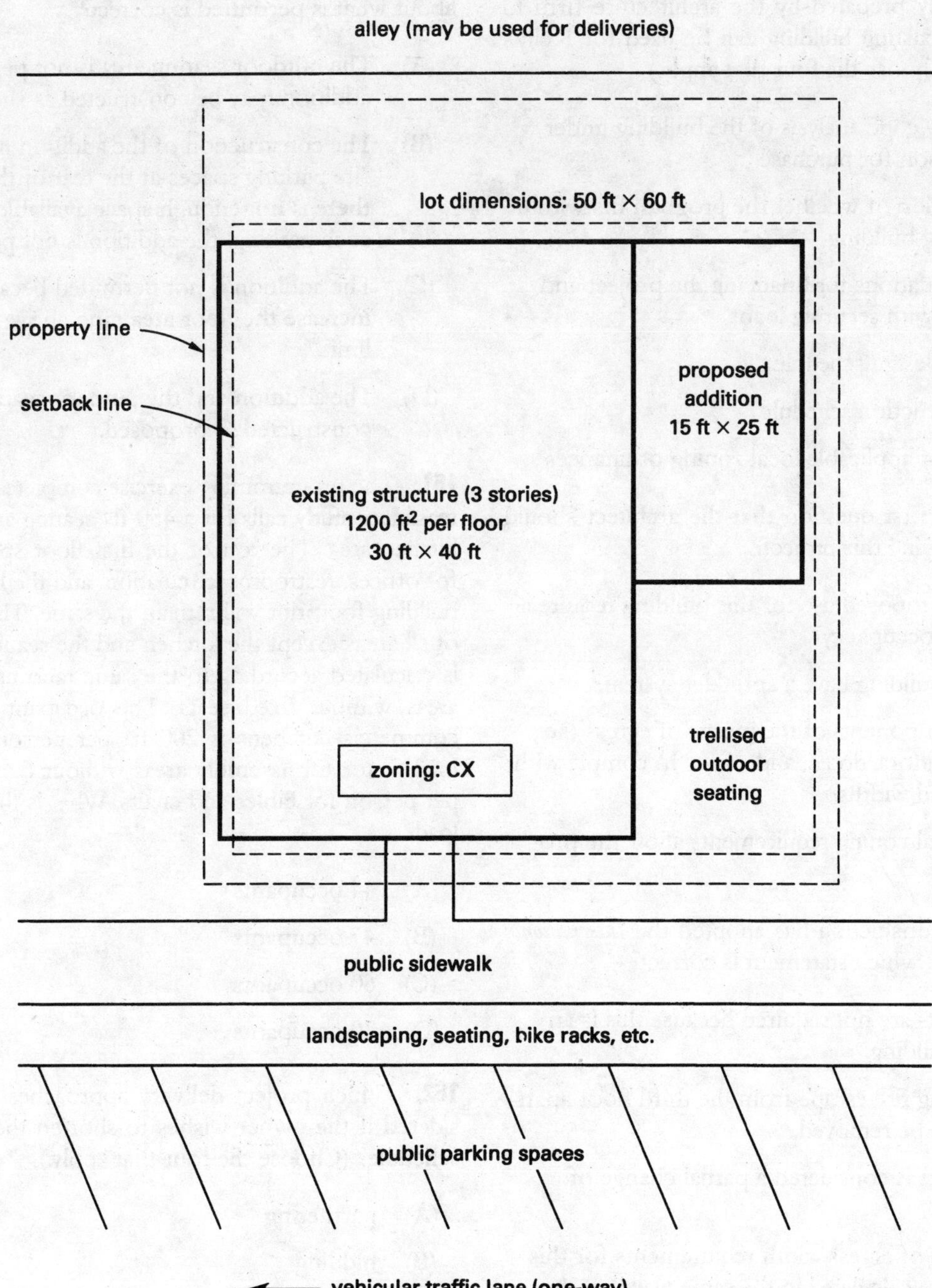
alley (may be used for deliveries)
lot dimensions: 50 ft × 60 ft
property line
setback line
proposed addition 15 ft × 25 ft
existing structure (3 stories)
1200 ft2 per floor
30 ft × 40 ft
trellised outdoor seating
zoning: CX
public sidewalk
landscaping, seating, bike racks, etc.
public parking spaces
vehicular traffic lane (one-way)

157. Which of the following items would be included in the feasibility study prepared by the architecture firm to determine if the existing building can be used for Kelly's new restaurant? (Choose the four that apply.)

(A) preliminary code analysis of the building under consideration for purchase

(B) determination of whether the program fits within the existing building

(C) recommendations for financing the project and assistance with securing loans

(D) proposed design schedule

(E) final construction schedule

(F) summary of applicable local zoning ordinances

158. What is the first question that the architect should address when studying this project?

(A) Does the proposed use for this building require a change of occupancy?

(B) Does the building have a sprinkler system?

(C) Do the components of the means of egress (i.e., stairs, corridors, doors, and so forth) comply with the required widths?

(D) Do the local zoning requirements allow the proposed use?

159. If the local jurisdiction has adopted the *International Building Code* (IBC), which statement is correct?

(A) Fire barriers are not required because this is an existing building.

(B) The existing fire escape from the third floor apartment must be removed.

(C) This project is considered a partial change of occupancy.

(D) The means of egress width requirements for this building are calculated in the same way that the requirements are calculated in new construction.

160. Kelly asks the architect to consider a single-story addition near the rear of the lot to house the freezer, cooler, and storage areas. The addition will allow more space in the existing building for serving and seating. She also wants to build an outdoor seating area that is visible from the street. The proposed locations of both of these improvements are shown on the site plan. According to the zoning requirements for this lot, which statement about what is permitted is correct?

(A) The outdoor seating area is not permitted, but the addition may be constructed as shown in the plan.

(B) The construction of the addition necessitates on-site parking spaces at the rear of the lot. Because there is not enough space available on the lot for such parking, the addition is not permitted.

(C) The addition is not permitted because it will increase the floor area ratio above the acceptable limit.

(D) The addition and the outdoor seating area can be constructed as proposed.

161. The programming exercise completed as a part of the feasibility study calls for a 450 ft^2 seating area and a 550 ft^2 kitchen area. The rest of the first floor space will be used for offices, restrooms, circulation, and the like. The existing building footprint will remain the same. The occupant load of all areas except the kitchen and the seating area specified is calculated according to the same ratio used for assembly areas without fixed seats. The occupant load factor for commercial kitchens is 200 ft^2 per person. The occupant load factor for assembly areas without fixed seats is 15 ft^2 per person for tables and chairs. What is the total occupant load?

(A) 44 occupants

(B) 47 occupants

(C) 60 occupants

(D) 80 occupants

162. Which project delivery approaches should be considered if the owner wishes to shorten the overall project schedule? (Choose the four that apply.)

(A) partnering

(B) bidding

(C) design-build

(D) construction manager as constructor

(E) construction manager as adviser

(F) bridging

163. The franchisor requires its franchisees to use the parent company's standard contracts for owner-architect and owner-contractor agreements. The information presented in the contracts is similar to that of the American Institute of Architects (AIA) Construction Manager as Adviser (CMa) family, but the content is not exact. Which of the following provisions in the company's standard agreements differs from the requirements of the AIA contracts?

(A) The architect is required to maintain professional liability insurance for the duration of the agreement.

(B) The architect is not responsible for the contractor's means and methods of construction.

(C) The architect is required to provide all site documentation such as surveys and geotechnical engineering reports.

(D) The owner's consultants must maintain professional liability insurance.

164. The available funding for a building project must cover construction costs, as well as all other project expenses that are classified as either hard or soft costs. Identify whether the expenses are considered to be hard or soft costs by placing an "X" in the applicable column.

expense	hard cost	soft cost
architecture and engineering fees		
fee to franchisor for construction manager's services		
landscaping		
ice cream freezer cabinet		
insurance		
interest paid on construction loan		
decor (artwork, signage, etc.)		
mechanical equipment		
light fixtures		
lighting design services		
installation costs associated with kitchen equipment		
sprinkler system		
contractor's overhead and profit		
fees for connecting to utilities (water, sewer, electricity, etc.)		
moving expenses		
contingency funds		
permit fees		
property taxes		

165. The project description states that the construction manager will be responsible for interviewing and choosing a general contractor, as well as negotiating a cost plus fixed fee construction contract with the selected firm. Why does the franchisor prefer to use this project award method?

(A) The price of the work is based on a specific scope as defined in the construction documents and will not change during the construction period.

(B) The contractor can be selected based on experience, reputation, and proposed schedule.

(C) The owner can obtain the lowest possible price for the work through negotiation with a contractor.

(D) The costs and risks associated with delays are allocated to the contractor if the project takes longer to complete than anticipated.

Project Management

Case Study 2

Problem 166 through Prob. 175 refer to the following case study. Refer to Resource 2.3 and Resource 2.4 to assist in solving the problems.

A large, cash gift from community leaders Milton and Doris Winter has been allocated to fund the design and construction of a new community park in the town of Summerville. The Winters also have donated a 100-acre parcel of land on which the park will be built. The Winter Family Foundation, led by the Winters' daughter, Rowan Winter Bradley, oversees the park's construction. When construction is complete, the facility will be turned over to the Summerville Parks Department.

Half of the cash contributed will finance the construction. The other half will be used to establish an endowment. The Summerville Parks Department will use the endowment's income to maintain and operate the center in perpetuity.

The Winter Family Foundation hired Parco Design & Planning to evaluate and document the site. Parco Design & Planning also organized a series of neighborhood charrettes to determine which amenities community members felt were the most important. The contract between Parco Design & Planning and the Winter Family Foundation is based on American Institute of Architects (AIA) Document C141, *Standard Form of Agreement Between Owner and Consultant for a Design-Build Project*. The information gathered in this phase is used by Parco Design & Planning and the Winter Family Foundation to develop a Request for Proposal (RFP), which includes a preliminary program for the project.

The Winter Family Center will be the centerpiece of the new park. This building will house the following spaces.

- four multipurpose community rooms with a centrally located catering kitchen
- gymnasium with full basketball court and mezzanine-level running and walking track
- 25 ft swimming pool and adjacent children's water play area
- two racquetball courts
- dance studio with sprung floor
- fitness center with cardiovascular and strength training equipment
- locker rooms (men, women, family)
- game room with air hockey, pool table, table tennis, and foosball
- arts and crafts center with kiln and pottery wheels
- child care area and play room
- vending and snack area
- staff offices and break room
- storage areas

The park's outdoor amenities will include the following areas.

- two soccer fields
- baseball and softball fields
- basketball court
- two tennis courts
- four picnic pavilions, each with a seating capacity of 50 people
- restrooms and vending area
- three-mile nature and fitness trail for pedestrians and bicyclists, which will be sponsored by the Summerville Community Hospital
- community garden plots and compost facility

- dog park
- playground
- catch-and-release fishing pond and dock
- on-site barn renovated to serve as a maintenance facility, storing tractors, lawnmowers, and other equipment
- parking areas as required by local zoning requirements

The RFP also includes an anticipated project schedule, which was developed by Parco Design & Planning on behalf of the Foundation.

The Winter Family Foundation has chosen the design-build method of project delivery and will base the construction contract on AIA Document A141, *Standard Form of Agreement Between Owner and Design-Builder.* The Winter Family Foundation has decided to retain Parco Design & Planning as an adviser to the owner during the design and construction phases of the project. During design, Parco Design & Planning will participate in progress reviews and evaluate the proposed design for compliance with the project objectives. In the construction phase, Parco Design & Planning will review the design-builder's applications for payment and perform periodic walk-throughs with the Foundation's representatives.

Multiple design-build teams submitted qualifications packages in response to the RFP. A committee including representatives of the Winter Family Foundation and Parco Design & Planning, the Summerville Parks Department, and community volunteers reviewed the packages. The Winter Family Foundation awarded the project to a team comprising Meadowfield Construction and Autumn Architects.

Meadowfield Construction will act as the design-builder for this project. As a general contractor, Meadowfield Construction will provide the majority of the construction services required, using its in-house resources. Meadowfield Construction will employ subcontractors for the site work and building services installation. Autumn Architects has been hired by Meadowfield to provide the required design services. Meadowfield Construction anticipates that Autumn Architects will have limited responsibilities in the construction phase because Meadowfield Construction believes these tasks can be performed by its in-house project managers. The contract between the firms is based on AIA Document B143, *Standard Form of Agreement Between Design-Builder and Architect.* Autumn Architects will team up with Verdure Engineering, a landscape and civil engineering firm that will design the site elements, and Equinox Building Systems, which will provide structural engineering and mechanical and electrical engineering design services. Their agreements will be based on AIA Document C441, *Standard Form of Agreement Between Architect and Consultant for a Design-Build Project.*

The listed program elements must be included in the final design. The designer may use judgment in arranging the site and building(s). Where not prescribed by a standard (such as the required dimensions of a sports court or field), various sizes of programmatic elements are acceptable. The finished space must accommodate the number of occupants or activity described in the program. The architect is responsible for determining the requirements for restrooms, circulation spaces, building services, and other support areas as necessary to support the programmatic elements. The design-builder may suggest a phasing plan, if advisable, or the design-builder may add elements to the program as long as the contracted work can be accomplished within the project budget and will be finished by the completion date.

Resource 2.3 Standard Form of Agreement Between Design-Builder and Architect

Agreement made as of the 2nd day of January
Between the Design-Builder: Meadowfield Construction
and the Architect: Autumn Architects
The Design-Builder has entered into the Design-Build Contract with the Owner dated: December 23
for the following Project: Design & Construction of the Winter Family Center and Grounds
The Owner: Winter Family Foundation

The Design-Builder and Architect agree as shown in the actual excerpt from the agreement.

§ 3.2 Design Services

The Architect shall provide only those Design Services listed in this Section 3.2 that are designated by an "X" in the adjacent box.

	§ 3.2.1	Multi-Discipline Coordination. Coordinate services provided by the Owner, the Owner's consultants, the Design-Builder, and the Design-Builder's consultants and contractors as they relate to the Architect's Portion of the Project.
X	§ 3.2.2	Project Design Presentations. Make presentations to explain the design of the Project to the Owner, Design-Builder, governmental authorities, or others.
X	§ 3.2.3	Governmental Authorities Submissions. Assist the Design-Builder in connection with the Design-Builder's responsibility for filing documents required for the approval of governmental authorities having jurisdiction over the Project.
	§ 3.2.4	Estimates of the Cost of the Work for the Architect's Portion of the Project. Prepare an estimate of the Cost of the Work, as that term is defined in Section 6.1, based on current area, volume, or similar conceptual estimating techniques. As the design progresses through the preparation of the Construction Documents, periodically update the estimate of the Cost of the Work.
X	§ 3.2.5	The Architect shall attend meetings with the Design-Builder and Owner to discuss and review the Owner's Criteria.
X	§ 3.2.6	The Architect shall provide to the Design-Builder a preliminary evaluation of the Owner's Criteria as it relates to the Architect's Portion of the Project. The preliminary evaluation shall discuss possible alternative approaches to design and construction and include the Architect's recommendations, if any, with regard to accelerated or fast-track scheduling, procurement, or phased construction. The preliminary evaluation shall consider cost information, constructability, and procurement and construction scheduling issues.
X	§ 3.2.7	After the Architect reviews the preliminary evaluation with the Design-Builder, the Architect shall provide a written report to the Design-Builder, summarizing the Architect's understanding of the Owner's Criteria as it relates to the Architect's Portion of the Project. The report shall include .1 allocations of program functions, detailing each function and their square foot areas .2 if necessary, recommendations to adjust the Owner's Criteria to conform to the Owner's budget .3 a preliminary schedule, conforming to the Owner's schedule, which shall include proposed design milestones; dates for receiving additional information from, or for work to be completed by the Owner; anticipated date for the Design-Builder's Proposal; and periodic design review sessions with the Owner; and .4 other, if any
X	§ 3.2.8	Preliminary Design. Upon the Design-Builder's issuance of a written notice to proceed, the Architect shall prepare and submit a Preliminary Design to the Design-Builder for the Architect's Portion of the Project. The Preliminary Design shall include a report identifying any deviations from the Owner's Criteria, or any other aspects of the Initial Information, and consist of drawings and other documents, including .1 Confirmation of the allocations of program functions .2 A site plan .3 Concept design, in diagrammatic form, allocating the functions and areas .4 Preliminary building plans, sections, and elevations; and may include some combination of study models, perspective sketches, or digital modeling .5 Structural system .6 Selections of major building systems, including but not limited to mechanical, electrical and plumbing systems, and .7 Outline specifications or sufficient drawing notes describing construction materials
	§ 3.2.9	Design-Builder's Proposal
X	§ 3.2.10	Construction Documents. Upon the Design-Builder's written notice to proceed, the Architect shall further develop the design in accordance with the Design-Build Amendment to the Design-Build Contract, as necessary, and prepare Construction Documents for the Architect's Portion of the Project. The Construction Documents shall set forth in detail the requirements for construction of the Architect's Portion of the Project. The Construction Documents shall include drawings and specifications that establish the quality levels of materials, systems, and performance criteria required. Construction Documents may include Drawings, Specifications, and other documents and electronic data setting forth in detail the requirements for construction of the Work, and shall be consistent with the Design-Build Documents, including the Design-Build Amendment.
	§ 3.2.11	Other Design Services

(continued)

Resource 2.3 Standard Form of Agreement Between Design-Builder and Architect (continued)

§ 3.3 Construction Procurement Services

The Architect shall provide only those Construction Procurement Services listed in this Section 3.3 that are designated by a check or "X" in the adjacent box.

	§ 3.3.1	Bidding/Proposal Information
	§ 3.3.2	Selection of Bidders/Proposers
	§ 3.3.3	Bidding/Proposal Document Reproduction
	§ 3.3.4	Bidding/Proposal Document Distribution
	§ 3.3.5	Substitutions
X	§ 3.3.6	Pre-Bid/Proposal Conference. Participate in, or at the Design-Builder's direction, organize and conduct a pre-bid conference for prospective bidders or pre-proposal conference for prospective proposers.
X	§ 3.3.7	Addenda. Prepare responses to questions from prospective bidders/proposers and provide clarifications and interpretations in the form of addenda.
	§ 3.3.8	Opening of Bids/Proposals
	§ 3.3.9	Bid/Proposal Evaluation
	§ 3.3.10	Bid/Proposal Negotiations

§ 3.4 Construction Contract Administration Services

The Architect shall provide only those Construction Contract Administration Services listed in this Section 3.4 that are designated by a check or "X" in the adjacent box. Duties, responsibilities, and limitations of authority of the Architect under this Section 3.4 shall not be restricted, modified, or extended without written agreement of the Design-Builder and Architect. The Architect shall have authority to act on behalf of the Design-Builder only to the extent provided in this Agreement unless otherwise modified in writing.

	§ 3.4.1	Requests for Information
	§ 3.4.2	Evaluations of the Work Related to the Architect's Portion of the Project
	§ 3.4.3	Review of Contractor's Applications for Payment
X	§ 3.4.4	Submittals (Architect shall review structural Shop Drawings only)
	§ 3.4.5	Review and Prepare Proposed Change Orders and Construction Change Directives
	§ 3.4.6	Minor Changes
	§ 3.4.7	Project Completion
	§ 3.4.8	Final Payment
	§ 3.4.9	Project Completion Documents
	§ 3.4.10	Project Anniversary Review

Resource 2.4 Project Schedule

project task	due date
RFP responses	November 18
shortlist and interviews	December 12–December 15
selection and contract negotiation	Completed before January 4
notice to proceed	January 4
review and evaluate owner's criteria and prepare report	January 4–March 1
design-builder review and pricing	March 2–March 18
owner review and comment	March 19–April 2
preliminary design phase	April 3–May 30
owner review and comment	May 31–June 15
prepare design-build amendment	June 15–June 22
construction documents phase	June 23–August 1
pricing and subcontractor agreements	August 2–August 31
permitting	August 2–August 31
construction begins	September 1
construction complete	August 31 of the following year

166. Early in the planning phase, representatives of the Winter Family Foundation and Parco Design & Planning meet to determine which delivery method best suits this project. They compare the characteristics of various delivery methods and decide to proceed with the work as a design-build project. The characteristics are listed.

- single point of contact for design and construction
- competitive pricing
- no contractor participation in pricing or design
- sequential design and construction phases
- owner has less control over design and construction quality
- cost unknown until design complete
- expedited project schedule
- contractor assumes more risk
- owner assumes risk of construction documents being complete and sufficient
- longer project duration
- fewer contractor-initiated change orders

Determine whether the project delivery methods' characteristics belong to a design-bid-build or design-build approach, and write them into the appropriate columns in the empty table.

design-bid-build ("traditional") approach	design-build approach

167. Two architecture firms are involved with this project. Parco Design & Planning has been hired by the owner as a consultant, and Autumn Architects has been hired by the design-builder to provide design and limited construction phase services. Project tasks include the following.

- Organize community design charrettes.
- Prepare outline specifications for the Winter Family Center building.
- Select type of mechanical system that will be used in the swimming pool area.
- Coordinate geotechnical studies.
- Prepare and submit qualifications data for RFP response.
- Review and comment on progress documents.
- Evaluate applications for payment.
- Prepare drawings to obtain building permit.
- Review structural shop drawings.
- Develop proposed overall project budget.
- Coordinate pre-proposal conference for subcontractors.

In the table shown, write the tasks each firm is responsible for in the appropriate column, indicating in which project phase each activity will occur.

	Parco Design & Planning	Autumn Architects
pre-design		
design		
construction		

168. Parco Design & Planning developed the initial project schedule, which was included in the RFP. After the project award, Meadowfield Construction has become responsible for developing the final project schedule.

Consider the following when preparing the schedule.

- The code enforcement officer requires contractors to have acquired the permit before any site work begins.
- Site clearing is anticipated to take two weeks.
- Excavation can overlap some of the site clearing work and is a four-week activity.
- Elevator installation and installation of the pool filtration equipment may take place concurrently.
- The building may be enclosed by the end of January.
- The contractor will provide temporary heat from January 15 to April 1.
- Interior framing and drywall installation will take place after the building is enclosed.
- Concrete work cannot begin until excavation is complete. Concrete work must be completed by November 1.
- Steel erection begins once concrete work is complete and is projected to take six weeks.
- Exterior wall framing may start at the beginning of December and may overlap part of the steel erection work.
- Windows and doors may be installed as the exterior cladding is being installed.
- The elevator cab is scheduled to be delivered to the site on April 1.

The tasks listed below must be completed during the construction phase. Using the information given, draw a bar on the chart to indicate each task's duration, place it at the appropriate calendar location, and write the task inside the bar.

- cladding
- clearing
- concrete
- elevator
- excavate
- filters
- framing
- framing/drywall
- permit
- steel
- temporary heat
- windows

jul	aug	sep	oct	nov	dec	jan	feb	mar	apr	may	jun

169. Which strategies can Autumn Architects employ to reduce the firm's risk on this project? (Choose the three that apply.)

(A) Team with engineering consultants with whom the firm has worked on previous projects.

(B) Accept the project only if the project structure is changed from contractor-led design-build to architect-led design-build.

(C) Delegate the design of curtain wall details to the subcontractor who will install the system.

(D) Ensure that the architecture firm's contracts with their consultants require the same responsibilities and obligations as the agreement between the architect and the design-builder.

(E) Include installation instructions in the specifications for each product used on the project and perform periodic inspections to ensure that workers are installing items correctly.

(F) Develop a project safety plan.

170. Which statements are true? (Choose the three that apply.)

(A) As a member of the design-build team, Autumn Architects assumes responsibility for determining appropriate construction methods for the project.

(B) The agreement between Meadowfield Construction and Autumn Architects defines the scope of the architecture firm's services.

(C) Autumn Architects' tasks during the design phase of a design-build project vary from those the architect assumes in a traditional design-bid-build project.

(D) Autumn Architects is required to coordinate work performed by the design-builder's consultants and the owner's consultants.

(E) The Winter Family Foundation is Autumn Architects' client.

(F) The Winter Family Foundation is Parco Design & Planning's client.

171. Which provisions are included in the agreement between Autumn Architects and Verdure Engineering? (Choose the four that apply.)

(A) The architect assumes toward the consultant the same obligations and responsibilities that the design-builder assumes toward the architect.

(B) The agreement between the architect and consultant creates a contract between the consultant and the design-builder.

(C) The architect's agreement with the design-builder is attached as an exhibit to this agreement.

(D) Communications between the consultant and the design-builder are to be through the architect.

(E) The consultant is required to carry liability insurance for the duration of the agreement.

(F) The architect is required to pay the consultant within 10 days of receipt of the consultant's invoice for services rendered.

172. Using the elements in the given illustration, create a diagram showing this project's contractual relationships. (Not all of the elements will be used.) Draw two contract party bubbles and draw a contract line between them.

contract parties		contract
Summerville Parks Department	Winter Family Foundation	A141
		A142
Autumn Architects	Meadowfield Construction	B143
		C141
Parco Design & Planning	Equinox Building Systems	C441

Project Management

173. Which responsibility is most likely to be assigned to Parco Design & Planning?

(A) Review and approve applications for payment.

(B) Expand the program defined in the request for proposal (RFP) to establish square footage requirements for each space.

(C) Provide value engineering services if the proposed project price exceeds the project budget.

(D) Certify that the design complies with applicable codes and regulations.

174. Which situation requires an amendment to Autumn Architects' contract with Meadowfield Construction?

(A) Meadowfield Construction phases construction of the project.

(B) Subcontractors request additional details for attachment of the cladding system planned for the exterior of the Winter Family Center building.

(C) The Winter Family Foundation asks Meadowfield Construction to organize an open house, where Autumn Architects will present conceptual drawings of the new facility to members of the community.

(D) The Winter Family Foundation includes the furniture and fixtures package in Meadowfield Construction's scope of work, and Autumn Architects is required to prepare the change order documentation.

175. Which strategy can the design-build team use to control scope creep?

(A) Request that the Winter Family Foundation approve the report prepared by the architect summarizing the design team's understanding of the owner's criteria.

(B) Allow project changes to be made by any of the Foundation's representatives.

(C) Keep a list of all changes requested by the owner and address the issues at the start of the construction documents phase.

(D) Assign additional construction management tasks to the architect so that the design-builder can focus on expediting the requested changes.

Solutions

Multiple Choice

81. (A) (B) (C) ●
82. ● (B) (C) (D)
83. ● (B) (C) (D) (E) ●
84. ● (B) (C) (D)
85. (A) (B) (C) ●
86. (A) (B) ● (D) ● ●
87. (A) ● (C) (D)
88. (A) ● (C) (D)
89. (A) (B) ● (D)
90. (A) (B) (C) ●
91. ● ● ● (D) (E) ●
92. ● (B) ● ● ● (F)
93. ● (B) (C) (D)
94. (A) ● (C) (D)
95. (A) ● (C) (D)
96. (A) (B) ● (D)
97. (A) (B) ● (D)
98. ● (B) (C) (D)
99. 14
100. ● (B) (C) (D)
101. ● (B) (C) (D)
102. (A) (B) ● (D)
103. ● (B) (C) (D)
104. (A) (B) (C) ●
105. (A) (B) (C) ●
106. (A) ● (C) ● ● (F)
107. (A) ● (C) (D)
108. (A) (B) ● (D)
109. (A) (B) ● (D)
110. (A) ● (C) (D)
111. ● (B) (C) (D)
112. (A) (B) ● (D)
113. ● (B) (C) (D)
114. (A) (B) ● (D)
115. (A) (B) (C) ●
116. (A) (B) (C) ●
117. (A) ● (C) (D)
118. ● ● (C) ● ● (F)
119. (A) ● (C) (D)
120. ● (B) (C) (D)
121. See Sol. 121.
122. ● (B) (C) (D)
123. (A) ● (C) (D)
124. (A) (B) ● (D)
125. (A) (B) (C) ●
126. (A) (B) (C) ●
127. (A) (B) ● (D)
128. (A) ● (C) (D)
129. (A) (B) (C) ●
130. See Sol. 130.
131. (A) (B) (C) ●
132. (A) (B) ● (D)
133. (A) (B) ● (D)
134. (A) (B) (C) ●
135. ● (B) (C) (D)
136. (A) (B) ● (D)
137. (A) (B) ● (D)
138. (A) ● (C) (D)
139. (A) (B) (C) ●
140. (A) ● ● ● ● (F)
141. (A) (B) ● (D)
142. ● (B) (C) (D)
143. (A) ● (C) (D)
144. (A) (B) (C) ●
145. (A) (B) (C) ●
146. (A) ● ● (D) ● ●
147. (A) ● (C) (D)
148. (A) (B) (C) ●
149. ● ● ● ● (E) (F)
150. (A) (B) (C) ●
151. (A) (B) ● (D)
152. (A) (B) (C) ●
153. (A) ● (C) (D)
154. (A) (B) ● (D)
155. (A) ● ● ● (E) (F)
156. ● (B) (C) (D)

Case Study 1

157. ● ● (C) ● (E) ●
158. (A) (B) (C) ●
159. (A) (B) ● (D)
160. (A) (B) (C) ●
161. (A) ● (C) (D)
162. ● (B) ● ● (E) ●
163. (A) (B) ● (D)
164. See Sol. 164.
165. (A) ● (C) (D)

Case Study 2

166. See Sol. 166.
167. See Sol. 167.
168. See Sol. 168.
169. ● (B) ● ● (E) (F)
170. (A) ● ● (D) (E) ●
171. ● (B) ● ● ● (F)
172. See Sol. 172.
173. ● (B) (C) (D)
174. (A) (B) (C) ●
175. ● (B) (C) (D)

81. The *International Building Code* requires interior finish materials applied to wall and ceiling surfaces to be categorized as Class A, B, or C. These materials are typically vinyl or textile wall coverings and fabrics that are applied over a substrate such as gypsum board. Each proposed material is assigned a class designation based on that product's performance in a series of flame spread and smoke developed tests.

The designer must consider the occupancy of the building, the location and method of installation of the material, and whether the building will be sprinklered to determine the minimum interior finish class required in a building or space within a building, and must ensure that the specified finish materials and systems comply.

The IBC does not consider exposed heavy timber structural members to be interior finish materials as long as the elements comply with the requirements for Type IV (Heavy Timber) construction. Combustible trim such as wood baseboards and cornices are not considered interior finish materials unless they cover more than 10% of the wall or ceiling area; however, these components are still required to have a minimum Class C flame spread and smoke-developed index. Solid wood flooring products must comply with the requirements for combustible materials in Type I and Type II construction.

Wainscoting is the only application listed in which the wood elements are considered interior finish materials and can be determined to have a Class A or Class B flame spread and smoke-developed index.

The answer is (D).

82. A change in floor level of $^1/_4$ in or less is acceptable; the beveled threshold helps to ease the transition and is beneficial at this location. The minimum width of the required clear floor area on the pull side of a door is 18 in when the when the door is approached from the front, so the provided space is greater than that required. A ramp that rises 6 in over 8 ft (96 in) has a slope of 1:16, which is less than the required 1:12 slope for ramps, and it complies with the accessibility requirements.

A wall-mounted object placed more than 27 in above the floor cannot protrude more than 4 in from the wall. It is reasonable to assume that the cabinet is mounted at a typical height and that the fixture or portions of the fixture are more than 27 in above the floor. Therefore, the fire extinguisher cabinet does not comply with the accessibility requirements and must be removed or replaced with a recessed model.

The answer is (A).

83. Lead may be found in paint in older buildings (pre-1978) and in plumbing pipes, solder, and roof flashings. It is linked to neurological problems, particularly in young children.

Polychlorinated biphenyls (PCBs) were outlawed in the 1980s but still can be found in older electrical equipment. PCBs are thought to cause a variety of types of cancer.

Radon is a naturally occurring, colorless, odorless, and carcinogenic gas that can be detected in spaces where a building comes in contact with the earth, such as a basement or crawlspace.

Crystalline silica is a natural material found in sand or stone and may be present in masonry products. It becomes respirable when the masonry is cut or ground and dust is released and can irritate the respiratory membranes. It is a carcinogen. Crystalline silica is also an ingredient in many latex paints.

Asbestos and glass fiber have been common components of insulation products. Asbestos was banned from most construction products in the 1970s and 1980s when it was determined that exposure to disturbed material causes cancer and related respiratory diseases. It can still be found in old buildings in wall and pipe insulation, floor and ceiling tiles, and equipment. Glass fiber requires special handling procedures to comply with Occupational Safety and Health Administration (OSHA) standards, such as protective clothing, respirators, and eye protection to keep the fibers away from the body. Prolonged unprotected exposure to glass fiber can irritate the skin and respiratory tract; it is undetermined if the material can cause cancer.

The answer is (A) and (F).

84. AIA Document A201 addresses issues of insurance and bonds in Article 11.

Section 11.2 requires the owner to carry standard liability insurance throughout the project, but an owner would not be required to carry professional liability insurance. This document does not require the owner to include the architect and the contractor as additional insureds on the owner's policies. (Section 11.1.4, however, does require the contractor to include the architect and owner as additional insureds on the contractor's commercial liability coverage.)

Section 11.3.3 discusses loss of use insurance. This coverage is optional; it is not required by AIA Document A201.

The owner is required to purchase all-risk property insurance per Sec. 11.3.1. Section 11.3.2 also requires the owner to carry boiler and machinery insurance until final acceptance of the work.

Architects are not qualified to give clients advice regarding insurance coverage. Owners should be advised to consult with an attorney or insurance agent if they have questions about insurance recommendations for the project. After this consultation architects can use AIA Document G612, *Owner's Instructions to the Architect*, to gather information about their client's insurance requirements for the purposes of preparing the contract documents.

The answer is (A).

85. The contract documents are the contract between the owner and the contractor according to American Institute of Architects (AIA) Document A201, *General Conditions of the Contract for Construction*, Sec. 1.1.2. This article goes on to explain that this contract is only between these two parties and that no other project participant is contractually obligated to another by this agreement.

The answer is (D).

86. AIA Document B101, Sec. 1.3.3, addresses changes in services and situations in which the architect is entitled to an adjustment to the schedule and compensation. The services defined in the agreement can be modified in writing and upon mutual agreement between the architect and the owner. If the architect is asked to assume additional responsibilities, or the scope of the project changes, the contract should be modified accordingly.

In circumstances where the owner delays the project because of indecision, changes to the project, or failure of performance on the part of consultants hired directly by the owner, the architect may request an adjustment of deadlines and fees. Appearing at public hearings on the owner's behalf is also cited in this subparagraph, as well as the adoption of new codes or regulations midway through the project that require revisions to previously prepared documents. The contract sum or time is not changed if the delay or error is the fault of the architect, such as the coordination error on the part of his consultants. The architect cannot receive compensation from the owner for additional time spent or expenses related to remedying the situation.

The answer is (C), (E), and (F).

87. AIA Document A201, Sec. 11.1.4, requires the contractor to include the owner, architect, and architect's consultants as additional insureds on the contractor's liability insurance policy for claims caused by the contractor's negligence. The owner is required to carry all-risk type property insurance per Sec. 11.3.1.1.

Property insurance deductibles are paid by the owner, not by the contractor, as explained in Sec. 11.3.1.3.

Section 11.3.1.2 states that if the owner chooses not to purchase property insurance and does not notify the contractor of this decision, the owner becomes responsible for all losses that the property insurance would have covered.

The answer is (B).

88. A proprietary specification is not the best choice in a situation where the owner and architect wish to encourage competitive bids. It specifies a particular product by brand name and allows no substitutions. This is the easiest type of specification for the architect to write, but puts all of the responsibility for choosing a material that is code-compliant and technically correct onto the architect.

A base bid with alternates specification is similar in format to the base bid with "approved equal" language specification. Both call for a specific product but allow substitution of other materials. However, an important difference between the two is that the base bid with alternates allows a contractor to substitute a product that he feels is equal, and does not require the architect's approval. The product he submits may not be comparable to the one defined in the specification but must be accepted due to the way the specification is written. This type of specification does not give the owner and architect control over the quality of the products used.

A descriptive specification defines the type of outcome desired but does not list specific products. It is the most difficult type of specification for an architect to write because it requires listing all of the criteria that a material or assembly must meet. The base bid with "approved equal" language lists the desired product and states that an alternative product proposed by a contractor will be considered by the architect. This establishes a minimum level of quality based upon the characteristics of the specified product, but it puts the responsibility on the contractor to find and submit an alternative product if he or she wishes. This type of specification will require the architect to evaluate the proposals during the bidding phase and issue addenda notifying all bidders of the decisions. When using a base bid with an "approved equal" type of specification, it is important to include a deadline for submission of proposed substitutions during the bidding phase to allow the architect enough time to research the products and issue notification to the bidders of the substitutions' acceptance or rejection.

The answer is (B).

89. If a penalty clause (a charge to the contractor for not completing work by the agreed-upon time of substantial completion) is included in an agreement, a bonus provision (payment to the contractor if the work is completed before the deadline) must also be included. Penalty clauses are generally disfavored and when they appear alone they are almost always held unenforceable by courts. Thus, a penalty clause must be accompanied by a bonus clause, and even this does not guarantee that it will be enforceable. A better way to cover the owner for potential losses is to include a liquidated damages clause.

Liquidated damages are damages agreed upon in advance; they are based upon estimated costs that will be incurred by the owner if the contractor does not complete the work by the agreed-upon completion date and the owner cannot use the building at the anticipated time. For example, if the owner estimates that he will lose $1000 in profits each day that he cannot occupy his new dry cleaning business, liquidated damages may be assessed to cover this expense. His actual losses may be less or greater; liquidated damages represent a reasonable average.

Clauses stipulating that liquidated damages will be assessed may also be accompanied by a bonus provision, but this is not required.

The answer is (C).

90. Arbitration is binding on all parties and, under ordinary circumstances, the decisions of arbitrators may not be appealed. Arbitration is completely separate from the judicial system. In rare instances, the courts may be called upon to respond to a case where allegations of fraud or partiality are made against an arbitrator or where there is reason to believe that the arbitration board made a decision on an issue that was not included in the agreement to arbitrate. In most circumstances, however, arbitration and litigation are two very distinct paths of dispute resolution and they do not cross.

Arbitration is generally less expensive than litigation but more expensive than negotiation or mediation. If the parties have agreed to arbitrate, they must abide by the arbitrator's decision. Arbitration places the disagreement into the hands of an objective third party, usually someone familiar with the construction industry, to render a decision. Because the IDM is not a neutral party, he or she would not be qualified to serve as an arbitrator. Both parties receive a list of potential arbitrators and have the opportunity to strike the names of persons to whom they object. An arbitrator or arbitration board is selected from the names that remain, or, under the Uniform Arbitration Act, each party chooses one arbitrator and together the arbitrators select a third. The arbitrator hears the evidence from both parties and upon conclusion of the hearings issues a statement with the arbitrator's findings and the amount due to the prevailing party. The decision is final, and unless the parties request a "reasoned" award, no explanation is provided.

The answer is (D).

91. The costs associated with preparing a response to a request for proposal and keeping office computer systems up to date are considered part of the architect's general overhead costs and may not be charged to the owner. AIA Document B101, Sec. 11.8, addresses the issue of reimbursable expenses. Reimbursable expenses are costs directly related to a project that are incurred by the architect and charged to the owner. Reimbursable expenses can include authorized travel, accommodations, and meals; reproductions and postage; overtime work (with prior owner authorization); additional insurance that the architect purchases specifically for this project or at the owner's request; renderings, models, and mock-ups; fees for jurisdictional approvals, such as permit fees; and taxes on professional services.

Usually, the architect includes a markup to reimbursable expenses to cover administrative expenses and the cost of advancing money on the owner's behalf. This multiplier is determined in AIA Document B101, Sec. 11.8.2.

The answer is (A), (B), (C), and (F).

92. AIA Document B101 does not require the owner to provide evidence that he or she has secured adequate funding for the project. The owner is also not required to provide information on regulations such as codes or zoning ordinances that apply at the project site; this research should be conducted by the architect. Section 5.1 requires the owner to provide a program, which includes information on the project objectives, criteria, and proposed schedule. Special requirements, such as an accelerated design or construction schedule or the desire to pursue a nontraditional construction delivery method, should be included in the program or documented at the beginning of the project to ensure that both parties have a clear understanding of the scope of the work. The owner is required to determine a budget for the project and to keep the architect apprised of any changes to this budget, per AIA Document B101, Sec. 5.2.

The answer is (A), (C), (D), and (E).

93. Contract time is measured in calendar days. The target date for substantial completion will be May 13, because it is 60 days from the date of commencement. No exceptions are made for weekends or holidays when calculating contract time.

The answer is (A).

94. When the dates included in the contract are firm, the contract will include the phrase "time is of the essence." By agreeing to the contract, the contractor is affirming that the construction period stated is a reasonable amount of time for completing the job and that the work will be completed by the specified date. If both parties (the contractor and the owner) do not fulfill their obligations by the dates stated in the contract, they may be in breach of the contract. This language is included in American Institute of Architects (AIA) Document A201, *General Conditions of the Contract for Construction*, Sec. 8.2.1. If the contractual deadlines are not met, the contractor may be forced to pay the owner liquidated damages if this provision has been agreed upon in advance.

The answer is (B).

95. AIA Document B101 requires the architect to have insurance coverage. If the owner requests more coverage than the architect normally carries, the architect may seek reimbursement for the additional insurance costs (Sec. 2.5). The owner is responsible for obtaining approvals from local authorities, but the architect is required to assist in this (Sec. 3.1.6). The contractor is responsible for preparing the punch list of items to be completed near the end of the project (Sec. 3.6.6.2).

Section 3.2.3 and Sec. 3.2.5.1 require the architect to discuss sustainable design technologies with the owner, but their use is not required if incorporating them into the project is not within the owner's budget or project scope. If the owner requests services such as design for Leadership in Energy and Environmental Design (LEED) certification, energy modeling, commissioning, or incorporation of innovative materials or systems, these additional services should be defined under Article 4.

The answer is (B).

96. AIA Document A201, Sec. 3.3.1, states that the contractor is solely responsible for the means and methods of construction, unless the contract documents give specific instructions to the contrary. However, upon determining that the instructions create an unsafe situation, the contractor must give timely written notice to the owner and architect and not proceed with the unsafe portion of the work until receipt of further written instructions from the architect. If the contractor is instructed to proceed regardless of the safety concerns raised, the owner becomes solely responsible for any resulting loss or damage.

The answer is (C).

97. The questions posed in AIA Document G612 deal with the owner-contractor contract. The form is divided into three sections: contract administration, insurance and bonds, and bidding procedures. This checklist provides a guide for the owner and the owner's attorney and insurance agent as they establish the requirements for a particular project and develop the specific language used to modify the contract. The architect may also furnish AIA Document A503, *Guide for Supplementary Conditions*, to further assist the owner and the owner's counsel in writing the supplementary conditions. Note that drafting the supplementary conditions is the responsibility of the owner, and the proper way to make revisions to the general conditions is to address the issues in the supplementary conditions.

It is preferable for the architect to request this information from the owner early in the project. The owner's preferences regarding project delivery methods and contracts will influence how the project is organized and how the documents are prepared.

The answer is (C).

98. Traditionally, real estate laws were based on the Latin phrase, *cuius est solum, ejus est usque ad caelum et ad inferos*, which means "whomever owns the land shall own the earth to its center and up to the heavens." Modern interpretations of land rights are a bit more complicated, particularly in states that separate surface and subsurface rights. Mineral interests pertain to oil, coal, natural gas, and other minerals found beneath the surface.

Air rights permit a party to use the open space above land or an existing structure. Air rights can be sold or transferred to another party. For example, in Boston, space above the Massachusetts Turnpike can be leased for development of buildings and parks constructed on massive platforms. Christ Church in New York City sold its air rights for $430 per square foot to developers who will "transfer" the unused vertical space to another building, so that structure can be built higher than zoning ordinances normally allow. Air rights do not give a property owner the right to prohibit aircraft from entering that space; in the United States, the Federal Aviation Administration controls where aircraft can and cannot fly, not individual property owners.

Riparian rights allow property owners whose lots abut a natural river the right to make use of that resource. Riparian rights are similar to riparian rights but apply to areas along the shores of bodies of water affected by tidal currents, such as oceans and navigable lakes. State laws vary, but generally, man-made bodies of water do not have the same usage rights attached to them as natural waterways.

The answer is (A).

99. The critical path is the path that takes the most amount of time to complete. In this diagram, the critical path is 1-2-3-4-5-6, and it will take 14 days to complete these activities.

The answer is 14.

100. Two major issues should be addressed in every agreement between an architect and a consultant: passing through rights and responsibilities of the architect to the consultant, and sharing risks and rewards.

Passing through responsibility and rights is often accomplished by incorporating the owner-architect agreement. American Institute of Architects (AIA) Document C401 may be used along with AIA Document B101, *Standard Owner and Architect Agreement*, to accomplish this. If the

AIA documents are not used, the architect should ensure that the consultant is aware of his or her duties in all phases of the project. The agreement should also establish responsibilities such as compensation, internal coordination, revisions on request of the architect, cost estimating, assistance with the bidding process, review of shop drawings, and site visits.

When undertaking a project, an architect assumes a certain amount of risk. This risk is appropriately shared with the consultant as a member of the project team, and the architect may require provisions addressing this risk to be a part of the agreement. For example, the architect can be held liable if consultant's duties are not performed with reasonable care; therefore, the architect may decide that it is prudent for the consultant to carry liability insurance.

The answer is (A).

101. A milestone chart is appropriate for this project schedule. Milestone charts are best for scheduling small projects with few participants. They consist of a list of deadlines and assignment of responsibility for each task. With only three people directly involved with this project, this type of schedule is a good way to set goals and keep the project on track.

Bar charts or Gantt charts show both start and finish dates and work well for larger architectural projects. CPM, or the critical path method, shows complex interrelationships between tasks. This scheduling method can be used for extremely large architectural projects, but more commonly is used by contractors to coordinate construction.

The answer is (A).

102. Budget prices are normally escalated to reflect the anticipated price at the midpoint of construction.

The answer is (C).

103. AIA Document B101, Article 1, allows incorporation of the project program as a part of the initial information, and Sec. 5.1 requires the owner to furnish this information.

The owner may choose to hire an architect to perform a programming study or to coordinate this process; these are considered changes to the architect's services for which additional compensation could be requested.

The answer is (A).

104. Daylighting, indirect lighting, and underfloor ventilation systems will add only a few feet, at most, to each floor. Interstitial spaces between occupied floors require the most additional height per floor and the most total building height because they must be high enough to accommodate a person accessing the space for maintenance duties, as well as the ducts and equipment servicing the occupied spaces below.

The answer is (D).

105. General obligation bonds are typically used to fund a specific project, such as a library or fire station. They are not used to encourage private development, although later private development could be a consequence of the new public facility being constructed (such as apartments or restaurants built in the vicinity of a publicly funded baseball stadium). Because all taxpayers in the jurisdiction issuing the general obligation bonds must pay off the bonds through a property tax, a voter majority is required.

Developer impact fees are generally used to fund infrastructure improvements made necessary by new development. Although these fees are a common method of raising money, they can have a negative effect because developers look for areas to build in where impact fees are not charged.

Business improvement districts are used to fund public space improvements, such as streetscapes, to enhance an area's appeal and, indirectly, its property values. Taxes are assessed on those property owners in the district who will benefit from the improvements, so this type of financing is not intended to encourage private development. Tax increment financing is a method cities use to issue bonds to pay for improvements (such as new sewers or streets) within a specified district. These improvements are intended to stimulate private development within the district by providing better infrastructure and city services. During the time of redevelopment, taxes are based on the assessed valuation of the properties prior to the redevelopment. (A tax based on the value of the property being taxed is known as *ad valorem* tax.) After the improvements are complete, the increase in tax revenue attributable to the development (the tax increment) is used to repay the bonds.

The answer is (D).

106. AIA Document B101 classifies services provided by the architect and his or her consultants as either basic services or additional services. Basic services are those tasks that must be performed to satisfy the requirements of Article 3, Scope of Architect's Basic Services. This includes architectural design and documentation as well as the structural, mechanical, and electrical engineering services necessary to support the architectural design, and would include preparation of the project manual, construction administration duties, and structural engineering.

Additional services are defined in Article 4. These are professional services that the architecture firm or consultants may provide to the owner for an additional fee.

Programming, existing facilities surveys and commissioning are examples of additional services.

The answer is (B), (D), and (E).

107. Subrogation is the legal technique whereby an insurer "steps into the shoes" of a party to whom it has made payment. The building owner has the right to try to collect compensation for the fire damage from the parties at fault. But when the insurance company pays the owner for the cost of repairing the damage, the company is subrogated to this right of the owner, and may sue the contractors in the owner's name. The insurer in this situation is called the subrogee; the insured party is the subrogor.

American Institute of Architects (AIA) Document A201, *General Conditions of the Contract for Construction*, Sec. 11.3.7, encourages the use of a waiver of subrogation clause in construction contracts in order to maintain relationships among project participants and minimize the opportunity for lawsuits. By agreeing to such a clause, the parties waive their rights against each other for any damage during construction that is covered by insurance. The rights obtained by the subrogee (the insurance company) cannot be any greater than the rights held originally by the subrogor (the owner), so if an owner and contractor have waived these rights in the contract between them, these rights cannot pass to the insurance company through subrogation.

Parties to such a contract must ensure that the waiver of subrogation clause does not conflict with the requirements of their insurance policies.

The answer is (B).

108. First determine the multiplying factor.

$$\begin{aligned}\text{cost index factor} &= \frac{\text{cost index of city B}}{\text{cost index of city A}} \\ &= \frac{1350}{1250} \\ &= 1.08\end{aligned}$$

Multiply this factor by the project cost in city A.

$$\begin{aligned}\begin{array}{l}\text{cost of similar}\\ \text{project in city B}\end{array} &= \begin{array}{l}(\text{cost in city A})\\ \quad\times(\text{cost index factor})\end{array} \\ &= (\$3{,}000{,}000)(1.08) \\ &= \$3{,}240{,}000\end{aligned}$$

Finally, increase for inflation.

$$\begin{aligned}\text{budget after inflation} &= \begin{array}{l}(\text{cost in city B})\\ \quad\times(\text{inflation factor})\end{array} \\ &= (\$3{,}240{,}000)(1.02) \\ &= \$3{,}304{,}800 \quad (\$3{,}305{,}000)\end{aligned}$$

There are two other methods that can be used to achieve the same result. Inflation can be calculated first and then the cost index factor can be used, or the inflation factor and cost index factor can be multiplied and applied to the cost in city A.

The answer is (C).

109. City B has a higher cost index, so divide the lower into the higher.

$$\frac{1517}{1440} = 1.053$$

Multiply this factor by the cost in city A ($1,500,000) to get $1,579,500. Then increase this by the 5% inflation factor.

$$(\$1{,}579{,}500)(1.05) = \$1{,}658{,}475 \quad (\$1{,}660{,}000)$$

Alternately, increase for inflation first, then use the cost index factor.

The answer is (C).

110. At the beginning of the schematic design phase the designer is probably estimating the cost of the project based on the number of square feet, multiplied by an assumed cost per square foot for the building type. At this very early stage in the project, there would probably not be enough information available about the specifics of the design to make adjustments to materials or levels of finish that would have much impact on the estimated price. These types of adjustments are more appropriate later in the design process as a part of a value engineering study.

Because the budget overage is small and the project is in the early schematic design phase, the budget discrepancy could probably be made up through a slight reduction in building area.

The answer is (B).

111. Labor unions have been a part of the United States economy since the country was founded. These organizations of workers, which began in the colonial era as systems of guilds, strive to improve working conditions, benefits, and wage rates for their membership.

However, the demands of labor unions come with a price, often raising the cost of labor and making union labor much more expensive than labor offered by open shops (businesses that use nonunion workers). This can put a contractor who uses union labor at a disadvantage when competing with a nonunion contractor on a project out for bid. If use of union labor is required by the owner, such as on some public construction projects, prices for the work may be significantly higher.

The other three answer choices have much less or no impact on labor costs. Interest rates affect the volume of construction as a whole, which in turn may affect the prices of labor and materials. Labor rates can vary by geographic location, and the cost of labor in suburban areas tends to be lower than in urban or extremely rural areas. Neither of these affects labor costs as much as a requirement to use union labor does. Overhead costs are not considered to be part of labor costs and are not included in calculations of labor rates.

The answer is (A).

112. Partnering is a management practice that encourages team members to work toward a common goal. It was originally tested on United States Army Corps of Engineers projects in the 1980s and was found to reduce project disputes and litigation costs compared to traditional project delivery methods.

The owner initiates a partnering agreement. The owner hires the architect and contractor and might also hire other consultants. The owner has a separate contract with each professional. In these contracts, the consultants agree to be a part of the partnering process, which means that they agree to participate in partnering activities and meetings and adhere to the dispute resolution terms defined by the team. The participants do not have a contractual relationship with each other (i.e., their contracts are with the owner) but they agree to cooperate and work together in good faith throughout the course of the project.

At the beginning of the project, the team members choose a third-party facilitator who leads a kick-off workshop in which the project goals are discussed, a work plan and schedule is developed, potential conflicts are identified, and the team determines the means of dispute resolution that will be used if required. The participants also develop an issue resolution ladder, which is a strategy for anticipating potential problems and a method for dealing with them.

The results of the kick-off workshop discussion are summarized in a partnering charter, to which all participants agree. Throughout the project, the facilitator will organize periodic partnering meetings to address and resolve issues that arise. At the end of the project, the facilitator will conduct an evaluation and summarize the advantages and disadvantages of the approach.

Partnering provides many advantages for the owner. Partnering projects are more likely to be completed on time and within budget, which saves time and money. Disputes are minimized and productivity and safety increase. The architect and other consultants will not necessarily see financial benefits or be exposed to additional risk. Moreover, these other team members will realize more intangible benefits because the process encourages greater interaction and project satisfaction.

The answer is (C).

113. Design-assist contracting is a strategy that an architect and owner can use when a portion of a project requires specialized detailing and specifications—often old or new technology about which the architect may not have sufficient technical knowledge. In this case, it is more efficient for the architect and owner to ask a manufacturer or a specialty craftsman to assist with the design and detailing of that system, rather than have the architect research the system from the beginning. The process is discussed in the AIA Best Practices document, *The Basics of Design-Assist Contracting.*

Design-assist contracting works well when it is incorporated into a project that will use a design-build or construction management at risk project delivery method. It is not appropriate for use on a project that will be bid.

Design-assist contracting is a three-phase process, not a four-phase process. First, the owner and architect identify portions of the project that will be approached in this way and write a request for proposal (RFP) for the required services. The RFP is issued to trade representatives, who prepare a proposal for providing design assistance based on the scope of work, design and construction budgets, and time frame outlined in the document. Second, the responses are reviewed and the architect and owner select a collaborator. Third, the selected subcontractor works with the architect to provide technical advice on construction details pertaining to the system and to write the specifications. The trade contractor is paid a design fee by the owner as compensation for the services. It is not a given, however, that the trade contractor will be awarded the contract.

The preliminary construction budget includes a placeholder amount for the system. If the owner is satisfied with the trade representative's performance, the company that assisted with the design receives the first opportunity to fulfill the scope, budget, and schedule requirements. If this subcontractor is awarded the contract, the subcontractor's documentation developed during the design phase may be used instead of preparing additional shop drawings. If the original subcontractor cannot provide the system within these constraints, the owner may choose to re-open the bid to other firms that can provide materials and labor that fulfill the contract requirements within the project parameters.

The answer is (A).

114. The Davis-Bacon Act requires workers to be paid local prevailing wages when public funds are used. The Clinger-Cohen Act allows the use of design-build contracting on federally funded projects. The Miller Act requires contractors to post performance and payment bonds.

The Brooks Act requires federal agencies to award projects to architecture and engineering firms based on qualifications-based selection processes. Firms submit evidence of their experience and qualifications but do not submit a cost proposal. After the firm is selected, the agency negotiates with the firm to determine the fee.

The answer is (C).

115. A hierarchical view of different types of work plans is shown.

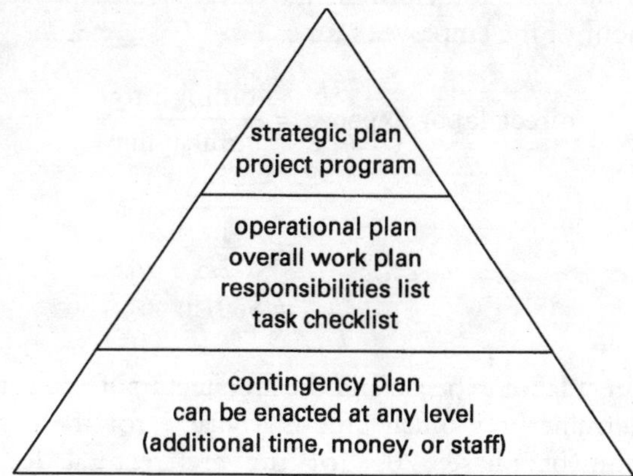

Strategic, tactical, and operational plans can be used to organize and schedule a design project. A contingency plan allows the project team to address unforeseen issues that may arise during the course of a project.

The firm principal or project architect takes the information from a strategic plan and uses it to develop a tactical plan, which is a list and schedule of the activities that must occur to accomplish the goals defined in the strategic plan. What architects generally call a project work plan is a type of tactical plan. This plan includes assigning responsibility for each task (i.e., to in-house staff or consultants), determining how much time and money is allocated for each task, and charting when tasks must be completed to keep the project on schedule, including deadlines or submission requirements. A tactical plan has a level of detail that falls in between a strategic plan and an operational plan. For example, a tactical plan lists "structural design by consultant" and may list review milestones or submission dates, but it does not break this topic into very specific tasks.

An operational plan is used by a designer or project manager who is responsible for a smaller part of the project. In a design project, an operational plan may be implemented through a responsibilities matrix or a task checklist. For example, a structural engineer may develop an operational plan that includes a list of the activities that the firm must complete to develop the design of the structural systems. The structural engineer begins by analyzing and applying the requirements and schedule defined in the architect's work plan. The engineer then lists the required engineering tasks, which may include receiving and reviewing the geotechnical report, choosing and designing the foundation system, completing wind and seismic loading analysis, selecting a material and calculating reactions for the structural frame, coordinating with the architect and other building systems engineers as their portions of the design are developed, and preparing the final documents and specifications.

A contingency plan is a way to rescue a troubled project, proposed in advance of a project being in trouble. Issues may arise for a variety of reasons but are usually attributable to a lack of time, money, or resources. A project may also encounter unforeseen issues or conditions related to the site, a delay in the approvals process, a change in the owner's direction or available resources, or a delay caused by a natural disaster. A contingency plan helps the architect respond to these issues quickly and thoughtfully. For example, a zoning approval board meeting is canceled because of a snowstorm, and the project does not receive land development plan approval until the next month. The design and construction schedules for the project may be adjusted to factor in this extra time. The architect may allow for these types of unforeseen conditions by including a design contingency in the project budget (e.g., usually 5–10%, determined by the architect), encouraging the owner to include a contingency in the construction budget (e.g., usually 5–10%, determined by the owner), and building extra time into the design and construction schedule.

A strategic plan is a high-level plan that outlines broad-scope project objectives. One example of a strategic plan is the program for an architectural project. The owner, with the assistance of a programmer or the architect, prepares the program. The architect becomes familiar with the requirements and determines both the design approach and the production plan to satisfy the program.

The answer is (D).

116. During the project's earliest stages, an architect may not fully understand the owner's desired scope of work, and the architect may not comprehend unforeseen conditions that make the project more complex. As the project progresses, the scope of work required to complete the design becomes clear. So as the project nears completion, the reserved contingency fee percentage may be reduced.

The traditional owner-architect agreement used for design-bid-build projects assigns a set of responsibilities to the architect that are fairly consistent from project to project. However, the architect's agreement with the design-builder determines the architect's responsibilities, and the design-builder has more flexibility in selecting the services that the contract will include. The design-builder may choose to use the architect's services in all phases of design and construction or may not require the architect to be as involved in the construction phase as during the design stages. The percentage of the fee that the architecture firm should allocate to each phase of the project varies depending on the tasks the architecture firm has been contracted to perform.

Most estimations of architectural fees can be grouped into two categories: top-down approaches or bottom-up approaches.

A bottom-up approach begins with a list of tasks and an estimate of how much time it will take to accomplish them. The anticipated hours are multiplied by the billing rate of the person to whom each responsibility is assigned. Any other expenses or allowances, such as consultant's fees and nonreimbursable project costs, are added. The total is the estimated fee that must be charged to cover the firm's expenses and generate the desired profit.

With a top-down approach, the architect either assumes the total proposed fee based on historical data gathered from other projects (e.g., through a per-square-foot calculation, a percentage of construction cost, a comparison to the fee earned for a similar project, etc.) or the owner sets the fee that will be paid. From the established fee, the architect first deducts the costs for consultants' services, the anticipated profit, and nonreimbursable costs. The remainder is the amount available for direct labor provided by the architecture firm's staff. A percentage of this amount is allocated to each phase of the project. The money available for each phase is divided by the direct labor cost for each person working on the project to determine the number of hours that can be devoted to the project.

The answer is (D).

117. The architecture firm's project manager determines how much time is available for the design team's work on the project. If the team can meet this goal, the architecture firm will earn the projected profit. If the project's completion time is less than anticipated, the profit increases. If it takes more time, the profit decreases.

The total design fee is \$312,500. Of this amount, \$162,500 will be paid to consultants or be used to cover other expenses related to the project. The remainder is the amount that the architecture firm will keep. This money will be used to pay for production expenses (i.e., direct labor).

$$\begin{aligned}\text{production fee} &= \text{design fee} - \text{other expenses}\\ &= \$312{,}500 - \$162{,}500\\ &= \$150{,}000\end{aligned}$$

Each employee's billing rate is \$125 per hour. The firm uses a multiplier of 2.5 times the direct labor expense to determine the billing rates. This information may be used to figure out direct labor expenses. Direct labor expenses include the salary, benefits, and other expenses to the firm associated with each employee. The billing rate is divided by the multiplier to determine the direct labor expense for each hour of the employee's time.

$$\begin{aligned}\text{direct labor expense} &= \frac{\text{billing rate}}{\text{multiplier}}\\ &= \frac{\frac{\$125}{\text{hr}}}{2.5}\\ &= \$50/\text{hr}\end{aligned}$$

The direct labor expense and the architectural fee are used to determine how much time is available for the design development phase. 20% of the architectural fee of \$150,000 is \$30,000—the amount that the project manager has budgeted for use during the design development phase.

$$\begin{aligned}\text{design development time} &= \frac{20\%\ \text{architectural fee}}{\text{direct labor expense}}\\ &= \frac{(0.2)(\$150{,}000)}{\frac{\$50}{\text{hr}}}\\ &= \frac{\$30{,}000}{\frac{\$50}{\text{hr}}}\\ &= 600\ \text{hr}\end{aligned}$$

The design development time is divided by the number of employees to determine how many hours each employee can work on the project.

$$\begin{aligned}\text{employee work time} &= \frac{\text{design development time}}{\text{no. of employees}}\\ &= \frac{600\ \text{hr}}{5\ \text{employees}}\\ &= 120\ \text{hr/employee}\end{aligned}$$

Each employee works 40 hours per week and is assigned solely to this project, so all of their billable time is devoted to this work. The utilization rate of 75% means that some time spent at work is not billable. The work week is multiplied by the utilization rate to determine the number of billable hours that each employee will record per week.

$$\text{billable time} = (\text{utilization rate})\left(\frac{\text{hr per wk}}{\text{employee}}\right)$$
$$= (0.75)\left(\frac{40\ \text{hr}}{\text{employee}}\right)$$
$$= 30\ \text{wk/employee}$$

To determine the minimum number of weeks that should be budgeted for the design development phase, the employee work time is divided by the billable time.

$$\text{design development phase time} = \frac{\text{employee work time}}{\text{billable time}}$$
$$= \frac{120\ \dfrac{\text{hr}}{\text{employee}}}{30\ \dfrac{\text{hr}}{\text{wk}}}$$
$$= 4\ \text{wk}$$

The answer is (B).

118. A project work plan includes a description of the project and a list of the owner's requirements, including the owner's program and the scope of work as defined in the project agreement. The plan summarizes anticipated deliverables such as drawings, specifications, business information modeling (BIM), and reports. In addition, a project work plan provides team structure and responsibilities of each member, including in-house staff and consultants to the architect and consultant's tasks to the owner outside of the architect's contract; contact information for team members; a project budget; and a project schedule, which includes all deadlines imposed by the owner and approvals authorities, plus key milestones, such as target completion dates for each phase of the design process.

The project manager conducts weekly design team meetings to check in with the team and monitor the progress of the work. Weekly team meetings are not part of the work plan.

The answer is (A), (B), (D), and (E).

119. Preliminary coordination regarding code compliance strategies should take place between the architect and consultants during the schematic design phase of a design-bid-build or design-build project. Communicating during this phase gives the engineer enough information about the proposed layout of the building, the construction type, anticipated occupant loads, exit paths, and fire ratings so that the engineer can evaluate options, suggest an appropriate system, and begin to incorporate the elements of that system into the initial design.

The owner usually develops the program before the design contract is awarded. If the architect waits until the design development or construction documents phase, there is no opportunity for the engineering consultants to offer suggestions about the building layout and overall design strategy. Providing information late in the project does not allow for proper design of systems and coordination of the work performed by all of the disciplines.

Several iterations of design changes occur between the architect and the engineer as the engineer develops the design. The engineer provides information about the required size and location of mechanical rooms, duct clearances, fire ratings, and connections to building utilities. The architect and the engineer must coordinate their work in all phases to ensure that the overall project goals are met. This work begins in the schematic design phase.

The answer is (B).

120. A utilization ratio is the ratio of time that a person spends working on billable tasks to the total amount of time worked.

The employee timesheet serves as a record of the time worked and the tasks accomplished, which the project manager can use as a tool to track project progress but not to assign responsibilities.

A work breakdown structure is the project's to-do list or the list of the tasks that must be performed to complete the project. This can take the form of a list, spreadsheet, or mind map, depending on the project manager's preferences. It is generally developed by breaking the project into sections (by discipline, phase, or both) and then further "decomposing" the project into smaller, single tasks. Unlike a responsibility matrix, a work breakdown structure does not assign the tasks to specific people. Unlike a critical path method (CPM) chart or other scheduling tool, it does not establish dependencies.

A responsibility matrix is a document that the project manager prepares that assigns tasks to specific team members. The matrix can be used on a micro level to clarify individuals' responsibilities and manage day-to-day workflow. Likewise, it can be used on a macro level to assess whether the firm or team has the resources available to complete the project within the proposed time frame.

The answer is (A).

121.

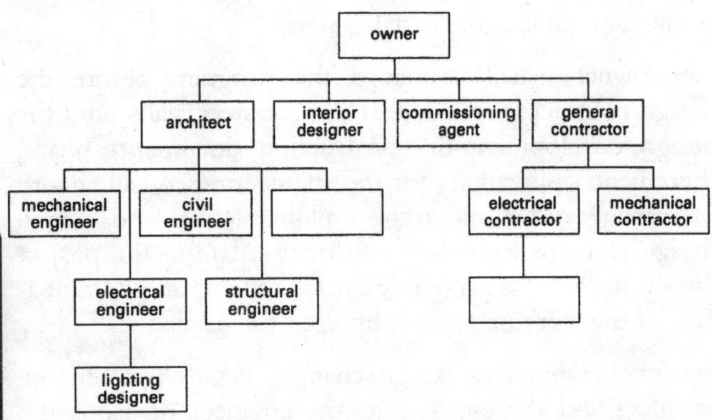

122. AIA Document C401 incorporates the prime agreement between the architect and owner into the architect-consultant agreement, which is advantageous when the consultant will be involved with the entire project.

AIA Document B142 may be used when the consultant—usually an owner's representative—is directly hired by the owner in a design-build project. This document can be used in a case where the owner chooses not to hire an architect to serve in this capacity.

AIA Document B206 is an owner-architect agreement to be used when an architecture firm provides security evaluation and design services that are classified as additional services. This form is intended to be used with either AIA Document B101, *Standard Form of Agreement Between Owner and Architect*, or with AIA Document G802, *Amendment to the Professional Services Agreement.* AIA documents in this series may be used to define the scope of services for many types of additional services, including design and construction contract administration, programming, site evaluation and planning, value analysis, and more.

The services of the security consultant's firm are provided in the design phase only. The services are limited, and it is anticipated that construction administration services will not be required from this consultant. The most appropriate form of agreement is AIA Document C727. This document allows the architect and consultant to define a limited scope of services but does not pass through the responsibilities assigned in the prime agreement between the owner and the architect.

The answer is (A).

123. AIA Document C401, Sec. 1.4, states that the architect is not responsible for the acts or omissions of the consultant.

AIA Document C401, Article 2, includes a place to define insurance requirements, but the agreement does not require the consultant to carry professional liability insurance in the same way that AIA Document B101, *Standard Form of Agreement Between Owner and Architect* requires the architect to carry insurance.

AIA Document C401, Sec. 11.6.2, states that the architect will pay the consultant after the architect is paid by the owner, in proportion to the amount received from the owner.

The architect is obligated to design a project that complies with the owner's budgetary requirements, as defined in the agreement. If the cost of the project exceeds the budget, the architect must modify the design with no additional compensation. This responsibility is passed to the consultant through the provisions in AIA Document C401, Article 6. The consultant must cooperate with the architect's efforts to bring the project within the constraints, which may include redesigning parts of the project as required to meet the budget.

The answer is (B).

124. In a project with multiple prime construction contracts, separate agreements are written between the owner and the general contractor; owner and mechanical contractor; owner and electrical contractor; owner and heating, ventilating, and air conditioning (HVAC) contractor; and owner and other specialty contractors, as applicable. Unlike a single prime project, the mechanical contractor is not a subcontractor to the general contractor.

The mechanical engineer is a subconsultant to the architect. The architect's contract is with the owner. Only the owner has a contract with the mechanical contractor. Therefore, communication between the mechanical contractor and the mechanical engineer should be facilitated through the architect and the owner.

The answer is (C).

125. An electrical engineer, a code compliance reviewer, and a specification writer may be required for a project, but the owner does not provide those consulting services.

AIA Document B101, Sec. 5.5, requires the owner to furnish the services of geotechnical engineers. Services include test borings, test pits, determination of soil bearing values, percolation tests, evaluations of hazardous materials, seismic evaluation, ground corrosion tests and resistivity tests, including necessary operations for anticipating subsoil conditions, with written reports and appropriate recommendations.

The answer is (D).

126. The AIA's design-build documents include AIA Document A141, *Standard Form of Agreement Between Owner and Design-Builder*, AIA Document A142, *Standard Form of Agreement Between Design-Builder and Contractor*, AIA Document A441, *Standard Form of Agreement Between Contractor and Subcontractor for a Design-Build Project*, AIA Document

B143, *Standard Form of Agreement Between Design-Builder and Architect*; AIA Document C141, *Standard Form of Agreement Between Owner and Consultant for a Design-Build Project*; and AIA Document C441, *Standard Form of Agreement Between Architect and Consultant for a Design-Build Project*.

The owner and the design-builder sign the prime contract. If the design-builder is a contractor, they sign a contract with an architect. If the design-builder is an architectural firm, they sign a contract with a contractor. As in a traditional project, the contractor may hire subcontractors and the architect may hire consultants as necessary to complete the work. The owner may also hire a third-party consultant to serve as an owner's representative or consultant acting independently of the design-builder. The architect's responsibilities in a design-build project differ from those assigned in a project where the architect is contracted to the owner. In a design-build project, the design builder determines the extent of the architect's responsibilities by choosing from a menu in AIA Document B143. The architect may have responsibilities from the beginning to the end of the project, or the architect may be called upon to provide design services only and may not be involved with construction administration.

The answer is (D).

127. AIA Document C103 is designed to allow the owner to contract directly with consultants. The document establishes the general terms of the agreement, such as ownership of copyright and licenses, requirements for compensation and schedule, dispute resolution, and termination of the contract. This document does not make the architect a party to the agreement between the owner and the consultant. AIA Document C103 also does not include the scope of work that the consultant will perform. One of two documents, AIA Document C201, *Standard Form of Consultant's Services: Land Survey*, or AIA Document C202, *Standard Form of Consultant's Services: Geotechnical Engineering*, may be attached as an exhibit to AIA Document C103 to define the responsibilities of these professionals. The owner can also use AIA Document C103 to contract directly with another engineering consultant, such as a mechanical or structural engineer, but the owner and engineer must develop a scope of work specific to the project.

The contract between the architect and owner should be formed using one of the sample agreements designed specifically for this purpose, such as AIA Document B101, *Standard Form of Agreement Between Owner and Architect* or a similar document describing the unique relationship between the architect and the owner.

The answer is (C).

128. Vicarious liability means that the architect is responsible for all services provided to the owner, whether those services are provided in-house or through a consultant. If the consultant is hired under the architect's contract, the architect bears responsibility for the work and may be held liable for errors or omissions committed by the consultant. If the architect is not confident in the owner-proposed consultant's abilities, the architect can minimize the risk by suggesting that the owner directly hire this consultant.

When an owner directly hires a consultant, the architect is still responsible for overall coordination of the architect's work with the consultant's work. Such coordination may require more time than when the consultant is hired under the architect's contract. The architect should ensure that the fee for services includes these coordination efforts. It is also important that the agreements include a statement that the architect can rely on the sufficiency and accuracy of the consultant's work. It is also advisable for the architect to request that the owner indemnify the architect for the services provided outside of the architect's contract. This situation should be addressed with an amendment to the owner-architect agreement. Sample text for this statement is available in American Institute of Architects (AIA) Document B503, *Guide for Amendments to AIA Owner-Architect Agreements*.

The answer is (B).

129. IBC is primarily a prescriptive code that states minimum requirements, some of which are based on referenced standards. The code, however, cannot cover all possible technologies or materials that can be used in construction. Following an alternative performance compliance path may be acceptable with the consent of the code official. A jurisdiction may adopt the International Code Council (ICC) *Performance Code for Buildings and Facilities* (ICCPC) to provide a framework for evaluating the types of designs.

The IECC offers a variety of compliance paths, including satisfying the requirements of ANSI/ASHRAE/IESNA 90.1, fulfilling the requirements outlined in IECC, or using energy consumption calculators or software if permitted by the code official. The mechanical designer must determine which approach is most appropriate for the building, in consultation with the code official, and follow this compliance path throughout design and construction. The ICC publishes new versions of the codes every three years. It is possible that the design phase of a project may be longer than three years and that code requirements may change while the work is still in progress. Some jurisdictions allow continued use of the previous code if the design is underway before the new code is adopted. If the code official requires modifications to the design to comply with the new code requirements, American Institute of Architects (AIA) Document B101, *Standard Form of Agreement Between Owner and Architect*, allows the architect to request additional services compensation from the owner for "changing or editing previously prepared Instruments of Service necessitated by the enactment or revision of codes, laws, or regulations or official interpretations."

The answer is (D).

130. The illustration shown contains the correct groups for each room.

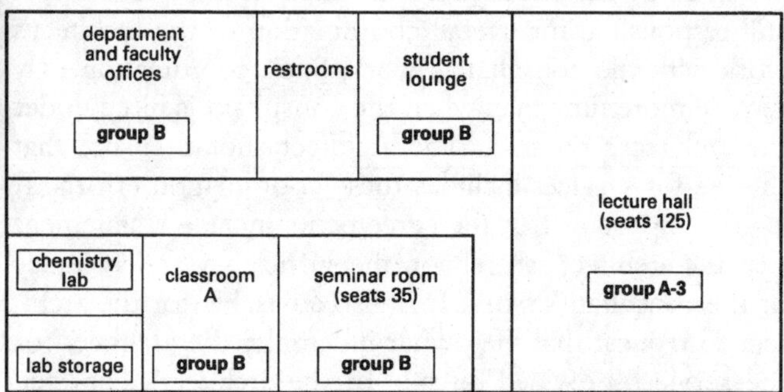

Classroom buildings on college campuses are classified as Group B (business) occupancies rather than Group E (educational) occupancies. The majority of the spaces shown on this plan are Group B occupancies. The seminar room functions like an assembly space, but its occupant load is fewer than 50, so according to the exceptions in the code, it also is classified as Group B. Fire-rated separation is not required between occupancies of the same classification.

The corridor walls must have a 1-hour fire rating because they serve an occupant load greater than 30 (assumed because the capacity of the Seminar Room alone is 35) and the building is not sprinklered.

The lecture hall seats greater than 50 people and occupies about one third of the total floor area of this story. This space is classified as Group A-3 (assembly occupancy). In a nonsprinklered building, the code requires a 2-hour separation between A and B occupancies. If the building is sprinklered, the required separation between these spaces is one hour.

The chemistry lab is a space where hazards exceed those found in the rest of the building, but these hazards do not contribute significantly to the overall fire hazard. The chemistry lab is classified as an incidental accessory occupancy. According to IBC, this space must be separated from adjacent spaces with 1-hour-rated construction because the building is not sprinklered. If an automatic fire extinguishing system is present, this rating is not required.

The lab storage room is typically classified as a storage occupancy. Because the size of the space is less than 10% of the total area of the story and the function of the space supports the spaces in which it is located, it is considered an accessory occupancy. No separation is required between Group B occupancies and accessory occupancies within.

131. Building code requirements represent the minimum standards that must be met to protect public health and welfare. The designer always has the option to exceed the code minimums. Building codes have undergone many revisions to reflect the introduction of new materials, building technologies, and challenges. The biggest changes to codes happen in response to disasters, when the shortcomings of the previous requirements become evident. The Chicago Fire of 1871, the 1906 San Francisco earthquake, the September 11, 2011 attacks on the United States, and other disasters have led to code requirement revisions that intend to make buildings safer and protect human life.

Anyone—contractors, architects, building code enforcement officers, lobbyist groups or manufacturer representatives, among others—may propose a change to the IBC according to the procedure available on the ICC website. The person making the proposal must complete forms identifying the text to be changed and explain the proposed modification and rationale for the change. State governments and some municipalities have the responsibility to decide which codes and which versions of codes are adopted for use in jurisdictions under their purview. A new edition of the code is not automatically adopted upon publication. There is usually a delay of a year or more to allow time for legislative approval. In some cases, provisions of the new edition are not acceptable to the legislature, and the new version is not adopted. Alternatively, the legislature may decide to adopt only parts of the code. The way to confirm which codes and which version of the codes are in effect in a specific jurisdiction is to contact that municipality's code enforcement office.

The answer is (D).

132. A state's statute of limitations establishes the amount of time that a party has to take legal action upon discovery of a design or construction defect. In contrast, a statute of repose establishes the time to take legal action once construction has completed. After the statute of repose period ends, an architect or contractor may be protected from third-party claims related to a project. However, some states include language that extends or modifies the length of time in cases of wrongful death or fraudulent activity. The statute of repose for a construction project usually begins at a fixed time (such as substantial completion, final inspection, or first use for the intended purpose, depending on the state), and the length of time varies by state. Current legislation sets the statute of repose in all states between 4 and 15 years.

The statute of limitation period and the statute of repose period for construction projects are often longer than those established for other types of claims not related to real property. It may take time for a design or construction date to become evident, but after a certain period of time, damage or deterioration of a building is more likely to be due to maintenance procedures or use.

The answer is (C).

133. A phased project is likely to have a greater overall cost because of the duplication of efforts required to construct the project in pieces. It can be a way to allow some construction to take place while other parts of a building remain occupied, which allows the building owner's staff to keep working during the project. Although the overall cost may be greater, it may be to the owner's benefit in terms of productivity or minimizing disruption of business operations. If access to the site is restricted, or if the site is in an environment where construction must stop during certain months of the year, phasing the project may be a logical approach.

Per American Institute of Architects (AIA) Document B101, *Standard Form of Agreement Between Owner and Architect*, Sec. 4.1.25, fast-track design services are an additional service. The local municipality may require a special permitting process and additional inspections for fast-track projects. This type of project delivery is inherently more complicated than other, more linear, project delivery methods. In a design-build, partnering, or integrated project management arrangement, some construction may begin before the design is complete. If a conflict or error is discovered during construction, correcting the error in the field will likely require more time and cost than if the issue were caught in design.

The answer is (C).

134. The contractor does not automatically receive compensation for severe weather conditions. The contractor must anticipate typical weather conditions and factor such conditions into the schedule. For example, if for the past three years, it snowed four days in January, it is reasonable to expect that will happen again in the year they are working. If in the January they are working it snows eight days, the contractor may have a good claim that this weather event is extraordinary and be compensated for those other four days. But the contractor must prove that it did affect specific work progress. For example, if they could not pour concrete outside because it was too cold, that is probably a valid claim. But if at the time they are working inside and the building is heated, that weather event claim is questionable because they probably could have continued to work.

AIA Document A201, Sec. 15.1.5.2, states that claims for adverse weather conditions require the contractor to submit data substantiating that weather conditions were abnormal for the period of time, the weather could not have been reasonably anticipated, and the weather had an adverse effect on the scheduled construction. Depending on the work scheduled at the time, severe weather conditions may bring a project to a halt if the work at the time is outdoors, or it may have no effect if the building is enclosed and the week's schedule calls for carpet installation and painting. The contractor must prove that the weather conditions were more severe than normal weather conditions anticipated at the project site at a similar time of year. The contractor's claims can be substantiated with records from the National Oceanographic and Atmospheric Administration (NOAA) for the dates in question and with historical data showing typical weather conditions. In addition, the contractor must show that the work was delayed because the activities scheduled for that time period were dependent upon typical weather conditions.

Although neither is specifically required by the AIA contracts, the owner and contractor may choose to add information to help define the requirements for a weather-related claim. The owner and contractor may include in the contract an anticipated number of weather delay days for each month of the project or include definitions of what constitutes adverse weather conditions (i.e., snow accumulation, rainfall, or temperature). These provisions can minimize disputes.

The answer is (D).

135. With the matrix costing method, various cost alternatives are drawn along one side of a matrix, and individual elements that combine to produce the total cost of the alternatives are drawn along the other side. The matrix costing method allows the designer to compare the factors that comprise the final cost. These factors might include the cost of custom-built versus pre-manufactured workstations, task lighting that will be planned with custom-built units versus higher-wattage ambient lighting, and so forth.

A cost plus overhead and profit method can be implemented with either a fixed fee or a nonfixed fee for overhead and profit. The owner usually chooses the cost-plus agreement to meet a deadline. For the owner, finishing the project at the deadline is worth paying the contractor overhead and profit. The fixed fee benefits the owner, but the owner often adds a bonus to the contractor as an incentive to finish the project early.

For the unit cost method, the project is broken down into its individual building components and the labor required to install them. Contractors typically use this method of estimation when they are determining a bid or negotiated price for the project. It is the most accurate method, but it can only be used when the construction drawings and specifications are complete and all the requirements of the project are known. The estimate should include not only material and labor costs, but also the cost of equipment, fees, and services necessary to complete the project, plus the contractor's overhead and profit. When subcontractors or vendors perform work, the fixed prices of the subcontractors are added to the general contractor's costs.

The parameter method calculates an estimated cost per square foot for many types of materials so that the designer can understand the cost implications of each, as well as mix and match materials or systems to arrive at a design that complies with the project budget. For example, if the architect is considering different types of exterior cladding materials, a cost per square foot may be calculated for wood clapboards, brick veneer, or stone veneer. The designer can then use this information to understand how changing the materials or combining materials with different costs in varying proportions can affect the overall cost of the project.

The answer is (A).

136. The architect may not delegate design responsibilities to the contractor because there is no contractual relationship between the two. However, the architect can specify that the contractor provide certain design services by a licensed design professional, in accordance with the requirements defined in a performance specification.

The initial decision maker (IDM) can be the architect or another person designated to hold this position. If no one is designated, this responsibility reverts to the architect according to AIA Document A101, Article 6. The contractor is not required to verify that the contract documents comply with code requirements, but according to AIA Document A201, Sec. 3.2.3, the contractor must notify the owner and architect if discrepancies are discovered. If the contractor does not do so in a timely manner and proceeds with the work as it is shown, liability for the costs of repairs is assigned to the contractor for failing to notify the owner of the issue, per AIA Document A201, Sec. 3.2.4.

The answer is (C).

137. Practical ways to adhere to the standard of care include preparing drawings and details in accordance with accepted industry standards, assigning responsibility for the coordination of documentation to a single person who has the knowledge and experience to manage the work effectively, keeping lines of communications between employees open and instructions clear, and using quality control checklists to ensure that all required tasks are completed.

The answer is (C).

138. A horizontal organization allows employees with differing levels of authority and experience to have similar input into how the organization is run. Instead of each person having clearly defined duties, employees may work in teams, with everyone on the team having input. Employees may perform many different functions and may report to several supervisors rather than one. Project managers or team leaders report to a team of supervisors, with members of each team being essentially equal in terms of power.

With a matrix organization, employees often report to more than one manager. Certain employees may have skill sets or duties that are useful to more than one group.

A firm that organizes its staff into studios employs a vertical organizational structure. In such an arrangement, a cross section of employees who have different levels of authority and experience are grouped into a team for a project. For example, a large firm may have a studio dedicated to educational projects, which deals with the design of K-12 schools only, or a commercial studio that handles retail and office design. Each of the studio groups includes a project manager or project architect who oversees the efforts of other architects, designers, and CAD operators.

The answer is (B).

139. Life-cycle cost analysis is an economic analysis tool that allows the designer and owner to evaluate the total cost of any project over a long period of time, usually 20 years or more. This type of review considers both the initial costs of building the structure and the long-term expenses associated with the operation and maintenance of the facility, such as equipment replacement, utility costs, and personnel costs. The long-term costs of a building usually outweigh the initial construction costs. The life cycle cost analysis also considers how the design of the building will affect employee productivity, because the cost of salaries and benefits for people working in the building will be greater than the costs of construction and maintenance of the facility. A life-cycle analysis is useful for many projects, not just government projects funded through bond issues.

To be the most effective, the analysis should account for more than one scheme, system, or approach and compare alternatives against a baseline design. The results are the most useful when they are used to determine which of two or more alternatives has the lowest long-term cost.

The answer is (D).

140. Placing the parking areas under the building makes sense in terms of sustainability because it disrupts less of the site and minimizes areas of imperviousness, but in terms of safety and security, it could be difficult to protect the building from vehicle bombs. Full-height glass walls for daylighting would be ideal for surveillance from the outside, but they would vulnerable to bomb or vehicle attacks.

Constructed wetlands are used to process wastewater, but they could also serve as an additional barrier to vehicular and pedestrian access to the building depending on where they are placed on the site. Integrated building automation and control systems help ensure that the mechanical systems in the building are operating efficiently; they can also be used to detect contaminants in the building. Trombe walls are used for passive solar heating, but their mass could also help the building resist a bomb impact. Natural landscaping and retention ponds, like constructed wetlands, could be used for limiting vehicular access as well as increasing standoff distance.

The answer is (B), (C), (E), and (F).

141. American Institute of Architects (AIA) Document A201, *General Conditions of the Contract for Construction*, Sec. 3.10, requires the contractor to prepare and submit a construction schedule for the owner's and architect's information. Often, Division 1, *General Requirements*, requires a contractor to use the critical path method (CPM) of scheduling to develop this plan for the construction period. The use of the critical path method is not limited to construction projects and can be a good way to organize any complex undertaking, including scheduling the preparation of contract documents within an architectural firm.

Sequencing cannot be shown accurately on a bar chart. Bar charts, also known as Gantt charts, are best for evaluating duration only, because they list the activities to be completed but do not explain interrelationships between the tasks. (For example, a bar chart does not show that concrete foundations must be poured before wall framing begins.) A bar chart is usually structured so that the activities occurring first are at the top of the chart and subsequent activities are listed later.

Items on the critical path must be accomplished by the time they are scheduled to be complete, and they must be completed in the specified order, or project completion will be delayed. Critical path items are defined by their earliest or latest possible start and finish dates and the duration of the activities. Not all construction activities listed in the schedule will be on the critical path.

Contractors prefer to have the duration of activities be within one payment period. This makes it easy to show the owner what has and has not been accomplished to date and simplifies preparing the application for payment. It is also advantageous to the contractor to keep the schedule up to date throughout the project to provide back-up for claims for extension of the contract time due to owner changes or other conditions such as inclement weather.

Float is the period of time between the end of an activity and the project completion date. Activities with float can be started or finished within a range of time prior to the project completion date, and they will not affect the completion of the project as long as these activities are completed before a subsequent activity. There is no float on the critical path.

The answer is (C).

142. Vertical cracking is usually an indication that the brick wall is not able to move laterally, which is a condition caused by lack of vertical expansion joints.

The answer is (A).

143. The Sears Tower in Chicago is a good example of how the influence of structural engineers can enhance the design of a building. Similarly, mechanical or electrical engineers may have a great impact on the appearance of a structure, particularly if they have designed elements that take advantage of natural heating and cooling techniques and daylighting.

The answer is (B).

144. The owner is responsible for determining the time limits for construction; this requirement should be stated in the contract documents. According to AIA Document A201, Sec. 3.10.1, the contractor is responsible for developing a construction schedule that documents the sequence of the work and allows the project to be completed within the owner's time frame. This schedule is submitted to the owner and architect for information only.

The answer is (D).

145. The general, supplementary, and special conditions, in addition to American Institute of Architects (AIA) Document A101, *Standard Form of Agreement Between Owner and Contractor*, establish the legal relationship between the two parties and define their rights and duties. The architect's duties in administering the construction contract are also defined by these documents. The administrative procedures for a project are established in Division 1 of the specifications, General Requirements. These sections explain exactly how the contractor is to perform the tasks assigned in the general, supplementary, and special conditions.

The answer is (D).

146. The indemnification provision, AIA Document A201, Sec. 3.18, requires the contractor to indemnify the owner, architect, architect's consultants, and any agents or employees of those parties from

> ... claims, damages, losses and expenses ... attributable to bodily injury, sickness, disease or death, or to injury to or destruction of tangible property (other than the Work

Project Management

Project Management

> itself), but only to the extent caused by the negligent acts or omissions of the Contractor, a Subcontractor, anyone directly or indirectly employed by them or anyone for whose acts they may be liable …

This part of the general conditions should be carefully reviewed by the owner's legal counsel, as indemnification statues vary by jurisdiction.

The answer is (B), (C), (E), and (F).

147. Although both the owner and the contractor are contractually required to carry insurance relative to a project, only the contractor is required to provide certificates of insurance per AIA Document A201, *General Conditions of the Contract for Construction*, Sec. 11.1.3. One of the most popular forms used to prepare this documentation is the ACORD Certificate of Insurance. ACORD, which stands for Association for Cooperative Operations Research and Development, is a nonprofit organization that develops standards for the insurance and financial services industries. If this document is used, it should be accompanied by AIA Document G715, *Supplemental Attachment for ACORD Certificate of Insurance*, which provides instructions for completing the ACORD form and contains additional space for information required by the construction contract that is not called for on the standard document.

The owner is required by AIA Document A201, Sec. 11.3.6, to file copies of required insurance policies with the contractor before any exposure to loss may occur.

All required insurance provisions mandate that one party give the other 30 days notice before any insurance is cancelled. This gives the other party time to consider the option of continuing the policy.

The architect and subcontractor are not parties to the owner-contractor agreement and are not required by this contract to carry insurance. However, insurance requirements may be detailed in their agreements with the owner or contractor, respectively. The 2009 version of AIA Document B101, *Standard Form of Agreement Between Owner and Architect*, Sec. 2.5, introduced the requirement that architects carry insurance.

The answer is (B).

148. AIA Document C401 may be used to form the contractual relationship between the architect and a consultant. It is most often used for consulting engineers but can also be used for relationships with consultants in other disciplines such as interior designers or specialty consultants. This document is coordinated with AIA Document B101, *Standard Form of Agreement Between Owner and Architect*, so that the architect's responsibilities to the owner are "passed through", and the consultant will assume similar obligations to the architect.

This contract does not require the mechanical contractor to perform a code compliance review of the architect's work or to assume responsibility for acts or omissions of the architect. Communication between the mechanical engineer and the contractor should be through the architect. Document C401 requires the consultant to prepare and coordinate the work relevant to the project with the work performed by the architect and other consultants, design within the budgetary guidelines established by the owner, and assist the architect with the preparation of the contract documents, bidding, and construction administration responsibilities.

The answer is (D).

149. The owner may choose any of the first four options listed, according to AIA Document B101, Sec. 6.6.

Abandoning the project is probably not the best decision. The owner presumably has already invested a significant amount of money in design fees, and the design that has been developed is extremely close in price to the budget. A $10,000 difference on a $1.5 million job is less than 1% of the total construction cost. It is probably be wise for the owner to ask the architect to identify areas of potential savings and revise the drawings or specifications, if necessary. (If the lowest bid exceeds the owner's budget, the architect must make revisions to the project documents without additional compensation.) The owner then has the option of rebidding the project or may be permitted to award the contract to the lowest qualified bidder, negotiate with the contractor, and modify the project through a change order to bring it in under the budget.

Rebidding the project generally does not result in much of a price difference unless there is reason to believe that market conditions will be very different at the time that the project goes out to bid the second time.

The answer is (A), (B), (C), and (D).

150. A pro forma is an analysis of the costs and revenues projected for a potential project and should be a part of the owner's initial planning. Generally this analysis and documentation is required to secure adequate funding for the project from lenders or investors.

The answer is (D).

151. AIA Document B101, Sec. 6.4, allows a 90-day grace period from the time that the construction documents are submitted to the owner. Delaying bidding can have a significant impact on construction prices. Given the volatility of the construction marketplace, even a 90-day grace period may be too long to insure that the prices used by bidders will be consistent with the prices used in estimating, especially for materials with great fluctuations in price, such as glass and steel.

The answer is (C).

152. Radon is a colorless, odorless gas found in the earth that has been shown to cause lung cancer. Testing is a relatively simple and inexpensive process. The Environmental Protection Agency (EPA) has determined that no action is required if the level of radon detected is less than 4 pCi/L (picocuries per liter). However, because this site shows an elevated radon reading, it should be monitored with periodic testing. Should an addition be constructed, steps should be taken to reduce radon levels by providing proper ventilation of spaces in direct contact with the earth.

Appropriate remedial actions for concentrations over 4 pCi/L include sealing any cracks in the foundation walls or floor slab and ventilating or depressurizing the basement or crawlspace area. The EPA recommends that new residences be built with radon-resistant techniques, which are explained in detail on its website, epa.gov.

The answer is (D).

153. A conditional covenant states that if the restrictions prescribed in the deed are not followed, the title to the land will revert to the original grantor or his or her heirs. A conditional use permit provides permission from a zoning board to use a property for a special purpose; the purpose may not comply with the zoning restrictions in force in that area, but the project is permitted because the use serves the public (such as a hospital in a residential neighborhood).

There is no clause in a deed known as a prescriptive covenant. An affirmative covenant commits a buyer to performing a specific duty in the future. By purchasing the grocery store, the owner agrees to maintain the garden and keep it available for public use. This type of covenant runs with the land, so the seating area will be open to the public in perpetuity.

The answer is (B).

154. Eminent domain is the right of a government to acquire private property for a use that is determined to be in the public interest. It is granted by the Fifth Amendment to the U.S. Constitution, which states, "...nor shall private property be taken for public use, without just compensation."

Eminent domain laws are intended to allow public projects to move forward while fairly compensating private property owners for their property and any other damages, such as relocation expenses. This process is sometimes referred to as condemnation.

A condemnor must be authorized by statute or ordinance to use the power of eminent domain for a specific purpose. The condemnor must first make an offer to buy the property from the property owner. If they cannot agree, eminent domain proceedings may be initiated, where the condemnor will be required to prove that the property is to be acquired for a public purpose. If the judge agrees that use of eminent domain is appropriate, hearings begin to determine the fair market value of the property. The judge may appoint a panel of "condemnation commissioners" who determine the fair market value or, if this is not satisfactory to either party, he or she may appoint a jury to determine the award. The property owner is then paid the determined fair market value plus any other damages the court deems appropriate. The power of eminent domain may be transferred to a private company, such as a utility company, railroad, port authority, and so on, when that entity is working on a project that is determined to serve the public interest. The U.S. Supreme Court's decision in *Kelo v. City of New London* determined that the power of eminent domain may be also used by a private, for-profit company when the project serves the public interest by promoting economic development.

The answer is (C).

155. The costs associated with a construction project are greater than just the costs associated with the building construction. The architect's estimate does not include professional fees (neither the architect's nor her consultants or those of any consultants the owner chooses to hire independently) and other project costs, such as purchase of the land; financing, insurance, and legal expenses; or the cost of furnishings, fixtures and equipment (not designed or specified by the architect) required to outfit the building. These items are more appropriately included in the project budget, which is developed by the owner.

The cost opinion prepared by the architect includes only the work designed by the architect and the architect's consultants. Hard costs are the costs of labor and materials. The contractor's overhead and profit allowances are included as well because that is a part of the expense of constructing the building. Also, contingency allowances should be included, particularly in early opinions, to cover design contingencies, unforeseen conditions, inflation, and potential changes in the marketplace.

The answer is (B), (C), and (D).

156. Unit prices are proposed by the contractor with the bid and are documented in AIA Document A101, Article 4.3.

The answer is (A).

157. The schedule for construction can be projected by the architect based on the scope of the work, but the contractor will develop the final construction schedule.

The architect should refrain from providing advice regarding ways to finance a project, or the project's anticipated profitability. The AIA contracts do not recognize providing financial advice as either a basic service or an additional service, and the architect's professional liability insurance may not cover the architect in a situation where he or she has offered such advice. The information included in the feasibility study may be referenced by the owner's attorney, accountant, or financial advisor to assist the owner with these types of decisions. The deliverables of a feasibility study generally include a statement of the project objectives, the development of the project program or comparison of an established project program to the available space or existing building configuration, information and a summary of research on zoning and code requirements that may apply to the project, and a preliminary estimate of the cost and schedule for the design work.

The answer is (A), (B), (D), and (F).

158. The designer must first confirm that the site's zoning classification will allow the proposed use. If the use is permitted according to the zoning requirements, the designer may then consider the structure and configuration of the building, the existing and proposed use, and the compliance strategies that may be employed to accomplish the owner's goals.

In this case, the information presented suggests that the proposed use is acceptable according to the zoning requirements for the site. The architect must confirm that the existing floor area ratio, setbacks requirements, parking, and site amenities are appropriate. If they are inappropriate, the architect must determine what changes must be made to comply with the municipality's requirements. Next, the architect should conduct a code review of the building, which will begin with considering the implications of the proposed change in use from residential to assembly functions. The determination of the sprinkler and means and egress requirements is a part of this review.

The answer is (D).

159. The IBC allows an existing fire escape to remain, and it is permitted to be a part of the means of egress but may not constitute more than 50% of the required exit capacity. The means of egress widths required in an existing building are calculated according to the means of egress width factors in use in the code under which the building was originally constructed. If the elements of the means of egress are altered, that new construction must be in compliance with current code requirements.

This project is a partial change of occupancy. The project description states that the building was formerly a single-family home that is being converted to an assembly occupancy on the first floor. If the occupant load of the first floor is less than 50, this assembly area may be considered a business occupancy. The second and third floors remain residential occupancies. Regardless of whether this area is considered an assembly occupancy or a business occupancy, the new first floor occupancy is considered a more hazardous occupancy than a residential occupancy. For this project, the designer has three options. The designer can separate the parts of the building that will house the more hazardous occupancy (i.e., the first floor) from the other occupancy (i.e., second and third floors) with fire barriers and fire-rated construction. Alternatively, the designer can provide an approved compliance alternative to fire barrier separation using IBC Chap. 34 or, if permitted in this jurisdiction, the *International Existing Building Code* (IEBC). Lastly, the designer can apply the requirements for the more hazardous occupancy to the entire building. The architect's code analysis, the owner's budget, and the interior configuration of the building will be used to determine which approach makes the most sense for this project.

The answer is (C).

160. To confirm whether the proposed addition and outdoor seating area can be constructed, verify compliance with the zoning requirements. (See *Table for Sol. 160.*)

The answer is (D).

161. The occupant loads are determined for each area. Occupant loads calculated for each area are always rounded up to the next whole number.

$$\text{occupant load}_{\text{kitchen, serving}} = \frac{550 \text{ ft}^2}{\frac{200 \text{ ft}^2}{\text{occupants}}} = 2.75 \quad \text{(3 occupants)}$$

$$\text{occupant load}_{\text{seating,other}} = 1200 \text{ ft}^2 - 550 \text{ ft}^2 = \frac{650 \text{ ft}^2}{\frac{15 \text{ ft}^2}{\text{occupant}}}$$
$$= 43.3 \quad \text{(44 occupants)}$$

Then the occupant loads are added together to determine the total occupant load for the first floor.

$$\begin{aligned}\text{total occupant load}_{\text{first floor}} &= 3 \text{ occupants} + 44 \text{ occupants} \\ &= 47 \text{ occupants}\end{aligned}$$

The answer is (B).

162. In the traditional design-bid-build delivery method, the design phase and the construction phase do not overlap because the design documents must be completed before contractors are asked to propose a price for the work.

The bid period itself also extends the project duration because sufficient time must be provided for issuing documents, responding to questions, receiving and reviewing bids, and finalizing the contract award.

A construction manager as adviser approach may increase the amount of time required for project delivery because additional time will be required for the third-party adviser to review and approve the design documents.

Partnering, design-build, bridging, and construction manager as constructor approaches may be used when a project schedule needs to be compressed. Each of these approaches allow portions of the design phase and the construction phase to overlap, which may shorten the overall project duration.

The answer is (A), (C), (D), and (F).

163. The Construction Manager as Adviser family of AIA documents is designed for use when a third-party construction manager is hired directly by the owner and will provide design advice and construction phase management services. The CMa family includes AIA Document B132, *Standard Form of Agreement Between Owner and Architect, Construction Manager as Adviser Edition*, and AIA Document A132, *Standard Form of Agreement Between Owner and Contractor, Construction Manger as Adviser Edition*, for use with AIA Document A232, *General Conditions of the Contract for Construction, Construction Manager as Adviser Edition*. Other documents in this family may be used to form the owner-architect and owner-contractor agreements for sustainable projects. The series also includes sample agreements between the owner and construction manager and construction phase forms such as change orders, construction change directives, certificates of substantial completion, and applications for payment.

AIA Document B132, Sec. 2.6, requires the architect to carry professional liability insurance as stated in the agreement, and Sec. 5.8 of this document, requires the owner's consultants to also be insured. AIA Document B132, Sec. 3.6.1.2, states that the architect is not responsible for the contractor's construction means and methods and safety procedures. These three requirements are the same as those included in the franchisor's standard agreements.

AIA Document B132, Article 5, outlines the owner's responsibilities to provide project information such as a program, budget, and survey, and the architect's right to rely upon the accuracy of this information. According to the question, the franchisor's standard agreement makes the architect responsible for providing surveys and other site documentation. This requirement is different from that included in the AIA contracts.

The answer is (C).

Table for Solution 160

zoning requirements	proposed addition	proposed construction	allowed
101	purpose		complies
102	allowed uses		permitted
103	size limits	proposed commercial establishment area = 1575 ft^2 gross floor area of proposed building (first floor area) = 1575 ft/3975 ft = 40% < 50%	
104	floor area	proposed commercial floor area = 1575 ft^2 > 1000 ft^2	complies
105	floor area ratio	lot area = (50 ft)(60 ft) = 3000 ft^2 existing building area = (30 ft)(40 ft) = (1200 ft^2)(3 floors) = 3600 ft^2 existing floor area ratio = (3600 ft^2)(3000 ft^2) = 1.2 < 2.0	FAR allowable
		proposed building area = 1575 ft^2 + 1200 ft^2 + 1200 ft^2 = 3975 ft^2 first floor area = (30 ft)(40 ft) + (15 ft)(25 ft) = 1575 ft^2 second floor area = 1200 ft^2 third floor area = 1200 ft^2 proposed floor area ratio = 3975 ft^2/3000 ft^2 = 1.325 < 2.0	FAR allowable
106	setbacks	addition within the setback	existing construction exempt
107	building height		complies
108	off-street parking	proposed commercial establishment area (first floor area) = 1575 ft^2; does not exceed 2000 ft^2 threshold where on-site parking spaces must be provided	
109	transparency		no information given
110	entrances	existing entrance faces public sidewalk	complies
111	driveway access		complies
112	operations	outdoor seating areas	permitted

164. Hard costs are expenses directly associated with construction, including materials, labor, and contractor's overhead and profit. Soft costs are other project expenses, such as design fees, legal fees, the cost of financing the project, insurance, administrative costs incurred by the owner, and moving expenses.

expense	hard cost	soft cost
architecture and engineering fees		X
fee to franchisor for construction manager's services		X
landscaping	X	
ice cream freezer cabinet	X	
insurance		X
interest paid on construction loan		X
decor (artwork, signage, etc.)	X	
mechanical equipment	X	
light fixtures	X	
lighting design services		X
installation costs associated with kitchen equipment	X	
sprinkler system	X	
contractor's overhead and profit	X	
fees for connecting to utilities (water, sewer, electricity, etc.)		X
moving expenses		X
contingency funds	X	
permit fees		X
property taxes		X

165. Although most public projects require owners to solicit bids, private owners have the opportunity to select a contractor for their project based on qualifications and experience, as well as negotiate with them to determine the price for the work. Negotiating the project offers the advantage of creating a team relationship with the contractor rather than creating an adversarial relationship between owner, architect, and contractor, as a bidding environment tends to create. Because the selection will be made based on the contractor's qualifications, not just the lowest price, preliminary interviews and estimating can take place while the design is being completed, and the pricing can be finalized when the documents are complete. When writing a contract, the owner and contractor negotiate a reasonable cost for additional work. The contract ensures that the contractor does not make up for bidding errors or shortcuts.

The answer is (B).

166. See *Table for Sol. 166.*

167. See *Table for Sol. 167.*

168. See *Table for Sol. 168.*

169. Whether the design-build team is led by a constructor or a design professional, managing risk on a design-build project requires thoroughly defining the responsibilities of each of the team members and encouraging communication between all parties throughout the course of the project. As the responsibilities and risks associated with a design-build project are different from those in a traditional design-bid-build project, it is important that the architect understand the way that the project is structured and consider how to perform their assigned duties while upholding their professional obligations.

Teaming with consultants with whom the architect has worked is one way to minimize risk. Facilitating communication and coordination between the consultants helps to reduce the number of conflicts that may arise. The architect and the design-builder must communicate frequently to ensure that the design work the architect is preparing can be built within the project budget. The agreement between the architect and consultant should place the same responsibilities and obligations upon the consultant as they exist between the architect and design-builder.

Delegating design of specific portions of the work to others who are more familiar with the construction and detailing can also reduce the architect's risk. In this case, the architect prepares a performance specification for the system and requires the contractor to arrange a licensed professional to design that system. The licensed engineer must submit stamped drawings documenting the system. The architect then reviews the other professional's work to ensure that it meets the design intent, but the engineer-of-record who designed that system bears responsibility for the engineering calculations and details specific to that system.

The prime design-builder assumes the majority of the risk associated with the project. The architect assumes more risk when leading the team. In this case, the proposed contractor-led design-build structure benefits the architect and changing the project's structure does not benefit the architect.

The architect must be careful not to assume responsibilities that are not covered by professional liability insurance, such as developing a project safety plan, performing inspections at the project site, or directing the means and methods through which the work is accomplished. These tasks are the contractor's responsibility.

The answer is (A), (C), and (D).

Table for Sol. 166

design-bid-build ("traditional") approach	design-build approach
competitive pricing no contractor participation in pricing or design design phase and construction phase are sequential cost unknown until design is complete owner assumes risk that construction documents are complete and sufficient longer project duration	single point of contact for design and construction owner has less control over design and construction quality expedited project schedule contractor assumes more risk fewer contractor-initiated change orders

Project Management

Table for Sol. 167

	Parco Design & Planning	Autumn Architects
pre-design	Organize community design charrettes. Coordinate geotechnical studies. Develop proposed overall project budget.	Prepare and submit qualifications data for RFP response.
design	Review and comment on progress documents.	Prepare outline specifications for the Winter Family Center building. Select type of mechanical system that will be used in the swimming pool area. Prepare drawings to obtain building permit.
construction	Evaluate applications for payment.	Coordinate pre-proposal conference for subcontractors. Review structural shop drawings.

Table for Sol. 168

jul	aug	sep	oct	nov	dec	jan	feb	mar	apr	may	jun	jul
	permit											
		clearing										
		excavate										
			concrete									
			steel									
					framing							
						cladding						
						windows						
							temporary heat					
							framing/drywall					
									filters			
									elevator			

170. Autumn Architects has a design-build contract with Meadowfield Construction. Meadowfield Construction is a client of Autumn Architects, not the Winter Family Foundation. The design-builder holds the primary contract with the owner and leads the project, including being responsible for determining the scope of Autumn Architects' services. This task is accomplished through the use of American Institute of Architects (AIA) Document B143, *Standard Form of Agreement Between Design-Builder and Architect.* This document includes a checklist of possible design services, requiring the parties to denote the specific tasks that will be performed by the architect in Sec. 3.2, Design Services; Sec. 3.3, Construction Procurement Services; Sec. 3.4, Construction Contract Administration Services; and Sec. 3.5, Sustainability Services. Additional responsibilities can be defined in Sec. 3.6, Description of Services and Sec. 3.7, Other Services. (An excerpt from this agreement is included in the project description.)

The design-builder may select as many or as few architectural services as necessary for the project. The scope of services required on a design-build project may be very different from the scope of services that are usually provided on traditional design-bid-build projects. The architect must be careful to provide only the services included in the contract, because only such work will be compensated. For example, coordination of work provided by the owner's consultants and design-builder's consultants (who are not under the architect's contract) may be performed by Autumn Architects, but only if this responsibility is assigned in the contract; otherwise, Meadowfield Construction will be responsible for performing this coordination. In this case, this responsibility belongs to the design-builder.

Autumn Architects does not assume responsibility for construction means and methods just because they are a member of the design-build team. According to AIA Document B143, Sec. 3.1.9, the contractor retains this responsibility.

Parco Design & Planning has a contract with the Winter Foundation. They are Parco Design & Planning's client.

The answer is (B), (C), and (F).

171. The agreement between Autumn Architects and their civil engineering consultant, Verdure Engineering, has been formed using American Institute of Architects (AIA) Document C441, *Standard Form of Agreement Between Architect and Consultant for a Design-Build Project.*

The architect's consultant and the design-builder do not have a contractual relationship. According to AIA Document C441, Sec. 1.1, the agreement between the architect and the design-builder (prime agreement) is attached to the architect-consultant agreement as an exhibit. Section 1.3 states that the architect assumes toward the consultant the same obligations and responsibilities that the design-builder assumes toward the architect.

Communications between the design-builder and the consultant are through the architect. The architect-consultant agreement requires the consultant to carry liability insurance. The limits of this insurance are determined by the parties and are stated in the contract. According to AIA Document C441, Sec. 11.7.1, the architect is required to notify the consultant of any questions or issues with an invoice within 10 days of receipt. Section 11.7.2 explains that the consultant will only be paid after the architect has received funds from the design-builder.

The answer is (A), (C), (D), and (E).

172. American Institute of Architects (AIA) Document C141, *Standard Form of Agreement Between Architect and Consultant,* is used as the contract between the Winter Family Foundation and Parco Design & Planning, who is acting as the owner's adviser throughout the project.

AIA Document A141, *Standard Form of Agreement Between Owner and Design-Builder,* is used as the contract between the Winter Family Foundation and Meadowfield Construction.

AIA Document B143, *Standard Form of Agreement Between Design-Builder and Architect,* is used as the contract between Meadowfield Construction and Autumn Architects to form their agreement.

Autumn Architects has hired Equinox Building Systems and Verdure Engineering to assist with the design of this project and may use AIA Document C441, *Standard Form of Agreement Between Architect and Consultant for a Design-Build Project,* for their contracts.

In this case, the design-build firm is a general contractor and can provide construction services using in-house forces. Therefore it is not necessary to use AIA Document A142, *Standard Form of Agreement Between Design-Builder and Contractor,* on this project. If Meadowfield Construction hires subcontractors for this project, they can use AIA Document A441, *Standard Form of Agreement Between Contractor and Subcontractor for a Design-Build Project,* to form this contract.

The Summerfield Parks Department is not a party to any of the construction contracts.

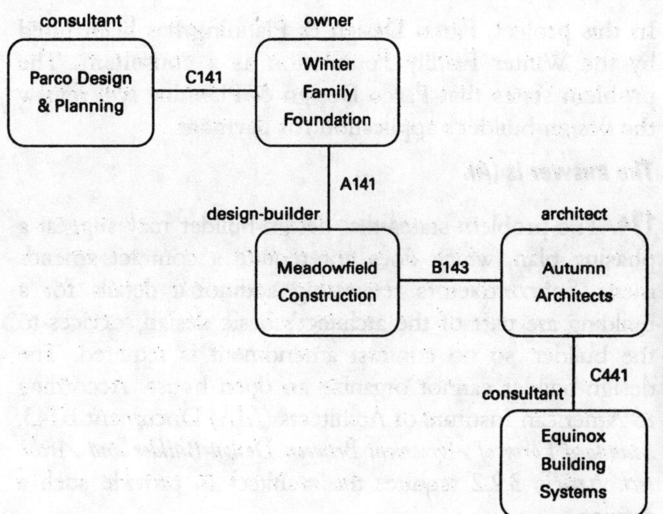

173. One of the greatest differences between a traditional design-bid-build project (in which the owner has separate contracts with the architect and contractor) and a design-build project (led by a constructor) is that in a design-build project, the architect hired by the design-builder does not act as the owner's agent or as the initial decision maker in the case of construction issues. The design-builder is the architect's client, not the owner.

Therefore, the checks and balances built into the traditional project (architect – owner – contractor) do not exist in a design-build project. The owner may elect to hire an independent consultant, who may assist with preparing initial project information, including developing a program, and providing additional services such as performing site evaluation and documentation; defining initial project parameters, such as proposed schedule and budget; acquiring and evaluating proposals from design-bid firms; preparing bridging documents; or providing construction phase services such as submittal review, site visits, recommendations for payment, and end of the project inspections.

The consultant may be an architecture firm, an engineering company, a construction management firm, or some other type of adviser. American Institute of Architects (AIA) Document C141, *Standard Form of Agreement Between Owner and Consultant for a Design-Build Project,* and Exhibit A to this document, *Consultant's Services,* may be used to form this contract, regardless of the consultant's discipline. This agreement between the owner and the consultant is independent from the agreement between the owner and the design-builder.

The design-builder has been assigned the responsibility of refining the program to determine square footage requirements. As a part of the design-build team, Autumn Architects will work with the contractor to modify the design if the price exceeds the budget. As the documents' author, Autumn Architects is responsible for code compliance.

In this project, Parco Design & Planning has been hired by the Winter Family Foundation as a consultant. The problem states that Parco Design & Planning will review the design-builder's application for payment.

The answer is (A).

174. The problem states that design-builder may suggest a phasing plan, which does not require a contract amendment. Subcontractors requesting additional details for a building are part of the architect's basic design services to the builder, so no contract amendment is required. The design-builder cannot organize an open house. According to American Institute of Architects (AIA) Document B143, *Standard Form of Agreement Between Design-Builder and Architect*, Article 3.2.2 requires the architect to provide such a service.

The furniture and fixtures package is not part of the contract between Autumn Architects and Meadowfield Construction. The agreement between Meadowfield Construction and Autumn Architects does not require the architecture firm to develop the documentation for change orders or other changes to the contract. If this task is assigned to Autumn Architects, it will be performed as an additional service and the contract should be modified accordingly.

The answer is (D).

175. Controlling scope creep depends on developing a clear scope of work statement approved by all parties and referring to this document often during the project. This process ensures that any additional items requested by the owner or added by the design-build team are considered and documented, including the effect the change will have on the project time and cost. At most, two designated owner's representatives may be authorized to modify the project scope. More than two representatives modifying the project scope leads to miscommunication. Changes to the project requirements need to be made earlier in the project rather than later. If the design team waits to address changes until the start of the construction documents phase, the number of modifications that must be made to incorporate the change take more time and cost more than changes made early on. A design-build project is particularly sensitive to the effects of scope modifications because the design-builder has already committed to delivering a specific product at an agreed-upon price within a compressed timeframe. Passing responsibilities off to the architect forces the designer to take on project management responsibilities that they may not be qualified or insured to perform and does not help to control scope creep.

The answer is (A).

DIVISION 3: PROGRAMMING & ANALYSIS

Multiple Choice

176. (A) (B) (C) (D)
177. (A) (B) (C) (D)
178. (A) (B) (C) (D)
179. (A) (B) (C) (D)
180. ______
181. (A) (B) (C) (D)
182. (A) (B) (C) (D) (E) (F)
183. (A) (B) (C) (D) (E) (F)
184. (A) (B) (C) (D)
185. (A) (B) (C) (D) (E) (F)
186. (A) (B) (C) (D)
187. (A) (B) (C) (D) (E) (F)
188. (A) (B) (C) (D)
189. (A) (B) (C) (D)
190. (A) (B) (C) (D)
191. (A) (B) (C) (D)
192. (A) (B) (C) (D)
193. (A) (B) (C) (D)
194. (A) (B) (C) (D) (E) (F)
195. (A) (B) (C) (D)
196. (A) (B) (C) (D)
197. (A) (B) (C) (D)
198. (A) (B) (C) (D) (E) (F)
199. (A) (B) (C) (D)
200. (A) (B) (C) (D) (E) (F)
201. (A) (B) (C) (D)
202. (A) (B) (C) (D)
203. (A) (B) (C) (D)
204. (A) (B) (C) (D)
205. (A) (B) (C) (D) (E) (F)
206. (A) (B) (C) (D)
207. (A) (B) (C) (D)
208. (A) (B) (C) (D)
209. (A) (B) (C) (D)
210. (A) (B) (C) (D)
211. (A) (B) (C) (D)
212. (A) (B) (C) (D)
213. (A) (B) (C) (D)
214. (A) (B) (C) (D) (E) (F)
215. (A) (B) (C) (D)
216. (A) (B) (C) (D)
217. (A) (B) (C) (D)
218. (A) (B) (C) (D)
219. (A) (B) (C) (D)
220. (A) (B) (C) (D)
221. (A) (B) (C) (D)
222. (A) (B) (C) (D)
223. (A) (B) (C) (D)
224. (A) (B) (C) (D)
225. (A) (B) (C) (D)
226. (A) (B) (C) (D)
227. (A) (B) (C) (D)
228. (A) (B) (C) (D)
229. (A) (B) (C) (D) (E) (F)
230. (A) (B) (C) (D)
231. (A) (B) (C) (D)
232. (A) (B) (C) (D)
233. (A) (B) (C) (D)
234. (A) (B) (C) (D)
235. (A) (B) (C) (D)
236. (A) (B) (C) (D)
237. (A) (B) (C) (D)
238. (A) (B) (C) (D) (E) (F)
239. (A) (B) (C) (D)
240. (A) (B) (C) (D) (E) (F)
241. (A) (B) (C) (D)
242. (A) (B) (C) (D) (E) (F)
243. ______
244. (A) (B) (C) (D)
245. ______
246. (A) (B) (C) (D) (E) (F)
247. (A) (B) (C) (D)
248. (A) (B) (C) (D)
249. ______
250. (A) (B) (C) (D)
251. (A) (B) (C) (D) (E) (F)
252. ______
253. (A) (B) (C) (D) (E) (F)
254. ______

Case Study 1

255. (A) (B) (C) (D)
256. (A) (B) (C) (D)
257. ______
258. (A) (B) (C) (D) (E) (F)
259. ______
260. (A) (B) (C) (D) (E) (F)
261. ______
262. (A) (B) (C) (D)
263. (A) (B) (C) (D)
264. (A) (B) (C) (D)

Case Study 2

265. (A) (B) (C) (D)
266. ______
267. ______
268. ______
269. ______
270. (A) (B) (C) (D) (E) (F)

176. A small gasoline station, built in the 1930s along Route 66 in Missouri, has been abandoned for 10 years. New owners have bought the property and want to fix it up so they can operate an automotive museum and small restaurant on the property. The building is listed on the National Register of Historic Places. The owners plan to apply for federal tax credits. According to the definitions established by the Secretary of the Interior's *Standards for the Treatment of Historic Properties*, which of the following treatments should be selected?

(A) preservation

(B) rehabilitation

(C) restoration

(D) reconstruction

177. An architect is designing an office building for a site in Minnesota and draws a profile of the site based upon a topographic survey provided by the client. The client asks the architect's opinion on the best location for the building. In order to take advantage of the most favorable microclimate on the site, where should the building be located?

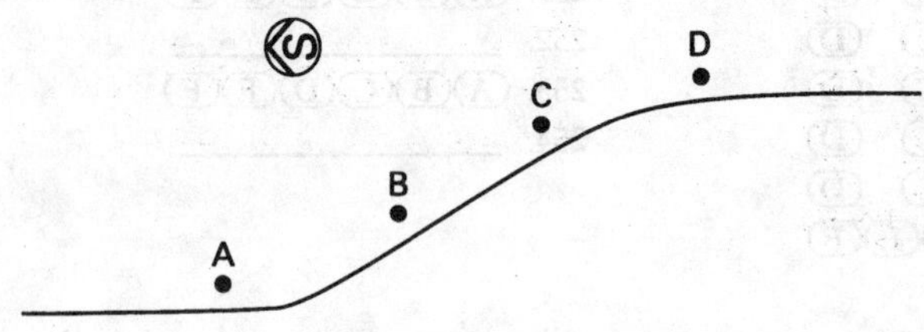

(A) point A

(B) point B

(C) point C

(D) point D

178. What is typically the maximum height building that can utilize an upfeed water supply system?

(A) 20–30 ft

(B) 30–40 ft

(C) 50–60 ft

(D) 70–80 ft

179. In what type of building is 120/208 voltage, three-phase power appropriate?

(A) industrial

(B) small commercial

(C) residential

(D) large commercial

180. A company is considering replacing its existing heating, ventilating, and air conditioning (HVAC) system with a new system at a total cost of $55,000. It is expected that the new, more efficient system will save the company $460 per month in utility costs. The simple payback period of their investment will be ______ years. (Fill in the blank.)

181. An architect is studying several sites for possible development by a client. Of the following sites, the one most likely to be buildable is

(A) a designated wetland

(B) a brownfield

(C) in a floodplain

(D) an endangered species habitat

182. Which of the following spaces should be acoustically "live"? (Choose the two that apply.)

(A) a talk radio recording studio

(B) a cathedral featuring an antique German pipe organ

(C) an opera house

(D) a community playhouse often used for poetry recitation

(E) a university lecture hall

(F) a movie theater

183. On the illustration shown, the three areas of negative wind pressure are ______. (Fill in the blank.)

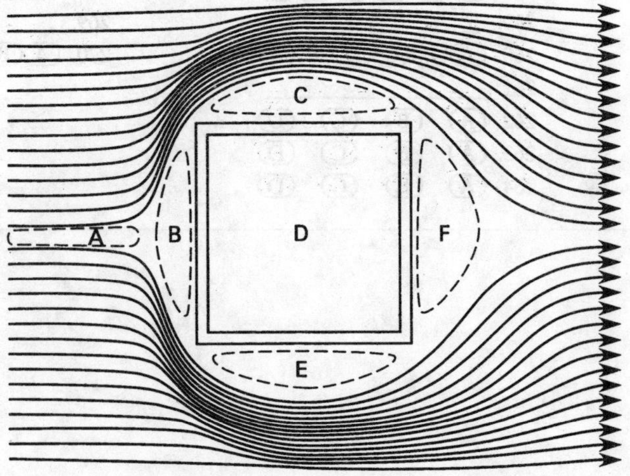

Used with permission from Fuller Moore, *Environmental Control Systems: Heating Cooling Lighting*, copyright © 2004 by Fuller Moore.

184. A developer plans to construct an office building on a previously undisturbed site. Each of the buildings shown has the same gross square footage. Which of the following diagrams represents the best planning approach?

(A)

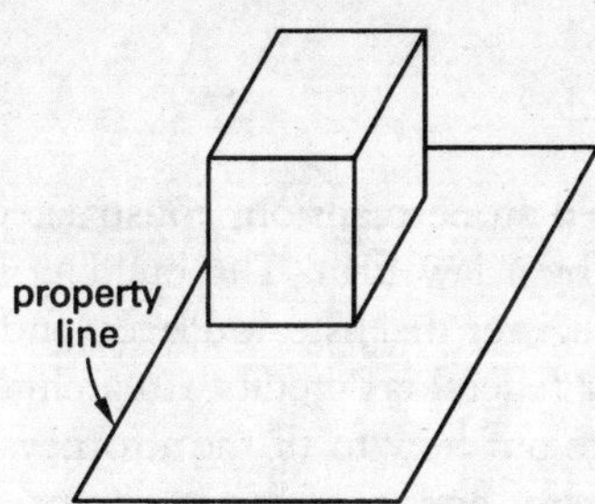

(B)

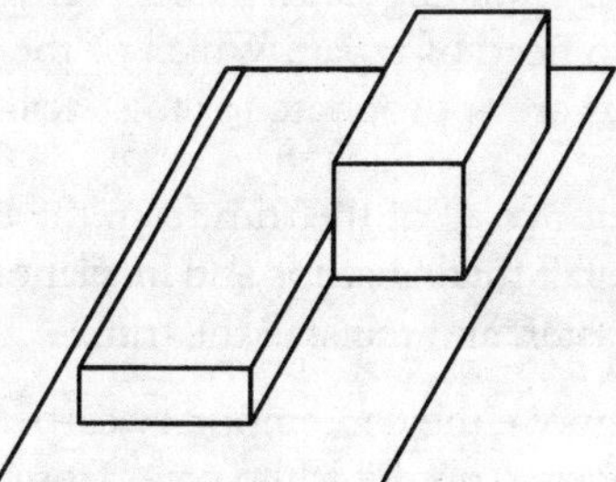

(C)

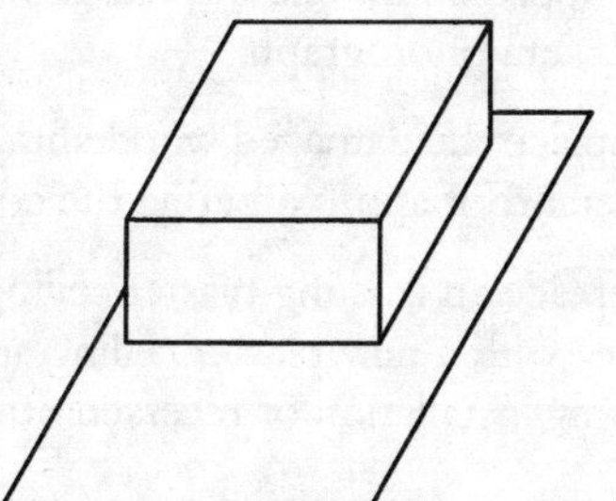

(D)

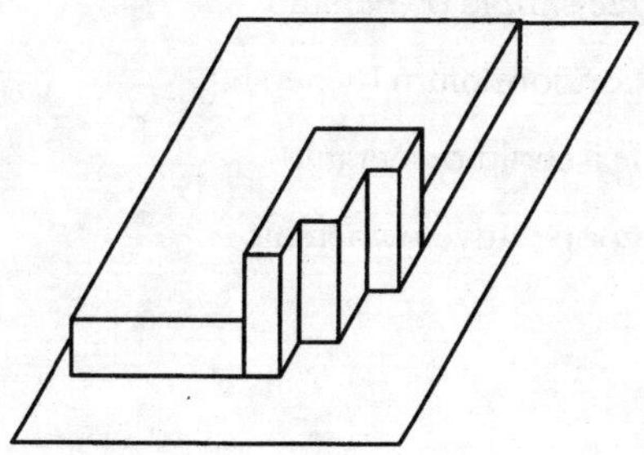

185. Which approaches are appropriate for passively cooling a building in Taos, New Mexico? (Choose the three that apply.)

(A) roof ponds

(B) evaporative coolers

(C) materials with high thermal mass

(D) limited windows on north side

(E) courtyards with fountains

(F) large windows on the east and west

186. A small one-story building in a temperate climate has been designed with its long side oriented to the south. If a southern view is not a concern, the best passive solar heating method will be

(A) direct gain space

(B) Trombe wall

(C) greenhouse

(D) convective loop

187. To conduct a preliminary code evaluation for a proposed project, the architect must possess a certain amount of information about the building. Which of the following are key pieces of information for the initial step of the code evaluation? (Choose the three that apply.)

(A) type of occupancy

(B) separation from adjacent buildings

(C) means of egress

(D) type of construction

(E) required type of fire suppression system

(F) fire district location

188. In the illustration shown, what is an appropriate use for the sloped region between points A and B?

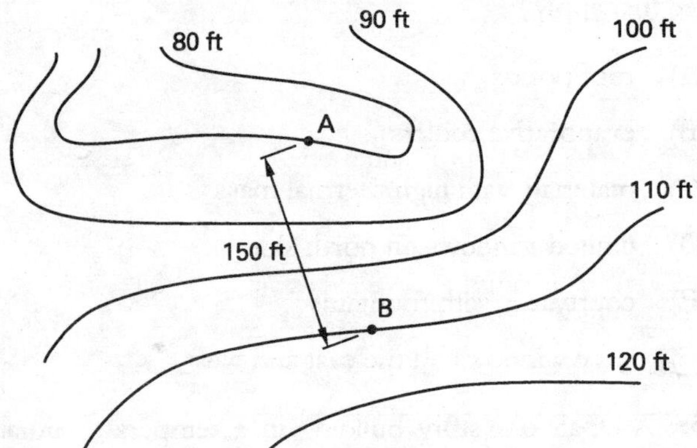

(A) Use it as a parking area.

(B) Plant it with grass.

(C) Use it as a detention area.

(D) Use it as a building site.

189. A family wishes to add a bedroom and bath to the first floor of their home to accommodate an elderly relative who will move in after she is discharged from a rehabilitation hospital. The family hopes to build the rooms adjacent to an existing but seldom-used sitting room, so that she may have her own living area. The site is tight, and the proposed addition may need to extend 2 ft into the property setback. The homeowners may choose to apply for

(A) an easement

(B) a covenant

(C) a conditional use permit

(D) a variance

190. The floor area ratio for a suburban property is 2.0. The lot is 50 ft wide (parallel to the street) by 100 ft deep (perpendicular to the street). The required front setback is 10 ft, and the back and side setbacks are 5 ft. Which of the following building configurations may be constructed?

(A) a two-story building that is 50 ft wide by 100 ft deep

(B) a three-story building that is 40 ft wide by 80 ft deep

(C) a three-story building that is 40 ft wide by 85 ft deep

(D) a four-story building that is 40 ft wide by 65 ft deep

191. The document that legally describes the layout of a subdivided piece of property is called a

(A) survey

(B) master plan

(C) plat

(D) deed

192. An old stone mansion, constructed in the 1850s, is purchased by a law firm. The building is eligible for the National Register of Historic Places, and the firm intends to apply for federal tax credits. An architect joins the project to figure out how to fit the attorneys' offices, support spaces, library, and conference rooms into the existing space. In addition, the architect has been asked to survey the existing building and identify any portions of the structure in need of repair. Which of the following recommendations are appropriate for this facility?

(A) Remove all of the trim from the interior walls, install furring strips and insulation, replace the plaster, and reinstall the trim.

(B) Remove the contemporary carpet in the dining room, strip the white paint from the mahogany paneling, and refinish the wood with a dark stain to approximate the way the room looked in a Civil War era photograph.

(C) Replace the damaged wood shingle roof with a metal roof approximating the color of the original.

(D) Replace an existing plaster ceiling in a common area with a new plaster ceiling at a lower level to allow installation of recessed downlights.

193. Absolute title to a portion of a structure is known as

(A) fee simple ownership

(B) condominium ownership

(C) leasehold ownership

(D) cooperative ownership

194. According to the affinity matrix shown, to which room or rooms must the kitchen be adjacent? (Choose the three that apply.)

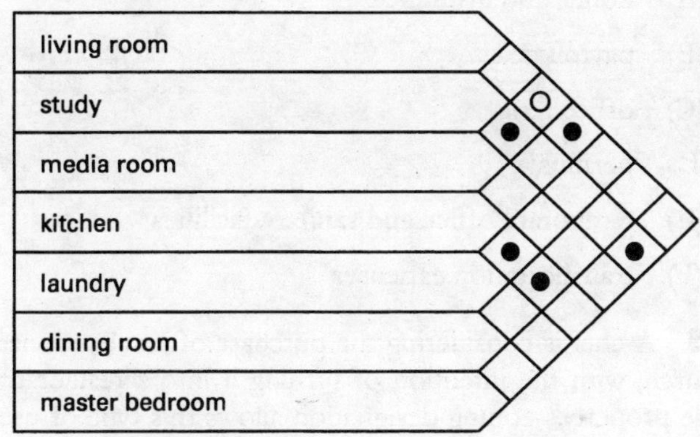

(A) living room

(B) study

(C) media room

(D) laundry

(E) dining room

(F) master bedroom

195. Which of the following cost opinions should include the highest contingency allowance?

(A) a cost opinion prepared just before the drawings are sent to contractors for bids on a small veterinary clinic

(B) a cost opinion prepared at the conclusion of the design development phase for an addition to a building designed by the architect two years ago

(C) a cost opinion prepared at the conclusion of the schematic design phase for converting an old warehouse into artists' studios and loft apartments

(D) a cost opinion prepared during the programming phase for a new elementary school

196. An architect is designing a small community theater that will feature musical and spoken word performances. The theater company's artistic director requests that the architect develop a design that will make it possible for the performer to have eye contact with every spectator in the theater while maximizing the number of seats from which the audience can see and hear most clearly. Which diagram represents the best approach to the theater layout?

(A)

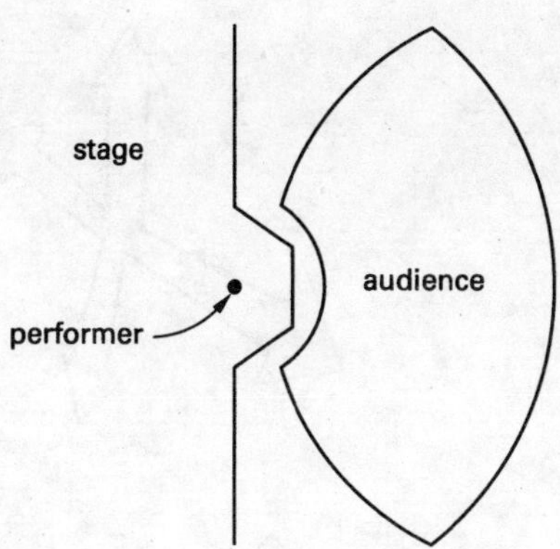

(B)

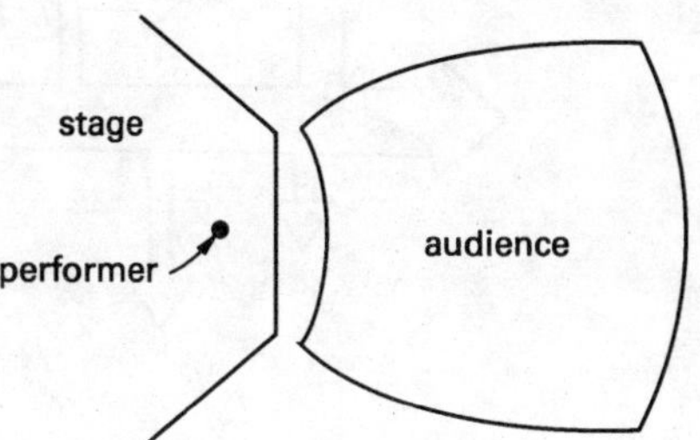

(C)

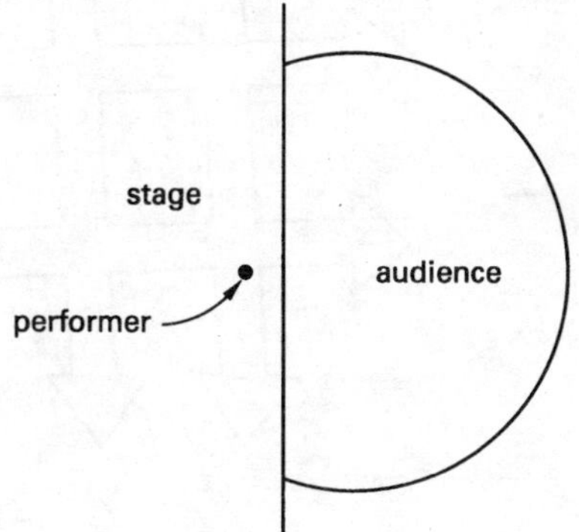

(D)

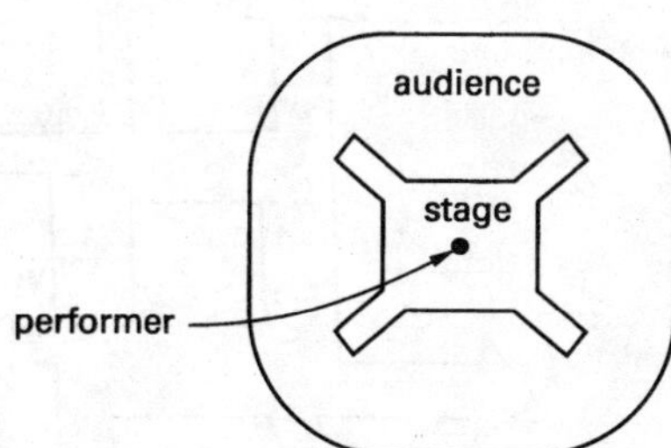

Programming & Analysis

197. Which organizational pattern for a space best facilitates social interaction?

(A)

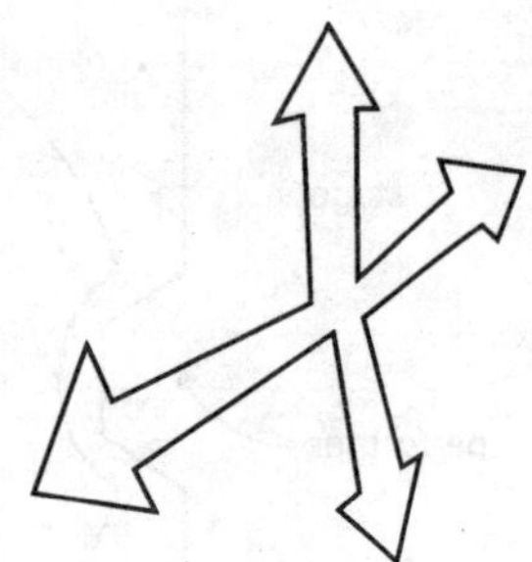

(B)

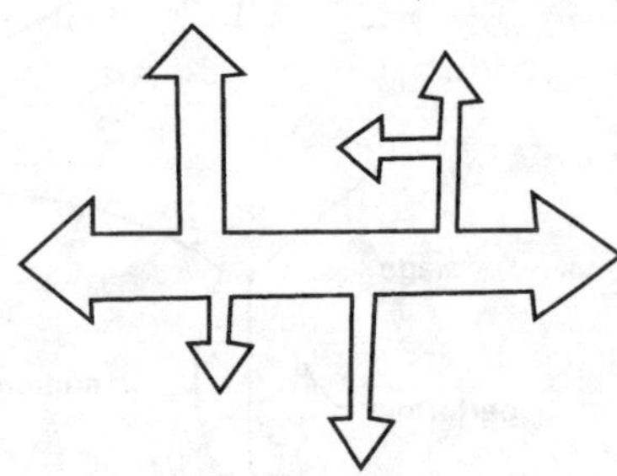

(C)

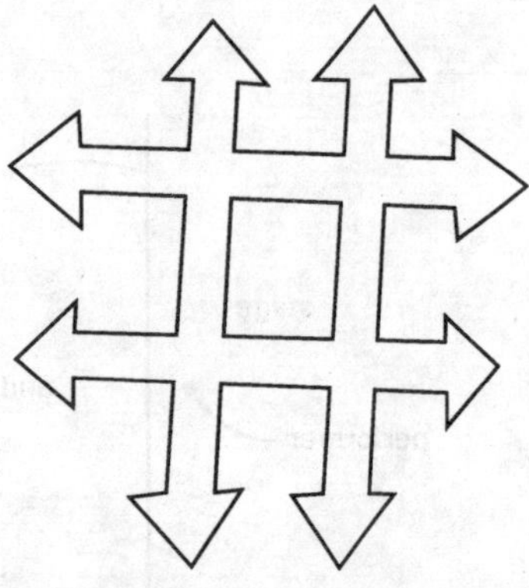

(D)

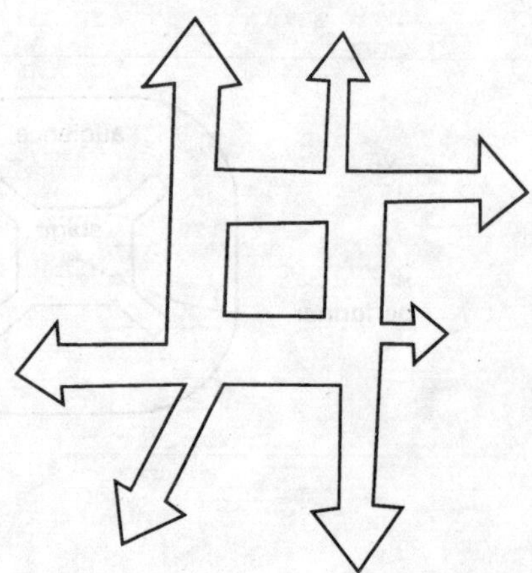

198. Which of the following are included in a contractor's project overhead costs? (Choose the four that apply.)

(A) bonds and insurance

(B) payroll taxes

(C) office rent

(D) permits

(E) temporary office and sanitary facilities

(F) transportation expenses

199. A chef is considering the purchase of an abandoned church, with the intention of turning it into a restaurant. The property's zoning designation allows this type of use. The chef has obtained a preliminary site plan and permission to access the site from the current owner, and hires an architect to assist with a feasibility study to examine the possibility of converting the old building to the new use. Which of the following should the architect do first?

(A) Check local zoning ordinances and analyze the site to determine if there is enough space available for the parking required.

(B) Assist the restaurateur in developing a program and check the space requirements against the area and layout of the existing structure.

(C) Research the history of the church.

(D) Complete a code review of the existing building and develop a preliminary plan for renovation.

200. Which of the following statements regarding building costs are true? (Choose the four that apply.)

(A) The greater the floor area of the building, the greater the cost.

(B) The longer the construction period, the greater the cost.

(C) The higher the perimeter-to-floor area ratio, the greater the unit cost.

(D) A cubic building costs less than a rectangular building of the same area.

(E) The greater the floor-to-floor height, the greater the unit cost.

(F) The taller the building, the greater the unit cost.

201. Which of the following factors increases a building's efficiency?

(A) a central mechanical plant

(B) small rooms

(C) a single-story building

(D) many offices requiring windows

202. According to *Design with Nature*, Ian McHarg's 1969 book on conservation and site planning, which of the following sites is most suitable for development?

(A) forest/woodland

(B) prime agricultural land

(C) marshland

(D) aquifer recharge area

203. For which of the following building types is the room data sheet approach to programming the most appropriate?

(A) a college dormitory

(B) a speculative office building

(C) a high school

(D) an assembly line area of a factory

204. A 100-year flood is defined as

(A) the most significant flood in a 100-year period

(B) a flood level with a 1% probability of being equaled or surpassed each year

(C) the highest water level recorded on a specific site during the past 100 years

(D) an area where development is not permitted

205. Which of the following approaches will fulfill sustainable design objectives and contribute to meeting a building's safety and security objectives? (Choose the four that apply.)

(A) parking areas under the building

(B) constructed wetlands

(C) integrated building automation and control systems

(D) full-height glass walls around the building lobby

(E) Trombe walls

(F) natural landscaping and rainwater retention ponds

206. An architect is preparing a cost evaluation for a project during the programming stage. The opinion is based upon a previous, similar project. Which of the following is a known factor that will add cost to the project?

(A) a contingency

(B) a premium

(C) an additive alternate

(D) an upcharge

207. Which of the following configurations of trees will be the most effective windbreak?

(A)

(B)

(C)

(D)

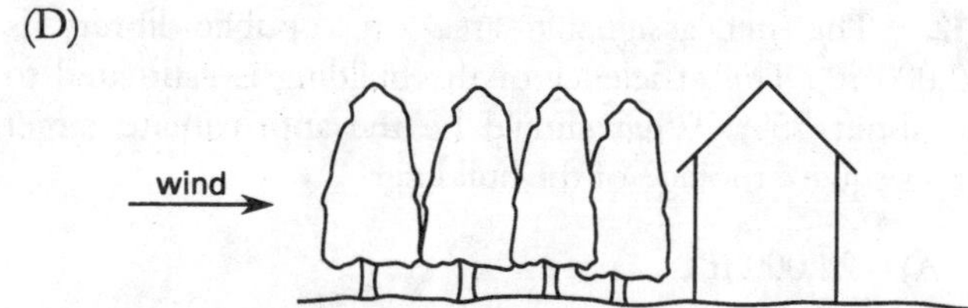

208. Which of the following detains water and allows it to be absorbed slowly by the ground?

(A) a bioswale

(B) an infiltration basin

(C) a catch basin

(D) a cistern

209. A town plans to build a small airport for commuter flights to the nearest metropolis. Which public works financing method will be most appropriate to use to fund the project?

(A) an ad valorem tax

(B) a general obligation bond

(C) a development impact fee

(D) a public enterprise revenue bond

210. A school district is an example of

(A) an overlay zoning district

(B) a catchment area

(C) a planned unit development

(D) a neighborhood

211. For which climate will these four design strategies be appropriate?

- using shade openings with moveable awnings
- selecting dark colors for exterior building finishes
- locating no windows on the north elevation
- using compact forms

(A) cool

(B) temperate

(C) hot-humid

(D) hot-arid

212. The net assignable area of a public library is 32,000 ft^2. The efficiency of the building is estimated to be about 75%. What should be the approximate target gross square footage of the building?

(A) 24,000 ft^2

(B) 40,000 ft^2

(C) 43,000 ft^2

(D) 44,000 ft^2

213. During "circle time" in a kindergarten class, the children arrange their chairs in a half circle with the teacher in the center, say their ABCs and count to 10, and read a book. The students then sing a song before going to their tables for snack time. This is an illustration of

(A) proximetrics

(B) territoriality

(C) personalization

(D) a behavior setting

214. Which of the following determines the allowable height of a building? (Choose the four that apply.)

(A) use group

(B) type of construction

(C) fire-suppression system

(D) means of egress

(E) occupant load

(F) zoning ordinances

215. A shopping center featuring a large grocery store, a few small take-out restaurants, a variety store, a greeting card shop, and a video rental store is classified as a

(A) neighborhood center

(B) community center

(C) regional center

(D) market center

216. A small business owner plans to build a factory and small warehouse to manufacture and distribute a line of diaper bags. A $75,000 loan is obtained to supplement the funds contributed by investors. Which calculation should be used to determine how much the monthly payments will be if the loan is to be repaid in 10 years?

(A) uniform present worth

(B) uniform sinking fund

(C) life-cycle cost analysis

(D) uniform capital recovery

217. Which foundation strategy is most likely to disturb natural surface drainage patterns?

(A) a raised pad

(B) piles

(C) piers

(D) columns

218. Which of the following building shapes will be most appropriate for a site with a hot-humid climate?

(A)

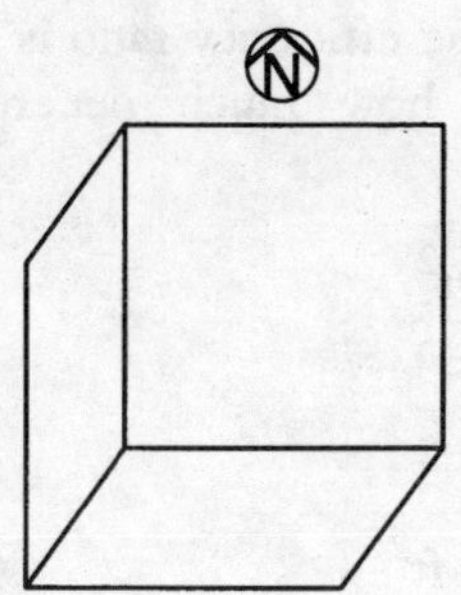

(B)

(C)

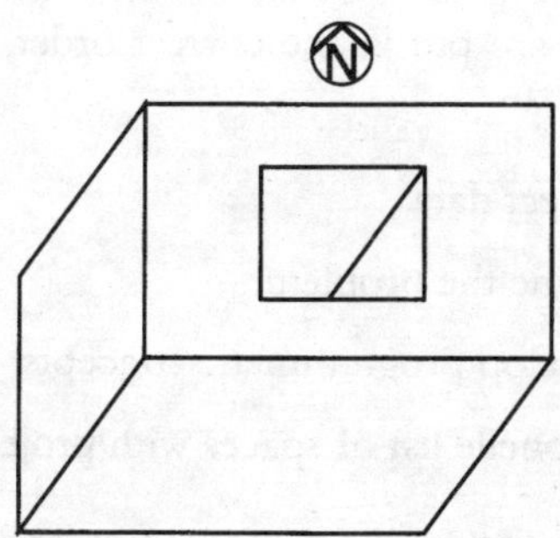

(D)

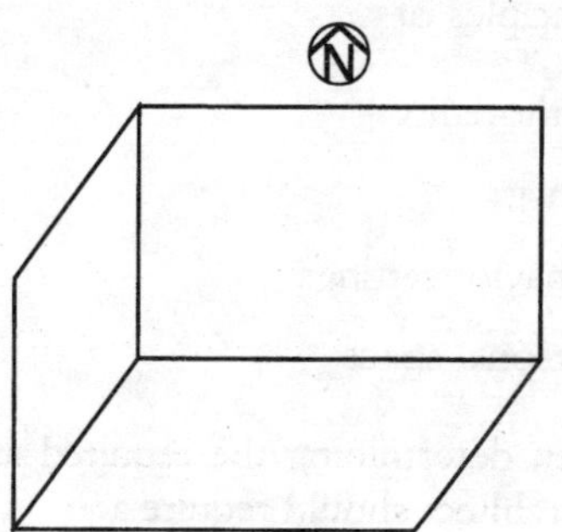

219. The science of designing objects and spaces so that they can be used most efficiently and comfortably by people is called

(A) anthropomorphism

(B) ergonomics

(C) primogentrics

(D) bionomics

220. Which of the following statements is true regarding soil mechanics?

(A) Coarse-grained soils are more likely to be affected by freeze/thaw cycles than fine-grained soils.

(B) A mix of organic soil and clay will have a suitable bearing capacity for a small residence.

(C) Silts and clays allow water to migrate above the water table on a site.

(D) A building's footings should be placed above the frost line so they will not be affected by heaving.

221. The statement "develop a multilevel system of pedestrian circulation" is an example of a

(A) need

(B) programming statement

(C) goal

(D) design concept

Programming & Analysis

222. Which of the programming diagrams shown will best record required space relationships just prior to initial space planning?

(A)

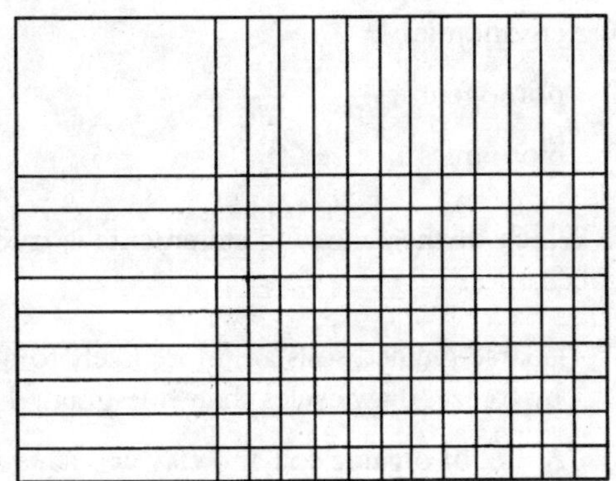

(B)

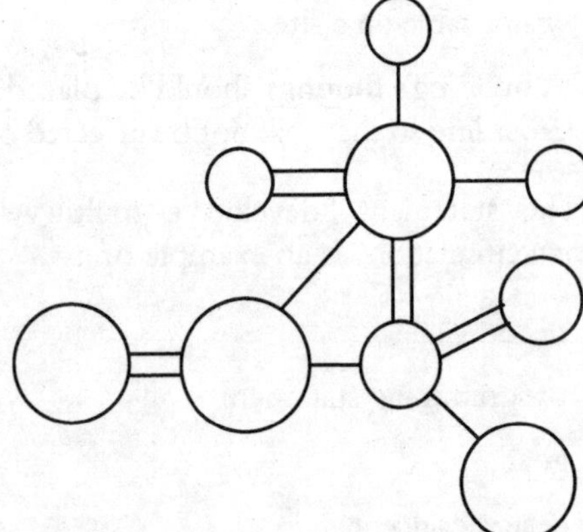

(C)

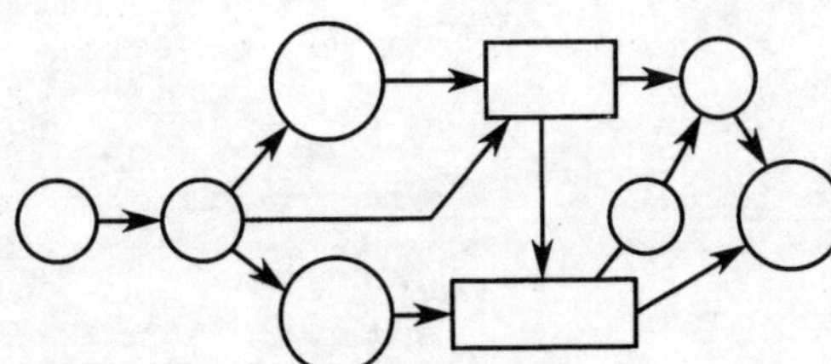

(D)

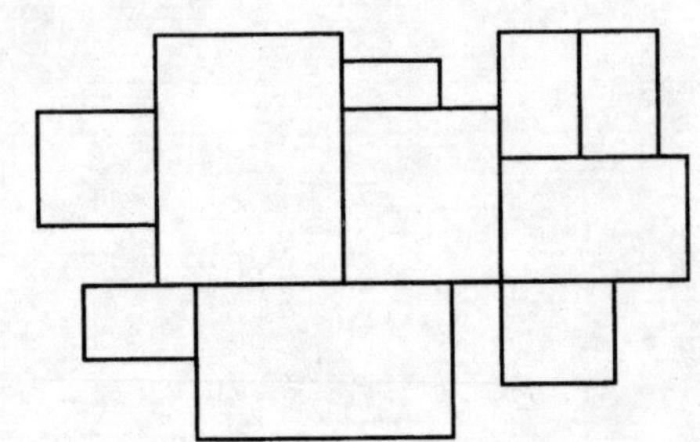

223. The developer of a retail shopping complex has estimated through an economic analysis that he can afford to build up to 85,000 ft^2 of gross building area. A central, enclosed pedestrian mall will occupy about 6% of the building, and the efficiency ratio is estimated to be 75%. Approximately how much net rentable area will be available?

(A) 59,900 ft^2

(B) 63,700 ft^2

(C) 67,600 ft^2

(D) 107,000 ft^2

224. The following five activities are completed during the programming phase.

- collect data
- define the problem
- develop programmatic concepts
- have owner describe project goals
- reconcile list of spaces with project budget

When they are put in the correct order, which will occur third?

(A) collect data

(B) define the problem

(C) develop programmatic concepts

(D) reconcile list of spaces with project budget

225. Designing environments so individuals can maintain a comfortable distance between them applies the psychological principles of

(A) territoriality

(B) density

(C) behavior settings

(D) personal space

226. When determining the required area for a leaching field, the architect should require a

(A) percolation test

(B) potability test

(C) topographic survey

(D) water table determination

227. If the contour interval on the map shown is 2 ft, what is the slope between point A and point B?

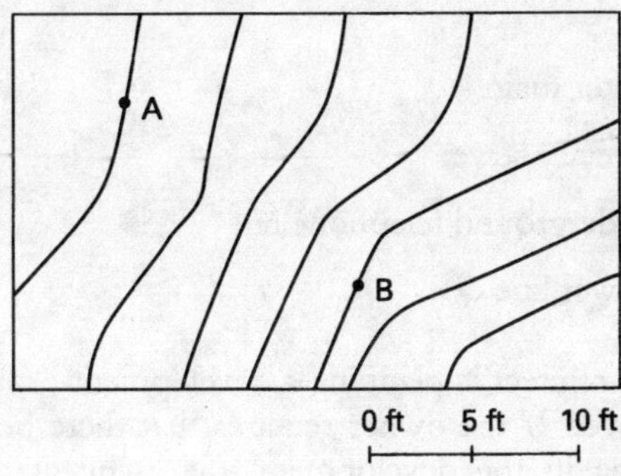

(A) 27%

(B) 53%

(C) 67%

(D) Not enough information is given to answer.

228. The abbreviated table shown includes requirements for occupancy loads. A restaurant on the ground floor contains 3500 ft^2 of dining area, a 1000 ft^2 kitchen, and a 1200 ft^2 bar area. What is the total occupant load?

use	occupant load factor (ft^2/occupant)
assembly areas, concentrated use	7
(without fixed seats)	
auditoriums	
dance floors	
lodge rooms	
assembly areas, less-concentrated use	15
conference rooms	
dining rooms	
drinking establishments	
exhibit rooms	
lounges	
stages	
hotels and apartments	200
kitchens—commercial	200
offices	100
stores, ground floor	30

(A) 202 occupants

(B) 319 occupants

(C) 380 occupants

(D) 409 occupants

229. Which of the following sustainable strategies best manages stormwater runoff? (Choose the three that apply.)

(A) bioswales

(B) catch basins

(C) cisterns

(D) infiltration basins

(E) pervious paving

(F) box culverts

230. What type of soil is best for slab-on-grade construction?

(A) clayey sand

(B) organic silt

(C) poorly graded gravel

(D) lean clay

231. Which schematic site section shown here demonstrates the best approach for reducing noise from an adjacent site?

(A)

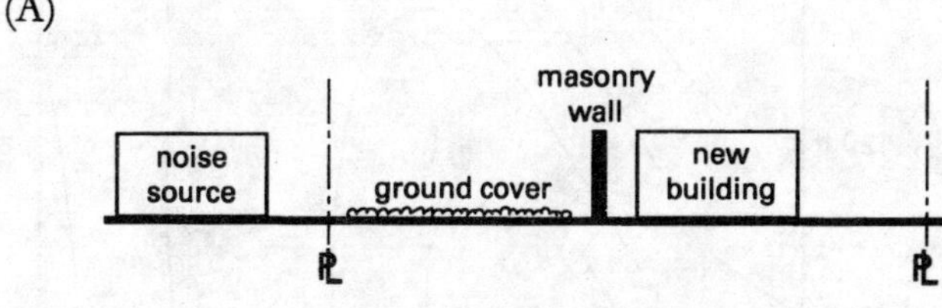

(B)

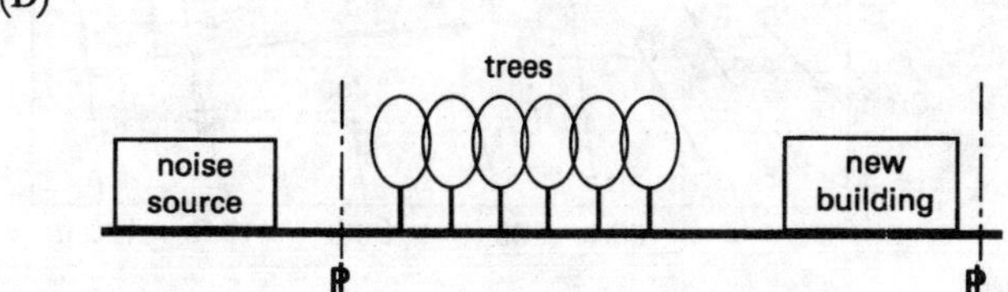

(C)

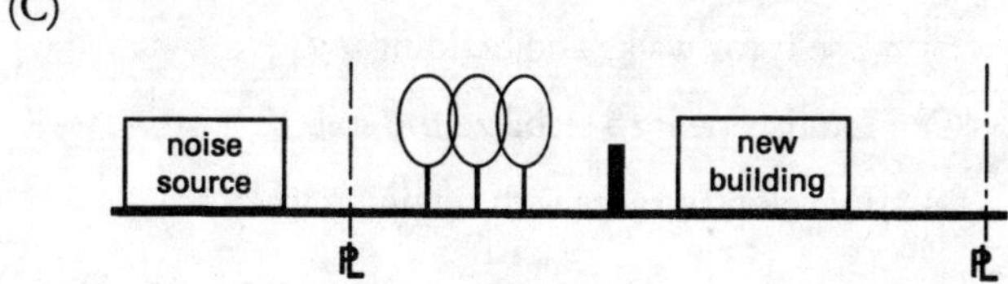

(D)

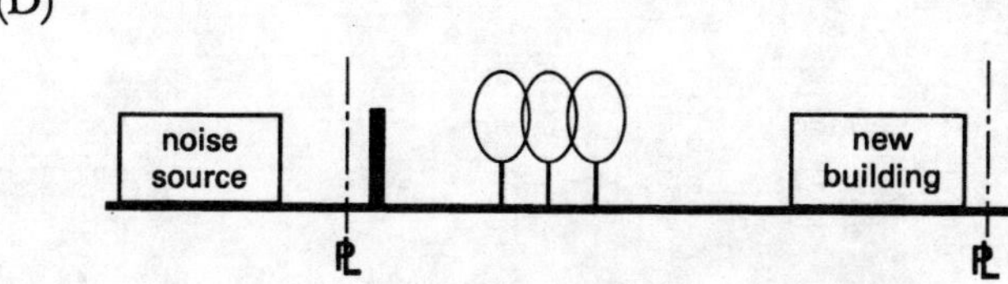

Programming & Analysis

232. In the diagram shown, which section represents a valley?

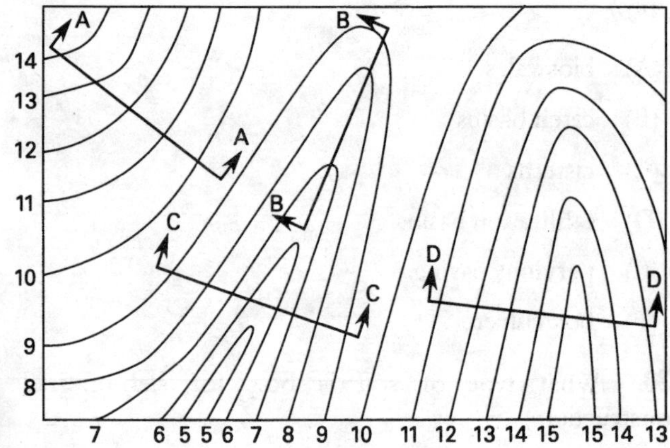

(A) section A-A

(B) section B-B

(C) section C-C

(D) section D-D

233. In the illustration shown, what will be the best use for the sloped region between point A and point B?

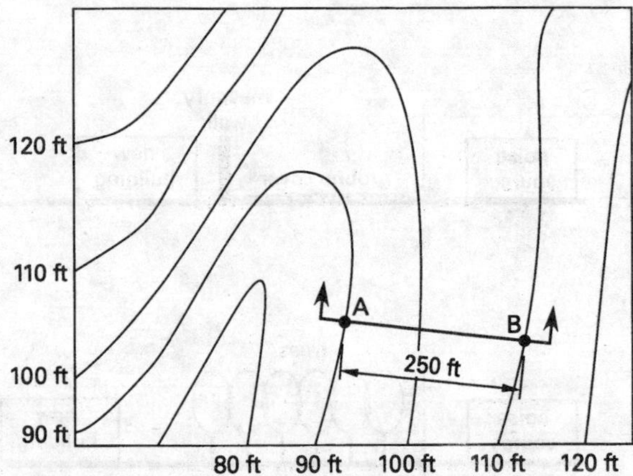

(A) Use it for parking.

(B) Use it for walks and buildings.

(C) Landscape it to stabilize the soil.

(D) Develop terraces with retaining walls.

234. In planning the location of a building on a site, the location of which of the following utilities should be considered first?

(A) water main

(B) sanitary sewer

(C) underground telephone line

(D) power line

235. An architect is planning a development project near a major river. If the owner requires that there be no risk of flooding in the development, the architect needs to determine the

(A) local flood plain regulations

(B) National Flood Insurance Program (NFIP) standards

(C) probable maximum flood (PMF)

(D) standard projected flood (SPF)

236. The basic allowable floor area of a planned building, as established by the building code in force, may be increased by adding a sprinkler system and

(A) increasing the hourly fire protection of exterior walls

(B) increasing the amount of open space between the building and the property lines

(C) decreasing the square footage of openings in the exterior walls

(D) reducing the height of the building

237. During the site design phase of an urban project, where does the architect most likely find information regarding the location of electrical and telephone lines?

(A) from the civil engineer

(B) from the electrical engineer

(C) from the utility companies

(D) from technical maps maintained by the municipal government

238. Leadership in Energy and Environmental Design (LEED) points for new construction can be earned for which of the following? (Choose the four that apply.)

(A) reducing construction activity pollution

(B) including building-level water metering

(C) redeveloping a brownfield

(D) reducing light pollution

(E) locating close to public transportation

(F) providing high-reflectance roofing

239. View plane restrictions are typically governed by

(A) building codes

(B) easements

(C) local ordinances

(D) zoning restrictions

240. Which of the following are requirements for making a site accessible for egress purposes? (Choose the four that apply.)

(A) An egress court or dispersal area must be provided.

(B) Abrupt changes in level cannot exceed $^1/_4$ in.

(C) Sidewalks must have a slope no greater than 1:20.

(D) The cross slope of accessible routes must be no greater than 1:50.

(E) Sidewalks must have handrail on at least one side.

(F) The clear width of walking surfaces must be a minimum of 36 in.

241. The illustration shown represents a plot of land.

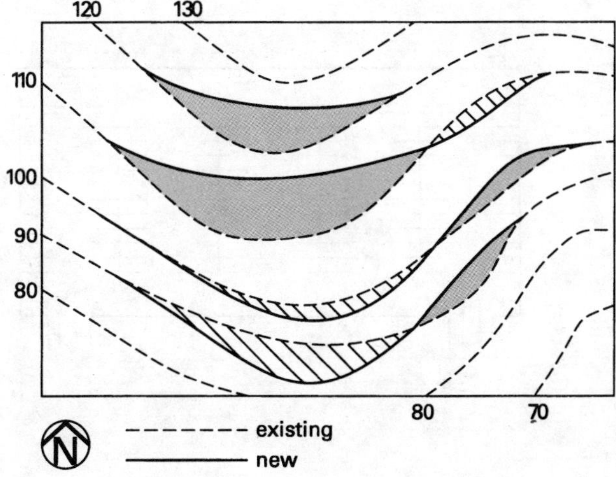

This illustration shows

(A) an earthwork diagram

(B) areas unsuitable for building

(C) desired positions for solar access

(D) regrading options

242. Which of the following are effective strategies for sustainability during preliminary site planning? (Choose the four that apply.)

(A) Select a suitable greenfield site.

(B) Minimize the building footprint.

(C) Position buildings along land contours.

(D) Provide maximum lawn area.

(E) Locate buildings and parking close to roads.

(F) Reserve areas for infiltration basins.

243. The slope between point A and point B is ____%. (Fill in the blank.)

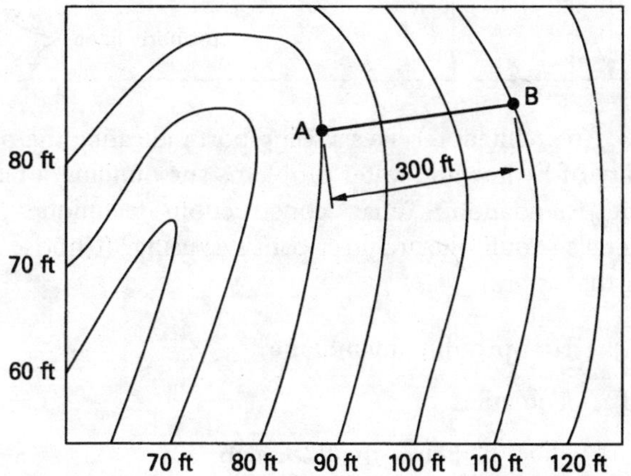

244. According to the Secretary of the Interior's *Standards for Rehabilitation*, which of the following modifications can usually be made to a historic property undergoing rehabilitation treatment?

(A) repairing an existing but damaged exterior cornice molding

(B) removing nonbearing interior walls to make larger spaces

(C) cleaning of brick and masonry using chemicals

(D) removing additions to the building that were made after original construction

245. In the lot shown, if the floor area ratio (FAR) is 2.0, the maximum allowable gross buildable area is ____ ft. (Fill in the blank.)

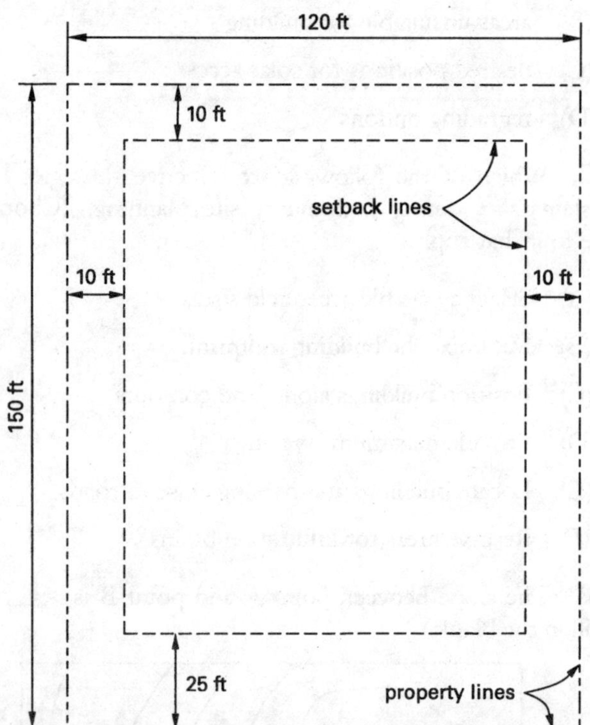

246. An architect receives a soil report indicating the possibility of hydrostatic water problems surrounding a basement foundation. What construction techniques or materials should the architect consider using? (Choose the four that apply.)

(A) dampproofing membrane

(B) geotextiles

(C) gravel fill below the floor slab

(D) pervious paving around the building

(E) positive slope away from the building

(F) sump pumps

247. Four schematic parking lot layouts are shown. Assuming all parking spaces, drives, and access aisles are sized correctly, which layout best serves a strip mall?

(A)

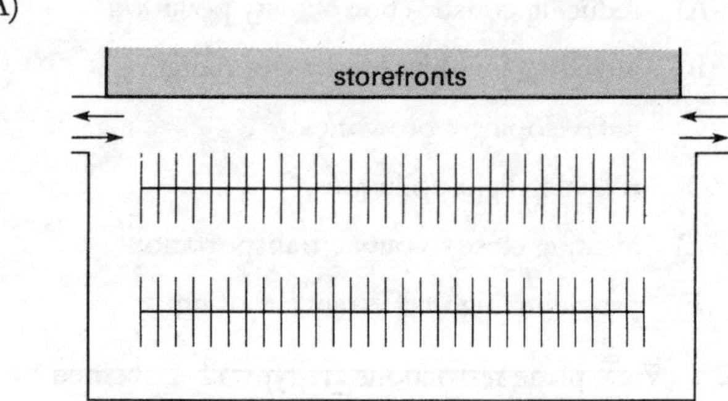

(B)

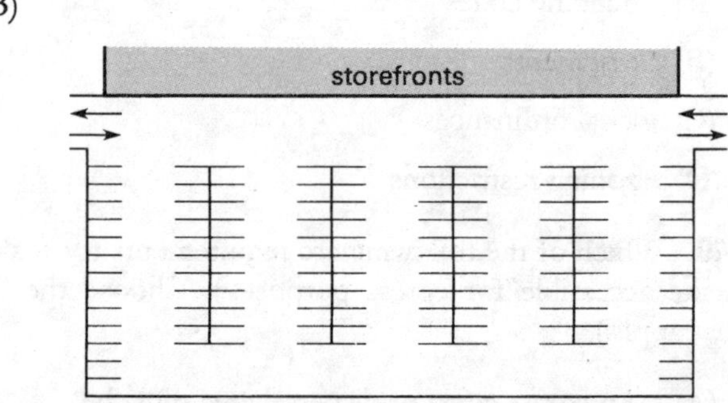

(C)

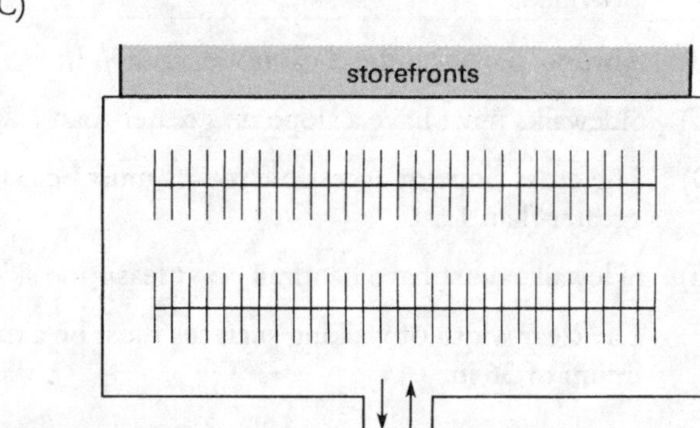

(D)

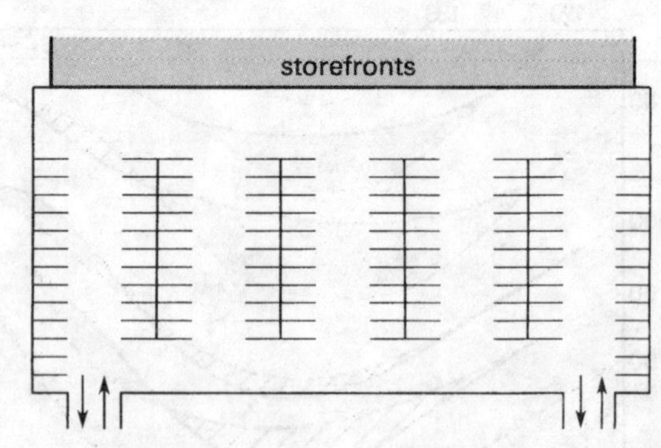

Programming & Analysis

248. A midsize college is constructing a center for ethnic studies. The single-story building will be used for group meetings and events and will include a specialized resource library.

program of spaces

tag	name	area (ft^2)	requirements
LB	lobby	400	direct access to meeting/activity room
R	reception area	150	exterior window; adjacent to lobby; near secretarial area
AO	administrator's office	200	exterior window, direct access to secretarial area
SO	secretarial area	150	exterior window
AA	administrative assistant's office	200	exterior window, direct access to secretarial area
S	storage room	150	near administrative offices
MA	meeting/activity room	2400	exterior windows and view, 15 ft ceiling, two exits
L	library	900	exterior window; near lobby
LO	librarian's office	200	exterior window; direct access to library
CR	classrooms	600	2 @ 300 ft^2 each; exterior windows; near seminar room
SR	seminar room	300	exterior window; near library
T	toilet rooms	300	2 @ 150 ft^2 each
ME	mechanical/electrical room	400	one side of room on exterior wall
	total program area	6350	

Based on the program summary given, what requirement has the greatest impact on building layout?

(A) adjacency of the lobby and meeting/activity room

(B) grouping of the reception area and administrative offices

(C) majority of rooms needing exterior windows

(D) proximity of the library to the lobby

249. The owner of the lot shown wants to develop a building with the maximum allowable gross area.

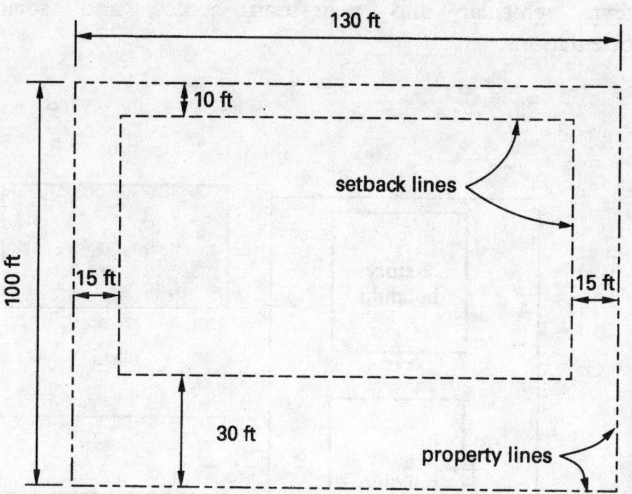

The floor area ratio (FAR) is 2.0. The owner wants to build each story fully to the setback lines shown. The building can have a maximum of _____ stories. (Fill in the blank.)

250. The maximum allowable area of a building is limited by a combination of

(A) floor area ratio and construction type

(B) occupancy group and setback requirements

(C) bulk plane limits and floor area ratio

(D) construction type and setback requirements

251. What factors determine the total allowable area and height of a building? (Choose the four that apply.)

(A) construction type

(B) occupancy group

(C) number of exits from the building

(D) separation between adjacent buildings

(E) combustibility of exterior materials

(F) whether or not the building has a sprinkler system

252. The site shown is to be developed with a two-story building consisting of retail shops on the first floor and office space on the second floor. A surface parking lot is also planned. The neighborhood is pedestrian friendly though the sidewalks and landscaping of the surrounding area are not shown. The shops can be accessed from any side of the building. Entry to the office lobby is indicated by the directional arrow, as shown in the "2-story building" blocks in the left side of the selection area. Any undeveloped area on the site will be landscaped open space.

On the illustration shown, place one building and one parking area in such a way that addresses community context, vehicular and pedestrian access, and solar orientations.

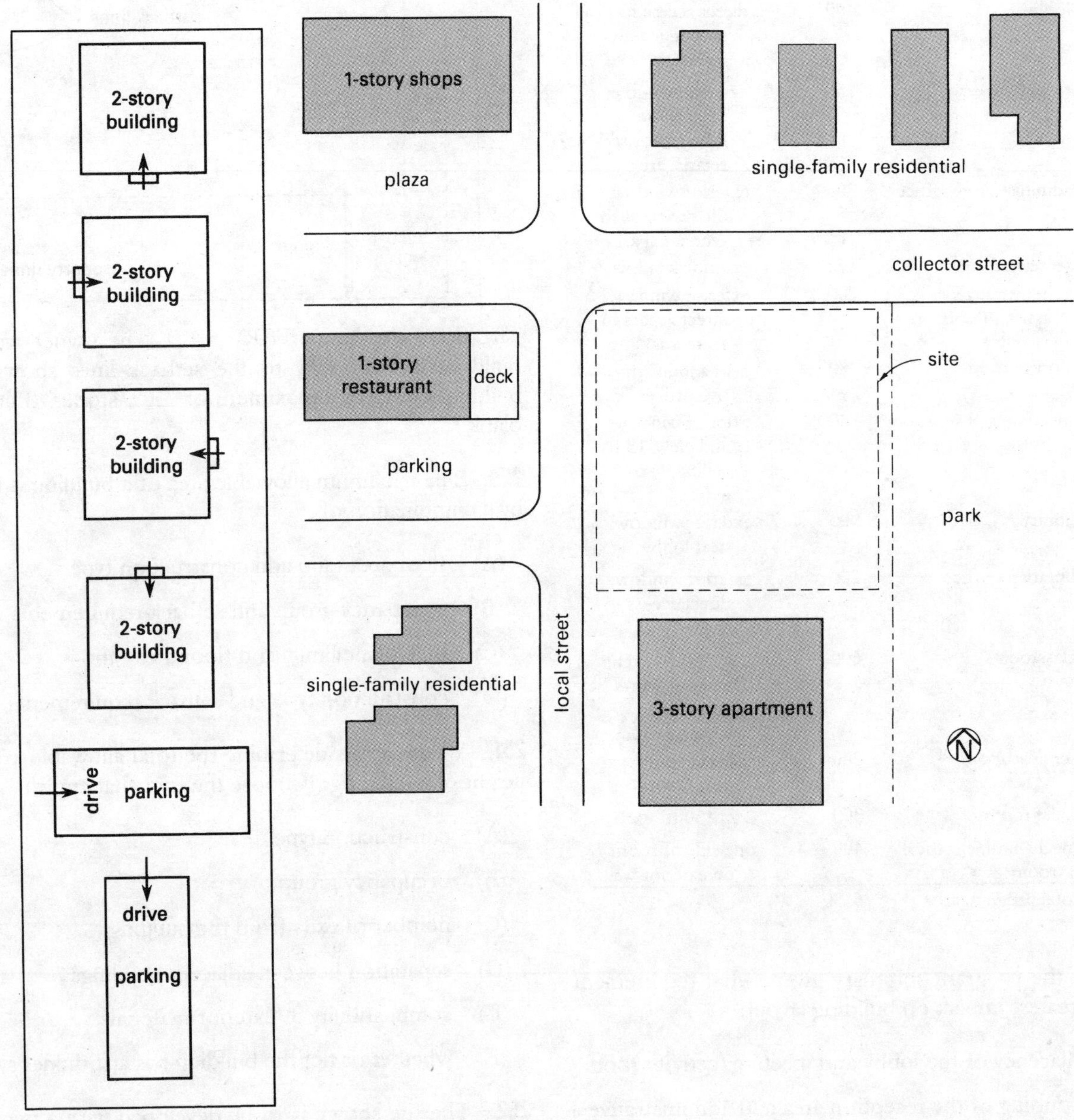

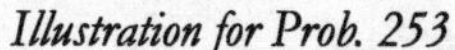

Illustration for Prob. 253

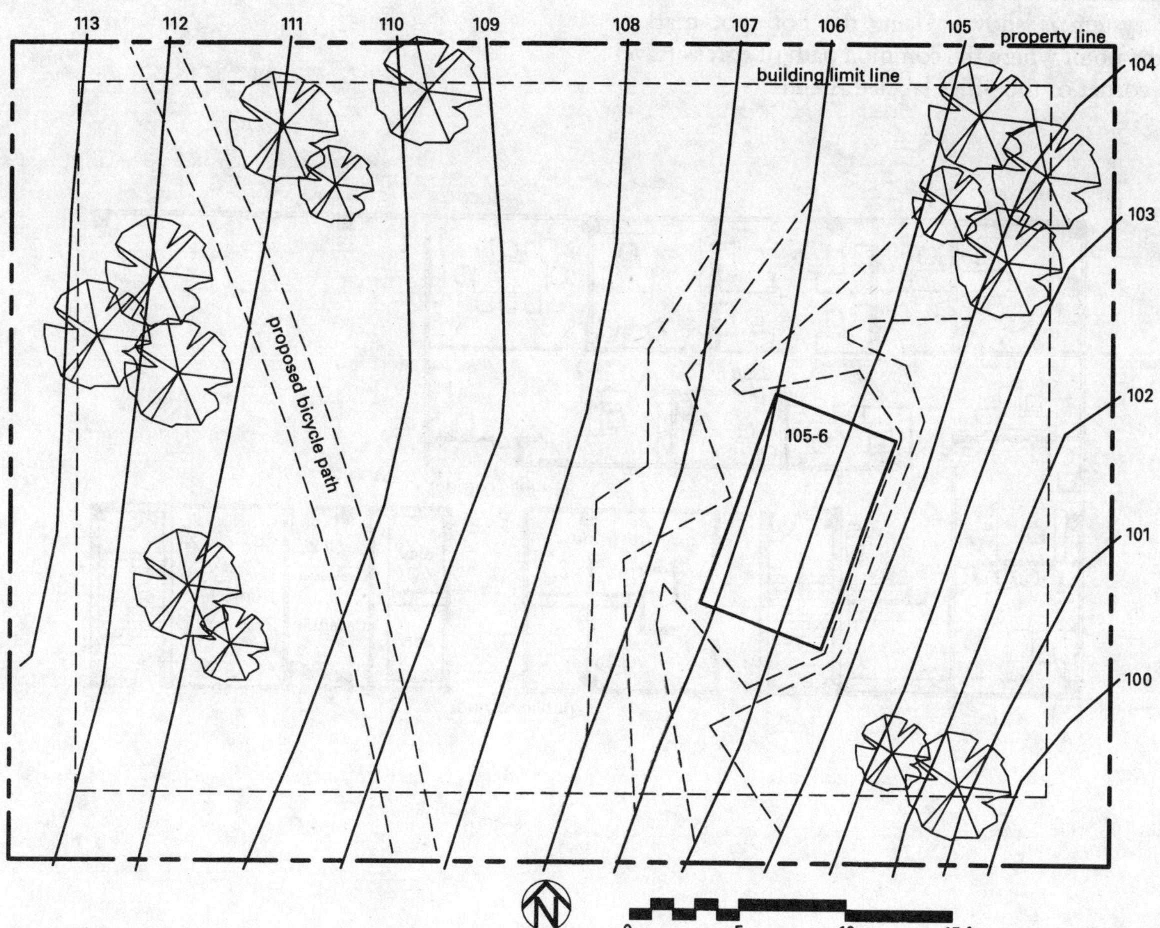

253. To make a picnic area level, the area needs to be regraded, allowing for installation of a pervious concrete slab, as shown.

The new grading changes—which are indicated by the dashed lines—must produce grades of a minimum of 1% and a maximum of 20%. What problems do this regrading present? (Choose the three that apply.)

(A) The new grading line is disturbed by the drip line of some trees.

(B) The swales do not adequately divert water away from the slab.

(C) The new grading lines are too close together.

(D) The graded area for the slab is not level.

(E) The graded area needs to be higher to improve the view.

(F) The grade line of 103 ft should also be modified.

254. A portion of a plan for an office building with a full sprinkler system is shown. Using the hot spot marker, identify the point where the common path of egress travel from the corner of the office labeled A ends.

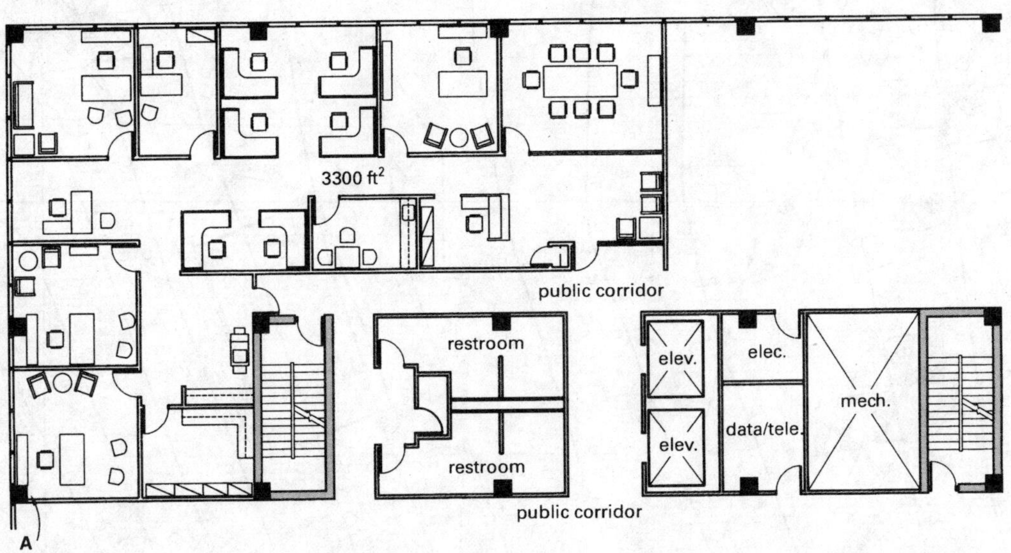

Case Study 1

Problem 255 through Prob. 264 refer to the following case study. Refer to Resource 3.1 through Resource 3.3 to assist in answering the problems.

A developer has purchased a temperate climate property located in a semi-urban area near bus and mass transit routes in zoning district M-1 with a floor area ratio (FAR) of 2.0. The lot is 350 ft wide and 315 ft deep with an area of 102,000 ft^2 on relatively flat topography. The front setback requirement is along 45th Street—which is a collector street, as compared to Perry Avenue, which is a local street. The developer plans to build a structure with retail space on the first floor and office space above. The owner also intends to lease part of the first floor and an outdoor deck to a small restaurant.

The architect sketches the site plan diagram shown in Resource 3.2 but, upon review, the city planning commission directs the architect to consider a layout that places the building closer to 45th Street and Perry Avenue in order to create a stronger urban edge. The suggested alternate proposal puts parking behind the building as much as possible and reduces the area devoted to surface parking, placing some of it under the building so more area can be devoted to landscaped open space. The architect's drafted configuration does not have parking under the structure.

Initially, the architect determined that a five-story, 120 ft × 210 ft building met the programming requirements. The structural engineer has suggested that the most economical base structure is a steel frame on a 30 ft × 40 ft grid and confirms that it will be possible to extend an underground parking area as much as 15 ft beyond the length of the building above, on both sides of the parking area. This extension allows for 40 parking spaces on one level below grade with the building shape shown in Resource 3.2. The *Americans with Disabilities Act* (ADA) *Accessibility Guidelines* requires two accessible parking spaces in the underground parking lot and four accessible spaces in the surface lot. Scheme A and Scheme B in Resource 3.3 show the architect's site plan sketches developed to meet the planning committee's suggestions. Landscaping is not shown.

Resource 3.1 Form and Parking Summary

zoning district[a]	setback			height limits		requirements per gross floor area or unit	
	front	side	rear	feet	stories	parking[c]	bicycle
R-1[b]	25	15	15	30[d]	2	2 spaces and 350 ft^2	NR
R-2[b]	25	10	5	45	3	2 spaces/unit	NR
R-3	10	5	10	65	5	1.25 spaces/unit	1/3 units
M-1	5	5	5	70	5	1/1000 ft^2	1/10,000 ft^2
M-2	0	0	5	110	8	2/1000 ft^2	1/10,000 ft^2
B-1	10	0	5	110	8	1/1000 ft^2	1/5000 ft^2
B-2	10	0	0	150	12	1/guest room or unit	1/5000 ft^2
B-3	5	0	0	250	20	2/1000 ft^2	1/10,000 ft^2
I-1	30	15	10	50	3	0.5/1000 ft^2	NR
I-2	30	10	5	55	3	0.5/1000 ft^2	NR
UE-1[b]	10	5	10	50[d]	3	2.5/1000 ft^2	NR
UE-2[b]	5	5	10	70[e]	5	2/1000 ft^2	1/5000 ft^2

[a]R: residential; M: mixed use; B: business; I: industrial; UE: urban edge

[b]The maximum height can be increased 1 ft for every 5 ft increase in lot width over 50 ft up to a maximum of 35 ft.

[c]See specific zone district requirements for additional information.

[d]Bulk plane limit required for side setbacks beginning on the property line at a point 10 ft above grade and extending at an angle of 45°.

[e]An upper story setback of 15 ft is required above 30 ft.

Resource 3.2 Site Plan Diagram

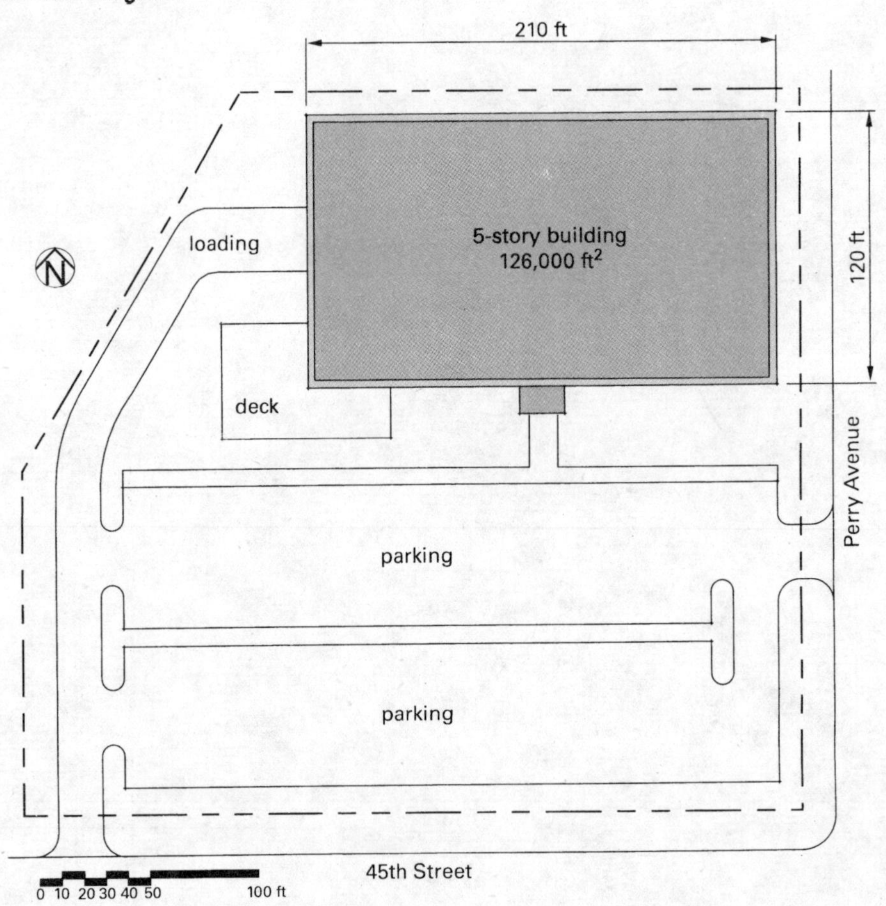

Resource 3.3 Site Plan Sketches

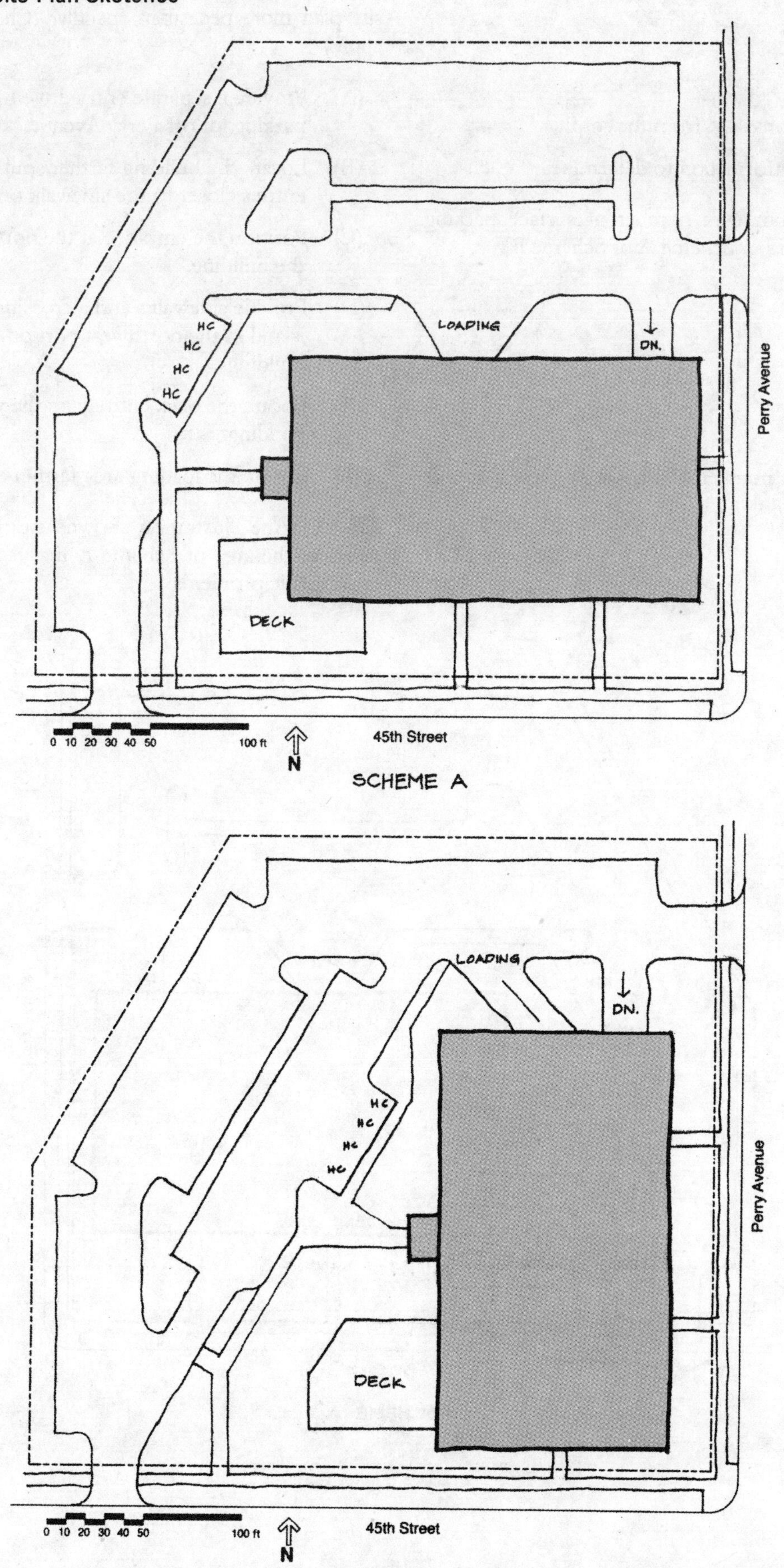

255. Which scheme is best for sustainability?

(A) Scheme A

(B) Scheme B

(C) building oriented 45° from the south

(D) not enough information to determine

256. What is the minimum number of surface parking spaces required for either Scheme A or Scheme B?

(A) 86

(B) 90

(C) 102

(D) 126

257. The minimum number of bicycle storage spaces is ______. (Fill in the blank.)

258. How can Scheme A be improved in order to make the site plan more pedestrian friendly? (Choose the three that apply.)

(A) Provide a separate entry drive for the underground parking lot off Perry Avenue.

(B) Locate the building farther south to position retail entries closer to the sidewalk on 45th Street.

(C) Position the entrance at the northwest corner of the building.

(D) Provide sidewalks and a crossing from the large island in the northwest portion of the lot to the building.

(E) Locate the deck entirely on the west side of the building.

(F) Locate the loading area farther east.

259. On the illustration shown, use the hotspot marker to select the area of Scheme A that is likely to create the most traffic problems.

Illustration for Prob. 259

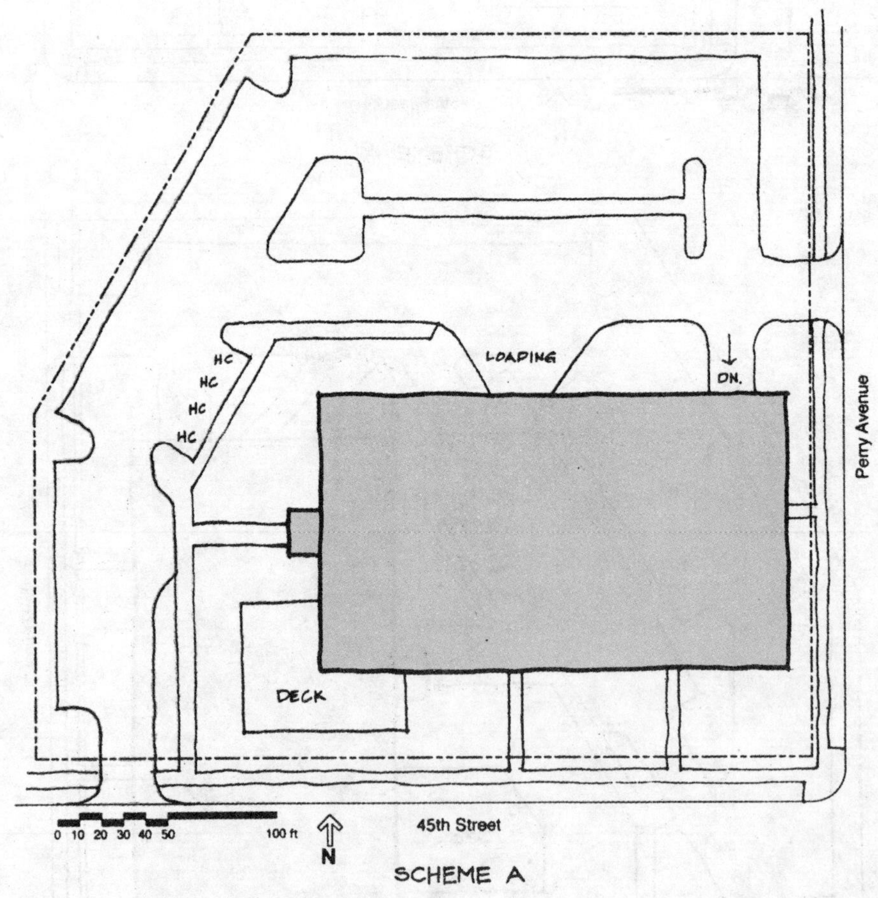

260. Using Scheme A and Scheme B, which areas are the best locations for a transformer vault in the basement of the building? (Choose the two that apply.)

(A) Scheme A, along the north side near the west end of the building

(B) Scheme A, along the north side between the loading area and the underground lot ramp

(C) Scheme A, along the south side, near the east end of the building

(D) Scheme B, along the north side, near the west end of the building

(E) Scheme B, along the east side, near the north end of the building

(F) Scheme B, along the east side, near the midpoint of the building

261. The maximum floor-to-floor distance that the architect should anticipate is _______. (Fill in the blank.)

262. In Scheme B, where is the bicycle storage best located?

(A) north of the entrance, east of the accessible parking

(B) between the entrance and the deck, close to the sidewalk

(C) west of the deck, near the sidewalk access

(D) on the north side of the building, next to the loading bays

263. For either scheme shown in Resource 3.3, in which direction should the 30 ft side of the engineer's suggested 30 ft × 40 ft steel frame column spacing be oriented?

(A) along the length of the building

(B) along the width of the building

(C) along either the length or width of the building

(D) not enough information given to determine

264. During the site and building planning phases, what additional zoning conditions given in Resource 3.1 should the architect consider in Resource 3.3 Scheme B?

(A) The building's height can be increased by 35 ft.

(B) The building's location will have to be moved west to meet requirements for bulk planes.

(C) The restaurant can be located in a separate building to increase retail space.

(D) The front setback will have to be increased.

Case Study 2

Problem 265 through Prob. 270 refer to the following case study. Refer to Resource 3.4 through Resource 3.8 to assist in answering the problems.

After the successful passing of a bond issue, a large Midwest city is proceeding with plans to build a new branch library in one of its underserved neighborhoods. The site is in a residential area and adjacent to a public park, as shown in Resource 3.5. The site's area is approximately 51,500 ft^2.

The building will be primarily one level, with a partial second story intended for a large community meeting room. The elevator and stairway must be located in a lobby that can be secured from the rest of the library for after-hours use. Because the site is between residential areas and offers the only access to the public park on the southern border of the park, pedestrian access is required from Spruce Street. In addition, the city wants the library to have views of and pedestrian access to the park. To achieve this, an approximately 1600 ft^2 plaza connected to the building is planned. The plaza is to be designed for use in the spring, summer, and fall and have views of and convenient access to the park. In addition to zoning restrictions, the local planning ordinance prohibits any building structure within 40 ft of a park. The site is in an R-4 district. A summary of the programmed spaces is given in Resource 3.4.

Resource 3.4 Summary of Programmed Spaces

space	area (ft^2)	notes
first floor		
book collection		
adult	1600	adjacent to adult reading area
children's	250	adjacent to children's reading area
reference	400	
periodicals	300	
reading rooms		
adult reading	1000	views to park required
computer terminals	400	
children's reading	300	adjacent to children's book stacks
meeting room	600	views to park required
staff		
circulation desk/lobby	250	includes catalog terminals
librarian	200	
assistant librarian	150	adjacent to librarian
administrative asst.	150	adjacent to librarian and admin. asst.
cataloging	200	
work room	300	adjacent to cataloging
staff lounge/lunch	200	
staff toilets	150	
public toilets (2 @ 200 ft^2)	400	
mechanical	400	
elevator	80	near entry and circulation desk
stairs, 150 ft^2 each	300	one stair near entry and elevator
total first floor net usable	7630	
circulation @ 18%	1370	
total gross first floor	9000	
second floor		
community room	2400	single, open space; 2 exits required
lobby	220	
elevator	80	
stairs, 150 ft^2 each	300	adjacent to elevator
total gross second floor	3000	
total building gross	12,000	

Resource 3.5 Site Plan

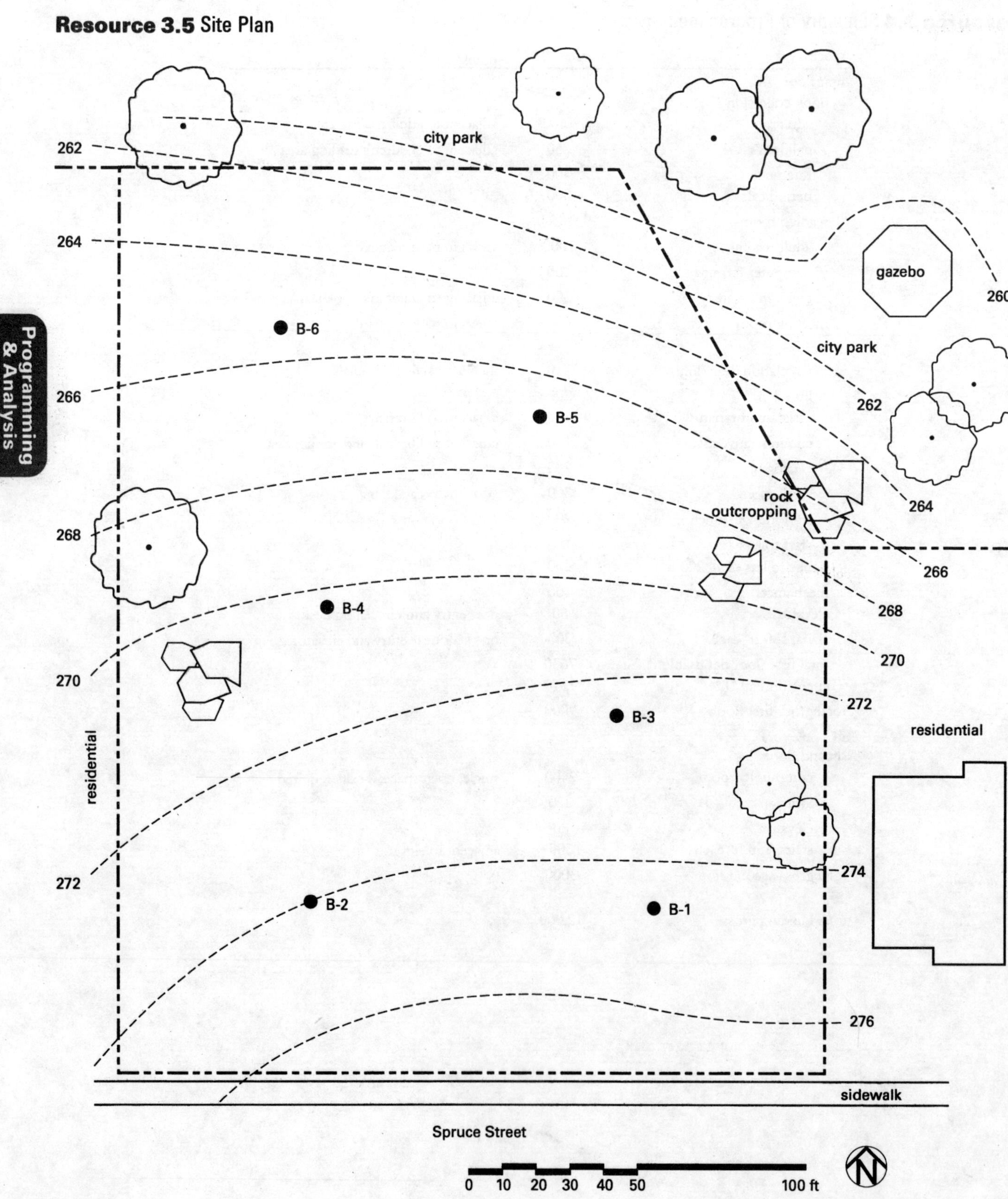

Resource 3.6 Zoning Ordinance Excerpt

3.4 building location and form

3.4.1 All development, except detached accessory structures meeting the requirements of other portions of this ordinance, must meet the setback and height requirements set forth in Resource 3.7.

3.4.2 Exceptions to the requirements of Resource 3.7 are described in the specific zone district requirements elsewhere in this ordinance.

3.4.3 The maximum number of structures on a zone lot must not be restricted except for zoning districts R-1, R-2, and UE-1, where the number of primary structures is limited to one (1).

Resource 3.7 Form and Parking Summary

zoning district[a]	setback			height limits		requirements per gross floor area or unit	
	front	side	rear	feet	stories	parking[c]	bicycle
R-1[b]	25	15	15	30[d]	2	2 spaces and 350 ft^2	NR
R-2[b]	25	10	5	45	3	2 spaces/unit	NR
R-3	10	5	10	65	5	1.25 spaces/unit	1/3 units
M-1	5	5	5	70	5	1/1000 ft^2	1/10,000 ft^2
M-2	0	0	5	110	8	2/1000 ft^2	1/10,000 ft^2
B-1	10	0	5	110	8	1/1000 ft^2	1/5000 ft^2
B-2	10	0	0	150	12	1/guest room or unit	1/5000 ft^2
B-3	5	0	0	250	20	2/1000 ft^2	1/10,000 ft^2
I-1	30	15	10	50	3	0.5/1000 ft^2	NR
I-2	30	10	5	55	3	0.5/1000 ft^2	NR
UE-1[b]	10	5	10	50[d]	3	2.5/1000 ft^2	NR
UE-2[b]	5	5	10	70[e]	5	2/1000 ft^2	1/5000 ft^2

[a]R: residential; M: mixed use; B: business; I: industrial; UE: urban edge
[b]The maximum height can be increased 1 ft for every 5 ft increase in lot width over 50 ft up to a maximum of 35 ft.
[c]See specific zone district requirements for additional information.
[d]Bulk plane limit required for side setbacks beginning on the property line at a point 10 ft above grade and extending at an angle of 45°.
[e]An upper story setback of 15 ft is required above 30 ft.

Programming & Analysis

Resource 3.8 Soil Report

Partial Soil and Foundation Investigation Branch Library

SUMMARY

(1) The subsurface conditions encountered in the exploratory borings generally consist of approximately 32 ft of silty, clayey sands to gravelly sands overlying claystone bedrock to the maximum depth investigated, 35 ft. Approximately 7 ft of sandy clay fill was encountered in borings B-1 and B-2. The extent of the existing fill was not known at the time of this report. Groundwater was not encountered in the exploratory borings at the time of drilling.

(2) Three rock outcroppings were found on the site consisting of large and moderate-size boulders. They are approximately 15 ft in diameter and extend approximately 6 to 8 ft below grade. Because of their size and depth, we recommend they remain in place.

(3) Based on the subsurface conditions encountered and considering the proposed construction is adjacent to roadway and/or existing structures, we recommend the building be founded on a straight shaft drilled pier (caissons) foundation system. However, as an alternative, the building may be supported on a shallow foundation system of spread footings placed on on-site natural undisturbed sands.

(4) Slab-on-grade recommendations are presented in the text of this report.

SCOPE OF STUDY

This report presents the results of a soil and foundation investigation for the proposed Branch Library located at 4567 Spruce Street, Middleton. The purpose of this study was to explore the subsurface conditions, obtain some data of the pertinent engineering characteristics of the underlying strata, recommend the most appropriate foundation system, develop specific foundation design criteria, attempt to evaluate risks of slab-on-grade construction, and address other geotechnical factors in the proposed development.

It should be understood that economic and practical constraints limit our sampling and laboratory testing to only a minuscule sample of the total mass of soil and/or bedrock, which lies within the zone of influence of the proposed structure.

Our analyses, conclusions, and recommendations are based upon the assumption that the samples of subsurface strata, which we observed and tested, are representative of the entire soil mass.

PROPOSED CONSTRUCTION

As we understand, the proposed construction on the site is to consist of a two-story building with no basement. The design loads are not known at the time of this report but are anticipated to be moderate. The floor slab elevation is anticipated to be near 270 ft.

FIELD INVESTIGATION

Six (6) exploratory test borings have been drilled at the site at the locations shown on the last page of this report. The borings were drilled with a 4 in diameter, continuous flight, solid-stem power augers or a 3.25 in inside diameter hollow-stem power augers using a truck-mounted drill rig.

At regular intervals, the drilling tools were removed from the boreholes and soil samples were obtained with a 2 in. I.D. California Spoon Sampler. The sampler was driven into the various subsoil strata with blows of a 140 lbm hammer falling 30 in. The number of hammer blows required to drive the sampler 1 ft, or a fraction thereof, constitutes the penetration test. This field test is similar to the standard penetration test described by ASTM Method D-1586. Penetration resistance values, when properly evaluated, are an index to the soil strength and density.

LABORATORY TESTING

All samples were carefully inspected and classified in the laboratory by the project engineer. Natural water contents, dry unit weights, Atterberg Limits, and a partial gradation analysis were performed on representative soil samples.

A swell-consolidation test was performed on typical specimen of potentially swelling and/or consolidating materials. This is to indicate the behavior of these materials upon wetting and loading.

SUBSURFACE CONDITIONS

The subsurface conditions encountered in the exploratory borings generally consist of approximately 32 ft of silty, clayey sands to gravelly sands overlying claystone bedrock to the maximum depth investigated, 35 ft. Approximately 7 ft of sandy clay fill was encountered in borings B-1 and B-2. The extent of the existing fill was not known at the time of this report.

The on-site existing fill consists of dark brown to brown, silty clay with sand and some brick fragments. As indicated by penetration resistance values, the existing fill was generally firm.

The on-site natural sands consist of light brown to brown, moist to wet, silty, clayey sand with occasional sandy clay lenses to gravelly sands. As indicated by penetration resistance values, the sands were generally loose to dense.

Bedrock was encountered at approximately 30 ft below the existing grade in the exploratory borings. The on-site bedrock typically consists of brown, moist to very moist claystone. As indicated by penetration resistance values, the claystone was hard to very hard.

Groundwater was not encountered in the exploratory borings at the time of drilling. However, based upon high moisture content of the recovered soil samples, perched groundwater may exist. It should be noted that the water table can vary with changes in precipitation, irrigation, and land use.

(continued)

Resource 3.8 Soil Report (continued)

DRILLED PIER FOUNDATIONS

Based on the subsurface conditions encountered and considering the proposed construction is adjacent to roadway and/or existing structures, it is recommended the building be founded on a straight shaft drilled pier (caissons) foundation system.

Using the drilled pier type of foundation, each column is supported on a single drilled pier or building walls are supported on a grade beam founded on a series of drilled piers. Load applied to a pier of this type is transmitted to the bedrock, partially through peripheral shear stresses, which develop on the sides of the pier and partially through end bearing pressure.

Design values for drilled piers are based on the field and laboratory test results and the supporting capacity of the average of the softest materials encountered. The strength of the bedrock increases with depth. For the portion of the pier in bedrock, we recommend the following maximum allowable end bearing and compressive side shear values. Estimated pier settlements at the site are on the order of less than 1 in.

depth into bedrock (ft)	end bearing pressure (psf)	compressive side shear (psf)
0–5	–	3000
5+	50,000	5000

A design value of 60% of the compressive side shear may be used for the tension shear.

Drilled piers should penetrate at least 5 ft into on-site nonweathered claystone bedrock and should have a minimum shaft length of 16 ft.

A minimum pier diameter of 16 in is recommended to facilitate proper cleaning and observation of the drilled pier hole.

Lateral pier design parameters would be horizontal modulus of subgrade reaction values of 40 tcf and 250 tcf for the on-site overburden soils and bedrock, respectively. The modulus values are based on a pier diameter of 1 ft. Values used should be the preceding divided by the actual pier diameter in feet.

Piers should have a center-to-center spacing of at least four pier diameters. If closer spacing is necessary, we can provide additional design criteria.

For uniform building code seismic analysis (per the *International Building Code*) the site is considered to be in Seismic Zone 1 and Soil Profile Type Sc. The soils at the site are not particularly prone to liquefaction. Site conditions do not require the use of structural ties between individual foundation elements.

SHALLOW FOUNDATIONS

As an alternative to the deep foundation system, the proposed building may be supported on a spread footing foundation system placed on natural on-site sands.

Footings placed at least 10 ft below the final grade on the natural, undisturbed sands will be designed using a maximum allowable soil bearing pressure of 3000 psf. Any footings placed from 3 to 10 ft below the final grade on the natural, undisturbed sands will be designed using a maximum allowable soil bearing pressure of 2000 psf. We recommend footings have a minimum width of 16 in for continuous footings and 24 in for isolated pads.

Prior to placement of spread footings, on-site existing fill and/or soft clay lenses are to be removed entirely beneath the bottom of footings.

If perched groundwater is encountered at the bottom of excavation, the subgrade must be stabilized prior to placement of spread footings. The subgrade stabilization will consist of placing and compacting 2 to 4 in diameter crushed stone or gravel until a stable subgrade is achieved. We highly recommend that this process be observed by a representative of our firm.

The footings need to be provided with adequate soil cover above their bearing elevation for frost protection. A cover of 36 in is typically considered adequate in Middleton.

SLAB-ON-GRADE CONSTRUCTION

Based on the subsurface conditions encountered, the following measures are recommended for the slab-on-grade construction:

1) All topsoil, organic materials, existing fill, and existing pavement sections are to be removed from the proposed building envelope. The floor slabs are to be placed on on-site natural sands. Any clay lenses, if encountered, are to be removed entirely beneath floor slabs.

2) Floor slabs need to be separated from all bearing walls and columns with expansion joints, which allow unrestrained vertical movement. Joints (construction joints/saw cuts) in the slabs are to be at maximum spacing in accordance with ACI requirements.

3) Place a minimum 1 in "void" above, or preferably below nonbearing partitions in slab-on-grade areas. Door jambs, drywall, heating and cooling equipment, and so forth, are to be similarly protected.

4) If perched groundwater is encountered at the bottom of excavation, any soft soils need to be removed entirely and the subgrade is to be stabilized prior to placement of any floor slabs. The subgrade stabilization is to consist of placing and compacting 2 to 4 in diameter crushed stone or gravel until a stable subgrade is achieved. We highly recommend that this process be observed by a representative of our firm.

5) It is important to keep any exposed clay material moist during construction by occasional sprinkling.

(continued)

Resource 3.8 Soil Report (continued)

6) No irrigation is to occur for a distance of 6 ft beyond the building limits. Those areas may be covered with decorative gravel or artificial lawn, or preferably pavement. All exterior joints (i.e., building-sidewalk, curb pavement, etc.) are to be well sealed. Roof downspouts will discharge on splashblocks, downspout extensions, or pavements to beyond the limits of the foundation backfill but not less than 6 ft from the buildings.

7) A polyethylene moisture barrier is to be used below the slabs in finished areas, especially if impermeable floor coverings are to be used. This moisture barrier is to be continuous and placed shortly before concrete placement. Any moisture/vapor barrier used is to be installed per recommendations of ASTM E-1643-94.

8) A modulus of subgrade reaction of 150 pci can be used for the on-site granular soils.

The slab-on-grade precautions generally limit potential floor slab movements on the order of 1 in.

EARTHWORK

All topsoil, organic materials, and existing pavement sections are to be removed from proposed building envelope. The topsoil depth is anticipated to be on the order of 4 to 6 in.

We recommend that cut and fill slopes generally be no steeper than 2 (horizontal) to 1 (vertical). Steeper slopes may be suitable but will need to be individually considered.

It is important to keep the exposed clays at or near the existing moisture content by properly moisture conditioning.

Structural fill refers to the fill material to be placed beneath the spread footings. We anticipate the use of structural fill to be limited during the proposed construction. However, if structural fill is needed, it will consist of inherently nonswelling, granular material and adhere to the following properties.

liquid limit	30 or less
plasticity index	10 or less
maximum particle size	2 in or less
passing no. 200 sieve	10% to 30%

Structural fill is to be placed in 8 in loose lifts, moisture conditioned and compacted to at least 98% of maximum Standard Proctor density (per ASTM D-698) within 2% of the optimum moisture content.

Select fill used beneath the floor slabs and pavement areas is to be a nonswelling material approved prior to its use. The select fill is to be placed in 8 in loose lifts and compacted to at least 95% of the maximum Standard Proctor density (per ASTM D-698) at a moisture content sufficient to minimize swell potential. The necessary moisture content of any material will be determined at the time of approval. The on-site sands, exclusive of topsoils and organic materials, are suitable to be used as select fill. The on-site existing fill is to be evaluated and approved prior to use as select fill.

Fill in landscaped areas may be placed at a minimum of 88% of the maximum Standard Proctor density with no moisture control.

265. What is the closest distance from the northeast property line that a structure can be constructed?

(A) 10 ft

(B) 15 ft

(C) 25 ft

(D) 40 ft

266. The architect is considering separating the library building into two sections with the north section built 3 ft lower than the south section in order to minimize earthwork. The north section will contain the book collection, reading rooms, and the meeting room; the south section will contain the staff areas as well as the second floor community room.

Place one block containing the book collection, reading rooms, and meeting room ("reading") on the site plan shown. In addition, place one block for the staff ("staff"), one block for the parking area ("parking"), and the block for the plaza ("plaza") such that they meet the requirements of the program, zoning, and the soil report.

267. On the site plan shown in Resource 3.5, place a hot spot marker where the parking area requires the least amount of earthwork and imported fill while conforming to the requirements of the program.

268. The head librarian has reviewed the program space assignments and wonders if there is sufficient stack space for the book collection, not including periodicals. The head librarian asks the architect to calculate the necessary space using a set of standard population-based guidelines for the library industry, so it can be compared with the current programmed area. The guidelines are as follows.

- number of books: 15,000 plus 2 books per capita for a base population over 5000
- linear feet of shelving required: 1875 ft plus 1 ft for every 8 books over 15,000
- standard shelving units: 12 in deep × 36 in long with 7 shelves per unit
- back-to-back shelving: 36 in space between units
- number of shelving units per module: 5
- Ignore space requirements for cross aisles at the ends of modules.

This branch library serves a population of 9000 people. The minimum floor area, rounded to the nearest 10 ft^2, is _________. (Fill in the blank.)

269. The architect is exploring several alternatives for parking. One alternative site plan is shown. On the site place shown in Resource 3.5, place a hotspot marker where a connection for service and delivery causes the least amount of conflict with automobile parking and access while responding to the requirements of the building program.

270. What structural elements are the least expensive to implement? (Select the three that apply.)

(A) spread footings

(B) drilled piers

(C) steel frame

(D) masonry bearing walls

(E) concrete on open-web steel joists

(F) concrete on steel beams

Solutions

Multiple Choice

176. (A) ● (C) (D)
177. (A) ● (C) (D)
178. (A) (B) ● (D)
179. (A) ● (C) (D)
180. 10 years
181. (A) ● (C) (D)
182. (A) ● ● (D) (E) (F)
183. C, E, and F
184. ● (B) (C) (D)
185. ● (B) ● (D) ● (F)
186. (A) ● (C) (D)
187. ● (B) (C) ● ● (F)
188. (A) ● (C) (D)
189. (A) (B) (C) ●
190. (A) ● (C) (D)
191. (A) (B) ● (D)
192. (A) ● (C) (D)
193. (A) ● (C) (D)
194. ● (B) (C) ● ● (F)
195. (A) (B) (C) ●
196. ● (B) (C) (D)
197. ● (B) (C) (D)
198. ● (B) (C) ● ● ●
199. (A) ● (C) (D)
200. (A) ● ● (D) ● ●
201. (A) (B) ● (D)
202. ● (B) (C) (D)
203. (A) (B) ● (D)
204. (A) ● (C) (D)
205. (A) ● ● (D) ● ●
206. (A) ● (C) (D)
207. (A) (B) (C) ●
208. (A) ● (C) (D)
209. (A) (B) (C) ●
210. (A) ● (C) (D)
211. ● (B) (C) (D)
212. (A) (B) ● (D)
213. (A) (B) (C) ●
214. ● ● ● (D) (E) ●
215. (A) ● (C) (D)
216. (A) (B) (C) ●
217. ● (B) (C) (D)
218. (A) ● (C) (D)
219. (A) ● (C) (D)
220. (A) (B) ● (D)
221. (A) (B) (C) ●
222. (A) ● (C) (D)
223. ● (B) (C) (D)
224. (A) (B) ● (D)
225. (A) (B) (C) ●
226. ● (B) (C) (D)
227. (A) ● (C) (D)
228. (A) ● (C) (D)
229. ● (B) (C) ● ● (F)
230. (A) (B) ● (D)
231. (A) (B) (C) ●
232. (A) (B) ● (D)
233. (A) ● (C) (D)
234. (A) ● (C) (D)
235. (A) (B) ● (D)
236. (A) ● (C) (D)
237. (A) (B) ● (D)
238. (A) (B) ● ● ● ●
239. (A) (B) ● (D)
240. (A) ● ● ● (E) ●
241. ● (B) (C) (D)
242. (A) ● ● (D) ● ●
243. 10%
244. ● (B) (C) (D)
245. 36,000 ft^2
246. (A) ● ● (D) ● ●
247. (A) ● (C) (D)
248. (A) (B) ● (D)
249. 4 stories
250. ● (B) (C) (D)
251. ● ● (C) ● (E) ●
252. See Sol. 252.
253. (A) ● ● ● (E) (F)
254. See Sol. 254.

Case Study 1

255. ● (B) (C) (D)
256. ● (B) (C) (D)
257. 13
258. (A) (B) ● ● (E) ●
259. See Sol. 259.
260. (A) ● (C) ● (E) (F)
261. 14 ft
262. ● (B) (C) (D)
263. ● (B) (C) (D)
264. (A) (B) ● (D)

Case Study 2

265. (A) (B) (C) ●
266. See Sol. 266.
267. See Sol. 267.
268. 1050 ft^2
269. See Sol. 269.
270. ● (B) ● (D) ● (F)

176. The Secretary of the Interior's *Standards for the Treatment of Historic Properties* are guidelines established for owners and architects contemplating projects at sites deemed to have historic value. They can be used for any project, but are only required to be followed when federal funding is sought for the project or if the owner plans to apply for Federal Historic Preservation Tax Incentives. Rehabilitation is the most lenient of the four approaches, and the one that best allows for new construction (additions or renovations) and adaptive reuse.

An electronic version of the *Standards* may be downloaded from the National Park Service website at cr.nps.gov. A current link to the document can be found at **ppi2pass.com/AREresources.**

The answer is (B).

177. In a cold climate, it is important to maximize exposure and warming effects of the sun while shielding the building from cold winter winds. Locating the building near the bottom of the slope will provide protection from the wind and exposure to the sun, and lifting the building to a higher elevation will avoid the effects of cold air collecting in the valley.

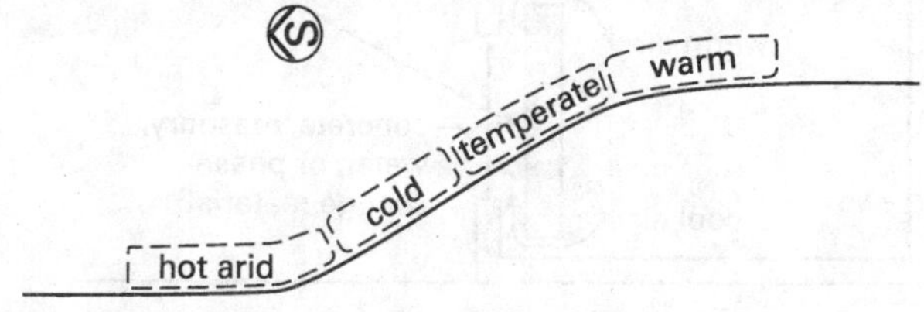

The answer is (B).

178. Upfeed water supply systems will work in buildings up to approximately 40–60 ft tall, so the most appropriate choice of the selections given is option (C), 50–60 ft. The exact height depends on a variety of factors, including losses due to static head as well as the pressure at the water main, which is generally anywhere from 40–80 psi.

Static head is the amount of pressure required to lift water through a piping system in a building. 0.433 psi can lift water 1 ft. For each foot of building height, then, 0.433 psi is lost. To determine water pressure at each floor of the building, multiply the static head by the building height and subtract this from the pressure at the building main. There must be enough pressure available to operate fixtures on the top floor. These calculations can help a designer to determine the most appropriate type of system for a project.

The answer is (C).

179. 120/208 voltage, three-phase power is appropriate for a small commercial building.

Residences typically have 120/240 voltage, single-phase systems. Larger buildings with greater demand require higher-voltage, three-phase services.

The answer is (B).

180. Calculate the initial (simple) rate of return.

$$\begin{aligned}\text{initial rate of return} &= \frac{\text{annual savings}}{\text{investment}} \\ &= \frac{\left(\frac{\$460}{\text{mo}}\right)\left(12\ \frac{\text{mo}}{\text{yr}}\right)}{\$55{,}000} \\ &= 0.1003/\text{yr}\end{aligned}$$

The simple payback period is the reciprocal of the initial rate of return.

$$\begin{aligned}\text{simple payback period} &= \frac{1}{\text{initial rate of return}} \\ &= \frac{1}{\frac{0.1003}{\text{yr}}} \\ &= 9.97\ \text{yr} \quad (10\ \text{yr})\end{aligned}$$

Although the simple rate of return and payback period are quickly calculated and can be used as a rough guideline, actual rate of return and discounted payback period calculations are much more valuable when assessing the return on investment and comparing alternative systems.

The answer is 10 years.

181. Each option listed has its own disadvantages. However, a brownfield probably would be the most buildable because, although it would take additional money and time, contaminates could be removed or otherwise mitigated. In addition, federal tax credits and incentive programs may be available to encourage the use of a brownfield site.

A floodplain would be very difficult to build on, assuming that the local, state, and federal regulations allowed it at all, because increased construction costs and continuing insurance costs could make it economically infeasible. Wetlands and endangered species habitats could not be used for development.

The answer is (B).

182. Generally, spaces intended to highlight spoken-word presentations should be "dead" spaces; that is, they should have short reverberation times. Musical presentations generally sound best in spaces with long reverberation times, or spaces that are "live."

Reverberation time is calculated as

$$T_R = \frac{0.049\,V}{A}$$

V equals the volume of the space, and A equals total absorptivity of the wall, floor, and ceiling surfaces along with other absorptive elements, such as upholstered seats, curtains, and so on. When a program or occupancy dictates the size of the room, dead spaces can often be created by specifying absorptive materials, and live spaces can be created by using materials that reflect sound.

The answer is (B) and (C).

183. Areas of positive pressure will occur on the windward side of the building as the wind pushes against the building wall. Areas of negative pressure occur on the sides of the building and on the leeward side. Because the building in the diagram has no fenestration, the pressure inside the building will be neutral.

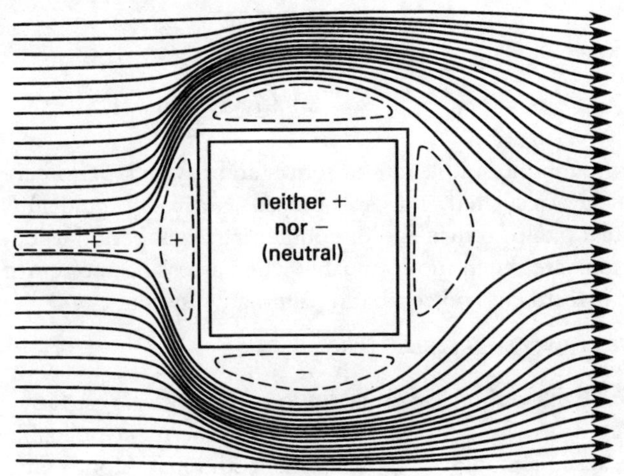

Used with permission from Fuller Moore, *Environmental Control Systems: Heating Cooling Lighting*, copyright © 2004 by Fuller Moore.

The answer is C, E, and F.

184. Designing a taller building with a smaller footprint to minimize site disturbance is the best approach to development on a previously undisturbed, or greenfield, site. A smaller footprint results in less area of impervious surfaces (which minimizes runoff) and limits the disturbance to existing landscaping and wildlife habitats. A smaller footprint generally results in a more energy- and resource-efficient building as well, with lower long-term maintenance costs.

The answer is (A).

185. Evaporative coolers are only effective in this type of climate, but this is not a passive cooling technique. Limited windows on the north side do little to cool a building passively. Windows on the east and west sides of the building may not help with cooling in this climate. All the other choices are good ways to cool a building passively in New Mexico's hot-arid climate. Roof ponds add thermal mass to the building; when used in tandem with high thermal mass building materials and night flushing, it is possible to take advantage of the cool nighttime temperatures. Courtyards help keep cooled air within the living space, and the fountains cool through evaporation and have a psychological effect of making the space seem cooler.

The answer is (A), (C), and (E).

186. A Trombe wall is a type of thermal storage wall used in passive solar design. It uses mass to collect and store heat from the sun during the day. When heating is required, the stored heat in the mass is circulated by natural convection to the rest of the building. A Trombe wall is very efficient, but because it is positioned directly behind glass on the south side of a building, it blocks the view from inside the building.

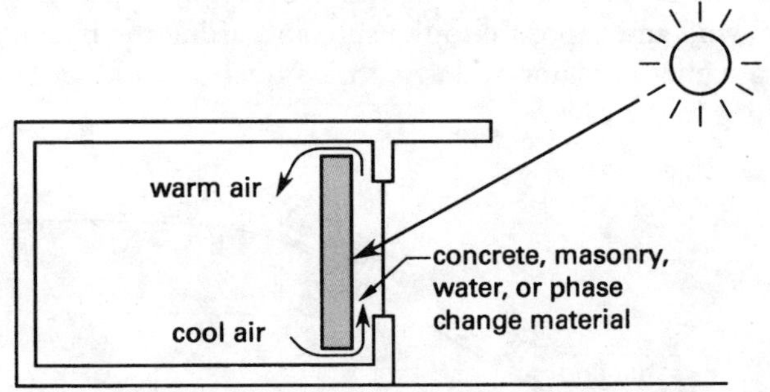

If view is a consideration, a direct gain space, greenhouse, or convective loop using mass in the flooring and wall materials will be a better choice.

The answer is (B).

187. There are three questions an architect must answer at the beginning of a project to determine the permitted size and layout of a building. The questions must be answered simultaneously, and the answers to each question are often dependent on the answers to the others (e.g., fully sprinklered buildings can often be larger and of a less fire-resistive type of construction than buildings for similar uses that do not include a sprinkler system). The questions are as follows.

- What is the occupancy of this building? The occupancy is determined according to the owner's program, which defines the size and use of the spaces within the building. A building can be comprised of many different types of occupancies, which must be separated with appropriately fire-rated walls or partitions. The *International Building Code* (IBC) lists the following occupancy classifications.

A	assembly
B	business
E	educational
F	factory and industrial
H	high hazard
I	institutional
M	mercantile
R	residential
S	storage
U	utility and miscellaneous

- What type of fire-suppression system will be required? This question ascertains whether or not the building will be sprinklered. This, in turn, can allow a larger building than a non-sprinklered one.
- What type of construction will be used? The IBC lists the following construction types.

types I and II	noncombustible materials
type III	exterior walls noncombustible, interior elements are of any materials complying with the code
type IV	heavy-timber construction
type V	exterior and interior elements are of any materials complying with the code

When the architect has determined the answers to these three questions, the information may be applied to the tables in the code to determine required means of egress, fire-separation requirements, and other code requirements that will govern design and materials selection.

The answer is (A), (D), and (E).

188. The first step in answering this problem is to calculate the slope between points A and B.

Grade is vertical distance over horizontal length, expressed as a percentage.

$$\begin{aligned} G &= \frac{d}{L} \times 100\% \\ &= \frac{30 \text{ ft}}{150 \text{ ft}} \times 100\% \\ &= 20\% \end{aligned}$$

The slope between the two points is 20%, which is difficult to climb and could be expensive to build on. The slope should be planted with grass to help to stabilize the soil.

Some typical slopes for various site elements are as follows.

sheet drainage	½% to 1%
adjacent to building, falling away from the structure	2% min.
parking areas	1½% to 5%
ditches	2% to 10%
ramps	5% to 8.33% max.
streets	10% max.
plant grass to stabilize soil	< 25%
plant ground cover that does not need to be mowed to stabilize soil (actual acceptable slope varies depending on soil composition)	25% to 50%
avoid slopes of 50% or greater because of the likelihood of erosion due to runoff	> 50%

The answer is (B).

189. The homeowners may choose to apply for a variance. A variance addresses situations where zoning requirements cause undue hardship for a property owner or where zoning requirements do not address a unique situation. Generally the application for a variance includes an explanation of the request and drawings depicting what will be built. The request is publicly advertised (often with a sign on the property) and then goes before a municipal board (such as a planning commission or zoning board), and comment is invited from neighbors and other interested parties. The board then makes a decision.

An easement allows a part of a site owned by one party to be used by another party for a specific purpose. Easements are noted on the deed and legal description of the property and may be granted for utility right-of-ways, access to an adjacent property, party walls, jointly used driveways, or conservation purposes.

A covenant is a restriction placed on a property by a clause in the deed. Covenants are often used to restrict the use of a property or to establish rules similar to zoning restrictions for private communities.

A conditional use permit allows a property to be used for a purpose that is normally not permitted, but only if the owner fulfills certain criteria. Often, conditional use permits are granted when the proposed use is in the public interest.

The answer is (D).

190.

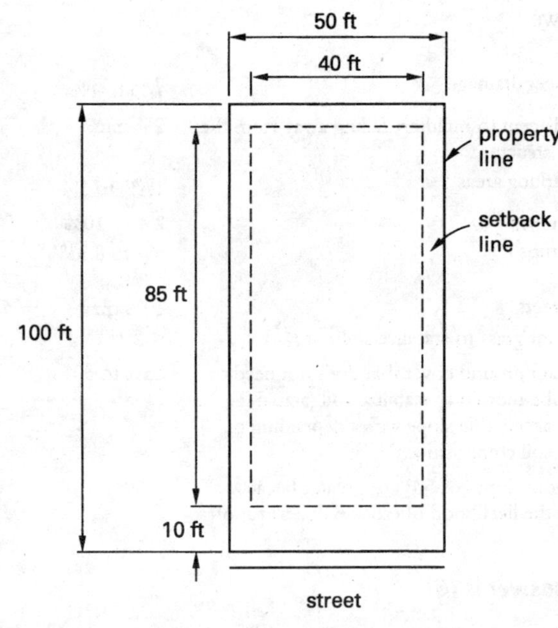

The floor area ratio (FAR) allowed for a specific site expresses the amount of building square footage that may be constructed relative to the total area of the site. In this case, the total area of the site is

$$A = wd$$

The floor area ratio is 2.0, so the buildable area is

$$A_{\text{buildable}} = A(\text{FAR})$$

$$A = wd = (50 \text{ ft})(100 \text{ ft}) = 5000 \text{ ft}^2$$

$$A_{\text{buildable}} = A(\text{FAR}) = (5000 \text{ ft}^2)(2.0) = 10{,}000 \text{ ft}^2$$

The three-story building, 40 ft wide by 80 ft deep, is the only answer option that complies with both the setback requirements and the floor area ratio requirements. Option (A) violates the site setbacks. Option (C) and option (D) exceed the total buildable area permitted.

The answer is (B).

191. A plat is prepared to legally define the layout of a subdivided piece of property. Plats depict new streets and rights-of-way, location and purpose of easements, lots or building sites, minimum setbacks, and any sites that are reserved for special purposes. A plat includes a statement from the owner dedicating any parts of the site that are reserved for public use. When approved, the plat becomes a part of the public land records.

A survey may contain much of the same information as a plat, such as location and purpose of easements, rights-of-way, and minimum setbacks, but surveys also define property boundaries and depict existing buildings and structures; utility lines on or serving the property; and remarkable natural features, such as streams, major trees, wooded areas, flood plains, and so on. The most notable difference between a survey and a plat is that a survey also includes topographical information, such as contour lines or spot elevations, that help to express the site in three dimensions.

A master plan may be prepared at the start of a project, during schematic design, as a tool for planning the amenities that will be included in the final plat for the property or to develop a plan for phasing the project.

A deed is a written document that describes the boundaries of the property and includes information about the owner and the party from whom the property was purchased.

The answer is (C).

192. The Secretary of the Interior's *Standards for Rehabilitation and Guidelines for Rehabilitating Historic Buildings* define the requirements for this type of work. To be eligible for federal historic preservation tax credits, these standards must be followed. The standards and additional information about historic preservation approaches are available on the National Park Service's website, nps.gov. A link can be found at **ppi2pass.com/AREresources.**

The standards advocate respecting the historic materials and character of the original building and treating them gently; repairing rather than replacing, but when replacement is necessary, replacing in kind; and recognizing that historic buildings are products of their own time and that they have evolved into their current state. When designing an addition to a historic building, the design should strive to match the historic structure in scale, materials, and character, but it should not attempt to replicate the historic structure exactly; there should be a clear distinction between old and new.

There are few black and white answers when it comes to the best way to approach a historic preservation project. Each scenario must be considered individually, within the context of that specific building, and in light of the approach selected (preservation, restoration, rehabilitation, or reconstruction). In this case, the project probably will be considered rehabilitation, and the least appropriate recommendation will be to remove the trim, install furring and insulation, replace the plaster, and reinstall the trim. The small amount of energy efficiency that might be gained through such a process will be far outweighed by the expense and the risk of destroying historic materials. The proportions of the spaces will be changed with the addition of a few inches of new wall, which will not be acceptable. In addition, it would not be appropriate to replace the roof with one of another material because new shingles could be found to approximate the original. Ceilings should be kept in their original condition as much as possible; another solution to lighting could be found.

The answer is (B).

193. Condominium is a form of ownership in which a buyer obtains absolute title to a portion of a structure. It can be used for either residential or commercial applications. Usually, a condominium owner has common tenancy of the land, parking areas and access roads, and site improvements (pools, tennis courts, etc.) associated with the property. Often fees are assessed to condominium owners to cover the expenses of maintaining these common areas. Owners can sell their properties and are responsible for paying their own property taxes.

Fee simple means that the owner has absolute title to the property and may sell it to another person, if desired.

A leasehold entitles the lessee to the use of the property for a specified period of time, during which the lessee pays rent. The lessee may not sell the property, but may sell the right to occupy the property, which is called a sublease.

Cooperative ownership means that the owner does not hold the title to the property, but owns a share of a corporation that owns the property. In return, the stockholder may occupy a portion of the property. The person may sell their stock to another individual or company, but the corporation always retains full ownership of the building and land.

The answer is (B).

194. An adjacency or affinity matrix is a way of graphically representing which spaces should be adjacent to one another. This simple diagram is read by following the lines representing the spaces to the box at which they meet. If there is a closed dot in the box, the rooms should be adjacent to one another. If the dot is open, the spaces have some relationship but need not be adjacent.

The answer is (A), (D), and (E).

195. When preparing cost opinions, it is a good idea to tack on a contingency allowance to provide for unforeseen conditions. The allowance usually varies from 5% to 20% (or more) of the estimated construction cost. The earlier the stage of the project, the higher the contingency should be. For example, a cost opinion prepared during the schematic design phase based on unit costs will have a much higher contingency factor than one prepared just before the project goes to bid, when the quantities and materials are better defined. In this problem, the highest contingency allowance should be tacked onto the cost opinion prepared during programming for the elementary school, as this project has the highest level of uncertainty.

The answer is (D).

196.

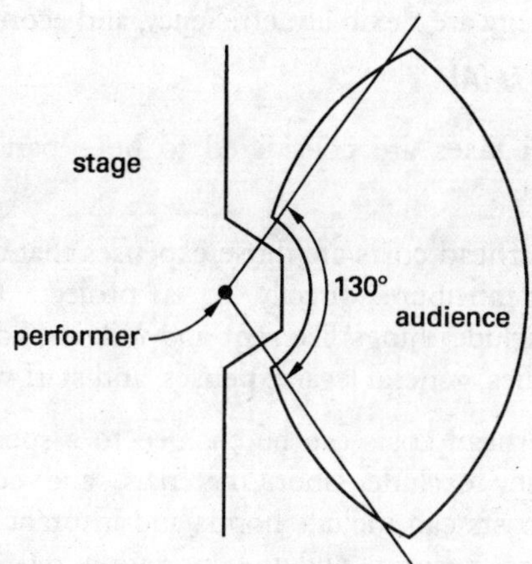

The human eye has a typical angle of vision of 130°. Therefore, a performer standing at the center of a stage will be able to make eye contact with spectators seated within this 130° range. Likewise, the spectators will be able to see the performer well as long as he or she is within their 130° range.

The open stage layout illustrated in option (A) locates the audience according to the performer's angle of encounter as measured from a point of command (a central point on the stage). The angle of encounter includes all of the spectators that the performer can make eye contact with while standing at this point. This arrangement will produce the greatest number of good seats, where spectators can both see and hear the performer clearly.

The answer is (A).

197. A radial organizational pattern best facilitates social interaction, because all inhabitants of a building pass through a central core to move to other spaces. This pattern is popular in secondary school design, where wings—a science wing, a humanities wing, the industrial arts shops, and so on—branch off from a central space housing common amenities like the library.

An axial pattern, option (B), connects two major spaces on the main axis with secondary paths branching off from either side. This organizational pattern is often used for shopping malls.

Most American cities are based on the grid pattern (option (C)). This strategy is easy to expand and easy to interpret, even for a first-time visitor. It can become monotonous, though, unless portions of the city or building break from the grid to form areas of surprise and complexity.

A precinctual pattern (option (D)) works well for buildings that house a number of dispersed activities. This organizational technique could be used for an office building housing several distinct companies. Advantages of this strategy are flexibility, efficiency, and economy.

The answer is (A).

198. Payroll taxes are considered to be a part of labor costs.

General overhead costs are those expenses that a contractor cannot attribute directly to a project. Overhead expenses include things like rent and utilities, advertising, office supplies, general legal expenses, and staff wages.

Project overhead costs can be charged to a specific project, but they exclude labor, materials, and equipment. Overhead costs can include bonds and insurance, temporary facilities, permits, and transportation related to the project, as well as other expenses the contractor may incur in the course of the work.

Total overhead costs vary from 5–20% of project costs. Overhead expenses are generally related to the size of the contractor's operation. For example, a general contractor working from his home, advertising through word of mouth, and coordinating the work through subcontractors rather than employing his own forces will have much lower overhead than a large construction company with hundreds of employees, large offices in a downtown highrise, and an advertising campaign that makes their firm a household word.

The answer is (A), (D), (E), and (F).

199. To determine if a site and its potential use are compatible, an architect and a client must first develop a program, a list of spaces needed in the building and their approximate sizes. This document will serve as the "instruction manual" for the project. The architect in this scenario should work with the client to develop this document and compare it against the existing space to see if the new use is compatible with the old structure. If it is determined to be a good fit, the process of site analysis can move forward. After that it will be important to study code issues, parking requirements, environmental concerns, and the historic value of the property to determine if the project is architecturally feasible. Simultaneously, the client should be developing the project pro forma, which examines the financial feasibility of the project. If the results of both studies indicate that the project should go ahead, the architect may begin to prepare schematic design concepts for the renovation.

The answer is (B).

200. As the floor area of the building increases, the cost per unit of area decreases. This decrease is attributable to better perimeter-to-floor area ratios (as mentioned in option (C); the exterior envelope is a costly building component) and more efficient utilization of the most expensive elements of the building, such as the heating, ventilating, and air conditioning (HVAC) system and elevators. In a similar vein, for the same area, a cubic building has the least amount of exterior envelope compared with a rectangular building. The contractor can also capitalize on economies of scale, which means that the more materials purchased, the better the deal.

Larger buildings tend to have lower unit costs. An exception is tall buildings: above six stories or so, costs per square foot tend to increase due to the need for elevators, additional fire protection measures, and specialized structural systems. As floor-to-floor heights increase, so do unit costs; this may be attributed to a need to use nonstandard building materials. In wood frame construction, for example, exceeding an 8 ft ceiling height requires that sheets of gypsum board must be cut to fit.

In addition to design factors mentioned, the cost per unit may also be affected by the length of the construction period, unusual contractual requirements, and the quality of the materials specified.

The answer is (B), (C), (E), and (F).

201. Efficiency is the ratio of net area to gross area and is always a number between zero and one. A building's program and design decisions made in the initial planning stages can have a great impact on a building's efficiency. Deciding to build a new building designed specifically to meet the program requirements generally leads to a more efficient building than retrofitting an existing building to meet new needs. The site has an effect as well; sites with lots of open space and gentle grades can help to increase building efficiency. Consultants' choices can also have a significant impact on efficiency; for example, placing mechanical units on the roof rather than in an interior mechanical room can help to increase efficiency. Furthermore, programs that require large rooms, specify flexible requirements regarding adjacencies and/or windows, and have a low population as defined by the code (requiring smaller means of egress) tend to be more efficient. A designer can further increase the efficiency of a building by limiting the design to one story with a central core and by using double-loaded corridors.

The answer is (C).

202. The forest/woodlands area is the most suitable site for development. Of the areas identified, the forest/woodland is the most tolerant to human use at appropriate densities and when developed in a way that retains many of the inherent characteristics of the land.

Design with Nature identifies eight categories of open space and lists them in order of the value of their natural processes and their degree of intolerance to development. The inverse of the list ranks the sites in order of their suitability for development. From least tolerant of development to most tolerant, these areas are

- surface water
- marshes
- floodplains
- aquifer recharge areas
- aquifers
- steep slopes
- forests and woodlands
- flat land excluding prime agricultural land

The answer is (A).

203. Room data sheets are questionnaires completed by end users or by programming team members based on interviews with end users of the spaces within a building. They are designed to help the programmer better understand the uses of the space, the people and things that the space is required to house (occupants, furniture, and equipment), unique finish or construction requirements, and any special mechanical, electrical, or acoustical requirements. The results of the surveys are then compiled into a document that helps the programmer to determine the appropriate area and location of each space within a building based on the established criteria.

Room data sheets are most effective for programming studies of buildings with many varying types of spaces. However, for buildings with lots of repetitive spaces or hard-to-define end users, they are not very helpful. Therefore, the best application of room data sheets listed is the high school, because the function and use of the rooms may vary greatly, and teachers and administrators could be interviewed about the needs of each space to determine appropriate sizes and relationships.

The answer is (C).

204. A 100-year flood is the maximum flood level with a 1% probability of occurring within a given year. This is the standard used by the National Flood Insurance Program for determining risk to a specific property and specifying which properties are required to have flood insurance to receive federally backed financing. Special hazard flood areas are shown on flood insurance risk maps, and properties within the boundaries must comply with special requirements for design and construction, particularly requirements for siting, lowest building elevations, and acceptable materials and construction methods.

The Federal Emergency Management Agency publishes a series of fact sheets discussing construction within flood-prone areas and along the coast, addressing both flooding and high winds. A link to them may be found at **ppi2pass.com/AREresources.**

The answer is (B).

205. Placing the parking areas under the building makes sense in terms of sustainability because it disrupts less of the site and minimizes areas of imperviousness, but in terms of safety and security, it could be difficult to protect the building from vehicle bombs. Full-height glass walls for daylighting would be ideal for surveillance from the outside, but they would vulnerable to bomb or vehicle attacks.

Constructed wetlands are used to process wastewater, but they could also serve as an additional barrier to vehicular and pedestrian access to the building depending on where they are placed on the site. Integrated building automation and control systems help ensure that the mechanical systems in the building are operating efficiently; they can also be used to detect contaminants in the building. Trombe walls are used for passive solar heating, but their mass could also help the building resist a bomb impact. Natural landscaping and retention ponds, like constructed wetlands, could be used for limiting vehicular access as well as increasing standoff distance.

The answer is (B), (C), (E), and (F).

206. Cost evaluations performed during the programming stage often compare a proposed project to a model project of similar size and scope. A premium is something that will add cost to a project in comparison to the model. Examples of premiums are short construction periods, unusual contract provisions (extra insurance, liquidated damages, etc.), challenging site conditions, and nonstandard programmatic elements or client requirements, such as the need to use prevailing wage rates or union labor.

Cost evaluation during programming is difficult because there are so many unknowns. Listing potential premiums helps the architect and owner to get a feel for how much the unknowns or unique conditions may add to the cost of the project. As the project progresses, it is necessary to reevaluate the costs attributed to the premiums as the design, materials, and conditions under which the project will be constructed become more defined.

The answer is (B).

207. Trees can have a variety of effects on the microclimate of a site. The cluster of trees that are all roughly the same height will be a more effective windbreak than any of the other configurations shown. When placed correctly to reduce the amount of winter wind reaching the structure, a windbreak such as this can create a more comfortable microclimate and reduce heating costs.

The answer is (D).

208. An infiltration basin is a pond that temporarily collects water and allows it to be released only through absorption into the earth. This helps to recharge the groundwater on the site rather than dumping it into a storm sewer, as a catch basin does.

A bioswale is a grassy sloped ditch that filters the storm runoff as it is directed away from a building or paved area. It allows the water to seep into the ground and also helps to recharge aquifers.

A cistern is a tank for collecting and storing water. It is often used with rainwater harvest systems that capture and store rainwater for use in irrigation or nonpotable building functions, such as flushing toilets.

The answer is (B).

209. A public enterprise revenue bond is issued to fund a public project that will produce revenue; the bond is repaid with the money generated by the facility. This type of bond may be issued to finance a project like an airport, a hospital, or a stadium.

A general obligation bond is used to fund public projects that will not produce revenue. These are often used to finance schools, public libraries, or municipal buildings. The bond is repaid through property, or ad valorem, taxes. General obligation bond measures must be approved by voters in the jurisdiction.

Development impact fees are charged to developers to pay for public improvements that are necessary because of the development. Fees may be assessed to cover the costs of road improvements, utility extensions, or other upgrades required for the private development project that must be provided by the municipality.

The answer is (D).

210. A school district could be considered a catchment area for a region's educational facilities. Master planning for a school district will begin with a study of the population of the area and how many children are living within the boundaries of the district. The schools could then be planned to accommodate the children and allow for future growth or decline, depending on population trends in the area.

The answer is (B).

211. The strategies listed will be most appropriate for a cool climate. A good example of a building type designed around these strategies is the New England saltbox, which has a blank north elevation and steep overhang to minimize the size of the wall, a taller south elevation, a tight, spare form, an economical design, and a dark shingled exterior. Cool climates in the United States are found in northern New England, the northern Midwest, the Rocky Mountains, and Alaska.

The answer is (A).

212. Efficiency expresses the ratio of net assignable area, or programmed space, to the gross area of the building.

$$\text{efficiency} = \frac{\text{net area}}{\text{gross area}}$$

$$\begin{aligned}\text{gross area} &= \frac{\text{net area}}{\text{efficiency}} \\ &= \frac{32{,}000\ \text{ft}^2}{0.75} \\ &= 42{,}667.67\ \text{ft}^2 \quad (42{,}667\ \text{ft}^2)\end{aligned}$$

The answer is (C).

213. A behavior setting is the "stage" for an event that occurs at a particular place on a regular schedule. The activities that happen within the behavior setting are definable, and the physical environmental facilitates that activity. Every building is designed around a sequence of behavior settings, whether that setting is a family's morning routine in their home, a classroom setting in a school, or an operating room in a hospital. The actions of the inhabitants can be analyzed to discover the best way for the physical environment to facilitate their activities.

The answer is (D).

214. The allowable height of a building is determined by the use group and type of construction and may be increased if a fire-suppression system or adequate street frontage is provided. Local zoning ordinances may also restrict the height of a structure.

The answer is (A), (B), (C), and (F).

215. The Urban Land Institute defines three types of shopping centers. The amount of retail sales area provided and the types of stores featured is determined primarily by the population of the catchment area. As a general rule, each person in the catchment area will support 3–5 ft^2 of retail space.

- Neighborhood centers provide daily convenience goods and services. Most have a grocery store or pharmacy as the anchor. Neighborhood centers serve about 7500–20,000 people within a six-minute driving radius. The center generally occupies about 4–10 acres, with a building area of about 30,000–75,000 ft^2 and an average building size of about 40,000 ft^2.
- Community centers are often anchored by a large supermarket and contain some type of variety store in addition to small services and specialty stores. This type of shopping center serves approximately

20,000–100,000 people. Community centers range in size from about 100,000–300,000 ft^2, with an average size of about 150,000 ft^2. The center generally occupies 10–30 acres.

- The typical American shopping mall is considered a regional center, as is a cluster of large "big box" retailers. Regional centers draw from a large geographical area and serve 100,000–250,000 people, generally with an average building area of about 40,000 ft^2. Total built area may range from 300,000 ft^2 to over 1,000,000 ft^2. The center generally occupies about 20–50 acres.

The answer is (B).

216. The calculations listed in option (A), option (B), and option (D) are a part of conducting a life-cycle cost analysis. Uniform capital recovery is used to calculate the annual value of a present value. Using a discount rate puts the future amount into terms of today's dollars.

Uniform present worth expresses a series of uniform annual amounts (such as an annual maintenance fee) in today's dollars. Uniform sinking fund is used to calculate the amount that will have to be invested today at a certain interest rate to have a specified amount of money at some point in the future (such as savings for a roof replacement in five years).

The answer is (D).

217. A raised pad will force drainage around a building, disrupting natural flow patterns. Elevating a structure on piles, piers, or columns preserves natural drainage patterns and allows a building to be constructed in areas prone to flooding, with unstable soil, or on a steep slope.

The answer is (A).

218. An elongated form stretched along the east-west axis is the most appropriate choice for a hot-humid climate. This shape minimizes east and west exposure. Overhangs or courtyards could be used to provide shade and enhance the cooling effects of the wind.

A square form is best suited to cold regions. A square or compact shape with courtyards is a good match for hot-arid regions. Rectangular buildings work well in temperate zones.

The answer is (B).

219. The science of designing things and spaces so that they can be used most efficiently and comfortably by people is called ergonomics. Ergonomics considers the size and proportions of the human body and analyzes how people interact with an object or their environment, with the goal of making objects and spaces easier to use, safer, and more efficient.

The answer is (B).

220. Because they are very porous, silts and clays allow water to migrate above the water table on a site.

Fine-grained soils are more likely to be affected by freezing and thawing than coarse-grained soils. Organic soil is never a suitable material for foundation support. Footings should always be placed below the frost line to protect them from the effects of freeze/thaw heaving.

The answer is (C).

221. A "multilevel system of pedestrian circulation" implies a definite type of physical solution and describes a design concept. This should not be confused with a programming statement, which states the problem but does not offer a solution or strategy. A programming statement that might precede the design concept is something like "separate incompatible circulation functions."

The answer is (D).

222. Option (B) illustrates a bubble diagram. These diagrams are often used to indicate required adjacencies and priorities of relationships. Although it is often derived from the matrix chart shown in option (A), the bubble diagram is best for showing relationships just prior to space planning, because the relative sizes and positions of the bubbles begin to give an indication of spatial relationships and sizes of the various spaces needed.

Option (C) is a flow diagram, as indicated by the arrows. This will be used as a scheduling chart or to show a flow of materials or some other kind of process from one point to another. Option (D) shows a block diagram, which represents the first results of spatial organization based on an adjacency diagram. It is not the correct answer because the question asks which diagram will be best just prior to the start of space planning.

The answer is (B).

223. None of the area of the enclosed mall will be rentable, so subtract the 6% right off the top. Then take 75% of the remainder.

$$(85{,}000\ \text{ft}^2)(0.06) = 5100\ \text{ft}^2$$

$$85{,}000\ \text{ft}^2 - 5100\ \text{ft}^2 = 79{,}900\ \text{ft}^2$$

$$(79{,}900\ \text{ft}^2)(0.75) = 59{,}925\ \text{ft}^2$$

The answer is (A).

224. The correct order of activities is

- have owner describe project goals

- collect data
- develop programmatic concepts
- reconcile list of spaces with project budget
- define the problem

Programming is a sequence of steps that leads the programmer and owner from a rough idea for a project to a clear statement of the problems and opportunities it presents. These challenges will be considered fully and resolved during the design phase.

First, to begin programming, it is first necessary to describe the project goals. This step includes a discussion of the owner's objectives for the building, problems that must be addressed, and space requirements.

Second, the programmer collects data. During this phase, the programmer organizes facts regarding the site, the occupants, the intended uses and characteristics of the spaces needed, the budget, and the local codes or ordinances that will affect and influence the project.

Third, the programmer develops schematic diagrams in order to organize the facts collected in the previous step and present them in a way that is visually clear and comprehensible. These diagrams, which can take many forms, display the sizes and spatial relationships (adjacencies) of the spaces that are needed or desired.

Fourth, the programmer must reconcile the list of programmed spaces with the project budget. Now is the time to adjust the program, the budget, or both, so that the project is feasible.

Finally, the programmer defines the problem. This is the goal of programming: to define the problem so that it can be solved during the design phase. What kind of building must be built? How are the spaces within it to be related? Where will it be built? How much will it cost? Programming is the process of seeking problems and defining objectives; design is the process of solving the problems and bringing physical form to those objectives.

The answer is (C).

225. The concept of personal space, as developed by Edward T. Hall, states that four basic distances can be understood to exist in the study of human behavior, each one appropriate for different private and social situations. These are the intimate distance, the personal distance, the social distance, and the public distance.

Review the theories of personal space as described by Edward T. Hall in *The Hidden Dimension* and by Robert Sommer in *Personal Space: The Behavioral Basis of Design*.

Some terms to know are as follows.

- *behavior setting*: A particular place, with definable boundaries and objects within the place, in which a standing pattern of behavior occurs at a particular time.
- *density*: The number of people per unit area.
- *proxemics*: A term coined by anthropologist Edward T. Hall and now used to describe the study of the spatial requirements of humans and the effects of population density on behavior, communication, and social interaction.
- *territoriality*: A behavioral system in which a person, animal, or group lays claim to an area and defends it against others.

The answer is (D).

226. When determining the required area for a leaching field, the architect should require a percolation test. A percolation test measures the amount of time it takes water in a test hole to drop 1 in. Based on this time, reference tables give the minimum length of piping and, therefore, the ground area, that is required to handle a project's projected sewage flow volume.

A potability test evaluates drinking water for bacteria, pH, color, odor, turbidity, hardness, and other commonly found elements.

A topographic survey is not necessary if the proposed leaching field is relatively flat. It is important to determine where the water table is, but a high water table is generally revealed in the percolation test.

The answer is (A).

227. Using the scale on the drawing, the horizontal distance between the two points is about 15 ft. The slope is the vertical distance divided by the horizontal distance.

$$G = \frac{(4)(2\text{ ft})}{15\text{ ft}} \cdot 100\% = 53\%$$

The answer is (B).

228. From the table, assembly areas, including restaurants and bars, have an occupant load of 15. Commercial kitchens have an occupant load of 200. Round up to an even number as appropriate. Therefore,

$$\text{dining area} = \frac{3500 \text{ ft}^2}{15 \frac{\text{ft}^2}{\text{occupant}}} = 234 \text{ occupants}$$

$$\text{kitchen} = \frac{1000 \text{ ft}^2}{200 \frac{\text{ft}^2}{\text{occupant}}} = 5 \text{ occupants}$$

$$\text{bar} = \frac{1200 \text{ ft}^2}{15 \frac{\text{ft}^2}{\text{occupant}}} = 80 \text{ occupants}$$

$$\text{total} = 319 \text{ occupants}$$

The answer is (B).

229. A bioswale is a shallow ditch lined with grass or other ground cover. It is designed to slow storm runoff and remove sediments and other contaminants while allowing the water to seep into the ground. An infiltration basin catches stormwater runoff and retains it until it can seep into the ground. Pervious paving allows stormwater to seep through the paving into the soil instead of running into storm sewers. All of these elements are sustainable approaches to reducing the amount of stormwater placed into storm sewers or natural waterways.

Catch basins, cisterns, and box culverts allow stormwater to run into the storm sewer system or off site.

The answer is (A), (D), and (E).

230. The best soil for slab-on-grade construction is poorly graded gravel (that is, gravel with uniform particle size). It has the highest bearing capacity of the four soil types listed and provides drainage to minimize water infiltration.

The other options have lower bearing capacities. Any soil containing clay is problematic because of the possibility of expansion and the poor drainage quality of clays. Soils containing organic material should also be avoided for slab bearing. Soils are defined according to the standards of the Unified Soil Classification System.

The answer is (C).

231. Option (D) includes three effective methods for minimizing noise to a building from an adjacent site. First, the building is placed as far away from the noise source as possible. Each doubling of the distance between a point source of noise and the receiver causes sound levels to drop by about six decibels. Next, a high, solid barrier is constructed as close to the noise source as possible. The effectiveness of a solid barrier increases as its height increases and as it is moved closer to the source. Finally, trees are used to attenuate the higher frequency sounds.

While the approaches shown in the other diagrams will help, none are as effective as option (D). The ground cover shown in option (A) is a nonreflective surface but is only marginally effective in attenuating noise. The deeper row of trees shown in option (B) is good for attenuating high-frequency noise and the building is located at a distance from the noise source, but there is no solid barrier. In option (C) the building is located closer to the source and the barrier is not as high as in option (D).

The answer is (D).

232. Because the contour lines in the middle of the section are at lower elevations and progress upward, section C-C represents a valley. Section A-A represents a uniform slope from elevation 10 up to elevation 14. Section B-B represents an upward slope from about elevation 6 to elevation 9. Section D-D represents a ridge.

The answer is (C).

233. In order to determine the appropriate use for the slope, first calculate the grade according to the following formula.

$$G = \frac{d}{L} \times 100\%$$

G is the grade measured as a percentage, d is the vertical distance between points in feet, and L is the horizontal distance between points in feet.

$$G = \frac{20 \text{ ft}}{250 \text{ ft}} \times 100\%$$
$$= 8\%$$

With an 8% grade, the site will best be used for buildings and walks. Parking should be planned for slopes from 1.5% to 5%. Slopes over 10% are difficult to walk on and building becomes more expensive. Slopes up to 25% should be landscaped to prevent erosion and slopes over 50% must be terraced to prevent erosion.

The answer is (B).

234. In planning the location of a building on a site, the location of the sanitary sewer should be considered before the locations of the water main, underground telephone line, and power line. Because the sanitary sewer needs gravity flow to work properly and because the elevation of the sanitary sewer in the street is established, the location of the building may be determined by the maximum distance from the building to the existing street sewer that still results in the minimum required slope of the sewer line.

The answer is (B).

Programming & Analysis

235. The PMF is the most severe flood that may reasonably be possible for a particular location. It results from a combination of the most critical meteorological and hydrological conditions in a drainage basin. The water level in this type of flood is higher than in a standard projected flood. PMFs are used for designing facilities and structures that must be subject to almost no risk of flooding.

A SPF is a flood that may be expected from the most severe combination of meteorological and hydrological conditions in a particular location, excluding extremely rare combinations as with a PMF. SPFs are typically expressed as a probability frequency, such as a 50-year flood, which means that there is a 2% probability in any one year that a flood will occur.

The NFIP standards require that local participating governments adopt minimum floodplain management plans. These plans include requirements for zoning, subdivision of buildings, and special-purpose floodplain ordinances. These requirements must be met in order for federal flood insurance to be available for property owners. The floodplain defined by the NFIP may not be as high as the PMF. Local flood regulations may be more or less strict than the NFIP requirements, but typically do not define a floodplain as high as the PMF.

The answer is (C).

236. The basic allowable height and floor area of a building is based on the construction type and the occupancy group. The floor area can be increased if an automatic sprinkler system is installed and if a prescribed minimum open space is maintained between the building and adjacent buildings or property lines. (The open space prevents fire from spreading from one building to another and allows emergency vehicle access.) The exact formula for determining the allowable increase in floor area varies depending on which code is being used, but the concept is similar for all codes.

Once the construction type is established and the distance from the building to property lines is known, the codes establish the required hourly fire protection of exterior walls and the required fire protection rating of openings. Reducing the allowable height of a building has no effect on the allowable area of the building.

The answer is (B).

237. Though municipal utility maps and the civil engineer may have information about the location of utility lines, an architect's primary source of such information is the utility companies, which maintain accurate and complete maps and other information regarding the services they provide. The electrical engineer uses utility location information gathered by the site survey or the architect, and requests additional technical information on power availability and the like from the utility company.

The answer is (C).

238. All the strategies listed will gain new construction project LEED points except reducing construction activity pollution and installing building-level water metering. These do not gain points but are prerequisites for applying for LEED credits.

The answer is (C), (D), (E), and (F).

239. Local ordinances typically establish view plane restrictions to protect scenic views from a specific point or area. Buildings cannot be built that obstruct these views. This is only possible through local control rather than through building codes or easements. Although zoning restrictions limit the height and bulk of buildings, they do so based on individual lot restrictions rather than with imaginary lines drawn through a site, or several sites, from some point.

The answer is (C).

240. An egress court, which is a type of exit discharge, is not required to make a site accessible for egress. An egress court is a court or yard on private property that provides access to a public way from one or more exits. When access to a public way cannot be provided, the *International Building Code* (IBC) allows an exception to provide dispersal areas if they are at least 50 ft away from the building, on the same lot, and provide at least 5 ft^2 for each person. These requirements are building code egress mandates, and they are not required by the *ADA/ABA Accessibility Guidelines.*

Abrupt vertical changes in level cannot exceed $^1/_4$ in as with all accessible routes. An accessible route such as a sidewalk cannot have a slope greater than 1:20 (5%) unless it is treated as a ramp and is in compliance with all ramp requirements, including handrails, curbs, and requirements for maximum rise and length. Cross slopes may be up to 1:50 (2%) for drainage. Walking surfaces must be at least 36 in wide.

The answer is (B), (C), (D), and (F).

241. An earthwork diagram is used to show approximately how much of a building site needs to be regraded. It is sometimes called a cut-and-fill diagram. In order to minimize construction costs, the areas of cut should approximately equal the areas that require fill so that earth does not have to be imported or hauled off the site. Using the area of each portion of the diagram and the vertical distance between contours, the volume of earth that has to be moved can be calculated fairly accurately.

The answer is (A).

242. During preliminary site planning, minimizing the building footprint is an effective sustainability strategy. It reduces the amount of site disturbance and provides more area for landscaping and porous paving, both of which reduce runoff. Positioning buildings along contours minimizes the amount of earthwork and site clearing required. Locating buildings and parking areas near roads minimizes the amount of paving required for access roads. An infiltration basin catches stormwater runoff and retains it until it can seep into the ground. This reduces the amount of stormwater added to the storm sewer system and avoids possible contamination of natural water courses.

A greenfield site is undeveloped land that may contain existing vegetation and native ecosystems. A better sustainable strategy is to remediate a brownfield site, which is previously developed land that may contain contaminated soil. Providing maximum lawn area is not a good strategy because lawns require significant amounts of water and maintenance.

The answer is (B), (C), (E), and (F).

243. To determine the slope, use the following formula.

$$G = \frac{d}{L} \times 100\%$$

G is the grade measured as a percentage, d is the vertical distance between points in feet, and L is the horizontal distance between points in feet.

$$\begin{aligned} G &= \frac{30 \text{ ft}}{300 \text{ ft}} \times 100\% \\ &= 10\% \end{aligned}$$

The answer is 10%.

244. According to the Secretary of the Interior's *Standards for Rehabilitation*, repairing an existing exterior cornice molding could be done to a historic property undergoing rehabilitation treatment. The *Standards for Rehabilitation* emphasize the retention and repair of historic materials but give some latitude for replacing damaged elements. Repairing a damaged or deteriorated historic element, rather than replacing it, is allowed.

Removing historic materials or altering internal spaces should be avoided. Chemical or physical treatments that could damage historic materials must not be used. If changes that have been made to the original structure also have historic significance, they must be retained and preserved.

The answer is (A).

245. The maximum allowable buildable area is the area of the lot multiplied by the FAR. In this case the total area of the site is

$$A = wd$$

The FAR is 2.0, so the buildable area is

$$A_{\text{buildable}} = w(\text{FAR})$$

$$A = wd = (120 \text{ ft})(150 \text{ ft}) = 18{,}000 \text{ ft}^2$$

$$A_{\text{buildable}} = A(\text{FAR}) = (18{,}000 \text{ ft}^2)(2.0) = 36{,}000 \text{ ft}^2$$

The area within the setbacks has nothing to do with the maximum allowable building area. However, it influences the number of stories of the building.

The answer is 36,000 ft².

246. Hydrostatic water problems are those that occur when water at the foundation is under pressure. To address hydrostatic water problems near a basement foundation, an architect should consider using geotextiles, gravel fill below the floor slab, positive slope away from the building, and sump pumps. These are in addition to the standard design elements such as using an appropriate waterproofing membrane and a foundation drain. Geotextiles and gravel fill use air space to interrupt the pressure between the water and the foundation or slab. A positive slope helps keep water away from the foundation. Sump pumps remove any water that may penetrate the structure.

Dampproofing is not appropriate if hydrostatic pressure may be present because dampproofing is not designed to stop water under pressure. Pervious paving allows water to seep into the soil around the foundation, exacerbating the problem.

The answer is (B), (C), (E), and (F).

247. Layout B sets the parking spaces perpendicular to the row of shops, making it easy for people to park relatively close to the stores they want and to reach the mall without walking through parked cars. The driveway locations and access aisle also allow for fire department access to the shops and easy pickup and dropoff.

Layout A forces people to walk through parked cars to get to the shops and creates conflict between circulation traffic and cars entering and exiting the row of spaces near the mall. Layout C concentrates incoming and outgoing traffic into one driveway, forces people to cross through parked cars, and doesn't provide easy building access for fire department and other emergency services. Although layout D distributes incoming and outgoing traffic from the street and sets parking spaces perpendicular to the

Programming & Analysis

row of shops, it forces emergency vehicles to travel through the parking area.

The answer is (B).

248. The requirement for many rooms and spaces to have exterior windows will influence the building layout the most because this building is conceived as a single-story structure. The layout will need to be spread out along a double-loaded corridor, resulting in a long and relatively narrow building. The other requirements can be easily achieved with any number of layout configurations.

The answer is (C).

249. If the FAR is 2.0, then the maximum amount of floor area that can be built is two times the area of the entire lot. The area of the lot is

$$\text{lot area} = (100\text{ ft})(130\text{ ft}) = 13{,}000\text{ ft}^2$$

Then the maximum floor area for the entire building is

$$\begin{aligned}\text{total floor area} &= (\text{lot area})(\text{FAR})\\ &= (13{,}000\text{ ft}^2)(2.0)\\ &= 26{,}000\text{ ft}^2\end{aligned}$$

Next, determine the available buildable area within the setbacks. The distance between the side setbacks is

$$130\text{ ft} - 15\text{ ft} - 15\text{ ft} = 100\text{ ft}$$

The distance between the front and rear setbacks is

$$100\text{ ft} - 30\text{ ft} - 10\text{ ft} = 60\text{ ft}$$

The available area for each floor, then, is

$$\begin{aligned}\text{floor area per story} &= (100\text{ ft})(60\text{ ft})\\ &= 6000\text{ ft}^2\end{aligned}$$

To find the allowable number of stories, divide the maximum floor area for each story into the maximum total area.

$$\begin{aligned}\text{number of stories} &= \frac{\text{total floor area}}{\text{floor area per story}}\\ &= \frac{26{,}000\text{ ft}^2}{6000\,\dfrac{\text{ft}^2}{\text{story}}}\\ &= 4.33\text{ stories}\end{aligned}$$

Each story will contain the full 6000 ft^2 allowed, so the building can have a maximum of four stories.

The answer is 4 stories.

250. Zoning regulations limit total building area based on floor area ratio and setbacks, while building codes limit building area by construction type and occupancy group. Bulk plane limits may affect the area by limiting height in some cases, but they are not a primary determinant. Of the choices given, the floor area ratio (from zoning codes) and construction type (from building codes) is the combination that limits maximum area.

The answer is (A).

251. The basic allowable floor area and height of a building are determined by the construction type and the occupancy group. This basic allowable floor area may be increased according to certain criteria, such as if the building is fully sprinklered and/or if there is a certain amount of space around the building.

The answer is (A), (B), (D), and (F).

252. The parking lot and entrance to the lot should be situated in the northeast corner of the site in order to minimize traffic conflicts with the intersection on the eastern side of the space. The shaded areas indicate the margin for error in locating the site features. (See *Illustration for Sol. 252.*)

The building should be positioned on the western side of the site for easy neighborhood access to the shops. Placing the building with the south-facing entry slightly south of center puts the entry in a sunny spot out of the shadow of the three-story apartment building. It also provides landscaped open space at the intersection of the streets while adding a plaza to the northwest, across from the single-story restaurant with a deck. There is easy access from the parking lot to the office building entrance, and the space between the building and the three-story apartment building can be used for access to the park.

Illustration for Sol. 252

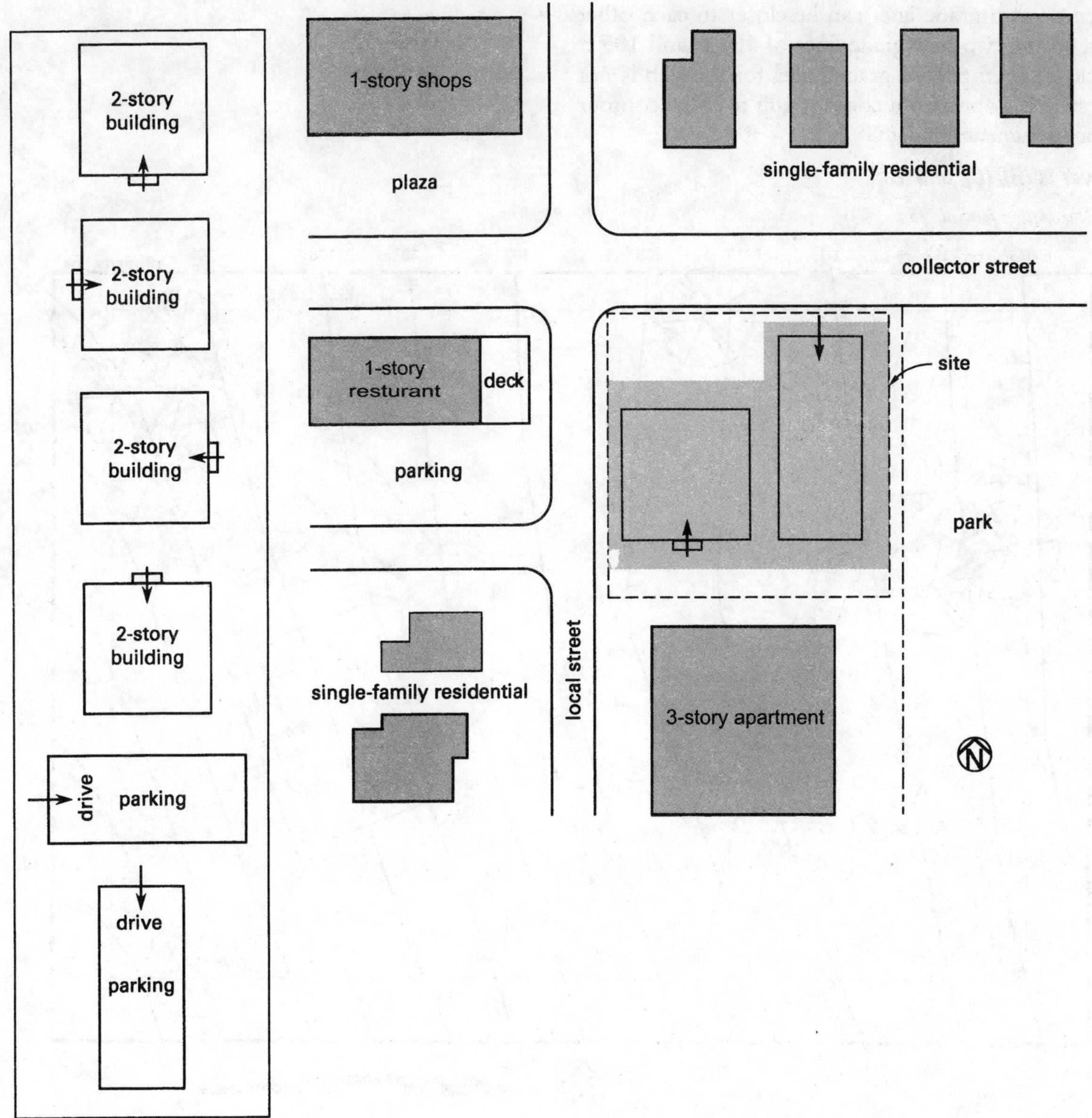

253. Although there is some attempt at creating a swale on the west side of the slab, water is still diverted onto it because there is a 106 ft grade adjacent to the slab with its elevation of 105 ft 6 in. If the maximum allowable slope is 20%, then no two grade lines can be closer to each other than 5 ft, so the two new grade lines of 104 ft and 105 ft are too close together. The graded area for the slab is not level because it slopes from contour 105 ft up to contour 106 ft. (See *Illustration for Sol. 253*.)

The answer is (B), (C), and (D).

Illustration for Sol. 253

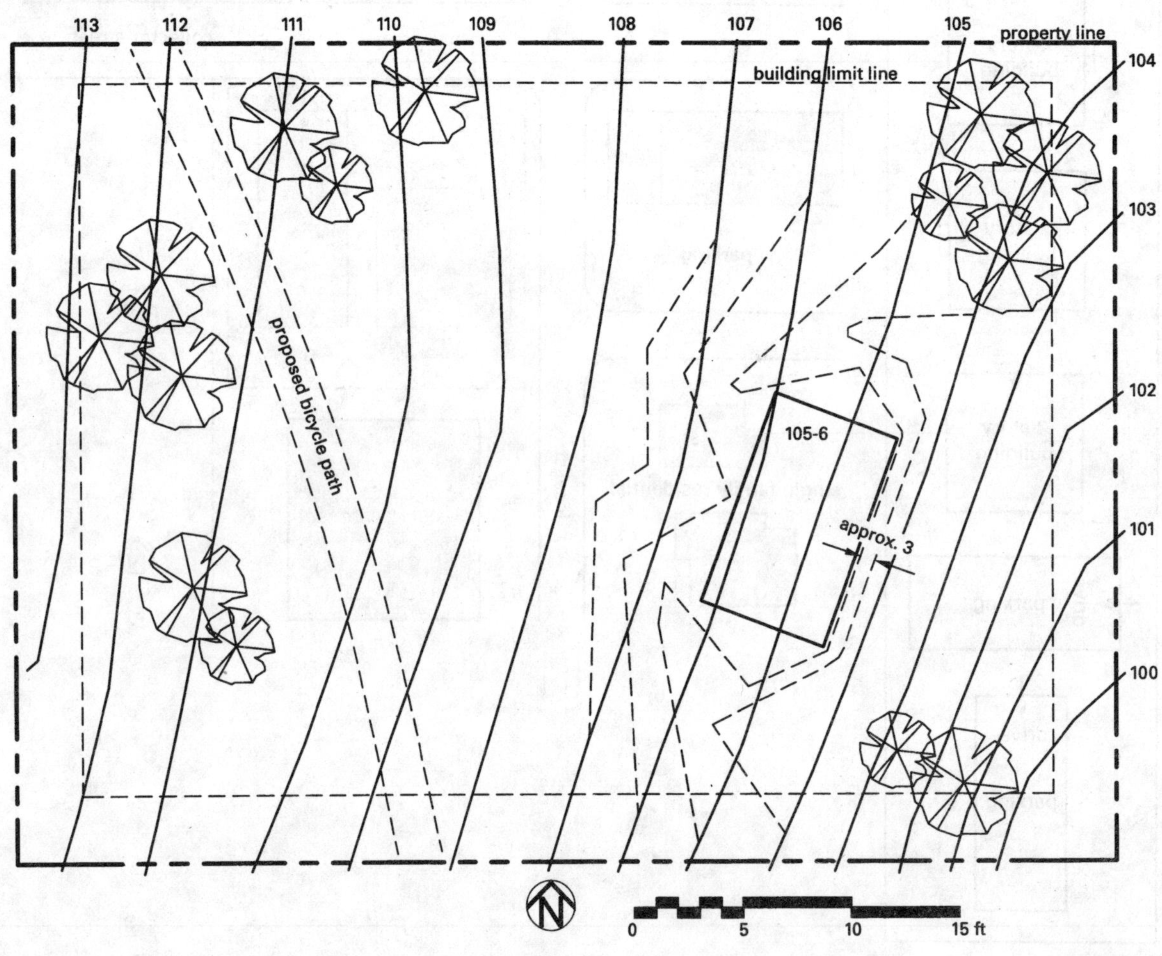

Illustration for Sol. 254

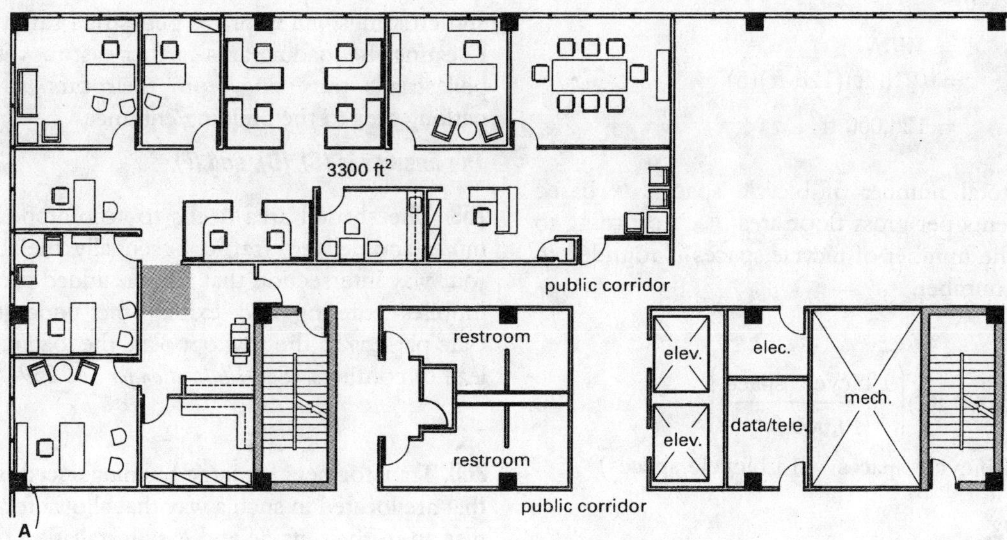

254. The common path of egress travel is the path that must be traversed before two separate and distinct paths of travel to two different exits are available. From the shaded area, an occupant has the choice of exiting through the nearest door into a stairway or by continuing through the main office corridor, out the main entrance of the office suite, and then through the public corridor to another stairway. (See *Illustration for Sol. 254.*)

255. In temperate climates, a rectangular building is best oriented in an east-west direction or as much as 17° east of south. This orientation provides daylight for much of the building, as well as the possibility of solar heat gain in the winter with minimized area exposed to low sun angles in the morning and afternoon. In the summer, high sun angles on the south side can be mitigated with shading devices.

The answer is (A).

256. According to Resource 3.1, one parking space is required for every 1000 ft^2 of gross floor area in zoning district M-1. The gross floor area of the building is 120 ft × 210 ft, or 25,200 ft^2 per floor. For five floors, the total gross square footage is 126,000 ft^2, which requires 126 parking spaces. Because 40 of these parking spaces are underground, the total required surface parking requirement is 86 spaces.

Calculate the building's gross floor area, A, with W as width, D as depth, and N as number of floors.

$$\begin{aligned} A &= WDN \\ &= (210 \text{ ft})(120 \text{ ft})(5) \\ &= 126{,}000 \text{ ft}^2 \end{aligned}$$

Calculate the total number of parking spaces, P, based upon requirements per gross floor area, R_P.

$$\begin{aligned} P &= AR_P \\ &= (126{,}000 \text{ ft}^2)\left(\frac{1 \text{ parking space}}{1000 \text{ ft}^2}\right) \\ &= 126 \text{ parking spaces} \end{aligned}$$

Calculate the surface parking spaces, S, using the underground parking spaces, U.

$$\begin{aligned} P &= S + U \\ S &= P - U \\ &= 126 \text{ parking spaces} - 40 \text{ parking spaces} \\ &= 86 \text{ parking spaces} \end{aligned}$$

The answer is (A).

257. According to Resource 3.1, one bicycle space is required for every 10,000 ft^2 of gross floor area in zoning district M-1. The gross floor area of the building is 120 ft × 210 ft, or 25,200 ft^2 per floor. For five floors, the total area is 126,000 ft^2, which requires 12.6 bicycle spaces. This number is rounded up to 13.

Calculate the building's gross floor area, A, with W as width, D as depth, and N as number of floors.

$$\begin{aligned} A &= WDN \\ &= (210 \text{ ft})(120 \text{ ft})(5) \\ &= 126{,}000 \text{ ft}^2 \end{aligned}$$

Calculate the total number of bicycle spaces, B, based upon requirements per gross floor area, R_B. According to Resource 3.1, the number of bicycle spaces is rounded to the next whole number.

$$\begin{aligned} P &= AR_B \\ &= (126{,}000 \text{ ft}^2)\left(\frac{1 \text{ bicycle space}}{10{,}000 \text{ ft}^2}\right) \\ &= 12.6 \text{ bicycle spaces} \quad (13 \text{ bicycle spaces}) \end{aligned}$$

The answer is 13.

258. A separate entry drive for the underground parking lot interferes with pedestrians on the sidewalk and creates traffic conflicts because the drive is too close to the intersection. Positioning retail entries closer to the 45th Street sidewalk makes pedestrian access easier but defeats the planning commission's desire to increase landscaping. Locating the deck on the west side of the building does not impact pedestrian access.

A northwest corner entry is closer to the majority of the parking to the north and to the accessible parking. Because there are many parking spaces along the north and northwest portion of the site, additional sidewalks and crossings will improve pedestrian safety and comfort. Locating the loading area farther east moves it away from pedestrians traversing from their cars in the northeast parking area to the building entrance.

The answer is (C), (D), and (F).

259. The shaded area needs to accommodate both commuter and delivery traffic. Essentially, the shaded area is a four-way intersection that has the added problem of automobiles entering and exiting the underground garage. Cars parking in the row opposite the loading area will also lead to conflicts. (See *Illustration for Sol. 259.*)

260. Transformers for large buildings need fireproof vaults that are located in such a way that allows for adequate ventilation to the outside and easy installation of and replacement of heavy equipment. The large vents and access grates should be located out of sight when feasible. The locations given in option (B) and option (D) provide the best opportunities to meet these criteria, assuming they are coordinated with the layout of the underground garage. The other locations are visible and less suitable for maintenance activities.

The answer is (B) and (D).

Illustration for Sol. 259

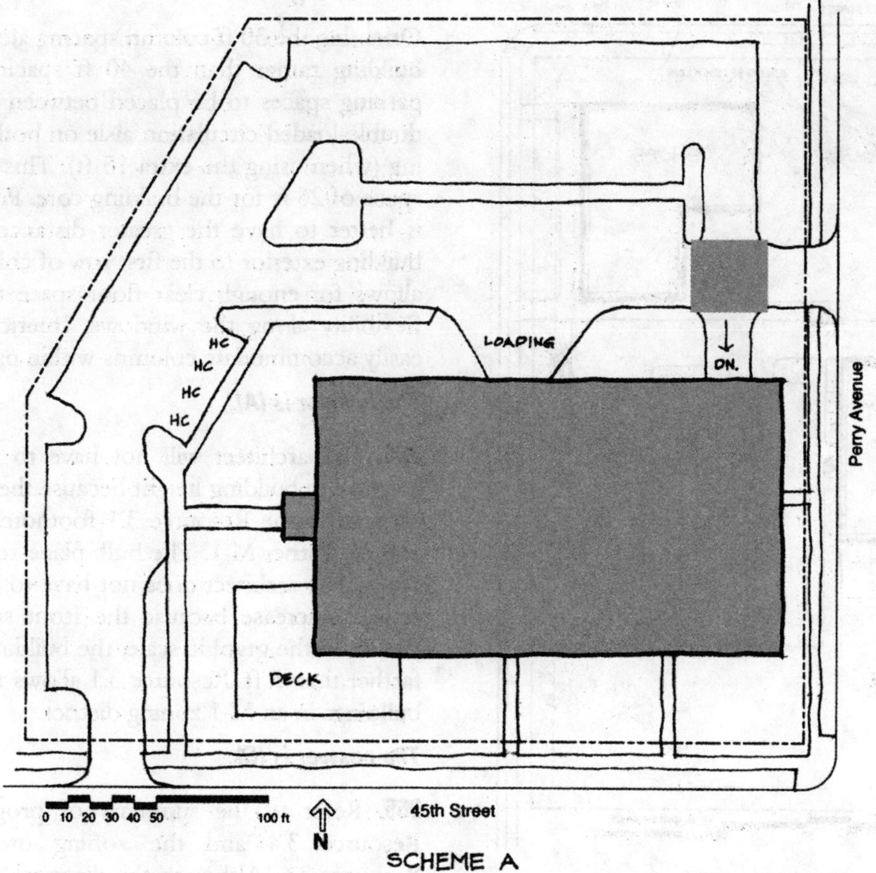

261. In Resource 3.2, a five-story building is proposed. Based on the limits given in Resource 3.3, the five-story building's maximum height is 70 ft. Building height is defined as the distance from grade to the average height of the highest roof surface. Calculate the maximum floor-to-floor distance, D, using the height limit, H, and the number of stories, N.

$$D = \frac{H}{N} = \frac{70 \text{ ft}}{5} = 14 \text{ ft}$$

Parapets, antennas, and mechanical equipment located on the roof may add to the height.

The answer is 14 ft.

262. According to the zoning regulations, bicycle storage must be publicly accessible near building entrances and walkways. Option (C) and option (D) put the bicycle storage area too far from the building entrance to meet zoning requirements. The areas on either side of the walkway leading to the main entrance, as in option (A) and option (B), satisfy the zoning requirements; however, the bicycle storage area should not be located between the restaurant deck or in place of any landscaping that may separate the deck from the building entrance. This makes a more pleasant environment for people using the deck.

The answer is (A).

263.

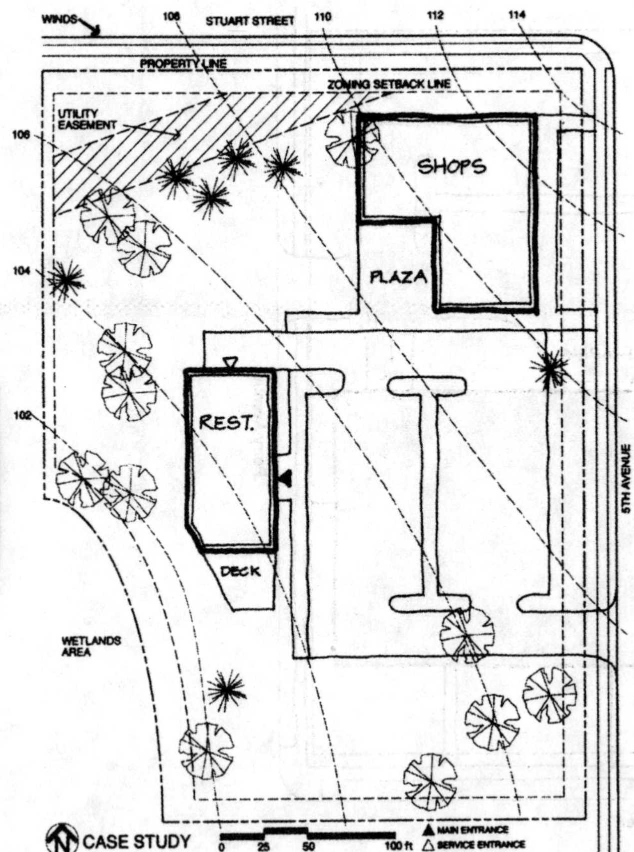

To answer this question, two aspects of the location are to be considered: the layout of the underground parking and the flexibility of space planning for the offices on the upper floors. Both Scheme A and Scheme B include one level of underground parking. The structural engineer has said that the underground level can extend as much as 15 ft beyond the edge of the building along the length of the building.

Orienting the 30 ft column spacing along the length of the building rather than the 40 ft spacing allows three 90° parking spaces to be placed between the columns with a double-loaded circulation aisle on both sides of the building (when using the extra 15 ft). This orientation leaves a space of 26 ft for the building core. For office planning, it is better to have the greater distance of 40 ft from the building exterior to the first row of columns. This distance allows for enough clear floor space to provide planning flexibility along the windows. Interior rooms can more easily accommodate columns within partitions.

The answer is (A).

264. The architect will not have to consider a possible increase in building height because the height increase referenced in the Resource 3.1 footnotes does not apply to zoning district M-1. The bulk plane requirement does not apply. The architect does not have to consider the a front setback increase because the front setback is only 5 ft. Based on the graphic scale, the building is clearly set back farther than 5 ft. Resource 3.1 allows for multiple primary buildings in an M-1 zoning district.

The answer is (C).

265. Refer to the summary of programmed spaces in Resource 3.4 and the zoning ordinance excerpt in Resource 3.6. Although the diagonal property line is normally considered a side setback line, the local planning office ordinance requires a minimum setback of 40 ft from any city park.

The answer is (D).

Illustration for Sol. 266

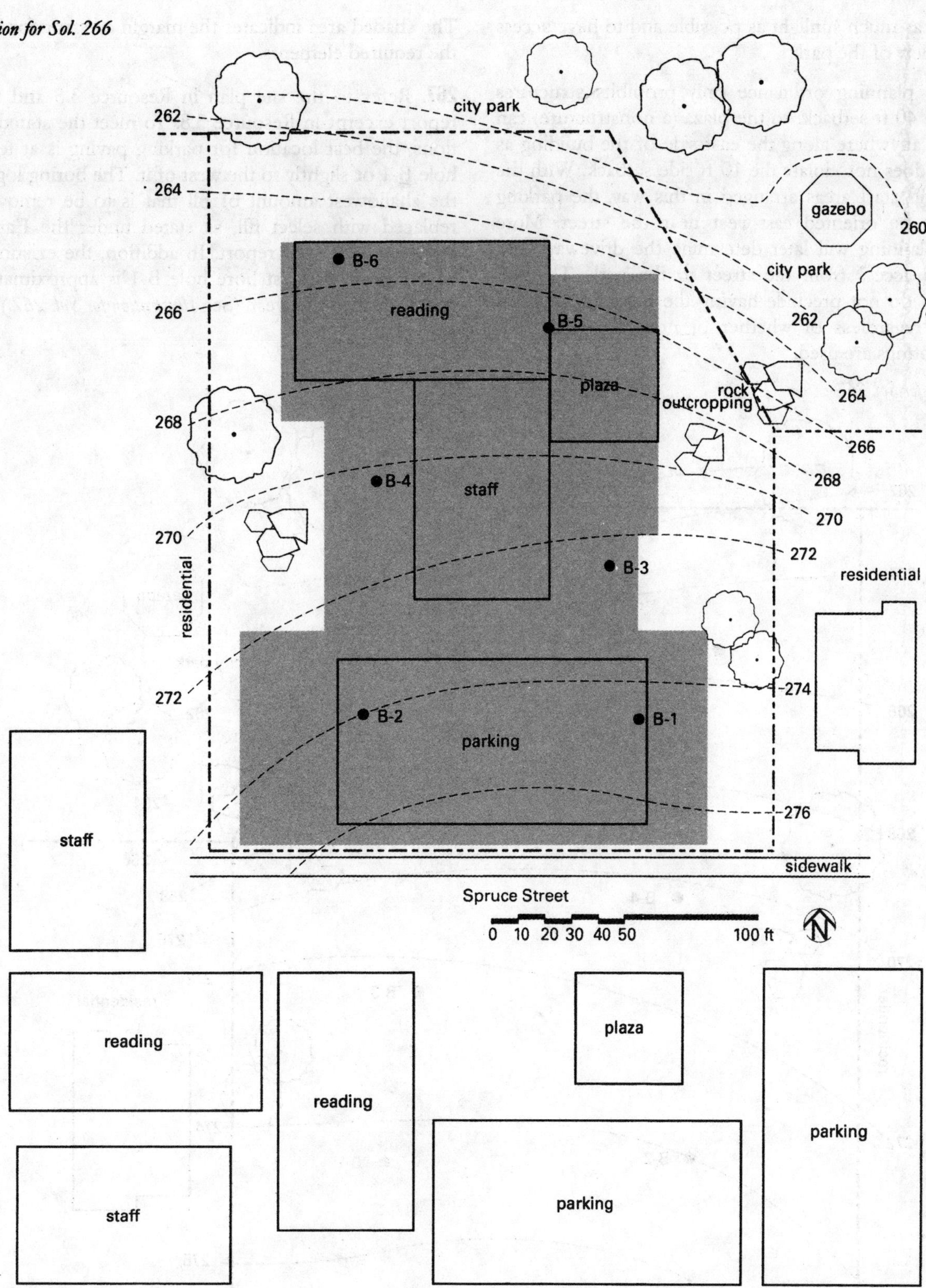

266. The best arrangement of the elements is shown. (See *Illustration for Sol. 266.*) Because the reading area needs to have a view of the park, it should be placed on the northernmost portion of the site oriented east-west without violating the 40 ft setback requirement. The other building must be placed in the north-south direction to avoid the rock outcropping, more or less aligned with the eastern edge of the reading area. This area could also be located slightly more to the west as long as the rock outcropping is avoided. The plaza should be placed east of the building to receive as much sunlight as possible and to have access to and a view of the park.

The local planning ordinance only prohibits structures within the 40 ft setback, so the plaza (a nonstructure) can be placed anywhere along the east side of the building as long as it does not violate the 10 ft side setback. With the reading and staff areas arranged in this way, the parking area must be oriented east-west near the street. More detailed planning will later determine the driveways and pedestrian access from the street to the park. The soil conditions do not preclude having the building arranged this way, regardless of whether or not drilled piers or spread footings are used.

Illustration for Sol. 267

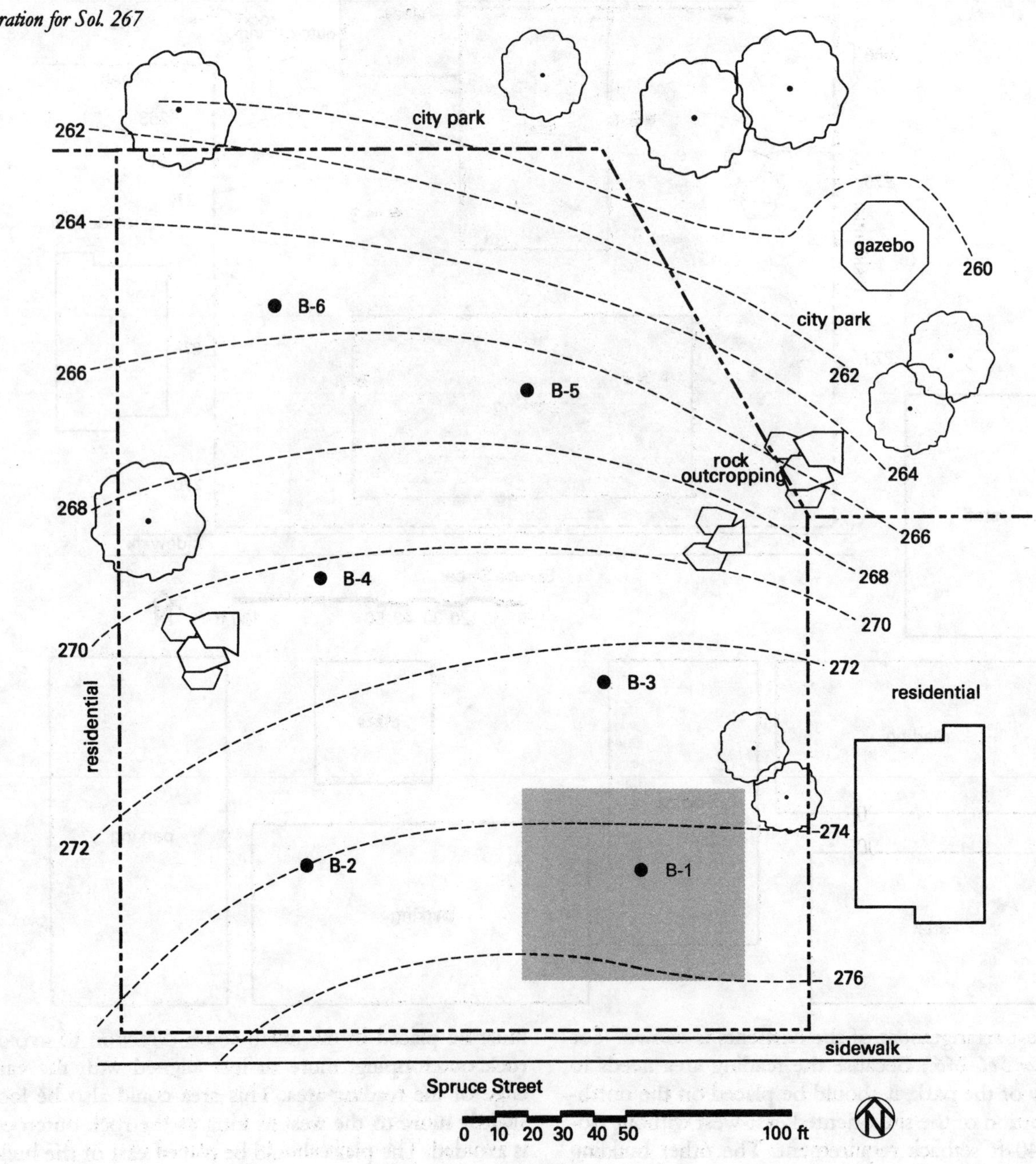

The shaded area indicates the margin of error for locating the required elements.

267. Refer to the site plan in Resource 3.5 and the soil report excerpt in Resource 3.8. To meet the stated conditions, the best location for parking paving is at test bore hole B-1 or slightly to the west of it. The boring log shows the shallowest amount of fill that is to be removed and replaced with select fill, as stated under the Earthwork section of the soils report. In addition, the existing slope of the land near test bore hole B-1 is approximately 5% and slightly to the west. (See *Illustration for Sol. 267.*)

While this value is the maximum recommended value for parking areas, only a small amount of grading is necessary to decrease the slope, if desired. If the parking area is extended to the north, the existing slope decreases to less than 4%. The location near test bore hole B-2 requires more removal of existing fill and the slopes are slightly greater. Other locations farther north require more fill to decrease the slope. Locating the parking in these areas does not allow enough room for the building or requires the building to be placed on the southern part of the site. Either results in long drives and more fill to achieve an acceptable slope for parking.

The shaded area indicates the margin of error for selecting the correct location.

268. Use the population size, the number of books, the linear feet of shelving required, and the shelving dimensions given to calculate how much space is needed.

The base population is given as 5000, and so there are 4000 more people in the actual population than the base population.

$$\begin{aligned}\text{no. of people} &= \text{actual population} - \text{base population}\\ &= 9000 - 5000\\ &= 4000\end{aligned}$$

Using the number of books per capita, the number of books for this population is

$$\begin{aligned}\text{no. of books} &= (2)(\text{books per capita})\\ &= (2)(4000)\\ &= 8000\end{aligned}$$

According to the guidelines given, there are 15,000 books for a population over 5000. The total number of books that the stack collection needs to accommodate is

$$\begin{aligned}\text{total no. of books} &= \begin{array}{l}\text{no. of books for population}\\ \quad\text{over 5000}\\ +\text{no. of books for population}\\ \quad\text{of 9000}\end{array}\\ &= 15{,}000 + 8000\\ &= 23{,}000\end{aligned}$$

The linear feet of shelving needed in addition to the base of 1875 ft is

$$\begin{aligned}\text{shelving} &= \frac{\text{no. of books for population of 9000}}{\frac{1\text{ ft}}{8\text{ books}}}\\ &= \frac{8000\text{ books}}{\frac{1\text{ ft}}{8\text{ books}}}\\ &= 1000\text{ ft}\end{aligned}$$

To find the total amount of shelving space needed, the additional linear feet of shelving is added to the base of 1875 ft.

$$\begin{aligned}\text{total shelving needed} &= 1875\text{ ft} + 1000\text{ ft}\\ &= 2875\text{ ft}\end{aligned}$$

Each module is 15 ft long. The linear feet of shelving in one module of five back-to-back shelving units is

$$\begin{aligned}\text{shelving per module} &= (10\text{ units})\left(7\ \frac{\text{shelves}}{\text{unit}}\right)\left(3\ \frac{\text{ft}}{\text{shelf}}\right)\\ &= 210\text{ ft}\end{aligned}$$

If the modules are placed 36 in apart, each module requires a floor area of 5 ft × 15 ft, or 75 ft^2, ignoring the space required for circulation at the ends of aisles. The number of modules needed in order to accommodate 2875 linear ft of shelving is calculated as

$$\begin{aligned}\text{no. of modules} &= \frac{\text{total shelving needed}}{\text{shelving per module}}\\ &= \frac{2875\text{ ft}}{210\text{ ft}}\\ &= 13.69\quad(14)\end{aligned}$$

The minimum floor area is

$$\begin{aligned}A &= (\text{no. of modules})\\ &\quad\times(\text{required floor area per module})\\ &= (14)(17\text{ ft}^2)\\ &= 1050\text{ ft}^2\end{aligned}$$

The answer is 1050 ft^2.

Illustration for Sol. 269

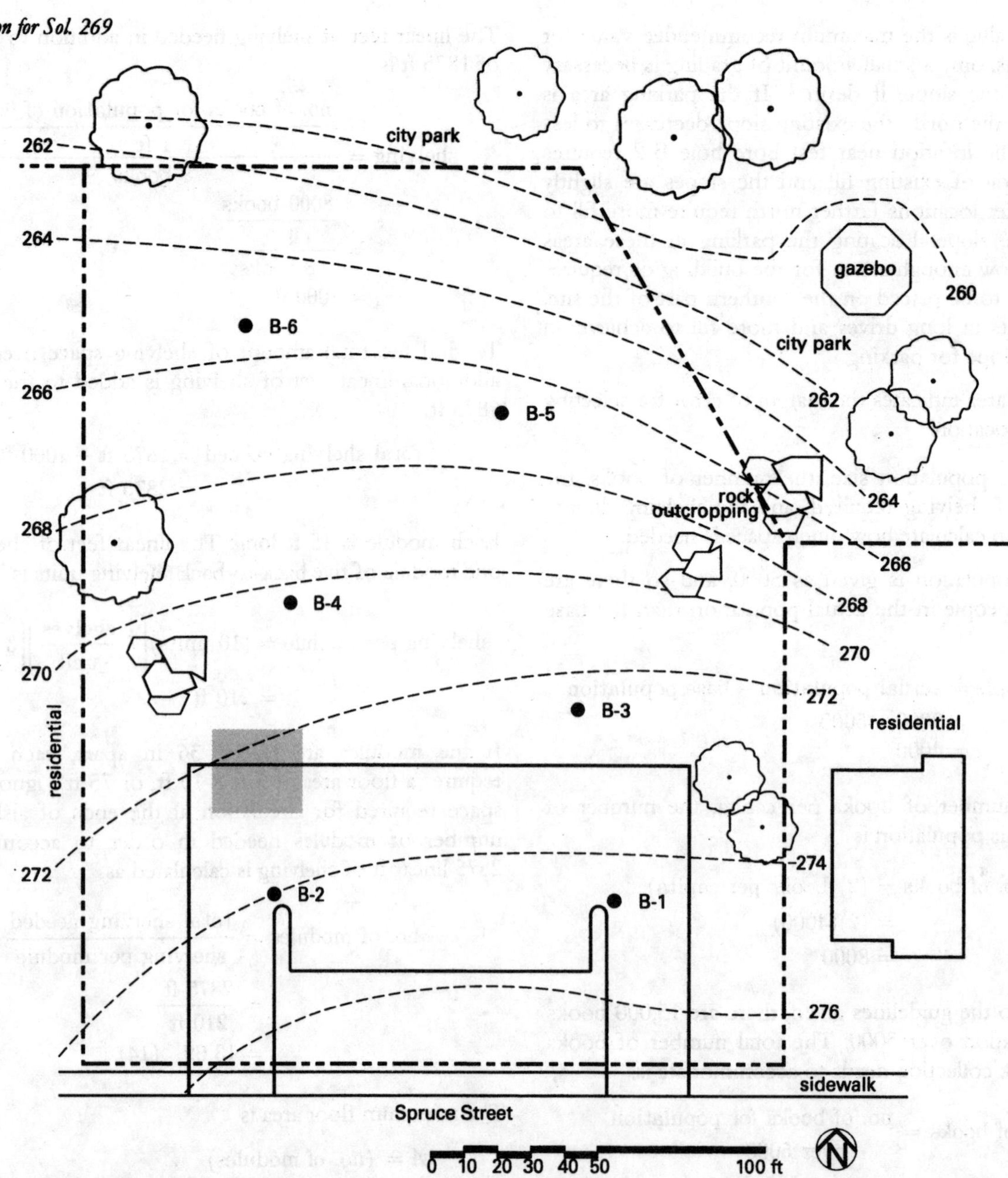

269. Given the program requirements of views to the park, sunlight for the plaza, and pedestrian access to the park from Spruce Street, the service access has to be along the west portion of the site near the property line. If the parking is oriented as in this configuration, any service drive connects at the west end of the parking area. Service vehicles drive directly toward a loading area on the west side of any building configuration that is developed. The only limitations to be avoided are the rock outcropping near the property line and to ensure that the required number of parking spaces is maintained.

The shaded area indicates the margin of error for selecting the correct location. (See *Illustration for Sol. 269.*)

270. The soil report recommends drilled piers to bedrock but also offers the alternative of spread footings if certain conditions are met. Shallow spread footings are less expensive than drilled piers. A steel frame is less expensive than masonry bearing walls while offering more flexibility for building configuration. Open-web steel joists provide for quick construction and easily span the required distances without the need for interior columns, which are essential for the second floor community meeting room. Joists are less expensive that heavier steel beams.

The answer is (A), (C), and (E).

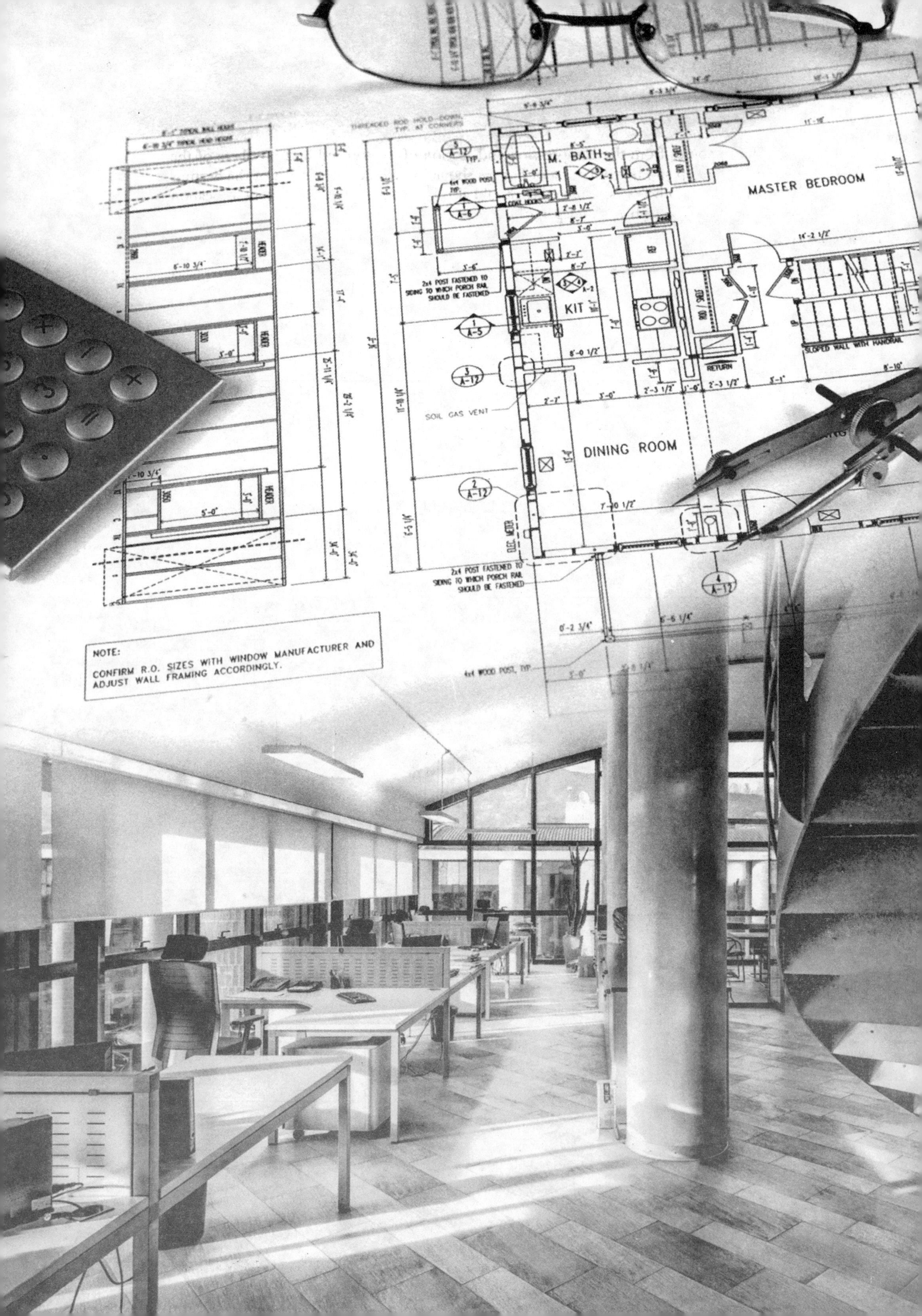
M. BATH
MASTER BEDROOM
KIT
DINING ROOM
SOIL GAS VENT
RETURN
SLOPED WALL WITH HANDRAIL
2x4 POST FASTENED TO SIDING TO WHICH PORCH RAIL SHOULD BE FASTENED
2x4 POST FASTENED TO SIDING TO WHICH PORCH RAIL SHOULD BE FASTENED
4x4 WOOD POST, TYP.
NOTE:
CONFIRM R.O. SIZES WITH WINDOW MANUFACTURER AND ADJUST WALL FRAMING ACCORDINGLY.

DIVISION 4: PROJECT PLANNING & DESIGN

Multiple Choice

271. (A) (B) (C) (D)
272. (A) (B) (C) (D)
273. (A) (B) (C) (D) (E) (F)
274. (A) (B) (C) (D) (E) (F)
275. (A) (B) (C) (D)
276. (A) (B) (C) (D)
277. (A) (B) (C) (D)
278. (A) (B) (C) (D)
279. (A) (B) (C) (D)
280. (A) (B) (C) (D) (E) (F)
281. (A) (B) (C) (D)
282. (A) (B) (C) (D)
283. (A) (B) (C) (D)
284. (A) (B) (C) (D)
285. (A) (B) (C) (D)
286. (A) (B) (C) (D)
287. (A) (B) (C) (D)
288. (A) (B) (C) (D)
289. (A) (B) (C) (D)
290. (A) (B) (C) (D)
291. (A) (B) (C) (D)
292. (A) (B) (C) (D)
293. (A) (B) (C) (D) (E) (F)
294. (A) (B) (C) (D)
295. (A) (B) (C) (D)
296. (A) (B) (C) (D)
297. (A) (B) (C) (D) (E) (F)
298. (A) (B) (C) (D) (E) (F)
299. (A) (B) (C) (D) (E) (F)
300. (A) (B) (C) (D)
301. (A) (B) (C) (D)
302. (A) (B) (C) (D) (E) (F)
303. (A) (B) (C) (D)
304. (A) (B) (C) (D)
305. (A) (B) (C) (D)
306. (A) (B) (C) (D)
307. (A) (B) (C) (D)
308. (A) (B) (C) (D)
309. (A) (B) (C) (D)
310. (A) (B) (C) (D)
311. (A) (B) (C) (D)
312. (A) (B) (C) (D)
313. (A) (B) (C) (D)
314. (A) (B) (C) (D) (E) (F)
315. (A) (B) (C) (D)
316. (A) (B) (C) (D)
317. (A) (B) (C) (D)
318. (A) (B) (C) (D)
319. (A) (B) (C) (D)
320. (A) (B) (C) (D)
321. (A) (B) (C) (D)
322. (A) (B) (C) (D)
323. (A) (B) (C) (D)
324. (A) (B) (C) (D)
325. (A) (B) (C) (D)
326. (A) (B) (C) (D)
327. (A) (B) (C) (D)
328. (A) (B) (C) (D)
329. (A) (B) (C) (D)
330. (A) (B) (C) (D) (E) (F)
331. (A) (B) (C) (D) (E) (F)
332. (A) (B) (C) (D) (E) (F)
333. (A) (B) (C) (D)
334. (A) (B) (C) (D)
335. (A) (B) (C) (D)
336. (A) (B) (C) (D)
337. (A) (B) (C) (D)
338. (A) (B) (C) (D)
339. (A) (B) (C) (D) (E) (F)
340. (A) (B) (C) (D)
341. (A) (B) (C) (D)
342. (A) (B) (C) (D)
343. (A) (B) (C) (D)
344. (A) (B) (C) (D)
345. (A) (B) (C) (D) (E) (F)
346. (A) (B) (C) (D) (E) (F)
347. (A) (B) (C) (D)
348. (A) (B) (C) (D)
349. (A) (B) (C) (D)
350. (A) (B) (C) (D)
351. (A) (B) (C) (D)
352. (A) (B) (C) (D)
353. (A) (B) (C) (D)
354. (A) (B) (C) (D) (E) (F)
355. (A) (B) (C) (D)
356. (A) (B) (C) (D)
357. (A) (B) (C) (D)
358. (A) (B) (C) (D) (E) (F)
359. (A) (B) (C) (D)
360. (A) (B) (C) (D)
361. (A) (B) (C) (D)
362. (A) (B) (C) (D) (E) (F)
363. (A) (B) (C) (D) (E) (F)
364. (A) (B) (C) (D)
365. ____________
366. ____________
367. (A) (B) (C) (D)
368. (A) (B) (C) (D)
369. ____________
370. ____________
371. (A) (B) (C) (D)
372. (A) (B) (C) (D)
373. (A) (B) (C) (D)
374. (A) (B) (C) (D)
375. (A) (B) (C) (D)
376. (A) (B) (C) (D)
377. (A) (B) (C) (D)
378. (A) (B) (C) (D)
379. ____________
380. (A) (B) (C) (D) (E) (F)

Case Study

381. ____________
382. (A) (B) (C) (D)
383. (A) (B) (C) (D)
384. (A) (B) (C) (D)
385. (A) (B) (C) (D)
386. (A) (B) (C) (D)
387. (A) (B) (C) (D)
388. (A) (B) (C) (D)
389. (A) (B) (C) (D)
390. (A) (B) (C) (D)

271. The type of lockset that is most secure is a

(A) unit lock

(B) cylindrical lock

(C) rim lock

(D) mortise lock

272. Identify the check rail on the pair of double-hung windows shown.

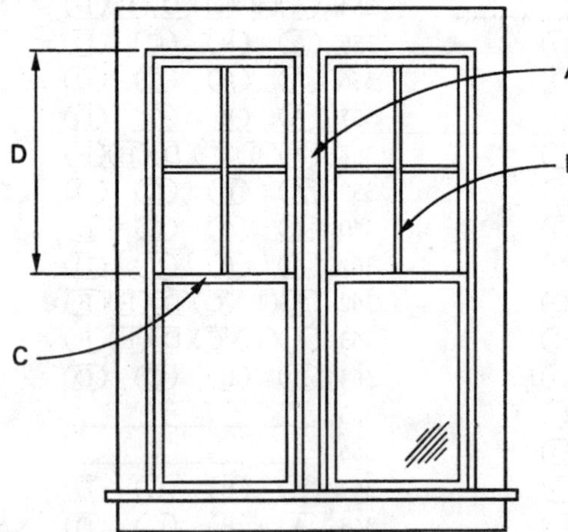

(A) A

(B) B

(C) C

(D) D

273. According to model codes, which of the following are considered parts of the means of egress? (Choose the three that apply.)

(A) common path of travel

(B) exit

(C) exit access

(D) exit discharge

(E) public way

(F) travel distance

274. Which of these are important considerations in designing a fire-rated ceiling? (Choose the two that apply.)

(A) hold-down clips

(B) structural slab

(C) thermal insulation

(D) composition of the floor/ceiling assembly

(E) sound absorption

(F) style of grid

275. An architect is designing custom oak cabinetry and wants the grain of the door frames to be as straight and consistent as possible. Which type of sawing should be specified?

(A) plain sawing

(B) quarter sawing

(C) flat sawing

(D) rift sawing

276. Which of the following statements is true?

(A) Dampproofing controls moisture that is under hydrostatic pressure.

(B) Membrane coatings should always be used for dampproofing.

(C) Waterproofing membranes may be easily punctured and require a protective covering.

(D) If hydrostatic pressure is present, foundation drains will be of no use.

277. An architect is asked to design an office suite that limits sound transmission into the surrounding corridor. Which of the following is the most important acoustical strategy to include in the design?

(A) Build walls with staggered studs and mount the gypsum board on resilient channels.

(B) Extend the partitions from deck to deck and provide acoustical seals at the top and bottom of the walls.

(C) Provide unfaced batt insulation in the partitions between the office and the corridor.

(D) Specify absorptive finish materials such as carpeting, draperies, and acoustical tile.

278. Which of the following materials is considered a rapidly renewable building material?

(A) chestnut flooring sawn from old barn beams

(B) mineral fiber insulation

(C) linoleum

(D) recycled cardboard paneling

279. An old warehouse is being converted into an apartment building. The project will be seeking Leadership in Energy and Environmental Design (LEED) certification, so a high priority will be placed on sustainable design. Which of the following existing building elements is most likely to be reused?

(A) masonry walls

(B) asbestos insulation

(C) roofing membranes and asphalt shingles

(D) windows

280. Which of the following is laminated glass commonly used for? (Choose the four that apply.)

(A) acoustical control

(B) decorative purposes

(C) fire protection

(D) insulation

(E) safety

(F) security

281. An architect has designed a bakery/coffee shop in Pittsburgh, Pennsylvania. The business is such a success that three years later, the owner decides to allow her sister, who lives in Durham, North Carolina, to open a similar store using the same name, logos, and decor. After consultation with the architect, they determine that a building of similar size and design will be appropriate for the Durham location. The sisters ask the architect for a rough projection of the cost to build the new bakery/coffee shop based upon the construction cost of the Pittsburgh store.

The location factor for Pittsburgh is 100. The cost factor for Durham is 75. The inflation rate has been 2% per year since the first building was built. The original construction cost was $300,000.

Based upon the information given, approximately how much will it cost to construct the new building?

(A) $225,000

(B) $239,000

(C) $306,000

(D) $318,000

282. A contractor is calculating how much lumber he needs to order to build a small addition on a client's house. The three exterior walls are to be framed with 2×6 studs at 16 in on center. The room is 12 ft by 12 ft, so he estimates that he will need nine 8 ft studs for each wall. The contractor will be charged by the board-foot for the lumber he purchases. How many board-feet will he need to buy?

(A) 108 board-feet

(B) 144 board-feet

(C) 216 board-feet

(D) 243 board-feet

283. An architect is designing a 10-story building and is analyzing the options for the cladding system. The architect has determined that the building will utilize a prefabricated system with a variety of glass vision and spandrel panels. Although the structural grid of the building is very regular, to add visual interest to the facade, the panels will be a variety of sizes. Which type of cladding system will be the best desirable choice for this application?

(A) curtain wall stick system

(B) substrate mounted composite metal and glass panels

(C) curtain wall panel system

(D) metallic finish EIFS system

284. What type of elevator should be specified for a 40-story office building?

(A) hydraulic

(B) gearless traction

(C) geared traction

(D) electric

Project Planning

285. An architect in Richmond, Virginia, has been asked to design a replacement roof for a hospital. The existing roof has a slope of approximately 1:12. The building supervisor requests a system that allows for additional insulation to be installed and includes paths of pavers for easy access to mechanical units and other equipment located on the roof. Which type of single-ply roofing system should be recommended?

(A) fully adhered ethylene propylene diene monomer (EPDM)

(B) loose-laid EPDM

(C) fully adhered polyvinyl chloride (PVC)

(D) mechanically attached PVC

286. Which type of passive solar heating strategy does the following illustration represent?

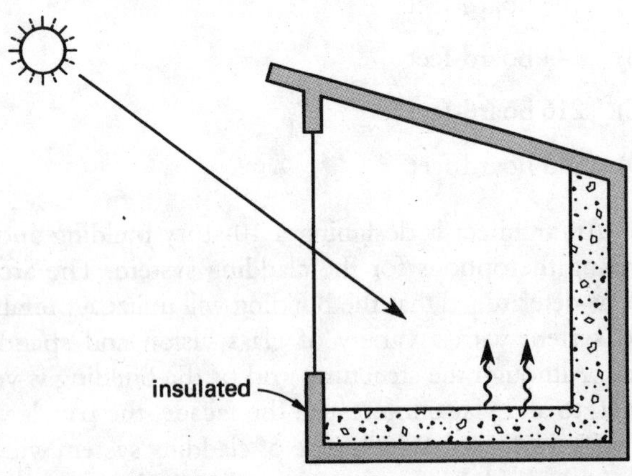

(A) Trombe wall

(B) sunspace

(C) roof panel

(D) direct gain

287. Which of the following is the most commonly used method to disinfect water to make it potable?

(A) chlorination

(B) ozonation

(C) ultraviolet light

(D) zeolite process

288. An architect is designing a new furniture gallery to be housed within an old bank building. The store will feature modern furniture and artwork and will display approximately one million dollars' worth of inventory. Which of these types of sprinkler systems will be the most appropriate choice for the store?

(A) wet pipe

(B) dry pipe

(C) preaction

(D) deluge

289. A photoelectric detector will warn of a fire when the fire reaches the

(A) incipient stage

(B) smoldering stage

(C) flame stage

(D) heat stage

290. The walls of a new coffee shop will be painted a rich pumpkin orange. What type of lighting will provide the best overall color rendering and accent the orange walls?

(A) cool white fluorescent

(B) warm white fluorescent

(C) incandescent

(D) daylight

291. What is typically the maximum height building that can utilize an upfeed water supply system?

(A) 20–30 ft

(B) 30–40 ft

(C) 50–60 ft

(D) 70–80 ft

292. In what type of building is 120/208 voltage, three-phase power appropriate?

(A) industrial

(B) small commercial

(C) residential

(D) large commercial

293. The energy cost budget method, as defined in ASHRAE/IESNA Standard 90.1, is recommended for which of the following types of buildings? (Choose the four that apply.)

(A) building that utilizes passive solar heating

(B) convenience store operating 24 hours a day, 7 days a week

(C) office building powered with photovoltaic panels

(D) retail store designed as a zero-net energy structure

(E) building with no mechanical system

(F) two-story apartment building

294. What is the minimum desirable width, x, of the lobby shown?

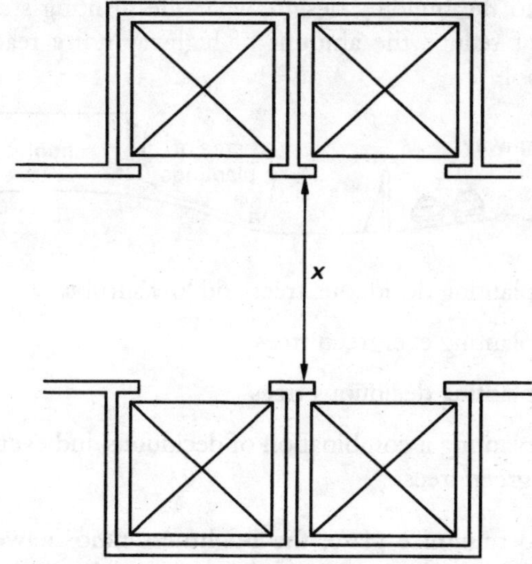

(A) 8 ft

(B) 10 ft

(C) 12 ft

(D) 14 ft

295. An architect is designing a nursing home with 150 beds. The patients have varying levels of mobility and independence. The building manager requests a heating, ventilating, and air conditioning (HVAC) system that permits each patient to control the temperature in his or her own room, that is quiet, and that requires minimal maintenance. Which type of system will be the most appropriate recommendation?

(A) packaged terminal units

(B) fan coil terminals

(C) variable air volume

(D) single duct, constant air volume

296. Which of the following principles is best exemplified by the "whispering arch" at Union Station in St. Louis, Missouri?

(A) focusing

(B) creep

(C) diffusion

(D) specular reflection

297. Which of the following statements regarding conduit and other pipes embedded in concrete slabs is true? (Choose the four that apply.)

(A) The minimum concrete cover over conduit and other pipes should be at least $^3/_4$ in.

(B) Conduit should always be placed in the lower half of the structural slab.

(C) Aluminum conduit may be used instead of steel conduit when it is fully embedded within a concrete slab.

(D) The outside diameter of the conduit should be no larger than $^1/_3$ of the thickness of the slab.

(E) Pipes carrying fluids or gases must be pressure tested prior to concrete placement.

(F) Plastic pipe cannot be used in concrete slabs.

298. Which of the following spaces should be acoustically "live"? (Choose the two that apply.)

(A) talk radio recording studio

(B) cathedral featuring an antique German pipe organ

(C) opera house

(D) community playhouse often used for poetry recitation

(E) university lecture hall

(F) movie theater

299. In case of a fire, which of these can be activated by building occupants? (Choose the three that apply.)

(A) fire extinguishers

(B) dry standpipes

(C) wet standpipes

(D) fusible links

(E) annunciators

(F) two-way communications devices

300. Which natural cooling technique is utilized by the Pantheon?

(A) stack ventilation

(B) pools of water

(C) thermal mass

(D) cross ventilation

301. What is the most likely location for a vernacular American home with the following first-floor plan?

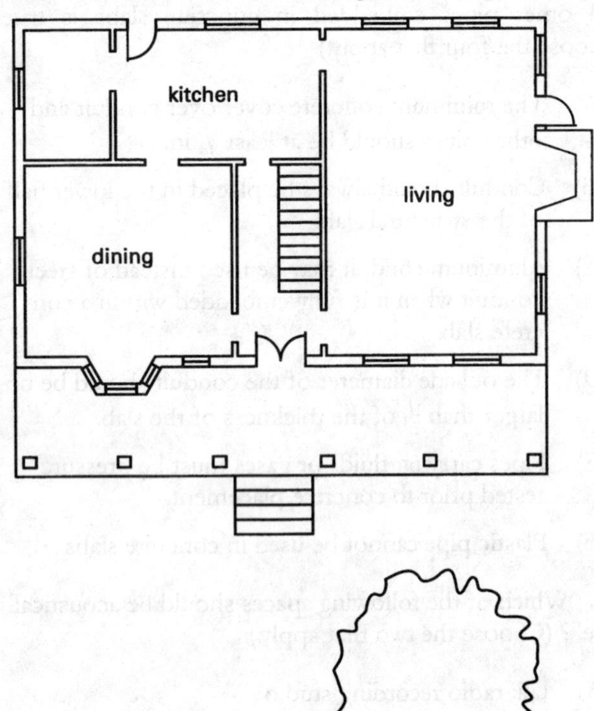

(A) Vermont

(B) Louisiana

(C) Montana

(D) Maryland

302. Production of which of the following refrigerants has been banned in the United States? (Choose the two that apply.)

(A) halon

(B) chlorofluorocarbon (CFC)

(C) hydrofluorocarbon (HFC)

(D) hydrochlorofluorocarbon (HCFC)

(E) volatile organic compound (VOC)

(F) Freon

303. A school is planned for a site near a major interstate. In addition to sound attenuation strategies to be incorporated into the building design, what site planting strategy will most reduce the amount of highway noise reaching the school?

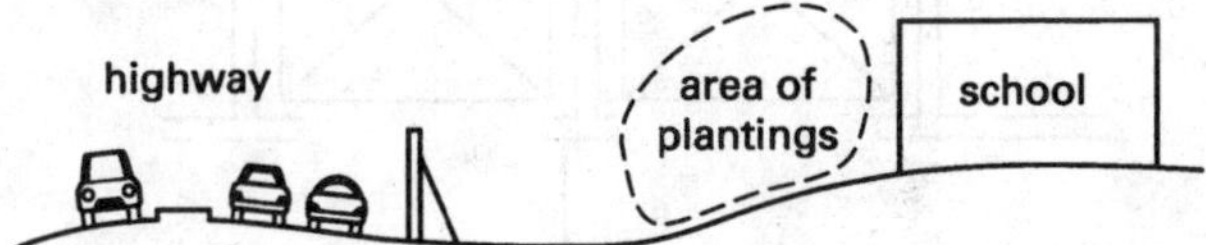

(A) planting deciduous trees and low shrubs

(B) planting evergreen trees

(C) planting deciduous trees

(D) planting a combination of deciduous and evergreen trees

304. To minimize glare, the brightness ratio between a task and its adjacent surroundings should be limited to approximately

(A) 1:½

(B) 1:⅓

(C) 1:⅕

(D) 1:$^1/_{10}$

Project Planning

305. Values in the area indicated on the following psychrometric chart call for

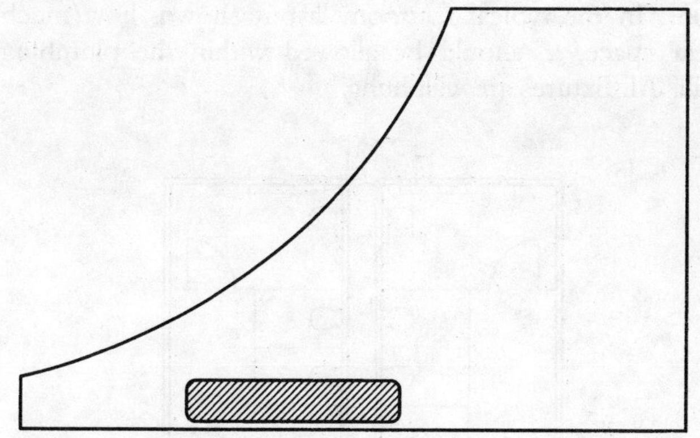

(A) dehumidification

(B) evaporative cooling

(C) passive solar heating

(D) humidification

306. Assuming that the capacity of each type of plant is the same, which type of heating, ventilating, and air conditioning (HVAC) system occupies the most space within the building?

(A) forced air

(B) radiant

(C) hydronic

(D) unitary

307. Which of the following buildings will be a good application of demand-controlled ventilation (DCV) technology?

(A) pet store

(B) locker room

(C) bowling alley

(D) dry cleaner

308. Which of the following is a type of perimeter security system?

(A) photoelectric cells

(B) pressure sensors

(C) ultrasonic detectors

(D) photoelectric beams

309. Which elevator operating system is the most appropriate choice for a four-story luxury apartment building with two passenger elevators?

(A) selective collective operation

(B) computerized system control

(C) single automatic push-button control

(D) collective control

310. Determine an appropriate spacing for ceiling diffusers in the space shown.

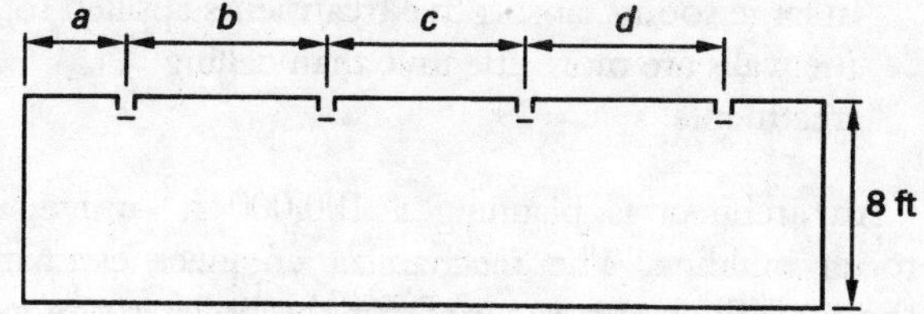

(not to scale)

(A) $a = 3$ ft, $b = 6$ ft, $c = 6$ ft, $d = 6$ ft

(B) $a = 2$ ft, $b = 4$ ft, $c = 4$ ft, $d = 4$ ft

(C) $a = 4$ ft, $b = 8$ ft, $c = 8$ ft, $d = 8$ ft

(D) $a = 3$ ft, $b = 6$ ft, $c = 8$ ft, $d = 6$ ft

311. A curtain board is

(A) used to block sunlight entering a space

(B) a part of a suspended wall assembly

(C) used to restrict movement of smoke and flame

(D) used to direct light toward the ceiling for even, reflected illumination

312. Which type of photovoltaic (PV) cell produces the most power?

(A) thin-film

(B) crystalline

(C) polycrystalline

(D) amorphous

313. Which of the following statements about absorption is true?

(A) The absorption coefficient of a room should be between 1.20 and 2.50.

(B) To produce a clearly noticeable reduction in noise, the absorption in a room should be doubled.

(C) Even a small hole in a 10 ft by 10 ft partition, such as that caused by unsealed electrical receptacles placed back to back, can make the partition effectively useless for blocking sound.

(D) In large rooms, absorptive treatments applied to the walls are more effective than ceiling treatments.

314. An architect is planning a 100,000 ft^2 university classroom building. The mechanical engineer estimates that the total floor area required for the boiler room and the chilled water plant will be about 3000 ft^2. Which of the following criteria should also be kept in mind when determining the location and design of the mechanical rooms? (Choose the three that apply.)

(A) Each mechanical room should have at least one exterior wall.

(B) The boiler room should be adjacent to the chilled water plant.

(C) Rooms should be as square as possible.

(D) Ceilings in both rooms should be at least 12 ft high.

(E) Mechanical rooms must be placed on the ground floor.

(F) The mechanical rooms should be equal in size.

315. Plumbing fixtures in large buildings are often placed back to back, and restrooms are stacked from floor to floor. In the typical restroom layout shown, how much clear space, x, should be allowed within the plumbing wall? All fixtures are wall hung.

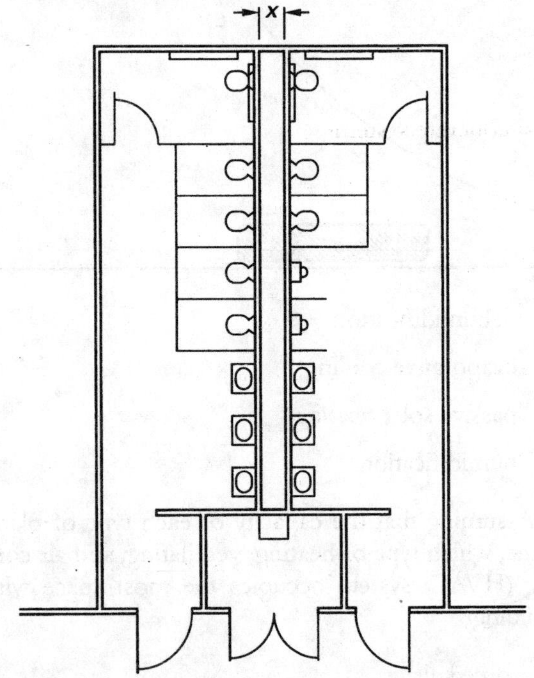

(A) 12 in

(B) 16 in

(C) 18 in

(D) 24 in

316. Which chart most accurately represents the distribution of energy use for a large office building?

(A)

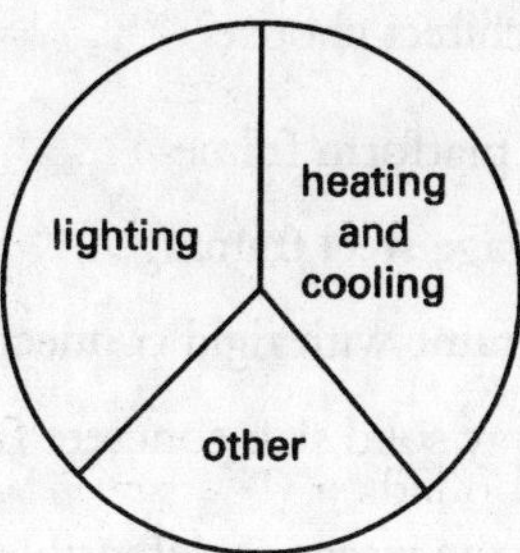

(B)

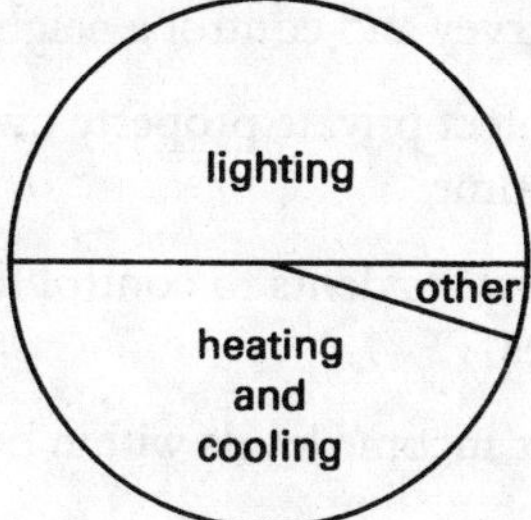

(C)

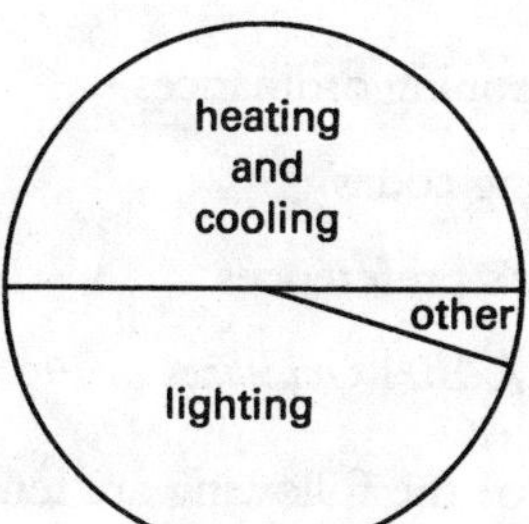

(D)

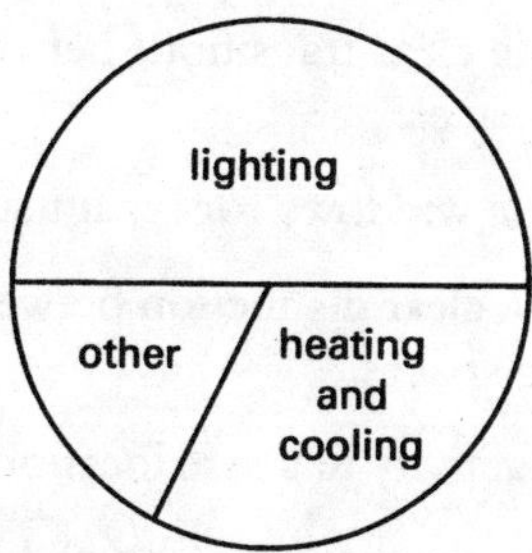

317. Which of the following building types has the highest percentage of total construction cost allocated for heating, ventilating, and air conditioning (HVAC)?

(A) full-service, sit-down restaurant

(B) climate controlled mini-warehouse

(C) hospital

(D) parking garage

318. A high school teacher is standing at the front of a classroom delivering a lecture to a class of 25 students. Students in the front row, 3 ft in front of the teacher's lectern, perceive the teacher's voice at 65 dB. What is the decibel level of the teacher's voice in the back row, 12 ft from the lectern?

(A) 53 dB

(B) 56 dB

(C) 59 dB

(D) 65 dB

319. Which type of glass is the most appropriate choice for a location in the northeastern United States?

(A) low-ε

(B) reflective

(C) tinted

(D) triple-pane

320. What is the best passive cooling strategy during the summer in a hot-humid climate?

(A) Design a series of pools and fountains to cool by evaporation.

(B) Include broad overhangs to shield glass and outdoor activities from the sun.

(C) Orient the building to catch summer breezes.

(D) Use light-colored surfaces to reflect sunlight and reduce solar gain.

321. The design occupant load of a hotel ballroom is determined by

(A) drawing proposed layouts of the room for receptions, meetings, and dining, and figuring out how many chairs will fit into the space in each scenario

(B) dividing the total square footage of the space by a factor that allocates space for each person

(C) multiplying the number of people expected to use the space by an assumed weight per person

(D) asking the conference services manager how many people must be accommodated in the space

Project Planning

322. Where does a common path of egress travel end?

(A) in an area of refuge

(B) at the exterior exit from the building

(C) at the point where an individual has a choice about which direction to go to reach an exit

(D) at a public way

323. Which of the following is most likely to be found in a local zoning ordinance?

(A) minimum setbacks from property lines

(B) maximum occupancy

(C) fire-rated assemblies

(D) types of materials that may be used for construction

324. When is the ideal time to "value engineer" a project?

(A) in the initial planning stages

(B) at the end of the design development phase

(C) after the construction documents have been completed

(D) after bids are received and they all exceed the owner's budget

325. In life-cycle cost analysis, costs incurred prior to the baseline date are referred to as

(A) uniform costs

(B) break-even costs

(C) sunk costs

(D) sensitive costs

326. Retainage at substantial completion is frequently equivalent to

(A) a percentage of incomplete items

(B) the contractor's overhead

(C) the cost of bonds

(D) the contractor's profit

327. An architect is designing a four-story hotel. The architect wishes to expose the structural system while maintaining a high fire-resistance rating and needs to minimize construction time. Which type of framing system should the architect choose?

(A) wood platform frame

(B) light-gage steel framing

(C) steel frame with rigid connections

(D) one-way solid slab concrete frame

328. What is the intent of defensible space?

(A) to design spaces so that law enforcement can better survey and control a neighborhood

(B) to protect private property owners from vandalism and crime

(C) to allow residents to control the areas around their homes

(D) to mix income levels within housing facilities

329. Which of the following determines minimum parking requirements for a specific site?

(A) local zoning ordinances

(B) building codes

(C) owner's preferences

(D) *ADA/ABA Guidelines*

330. Which of the following are tenets of Crime Prevention Through Environmental Design (CPTED)? (Choose the four that apply.)

(A) Provide clear transitions between public and private spaces.

(B) Provide windows for tenant surveillance.

(C) Make a clear distinction between public and semipublic spaces.

(D) Place activity in a safe location.

(E) Encourage the use of keypad locks.

(F) Locate stairways near heavily used areas.

Project Planning

331. Which of the following generally is required to comply with a site setback? (Choose the four that apply.)

(A) bay window

(B) roof overhang

(C) fence

(D) detached garage

(E) landscaping

(F) deck

332. The approach to town planning known as "new urbanism" advocates which of the following design strategies? (Choose the four that apply.)

(A) narrow streets and frequent intersections

(B) mixed-use occupancies, such as apartments over retail shops

(C) parallel parking

(D) front porches on houses

(E) parallel parking

(F) large parks to serve a district

333. The height of a proposed building will be most influenced by the decision to use

(A) daylighting

(B) indirect lighting

(C) underfloor ventilation systems

(D) interstitial spaces

334. A new restaurant has a maximum occupancy of 300 people. For all exits, the building code requires an allowance of 0.2 in per occupant. Calculate the minimum number and size of exits.

(A) one exit, 5 ft 0 in pair of doors

(B) one exit, 6 ft 0 in pair of doors

(C) two exits, two 30 in doors

(D) two exits, two 3 ft 0 in doors

335. The architect can minimize the heat island effect of impervious site paving by selecting a material with

(A) low albedo

(B) high albedo

(C) low conductivity

(D) high conductivity

336. Which of the following statements regarding blast-resistant design is true?

(A) L-shaped buildings can minimize blast effects.

(B) Float glass can be used if properly framed.

(C) Blast energy decreases in inverse proportion to the square of the distance.

(D) Standoff distance should be maximized.

337. An architect is laying out the house sewer for a small commercial building. The sewer has been sized at a 6 in diameter with a $1/8$ in/ft slope. The architect discovers that the original information on the invert of the main sewer line, which is approximately 300 ft away, was incorrect and that it is actually 1 ft higher than planned. In order to minimize cost, what is the best course of action?

(A) Decrease the slope and increase the size of the house sewer.

(B) Angle the house sewer to connect farther down the main line.

(C) Change the location of the building.

(D) Decrease the slope of the sewer and add an intermediate manhole.

338. The maximum area of signage on the exterior of a building is most commonly regulated by

(A) building codes

(B) restrictive covenants

(C) state laws

(D) zoning ordinances

339. To determine the regulations that pertain to a planned development around a wetlands area, which of the following should the architect investigate? (Choose the three that apply.)

(A) local governmental rules

(B) local building codes

(C) state governmental rules

(D) U.S. Army Corps of Engineers regulations

(E) development covenants

(F) zoning ordinances

340. Which schematic layout is most appropriate for a site in a neighborhood dominated by Baroque planning concepts?

(A) 

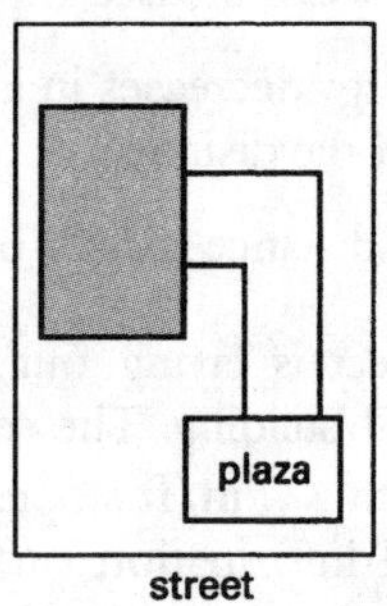

(B)

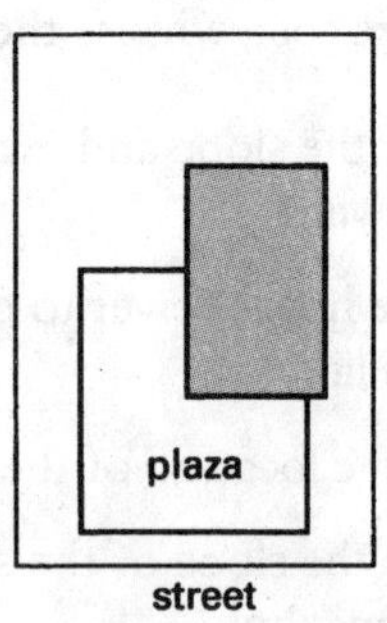

(C)

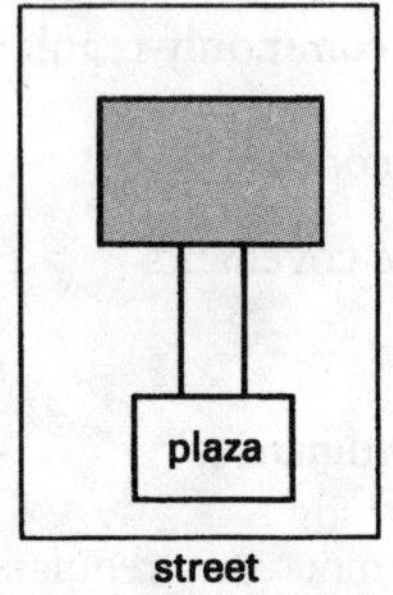

(D)

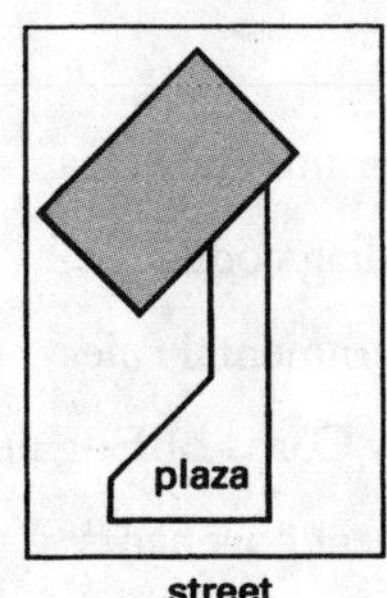

341. Which building type is most appropriate for a retail store in an urban setting?

(A) courtyard building

(B) perimeter yard building

(C) rear yard building

(D) side yard building

342. Which of the following is a good strategy for minimizing light pollution on a site?

(A) eliminate parking lot lighting

(B) employ light bollards instead of pole-mounted luminaires

(C) specify high-reflectance surfaces

(D) reduce light trespass at night from inside buildings on the site

343. An architect is designing an exterior pedestrian walk. In one area, there is a change in level of 12 in. The transition must be made within a horizontal distance of no more than 14 ft. Which of the following design solutions is most appropriate?

(A) two steps with 6 in risers

(B) three steps with 4 in risers

(C) a ramp 14 ft long

(D) two steps with 6 in risers and a ramp 12 ft long

344. What type of electronic security system best protects the exterior of an office building?

(A) audio alarms

(B) motion sensors

(C) thermal detectors

(D) video surveillance

345. Which site design elements for fire protection are the responsibility of the architect? (Choose the four that apply.)

(A) position and size of building canopies

(B) surface material outside of the building

(C) traffic control fences and bollard positions

(D) maximum fire hydrant spacing on the street

(E) utility poles and overhead utility lines

(F) width of fire apparatus access drives

346. In a residential subdivision, which of the following are the most effective in reducing the potential for criminal activity? (Choose the four that apply.)

(A) using low plantings to define property lines

(B) positioning exterior entry doors visible to the street or neighbors

(C) designing stairways within solid structures

(D) locating common areas within the view of a number of residential windows

(E) orienting living areas toward the backyard

(F) making walks from the street to the houses as short and direct as possible

347. Which of the following is an ideal design strategy for a building in a hot-arid climate?

(A) minimizing thermal mass

(B) locating large windows for cross ventilation

(C) shading east and west facing windows

(D) using a compact form

348. The most important characteristic of an on-site road designed to serve parking areas and service vehicles is the

(A) slope

(B) tangent

(C) horizontal alignment

(D) vertical alignment

349. Which of the following outdoor deck materials is most comfortable and best moderates the microclimate around a house in a temperate zone?

(A) red brick pavers

(B) light colored concrete

(C) grass between stone pavers

(D) dark wood decking

350. What is especially important in designing roads for drainage?

(A) curbs and gutters

(B) crown

(C) catch basin

(D) superelevation

351. Wastewater flows because of differences in elevation

(A) between catch basin entrances

(B) between storm sewer vents

(C) between drain inlets

(D) along inverts

352. Reinforced concrete or masonry retaining walls are usually necessary when

(A) the height of the wall exceeds 4 ft

(B) expansive clay soil is present

(C) the groundwater level is above the lowest exposed portion of the wall

(D) drainage behind the retaining wall is a problem

353. Corners and eaves are generally

(A) subject to higher wind forces

(B) subject to lower wind forces

(C) subject to the same amount of wind forces as the rest of the building

(D) not affected by wind forces

354. Which of the following factors affect the wind pressure on a building? (Choose the four that apply.)

(A) wind speed

(B) terrain surrounding the building

(C) soil type

(D) building height

(E) building weight

(F) building shape

355. The moment-resisting frame is an appropriate system to use for resisting wind forces in

(A) low-rise buildings only

(B) low-rise buildings and high-rise buildings of 30 stories or less

(C) high-rise buildings of approximately 50 stories

(D) high-rise buildings of any height

356. Wood I-joists generally can be used for spans

(A) up to about 20 ft

(B) up to about 30 ft

(C) up to about 45 ft

(D) exceeding 100 ft

357. What types of buildings are most suited for a pan joist concrete system?

(A) industrial and storage buildings

(B) residential buildings

(C) hotels

(D) office buildings

358. Which of the following factors affect a building's response to an earthquake? (Choose the four that apply.)

(A) soil type

(B) local temperature

(C) building form

(D) building orientation

(E) building weight

(F) structural materials and system

359. Which of the following floor plans represents the best design for lateral loads?

(A)

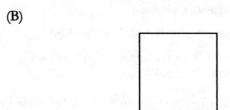

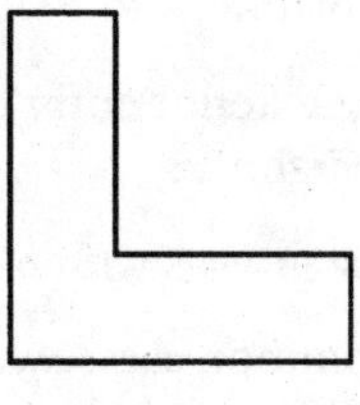

(B)

(C)

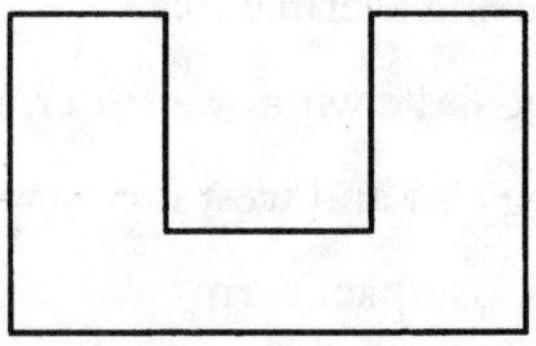

(D)

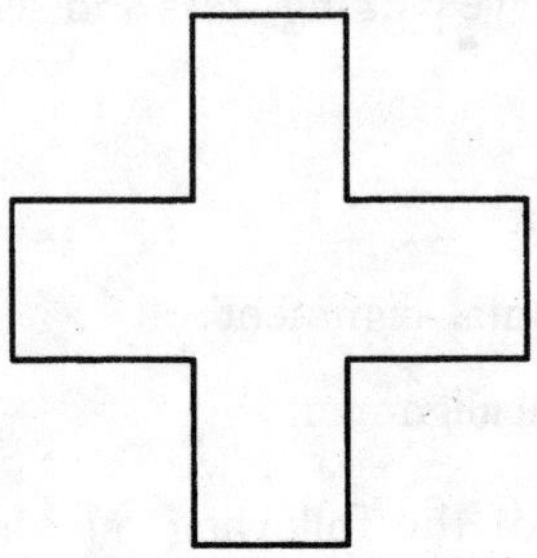

360. Which of the following building elevations is problematic for lateral loads and must be avoided?

(A)

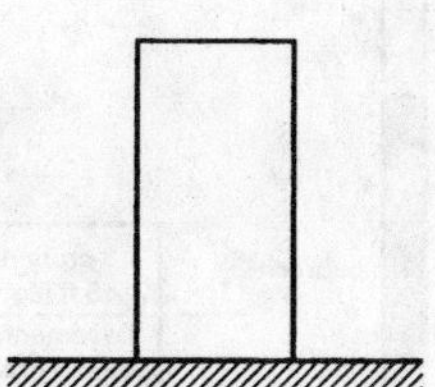

(B)

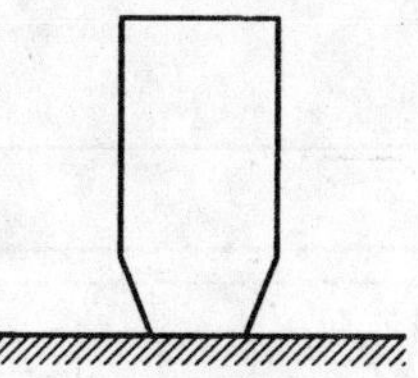

(C)

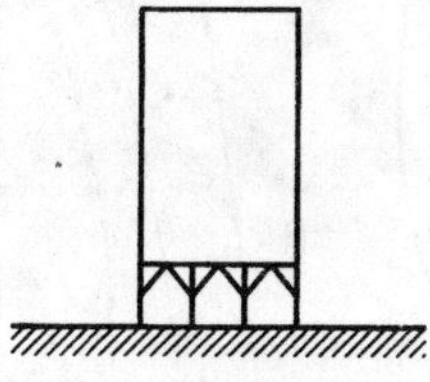

(D)

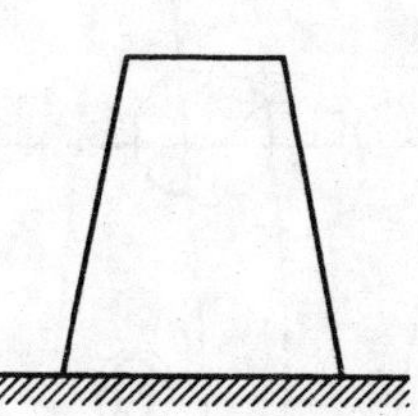

361. Which of the following types of piles has the lowest initial cost and least load-bearing capacity?

(A) steel piles

(B) precast concrete piles

(C) cast-in-place concrete piles

(D) timber piles

362. Which of the following earthquake effects or damages are covered by the building code? (Choose the three that apply.)

(A) ground shaking

(B) landslides

(C) avalanches

(D) horizontal movement

(E) soil liquefaction

(F) vibration effects

363. An architect is designing and detailing an exterior cladding system. Which constraints and issues should the architect consider? (Choose the three that apply.)

(A) zoning ordinance

(B) building code

(C) state energy code

(D) ASTM standards

(E) local fire department

(F) city planning board

364. During the design of a restaurant, the architect discovers that a local building code amendment conflicts with state health department requirements. What action should the architect take?

(A) Appeal to the health department.

(B) Ask for a ruling from the building department.

(C) Have the client resolve the issue.

(D) Design to the most restrictive requirement.

Illustration for Prob. 365

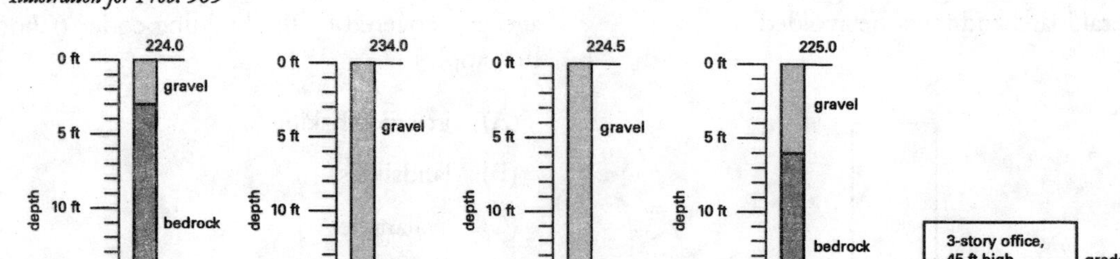

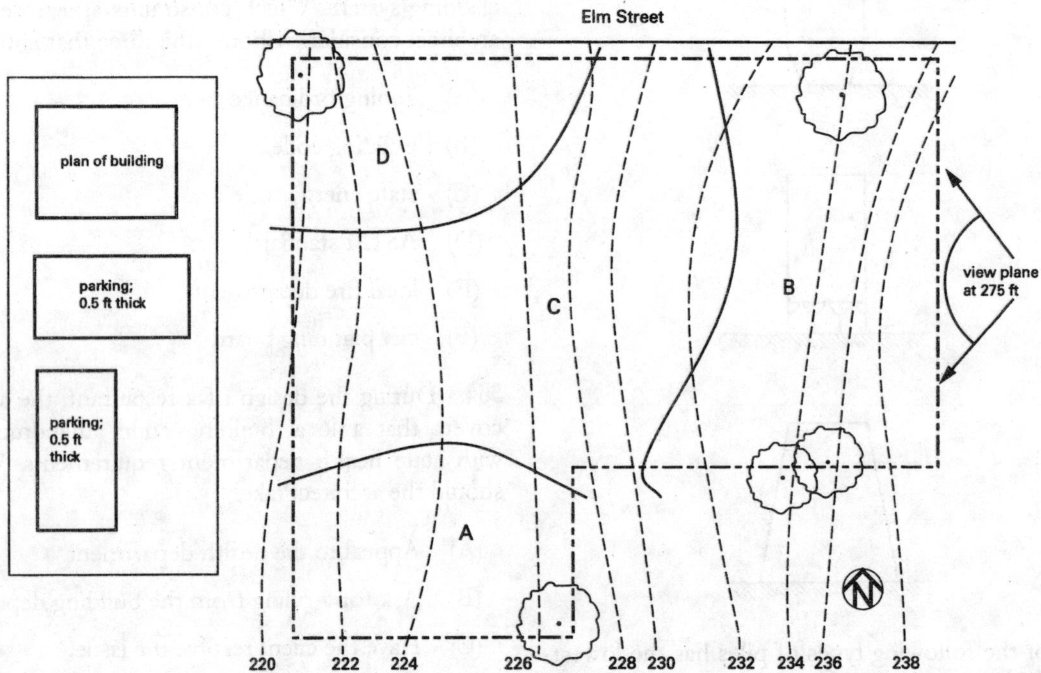

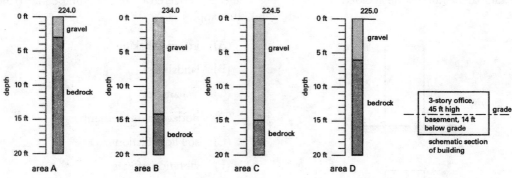

365. A new building and a parking lot are being planned on an empty lot, as shown. Elm Street borders the north side of the empty lot. The test borings show the approximate soil conditions in the four parts of the site labeled A, B, C, and D. No building can encroach above the view plane on the east side of the site. The parking area must have 2 ft of new fill below a slab 0.5 ft thick. The remaining area on the site will be landscaped open space.

Consider community context, vehicular and pedestrian access, and solar orientation. On the illustration shown, place one building and one parking area in such a way that minimizes site development costs.

366. The site plan shown borders Decatur Street to the south and 13th Avenue to the east. A lake borders the site to the west. An existing shopping center borders the site to the north. The site contains a five-story apartment building, a connecting plaza, and a cafe/bookstore. To the east of the buildings is a parking lot, with three accessible parking spaces nearest the apartment building. The site plan shown poses a potential problem for *Americans with Disabilities Act* (ADA) accessibility and community development. Place the hot spot marker in the site area where an element should be included to meet ADA requirements.

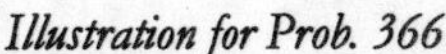

Illustration for Prob. 366

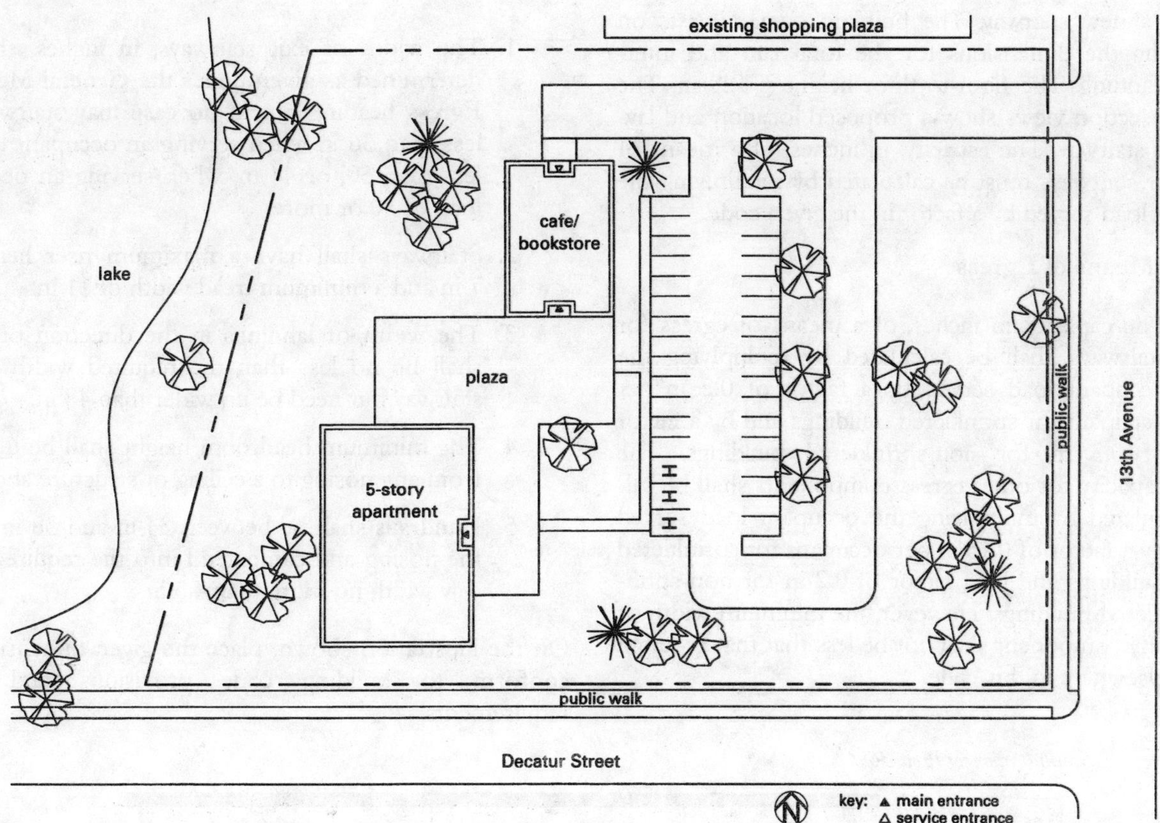

367. When determining the massing of a building during preliminary design, what should the architect research first?

(A) view ordinances

(B) zoning regulations

(C) utility easements

(D) municipal master plan

368. During preliminary planning for a middle school, the architect realizes that the school district facilities management department requires a larger building than is allowed by current zoning setbacks. How can the architect resolve the conflict?

(A) Ask the school board to reduce the space needs.

(B) Appeal to the planning commission.

(C) Suggest the school apply for a variance.

(D) Apply for a conditional use permit.

369. Inside a two-story building, a building owner wants to build a new stairway. The building owner insists on minimizing the dimensions for the total run and intermediate landing. The floor-to-floor height is 129 in. The plan and section views show a proposed location and layout for a stairway. The capacity, in inches, of a means of egress for stairways must be calculated by multiplying the occupant load served by a factor in the given code.

General Means of Egress

1. The capacity, in inches, of a means of egress for stairways shall be calculated by multiplying the occupant load served by a factor of 0.2 in per occupant for sprinklered buildings and by a factor of 0.3 in for non-sprinklered buildings. The capacity for other egress components shall be calculated by multiplying the occupant load served by a factor of 0.15 in per occupant for sprinklered buildings and by a factor of 0.2 in for non-sprinklered buildings. However, the minimum width of any component shall not be less that that required elsewhere in this code.

Stairways

1. The width of exit stairways, in inches, shall be determined as given under the General Means of Egress heading but in no case may stairways be less than 36 in when serving an occupant load of less than 50, or 44 in, when serving an occupant load of 50 or more.
2. Stairways shall have a maximum riser height of 7 in and a minimum tread width of 11 in.
3. The width of landings in the direction of travel shall be no less than the required width of the stairway but need be no wider than 48 in.
4. The minimum headroom height shall be 6 ft 8 in from any nosing to a ceiling or structure above.
5. Handrails shall be between 34 in and 38 in above the nosing and can extend into the required stairway width no more than 4.5 in.

On the illustration shown, place the given dimensions to conform to building code provisions and meet requirements.

Illustration for Prob. 369

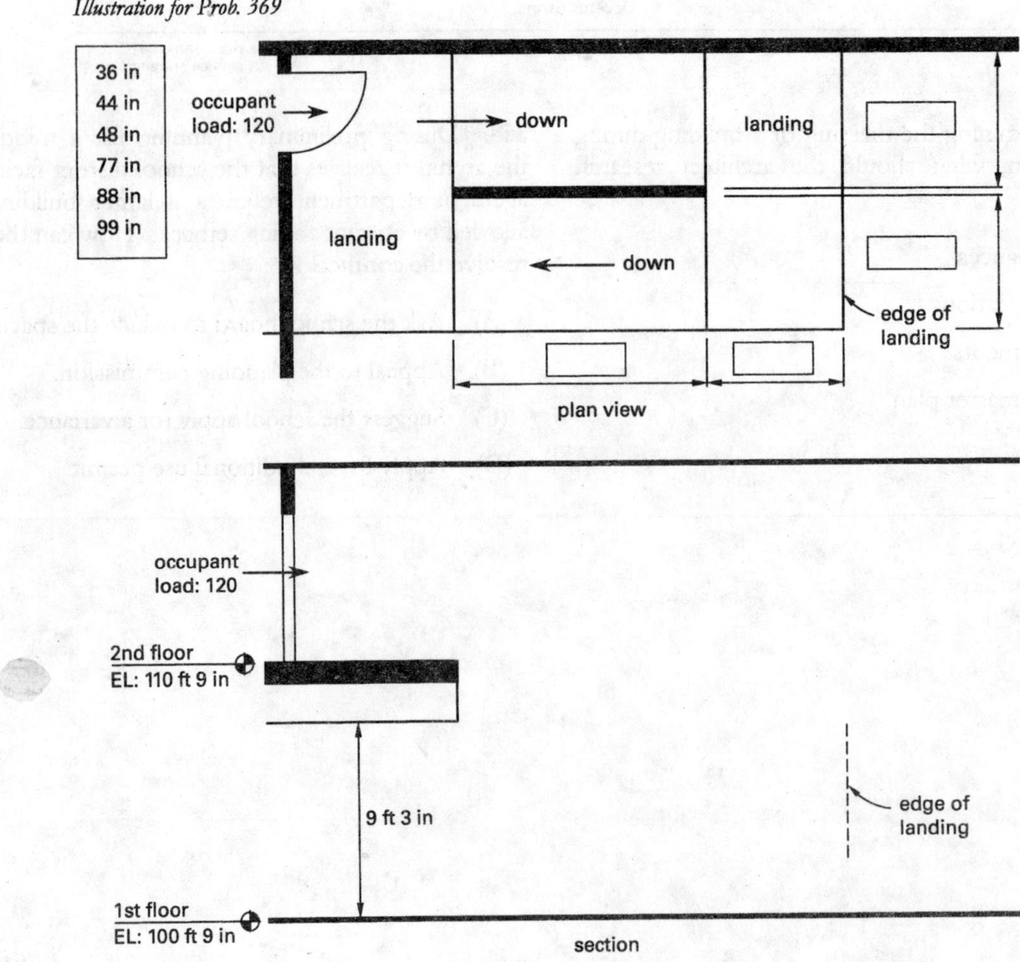

Project Planning

Table for Prob. 370

zoning district[a]	setback			height limits		requirements per gross floor area or unit	
	front	side	rear	feet	stories	parking[b]	bicycle
R-1[c]	25	15	15	30[d]	2	2 spaces and 350 ft^2	NR
R-2[b]	25	10	5	45	3	2 spaces/unit	NR
R-3	10	5	10	65	5	1.25 spaces/unit	1/3 units
M-1	5	5	5	70	5	1/1000 ft^2	1/10,000 ft^2
M-2	0	0	5	110	8	2/1000 ft^2	1/10,000 ft^2
B-1	10	0	5	110	8	1/1000 ft^2	1/5000 ft^2
B-2	10	0	0	150	12	1/guest room or unit	1/5000 ft^2
B-3	5	0	0	250	20	2/1000 ft^2	1/10,000 ft^2
I-1	30	15	10	50	3	0.5/1000 ft^2	NR
I-2	30	10	5	55	3	0.5/1000 ft^2	NR
UE-1[b]	10	5	10	50[d]	3	2.5/1000 ft^2	NR
UE-2[b]	5	5	10	70[e]	5	2/1000 ft^2	1/5000 ft^2

[a]R: residential; M: mixed use; B: business; I: industrial; UE: urban edge
[b]See specific zone district requirements for additional information.
[c]The maximum height can be increased 1 ft for every 5 ft increase in lot width over 50 ft up to a maximum of 35 ft.
[d]Bulk plane limit required for side setbacks beginning on the property line at a point 10 ft above grade and extending at an angle of 45°.
[e]An upper story setback of 15 ft is required above 30 ft.

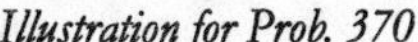

Illustration for Prob. 370

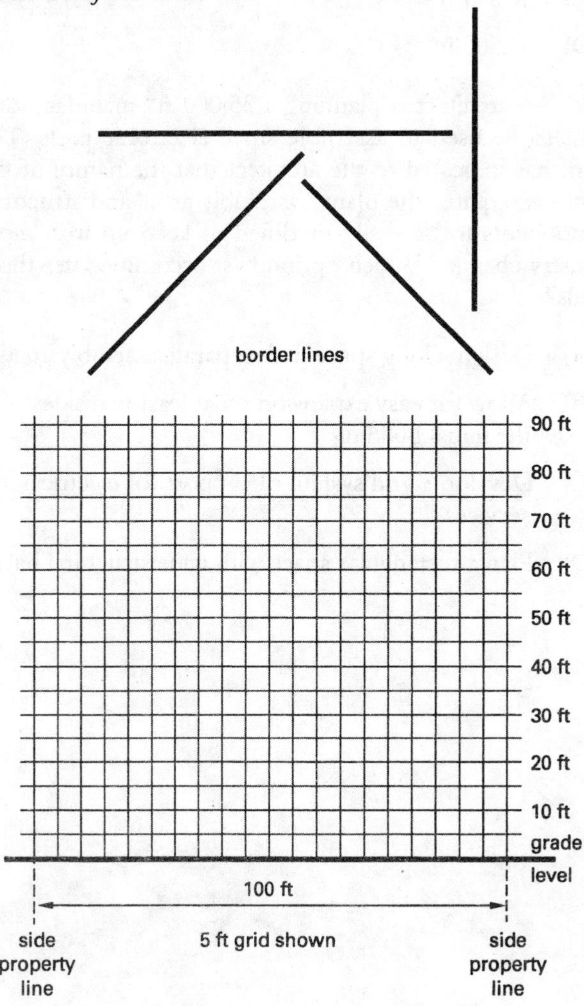

370. A five-story mixed-use building is being planned in a UE-2 zoning district. The zoning requirements are given in the table.

Using the zoning information given in the table, draw lines on the elevation diagram grid to indicate the maximum allowable profile of the building. The lines may overlap or cross, and as many lines as are required may be used.

371. An architect is designing a medium-sized urgent care center. During the project's programming phase, the client asks the architect to design the site so that visitors always know where they are in the building and how to get to their destination. Which design concept does the architect use to meet the client's request?

(A) Establish the floor plan as a grid system to provide multiple paths to destinations.

(B) Develop a signage system with large graphics to orient visitors to their position.

(C) Use color-coded stripes in the flooring to direct visitors to the correct department.

(D) Centralize the reception space and waiting lobby with corridors radiating from it.

372. An architect is incorporating a circulation scheme into a building layout with certain mechanical and structural constraints. The circulation scheme must provide the location for mechanical system distribution and must allow for a simple post-and-beam or bearing wall structural system. Which scheme is the most effective?

(A) grid system

(B) circular loop

(C) radial configuration

(D) linear layout

373. An architect is designing an office building in a long, narrow shape, with as much open space and glass as possible. Creating such a building configuration is an example of

(A) structural efficient design

(B) evidence-based design

(C) social hierarchy minimization

(D) current cultural precedence

374. An architect is sketching ideas for a new mixed-use project in a downtown historic area dominated by two-story buildings built to the sidewalk and the side lot lines. The program for the new building requires four stories. The lot has enough area to allow some open space. Although there are no historic district restrictions, how can the architect respect the neighborhood and still provide the required programmed space?

(A) Match the two-story height along the existing building line and set back the upper stories.

(B) Set the new building back from the sidewalk by 10 ft to de-emphasize its presence.

(C) Build the full height of the new building at the sidewalk line to provide contrast.

(D) Re-create the materials, colors, and details of the existing buildings in the new structure.

375. An architect is asked to design a program requiring many primary adjacencies and easy movement of people and supplies. This program does not allow for easy expansion. What organization layout works for such a program?

(A) central

(B) grid

(C) linear

(D) radial

376. Programming for a neighborhood library has determined that the building will need 25,000 ft^2 of net assignable space. The program calls for all spaces to be on one level with minimal circulation space estimated at 10%. Historical planning for the city's libraries has shown an average efficiency ratio of 80%. The architect should plan for ____ of total building area when doing initial site planning. (Fill in the blank.)

(A) 28,500 ft^2

(B) 30,000 ft^2

(C) 31,250 ft^2

(D) 35,500 ft^2

377. An architect is planning a 35,000 ft^2 manufacturing plant to be used to assemble small electronic parts. The client has indicated to the architect that the nature of the business requires the plant's assembly areas and structural components to be easily modified to keep up with rapid industry changes. Which option best accommodates these needs?

(A) Design a long space with separate assembly areas.

(B) Allow for easy expansion on at least two sides of the initial building.

(C) Develop a grid system of support for electrical services.

(D) Plan a rectangular space with wide structural bays.

378. A two-story office building is being planned in a temperate climate zone for the site shown. The site is bounded on two sides by streets.

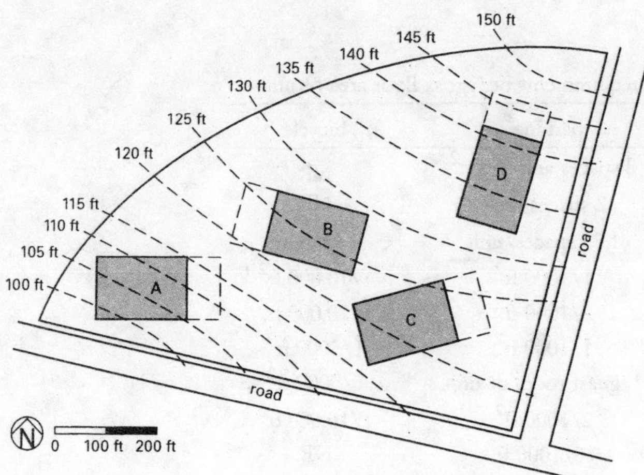

The program requires a sustainable design, the ability to integrate both passive and active solar design into the building, an expansion of the building in the lengthwise direction, and the addition of more buildings as the site is fully developed. The architect is considering four locations for the building. The remainder of the site will be used for the additional buildings, landscaping, and parking. Which building location meets the program requirements?

(A) A

(B) B

(C) C

(D) D

379. An architect is working on a preliminary planning study for an elementary school. The school is being designed for 750 students: 400 girls and 350 boys. From the following sample code, a total of ____ water closets are required. (Fill in the blank.)

Plumbing fixture requirements for pupils' use:

water closets:
- 1 per 100 males
- 1 per 35 females

lavatories:
- 1 per 50 students

urinals:
- 1 per 30 male students

drinking fountains:
- 1 per 150 students

380. An architect is planning a small day care center for three- to six-year-old children. The space needs are given in the table.

space	area (ft^2)	location requirements
administrator office	150	near entry
assistant's office	150	directly adjacent to administrator's office
staff lounge	200	–
children's toilets	200	adjacent to classrooms and outdoor play area
kitchen	250	adjacent to multipurpose room
storage	250	–
adult toilets	300	–
entry and reception	400	at drop-off area
classroom I	500	directly adjacent to outdoor play area
classroom II	500	directly adjacent to outdoor play area
multipurpose room	600	adjacent to storage
outdoor play area	3000	–

When designing the center, what are the most important issues that the architect must consider? (Choose the three that apply.)

(A) educational needs

(B) relationship to outdoor spaces

(C) toilet rooms

(D) exits

(E) children's storage areas

(F) multipurpose room location

381. An architect has designed a parking lot and landscaping around the lot's west and south sides. Minimum dimensions are required along the drive, the standard stalls, and the right-of-ways.

Form and Parking Summary

zoning district[a]	setback: front	setback: side	setback: rear	height limits: feet	height limits: stories	requirements per gross floor area or unit: parking[b]	requirements per gross floor area or unit: bicycle
R-1[c]	25	15	15	30[d]	2	2 spaces and 350 ft^2	NR
R-2[b]	25	10	5	45	3	2 spaces/unit	NR
R-3	10	5	10	65	5	1.25 spaces/unit	1/3 units
M-1	5	5	5	70	5	1/1000 ft^2	1/10,000 ft^2
M-2	0	0	5	110	8	2/1000 ft^2	1/10,000 ft^2
B-1	10	0	5	110	8	1/1000 ft^2	1/5000 ft^2
B-2	10	0	0	150	12	1/guest room or unit	1/5000 ft^2
B-3	5	0	0	250	20	2/1000 ft^2	1/10,000 ft^2
I-1	30	15	10	50	3	0.5/1000 ft^2	NR
I-2	30	10	5	55	3	0.5/1000 ft^2	NR
UE-1[b]	10	5	10	50[d]	3	2.5/1000 ft^2	NR
UE-2[b]	5	5	10	70[e]	5	2/1000 ft^2	1/5000 ft^2

[a]R: residential; M: mixed use; B: business; I: industrial; UE: urban edge
[b]See specific zone district requirements for additional information.
[c]The maximum height can be increased 1 ft for every 5 ft increase in lot width over 50 ft up to a maximum of 35 ft.
[d]Bulk plane limit required for side setbacks beginning on the property line at a point 10 ft above grade and extending at an angle of 45°.
[e]An upper story setback of 15 ft is required above 30 ft.

Parking Dimensions[a,b]

angle	A	B	C	D	E	F	G	H
parking angle	stall width	stall length	projection	aisle width: one-way/ two-way	module: one-way	module: two-way	stall width projection	interlock
standard parking space: 9 ft × 19 ft								
0°	9	23	9	13/24	21	33	23	–
30°	9	19	17.3	13/20	47.6	54.6	18	7.8
45°	9	19	19.8	13/20	52.6	59.6	12.7	6.4
60°	9	19	21	16/20	58	62	10.4	4.5
90°	9	19	19	24/24	62	62	9	–

[a]All dimensions are given in feet.
[b]The minimum internal drive width shall be 10 ft for one-way traffic and 20 ft for two-way traffic. Internal drives are those used for vehicular circulation, but which do not abut parking stalls in a way that allows for their use for vehicular access to the parking stalls.

Illustration for Prob. 381

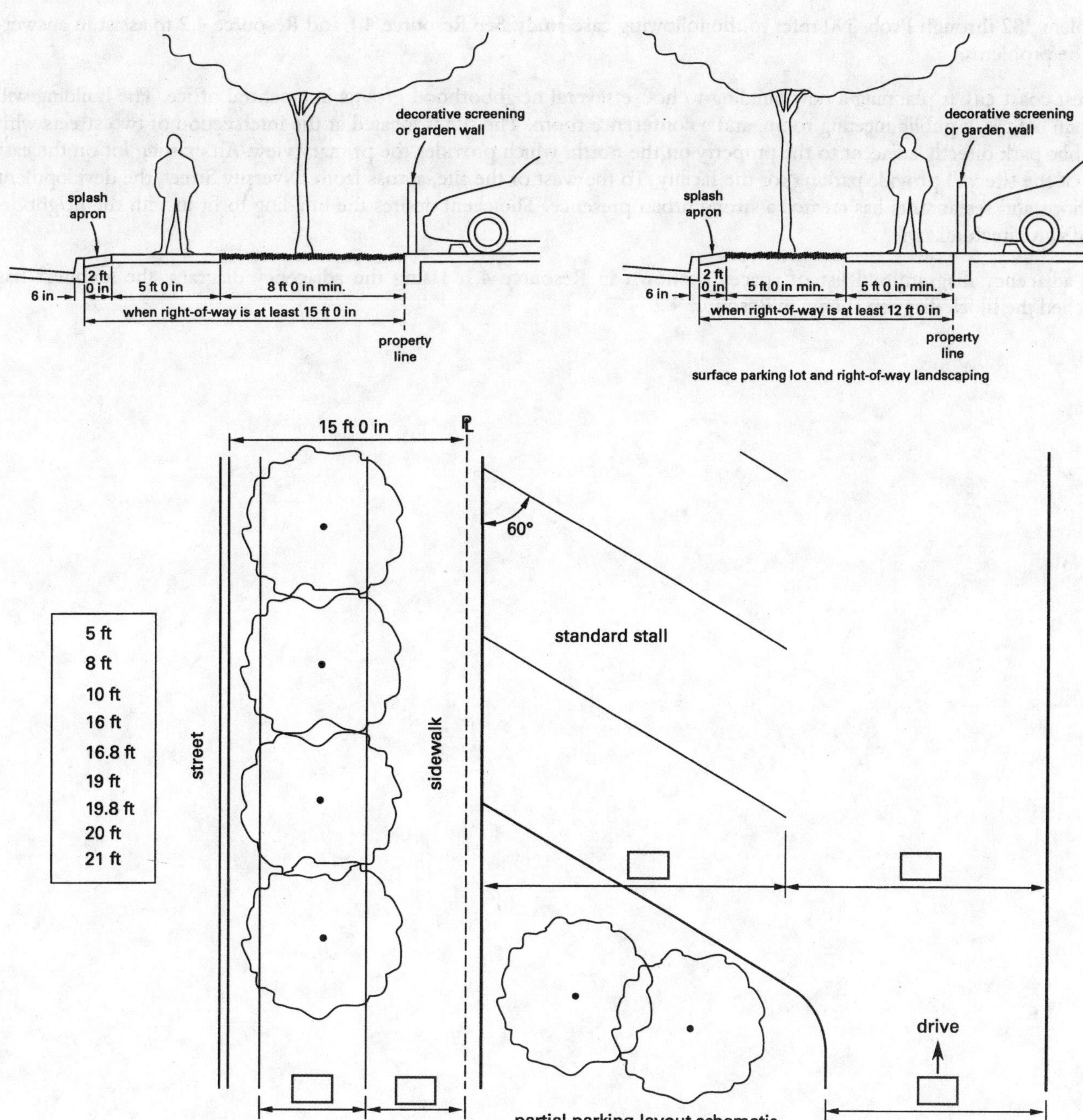

Using the parking dimensions, surface parking lot and right-of-way landscaping (see *illustration for Prob. 381*), and the form and parking summary table, place the minimum required dimensions in the boxes provided on the partial parking layout schematic. Each dimension may be used more than once.

Case Study

Problem 382 through Prob. 390 refer to the following case study. See Resource 4.1 and Resource 4.2 to assist in answering the problems.

A west coast city is planning a new building to house several neighborhood groups in a central office. The building will contain offices, a public meeting room, and a conference room. The site is located at the intersection of two streets with a public park directly adjacent to the property on the north, which provides the primary view. An existing lot on the east side of the site will provide parking for the facility. To the west of the site, across from Diversity Street, the development of shops and restaurants has created a strong urban presence. The client desires the building to fit in with the neighborhood's architectural style.

The adjacency diagram and list of spaces is shown in Resource 4.1. Using the adjacency diagram, the architect has sketched the block diagram shown in Resource 4.2.

Resource 4.1 Adjacency Diagram

L	lobby (400 ft^2)
C	conference room (400 ft^2)
MR	meeting room (1500 ft^2,15 ft ceiling)
MS	meeting storage room (500 ft^2)
R	reception area (150 ft^2)
FC	facility coordinator office (200 ft^2)
AC	asst. facility coord. office (150 ft^2)
CR	community relations office 150 ft^2)
SO	secretarial area (200 ft^2)
S	storage room (100 ft^2)
NO	neighborhood dir. office (150 ft^2)
W	work room (150 ft^2)
B	break room (150 ft^2)
ME	mechanical/electrical room (300 ft^2)
T	toilet room (2 @ 150 ft^2 ea.)

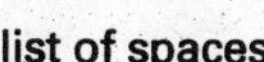

list of spaces

S
W
B
ME
NO
C
CR
SO
T
AC
FC
MR
L
R
MS
direct adjacency
secondary adjacency
view to park required

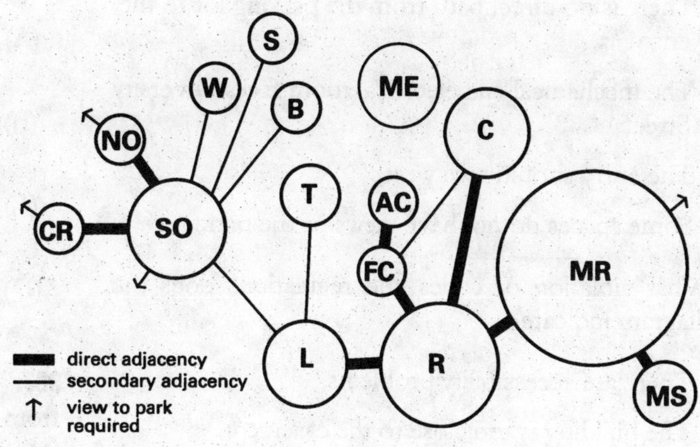

adjacency diagram

Resource 4.2 Block Diagram

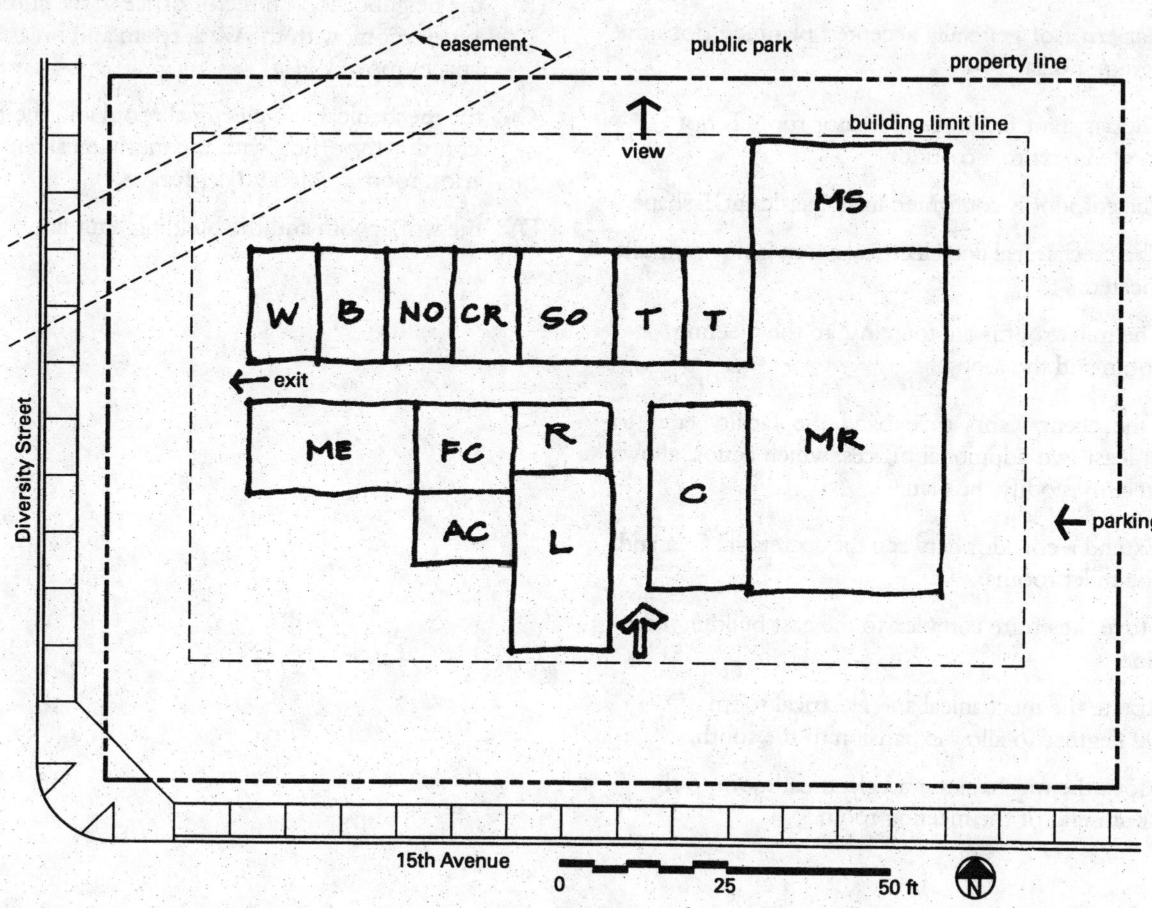

easement
public park
property line
building limit line
view
MS
W
B
NO
CR
SO
T
T
exit
ME
FC
R
MR
C
AC
L
parking
Diversity Street
15th Avenue
0
25
50 ft
N

block diagram

382. What neighborhood context is missing in the block diagram?

(A) There is no direct path from the parking lot to the entry.

(B) The mechanical and electrical room faces Diversity Street.

(C) The entry should face west.

(D) Some spaces do not have views of the park.

383. What violation of codes and regulations does the block diagram indicate?

(A) There are accessibility problems.

(B) The building is too close to the easement.

(C) There are not enough exits.

(D) There are zoning setbacks, which makes expansion difficult.

384. What error of generally accepted planning does the block diagram indicate?

(A) The assistant facility coordinator room is not located next to a corridor.

(B) The corridor is configured in an inefficient T-shape.

(C) The mechanical and electrical room is not centrally located.

(D) The toilet rooms are too close to the meeting room and the lobby.

385. If the client wants to expand the facility later to include at least two additional offices, which action allows the architect to modify the plan?

(A) Extend a corridor between the secretarial area and the toilet rooms.

(B) Move the entire complex to the east building limit line.

(C) Rotate the mechanical and electrical room 90 degrees to allow expansion to the south.

(D) Move the mechanical and electrical room to the south end of the meeting room.

386. The adjacency diagram and the block diagram address adjacency requirements for the project design. Which action accurately satisfies adjacencies?

(A) Locate the meeting storage space on the east side of the meeting room.

(B) Reverse the location of the conference room and the lobby area.

(C) Move the community relations office closer to the conference room.

(D) Locate the neighborhood director office next to the secretarial area.

387. 100 ft^2 of programmed storage space is missing from the block diagram. To correct this deficiency, the storage room should be located between

(A) the toilet rooms and the secretarial space, with the remaining rooms moved to the west

(B) the neighborhood director office space and the break room, with the work room and break room spaces moved west

(C) the mechanical and electrical room and the facility coordinator office, with the mechanical and electrical room rotated 90 degrees

(D) the work room and the building limit line

Project Planning

388. Because of problems with the initial block diagram layout and client comments, the architect has developed an alternative block diagram, as shown.

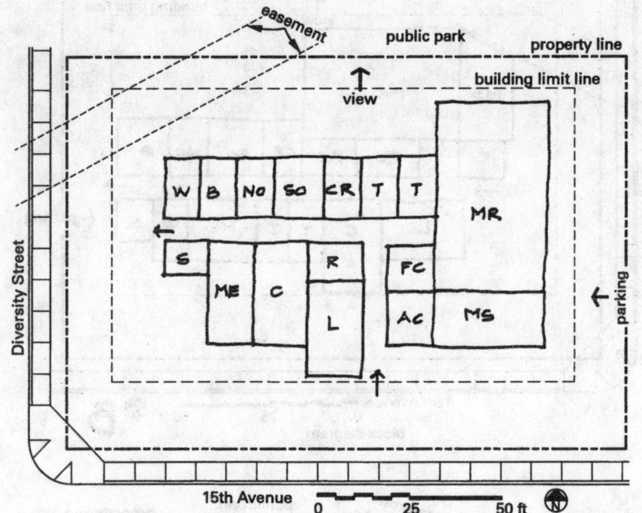

Which of the following actions would improve a program issue with this alternative block diagram?

(A) Strengthen the connection to the urban neighborhood to the west.

(B) Relocate the storage space because it appears to be an afterthought.

(C) Place the facility coordinator office directly adjacent to the reception space.

(D) Do not have the facility coordinator office and assistant facility coordinator offices directly open to the lobby.

389. The client and architect discuss alternatives for improving the pedestrian connection to the urban neighborhood to the west and improving the urban design aspects of the building on both Diversity Street and 15th Avenue.

As possible plans, the architect has developed the four block diagram schemes shown. Which of the four schemes achieves these goals?

(A) A

(B) B

(C) C

(D) D

390. Analyze the block diagram in Resource 4.2. To minimize construction costs without extensive re-planning, how should the block diagram be modified?

(A) Rotate the mechanical and electrical room and lobby space 90 degrees, and then relocate the assistant facility coordinator office along the corridor.

(B) Place the meeting storage space to the east of the meeting room.

(C) Shorten the span of the meeting room by using two columns in the middle of the room.

(D) Re-plan to eliminate as many corners as possible.

Project Planning

Illustration for Prob. 389

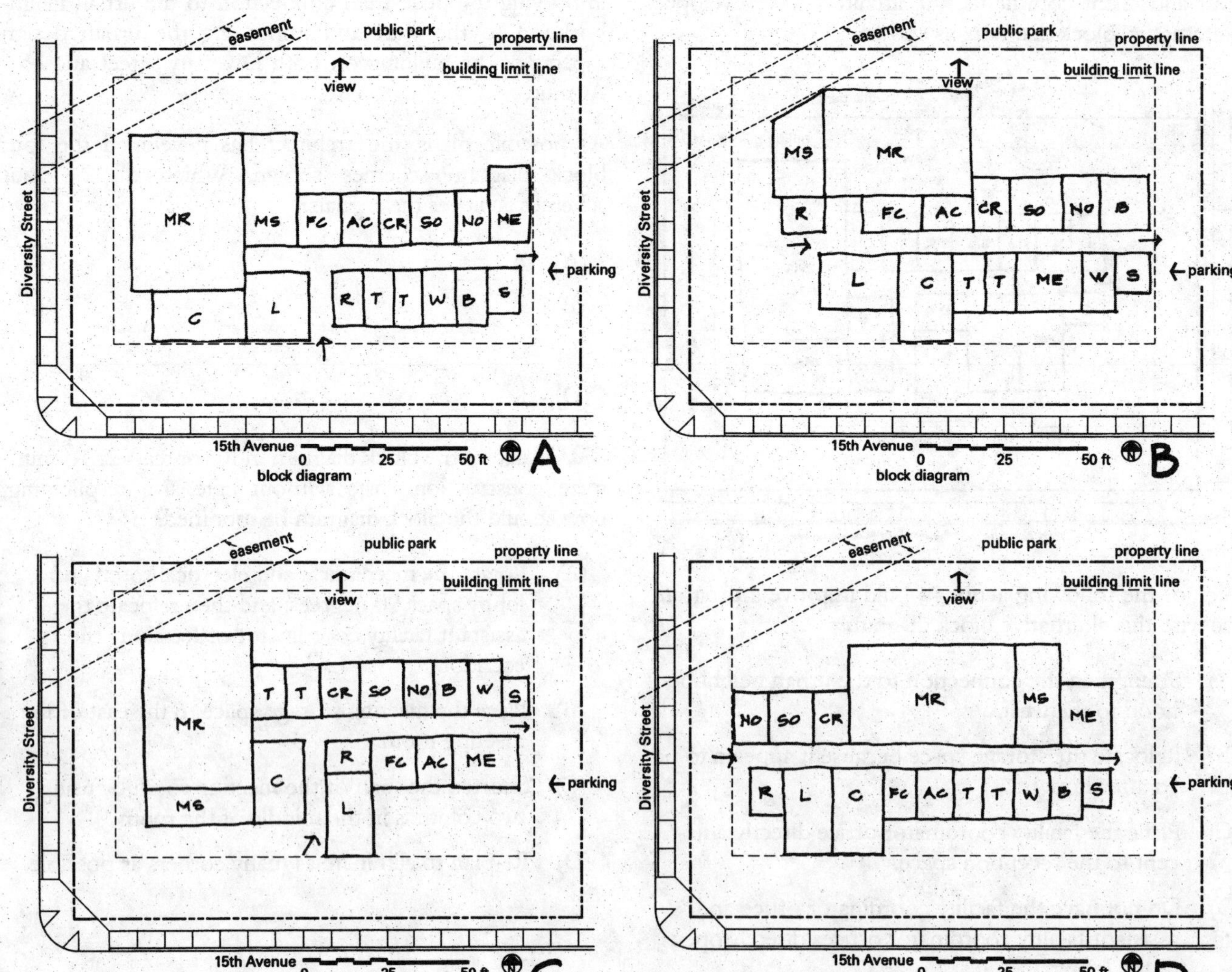

Solutions

Multiple Choice

271. (A) (B) (C) ●

272. (A) (B) ● (D)

273. (A) ● ● ● (E) (F)

274. ● (B) (C) ● (E) (F)

275. (A) (B) (C) ●

276. (A) (B) ● (D)

277. (A) ● (C) (D)

278. (A) (B) ● (D)

279. ● (B) (C) (D)

280. ● ● (C) (D) ● ●

281. (A) ● (C) (D)

282. (A) (B) ● (D)

283. ● (B) (C) (D)

284. (A) ● (C) (D)

285. (A) ● (C) (D)

286. (A) (B) (C) ●

287. ● (B) (C) (D)

288. (A) (B) ● (D)

289. (A) ● (C) (D)

290. (A) (B) ● (D)

291. (A) (B) ● (D)

292. (A) ● (C) (D)

293. ● ● ● ● (E) (F)

294. (A) ● (C) (D)

295. (A) (B) ● (D)

296. ● (B) (C) (D)

297. ● ● (C) ● ● (F)

298. (A) ● ● (D) (E) (F)

299. ● (B) ● (D) (E) ●

300. ● (B) (C) (D)

301. (A) (B) (C) ●

302. ● ● (C) (D) (E) (F)

303. (A) (B) (C) ●

304. (A) ● (C) (D)

305. (A) (B) (C) ●

306. ● (B) (C) (D)

307. (A) (B) ● (D)

308. ● (B) (C) (D)

309. ● (B) (C) (D)

310. (A) (B) ● (D)

311. (A) (B) ● (D)

312. (A) ● (C) (D)

313. (A) (B) ● (D)

314. ● ● (C) ● (E) (F)

315. (A) (B) (C) ●

316. (A) (B) (C) ●

317. ● (B) (C) (D)

318. ● (B) (C) (D)

319. ● (B) (C) (D)

320. (A) (B) ● (D)

321. (A) ● (C) (D)

322. (A) (B) ● (D)

323. ● (B) (C) (D)

324. ● (B) (C) (D)

325. (A) (B) ● (D)

326. (A) (B) (C) ●

327. (A) (B) (C) ●

328. (A) (B) ● (D)

329. ● (B) (C) (D)

330. ● ● ● (D) (E) ●

331. ● ● (C) ● (E) ●

332. ● ● (C) ● ● (F)

333. (A) (B) (C) ●

334. (A) (B) (C) ●

335. (A) ● (C) (D)

336. (A) (B) (C) ●

337. ● (B) (C) (D)

338. (A) (B) (C) ●

339. ● (B) ● ● (E) (F)

340. (A) (B) ● (D)

341. (A) (B) ● (D)

342. (A) ● (C) (D)

343. (A) (B) ● (D)

344. (A) (B) (C) ●

345. ● ● ● (D) (E) ●

346. ● ● (C) ● (E) ●

347. (A) (B) (C) ●

348. ● (B) (C) (D)

349. (A) (B) (C) ●

350. (A) ● (C) (D)

351. (A) (B) (C) ●

352. ● (B) (C) (D)

353. ● (B) (C) (D)

354. ● ● (C) ● (E) ●

355. (A) ● (C) (D)

356. (A) (B) ● (D)

357. ● (B) (C) (D)

358. ● (B) ● (D) ● ●

359. (A) ● (C) (D)

360. (A) ● (C) (D)

361. (A) (B) (C) ●

362. ● (B) (C) ● (E) ●

363. (A) ● ● (D) (E) ●

364. (A) (B) (C) ●

365. See Sol. 365.

366. See Sol. 366.

367. (A) ● (C) (D)

368. (A) (B) ● (D)

369. See Sol. 369.

370. See Sol. 370.

371. (A) (B) (C) ●

372. (A) (B) (C) ●

373. (A) ● (C) (D)

374. ● (B) (C) (D)

375. ● (B) (C) (D)

376. (A) (B) ● (D)

377. (A) (B) (C) ●

378. (A) (B) ● (D)

379. 16 water closets

380. ● ● (C) ● (E) (F)

Case Study

381. See Sol. 381

382. (A) (B) (C) ●

383. (A) (B) ● (D)

384. ● (B) (C) (D)

385. (A) ● (C) (D)

386. (A) (B) (C) ●

387. (A) (B) ● (D)

388. ● (B) (C) (D)

389. (A) ● (C) (D)

390. (A) (B) (C) ●

271. Mortise locks are the most secure type of lockset because the mechanism is concealed within the leaf of the door.

Unit locks are installed into a notch cut into the leaf of the door. Cylinder locks are installed through a hole drilled in the leaf. Rim locks are mounted on the face of the leaf. Because each of these types of locksets leaves portions of the mechanism exposed, they can be more easily tampered with and are not as secure as the mortise lockset.

The answer is (D).

272.

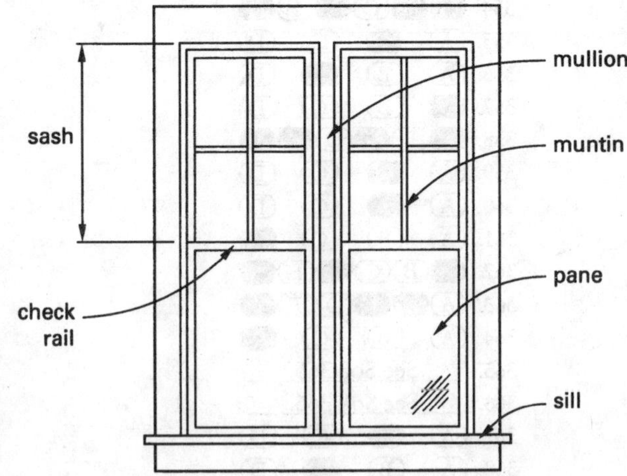

The answer is (C).

273. By definition, the means of egress consists of the exit access, the exit, and the exit discharge.

The means of egress must lead to a public way, but the public way is not part of the means of egress. The common path of travel (or common path of egress travel) is that portion of exit access that the occupants are required to traverse before two separate and distinct paths of egress travel to two exits are available. Although an important feature, this is not a part of the means of egress. The travel distance is the distance from any point in the exit access to the nearest exit.

The answer is (B), (C), and (D).

274. The structural slab is a consideration only as part of the entire floor/ceiling assembly. Neither thermal insulation nor sound absorption is a consideration in a ceiling's fire resistance. Style is not as important as whether or not the grid is rated.

The answer is (A) and (D).

275. In rift sawing, boards are cut radially from the center of the log. This produces a very straight and consistent vertical grain, and this type of cut is typically only used for sawing oak. However, the log must be repositioned for each cut, so the process is very labor intensive. Also, because the boards are not cut perpendicular to one another, there is a great deal of waste in rift sawing. For these reasons, it is the most expensive sawing technique.

Quartersawing involves dividing a log into quarters and then cutting boards perpendicular to the grain. Like rift sawing, it produces boards with straight grain running parallel to the length of the board. However, the grain is not as straight with quartersawing as it is with rift sawing.

Plain sawing and flat sawing are the same thing. The boards are cut in straight lines across the grain of the log. The grain tends to be more uneven than quartersawn or rift-sawn boards, but it is this technique that produces the "curvy" grain often seen on framing members. Boards cut from the periphery of the log tend to cup or warp a little more than quarter- or rift-sawn boards because of the curve of the grain.

The answer is (D).

276. Waterproofing membranes—usually building felt saturated with bituminous material, sheet plastics, or thin sheets of bentonite clay—can be easily punctured when the foundation is backfilled. As their effectiveness is entirely dependent on their watertightness, it is prudent to provide a protection board to prevent rocks or machinery from damaging the surface.

Dampproofing controls moisture that is not under hydrostatic pressure, while waterproofing is required to control moisture that is affected by hydrostatic pressure. Waterproofing techniques are generally more costly and difficult to apply. Membrane coatings are an excellent choice for waterproofing but are not generally required for dampproofing. In a situation where waterproofing is required, hydrostatic pressure against the wall can be lessened by providing geotextile matting ("filter fabric") and a foundation drain set in gravel at the footing.

The answer is (C).

277. Although option (A), option (B), and option (C) are all valid approaches to reducing the sound transmission from one space to another and option (D) is a good approach for increasing the absorption of sound within an office, the most critical strategy to employ is to extend the partition walls from floor deck to floor deck and seal the connections well (option (B)). Any gaps, such as a partition that only extends a few inches above a suspended ceiling, will allow sound to pass freely from the office to the corridor and vice versa.

The answer is (B).

278. Rapidly renewable building materials are made from plants that can be grown and harvested relatively quickly, generally within 10 years. Wheat board cabinetry, linoleum (which is made from jute, linseed oil, and other natural

Project Planning

and sustainable materials), and bamboo paneling are considered rapidly renewable resources.

Recovering materials to be reused for a new purpose (such as flooring manufactured from reclaimed barn beams or paneling manufactured from recycled cardboard) will help prevent the harvesting of other materials and may be considered "green." Recovered materials, however, do not count as rapidly renewable. Mineral fiber insulation is not from a renewable source.

The answer is (C).

279. Windows are rarely reused in sustainable design projects that convert old buildings to a new use. Old windows do not possess the energy efficiency of a new window that could be installed in the existing masonry opening. The exterior building envelope and structural framing of an old building is often intact and can be reused without diminishing the building's energy efficiency.

Another material that is almost always replaced in a green building reuse project is the nonstructural roofing material (membrane roofing, shingles, etc.). Again, newer materials far surpass the older, existing materials in terms of building energy efficiency.

Asbestos is a known carcinogen and should never be reused.

The answer is (A).

280. Laminated glass is good for acoustical control because of its mass and the damping quality of the plastic interlayer. Laminated glass can be used for decorative purposes by using a decorative interlayer between the sheets of glass. It is also considered to be safety glazing and provides excellent resistance to breaking, as a security measure. With the correct thickness and types of interlayers, laminated glass can also provide bullet resistance.

Although some laminated glass can carry a 30-minute fire rating, fire protection is not a common use of this material. The insulation value of laminated glass is negligible unless the glass is used with other glazing in an insulated glass unit.

The answer is (A), (B), (E), and (F).

281. Information provided in resources such as the series of publications from R.S. Means provides valuable information about construction costs, including labor, materials, and how these costs compare in different regions of the country. Location factors can very greatly depending on the local economy, prevailing wage rates, difficulty of transporting materials to the site, demand for construction services, and numerous other factors.

Begin by increasing the $300,000 original construction cost to today's dollars using the inflation rate given, 2%, for three years.

$$\begin{aligned} C_{\text{today}} &= C_{3\,\text{yr ago}}(1+i)^n = (\$300{,}000)(1.02)^3 \\ &= \$318{,}362.40 \quad (\$318{,}362) \end{aligned}$$

It costs about $318,362 to build the same building in Pittsburgh today.

Next, calculate the cost of construction in Durham. The ratio of the construction costs in the two cities is equivalent to the ratio of their location factors.

$$\frac{C_{\text{Pittsburgh}}}{C_{\text{Durham}}} = \frac{f_{\text{Pittsburgh}}}{f_{\text{Durham}}}$$

$$\begin{aligned} C_{\text{Durham}} &= \left(\frac{f_{\text{Durham}}}{f_{\text{Pittsburgh}}}\right) C_{\text{Pittsburgh}} \\ &= \left(\frac{75}{100}\right)(\$318{,}362) \\ &= \$238{,}771.50 \quad (\$239{,}000) \end{aligned}$$

It can be estimated that it will cost about $239,000 to build the same building in Durham, North Carolina, today.

The answer is (B).

282. Nine 2 × 6 studs will be needed for each of the three walls, so 27 studs will be needed in all.

Each 2 × 6 stud will be 8 ft long, and 27 studs are needed, so the total length needed is 27 times 8 ft, or 216 ft.

Board-feet is a measurement that refers to a piece of lumber 1 in thick by 12 in wide by 12 in long, or 144 in^3. A piece of wood 2 in thick by 6 in wide by 12 in long is equivalent to a board-foot. Therefore, the contractor will need to purchase 216 board-feet of lumber to complete the project.

The answer is (C).

283. The substrate mounted system provides a lot of flexibility but requires the building to be covered with a supporting substrate. This is an unnecessary expense and will complicate the installation of vision panels. The curtain wall panel system is economical and practical only for structures with large numbers of identical panels, and it would not be desirable for this building. A metallic EIFS may provide a similar look but requires additional construction and would be separate from any spandrel or vision panel installation.

The answer is (A).

284. A gearless traction elevator will be an appropriate choice for the office building. Gearless traction elevators can travel at the highest speeds of the types listed, and to accommodate the rush of people entering and exiting the building in the morning, at lunch time, and in the evening, the quick cycles will be a necessity.

Gearless traction and geared traction are two different types of electric elevators. Both operate on DC current. The geared traction elevator travels at slower speeds but offers many options for adjusting the speed to suit the building conditions.

Hydraulic elevators are lifted by a ram, which must be sunk into the ground the same distance as the height of the elevator's path of travel. Therefore, they are used only in low-rise buildings (generally less than six stories). They travel much more slowly than electric elevators and are better used for freight or for low-occupancy passenger elevators where speed is not an issue.

The answer is (B).

285. A loose-laid, single-ply EPDM roofing system will be a reasonable choice in this situation. The summers in Richmond are hot while the winters can be cold, and EPDM rubber weathers extreme temperature fluctuations well. The existing roofing material should be removed down to the roof deck to allow new insulation board to be installed. The EPDM will be installed over the insulation board and topped with a layer of roof pavers or a combination of pavers and ballast.

The answer is (B).

286. The strategy pictured is direct gain. Heat from the sun passing through the window is absorbed by the mass of the concrete and distributed thoughout the space.

The answer is (D).

287. Chlorination is the most common process used to disinfect drinking water. The chlorine kills bacteria and viruses that may be in the water. Ozonation and exposure to ultraviolet light are two other methods of removing harmful organisms from drinking water, but they are not as common as chlorination. A zeolite process is not used to disinfect potable water. It is used to soften water that has a high mineral content.

The answer is (A).

288. A preaction sprinkler system will be a good choice for the store. Preaction systems admit water to the sprinkler pipes after the system detects a fire. As the water enters the pipes, the system sounds an alarm. The delay between detection and activation allows a little time for the fire to be found and extinguished before the sprinkler heads open. This type of system is a popular choice for applications where there will be a great deal of water damage to building contents if the sprinklers were activated.

Wet pipe systems are always filled with water and are activated by the sprinkler heads through use of a fusible link or other heat sensitive controls. The water is immediately discharged in the area wheWre the fire is detected. Dry pipe systems are filled with compressed air until the system is activated, and then water fills the pipes and exits through the sprinkler heads. They are a good choice for unheated buildings where water in the pipes could potentially freeze and render the system useless. A deluge system is filled with water, like a wet pipe system, but all of the heads discharge at the same time. They are used where flammable materials are stored, or where a fire could spread very rapidly. However, if the system activates, the potential for severe water damage is high.

The answer is (C).

289. Photoelectric smoke detectors (like the ones often found in homes) pass a beam of light onto a sensor; if the beam is obscured by smoke, the alarm sounds. Smoke begins to form when a fire reaches the smoldering stage.

The answer is (B).

290. Incandescent light will make the orange walls appear more vibrant and will provide good color rendering for other colors.

However, incandescent lamps do not have a very long life span and tend not to be as efficient as fluorescent lamps. Warm white fluorescent lamps are the next best choice, and though their color rendering is not quite as accurate, the owner might select them over the incandescent lamps when other factors are taken into consideration.

Both daylight and cool white fluorescent lamps tend to make things seem a little bluish. These types of light will give the orange a grayer appearance and are not good selections for this application.

The answer is (C).

291. Upfeed water supply systems will work in buildings up to approximately 40–60 ft tall, so the most appropriate choice of the selections given is option (C), 50–60 ft. The exact height depends on a variety of factors, including losses due to static head as well as the pressure at the water main, which is generally anywhere from 40–80 psi.

Static head is the amount of pressure required to lift water through a piping system in a building. 0.433 psi can lift water 1 ft. For each foot of building height, then, 0.433 psi is lost. To determine water pressure at each floor of the building, multiply the static head by the building height and subtract this from the pressure at the building main. There must be enough pressure available to operate fixtures on the top floor. These calculations can help a designer to determine the most appropriate type of system for a project.

The answer is (C).

292. 120/208 voltage, three-phase power is be appropriate for a small commercial building.

Residences typically have 120/240 voltage, single-phase systems. Larger buildings with greater demand require higher-voltage, three-phase services.

The answer is (B).

293. The building energy cost method allows the designer to compare the annual energy costs of the design building to a baseline building. If the design energy costs are less in the design building, the building complies with the standard. This method must be used to obtain LEED credit. It cannot be used to analyze a building that does not have a mechanical system or a low-rise residential building.

Two alternative approaches to analyzing annual energy costs are the system performance method and the prescriptive criteria method. The system performance method requires complex calculations based upon the site's climate. A computer model of the design building is often necessary to complete these calculations. The prescriptive criteria method allows calculations to be completed relatively quickly but tends to be more restrictive than the other methods.

The answer is (A), (B), (C), and (D).

294. The minimum width of the lobby should be 10 ft. As a general rule, it is most economical and efficient to group elevators into "banks." A 10 ft wide lobby will allow sufficient space for a group of passengers to gather, but is small enough that a person in the lobby can see all of the elevators while waiting for an available car.

The answer is (B).

295. A variable air volume (VAV) system will be the best choice for this application. VAV systems allow for individual control of temperature, quiet operation, and minimal maintenance.

Packaged terminal units and fan coil terminals permit control over the temperatures of individual spaces but do not operate as quietly or require as little maintenance as VAV systems.

Single duct, constant air volume (CAV) units are relatively inexpensive to install and maintain but do not offer occupants the ability to control the temperatures of individual spaces.

The answer is (C).

296. A person standing along the marble wall near the entrance to Union Station and who is speaking softly can be heard clearly from across the lobby. The arch works because the sound is focused by the concave surfaces and directed into a specific part of the room—in this case, the niche on the other side of the lobby.

Creep is the reflection of sound along a curved surface, such as a dome. The sound can be understood at points along the way but cannot be heard across the room. Diffusion is the opposite of focusing, where sound is scattered all around a room as it is reflected from convex surfaces. Specular reflection is the reflection of sound off hard, polished surfaces.

The answer is (A).

297. Aluminum conduit should not be used in concrete slabs because it tends to cause spalling and cracking if it reacts with ingredients in the concrete admixtures. Plastic pipe may be used in concrete slabs if properly installed.

Many of the rules for placing conduit in concrete slabs are similar to those for reinforcing bars. Conduit always should be placed in the part of the slab that is in tension. It is important to cover the conduit with at least $^3/_4$ in of concrete, and in locations where heavy loads will be applied to the slab, the coating should be even thicker. The designer must take care to specify conduit of an appropriate size relative to the thickness of the slab. The outside diameter of the conduit should be no greater than $^1/_3$ of the slab thickness. It is also important to allow an adequate amount of space between parallel runs of conduit—at least three times the outside diameter of the largest tube. Pipes carrying fluids and gasses must be pressure tested prior to the placement of the concrete.

The answer is (A), (B), (D), and (E).

298. Generally, spaces intended to highlight spoken-word presentations should be "dead" spaces; that is, they should have short reverberation times. Musical presentations generally sound best in spaces with long reverberation times, or spaces that are "live."

Reverberation time is calculated as

$$T_R = \frac{0.049\,V}{A}$$

V equals the volume of the space, and A equals total absorptivity of the wall, floor, and ceiling surfaces along with other absorptive elements, such as upholstered seats, curtains, and so on. When a program or occupancy dictates the size of the room, dead spaces can often be created by specifying absorptive materials, and live spaces can be created by using materials that reflect sound.

The answer is (B) and (C).

299. Fire extinguishers should always be available in buildings to combat a fire as quickly as possible. They should be located a maximum of 75 ft from every building

Project Planning

occupant or as required by local building codes. Wet standpipes may also be available for building occupants' use. They consist of a large pipe running vertically through a building and connected to at least one hose on each floor (the exact number of hoses is determined by building layout and local codes). The occupants can access the hose and release the water as necessary. Two-way communications devices are installed for building occupants' use so that those who are having difficulty evacuating the building may call for help.

Dry standpipes must be connected to a pumper truck in order to be filled with water. They are designed to be used by the fire department to distribute water throughout a building. The firefighters enter the building and attach their hoses to the standpipe outlets on each floor to fight the fire.

A fusible link is a sensor in a sprinkler head and is not activated by building occupants but rather by a rise in ambient temperature indicating the presence of fire. Annunciators are used to give instructions to building occupants. They are used by firefighters or others authorized to assist with evacuation efforts.

The answer is (A), (C), and (F).

300.

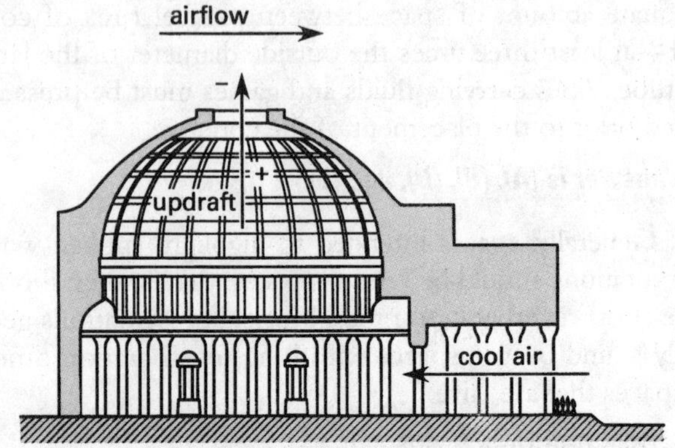

The Pantheon is naturally cooled through stack ventilation. Cool air is drawn into the building through the portico and travels through the drum to cool the interior space before being vented through the oculus at the top of the dome. Wind flowing over the top of the building creates negative pressure that sucks the air through the building, so the system is effective regardless of the direction of the wind.

The other three options are also natural cooling techniques. Pools of water can be placed in courtyards or near building openings in hot-arid climates to cool the air entering the interior spaces through evaporation.

In the thermal mass strategy of natural cooling, heat is stored during the day and the building is opened for ventilation at night. The mass is cooled and ready to absorb heat the next day.

Placing openings on parallel walls and orienting them to the prevailing winds creates cross ventilation and increases the velocity of the air moving through a space. This is an effective cooling technique for hot-humid climates.

The answer is (A).

301. The house depicted is appropriate for a temperate climate, such as that of Maryland. The longest facade is oriented east-west, exposing most windows to the south to take advantage of winter sun. The porch on the south side shades the first-floor windows in the summer, as does the deciduous tree to the south, which blocks the sun's rays in the hottest months and allows the sun to shine through during the winter when the tree is bare. Sometimes evergreen trees are planted to the north to block the winter winds. The heat source (fireplace) is located at the end of the building, and the kitchen is located to the north since it will create its own heat.

The answer is (D).

302. Because of their ability to deplete the earth's ozone layer, the production of certain refrigerants has been discontinued in the United States in compliance with the Montreal Protocol on Substances that Deplete the Ozone Layer. Halon production ceased in 1994. U.S. production of CFCs stopped in 1995. HFCs will continue to be produced, but they are not without their own environmental challenges, as they have a high global warming potential. HCFCs will be phased out by 2030.

More information about ozone-depleting substances can be found on the Environmental Protection Agency's website, epa.gov/ozone.

The answer is (A) and (B).

303. Planting a combination of deciduous and evergreen trees is the most effective sound attenuation strategy. Planting the trees on an earth mound will further improve the effectiveness of the buffer.

The answer is (D).

304. A brightness ratio is the relationship between the illumination levels of the surfaces within a person's field of vision. The maximum ideal brightness level ratio between a task and the adjacent surroundings should be under 1:$\frac{1}{3}$.

The answer is (B).

305. Values in the zone indicated on the chart necessitate humidification, or adding moisture to the air, to prevent static electricity, uncomfortable breathing, and the potential for nosebleeds and dry skin. Humidification can be accomplished either with a central humidification system at the HVAC unit, which treats the air before it is distributed throughout the building or, in smaller buildings or residences, with point-of-use humidifiers.

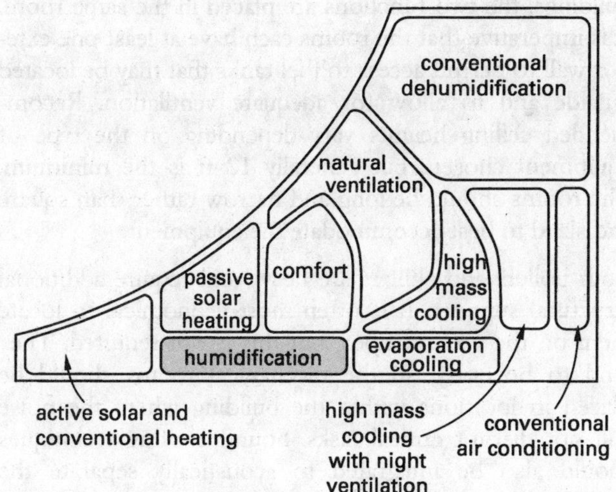

This extremely simplified diagram of the psychrometric chart provides a quick reference to the best approaches for each region of the chart. Note that they are not the only strategies that will work for a specific reading, and that the areas of the chart where the strategy can be successful overlap more than this diagram implies. A more detailed chart that illustrates the overlap can be found in *Mechanical and Electrical Equipment for Buildings*, by Grondzik, et al.

The answer is (D).

306. Forced air systems occupy the most space within the building because of the size of the mechanical unit itself and the amount of ductwork necessary to distribute the conditioned air.

The answer is (A).

307. DCV technology uses a carbon dioxide sensor to increase or decrease ventilation of a space according to occupancy. This technology is best used for spaces where the occupancy of the space can vary greatly at different times during the day or week and where there is not a high concentration of air contaminants that need to be exhausted through a continuously operating heating, ventilating, and air conditioning (HVAC) system. A bowling alley will be a good application of DCV because it has long operating hours but widely varying occupancy levels. Although the bowling alley may be open during the afternoon during the week, there probably will not be as many people present then as there will be on a Friday or Saturday night. A DCV system will increase ventilation of the space when necessary and decrease it when the building is less full.

DCV technology is not a good choice for spaces where there are odors or contaminants that must be constantly exhausted or for spaces that are always occupied. Therefore, the pet store, the locker room, and the dry cleaner will not be good applications of this technology because there are air quality issues to be addressed beyond those determined by occupancy.

Demand-controlled ventilation is a relatively new technology. A good primer on its best applications and potential cost savings is available from E Source, a clearinghouse of energy information.

The answer is (C).

308. Photoelectric cells are a type of perimeter security system. Perimeter systems secure building entry points such as doors and windows. Photoelectric cells pass a beam from one point to another and sound an alarm when the beam is broken.

The other three types of security systems are area or room protection systems. They sense when an intruder is in a protected room and sound an alarm. Pressure sensors detect changes in pressure on the floor caused by a person walking. Ultrasonic detectors use a high-frequency sound wave to sense intruders. Photoelectric beams use infrared technology to protect a space. If the photoelectric beam is broken by an intruder's movements, an alarm sounds.

The answer is (A).

309. Selective collective operation is a good choice for the apartment building. It collects calls and answers the up calls on the up trip, travels to the floor level with the highest call, then collects and answers the down calls on the return trip to the floor level with the lowest call. This type of operating system works best with more than one car because cars can be making separate trips and answering calls simultaneously, reducing waiting time at the stops.

Computerized controls are much more sophisticated (and more expensive) than the other three types. They are programmed based on data about building traffic patterns and analysis of the most important calls. Single automatic control answers one call at a time, delivers that passenger to the destination, and then responds to the next call. Collective control answers all calls without differentiating between up and down calls, so waiting time and time spent on the elevator can be unacceptably long. This type of system is rarely used in new projects in the United States.

The answer is (A).

310.

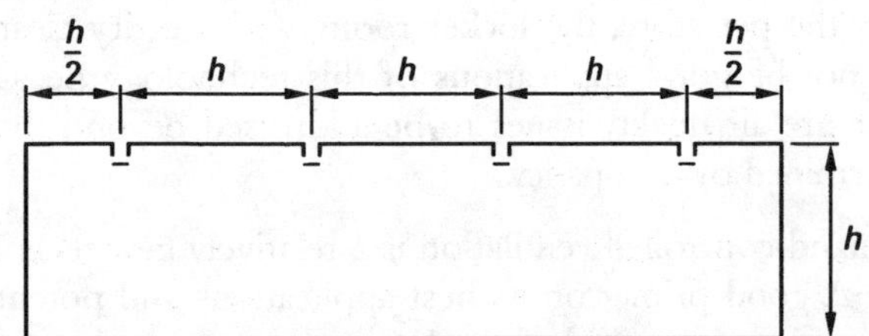

A good guideline for the initial layout of ceiling diffusers in a room is to space them approximately the same distance apart as the room is high. The height of the room is considered to be the distance from the floor to the nearest ceiling element. Diffusers at the edge of the space should be placed about half that distance from the perimeter walls.

The answer is (C).

311. A curtain board, also called a draft curtain, is an assembly suspended from the ceiling to prohibit movement of smoke and flame. Since smoke rises and gathers at the ceiling, the curtain board helps to block it from entering an adjacent space. Curtain boards are often used to protect openings in the floor, such as escalators and mezzanines. The depth of the curtain board varies and must be confirmed for a specific project.

The answer is (C).

312. There are three types of PV cells: crystalline, polycrystalline, and amorphous (also known as thin-film). Crystalline cells are the best power generators. They also tend to be the most expensive. Polycrystalline cells produce less power but are more competitively priced. Amorphous PV cells produce the least power, but are unique in that they can be applied onto other building materials (such as roofing materials) to capture solar energy with a less obtrusive appearance.

The answer is (B).

313. The absorption coefficient is a fractional number and cannot exceed 1.0. The correct room absorption coefficient should be between 0.20 and 0.50.

Doubling the absorptive surfaces in a room results in a noise reduction of only 3 dB, which is barely perceptible. To justify the expense of adding more absorptive materials, the absorption should be tripled. With three times the amount of absorption, the change is about 5 dB and the level of noise reduction is clearly noticeable.

In large rooms, there is typically more ceiling area than wall area. Therefore, absorptive treatments to the ceiling will have a more efficient impact than similar treatments to the walls.

The answer is (C).

314. Boiler rooms and chilled water plants should be located adjacent to one another when possible; in some buildings, the two functions are placed in the same room. It is imperative that the rooms each have at least one exterior wall to permit access to fuel tanks that may be located outside and to allow for adequate ventilation. Recommended ceiling heights vary depending on the type of equipment chosen, but generally 12 ft is the minimum. The rooms should be long and narrow rather than square and sized to best accommodate the equipment.

Both boilers and chillers are heavy and require additional structural support. It is often most economical to locate them on the ground floor, but this is not required. They tend to be noisy, so the mechanical rooms should be placed in locations within the building where the noise will not disrupt critical tasks. Soundproofing techniques should also be integrated to acoustically separate the mechanical rooms from the occupied spaces.

The answer is (A), (B), and (D).

315. The fixtures shown in this typical restroom layout are all wall-hung, so at least 24 in of clear space should be allowed within the plumbing wall to accommodate the plumbing and the carriers that support the fixtures.

If there are fixtures on only one side of the wall, a 12 in space will be adequate. If the fixtures are not wall-hung (tank-type toilets and pedestal sinks, for example), a 16 in space will be sufficient.

The answer is (D).

316. Electric lighting generally demands half of the total energy consumed by an office building. Heating and cooling systems demand about 30%. The remaining 20% is used to operate equipment in the building (such as copy machines, computers, and so on) and for other uses. Since offices are typically used most heavily during the daytime, a good case can be made for integrating daylighting techniques into the design of the building. Daylighting may also reduce the building's total energy consumption because the cooling load contributed by the electric lights is greatly reduced.

The answer is (D).

317. Nearly 40% of a restaurant's construction budget are allocated for HVAC. This includes ventilation of the kitchen in addition to multizone climate control for the dining areas.

A hospital's construction budget includes a 20% allowance for HVAC. About 10% of the total construction cost for the climate controlled mini-warehouse is related to heating, ventilation, and cooling. A typical parking garage contains no HVAC systems.

More information about typical costs for building construction can be found in *Square Foot Costs*, published by RSMeans, a division of Reed Construction Data, Inc.

The answer is (A).

318. The sound intensity level at the back row of the classroom is 53 dB. Sound intensity levels decrease 6 dB for every doubling of distance. The simple math in this problem makes it easy to solve in this manner, as 3 ft doubled is 6 ft, and 6 ft doubled is 12 ft. The total drop is 12 dB, and 65 dB − 12 dB = 53 dB.

The answer is (A).

319. Low-ε (low-emittance) glass is a good choice for a cold climate because it has a low *U*-value, which means that it can minimize heat loss while still allowing some solar heat gain. The low-ε film or coating allows both visible and near-infrared radiation to be transmitted through the glass but prevents long-wave radiation (heat) from escaping the room.

Reflective, tinted, and triple-pane glass is not as efficient as the newer technologies of low-ε glass or "super windows." Reflective and tinted glass reduces heat gain in the summer but does not allow desirable heat gain during the cold months.

The answer is (A).

320. When the temperature is above about 85°F, the body loses more heat through evaporation than through convection or radiation. In a humid climate this process is retarded, so encouraging air movement is the best strategy. Overhangs and light-colored surfaces help minimize heat buildup in the structure itself, and water features contribute to a feeling of comfort by cooling through evaporation and having a psychological cooling effect.

The answer is (C).

321. Occupant load determines means-of-egress requirements: how many exits must be provided to evacuate a space in case of an emergency, how large the exits must be, and where they must be located. Design occupant load for assembly occupancies is calculated under the *International Building Code* (IBC) by using the following guidelines.

standing space	5 net ft^2 per occupant
concentrated (chairs only)	7 net ft^2 per occupant
unconcentrated (tables and chairs)	15 net ft^2 per occupant

The largest occupancy determines the egress requirements.

The answer is (B).

322. A common path of egress travel is the part of the path of egress travel that occupants are required to move through before they reach a point where they have a choice to follow one of two distinct paths of travel to an exit.

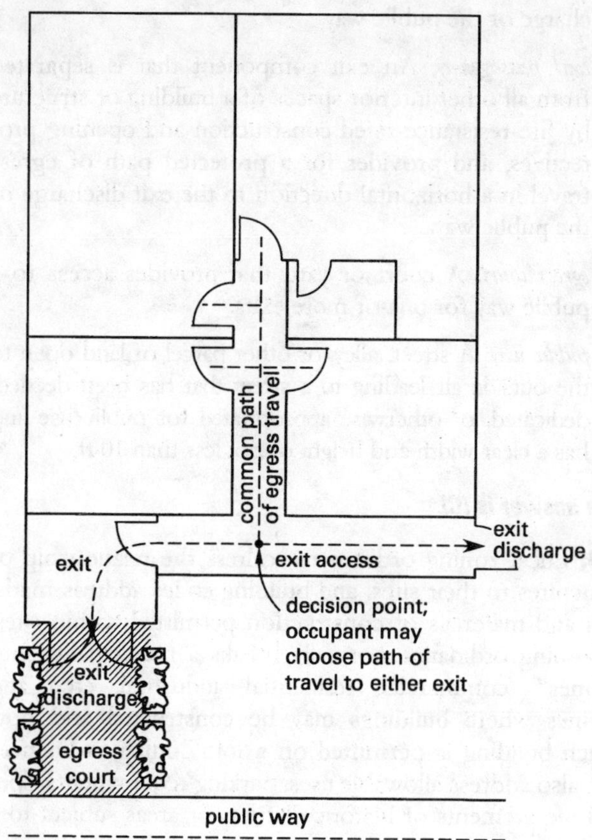

The *International Building Code* (IBC) uses specific terms to describe different parts of the path from a point inside a building to a safe point outside the building. These terms include the following.

- *area of refuge*: An area where people who are unable to use stairways can remain temporarily to await instructions or assistance during emergency evacuations.
- *exit*: That portion of a means-of-egress system that is separated from other interior spaces of a building or structure by fire-resistance-rated construction and opening protectives as required to provide a protected path of egress travel between the exit access and the exit discharge.
- *exit access*: That portion of a means-of-egress system that leads from any occupied portion of a building or structure to an exit.
- *exit discharge*: That portion of a means-of-egress system between the termination of an exit and a public way.

Project Planning

- *exit enclosure*: An exit component that is separated from all other interior spaces of a building or structure by fire-resistance-rated construction and opening protectives, and provides for a protected path of egress travel in a vertical or horizontal direction to the exit discharge or the public way.
- *exit passageway*: An exit component that is separated from all other interior spaces of a building or structure by fire-resistance-rated construction and opening protectives, and provides for a protected path of egress travel in a horizontal direction to the exit discharge or the public way.
- *egress court*: A court or yard that provides access to a public way for one or more exits.
- *public way*: A street, alley, or other parcel of land open to the outside air leading to a street that has been deeded, dedicated, or otherwise appropriated for public use and has a clear width and height of not less than 10 ft.

The answer is (C).

323. Local zoning ordinances address the relationship of structures to their sites, and building codes address methods and materials of construction permitted within sites. A zoning ordinance normally breaks a municipality into "zones" (commercial, residential, industrial, etc.) and defines where buildings may be constructed and how much building is permitted on a lot. Zoning ordinances can also address allowable uses, parking requirements, special requirements of historic districts or areas subject to a design or architectural review board, and site planning issues.

Information regarding maximum occupancy, fire-rated assemblies and types of materials that may be used for construction is commonly found in building codes.

The answer is (A).

324. Value engineering is a process that identifies areas of potential savings, analyzes their potential cost impact, and selects the preferred options. An informal form of value engineering can be completed in-house by the architect after an initial opinion of probable cost has been generated, and provides a good way for the architect to communicate to the owner that a design in the owner's best interest is being generated. Based upon this information, the architect and owner can make decisions and set priorities that reflect the goals of the project. Ideally, this analysis should be a standard part of every architectural project and should be ongoing as the architect makes choices about the optimal types of materials and construction methods for this particular building.

Ideally, value engineering should be undertaken as early in the project as possible. In practice, however, it often occurs much later, giving it a bad reputation among architects for stripping all of the "good stuff" out of a design and requiring extensive (and expensive) revision of work that had been "complete."

Often, a third-party value engineer is hired by the owner to determine appropriate methods of reducing cost. The value engineer may facilitate a workshop including representatives of the architect, owner, consultants, and cost estimators. The participants will evaluate the design and propose cost-saving methods. This can be very effective if it is done early in the design process, but the closer the project is to completion, the less advantageous the process will be for the owner. The changes suggested may have serious ramifications in other parts of the design, forcing up the prices of those elements. It is critical that the architect evaluate these late proposals very carefully. If elements from the proposal are to be incorporated into the design, the architect should pay special attention to other parts of the design that may be affected by the changes and carefully coordinate the construction documents to avoid errors or omissions.

The answer is (A).

325. Sunk costs are expenses that have been incurred on a project prior to the baseline date and cannot be recovered. Generally these costs are disregarded when analyzing life-cycle costs, because it is impossible to make decisions about the best way to spend money that has already been spent. Sunk costs are incorporated into analyses of total project costs.

The answer is (C).

326. The amount of retainage at substantial completion frequently is comparable to the contractor's profit for the job—anywhere from 5% to 20%; commonly about 10%. Therefore, the contractor is often anxious to establish a substantial completion date and resolve any outstanding punch list items or other unresolved issues expeditiously, so that they may receive final payment.

The answer is (D).

327. Cast-in-place concrete one-way solid slab systems allow the designer to expose the structural system while maintaining a high fire-resistance rating. Construction time can be minimized with this system by designing repetitive elements so formwork can be reused. The system can be used with either bearing walls (less expensive, good for multiple repetitive elements) or beams and girders (more expensive, but more flexible for longer spans or greater loads).

Neither wood platform framing nor either type of steel framing permits the structure to be exposed and maintain required fire ratings. While the steel frame with rigid connections may help to reduce construction time, neither the light-gage steel framing system nor the wood platform frame helps to speed up construction of a four-story building.

The answer is (D).

328. Defensible space is a concept originally explored by Oscar Newman in the 1970s. Through a partnership with the Department of Housing and Urban Development, Newman expanded and updated his ideas in a book called *Creating Defensible Space*, which can be downloaded for free from defensiblespace.com.

Newman's work was sparked by the demise of Pruitt-Igoe, a housing complex in St. Louis, Missouri, which was planned according to the most contemporary architectural thinking but was a disaster in terms of vandalism and crime. The complex was imploded about 10 years after it was constructed. The book's thesis is that designing a space that allows residents a sense of ownership and control (unlike Pruitt-Igoe) leads to an environment that people care about and will work to maintain and protect. In his book, written in cooperation with the Department of Housing and Urban Development (HUD), Newman examines these ideas through case studies of three projects.

In low- to moderate-income housing facilities, large public spaces (such as common rooms or elevator lobbies) feel anonymous and are more likely to be vandalized. Newman's research indicates that the crime rate in a housing project increases as the number of units per entry (building height) increases and as the size of the building project increases. In contrast, a few families sharing a common entry vestibule creates a semiprivate space that those occupants can monitor. When residents have the ability to oversee the street, their feelings of association with the neighborhood, and thus of "neighbors looking out for one another," are further increased.

The answer is (C).

329. Minimum parking requirements for a site are generally determined by a local zoning ordinance. In the absence of such an ordinance, they may be determined by the program (one space for every two seats in a movie theater, for example). If the owner wishes to provide more parking than is required by the zoning ordinance, the quantity of the additional parking spaces is at his or her discretion provided that the site will accommodate them. The *ADA/ABA Guidelines* require that a percentage of the parking spaces provided be accessible, but they do not establish overall parking requirements.

The answer is (A).

330. CPTED is a concept of the National Crime Prevention Institute. CPTED evolved from defensible space ideas, and it relies on the inhabitants to police their own surroundings. The goal is to design an environment that encourages them to do so by clearly defining public and private spaces and by making streets, parking areas, and building entrances more visible to those who live in the area.

CPTED is focused on influencing behavior in positive ways through a neighborhood's design. Regulating behavior, such as by placing activities in particular locations, is outside its scope, as is suggesting materials such as hardware.

For more information on CPTED, see American Institute of Architects (AIA) Best Practices 17.07, *Understanding Human Behavior Leads to Safer Environments*, or *Crime Prevention Through Environmental Design*, by Timothy D. Crowe, available through the AIA Bookstore at aia.org.

The answer is (A), (B), (C) and (F).

331. Most zoning setback regulations affect buildings, accessory buildings, and their various components. These include bay windows, roof overhangs, and decks. However, some zoning ordinances are written to allow exceptions such as roof overhangs, if they don't project more than a certain distance into the setback, or decks that are close to the ground and do not include a roof structure. Landscaping and fences are generally excluded from setback requirements.

Each jurisdiction interprets setback requirements a little differently, so it is important to research the requirements governing a specific site.

The answer is (A), (B), (D), and (F).

332. New urbanism is an approach to town planning that advocates more diverse housing opportunities and less dependence on cars. It is a reaction to "suburban sprawl," which is characterized by congested roadways, developments of "cookie cutter" houses, and wasteful use of land and resources. New urbanism is sometimes referred to as "smart growth," and the primary force behind the movement is the Congress of the New Urbanism (cnu.org), which has compiled the basic tenets into the Charter of the New Urbanism.

Hallmarks of new urbanism include the following.

- mass transit within walking distance of homes and businesses
- mixed-use zoning with multi-family housing, single family housing, and commercial uses in proximity to one another
- a blend of single-family homes and apartments in the same neighborhood, which allows people to choose a housing type that fits their needs so they are not forced

- to relocate out of the neighborhood as their needs change
- more independence for those who cannot drive or do not own a car
- narrow streets and frequent 90° intersections, which encourage drivers to be alert and make pedestrian paths safer while making the neighborhood easier to navigate
- on-street or small-lot parking rather than vast parking lots, which encourages more interaction between the businesses and the street and while also reducing the impervious area on the site
- streets that are safe and interesting to pedestrians, which encourage walking and enable neighbors to know each other and protect their communities

The answer is (A), (B), (D), and (E).

333. Interstitial spaces between occupied floors require the most additional height per floor and the most total building height because they must be high enough to accommodate a person accessing the space for maintenance duties, as well as the ducts and equipment servicing the occupied spaces below. Daylighting, indirect lighting, and underfloor ventilation systems will add only a few feet, at most, to each floor.

The answer is (D).

334. Because there are more than 50 occupants in this space, two exits must be provided. These exits must be separate and a certain minimum distance apart so that a fire is unlikely to block both. To calculate the minimum size of the required exits from the space, multiply the maximum number of occupants by 0.2 in per occupant.

$$(300 \text{ occupants})\left(0.2 \frac{\text{in}}{\text{occupant}}\right) = 60 \text{ in}$$

Because two exits must be provided, the minimum width per exit is 30 in. However, accessibility standards and component requirements both call for a minimum clear opening width of 32 in for each door. This width is generally achieved by using a 36 in door. Therefore, the best answer is two exits, two 3 ft 0 in doors.

The answer is (D).

335. The heat island effect is the tendency for architectural materials and paving to increase the temperature of their immediate environment. A paving material with a high albedo will reflect more of the sun's heat, thereby reducing the heat island effect.

Albedo is a measure of how much of the radiant energy that a surface receives is reflected rather than absorbed. It is expressed as a fraction from zero to one. A surface that reflects three-fourths of the energy it receives (and therefore absorbs the other one-fourth) has an albedo of 0.75.

Selecting a material with a low conductivity will not have as much of an effect on the site's temperature.

The answer is (B).

336. Building shapes that can focus or amplify blast energy should be avoided. This includes L-shaped and U-shaped buildings and buildings with reentrant corners or second-floor overhangs. Because a great deal of injury can be caused by flying glass, standard float glass should not be used. Instead, injury can be minimized by using laminated glass and by properly designing glazing framing. Blast energy decreases in inverse proportion to the cube of the distance.

Blast energy decreases exponentially with increased distance between the source of the blast and the building. Because of this, one of the most effective site planning strategies is to maximize the distance between the building and the outermost secured perimeter.

The answer is (D).

337. For a change in elevation of only 1 ft in a distance of 300 ft, the slope of the house sewer can be easily decreased. However, the size of the sewer must be increased to maintain proper flow. As the slope of drainage pipe decreases the size must increase. The *International Plumbing Code* (IPC) requires a minimum slope of $^1/_4$ in/ft for pipes with a diameter of 2 $^1/_2$ in or less, $^1/_8$ in/ft for pipes from 3 in to 6 in in diameter, and $^1/_{16}$ in/ft for pipes with a diameter of 8 in or larger. In this case, the pipe could be increased from 6 in to 8 in without much increase in cost because the cost of trenching, installation, and backfill is the same.

Changing the angle of the house sewer to intercept the main line farther down the slope might be possible, but additional trenching is more expensive than increasing the pipe size. In addition, option (B) is a poor choice because there is no information about the position or the slope of the main line. Changing the location of the building may not be possible due to setback requirements or other site planning decisions. Adding a manhole does not solve the problem of slope.

The answer is (A).

338. Zoning ordinances commonly regulate the maximum area of exterior signage to control the overall amount of signage in a given zone district. The *International Building Code* (IBC) does have an appendix on signage, but this appendix is not mandatory unless specifically adopted by the local ordinance adopting the IBC. The IBC appendix primarily regulates signs' structural aspects, which may depend on the material and size. Restrictive covenants generally do not regulate signs except in residential areas. State laws do not regulate exterior building signage.

The answer is (D).

339. To determine the regulations that pertain to a planned development around a wetlands area, the architect should investigate local and state governmental rules, and U.S. Army Corps of Engineers regulations.

Regulations for wetlands are established at the federal level and can be set by local and state governments. At the federal level the U.S. Army Corps of Engineers administers provisions of the Clean Water Act of 1972, which, among other things, regulates the discharge of dredged or fill material into United States waters, including wetlands. When wetlands do not fall under the jurisdiction of the Clean Water Act, as with isolated wetlands, then state and local governments may have established rules and regulations.

LEED credit may be earned for preserving portions of the site that are within 100 ft of any wetland as defined by the *U.S. Code of Federal Regulations*, or of any isolated wetlands identified by state or local rule or within setback distances from wetlands prescribed in state or local regulations.

The answer is (A), (C), and (D).

340. The diagram shown in option (C) indicates a symmetrical layout on the site with the building visually connected with the plaza on a strong axis. Both of these are commonly used Baroque planning concepts, in which grand boulevards were used to connect palaces and other major buildings.

Although diagonal avenues were used in Baroque planning, the diagonal lines shown in option (D) are not strong enough to pick up the theme of diagonal avenues or boulevards.

The answer is (C).

341. In an urban setting, a rear yard building is most appropriate for a retail store. In urban site planning, there are four basic types of site utilization based on where the building is located. With a rear yard type, the front of the building is placed on the lot line. Open space at the rear of the lot is used for parking, service, or other functions. This type is a good way for retail stores to expose a maximum amount of storefront to the street while defining an edge of an urban space.

A courtyard building occupies all or nearly all of the edges of a lot with a private interior courtyard. This building type is good where security or privacy is needed for the outdoor space. A perimeter yard building is located in the middle of the lot with open space surrounding it. It is often utilized in semi-urban or suburban locations for residential use or where a monumental appearance is desired. A side yard building occupies one side of the lot with the other side open. This configuration can be used to create a semiprivate yard or to orient the building for solar access.

The answer is (C).

342. Eliminating parking lot lighting is a poor strategy for minimizing light pollution. Although eliminating any site lighting will reduce light pollution, some light is necessary for circulation and safety. High-reflective surfaces will increase the possibility of light pollution. Changing the light trespass from the inside of buildings could be used in conjunction with other strategies, but that will not likely minimize light pollution by itself.

The answer is (B).

343. An exterior pedestrian walk must be accessible, so the design solution must include a ramp. Option (A) and option (B) do not include a ramp, and so are not viable options. Either option (C) or option (D) work, but of the two, option (C) is the better design solution. A single ramp for such a short distance works for all people and be safer. Further, if the ramp is 14 ft long, the slope is less than the maximum 1:12, which is generally recommended. For option (D), it is also difficult to locate the beginning and end of the ramp at the recommended location near the bottom and top of the steps.

Option (A) is incorrect not only because it does not include a ramp, but also because it has only two steps, which is dangerous. There should be a minimum of three steps in a flight of stairs.

The answer is (C).

344. Of the options listed, video surveillance monitored by a central station is the best electronic security system to protect the exterior of an office building. Audio alarms are not appropriate to protect the exterior of a building because of possible false alarms caused by on- and off-site noises. Motion sensors are not useful because of possible false alarms caused by animals, air turbulence, and other interferences. Thermal detectors are only useful in relatively small rooms and are used to detect torches and other high-heat sources.

The answer is (D).

345. The site design elements that influence fire protection and are the responsibility of the architect include the position and size of building canopies, surface material outside of the building, traffic control fences and bollard positions, and the width of fire apparatus access drives. While the local fire department may have suggestions or requirements for these features, the exact design is the responsibility of the architect.

The position of fire hydrants on streets and the size and position of other utility elements are the responsibility of the various municipal utilities.

The answer is (A), (B), (C), and (F).

346. In a residential subdivision, designing stairways within solid structures is counter to reducing the potential for criminal activity. According to the principles of Crime Prevention Through Environmental Design (CPTED), stairways and elevators should be located within view of other areas.

Using low plantings or post-and-rail fences helps to define private areas and gives a sense of territorial reinforcement. Locating entry doors and common areas within view of the street or other neighbors provides natural surveillance. Short walks also make natural surveillance possible.

The answer is (A), (B), (D), and (F).

347. For a hot-arid climate, a building's thermal mass should be maximized, not minimized. (Minimizing the thermal mass is a suitable strategy in a hot-humid climate.) Openings should be minimized to reduce heat infiltration. For a hot-arid climate, all windows should be shaded. A compact form is ideal for minimizing heat gain.

The answer is (D).

348. The most important characteristic of an on-site road designed to serve parking areas and service vehicles is the slope. An on-site road should be laid out to avoid steep slopes, which may be difficult to drive on, especially when the surface is icy. A tangent is the straight portion of a road connected to the curved portions. Horizontal alignment is the road layout in the horizontal direction and vertical alignment is the layout in the vertical direction. While all are important in the design of roads for higher speed traffic, slope is the most critical for slow speed service use such as parking and service roads.

The answer is (A).

349. A material with a low albedo and a low conductivity such as dark wood is most comfortable and moderates the microclimate best. Brick, concrete, and stone have higher albedos and make the surrounding area hotter in the summer. Their high conductivity also make them feel hot to the touch. Planting grass around the pavers will improve the albedo of a brick deck slightly, but dark wood still has a lower albedo. Also, wood has the lowest conductivity of the materials listed and will feel less hot in the summer.

The answer is (D).

350. All roads should have a crown, or high point, in the center to ensure positive drainage to either side.

The answer is (B).

351. The difference in elevation between two points at the bottom, or invert, of a sewer line is what causes the water flow. The term invert is also used to call out the bottom of drains, catch basins, and manholes.

The answer is (D).

352. Retaining walls less than 4 ft high can usually be constructed of any suitable material, such as stones, loose-laid blocks, or preservative-treated wood. Higher walls become subject to sliding and overturning forces and must be engineered to resist the expected loads. Typically these engineered retaining walls are constructed of concrete or masonry and are built on footings.

The type of soil, the groundwater level, and the soil porosity alone do not dictate the use of reinforced concrete or masonry.

The answer is (A).

353. Corners and eaves generally receive higher wind forces than the rest of a building. This is why most wind damage occurs at corners and eaves.

The answer is (A).

354. Wind pressure on a building is affected by wind speed, surrounding terrain, and the building's height and shape. The weight of the building and the soil type do not affect it.

The answer is (A), (B), (D), and (F).

355. The moment-resisting frame has rigid moment-resisting connections between beams and columns. It is an appropriate system to use for resisting lateral forces, not just in low-rise buildings, but also in high-rise buildings with 30 stories or less. For taller buildings, other systems should be considered, or some additional type of bracing, such as X or chevron bracing, should be used.

The answer is (B).

356. Wood I-joists generally can used for spans larger than 20 ft, up to about 45 ft or a little more, depending on the manufacturer.

The size of lumber is limited by the size of the trees from which it is made. For this reason, regular sawn lumber joists are usually available for spans up to about 20 ft. In wood buildings and for spans larger than 20 ft, sawn lumber joists cannot be used and other options must be considered, such as I-joists and other engineered wood products like laminated veneer lumber (LVL) and glulam (glued laminated construction).

Wood I-joists have an I-section, with flanges made of lumber and a web made of plywood or oriented strand board (OSB). They are generally spaced like sawn lumber beams, and often frame into an LVL or a glulam beam in the perpendicular direction. They are usually available for spans up to about 45 ft.

The answer is (C).

357. The pan joist is a reinforced concrete slab system that is ribbed in one direction only. This system is strong compared to the other traditional concrete slab systems and is therefore best suited for buildings with heavy live loads, such as industrial and storage buildings (option (A)). Hotels are similar to residential buildings in terms of live loads. Live loads are relatively light in these buildings, so option (B) and option (C) are incorrect. Live loads in office buildings are generally lower compared to the industrial and storage buildings, so option (D) is also incorrect.

The answer is (A).

358. All the listed factors affect a building's response to an earthquake except for the local temperature and the orientation of the building. Other factors that have an effect are the quality of the construction and the distance from the epicenter of the quake.

The answer is (A), (C), (E), and (F).

359. The square floor plan (option (B)) is the best shape for lateral loads. The figures in option (A) (L-shaped), option (C) (U-shaped), and option (D) (cross-shaped) show floor plans with reentrant corners, which should be avoided when possible. If reentrant corners cannot be avoided, then drag struts or seismic separations must be considered.

The answer is (B).

360. The problematic building elevation is shown in option (B). This configuration is unstable because the weight of the building is resting on a base that is smaller than the rest of the structure.

An opposite design is shown in option (D). Here the base of the building is wider than the top, which helps with the general stability of the building. Option (A) is regular in shape, and no problems are to be expected with it. In option (C), the building is supported on columns, which suggests a soft story; however the columns are braced as shown, which constitutes an acceptable design practice.

One of the most important design recommendations for lateral loads is regularity. Buildings and structures must be regular in stiffness and shape both in plan and in vertical configuration. Symmetry is another good rule of design, as it helps in the general structural stability of a building.

Reentrant corners as well as sudden changes in shape or stiffness must be avoided. In a vertical configuration, pyramidal shapes should have the wide side at the base. The load path must always be continuous, and the lateral load-resisting elements should not be interrupted.

The answer is (B).

361. Timber piles have the lowest initial cost and least load-bearing capacity. The general depth range of these piles is 25 ft to 40 ft. Their safe load-bearing capacity varies from 30 kips to 80 kips.

The answer is (D).

362. The earthquake effects or damages not covered in the building codes are landslides, avalanches, and soil liquefaction. Building codes cover ground shaking, horizontal movement, and vibration effects. Vibration generally covers a large area and can occur in any direction, including the vertical direction.

The current practice, however, is to consider only the horizontal or lateral movement; the vertical component of the vibration is ignored because the component is small compared to the horizontal component, and the weight of the building tends to counterbalance the vertical forces.

The answer is (A), (D), and (F).

363. The architect does not need to consider the zoning ordinance, ASTM standards, or the local fire department. The zoning ordinance does not set forth specific requirements for claddings. Although the architect should be aware of ASTM standards, any that are required are referenced in the code or the state energy code. Moreover, the local fire department is concerned with the fire resistance of exterior walls. The building code specifies these requirements along with the required construction types based on the building's size and height plus the fire zone in which the building is located.

The design of an exterior cladding system requires the architect to consider a variety of constraints and issues. The building code gives requirements for insulation, fire resistance, air barriers, structural attachment, durability, and tolerances. The state energy code may place additional requirements on elements such as insulation. The city planning board may have specific requirements for the appearance and detailing of cladding. For example, the city may require specific adopted design goals for buildings in a certain neighborhood.

The answer is (B), (C), and (F).

364. Although any of the options might be a possibility, the most restrictive requirement usually takes precedence when regulations are in conflict. Appealing a requirement takes time and costs money. Appealing a requirement is typically not worth the effort compared with designing to

Project Planning

the most restrictive requirement. It could also delay the project.

The answer is (D).

365. The site plan shown borders Decatur Street to the south and 13th Avenue to the east. A lake borders the site to the west. An existing shopping center borders the site to the north. The site contains a five-story apartment building, a connecting plaza, and a cafe/bookstore. To the east of the buildings is a parking lot, with three accessible parking spaces nearest the apartment building. The site plan shown poses a potential problem for Americans with Disabilities Act (ADA) accessibility and community development. Place the hot spot marker in the site area where an element should be included to meet ADA requirements.

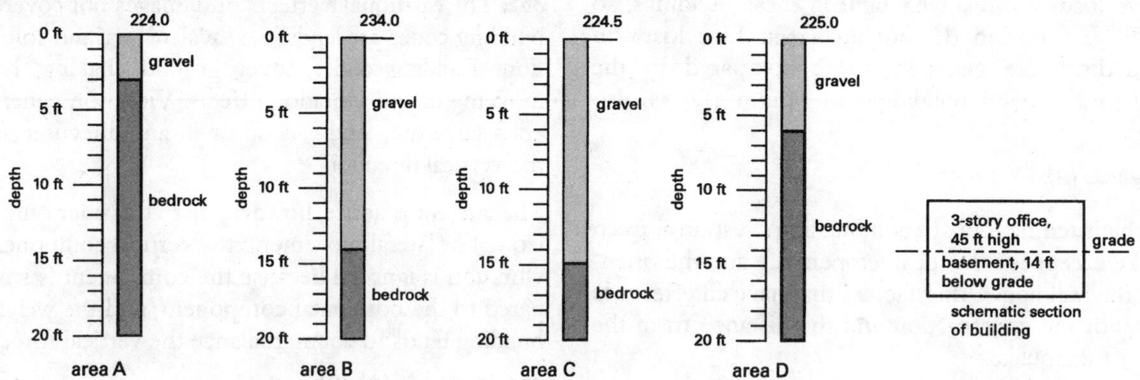

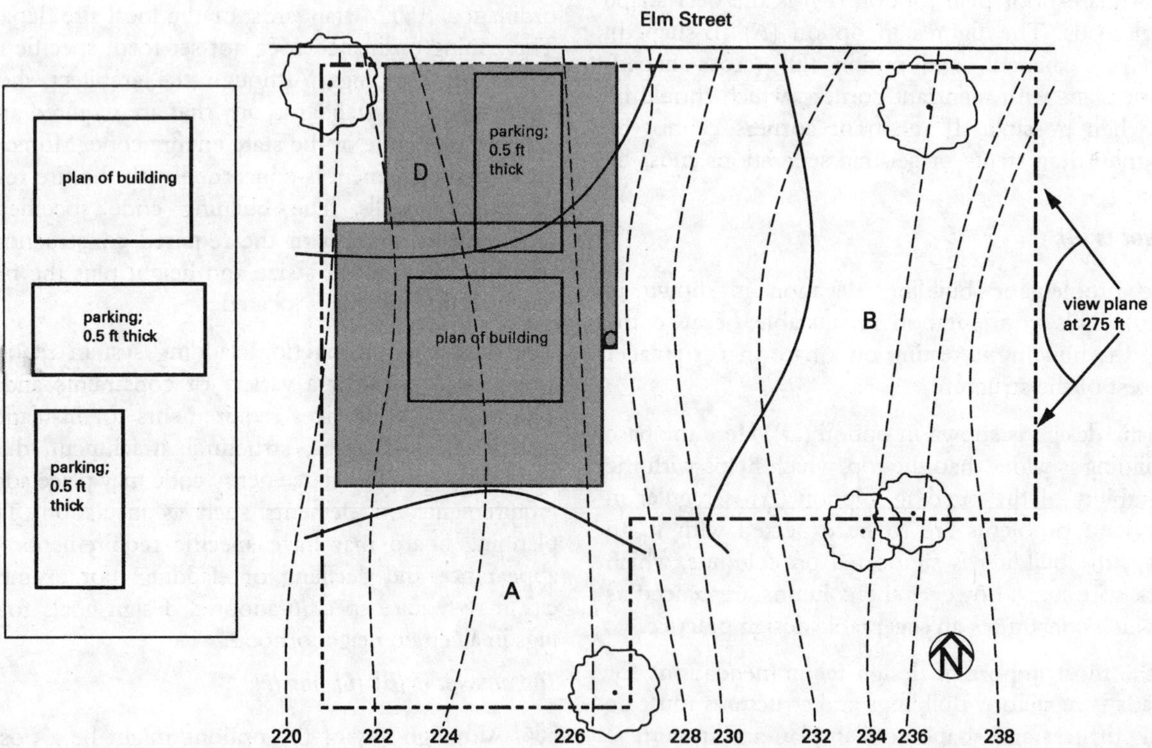

366. There must be ADA accessibility from the public walks to the site. In this case, such access is the area between the sidewalk from Decatur Street and the plaza. The access is needed for a direct connection to the sidewalk and neighborhood in general. The parking lot and access from the parking lot to the plaza and buildings are acceptable as shown. The shaded area in the site plan indicates the allowable margin for error. The correct place for the hot spot marker is somewhere in this shaded area. (See *illustration for Sol. 366.*)

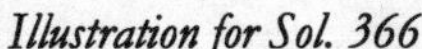

Illustration for Sol. 366

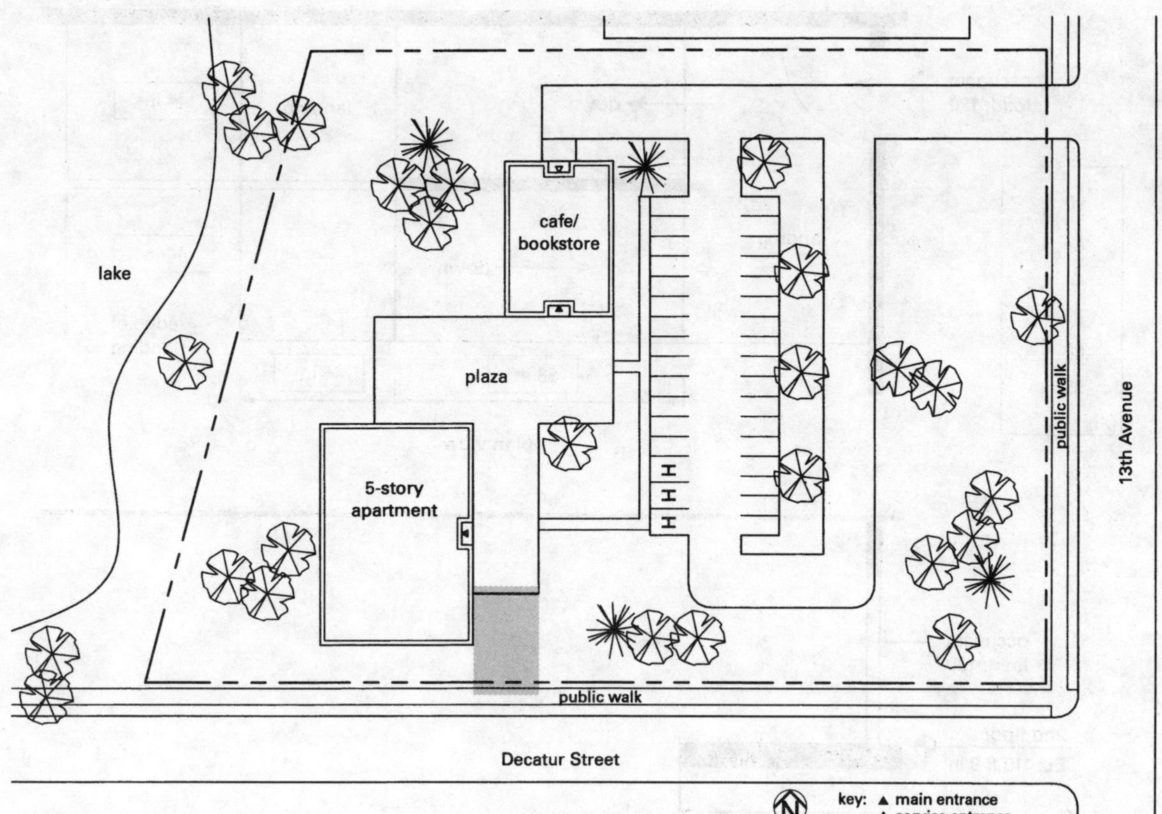

367. View ordinances, utility easements, and municipal master plans affect the massing, but they are investigated after zoning. Because zoning regulations significantly affect building massing—including floor area ratio, setbacks, and bulk plane restrictions—the architect should research zoning regulations first.

The answer is (B).

368. The school board is unlikely to reduce space needs. The local planning commission is not involved with setback issues. A conditional use permit typically is used to allow a nonconforming use in a zoning district, which is not the appropriate way to solve the conflict. A variance is a deviation from zoning regulations. The architect can assist the school district in applying for a variance and present the case to the zoning board. When a school requests a setback variance, the hardship is likely to be recognized and a variance granted.

The answer is (C).

369.

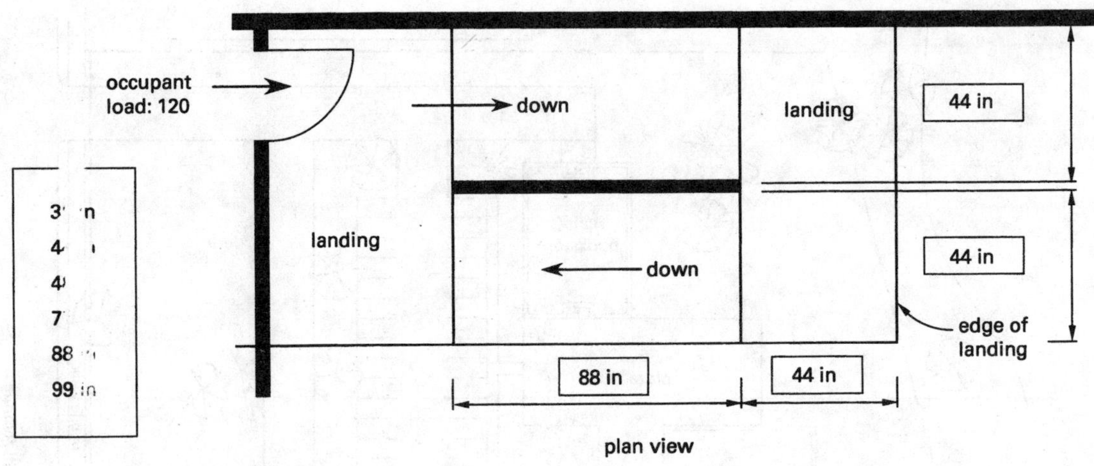

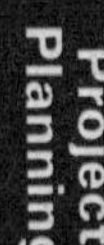

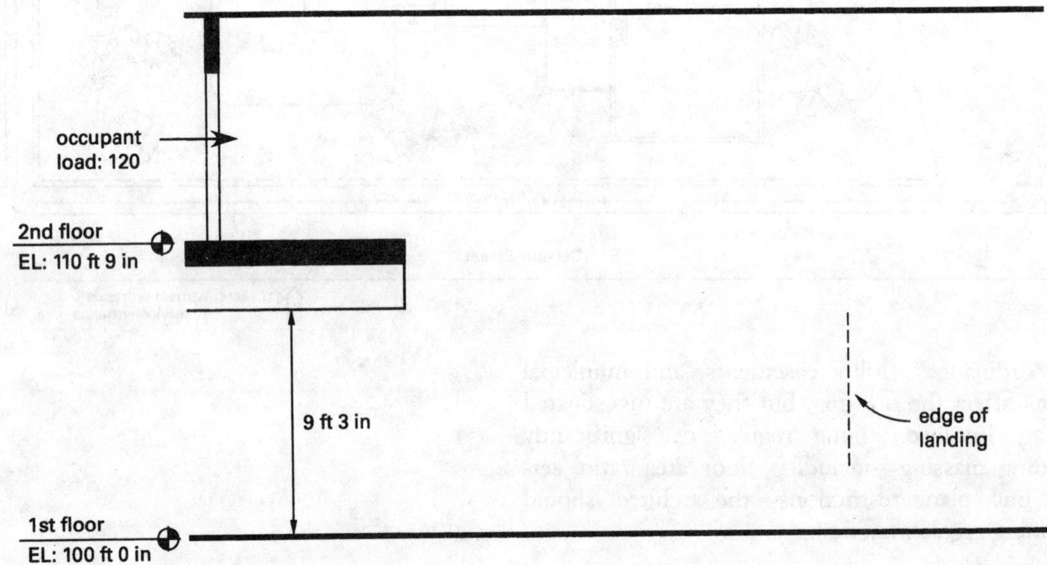

The number of risers must be determined to establish the number of treads and total run. The maximum allowable riser dimension is used to calculate the necessary number of risers.

$$\begin{aligned}\text{no. of risers} &= \frac{\text{riser height}}{\text{floor-to-floor height}}\\ &= \frac{7\text{ in}}{129\text{ in}}\\ &= 18.43 \quad (19)\end{aligned}$$

19 is an odd number, so there will be an unequal number of risers and treads in the two flights of stairs. If 9 risers are used in the upper flight and 10 risers in the lower flight, the last tread on the first floor will extend beyond the edge of the upper landing, which is acceptable because there will still be sufficient head clearance below the ceiling. This configuration will result in the minimum total run.

The minimum tread dimension for 9 risers is used to calculate the minimum total run.

$$\begin{aligned}\text{total run}_{\text{minimum}} &= (\text{tread dimension}_{\text{minimum}})\\ &\quad\times(\text{tread width}_{\text{minimum}})\\ &= (8\text{ treads})(11\text{ in})\\ &= 88\text{ in}\end{aligned}$$

The required width of the stair is calculated from the occupant load and the non-sprinklered factor.

$$\begin{aligned}\text{stair width} &= (\text{occupant load})(\text{non-sprinklered factor})\\ &= (120)(0.3\text{ in})\\ &= 36\text{ in}\end{aligned}$$

For an occupant load greater than 50, however, the minimum required width is 44 in. The landing must be at least the same width as the stair, which is also 44 in.

370. The three parts of the zoning ordinance that affect the building configuration are the side setback requirement, the allowable maximum height, and the upper story setback requirement. The side setback requirement is 5 ft. For lots wider than 50 ft, if an additional foot is allowed for each 5 ft in lot width (up to a maximum of 35 ft), then the maximum height increase on a 100 ft wide lot is 10 ft, which is in addition to the basic 70 ft height limit. The upper story must be set back 15 ft for a story higher than 30 ft. The zoning requirements determine the allowable building configuration as shown in the elevation diagram grid.

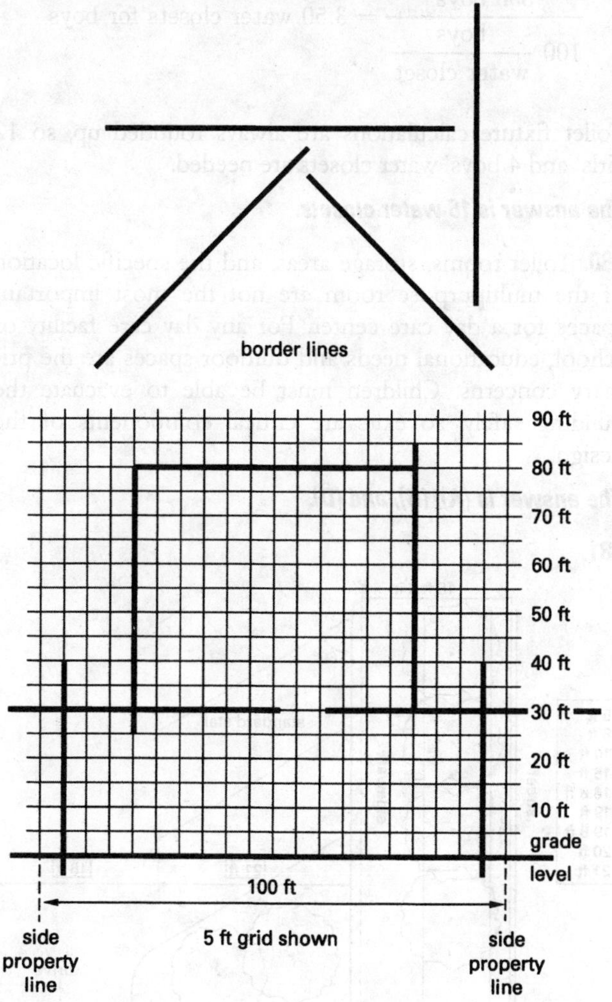

371. A grid floor plan is confusing and is not appropriate for visitors not familiar with the building. Although signage is critical to orient visitors in an unfamiliar facility, signage alone can become confusing. Color-coded stripes in the floor are useful, but they only help direct people to a particular area and generally do not assist in overall orientation in a building. The correct orientation method is a spatial one. A waiting lobby is a central space that allows visitors to access corridors easily.

The answer is (D).

372. The grid system, circular loop, and radial configuration result in a circulation system that is spread out and more complicated to integrate with mechanical systems, although structural systems may be easily integrated with them. The linear layout, or dumbbell scheme, establishes a single corridor with spaces on either side. The scheme can be in a straight line, bent in an L-shape, or in another configuration.

The answer is (D).

373. The shape of the building described does not necessarily result in structural efficiency. Similarly, open planning does not necessarily minimize social hierarchy. Although the design of open space with maximum window exposure is popular for other reasons (such as increased efficiency and daylighting), it is not a result of cultural popularity or precedence. Evidence-based design suggests that having access to views and ample daylight contributes to increased efficiency and the satisfaction of office workers.

The answer is (B).

374. Setting the building back from the sidewalk a short distance is not effective because a four- or five-story building is a dominating presence in the neighborhood. Building at the sidewalk is disruptive to the scale of the neighborhood. Trying to re-create historic buildings with materials and detailing is seldom successful. In a downtown area with dense development and little open space, the scale of the new building is important. One approach is to build no higher than the existing buildings along the sidewalk, and then set back upper stories so they are not be seen from the street. This approach also allows for ample sunlight and views to the sky.

The answer is (A).

375. Grid, linear, and radial layout options tend to spread out spaces and allow for fewer primary adjacencies, even though they do allow for expansion. For example, a grid system requires many corridors to connect the spaces in the grid, increasing size and making direct adjacencies difficult. A linear layout extends the building and necessarily places some spaces far away from others along a corridor, making primary adjacencies difficult. A radial layout does the same. A central layout of spaces and activities provides immediate adjacencies between spaces next to each other and across the central organizing space. Central layouts also allow for short walking distances between spaces for both people and supplies. If the entire area around the central space is used, however, expansion can be problematic because corridors must be made to connect the expansion with the original layout.

The answer is (A).

Project Planning

376. The net assignable space includes the spaces used for specific functions (i.e., book stacks, reading rooms, offices, meeting rooms, and similar spaces). It does not account for circulation, toilet rooms, mechanical rooms, walls, and the like. The estimated 10% circulation space is part of the 80% efficiency ratio and is not included in the calculation.

The total gross area required is determined by dividing the net assignable area by the efficiency ratio.

$$\text{gross area} = \frac{\text{net assignable area}}{\text{efficiency ratio}} = \frac{25{,}000\ \text{ft}^2}{0.80} = 31{,}250\ \text{ft}^2$$

The answer is (C).

377. A long space can function for the initial design but a long space with separate assembly areas is not as flexible as a rectangular or square plan. Expansion is not mentioned. Although a flexible system of electrical and mechanical services is a good idea for any building shape, a grid system of support does not fully accommodate the needs.

The portion of the program given relates to providing timely flexibility as needs change. Future requirements are not known, except for electronics manufacturing. The architect plans for this facility by providing a large open space that can be reconfigured as required. A rectangular space most likely serves a linear assembly line and wide structural bays keep the space as unencumbered as possible.

The answer is (D).

378. Building location A is oriented in a suitable direction for passive solar design. Because it is located on a steeper slope, however, construction on location A is difficult and costly. Building location B allows for easy expansion and allows an adequate though not ideal orientation for passive and active solar design. Location B is in the middle of the site, however, making future development difficult. Building location D is oriented in the wrong direction for solar design (the length-oriented north to south) and runs across the contour lines, making construction difficult and costly.

Building location C integrates the given program requirements. It is oriented with the long direction slightly to the east of south, which is ideal for passive solar design in a temperate climate and active solar design. Placing the building at location C also allows for easy expansion. The building lies on a gentle slope, and the remainder of the site remains clear for future expansion. The possibility of placing the first building of the development in a prominent corner location is an added advantage.

The answer is (C).

379. This problem asks only for a calculation of water closets, so the information on lavatories, urinals, and drinking fountains can be disregarded.

$$\frac{400\ \text{girls}}{35\ \dfrac{\text{girls}}{\text{water closet}}} = 11.42\ \text{water closets for girls}$$

$$\frac{350\ \text{boys}}{100\ \dfrac{\text{boys}}{\text{water closet}}} = 3.50\ \text{water closets for boys}$$

Toilet fixture calculations are always rounded up, so 12 girls' and 4 boys' water closets are needed.

The answer is 16 water closets.

380. Toilet rooms, storage areas, and the specific location of the multipurpose room are not the most important spaces for a day care center. For any day care facility or school, educational needs and outdoor spaces are the primary concerns. Children must be able to evacuate the building safely, so exits are critical components of the design.

The answer is (A), (B), and (D).

381.

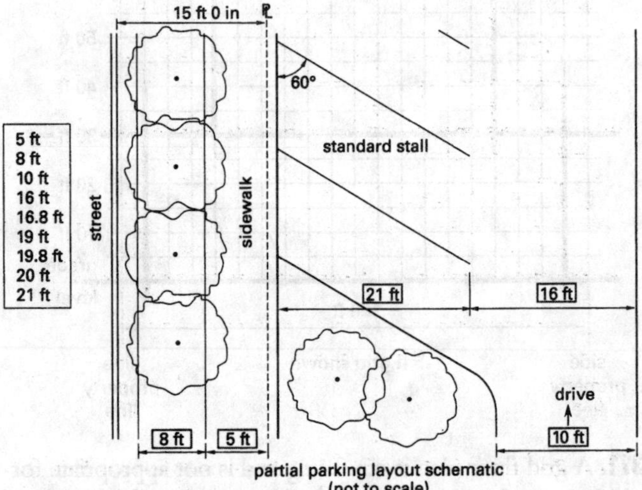

partial parking layout schematic
(not to scale)

For right-of-ways that are at least 15 ft, the surface parking lot and landscaping figure shows that walks must be a minimum of 5 ft and landscaped areas must be a minimum of 8 ft. For standard parking spaces, the required dimensions are given in the table row labeled 60° Although the required width of the parking row access is 16 ft, the minimum required width of a one-way internal drive is 10 ft, as stated in the parking dimensions table footnote.

382. The block diagram does not provide any indication of site development, and any connection will not be present in the block diagram. Presumably, a well-designed connection will be developed from the parking to the indicated entrance to the building. Although the mechanical and electrical room does present a blank, uninviting wall toward the important urban portion of the site, it is not missing in the block diagram. The entry faces west to respond to the urban development, but there must still be a connection to the parking area to the east. According to the adjacency diagram, both the meeting room and the conference room must have views of the park.

The answer is (D).

383. The block diagram and site plan are too general to determine whether there are accessibility problems. The building is clearly outside of the easement. The block diagram shows no violations of any setback requirements. There is enough space to the north and south for expansion. The list of spaces in Resource 1 indicates that the meeting room is 1500 ft^2. According to the *International Building Code* (IBC), this space requires two exits and only one is shown. Another exit can be located on the east wall of the space for direct access to the exterior.

The answer is (C).

384. The T-shape makes it awkward for the assistant coordinator to access the corridor directly either through the facility coordinator office or through the lobby; there is still corridor access. The mechanical and electrical room does not need to be centrally located. It should be located at one edge of the building. The restrooms are located in a convenient location. Although the adjacency diagram only indicates that the assistant facility coordinator office needs to be directly adjacent to the facility coordinator office, good planning suggests that each office have direct access to a corridor.

The answer is (A).

385. A corridor may become a dead end before the expansion is completed. Rotating the mechanical and electrical room 90 degrees only provides space for one office without extending the corridor or creating another awkward dead-end corridor. Although moving the mechanical and electrical room to the south of the meeting room allows for expansion space along the south side of a corridor, placing the mechanical and electrical room at this location makes it difficult to create a direct and pleasant path from the parking area. Having a mechanical and electrical room at the entry to a building also exposes air intakes, exhausts, and similar wall penetration to the public face of the facility.

The easiest and most direct way to allow for expansion is to plan for the new offices on the building's west end, by extending the corridor. This initial phase of construction must be located as far east as possible.

The answer is (B).

386. Although the plan could be improved by placing the meeting storage space on the east side of the meeting room, the block diagram shows this same adjacency requirement. The plan allows a view from the meeting room to the park, but the view requirement is not a necessary consideration in this case. Switching the conference room and the lobby creates the same adjacency relationship that the block diagram shows. The community relations office is not required to be close to the conference room. A secondary adjacency is not indicated. The adjacency diagram shows a direct adjacency requirement between the neighborhood director office and the secretarial space. By switching the location of the secretarial space and community relations office, the adjacencies are accurately satisfied as compared to placing the storage space on the east side of the meeting room.

The answer is (D).

387. Putting the storage space in a prominent position between the toilet rooms and secretarial space is unnecessary and undesirable. Likewise, placing the storage space between the neighborhood director office space and the break room is not ideal because there is little available space at the building limit line and the corridor must be extended for this one space. There is little space for the storage room between the mechanical and electrical room and the facility coordinator office as well.

According to the adjacency diagram, the storage space should have a secondary adjacency with the secretarial space. If the storage space is placed next to the facility coordinator office, the storage space is nearby, across the corridor from the secretarial space. According to the adjacency diagram, the secretarial space should be switched with the community relations office, which makes the secretarial space closer to the storage space. The corridor and the mechanical and electrical room align when the mechanical and electrical room is rotated 90 degrees from the west walls of the work room.

The answer is (C).

388. The adjacency diagram does not require moving the storage space because it meets the adjacency requirements. The facility coordinator office is already directly across from the reception space. The facility coordinator office and assistant facility coordinator office are allowed to open directly to the lobby. Although this alternate plan corrects many of the problems in the original layout in Resource 4.2, the plan still has a weak connection to the developing urban neighborhood to the west. The entrance is not visible from the west. In addition, the location of

Project Planning

the work room, storage space, and mechanical and electrical room display a blank image of the building to the west.

The answer is (A).

389.

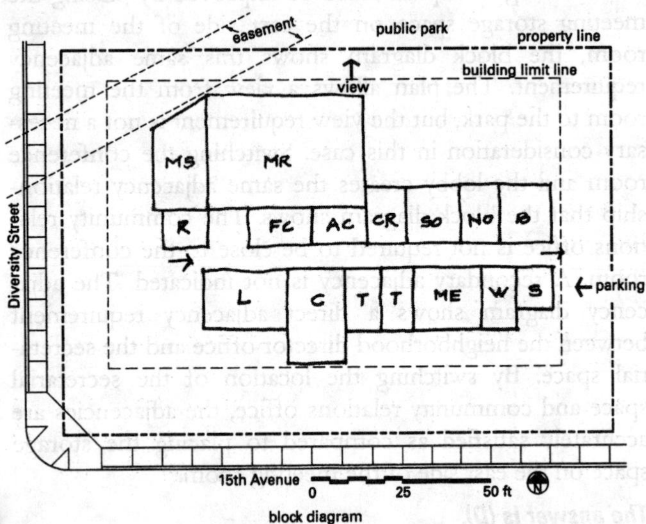

block diagram

Improving the connection to the west conflicts with creating easy building access from the parking lot on the opposite end of the property. The sides of the meeting room, as well as the sides of the meeting storage space, present a large blank face toward Diversity Street. In addition, the entrance is somewhat removed from the urban neighborhood to the west, making option (C) incorrect. Although option (A) is a slight improvement, the meeting room still presents a large, mostly blank facade to the west. The entry is also removed from the west side.

Both option (B) and option (D) provide pedestrian entrance access from the building's west side. Option (D), however, from an urban design point of view, does not allow as much aesthetic appeal along the building's west side. Because option (B) allows for easy pedestrian access while giving an urban open space on the corner, the reception space, entry, lobby space, and conference room can be designed as open, inviting spaces.

The answer is (B).

390. Rotating the mechanical and electrical room and lobby spaces and relocating the assistant facility coordinator office still result in as many corners, with similar costs. Placing the meeting storage space east of the meeting room actually increases construction costs by adding two additional corners to the building. Although shortening the span of the meeting room reduces costs by reducing the size of structural members, two awkward columns are placed in the middle of the meeting room. Costs are often reduced by eliminating as many corners as possible. Eliminating corners reduces foundation wall construction costs and exterior wall costs. Such a strategy is a general approach to minimizing costs.

The answer is (D).

DIVISION 5: PROJECT DEVELOPMENT & DOCUMENTATION

Project Development

Multiple Choice

391. (A) (B) (C) (D) (E) (F)
392. (A) (B) (C) (D)
393. (A) (B) (C) (D) (E) (F)
394. (A) (B) (C) (D)
395. (A) (B) (C) (D)
396. (A) (B) (C) (D)
397. (A) (B) (C) (D)
398. (A) (B) (C) (D)
399. (A) (B) (C) (D)
400. (A) (B) (C) (D)
401. (A) (B) (C) (D)
402. (A) (B) (C) (D)
403. (A) (B) (C) (D)
404. (A) (B) (C) (D)
405. (A) (B) (C) (D)
406. (A) (B) (C) (D)
407. (A) (B) (C) (D)
408. (A) (B) (C) (D)
409. (A) (B) (C) (D)
410. (A) (B) (C) (D)
411. (A) (B) (C) (D)
412. (A) (B) (C) (D)
413. (A) (B) (C) (D)
414. (A) (B) (C) (D)
415. (A) (B) (C) (D)
416. (A) (B) (C) (D)
417. (A) (B) (C) (D)
418. (A) (B) (C) (D)
419. (A) (B) (C) (D)
420. (A) (B) (C) (D)
421. (A) (B) (C) (D)
422. (A) (B) (C) (D)
423. (A) (B) (C) (D)
424. (A) (B) (C) (D)
425. (A) (B) (C) (D)
426. (A) (B) (C) (D) (E) (F)
427. (A) (B) (C) (D)
428. (A) (B) (C) (D) (E) (F)
429. (A) (B) (C) (D)
430. ____________
431. ____________
432. (A) (B) (C) (D)
433. (A) (B) (C) (D)
434. (A) (B) (C) (D) (E) (F)
435. (A) (B) (C) (D) (E) (F)
436. (A) (B) (C) (D)
437. (A) (B) (C) (D)
438. (A) (B) (C) (D)
439. (A) (B) (C) (D) (E) (F)
440. (A) (B) (C) (D) (E) (F)
441. (A) (B) (C) (D) (E) (F)
442. (A) (B) (C) (D)
443. (A) (B) (C) (D)
444. (A) (B) (C) (D)
445. (A) (B) (C) (D)
446. (A) (B) (C) (D) (E) (F)
447. (A) (B) (C) (D) (E) (F)
448. (A) (B) (C) (D)
449. (A) (B) (C) (D)
450. (A) (B) (C) (D)
451. (A) (B) (C) (D)
452. (A) (B) (C) (D)
453. (A) (B) (C) (D)
454. (A) (B) (C) (D)
455. (A) (B) (C) (D) (E) (F)
456. (A) (B) (C) (D)
457. (A) (B) (C) (D)
458. (A) (B) (C) (D) (E) (F)
459. (A) (B) (C) (D) (E) (F)
460. (A) (B) (C) (D)
461. (A) (B) (C) (D) (E) (F)
462. (A) (B) (C) (D)
463. (A) (B) (C) (D)
464. (A) (B) (C) (D)
465. (A) (B) (C) (D)
466. (A) (B) (C) (D)
467. (A) (B) (C) (D)
468. (A) (B) (C) (D)
469. (A) (B) (C) (D)
470. (A) (B) (C) (D)
471. (A) (B) (C) (D)
472. (A) (B) (C) (D)
473. (A) (B) (C) (D) (E) (F)
474. (A) (B) (C) (D) (E) (F)
475. (A) (B) (C) (D)
476. (A) (B) (C) (D)
477. (A) (B) (C) (D) (E) (F)
478. (A) (B) (C) (D) (E) (F)
479. ____________
480. (A) (B) (C) (D)
481. (A) (B) (C) (D) (E) (F)
482. (A) (B) (C) (D)
483. (A) (B) (C) (D) (E) (F)
484. (A) (B) (C) (D)
485. (A) (B) (C) (D)
486. (A) (B) (C) (D)
487. (A) (B) (C) (D)
488. (A) (B) (C) (D)
489. (A) (B) (C) (D) (E) (F)
490. (A) (B) (C) (D) (E) (F)
491. (A) (B) (C) (D) (E) (F)

Case Study 1

492. (A) (B) (C) (D)
493. (A) (B) (C) (D)
494. (A) (B) (C) (D)
495. (A) (B) (C) (D)
496. ____________
497. ____________
498. ____________
499. (A) (B) (C) (D) (E) (F)

Case Study 2

500. (A) (B) (C) (D)
501. (A) (B) (C) (D)
502. (A) (B) (C) (D)
503. (A) (B) (C) (D)
504. (A) (B) (C) (D)
505. ____________
506. ____________
507. ____________
508. (A) (B) (C) (D)
509. (A) (B) (C) (D) (E) (F)
510. (A) (B) (C) (D)

391. Which of the following statements about precast concrete are true? (Choose the three that apply.)

(A) Type III cement (high-early-strength) is often used for precast concrete members.

(B) Precast concrete members can be a maximum of 14 ft wide.

(C) Concrete used in precast members is typically 3000 psi.

(D) Conditions are more controlled during the production of precast concrete members than they would be for similar structural systems built in the field.

(E) Precast concrete can be used only with white aggregate.

(F) Precast concrete shapes include flooring planks, wall panels, and door modules.

392. A slip joint is used in the head of an aluminum storefront system to

(A) allow for expansion and contraction

(B) accommodate the deflection of the structure

(C) facilitate the installation of the mullions

(D) provide a way to install and remove the glazing

393. Which of the following will effectively reduce the possibility of termite infestation? (Choose the three that apply.)

(A) Design the slope of the grade near the foundation to fall away from the structure.

(B) Specify pressure-treated lumber.

(C) Require that soil poison be applied to the footprint area of the building before construction operations begin.

(D) Provide a gravel drainage area where the foundation wall meets the surrounding grade.

(E) Wood members are located above ground.

(F) Provide adequate attic ventilation.

394. The energy required to turn a raw material into a finished building product is known as

(A) manufacturing energy

(B) embodied energy

(C) production energy

(D) commissioning energy

395. Materials or assemblies with a high noise reduction coefficient (NRC) generally have a

(A) high sound transmission class (STC)

(B) low STC

(C) high reverberation time

(D) low absorption coefficient

396. Which of these statements about reinforcing bar (rebar) sizes is true?

(A) American and metric sizes are now based on a unitless number.

(B) American bar numbers equal the number of eighths of an inch across the diameter.

(C) Reinforcing bars are available only in Grade 40.

(D) Epoxy-coated reinforcing steel bars are used only on interior concrete floor slabs.

397. The portion of the roof indicated at A is a

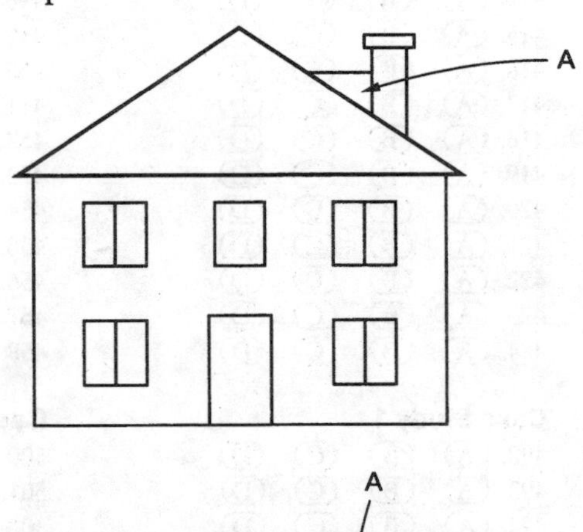

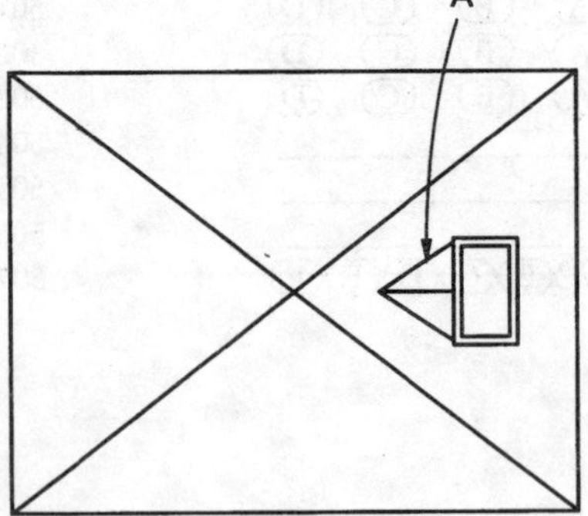

(A) cricket

(B) hip

(C) gable

(D) dormer

398. A section of a precast concrete panel attached to a cast-in-place concrete structure is shown.

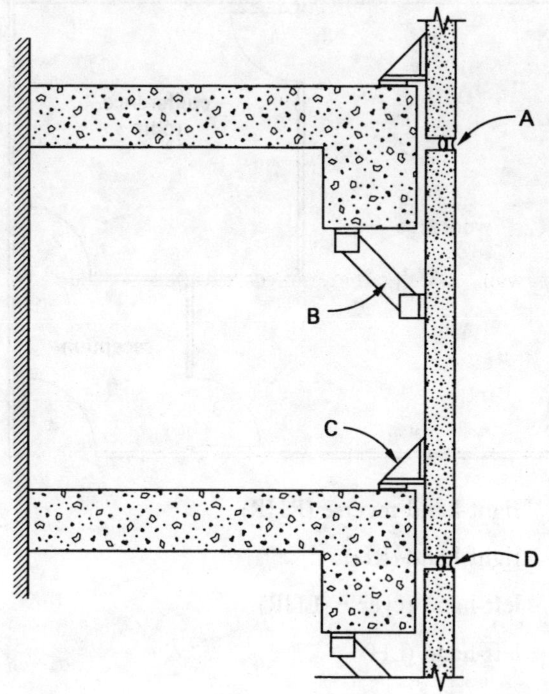

Which connection point should allow for both vertical and lateral movement?

(A) A

(B) B

(C) C

(D) D

399. What is used to minimize corner chipping of concrete?

(A) chamfer strips

(B) hardeners

(C) rustication strips

(D) walers

400. In masonry walls, water is prevented from seeping back into the wall through capillary action by using

(A) base flashing

(B) coping

(C) drips

(D) weep holes

401. Which area in the masonry wall assembly shown is the most susceptible to water penetration?

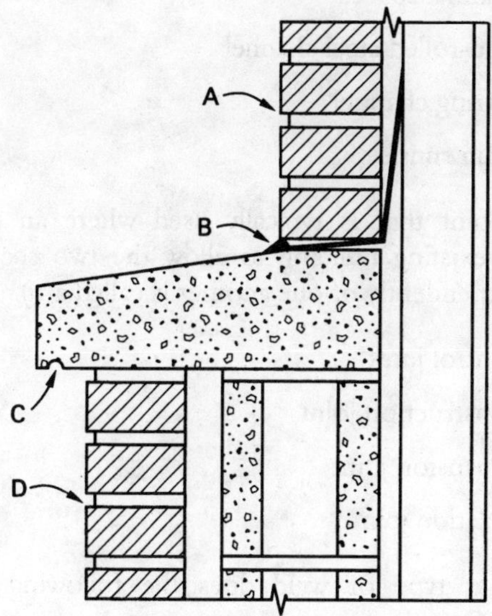

(A) area A

(B) area B

(C) area C

(D) area D

402. Asphalt-impregnated building paper is used under siding primarily to

(A) improve thermal resistance

(B) increase the water resistance of the wall

(C) act as a vapor barrier

(D) all of the above

403. A gypsum wallboard ceiling detail is shown.

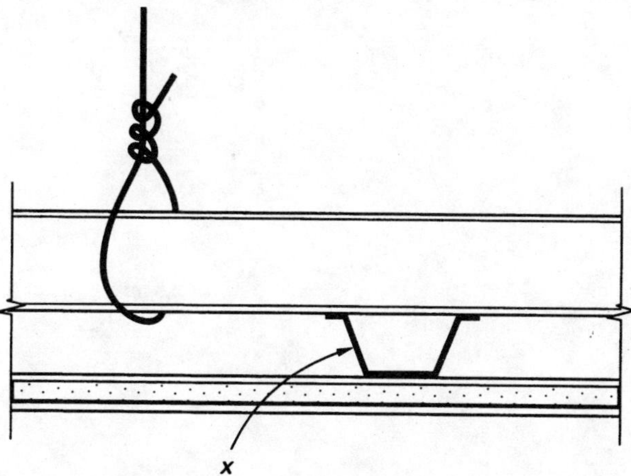

The component labeled x is the

(A) channel spacer

(B) cold-rolled steel channel

(C) furring channel

(D) main runner

404. A joint that is typically used where an addition meets an existing building to allow the two sections to move independently of one another is called a(n)

(A) control joint

(B) construction joint

(C) expansion joint

(D) isolation joint

405. What type of weld does the following symbol represent?

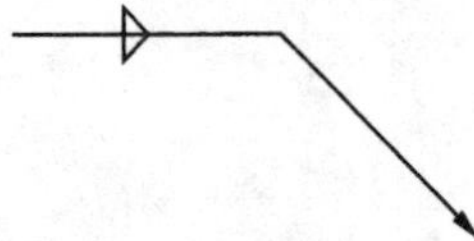

(A) V-groove weld with back-up bar

(B) double-bevel groove weld

(C) double-fillet weld

(D) fillet weld all around

406. In the following illustration, what is the hand of door 3?

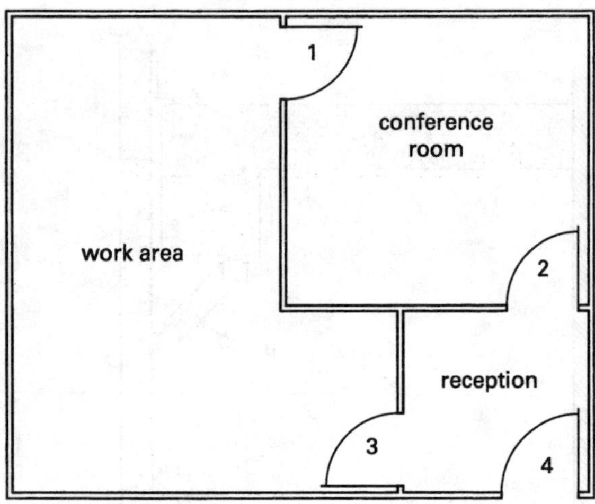

(A) right-hand reverse (RHR)

(B) right-hand (RH)

(C) left-hand reverse (LHR)

(D) left-hand (LH)

407. What type of cement is used in slip form construction?

(A) Type I

(B) Type II

(C) Type III

(D) Type IV

408. Which type of masonry cement mortar has the highest compressive strength?

(A) Type M

(B) Type N

(C) Type O

(D) Type S

409. What type of brick would be most likely specified for an eastern exposure in New Hampshire?

(A) NW

(B) FBX

(C) MW

(D) SW

410. An architect is writing specifications for a small clothing boutique. The architect has worked closely with the owner and fashion designer to plan an intricately detailed tile floor for the main showroom. The designer wishes to use a type of marble she saw installed in a friend's home in Rome. Which type of tile specification is most appropriate?

(A) prescriptive

(B) proprietary

(C) descriptive

(D) reference standard

411. Devices that hold reinforcing steel in position and prevent the rebar from slipping out of place as concrete is placed are called

(A) props

(B) lifts

(C) shims

(D) chairs

412. What type of plywood is used for roof sheathing?

(A) A-B Exterior

(B) B-C Exterior

(C) C-D Exterior

(D) A-D Exterior

413. Architectural woodwork for installation in the southwestern United States should have a moisture content of

(A) less than 5%

(B) 4% to 9%

(C) 5% to 10%

(D) 8% to 13%

414. A 6 in thick concrete slab is reinforced with no. 4 rebar placed in a horizontal grid and spaced 4 in on center. The maximum size of the aggregate shall not exceed

(A) $1\frac{1}{2}$ in

(B) 1 in

(C) 2 in

(D) $2\frac{5}{8}$ in

415. Calculate the equivalent thickness of a 12 in concrete block that is 75% solids.

(A) $8\frac{1}{2}$ in

(B) $8\frac{3}{4}$ in

(C) 9 in

(D) $9\frac{1}{4}$ in

416. Aluminum windows are specified for installation in a masonry wall. Which material is the least desirable choice for flashing at the head of the window?

(A) aluminum

(B) copper

(C) stainless steel (passive)

(D) lead

417. When selecting a fire extinguisher cabinet, the most critical design feature is the

(A) projection distance from the wall

(B) size of the glazing

(C) height of the cabinet enclosure

(D) finish

418. A fire-rated gypsum board partition must

(A) be Type X gypsum board

(B) stop at the ceiling

(C) be attached with screws

(D) be non-bearing

419. What is the building code requirement for pairs of exit doors with astragals?

(A) weather stripping

(B) door stop

(C) coordinator

(D) flush bolts

420. According to most building codes, horizontal masonry reinforcement is required every

(A) 8.0 in

(B) 16 in

(C) 24 in

(D) 32 in

Project Development

421. What is the most important fire-resistance property of a concrete masonry unit (CMU) partition?

(A) overall width

(B) density

(C) joint reinforcement

(D) equivalent thickness

422. The allowable stress ratings for lumber in the building codes are based primarily on

(A) the length of the lumber

(B) species

(C) the cross sectional area of the lumber

(D) whether the lumber is used as a floor or ceiling joist

423. Which of the following pedestrian walk materials provides the best positive grade-level drainage away from a building?

(A) asphaltic concrete

(B) brick pavers

(C) cobblestones

(D) concrete

424. Radon testing is conducted in the basement of an elementary school that is under study for a renovation and addition project. The results show a concentration of 3 pCi/L. Determine an appropriate course of action.

(A) Demolish the existing slab, and install a new 4 in slab on a vapor barrier placed on top of a 4 in base course of gravel.

(B) Seal any cracks in the foundation walls and floor slab, and ventilate the basement to the exterior.

(C) Install a membrane on the floor and ventilate beneath it.

(D) No action is required at this time, but the site should be monitored.

425. A massive brick wall behind glazing on the south side of a house would act as a

(A) direct gain system

(B) greenhouse design

(C) passive system with active assist

(D) Trombe wall

426. Air barriers are designed to stop infiltration and exfiltration caused by which of the following? (Choose the three that apply.)

(A) wind pressure

(B) stack pressure

(C) heating, ventilating, and air conditioning (HVAC) fan pressure

(D) vapor pressure

(E) pressure in an elevator shaft

(F) pressure in a built-up roofing system

427. The surface of a water tank is 100 ft above the lowest plumbing fixture in a building. Ignore friction loss. The water pressure available at the lowest fixture is most nearly

(A) 23 psi

(B) 31 psi

(C) 36 psi

(D) 43 psi

428. Which statements about drainage are correct? (Choose the three that apply.)

(A) The vent stack connects with the stack vent above the highest fixture served by the stack.

(B) The vent stack extends through the roof.

(C) Vents help prevent the drainage of water from traps.

(D) The house drain cannot also serve as the building sewer.

(E) Cleanouts are always a necessary part of a drainage system.

(F) Vents have a maximum size of 1 in.

429. Energy transfer wheels

(A) temper incoming air with exhaust air

(B) use ground temperature for heating or cooling

(C) capture the heat of flue gases to warm cold water

(D) exchange heat from solar panels to an airstream

430. The heat gain for a building has been calculated at 108,000 Btu/hr. A compressive refrigeration machine of ___ tons should be specified. (Fill in the blank.)

431. An architect is assisting with the renovation of a 1780 farmhouse in Virginia. The total floor area of the farmhouse is approximately 1500 ft^2. The owner requests a central air conditioning system. The cooling capacity required, rounded to the nearest ton, will be ____ tons. (Fill in the blank.)

432. Which of the following types of conduit is best suited for use when connecting to a motor?

(A) flexible metal conduit

(B) electric metallic tubing

(C) intermediate metal conduit

(D) rigid steel conduit

433. What is the voltage of the service obtained at each tap?

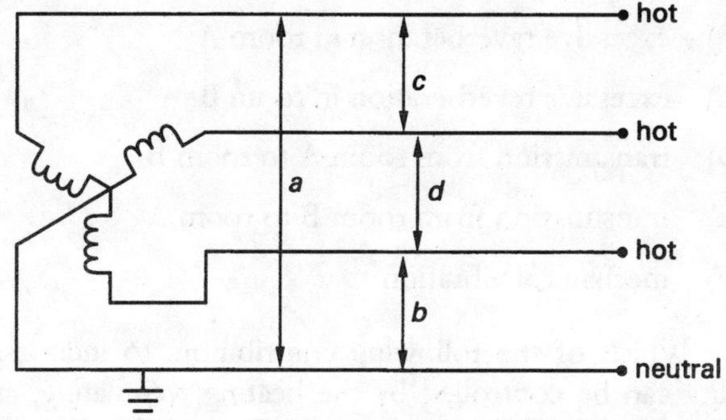

(A) $a = 120$ V, $b = 120$ V, $c = 240$ V, and $d = 240$ V

(B) $a = 277$ V, $b = 277$ V, $c = 480$ V, and $d = 480$ V

(C) $a = 208$ V, $b = 208$ V, $c = 120$ V, and $d = 120$ V

(D) $a = 120$ V, $b = 120$ V, $c = 208$ V, and $d = 208$ V

434. Which of the following are included in a typical transformer specification? (Choose the four that apply.)

(A) sound level in decibels

(B) the type of cooling medium

(C) physical dimensions

(D) voltage

(E) insulation class

(F) kVA rating

435. Two adjacent rooms separated by an acoustical partition are shown. There is a noise-producing source in room B.

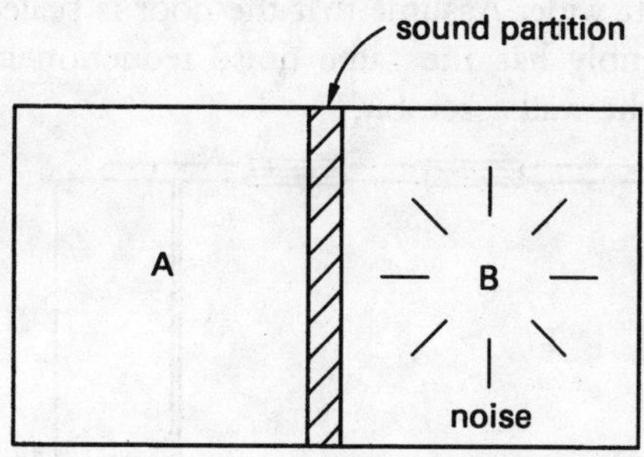

The noise reduction in room A is dependent on which of the following? (Choose the three that apply.)

(A) area of the partition

(B) thickness of the partition

(C) transmission loss of the partition

(D) absorption of surfaces in room A

(E) noise source in room B

(F) floor area of room A

436. The goal of a lightning protection system is to

(A) provide a continuous path to the ground for a lightning strike

(B) prevent a lightning strike

(C) prevent damage to computer equipment

(D) attract lightning

437. Which of the following statements about detectors is true?

(A) Smoke detector covers should be used in areas under construction.

(B) Ionization detectors should be installed in a restaurant kitchen.

(C) Smoke detectors may be installed in ductwork in lieu of installation in occupied areas of a building.

(D) Spot heat detectors can detect a fire before any other type of detector.

438. Determine the total absorption of an office 12 ft wide and 15 ft long with a 9 ft ceiling. Each window is 5 ft tall and 3 ft wide. Assume that the door is sealed and the door assembly has the same noise reduction coefficient (NRC) as the wall assembly.

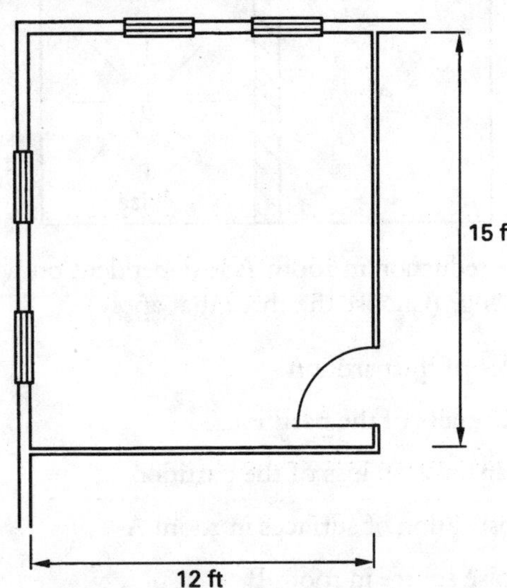

surface	description	NRC
walls	½ in gypsum board on metal studs at 16 in o.c.	0.05
ceiling	acoustical ceiling tile	0.60
floor	carpet on pad	0.55
windows	standard window glass	0.15

(A) 225.3 sabins (ft^2)

(B) 237.3 sabins (ft^2)

(C) 240.3 sabins (ft^2)

(D) 245.3 sabins (ft^2)

439. Which of the following is a recommended connection for a three-phase transformer? (Choose the three that apply.)

(A) delta to delta

(B) delta to wye

(C) wye to delta

(D) wye to wye

(E) alpha to delta

(F) delta to alpha

440. The partition assembly shown would be best for controlling which of the following kinds of acoustic situations? (Choose the two that apply.)

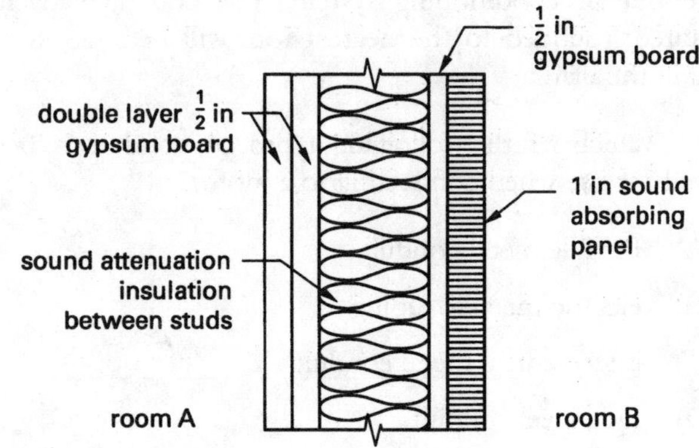

(A) impact noise

(B) excessive reverberation in room A

(C) excessive reverberation in room B

(D) transmission from room A to room B

(E) transmission from room B to room A

(F) mechanical vibration

441. Which of the following contributors to indoor air quality can be controlled by the heating, ventilating, and air conditioning (HVAC) system? (Choose the four that apply.)

(A) outgassing

(B) air change effectiveness

(C) volatile organic compound (VOC) content of building materials

(D) carbon dioxide levels

(E) humidity

(F) mold growth

442. An economizer cycle

(A) cools only as much chilled water as required by the demand load

(B) uses outdoor air to cool a building

(C) automatically reduces the amount of time the compressor runs

(D) uses air and water to cool the condenser coils

443. An architect wants to increase the expected lighting level of a room. Which of the following steps could accomplish this?

(A) Change to a lamp type with a lower efficiency.

(B) Suggest to the owner that the lamps be replaced infrequently.

(C) Use finishes with a lower light reflectance value.

(D) Change to luminaires with a higher coefficient of utilization.

444. Which type of pipe is typically used for sanitary lines in nonresidential buildings?

(A) PVC

(B) copper

(C) ABS

(D) cast iron

445. Which type of fire extinguisher should be provided in an electrical room?

(A) class A

(B) class B

(C) class C

(D) class D

446. Which of the following receptacle locations would require ground fault circuit interrupter (GFCI) protection? (Choose the four that apply.)

(A) an exterior receptacle for holiday lights

(B) a coffeemaker receptacle on a kitchen counter

(C) a receptacle located in a finished living area in a basement

(D) a receptacle for a chest freezer located in a garage

(E) a receptacle next to a bathroom lavatory

(F) a receptacle in an upstairs bedroom

447. Which of the following are required of lavatories to meet *ADA Accessibility Guidelines*? (Choose the four that apply.)

(A) The lavatory rim shall be no more than 34 in above the finish floor.

(B) Clear floor space of 30 in by 48 in must be provided in front of the lavatory.

(C) All piping must be concealed within cabinetry.

(D) The bowl of the sink must be no greater than $6\frac{1}{2}$ in deep.

(E) A minimum vertical clearance of 29 in must be provided in front of the lavatory.

(F) All piping must be insulated.

448. While the architect is coordinating a set of construction documents, the interior designer submits the drawing shown.

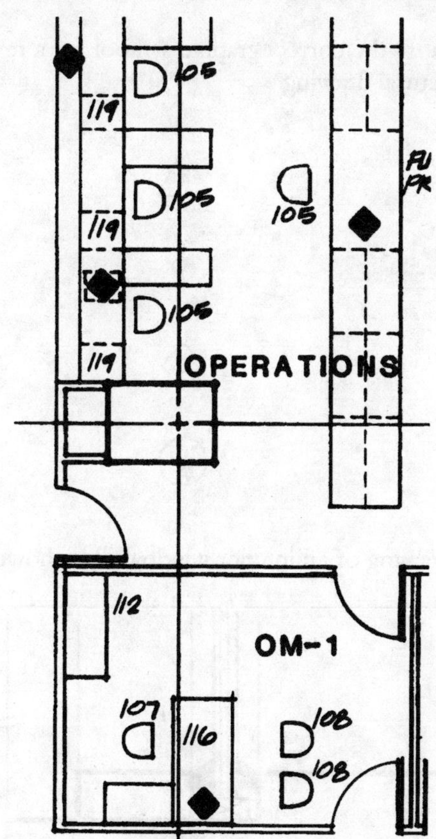

The drawing is a portion of a(n)

(A) finish plan

(B) furniture location plan

(C) telecommunications plan

(D) equipment layout

449. During the final stages of contract document development, the electrical engineer discovers that mechanical ductwork is shown on the mechanical engineering drawings in a position that interferes with electrical conduit. The person responsible for resolving this conflict is the

(A) electrical engineer

(B) mechanical engineer

(C) contractor

(D) architect

450. Plans, sections, and elevations are examples of

(A) isometric drawings

(B) axonometric drawings

(C) orthographic drawings

(D) oblique drawings

451. Identify the correct graphic symbol for a revision to an architectural drawing.

(A)

(B)

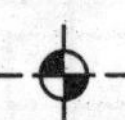

(C)

(D)

452. A drawing of an interior windowsill is shown.

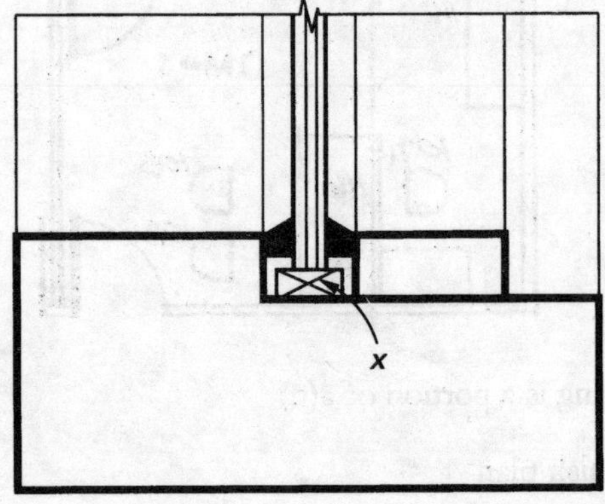

What is the element labeled *x*?

(A) anti-walk block

(B) glazing bead

(C) setting block

(D) removable stop

453. An architect is designing a decorative wood grille wallcovering in a building lobby. The grille is attached to a gypsum board partition with metal clips. Which item should be checked first?

(A) spacing and size of the screws holding the clips to the partition

(B) possibility of splintering due to the way the exposed surfaces are milled

(C) flame-spread rating

(D) method of cleaning the grille based on design and finish techniques used

454. The following are pages in a set of construction drawings for a small conference room renovation in a large office building: electrical and data plan, finish schedule, demolition and new work plans (on the same sheet), reflected ceiling plan, and interior elevations. If the drawings are arranged properly in a set, which drawing from the list will be the third drawing to be placed in the set?

(A) electrical and data plan

(B) interior elevations

(C) demolition and new work plans (on the same sheet)

(D) reflected ceiling plan

455. Which of the following is a part of the contract documents? (Choose the three that apply.)

(A) an addendum

(B) bidding documents

(C) general conditions of the contract for construction

(D) change orders

(E) specifications

(F) instructions to bidders

456. According to the U.S. National CAD Standard system of organizing construction documents, what type of drawings would one expect to find on sheet A-302?

(A) wall sections

(B) fourth-floor plan

(C) exterior elevations

(D) reflected ceiling plans

457. The owners of a residential project plan to shop for and purchase all the kitchen appliances in their new home. They want the contractor to be responsible for coordinating the electricity, gas, and plumbing, and for installing the equipment. How should these items be noted on the drawings?

(A) "N.I.C."

(B) "owner furnished-contractor installed"

(C) "cash allowance"

(D) by name, as "range," "refrigerator," and so on

458. When incorporating the mechanical engineer's specifications into the project manual, the architect should establish which of the following? (Choose the four that apply.)

(A) exact numbering system of the specification sections

(B) type of header and footer used on each page

(C) content of each specification section

(D) page layout of the specification sections

(E) type of mechanical equipment to be specified

(F) where the cooling tower should be located

459. Which of the following statements about specifications are true? (Choose the two that apply.)

(A) Both narrowscope and broadscope sections can be used in the same project manual.

(B) Drawings are more binding than specifications if there is a conflict.

(C) Specifications show quality; drawings show quantity.

(D) Proprietary specifications encourage competitive bids.

(E) Specifications should not be open to interpretation if they are the "base bid with alternates" type.

(F) Proprietary specifications are the most difficult for an architect to write.

460. The procedure for submitting shop drawings for architectural woodwork is specified in MasterFormat Division

(A) 01

(B) 06

(C) 09

(D) 12

461. Which of the following are parts of the contract documents? (Choose the four that apply.)

(A) an addendum

(B) a change order

(C) special supplementary conditions

(D) the contractor's bid

(E) a written amendment signed by owner and contractor

(F) instructions to bidders

462. Which of the following items should be addressed in the supplementary conditions?

(A) bidding instructions

(B) demolition requirements

(C) administrative procedures

(D) legal requirements of the jurisdiction in which the project is located

463. A reference to 3000 psi concrete alludes to the concrete's

(A) ultimate strength in psi

(B) strength in tension

(C) flexural strength without reinforcing

(D) design strength in psi after curing for 28 days

464. It would be appropriate for an architect to specify a mockup for

(A) a concrete masonry unit (CMU) foundation wall for a small warehouse

(B) kitchen cabinetry, granite countertops, and mosaic tile backsplashes for a series of identical apartments

(C) a custom-designed carpet inlay in the lobby of a hotel

(D) a portion of a brick wall for an addition to a 1760s building

465. According to the *ADA/ABA Guidelines*, what is the minimum clear floor space for one stationary wheelchair?

(A) 24 in by 36 in

(B) 30 in by 48 in

(C) 32 in by 48 in

(D) 60 in by 60 in

466. Stress in a body

(A) is an internal resistance to deformation

(B) is the change in size due to force

(C) is the tendency of the body to rotate

(D) happens where the moment is zero

467. The direct wind pressure on a vertical surface is

(A) directly proportional to the wind velocity

(B) inversely proportional to the wind velocity

(C) directly proportional to the square of the wind velocity

(D) not related to the wind velocity

468. A beam is loaded as shown.

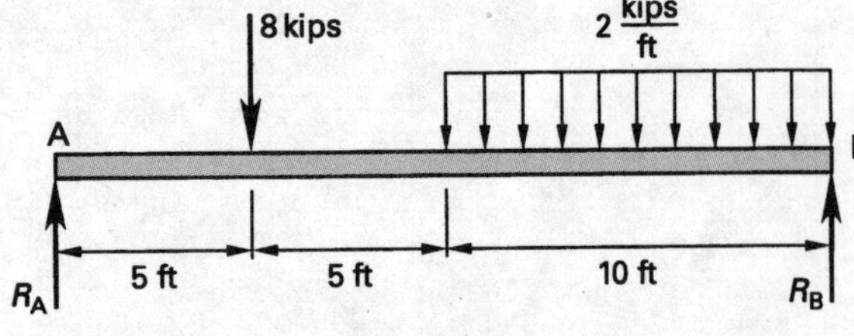

Which is the correct shear diagram?

(A)

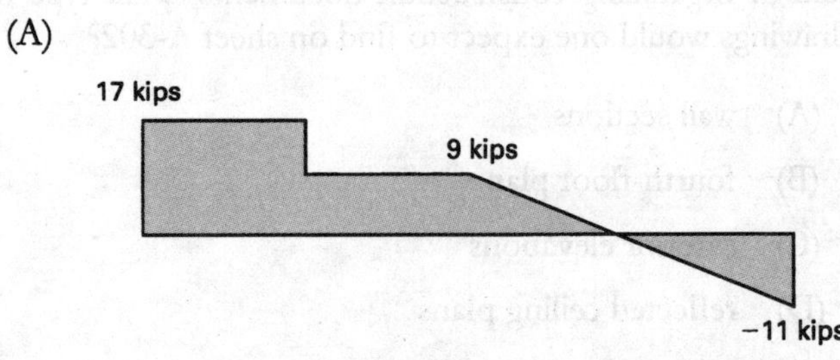

(B)

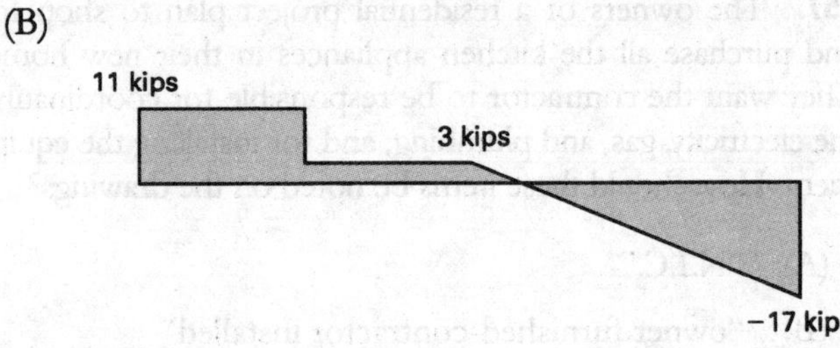

(C)

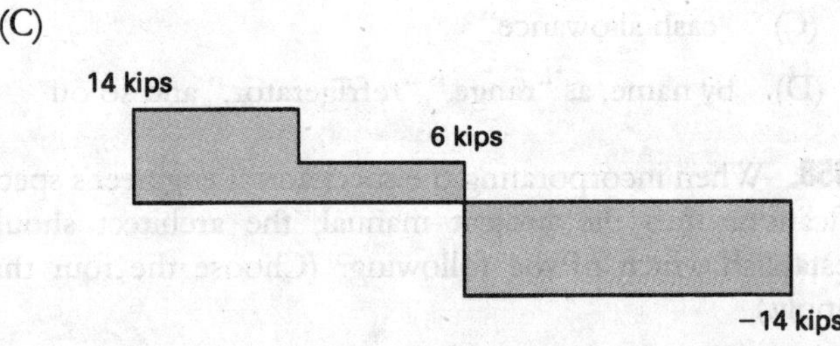

(D)

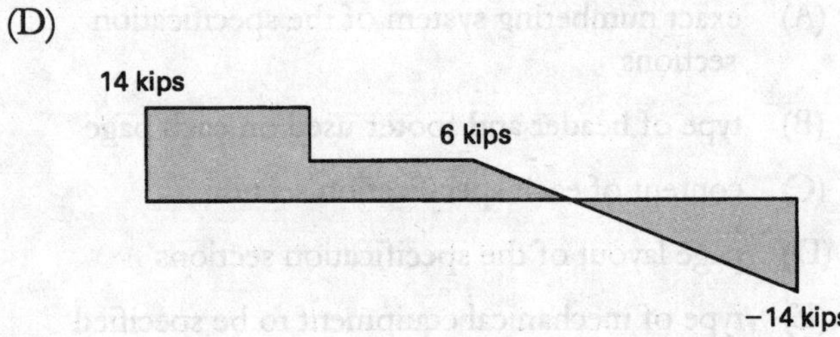

469. In the open-web steel joists structural system, the deep-long span joists of the DLH-series have depths up to

(A) 30 in

(B) 4.0 ft

(C) 6.0 ft

(D) 10 ft

470. In order to limit the horizontal deflection of a plywood diaphragm system, most building codes limit the span-to-depth ratio of the diaphragm to

(A) 2:1

(B) 3:1

(C) 4:1

(D) 5:1

Project Development

471. Which statement about designing for wind forces is correct?

(A) Maximum drift should be limited to 1/500 of a building's height.

(B) Maximum drift should be limited to 1/100 of a building's height.

(C) Drift between adjacent stories should be limited to 0.025 times the story height.

(D) Drift between adjacent stories should be limited to 0.0025 times the story height.

472. The overall thickness of a one-way reinforced concrete slab is often determined based on American Concrete Institute (ACI) 318 provisions for minimum thickness. According to these provisions, what should be the overall thickness for a cantilevered concrete slab if the slab span is 11 ft?

(A) 5.0 in

(B) 5.5 in

(C) 7.0 in

(D) 13 in

473. Which of the following structures require some complex wind calculations and possibly some wind tunnel testing? (Choose the three that apply.)

(A) commercial building with a total height of 50 ft

(B) residential building with a height of 200 ft

(C) office building with a height of 450 ft

(D) building with a height-to-width ratio of 3

(E) building with a height-to-width ratio of 7

(F) extra-long span suspension bridge

474. Which of the following statements about tilt-up walls is correct? (Choose the four that apply.)

(A) Tilt-up walls are reinforced concrete walls that are precast generally in a flat position and later tilted up to a vertical position.

(B) Tilt-up walls are subject to high stresses during construction.

(C) Exterior columns used with tilt-up walls must be precast concrete columns.

(D) Tilt-up walls provide a good fire resistance, great strength, and low maintenance.

(E) Tilt-up walls are delivered on a truck.

(F) Tilt-up walls can be supported by a structural steel frame.

475. For earth of a depth between 10 ft and 20 ft, the most efficient type of retaining wall is

(A) a gravity wall

(B) a cantilever wall

(C) a counterfort wall

(D) either a gravity or a counterfort wall

476. A contractor is purchasing a high-efficiency chiller for a small suite with four offices, as shown in the following floor plan.

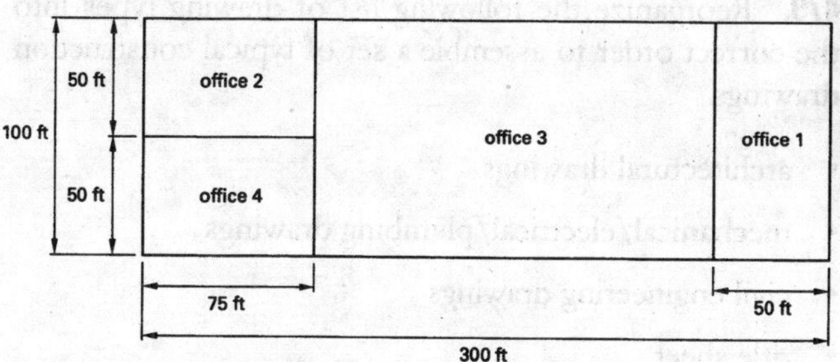

To distribute cool air throughout the space, the high-efficiency chiller must have a per-ton cooling capacity of 500 ft^2. What is the size of the unit(s) needed to cool office 1 and office 2?

(A) one 20 ton unit

(B) two 7.5 ton units

(C) one 10 ton unit and one 7.5 ton unit

(D) one 15 ton unit

477. Which statements about heat pumps are true? (Choose the four that apply.)

(A) Heat pumps use the refrigeration cycle to heat and cool.

(B) Heat pumps can be connected to solar collectors and water storage tanks.

(C) Air-to-air heat pumps are appropriate for areas with cold winters.

(D) Heat pumps have a relatively low initial cost.

(E) Air-to-air heat pumps are the most common types of pumps used for small buildings.

(F) Heat pumps minimize operating costs in moderate climates.

478. Which statements about a passive solar water heating system are correct? (Choose the four that apply.) Such a system has a

(A) storage tank that is placed above the collector

(B) low initial cost

(C) high operation cost

(D) reliable mechanical system

(E) pump

(F) storage tank that can cause structural costs

479. Reorganize the following list of drawing types into the correct order to assemble a set of typical construction drawings.

- architectural drawings
- mechanical/electrical/plumbing drawings
- civil engineering drawings
- title sheet
- structural drawings

480. What structural data must be included in both structural and architectural drawings?

(A) footing details

(B) rebar layouts

(C) pier reinforcing schedules

(D) elevations for tops of beams and structural walls

481. Which site features shown will need additional documentation to preserve and/or demolish? (Choose the four that apply.)

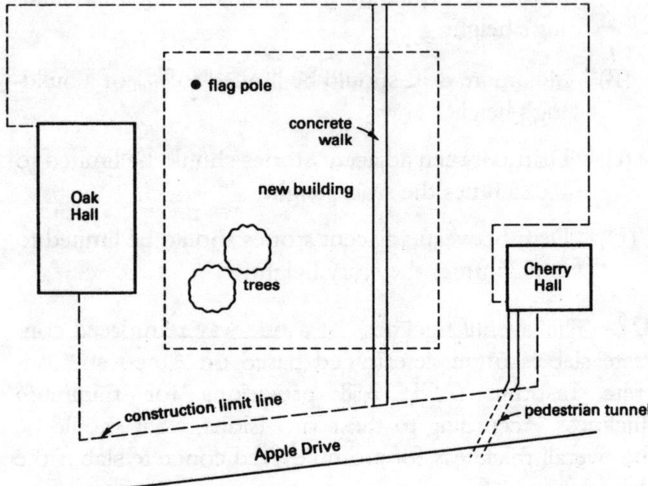

(A) preservation of trees

(B) pedestrian tunnel

(C) Oak Hall

(D) concrete walk

(E) Cherry Hall

(F) flagpole

482. For site grading on a project, slopes for permanent fill are not be steeper than 1 vertical unit for how many horizontal units?

(A) 2

(B) 3

(C) 4

(D) 5

483. What information is needed by building departments? (Choose the three that apply.)

(A) construction documents

(B) site plans

(C) fire protection shop drawings

(D) structural calculations

(E) structural drawings

(F) occupant load calculations

484. An architect is consulting with an electrical engineer for a reflected ceiling plan. Which information must be given to the electrical engineer?

(A) grille and register location

(B) sprinkler head location

(C) luminary location

(D) lighting and power outlet circuiting

485. Which statement about an architect's responsibilities is correct?

(A) An architect is responsible for continuous site inspections and safety conditions on the job site.

(B) An architect is responsible for methods and means of construction.

(C) An architect is responsible for failures to implement design changes in construction.

(D) An architect is responsible for construction time, cost overruns, and contractor failures in construction.

486. American Institute of Architects (AIA) Document A201, *General Conditions of the Contract for Construction*, Article 7, allows the owner to make changes in the work once a construction contract is signed. The present construction environment is such that labor and material prices are changing almost daily. If the owner wants to make changes and cannot agree with the contractor on the cost adjustment to the work, the work may stop. How can the owner make changes to the work without invalidating the contract or stopping the work?

(A) The architect can issue a change order.

(B) The architect can issue a construction change directive.

(C) The architect can issue minor changes to the work without the approval of the owner or contractor.

(D) The owner must negotiate with the contractor.

487. In preparing the contract documents, the owner asks what the architect's responsibility is if the architect finds a safety violation during a job site visit. The architect should

(A) do nothing

(B) prepare a change order to correct all safety violations

(C) notify the owner and follow up in writing

(D) write to the contractor to suggest how to correct the problem

488. A project's contract documents require concrete samples to be tested. Who makes the necessary arrangements with the appropriate testing agencies?

(A) contractor

(B) owner

(C) architect

(D) structural engineer

489. A project design team for a speculative office building owned by a real estate development company is in the construction document phase. The development company informs the architect that the project has been sold to a software development company. The new owner intends to be the sole tenant and to make this new building the corporate headquarters for the company. How will this change impact the completion of the design and construction documents? (Choose the four that apply.)

(A) Mechanical and electrical systems must be redesigned and redocumented.

(B) On-site parking must be redesigned.

(C) Structural design for the building can proceed with construction documents.

(D) Site drainage must be redesigned.

(E) The elevator consultant must redesign the elevator controls.

(F) The fire protection system must be redesigned.

490. The design team has completed the design development documents for a new two-story tenant commercial office building on a site zoned with a height limit of three stories. As the team begins the construction document phase, the owner announces to the team that the project has been changed to include a third story to the building. Which of the following is included in an amendment to the design contract? (Choose the two that apply.)

(A) site planning

(B) floor plan core elements

(C) building setbacks from the property line

(D) facade design

(E) door hardware

(F) roofing system

491. Which of these statements about mediation and arbitration are correct? (Choose the three that apply.)

(A) Both mediation and arbitration or litigation are legally binding.

(B) Arbitration is more formal than mediation.

(C) The decisions for both mediation and arbitration cannot be appealed.

(D) An arbitrator can be either a single party or a panel.

(E) Litigation is typically more expensive than mediation or arbitration.

(F) A professional liability insurance policy will cover all of the costs for litigation.

Case Study 1

Problem 492 through Prob. 499 refer to the following case study. Refer to Resource 5.1 and Resource 5.2 to assist in answering the problems.

An architect has designed a two-story addition to a home in West Orange, New Jersey. The addition is 20 ft × 20 ft 6 in. The second floor plan of this addition is shown in Resource 5.1. It will be constructed using light wood framing and a concrete masonry unit (CMU) wall foundation system. The roof will be gabled and will connect to the existing roof. The addition will have a new basement with slab-on-grade concrete. The architect wants the height of the basement to be 3 ft taller than that of the existing basement, so the contractor will need to excavate the soil and dig deeper than the depth of the existing basement for the addition.

The distance from the foundation wall to the property line is 10 ft.

Due to the increased impervious clay-type soil in the area of the addition combined with stormwater runoff issues, the architect has recommended the addition of a simple dry well to the site. (See Resource 5.2.) The dry well has a diameter of 30 in and is 6 ft deep.

The option of creating a rain garden to connect to the downspout in lieu of the dry well is being considered. The rain garden will be designed to hold a 1 ft deep amount of water.

Project Development

Resource 5.1 Second Floor Plan

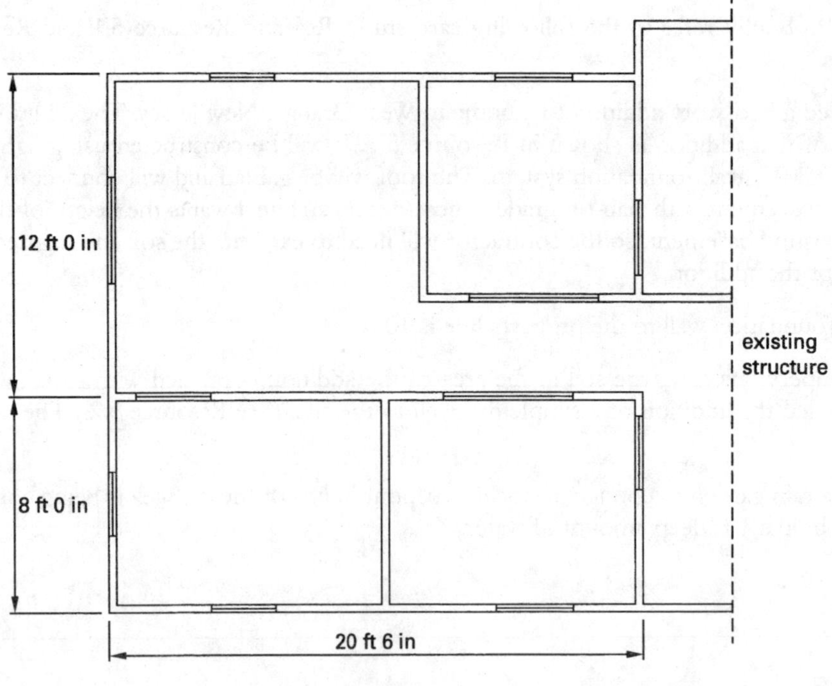

Resource 5.2 Dry Well Detail

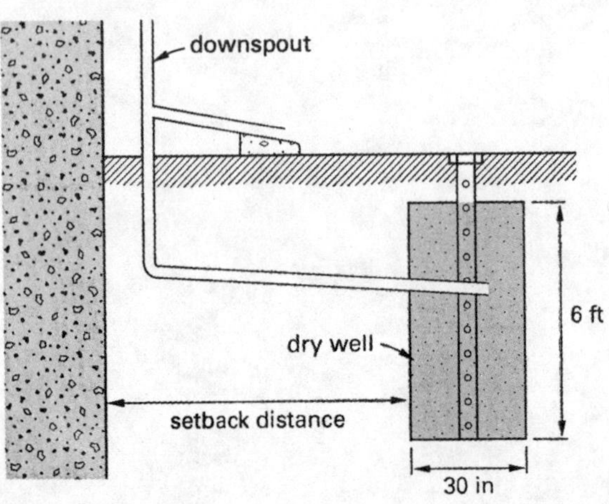

492. What distance from the foundation wall to the centerline of the dry well, as shown in Resource 5.2, should be used?

(A) 2 ft

(B) 5 ft

(C) 8 ft

(D) 9 ft

493. The simple dry well selected for this project must be

(A) empty

(B) filled with sand

(C) filled with clay

(D) filled with stone and gravel

494. A rain garden can help manage stormwater and reduce runoff pollution. Designed to absorb some or all roof runoff, a rain garden consists of a depression in the soil that is populated with plants and is located 9 ft from the foundation wall. If the architect uses a rain garden in the design of the new addition and the capacity matches the volume of the dry well, how long is the rain garden?

(A) 8 ft

(B) 10 ft

(C) 12 ft

(D) 15 ft

495. The architect wants to draw a building section through the existing structure. So that the existing structure and the new structure are stable, the new foundation wall footing must be

(A) drawn 3 ft deeper than the existing footing

(B) drawn immediately beneath the frost depth

(C) shown at the new depth, and the existing foundation footing must be shown as underpinned

(D) no deeper than the existing footing so the architect must revise the design before drawing both footings at the same depth

496. The second floor plan is shown in Resource 1. Designate the load-bearing walls by drawing the load-bearing wall symbol in the appropriate locations.

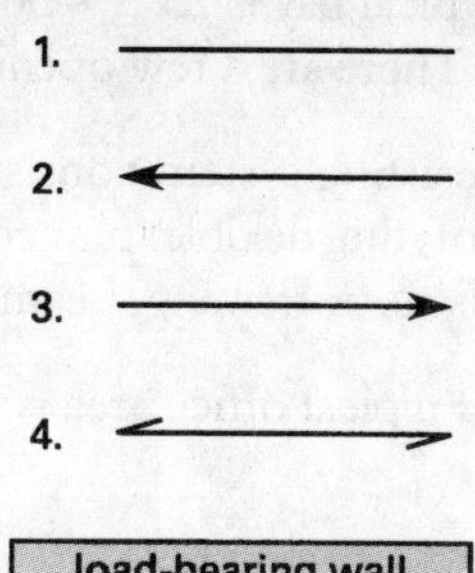

497. On the second floor plan shown in Resource 5.1, draw the correct joist span symbol in the appropriate framing span direction (horizontal, vertical, or diagonal).

498. In ascending order, place the uniform live load requirements of various elements of the residence.

- pitched roof
- second floor
- uninhabitable attics without storage

499. To support the second floor plan shown in Resource 5.1, the joists will be constructed of which types of products? (Choose the two that apply.)

(A) lumber joists

(B) wood I-joists

(C) laminated veneer lumber (LVL)

(D) parallel strand lumber (PSL)

(E) glued laminated members (glulam)

(F) steel

Case Study 2

Problem 500 through Prob. 510 refer to the following case study. Refer to Resource 5.3 through Resource 5.6 to assist in answering the questions.

A typical steel floor framing plan for a two-story office building with a footprint of 75 ft × 120 ft is shown in Resource 5.3. A typical bay is 25 ft × 30 ft. The structural system consists of a classical skeleton framing with beams, girders, and columns. There are a few openings in the floor as shown on the framing plan.

The lateral load resisting system consists of moment resisting frames along the perimeter of the building. All other steel connections are of the flexible pinned type. All steel beams, A-girders, and columns are to be wide-flange sections (W-shapes). In this floor framing, beams are spaced at 10 ft and are spanning in the 25 ft direction.

The live load for a typical office area is 50 psf. The total dead load is 54 psf.

Resource 5.3 Floor Framing Plan

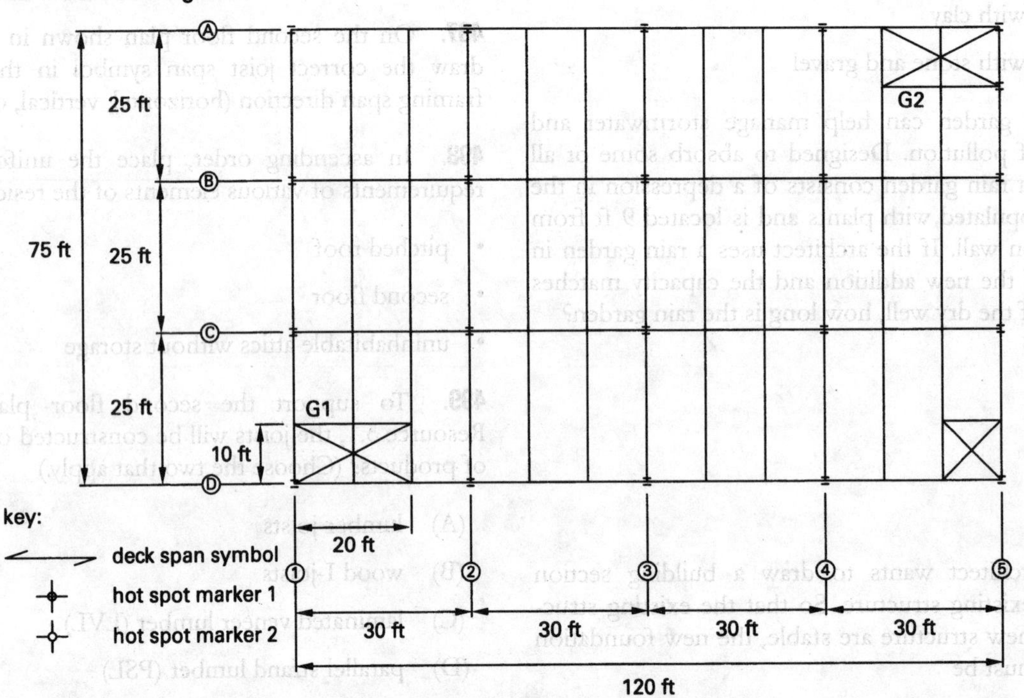

Resource 5.4 Nomenclature

DL	dead load	lbf/ft^2
f	modified or allowable bending stress	lbf/in^2
L	tributary width	ft
LL	live load	lbf/ft^2
M	moment of inertia	in-lbf
S	section modulus	in^3
TL	total load	lbf/ft^2
w	uniformly distributed load	lbf/ft
W	weight	lbf

Resource 5.5 Formulas

$$M = \frac{wL}{8}$$

$$S = \frac{M}{f}$$

$$w = (\mathrm{TL})L$$

$$W = wL$$

Resource 5.6 Steel Types

ASTM	tensile yield strength (kips/in^2)
A36	36
A242	50
A514	100
A992	50

Resource 5.7 Beams

designation	depth (in)	S^3
W14 × 22	13.72	28.9
W12 × 19	12.16	21.3
W12 × 16.5	12.00	17.6
W12 × 14	11.91	14.8
W10 × 21	9.90	21.5
W8 × 24	7.93	20.8
W8 × 20	8.14	17.0

500. Using the information given in the case study, what is generally the steel type to specify for the beams, girders, and columns?

(A) A36

(B) A242

(C) A514

(D) A992

501. In typical steel buildings such as the office building described in the case study, what is the general range of beam spacing?

(A) 4–6 ft

(B) 6–10 ft

(C) 13–17 ft

(D) 18–20 ft

502. In the floor framing plan given in the case study, which beam has the minimum depth that is spanning in the 25 ft direction?

(A) W12 × 19

(B) W8 × 20

(C) W10 × 21

(D) W8 × 24

503. The steel columns for this building have been calculated to fall within a range of 6–14 in, depending on the location of the steel columns in the building. Based on the layout of the framing plan, what is the depth range of the steel columns on the first floor?

(A) 4–6 in

(B) 6–8 in

(C) 8–10 in

(D) 12–14 in

504. According to the allowable stress design (ASD) method for steel structures, what is the total design load in pounds per linear foot for a typical interior beam in this framing plan?

(A) 104 lbf/ft

(B) 520 lbf/ft

(C) 1040 lbf/ft

(D) 2080 lbf/ft

505. Refer to Resource 5.3. On the floor framing plan, place hot spot marker 1 where the columns should be designed as concentrically loaded columns.

506. Refer to Resource 5.3. On the floor framing plan, place the metal deck span symbol in the appropriate direction in one of the 25 ft × 30 ft bays.

507. The architect needs to coordinate the various building systems and to identify the deepest girders on the floor framing plan. Refer to Resource 5.3. On the floor framing plan, place hot spot marker 2 where the grid lines of the largest girders on the framing plan are located.

508. In addition to the selfweight, for what type of load should the short girder labeled G1 near the stair openings on the floor framing plan be designed?

(A) one concentrated load at the center

(B) two concentrated loads

(C) three concentrated loads

(D) a uniformly distributed load

509. The lateral load-resisting system consists of moment-resisting frames along the perimeter of the building. What other options does the architect have for a lateral load resisting system? (Select the four that apply.)

(A) Use a moment beam.

(B) Use braced frames.

(C) Include shear walls.

(D) Use a combination of shear walls and moment frames in different directions.

(E) Use a combination of braced frames and shear walls in different directions.

(F) Use moment frames in one direction only.

510. The architect wants a large bay window between grid lines B and C on the left and right side of the floor framing plan. Which is the most appropriate lateral load-resisting system along the left and right sides of the building between grid lines B and C?

(A) shear wall

(B) braced frame

(C) moment-resisting frame

(D) combination of a braced frame and a moment-resisting frame

Solutions

Multiple Choice

391. ● ● (C) ● (E) (F)
392. (A) ● (C) (D)
393. ● (B) ● (D) ● (F)
394. (A) ● (C) (D)
395. (A) ● (C) (D)
396. (A) ● (C) (D)
397. ● (B) (C) (D)
398. (A) ● (C) (D)
399. ● (B) (C) (D)
400. (A) (B) ● (D)
401. ● (B) (C) (D)
402. (A) ● (C) (D)
403. (A) (B) ● (D)
404. (A) (B) (C) ●
405. (A) (B) ● (D)
406. (A) (B) (C) ●
407. (A) (B) ● (D)
408. ● (B) (C) (D)
409. (A) (B) (C) ●
410. (A) ● (C) (D)
411. (A) (B) (C) ●
412. (A) (B) ● (D)
413. (A) ● (C) (D)
414. (A) (B) ● (D)
415. (A) ● (C) (D)
416. (A) (B) ● (D)
417. ● (B) (C) (D)
418. ● (B) (C) (D)
419. (A) (B) ● (D)
420. (A) ● (C) (D)
421. (A) (B) (C) ●
422. (A) ● (C) (D)
423. (A) (B) (C) ●
424. (A) (B) (C) ●
425. (A) (B) (C) ●
426. ● ● ● (D) (E) (F)
427. (A) (B) (C) ●
428. ● ● (C) ● (E) (F)
429. ● (B) (C) (D)
430. 9 tons
431. 3 tons
432. ● (B) (C) (D)
433. (A) (B) (C) ●
434. ● (B) (C) ● ● ●
435. ● (B) ● ● (E) (F)
436. ● (B) (C) (D)
437. ● (B) (C) (D)
438. (A) ● (C) (D)
439. ● ● ● (D) (E) (F)
440. (A) (B) ● ● (E) (F)
441. (A) ● (C) ● ● ●
442. (A) ● (C) (D)
443. (A) (B) (C) ●
444. (A) (B) (C) ●
445. (A) (B) ● (D)
446. ● ● (C) ● ● (F)
447. ● ● (C) ● ● (F)
448. (A) ● (C) (D)
449. (A) (B) (C) ●
450. (A) (B) ● (D)
451. ● (B) (C) (D)
452. (A) (B) ● (D)
453. (A) (B) ● (D)
454. (A) ● (C) (D)
455. ● (B) ● ● ● (F)
456. ● (B) (C) (D)
457. (A) ● (C) (D)
458. ● ● (C) ● ● (F)
459. ● (B) ● (D) (E) (F)
460. ● (B) (C) (D)
461. ● ● ● (D) ● (F)
462. (A) (B) (C) ●
463. (A) (B) (C) ●
464. (A) ● (C) (D)
465. (A) ● (C) (D)
466. ● (B) (C) (D)
467. (A) (B) ● (D)
468. (A) ● (C) (D)
469. (A) (B) ● (D)
470. (A) (B) ● (D)
471. ● (B) (C) (D)
472. (A) (B) (C) ●
473. (A) (B) ● (D) ● ●
474. ● ● (C) ● (E) ●
475. (A) ● (C) (D)
476. (A) (B) ● (D)
477. ● ● (C) (D) ● ●
478. ● ● (C) ● (E) ●
479. See Sol. 479.
480. (A) (B) (C) ●
481. ● ● ● (D) ● (F)
482. ● (B) (C) (D)
483. ● ● (C) (D) ● (F)
484. (A) (B) (C) ●
485. (A) (B) ● (D)
486. (A) ● (C) (D)
487. (A) (B) ● (D)
488. ● (B) (C) (D)
489. ● (B) ● (D) ● ●
490. ● (B) (C) ● (E) (F)
491. (A) ● (C) ● ● (F)

Case Study 1

492. (A) (B) ● (D)
493. (A) (B) (C) ●
494. (A) (B) ● (D)
495. (A) (B) ● (D)
496. See Sol. 496.
497. See Sol. 497.
498. See Sol. 498.
499. ● ● (C) (D) (E) (F)

Case Study 2

500. (A) (B) (C) ●
501. (A) ● (C) (D)
502. (A) (B) (C) ●
503. (A) (B) (C) ●
504. (A) (B) ● (D)
505. See Sol. 505.
506. See Sol. 506.
507. See Sol. 507.
508. ● (B) (C) (D)
509. (A) ● ● ● ● (F)
510. (A) (B) ● (D)

Project Development

391. Concrete used in precast members is generally a higher-strength mix than the 3000 psi concrete typically used for site cast applications.

Precast concrete can have many different appearances by using colored or gray aggregate, formed surfaces or patterns. Precast concrete shapes include floor planks, beams, columns, wall panels, and domes.

Type III (high-early-strength) cement and steam curing allows prestress plants to get finished beams and tees out of the beds and into the yard more quickly so that production can continue. They are then warehoused in the yard until they have passed 28-day cylinder testing.

Precast members are generally transported over the highway, so their width is limited to the width of a travel lane.

In general, conditions can be better controlled during the production of precast concrete than they can in the field. Forms can be used repeatedly, and curing can take place under shelter and in controlled conditions, making precast concrete products both economical and consistent.

The answer is (A), (B), and (D).

392. Any deflection of the structure above a storefront could possibly break the glass or bend the mullions. A slip joint is used to prevent the weight of the structure above from bearing on the framing or the glazing.

The answer is (B).

393. There is no way to completely prevent termites from entering a structure, but there are many elements that architects can include in their designs to make the environment less hospitable to insects and, therefore, less prone to the damage they can cause.

Termites, along with many other damaging insects such as carpenter ants, bees, and powderpost beetles, flourish in moisture and wood, and they generally enter buildings at the ground level. (Other types of wood-destroying insects are found in different parts of the country and favor varying environments, so it is important to research the most common types of infestation and design an insect control plan accordingly.) Preventing wooden parts of the structure from coming in contact with the ground is one of the keys. Foundations should also be kept as dry as possible; designing the grade to fall away from the building will help to keep the area well drained. It is important to specify that an appropriate soil poison be applied to the area of the building footprint before construction begins. The type of insecticide used varies depending on the type of insect it is to combat.

Pressure-treating lumber makes the wood more resistant to damage from water but does not make it more resistant to insect damage.

One of the most common errors building owners make is to pile mulch around the base of shrubbery planted at the perimeter of the building. The mulch, whether made of pine bark, cocoa bean shells, gravel, or any other material, holds in the moisture, which is good for plants but bad for the structure. Termites thrive in the warm, moist soil underneath the gravel and can use that as an access point to enter the basement or crawlspace. Using a gravel drainage area in lieu of gutters and downspouts can have the same consequences if the system is not designed to carry the water away from the perimeter of the building.

The answer is (A), (C), and (E).

394. The amount of embodied energy in a building material is a measure of the resources that went into its acquisition (mining, harvesting, etc.), processing (transportation, the mechanical processes necessary to convert the material from one form to another, etc.), and final production and delivery (packaging, transportation, etc.).

The answer is (B).

395. Materials or assemblies with a high NRC generally have a low STC. The NRC, or noise reduction coefficient, is a measure of how absorptive a material is to sound. Materials with a high NRC are generally very porous materials such as acoustical ceiling tile, fabrics, carpet, and so on. The STC, or sound transmission coefficient, measures how well a material blocks sound transmission from one space to the next.

The absorption coefficient is linked to the NRC, but they are directly proportional; high NRCs equal high absorption coefficients. Reverberation time is a calculation for a space rather than a property of a material or an assembly.

The answer is (B).

396. The designation system for American standard sizes of rebar is based on the number of eighths of an inch in the nominal diameter of a bar, up to 1 in.

The soft metric sizes are based on the approximate number of millimeters in the nominal diameter. For example, a no. 5 bar in the American designation is $\frac{5}{8}$ in, which in soft metric is 15.9 mm or a no. 16 bar. In hard metric, the actual size is different, and the numbering system is based on round numbers of the cross-sectional area, using the letter "M" as a suffix. For example, the nearest size to an American no. 5 bar is a 15M with an area of 200 mm^2.

Epoxy-coated rebar is typically used in exterior concrete construction to slow down or prevent the steel from rusting. Steel reinforcing bars are typically manufactured in grade 40, grade 60, and grade 75.

The answer is (B).

397. A cricket is a small gable placed directly behind a chimney to direct water away from the masonry and encourage it to drain from the roof rather than allowing it to accumulate behind the chimney.

The answer is (A).

398. A precast panel should have only two points of bearing on the structure. These are indicated at point C. One point should be a rigid connection and the other should provide for lateral movement. The remaining points of connection to the structure, or tiebacks as they are often called, should allow for both vertical and lateral movement of the panel due to differential movement of the structure and panel, and due to expansion and contraction caused by temperature differences.

The answer is (B).

399. A chamfer strip is a small, triangular piece of material placed in the corners for forms to prevent sharp 90° corners, which are difficult to cast and have a tendency to break off during use or when the forms are removed.

The answer is (A).

400. Drips are extensions of through-wall flashing or projections below masonry units that extend beyond the primary plane of the wall. The purpose of a drip is to force water that is draining off flashing or a sill to fall down and away from the wall rather than to adhere to the wall and possibly flow back into the wall through capillary action or cracks below the flashing.

The question asks for the solution that will prevent water from seeping back into the wall, so it can be assumed that the water is already outside, precluding option (A) and option (D). Option (B) is incorrect because coping simply covers a parapet and may include drips.

Study the basic components of masonry construction, including multi-wythe construction, flashing, reinforcing, opening details, and connections to backup walls or the superstructure. Also know the methods of repairing masonry walls and grout for renovations.

The answer is (C).

401. A raked joint like that shown in the masonry wall above the ledge (area A) is not a good one to use because water running down the wall can seep into the joint by capillary action. The details at areas B and C are correctly executed. The flashing and sealant at area B would keep water out, and the drip at area C would prevent water from running under the ledge and into the masonry joint at area D.

The answer is (A).

402. Although asphalt-impregnated paper can act as a vapor barrier, the fact that it is placed on the outside of the sheathing precludes option (C) and option (D) from being correct. It does add a little to the thermal resistance, but its primary purpose is to prevent any water that seeps behind the siding from getting into the structure. It also serves to prevent air infiltration.

The answer is (B).

403. The illustration shows a standard method of installing gypsum wallboard ceilings. The components shown include the gypsum wallboard attached to the furring channel. Furring channels are normally installed 24 in on center and are attached to $1\frac{1}{2}$ in cold-rolled steel channels placed 48 in on center. The cold-rolled steel channels are suspended from the structure above with wire.

The answer is (C).

404. An isolation joint allows two sections of a building to move independently, and is typically used where an addition meets an existing building or where two different materials meet. It is also called an abutment joint.

A control joint is a groove or saw cut that provides an area of weakness so that expected cracking caused by expansion and contraction can be limited to a predetermined area. A construction joint is a break between two successive concrete pours; the concrete is generally keyed at this location, and reinforcing extends from the first pour to the second. Expansion joints allow for the natural movement of a building due to expansion and contraction. Expansion joints must be covered with a watertight barrier and are located at regular intervals in long expanses of masonry or concrete, where taller building forms meet shorter ones, at corners, and at openings.

The answer is (D).

405. This symbol represents a double-fillet weld. The arrow would point to the location of the weld. The triangle is the symbol for a fillet weld; two indicate a double-fillet weld. Symbols below the horizontal line refer to welds on the arrow side; symbols above the line refer to welds on the other side.

The American Institute of Steel Construction's *Steel Construction Manual* features a full explanation of basic and supplementary weld symbols and instructions for using this symbol system to explain what type of weld is required.

The answer is (C).

406. When preparing door and hardware schedules, it is important to note the hand of the door. Referring to the hand is a standard method of describing the location of the hinges and which way the door swings. If a person standing on the outside of a door cannot see the hinges and the door swings away, it is either right-hand (RH) or left-hand (LH), depending upon which side the hinges are located. If the door swings toward the person, it is either

Project Development

right-hand reverse (RHR) or left-hand reverse (LHR), again depending upon the location of the hinges.

The answer is (D).

407. Type III cement is high-early-strength—the type needed for rapid slip form construction. Type I is normal cement. Type II is low heat and sulfate resistant, and Type IV is slow setting and low heat for massive structures.

The answer is (C).

408. Type M mortar has a minimum average 28-day compressive strength of 2500 psi. Type O has the lowest compressive strength, 350 psi.

For exterior walls and interior walls under normal loads, Type N mortar is commonly used. Type S mortar is used for heavier loading on interior walls and for exterior walls at or below grade, such as foundation walls, retaining walls, pavements, walks, and patios. When high-strength mortar is required for heavy loads or for cases where the mortar will be exposed to severe, saturated freezing, Type S or M mortar is used. Type O mortar is used only for light loads and where freezing is not expected.

The answer is (A).

409. SW stands for severe weathering and would be the type that should be specified for the northeastern United States. NW is negligible weathering, and MW is moderate weathering. FBX refers to the finish appearance.

The answer is (D).

410. A proprietary specification is appropriate in this situation because it gives the architect the most control over the product provided and installed by the contractor. The architect and owner will have the opportunity to select the products they want to use for the floor and will refer to those specific products in the specification. A proprietary specification is a type of closed, or prescriptive, specification.

Descriptive and reference standard specifications are types of open specifications. They outline the final results desired but do not specifically tell the contractor what materials to use. Descriptive specifications require the architect to list all of the desired characteristics of the material and put the onus on the contractor to find a product that will satisfy the requirements. They can be difficult to write because of the level of detail that must be included to ensure that an appropriate product is chosen. A reference standard specification is much simpler to write. It refers to industry standards to define the desired characteristics of materials and installation systems.

The answer is (B).

411. Chairs are small wire supports that help to keep rebar a specified distance from the outside of the concrete and help to ensure adequate concrete cover. A bolster is a type of chair used in broad slabs or beams.

The answer is (D).

412. The most common grade of plywood used for roof sheathing is C-D Exterior, sometimes referred to as CDX. The Engineered Wood Association classifies plywood veneers into six grades, as follows.

N	natural finish, free of defects
A	smooth and paintable
B	solid-surface veneer
$C_{plugged}$	splits limited to 1/8 in width and knot/borer holes limited to 1/4 in by 1/2 in
C	knotholes permitted to 1 in, limited splits permitted, minimum grade for exterior plywood
D	knots/knotholes to 3 in permitted, limited splits permitted

The first letter indicates the classification of the face ply (the highest-grade side) of the plywood. (If both sides have the same classification, they are both referred to as faces.) The second letter indicates the classification of the back ply (the lower-grade side) of the material. If the plywood is marked exterior, it contains plies bonded with exterior glue.

More information about plywood, including the *Panel Handbook and Grade Glossary,* can be downloaded in electronic format from The Engineered Wood Association's website, apawood.org. (Registration is required.)

The answer is (C).

413. The southwestern portion of the United States is the driest, so moisture content should approximate the conditions in which the lumber will be used. However, it is difficult to reduce the moisture content much below 5%, so option (A) is an unrealistic answer.

The answer is (B).

414. Aggregate shall not be larger than one-third of the slab thickness or three-quarters of the minimum space between reinforcing bars, whichever is smaller.

The slab thickness is 6 in, and one-third of this is 2 in.

The rebar is spaced 4 in apart. Number 4 rebar has a diameter of 1/2 in, so the minimum space between reinforcing bars is 4 in − 1/2 in = 3 1/2 in. Three-quarters of this is

$$(3.5\text{ in})(0.75) = 2.625\text{ in} \quad (2\tfrac{5}{8}\text{ in})$$

The aggregate must not be larger than the smaller of the two values, which is 2 in.

The answer is (C).

415. The equivalent thickness is a measurement of the amount of concrete in a hollow core block. It is equal to the thickness that the block would be if it were the same height and length but cast without holes. This information is often necessary for calculating fire resistance of assemblies.

A nominal 12 in concrete block is actually $11\frac{5}{8}$ in thick. Multiply the actual thickness by the percentage of solids to arrive at equivalent thickness. The equivalent thickness of this block is 75% of $11\frac{5}{8}$ in, or $8\frac{3}{4}$ in.

The answer is (B).

416. Stainless steel would be the least desirable choice for flashing material when used near an aluminum window assembly because of the metals listed, it is furthest from aluminum on the galvanic action table, even further than copper. The more dissimilar the materials, the more current that will flow between the two and speed corrosion. This process is called electrolysis.

The best choice would be to use aluminum flashing and aluminum fasteners and accessories. However, aluminum can also react with alkaline materials, so it must be protected from mortar and concrete. Nonreactive materials such as plastics are also an option, but they should be carefully researched, as plastics tend to degrade more quickly than metals. Any dissimilar materials in proximity to one another must always be carefully separated with a layer of nonreactive material such as rubber or neoprene.

The answer is (C).

417. The *ADA/ABA Guidelines* limit the projection of any construction element to a maximum of 4 in from a wall when the element is located between 27 in and 80 in above the floor. Because extinguisher cabinets fall within this range, they must be recessed or semi-recessed to meet the 4 in requirement.

Glazing is not necessarily required, and if it is used there are no requirements for size. The height of the cabinet itself depends on what is installed within it. The type of finish is not critical. For example, painted stainless steel or bronze can be used. However, local jurisdictions may have requirements for the color and lettering type used for identification.

In addition to meeting the 4 in projection requirement, the height of the cabinet above the floor must also meet the *ADA/ABA Guidelines* requirement of 48 in for unobstructed forward and side reach. National Fire Protection Association (NFPA) guidelines require that the maximum height to the top of a mounted cabinet be no more than 5 ft above the floor.

The answer is (A).

418. Fire-rated partitions must be constructed according to tested and approved methods that include using Type X gypsum board, the method of attachment to the framing, how the joints are finished, the type and size of studs, and other details. In addition, the fire separation must extend from the slab to the rated slab above, not just to a suspended, finish ceiling.

Fire-rated partitions can be bearing or non-bearing.

The answer is (A).

419. A coordinator prevents the door leaf with the astragal from closing before the other leaf, so the pair of doors seals properly.

The answer is (C).

420. Most building codes require horizontal reinforcement in both brick and concrete masonry walls a minimum of every 16 in. The reinforcing may be a continuous truss or ladder type laid in the mortar joints.

The answer is (B).

421. Concrete masonry partitions are usually hollow, so the actual thickness of the solid material, not the actual overall width, is used to rate the fire resistance of the unit.

The answer is (D).

422. The allowable stress ratings for lumber in the building codes are based primarily on species. The stress ratings are not dependent on the span, the area of the section, or the framing use.

The answer is (B).

423. A safe pedestrian walk should not have a slope exceeding $\frac{1}{4}$ in/ft perpendicular to the direction of travel. This allows for drainage without creating a dangerous cross slope. Of the materials listed, concrete could be finished to provide a continuous, uniform slope for drainage in conjunction with a smooth walking surface.

Asphalt could be used, but it is more difficult to smooth uniformly at such a low slope. Minor dips and surface irregularities in the asphalt might cause ponding of water against or toward the building. Both brick pavers and cobblestone would allow water to seep into the joints near the building.

The answer is (D).

424. Radon is a colorless, odorless gas that has been shown to cause lung cancer. It is found in the earth. Testing is a relatively simple and inexpensive process. The

Project Development

Environmental Protection Agency (EPA) has determined that no action is required if the level of radon detected is less than 4 pCi/L (picocuries per liter). However, because this site shows an elevated radon reading, it should be monitored with periodic testing. Should an addition be constructed, steps should be taken to reduce radon levels by providing proper ventilation of spaces in direct contact with the earth.

Appropriate remedial actions for concentrations over 4 pCi/L include sealing any cracks in the foundation walls or floor slab and ventilating or depressurizing the basement or crawlspace area. The EPA recommends that new residences be built with radon-resistant techniques, which are explained in detail on its website, epa.gov.

The answer is (D).

425. A Trombe wall is a type of thermal storage wall that is placed directly behind glass on the south side of a building to store solar energy during the day for release at night.

A direct gain system uses various types of massive materials (masonry, concrete, or even gypsum board) in different locations inside a building to store heat. A greenhouse uses a south-facing room enclosed with extensive glass, not masonry. A passive system with active assist includes mechanical devices in addition to thermal mass.

The answer is (D).

426. Wind pressure, stack pressure, and HVAC fan pressure can all influence infiltration and exfiltration rates. Vapor pressure does not cause air movement; rather, vapor pressure is a movement of moisture. Pressure in an elevator shaft does not influence air barriers in an exterior wall.

The answer is (A), (B), and (C).

427. 0.433 psi is required to lift water a vertical distance of 1 ft. Viewed another way, 0.433 psi of pressure is developed for every 1 ft of height. This is called the static head. To determine the static head in this problem, use the following formula.

$$\text{pressure} = \left(0.433\ \frac{\frac{\text{lbf}}{\text{in}^2}}{\text{ft}}\right)h = \left(0.433\ \frac{\frac{\text{lbf}}{\text{in}^2}}{\text{ft}}\right)(100\ \text{ft})$$

$$= 43.3\ \text{lbf/in}^2 \quad (43\ \text{psi})$$

Another way to view the relationship is to remember that 1 psi will lift water 2.3 ft.

The answer is (D).

428. The minimum slope of drains depends on the size of the pipe. The vent stack may extend through the roof, but this is not required. In many cases, the vent stack connects with the stack vent above the highest fixture served by the stack.

The answer is (A), (B), and (D).

429. An energy transfer wheel transfers heat between two airstreams (incoming air and exhaust air) using a lithium-chloride-impregnated heat exchanger. These devices transfer both latent and sensible heat and can be used to either heat or cool the incoming air.

Option (B) describes a ground-source heat pump. This type of system uses the constant temperature of the ground to heat or cool a building. Option (C) describes a boiler fuel economizer. Option (D) describes a standard heat exchanger.

Understand the various types of mechanical techniques and devices used to conserve energy that are not necessarily active solar systems, photovoltaic systems, or wind systems. These include the economizer cycle, boil fuel economizers, heat pipes, runaround coils, energy transfer wheels, ground-source heat pumps, and dual-condenser chillers.

The answer is (A).

430. A ton of air conditioning is equivalent to 12,000 Btu/hr. Dividing 108,000 Btu/hr by 12,000 Btu/hr gives 9 tons.

Modern refrigeration has its roots in the ice-making industry. 12,000 Btu/hr is the amount of refrigeration needed to make one ton of ice per day from 32°F water.

The answer is 9 tons.

431. A good guideline when selecting a cooling system for an older home is to assume that approximately 1 ton of cooling capacity will be necessary for each 500 ft^2 of living space. This old farmhouse presumably has drafty windows and lots of air infiltration, so a 3-ton unit would be a reasonable choice.

If this project were a residence of similar size but new construction, a more appropriate guideline would be about 1 ton for each 1000 ft^2 of floor area. New construction materials and methods, such as house wrap and vapor barriers, additional insulation, improved windows, caulking and sealants, and so on, make it much easier to control the environment within the residence and require less cooling capacity.

The answer is 3 tons.

432. Flexible metal conduit should be used to connect to a motor because it can "give" with the movement of the machinery. It is a good choice for any location where there is vibration or where it is impossible to use a straight run of rigid conduit.

The answer is (A).

433. The system shown in the diagram is a 120/208 voltage, three-phase, four-wire electrical system. Taps that connect to a hot wire and a neutral wire produce 120 V service (such as at convenience receptacles); *a* and *b* are 120 V taps. Taps that connect to two hot wires produce 208 V service; *c* and *d* are 208 V taps.

120/240 V power is produced by a single-phase, three-wire system. It is found primarily in residences, with the 120 V power directed to convenience receptacles and light fixtures and the 240 V reserved for equipment such as air conditioners or clothes dryers. 277/480 V power systems are diagrammatically similar to the 120/208 V system shown, but step-down transformers are required to convert the higher voltages to 120 V for receptacles.

The answer is (D).

434. Transformer specifications should include the type of transformer, phase, voltage, kVA (kilovolt-ampere) rating, sound level, and insulation class.

It is unlikely that the physical dimensions of a transformer would be included in the specification, as the size tends to be determined by the technical criteria, particularly by the capacity and insulation type. The size of units can vary greatly from one manufacturer to the next.

The answer is (A), (D), (E), and (F).

435. The thickness of a partition or other acoustical separation is irrelevant to the total noise reduction within a space. Factors which would influence the effectiveness of the partition are transmission loss, the area of the barrier, and the total sound absorption within the "quiet" space.

Understand the difference between transmission loss and noise reduction. Transmission loss (TL) is the difference (in decibels) between the sound power incident on a barrier in a source room and the sound power radiated into a receiving room on the opposite side of the barrier. It is typically a laboratory measurement. Noise reduction (NR) is the arithmetic difference (in decibels) between the intensity levels in two rooms separated by a barrier having a given transmission loss level.

The formula for calculating the noise reduction is

$$\text{NR} = \text{TL} + 10\log\frac{A}{S}$$

A	total acoustical absorption of the receiving room, in sabins (ft^2)
NR	noise reduction, in decibels (dB)
S	area of the barrier, in ft^2
TL	transmission loss level of the barrier, in decibels (dB)

The answer is (A), (C), and (D).

436. A lightning protection system is designed to provide a continuous path from a building (most often from the highest points of the building) to the ground. Unfortunately, no method exists for preventing lightning strikes. The best that can be achieved is to route the energy from the strike to a point where the strike is least likely to damage mechanical, electrical, and computer systems or cause a fire.

The answer is (A).

437. When a portion of a building is under construction or undergoing renovation, smoke detector covers should be used to protect the detectors from damage, from accumulating dust that could destroy the sensors, and from sounding false alarms.

Ionization detectors would be a poor choice for a restaurant kitchen or any other location that tends to be hot, because of the high likelihood of false alarms.

Smoke detectors are normally installed in ductwork to direct the heating, ventilating, and air conditioning (HVAC) system to shut down in case of a fire, so that smoke and other toxic gases are not transported throughout the building through the ventilation system. They are not an acceptable substitute for detector systems installed throughout the occupied areas of the building.

Of all types of detectors, spot heat detectors would detect a fire last, and after the most deadly smoke stage. They detect changes in the temperature of the space.

The answer is (A).

438. A material's absorption, A, is equivalent to its area, S, multiplied by its coefficient of absorption, α. For convenience, the NRC is used for the coefficient of absorption. The total absorption of the room is equivalent to the sum of all materials' absorptions.

$$A_{\text{material}} = S\alpha$$
$$A_{\text{total}} = S_1\alpha_1 + S_2\alpha_2 + S_3\alpha_3 \ldots$$

When calculating the area of the walls, remember to subtract the area of the windows.

Project Development

The total area of the walls (including the windows) is

$$\begin{aligned} S_{\text{total}} &= 2S_{12\text{ ft}} + 2S_{15\text{ ft}} \\ &= (2)(12\text{ ft})(9\text{ ft}) + (2)(15\text{ ft})(9\text{ ft}) \\ &= 486\text{ ft}^2 \end{aligned}$$

The area of the walls without the four windows is

$$\begin{aligned} S_{\text{walls}} &= S_{\text{total}} - 4S_{\text{window}} \\ &= 486\text{ ft}^2 - (4)(5\text{ ft})(3\text{ ft}) \\ &= 426\text{ ft}^2 \end{aligned}$$

The absorptions of the materials in the office are

$$\begin{aligned} A &= S\alpha \\ A_{\text{walls}} &= (426\text{ ft}^2)(0.05) = 21.3\text{ sabins (ft}^2) \\ A_{\text{ceiling}} &= (12\text{ ft})(15\text{ ft})(0.60) = 108\text{ sabins (ft}^2) \\ A_{\text{floor}} &= (12\text{ ft})(15\text{ ft})(0.55) = 99\text{ sabins (ft}^2) \\ A_{\text{windows}} &= (4)(5\text{ ft})(3\text{ ft})(0.15) = 9\text{ sabins (ft}^2) \end{aligned}$$

The total absorption is the sum, or 237.3 sabins (ft^2).

The answer is (B).

439. Wye-to-wye connections are rarely used because they can cause problems with harmonics and can interfere with communications systems within the building.

The answer is (A), (B), and (C).

440. The sound absorbing panel in room B would help control excessive reverberation in this space. The hard surface on the room A side of the partition would not control excess reverberation in room A. The double layer of gypsum board would help improve the transmission loss of the wall. Because noise reduction between two spaces is dependent on the transmission loss of the wall, the area of the wall, and the absorption of the surfaces in the receiving room, this assembly would do a better job of reducing sound transmission from room A to room B (because the absorptive panel is in room B) than from room B to room A. The partition would do little to control impact noise or mechanical vibration.

The answer is (C) and (D).

441. Mechanical systems cannot control outgassing (the release of undesirable odors and chemicals) or the level of VOC emissions from materials already incorporated into a building. These will exist regardless of the type of HVAC systems used. The HVAC system can provide continuous ventilation to remove VOCs and other undesirable chemicals from a building.

The HVAC system can control air change effectiveness and the levels of carbon dioxide found within the building. The HVAC system can also be relied on to keep humidity within human comfort range at acceptable levels to minimize mold growth.

The answer is (B), (D), (E), and (F).

442. An economizer cycle introduces outdoor air when the ambient temperature is low enough to assist in cooling.

The answer is (B).

443. Luminaires with a higher coefficient of utilization (CU) allow more light from the lamps to reach the desired surfaces. Lamps with a higher efficiency (not lower) should be selected, although the selection of this type of fixture would have to be balanced against the change in color temperature. Lumen output decreases as lamps age and as dirt accumulates on them. Changing lamps often would help maintain the initial footcandle level. Room finishes with high light reflectance values can make a significant increase in the total light level in a room.

The answer is (D).

444. Cast iron pipe is typically used for sanitary lines in nonresidential buildings. It is noncorrosive in most soils and resists abrasion from waste materials that may be drained through the pipe as well as from rock and soil on the outside of the pipe in underground installations. Cast iron pipe is quick to install, readily available, and economical. Because of the thickness of the material and the way that it is joined, cast iron pipe typically muffles sound.

PVC pipe is a white plastic pipe often used for cold water supply lines. PVC pipe is another option for sanitary lines. It is typically less expensive and easier to install, but it cannot be used for exterior applications or where noise reduction is a consideration.

Copper pipe is generally used for supply lines. ABS is a rigid black plastic pipe used primarily for drainage lines in residential buildings.

The answer is (D).

445. Class C fire extinguishers are for electrical fires. They contain an extinguishing chemical, often halon or carbon dioxide, that will not conduct electricity. After the electricity has been disconnected, Class A or B fire extinguishers may be used on a fire that was originally electrical in nature. Class C fire extinguishers are marked with an illustration of a flaming electrical receptacle and a plug. (In the former labeling system, they were marked with a blue circle and the letter C.)

Class A fire extinguishers are for ordinary combustible materials such as paper or wood and usually use water or a dry chemical as the extinguishing agent. They are marked with an illustration of a burning stack of firewood and a trash can. (Older models may be marked with a green triangle and the letter A.) Class B extinguishers are for flammable gases and are marked with an illustration of a flaming can of gasoline. (The older labeling system marks them with a red square and the letter B.) Class D extinguishers are for combustible metals and are not marked with an illustration. Multi-class extinguishers are available that can be used for a variety of types of fires.

Fire extinguishers are covered in depth in National Fire Protection Association (NFPA) 10: *Standard for Portable Fire Extinguishers.*

The answer is (C).

446. The receptacle in the finished living area of a basement or bedroom would not be required to be GFCI-protected because it is not located in an exterior space, in a space that could potentially be damp (such as a crawlspace), or in a place where water will be present.

GFCI protection is available on both receptacles and breakers. The devices constantly monitor the amount of electricity flowing through the circuit. If the GFCI detects any variation, indicating that there is a "leak" and current is flowing out of the circuit and into the ground (potentially through a person), it instantly shuts off the power to that circuit. The person may still be shocked but will not be electrocuted.

The answer is (A), (B), (D), and (E).

447. Hot water and drain pipes must be protected with an enclosure, wrapped with insulation or plastic covers, or concealed within cabinetry—so that a disabled person cannot come in contact with them and be burned.

The *ADA Accessibility Guidelines* require the following for accessible lavatories. (Note that some of these guidelines are different for lavatories designed primarily for children's use. Review the *ADA Accessibility Guidelines* for more information.)

- The rim of the lavatory should be no higher than 34 in above the finish floor.
- There should be a vertical clearance of at least 29 in in front of the lavatory.
- There must be 30 in by 48 in area of clear floor space for forward approach extending a maximum of 19 in under the lavatory. This clear floor space must adjoin or overlap an accessible route.
- Each sink shall be a maximum of 6½ in deep.
- All plumbing pipes are to be insulated or otherwise protected against contact, with no sharp or rough edges under the sink.

The *ADA Accessibility Guidelines* can be reviewed at access-board.gov. A link can also be found at **ppi2pass.com/AREresources.**

The answer is (A), (B), (D), and (E).

448. This partial drawing shows furniture locations and the individual pieces identified with numbers. It would be coordinated with a schedule that would specify each piece of furniture.

The answer is (B).

449. The architect is responsible for the overall coordination of all consultants' drawings and for resolving disputes and conflicts. The electrical engineer should bring the conflict to the architect's attention. The architect can then coordinate with both consultants to resolve the conflict.

The answer is (D).

450. Plans, sections, and elevations are examples of orthographic projections. These drawings "project" the building onto a drawing surface parallel to the object. This allows the elements of the building to be shown to scale but eliminates depth from the drawing. Other drawing conventions, such as lineweight, must be used to communicate which parts of the building are closest to the viewer and which portions recede.

Axonometric drawings are prepared by rotating the plan at an angle (usually 45°/45°, 30°/60°, or 60°/30°) and drawing the horizontal and vertical elements of the elevations to scale. They are sometimes called paraline drawings. An isometric drawing is a type of axonometric drawing that projects the view along *x*-, *y*-, and *z*-axes that are 120° apart.

Oblique drawings can be drawn relative to either the plan or the elevation. A plan oblique is another term for an axonometric drawing. An elevation oblique is projected from an elevation; the elevation closest to the viewer is shown to scale and actual shape, but the other sides of the building are foreshortened.

The answer is (C).

451. Standard symbols on architectural drawings make it possible for architects, consultants, and contractors to communicate with a common, consistent language.

The answer is (A).

452. In all windowsill details, the glass is placed on two or more setting blocks to support the weight of the glass and cushion it from the frame.

Anti-walk blocks are sometimes used in jamb frames to prevent the glass from touching the jambs. A glazing bead describes a material used to cushion and seal the glass against the stop and the frame. A stop is a removable piece used to hold the glass in place after it has been installed in the frame. A stop makes it possible to replace the glass when necessary.

The answer is (C).

453. Of the four detailing considerations implied by the choices (structural integrity, safety from contact, fire safety, and maintainability), fire safety is the most important, which would include verifying the code requirements for the actual flame-spread rating of the specified material. Next, the architect should verify the attachment method and structural integrity of the grille. Subsequently, the reviewer should verify the finish of the material to ensure it will not splinter or break, which could cause injury. Finally, the architect may choose to examine the material's maintainability.

The answer is (C).

454. Construction drawings are generally organized in the following sequence.

- title sheet and identifying information
- civil or site drawings
- architectural drawings
- structural drawings (on some projects, structural drawings are placed before architectural drawings)
- plumbing, mechanical, and electrical drawings (order may vary by office)
- other consultants' drawings

Within the category of architectural drawings, the sheets are generally placed in the following order.

- demolition plans (if applicable)
- floor plans
- reflected ceiling plans
- roof plans
- elevations: exterior and interior
- sections: building sections and wall sections
- details: exterior and interior
- schedules

A project of this scope would involve rewiring, so the electrical and data plan would be created by an electrical engineer and be included with the plumbing, mechanical, and electrical drawings.

The answer is (B).

455. The contract documents form the contractual relationship between the owner and contractor and are defined in American Institute of Architects (AIA) Document A201, *General Conditions of the Contract for Construction*, Sec. 1.1.1.

> The Contract Documents are enumerated in the Agreement between the Owner and Contractor (hereinafter the Agreement), and consist of the Agreement, Conditions of the Contract (General, Supplementary and other Conditions), Drawings, Specifications, Addenda issued prior to execution of the Contract, other documents listed in the Agreement, and Modifications issued after execution of the Contract…

Modifications issued after execution of the contract can include change orders, construction change directives, a written amendment to the contract signed by both parties, or a written order for a minor change in the work issued by the architect.

Anything associated with bidding—including sample forms, the advertisement or invitation to bid, instructions to bidders, and the bid itself—is not a part of the contract documents. The contract documents represent the entire agreement between the owner and contractor, so anything that was negotiated or discussed prior to the agreement but not integrated into the written document is not a part of the contract.

The answer is (A), (C), (D), and (E).

456. The U.S. National CAD Standard was developed to simplify and standardize the way that a set of documents is assembled and cross-referenced, with the intention of making it easier for someone unfamiliar with the documents to find information expeditiously. Each sheet is given a letter and number designation corresponding to the information that is located on the sheet.

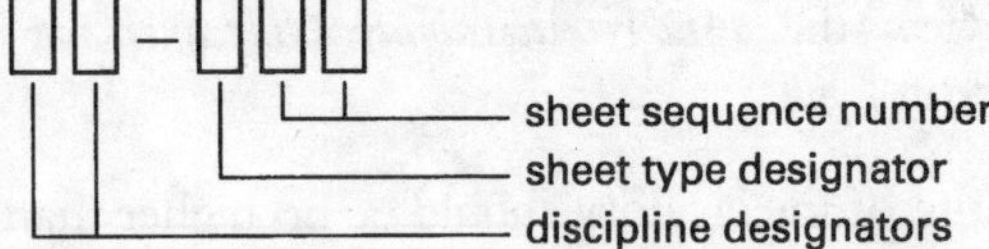

Architectural sheets are given the discipline designator of A. The second space for a discipline designator is often omitted but can be used to further define the discipline that developed the documents.

Level 1 discipline designators are

A architectural
B geotechnical
C civil
D process
E electrical

F fire protection

G general

H hazardous materials

I interiors

L landscape

M mechanical

O operations

P plumbing

Q equipment

R resource

S structural

T telecommunications

V survey/mapping

W civil works

X other disciplines

Z contractor/shop drawings

The sheet type designators are

0 schedules, master keynote legend, general notes

1 plans

2 elevations

3 sections

4 large-scale views

5 details

6 schedules and diagrams

7 user-defined

8 user-defined

9 three-dimensional representations

Each sheet is divided into a grid like a map, with numerical coordinates across the top of the sheet and alphabetical coordinates on the side. Title block information is located at the right side of the sheet in either a horizontal or vertical format. Each drawing is placed within the grid and referred to by its coordinates and sheet number. For example, a column detail may be placed in the lower right corner of one of the A-500 detail sheets; the marker on the plan sheet will refer to the detail as A-14/A-500, and the person reading the drawings will know exactly where to go to find that particular detail.

Another hallmark of the U.S. National CAD Standard system is the use of keynotes. Keynotes are abbreviations that may be coordinated with CSI MasterFormat divisions and that identify particular building elements in lieu of written notes. For example, fire-rated gypsum board may be designated "09 21 16.A." A keynote symbol will point to that element on the drawings, and a full definition of the material, such as "09 21 16.A—$^5/_8$ in fire-rated (type X) gypsum board" will be listed in a note block. The master list of keynotes for a project can be used as a checklist for preparing the specifications to ensure that all materials are properly defined.

Additional information on the U.S. National CAD Standard is available at nationalcadstandard.com.

The answer is (A).

457. Indicating that the items are to be furnished by the owner and installed by the contractor requires the contractor to be responsible for coordination and installation. N.I.C. means "not in contract" and the contractor has no responsibility for those items; they are indicated on the drawings for information only. Cash allowances are used when an owner wishes to include an item in the contract but has not yet selected something to be specified. If the items were noted by name, such as "range" or "refrigerator," it would imply that the contractor is responsible for providing, coordinating, and installing the equipment.

The answer is (B).

458. The architect is responsible for developing the overall format and appearance of the project manual and the specification sections. Each consultant is responsible for the content of their respective specifications. The location of the cooling tower is found on the drawings.

The answer is (A), (B), (D), and (E).

459. It is possible to use both narrowscope and broadscope specifications in the same project manual. It may be necessary to provide a more in-depth specification for an innovative construction technique, for example, than for concrete block or some other common construction material. Specifications are used to define the quality of products to be used in the project, while the drawings define the quantities of materials and where they are to be used.

American Institute of Architects (AIA) Document A201, *General Conditions of the Contract for Construction*, states that the drawings and specifications are to be considered equally binding. Proprietary specifications do not encourage competitive bids because they refer to a specific product and do not allow substitutions. They are the easiest for an architect to write because they simply call out a product

Project Development

by name. A base bid with alternates allows a contractor to substitute products he or she deems equal without requiring the architect's approval. Therefore, they could be considered to be open to interpretation.

The answer is (A) and (C).

460. Procedures for submittals are found in Division 01, General Requirements. The requirements in individual technical sections refer to Division 01 to define procedural requirements, and each section includes a list of the specific types of samples required for that product.

The answer is (A).

461. The contractor's bid form, like other bidding documents, is not part of the contract documents unless specifically stated in the agreement. The amount of the bid, or contract amount, would be incorporated into the agreement, but the bid form itself is not included.

The answer is (A), (B), (C), and (E).

462. The supplementary conditions should include information about basic legal rights and responsibilities that may vary from one project to another. This includes insurance, indemnification, liquidated damages, legal requirements of the jurisdiction that may differ from the standard language in the general conditions, and fiduciary obligations. Instructions for preparing the supplementary conditions are available in American Institute of Architects (AIA) Document A503, *Guide for Supplementary Conditions.* The owner and the owner's legal and/or insurance counsel are responsible for preparing these modifications, not the architect.

Administrative procedures are properly addressed in the specifications in Division 01, General Requirements. Demolition Requirements are addressed in Division 02, Existing Conditions.

The answer is (D).

463. The design strength of the final mix of concrete is specified by the compressive strength of the concrete in pounds per square inch after it has cured for 28 days, indicated with the variable f'_c. Common strengths are 3000 psi and 4000 psi, although high-strength concrete is available up to 22,000 psi.

The answer is (D).

464. A mock-up is a full-scale preview of a building assembly. Mock-ups can be very expensive, so it is important to specify them only where they are truly necessary. Approved mock-ups can often be integrated into the work, making them more cost-effective.

In this problem, the best application of mock-up would be the apartment kitchens. In the case of the cabinetry, the mock-up would allow the architect and owner to see the kitchen in place and sign off on it before the contractor orders the materials for the other apartments. Modifications could be made relatively inexpensively based upon the mock-up, as opposed to waiting until all of the cabinets and countertops have been fabricated to make a change.

There is no need to specify a mock-up for a CMU foundation wall, as this is a relatively standard detail. The carpet inlay would be an extremely expensive mock-up and could probably be more economically represented using a computer modeling program or a paper version of the design.

The answer is (B).

465. The minimum clear floor space required for one stationary wheelchair is 30 in by 48 in. This critical dimension is the basis for many other accessibility guidelines, such as the amount of clear floor space required at a lavatory and the width of a hallway required to allow two wheelchairs to pass (60 in, which is 30 in times two).

The answer is (B).

466. Stress in a body is the internal resistance to deformation or to the action of the external force.

The answer is (A).

467. The direct wind pressure on a vertical surface is directly proportional to the square of the wind velocity. This pressure, *p*, also called "stagnation pressure," is related to the basic wind velocity, v, by the following formula.

$$p_{\text{psf}} = 0.00256\text{v}_{\text{mph}}^2$$

In this formula, the wind pressure is measured in pounds-force per square foot, and the basic wind velocity is measured in miles per hour.

The answer is (C).

468. Calculate the support reactions of the beam by solving the equations of equilibrium.

$$\sum M = 0$$
$$\sum F_y = 0$$

The sum of moments can be calculated either about support A or about support B. The uniform load is replaced by its resultant (R), which is considered to act at the center of the load 5 ft from support B.

$$R = (2)(10) = 20$$

Project Development

Calculating the sum of moments at support B, with clockwise being positive,

$$\begin{aligned}\sum M_B &= 0\\ R_A(20) - (8)(15) - (20)(5) &= 0\\ R_A &= 11\end{aligned}$$

Balancing forces,

$$\begin{aligned}\sum F_y &= 0\\ 11 - 8 - 20 + R_B &= 0\\ R_B &= 17\end{aligned}$$

The answer is (B).

469. In the open-web steel joists structural system, the deep-long span joists of the DLH-series have depths of up to 6.0 ft.

Option (A) is the limit depth for the open-web joists of the K-series. Option (B) is the limit depth for open-web joists of the LH-series.

The answer is (C).

470. Most building codes limit the span-to-depth ratio of a plywood diaphragm to 4:1. This prevents excessive horizontal deflection of the diaphragm. Codes also require that diaphragm deflection be controlled in a way that will not exceed the limits for structural integrity of the diaphragm and the attached load-resisting elements. Excessive horizontal deflection of the diaphragm might lead to damage or failure of the attached resisting elements.

The answer is (C).

471. Maximum drift should be limited to $\frac{1}{500}$ of a building's height.

The answer is (A).

472. According to ACI 318, provisions for minimum slab thickness, the minimum overall thickness of a cantilevered slab of span L is $L/10$.

The minimum thickness, h, is

$$\begin{aligned}h &= \frac{L}{10} = \left(\frac{11 \text{ ft}}{10}\right)\left(12 \ \frac{\text{in}}{\text{ft}}\right)\\ &= 13 \text{ in}\end{aligned}$$

The answer is (D).

473. An office building with a height of 450 ft, a building with a height-to-width ratio of 7, and an extra-long span suspension bridge would require some complex wind calculations and possibly some wind tunnel testing.

Generally, complex wind calculations and wind tunnel testing are required for buildings with heights exceeding 400 ft, for buildings subject to dynamic effects, those sensitive to wind vibrations, and for buildings with a height-to-width ratio of 5 or more. Wind tunnel testing is often carried out on reduced-scale models of long-span suspension bridges.

The answer is (C), (E), and (F).

474. Exterior columns used with tilt-up walls do not necessarily have to be precast concrete. These columns can also be cast-in-place concrete or steel columns.

The answer is (A), (B), (D), and (F).

475. For depths between 10 ft and 20 ft, the most efficient retaining wall type would be the cantilever wall. A gravity wall is not economical beyond a depth of about 4 ft. A counterfort wall is a stronger retaining wall that is generally used for depths of about 25 ft or more.

The answer is (B).

476. The two offices are located on either side of the floor plan, so each office space has a separate unit to accommodate future tenant needs. The cooling requirements of office 1 and office 2 are calculated using the area, A, width, W, and length, L, of each office.

$$\begin{aligned}A_1 &= W_1L_1\\ &= (50 \text{ ft})(100 \text{ ft})\\ &= 5000 \text{ ft}^2\end{aligned}$$

$$\begin{aligned}A_2 &= W_2L_2\\ &= (75 \text{ ft})(50 \text{ ft})\\ &= 3750 \text{ ft}^2\end{aligned}$$

Using cooling capacity, c, the unit size, U, for office 1 and office 2 is

$$\begin{aligned}U_1 &= \frac{A_1}{c}\\ &= \frac{5000 \text{ ft}^2}{500 \ \frac{\text{ft}^2}{\text{ton}}}\\ &= 10 \text{ tons}\end{aligned}$$

$$\begin{aligned}U_2 &= \frac{A_2}{c}\\ &= \frac{3750 \text{ ft}^2}{500 \ \frac{\text{ft}^2}{\text{ton}}}\\ &= 7.5 \text{ tons}\end{aligned}$$

The answer is (C).

Project Development

477. Air-to-air heat exchangers reclaim waste energy from the exhaust air stream and use it to condition the incoming fresh air. The coefficient of performance (COP) of an air-to-air heat pump decreases as the temperature approaches the freezing mark, so it is not appropriate for colder climates.

Air-to-air heat pumps generally have a high initial cost compared to evaporative cooling or through-the-wall units. Heat pumps can both heat and cool by transferring heat from one place to another. To extend their efficiency, heat pumps can be connected to either solar energy systems or water storage tanks. Heating or cooling incoming air needs the use of a reversible refrigeration cycle, which is very economical to operate. Heat pumps are the most common type of pumps in small buildings because they are the most efficient and economical to operate.

The answer is (A), (B), (E), and (F).

478. Because a passive solar water heating system has no pump, gravity is used to circulate the water, and the storage tank must be placed above the collector. In general, a passive solar water heating system has both a low initial cost and a low operation cost. A passive solar water heating system has a high mechanical reliability because it has no pump that can fail or malfunction. Placing the storage tank on the roof can cause structural problems if it is heavy and the roof framing is inadequate. The placement of the storage tank on the roof may be subject to local design review and additional costs may be incurred to shield the tank from the street view.

The answer is (A), (B), (D), and (F).

479. A set of typical construction drawings is organized in the following order.

- title sheet
- civil engineering drawings
- architectural drawings
- structural drawings
- mechanical/electrical/plumbing drawings

Construction drawings must be accurately produced and organized to communicate the architect's intent. The drawings are typically organized in a standardized sequence based on the normal sequence of construction tasks, so that contractors and other working professionals can find what they need without confusion.

The standardized sequence is the title sheet, civil engineering drawings, architectural drawings, structural drawings, and mechanical/electrical, and plumbing drawings.

480. Footing details, rebar layout, and pier reinforcement schedules must be in only the structural drawings because only the reinforcing steel and concrete subcontractors use this information. Elevations for tops of beams, structural walls, and floors must be in both architectural and structural drawings. Various construction trades will use this information for constructing the beams, walls, and floors.

The answer is (D).

481. The landscape specification section should include instructions on the preservation of existing trees. Any existing structures (Oak Hall, Cherry Hall, and pedestrian tunnel) that are located within the construction limit line include documentation. Both a demolition specification and a site demolition drawing further delineate the needed work to alter or protect the buildings or structures from damage. A concrete walk or a flagpole can be demolished without additional documentation.

The answer is (A), (B), (C), and (E).

482. Slopes for permanent fill are not to be steeper than 1 vertical unit for every 2 horizontal units, or 50% slope. The same limit applies to cut slopes for permanent excavations. Deviation from the limit is allowed only with the presentation of a soil report. This limit is expressed in the building code, state transportation agency standards, and accepted practice by civil engineers for typical soil conditions.

The answer is (A).

483. Fire protection shop drawings, structural calculations, and occupant load calculations may or may not be requested depending on local authorities' jurisdiction. Occupant load calculations are not performed for single family residences.

The answer is (A), (B), and (E).

484. The exact circuiting of lighting and power outlets does not have to be shown on the architect's reflected ceiling plan. Rather, electrical drawings must contain this information. In some cases, such as an office tenant improvement project, the architect shows the location of switches on the reflected ceiling plan if the electrical construction work will be subcontracted out as design-build work and no electrical engineer is consulting on the project.

The answer is (D).

485. An architect is not responsible for any of these items, except for interpreting the design intent of the drawings. All items are included in American Institute of Architects (AIA) Contract Document A201, *General Conditions of the Contract for Construction.* The job site safety conditions, methods, and means of construction are the sole responsibility of contractors. An architect is not responsible for the contractors' failures and is not required to perform continuous site inspections.

The answer is (C).

486. A change order requires the owner to accept the cost proposal from the contractor before it can be issued. Minor changes to the work are limited to the intent of the contract documents. The owner cannot make changes to the work directly through the contractor. The architect can issue a construction change directive with only the owner's and architect's signature, requiring the contractor to proceed with the change prior to an agreement on the cost and/or time adjustment.

The answer is (B).

487. Safety violations, when discovered, must not be ignored. Although the architect is not responsible for safety issues on the job site, the matter is to be brought to the attention of the owner without a suggestion for correction. The architect also follows up with a notice in writing. It is the responsibility of the contractor to rectify safety problems as described in American Institute of Architects (AIA) Document A201, *General Conditions of the Contract for Construction.*

The answer is (C).

488. Because the testing is required by the building code and is included in the contract documents, it is the contractor who is responsible for making arrangements with the acceptable testing agencies to test the concrete samples.

The answer is (A).

489. The changes needed to convert a speculative office building into a corporate headquarters are significant. The building team must upgrade and redesign the building's mechanical and electrical systems, elevator, fire protection system, and interior finishes to corporate level standards that meet tenant requirements. Because the use of the building remains as an office, the structural design, site drainage, and on-site parking will remain unchanged.

The answer is (A), (C), (E), and (F).

490. The typical design approach to adding a third story to a tenant office building is to extrude the plan vertically. The plan view will remain the same so the floor plan core elements and the roof plan are not affected and the building setbacks are required by the basic zoning code. The façade will be redesigned to add the third floor. Site planning will be altered to accommodate the additional parking. This building type does not require special hardware.

The answer is (A) and (D).

491. Mediation and arbitration are methods of resolving claims and disputes without the lengthy and costly procedure of litigation. Both methods make use of neutral third parties to help the parties reach a resolution. Unlike litigation, the decisions of mediation can be appealed. Arbitration is a more formal process than mediation in that arbitration is carried out under state laws and proceedings as conducted under the Construction Industry Arbitration Rules of the American Arbitration Association. The arbitrator can be a single party or a panel of three. The mediation process is required before arbitration or litigation can be pursued. The decision in mediation is not legally binding, while arbitration can be binding or nonbinding depending on the terms of the agreement.

The answer is (B), (D), and (E).

492. A dry well is an underground tank or structure designed to dissipate excess water into the ground. In order to protect the basement foundation from this dissipated water, it is important to maximize the distance between the dry well and the building without encroaching beyond the property line. One-half the diameter of the dry well is 8 ft + 1 ft, 3 in, which is equal to 9 ft, 3 in, which is less than the 10 ft distance to the property line.

The answer is (C).

493. An empty soil pit can collapse. Sand and clay retain water. The type of simple dry well selected for this project generally has a filter fabric liner and is filled with stone, gravel, or rubble to help drain and store the water until it can be dissipated into the surrounding clay soil.

The answer is (D).

494. First, calculate the dry well volume, V_D. The radius, r, is one-half of the dry well diameter given and d_D is the depth.

$$\begin{aligned} V_D &= \pi r^2 d_D \\ &= (3.14)\left(\frac{30 \text{ in}}{2}\right)^2 (6 \text{ ft})\left(12 \ \frac{\text{in}}{\text{ft}}\right) \\ &= \frac{50{,}868 \text{ in}^3}{\left(12 \ \frac{\text{in}}{\text{ft}}\right)^3} \\ &= 29.44 \text{ ft}^3 \end{aligned}$$

The dry well garden volume also equals the rain garden volume, V_R, with width, w, depth, d_R, and length, L.

Project Development

Solve for length.

$$V_R = wd_R L$$
$$L = \frac{V_R}{wd_R}$$
$$= \frac{29.44 \text{ ft}^3}{(2.5 \text{ ft})(1 \text{ ft})}$$
$$= 11.78 \text{ ft} \quad (12 \text{ ft})$$

The answer is (C).

495. Because the new basement is designed to be deeper than the existing one, the existing adjacent foundation footing must be underpinned so as to not destabilize the structure. The contractor will need to underpin in alternate sections of approximately 3 ft. Concrete with rebar will be cast under the existing footing to a depth that matches the new footing depth. The new footing will also need to connect to the underpinning concrete using rebar.

The existing footing is below the frost depth. To remain economical, the new foundation should not be deeper than needed to underpin the existing foundation. Option (D) will not allow the existing footing to be underpinned properly.

The answer is (C).

496. The load-bearing walls are the long walls running in the horizontal direction of the addition. It is better not to overload the existing wall on the right side of the plan.

497. The new floor joists run perpendicular to the load-bearing walls. It is better to support the joists of the new framing on the new foundation and load-bearing walls running in the horizontal direction of the plan. The correct framing span symbol is shown. The symbol must be placed vertically and perpendicular to these new bearing walls.

Illustration for Sol. 496

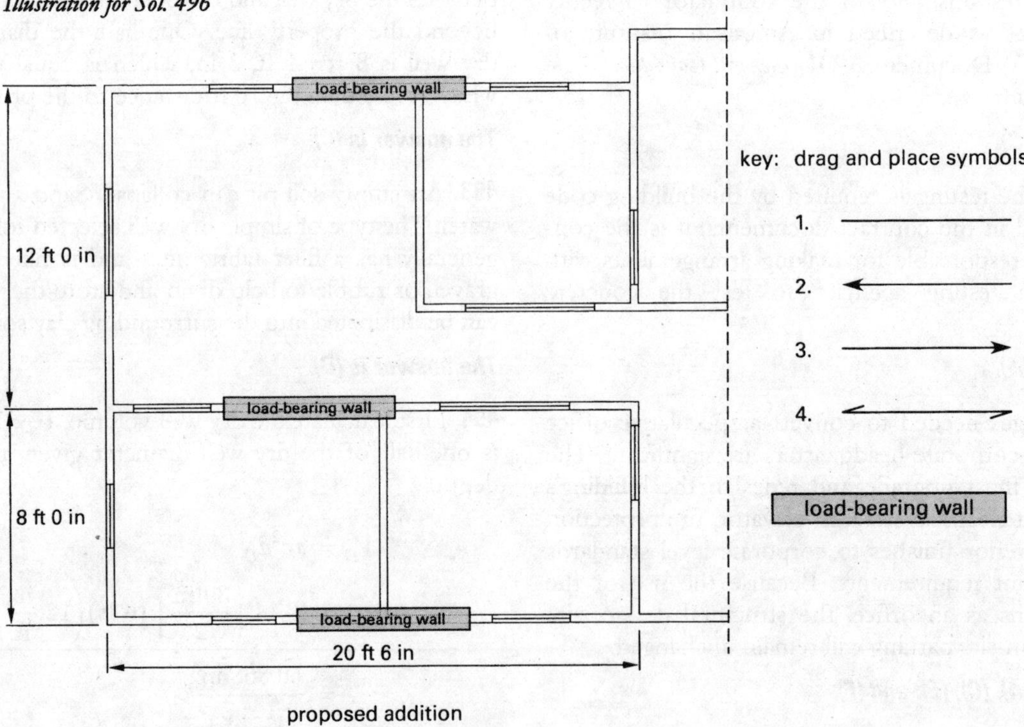

Illustration for Sol. 497

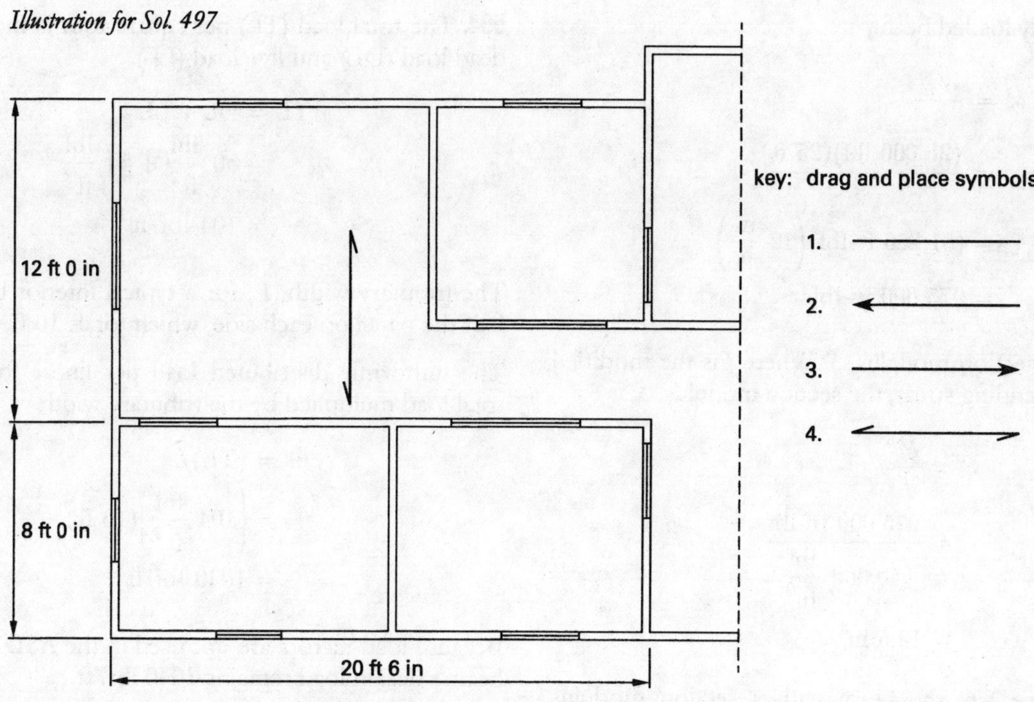

498. The *International Building Code* (IBC) gives the uniform live load requirements: uninhabitable attics without storage is 10 ft^2, pitched roof is 20 ft^2, and second floor is 40 ft^2.

Therefore, the correct order of the uniform live load requirements is as follows.

- uninhabitable attics without storage
- pitched roof
- second floor

499. LVL, PSL, and glulam are considered for any necessary beams but not for joists because they can carry heavier loads. Steel elements such as steel beams are sometimes used in wood residential construction, but not as joists. The most appropriate products to use in this case for the given spans are lumber and wood I-joists because they are the most cost-effective.

The answer is (A) and (B).

500. A36 is no longer commonly used to fabricate W-shapes. A242 is a high-strength, corrosion-resistant steel that is mostly used when the steel is exposed to the elements. A514 is a very high-strength steel that is typically used to make plates and bars only. Most wide-flange sections are fabricated using A992 grade 50 (yield stress of 50 kips/in^2).

The answer is (D).

501. In typical steel buildings, using regular metal decks, the range of beam spacing is 6–10 ft because the metal decks cannot sustain the loads over a larger deck span. This spacing can be increased to as much as 14 ft when using composite metal decks that are stronger and able to support loads over larger deck spans.

The answer is (B).

502. Use the formulas in Resource 5.5 and the allowable stress design (ASD) method.

The uniformly distributed load per linear foot, w, is the total load multiplied by the tributary length.

$$\begin{aligned} w &= (\mathrm{TL})L \\ &= \left(104\ \frac{\mathrm{lbf}}{\mathrm{ft}^2}\right)(10\ \mathrm{ft}) \\ &= 1040\ \mathrm{lbf/ft} \end{aligned}$$

Take the uniformly distributed load, w, and solve for weight, W.

$$\begin{aligned} W &= wL \\ &= \left(1040\ \frac{\mathrm{lbf}}{\mathrm{ft}}\right)(25\ \mathrm{ft}) \\ &= 26{,}000\ \mathrm{lbf} \end{aligned}$$

For a uniformly loaded beam,

$$\begin{aligned} M &= \frac{WL}{8} \\ &= \frac{(26{,}000\ \text{lbf})(25\ \text{ft})}{8} \\ &= (81{,}250\ \text{ft-lbf})\left(12\ \frac{\text{in}}{\text{ft}}\right) \\ &= 975{,}000\ \text{in-lbf} \end{aligned}$$

Solve for the section modulus, S. Where f is the modified or allowable bending stress, the section modulus, S, is

$$\begin{aligned} S &= \frac{M}{f} \\ &= \frac{975{,}000\ \text{in-lbf}}{50{,}000\ \frac{\text{lbf}}{\text{in}^2}} \\ &= 19.5\ \text{in}^3 \end{aligned}$$

From Resource 5.6, the beam with a section modulus greater than 19.5 in^3 and the minimum depth of 7.93 in is W8 × 24.

This formula gives the designer the correct section modulus regarding a preliminary beam depth but the most economical beam section that is used in the final structural analysis may actually be a deeper section.

The answer is (D).

503. Columns on the upper floors are generally smaller in size compared to columns on the lower floors. First floor columns are the largest and are likely to be about W12 to W14, while upper floor columns are closer to W8. The depth range for the columns on the first floor is 12–14 in.

The answer is (D).

504. The total load (TL) per square foot is the sum of the dead load (DL) and live load (LL).

$$\begin{aligned} \text{TL} &= \text{DL} + \text{LL} \\ &= 50\ \frac{\text{lbf}}{\text{ft}^2} + 54\ \frac{\text{lbf}}{\text{ft}^2} \\ &= 104\ \text{lbf/ft}^2 \end{aligned}$$

The tributary width, L, for a typical interior beam is one-half the panel on each side, which totals 10 ft.

The uniformly distributed load per linear foot, w, is the total load multiplied by the tributary width.

$$\begin{aligned} w &= (\text{TL})L \\ &= \left(104\ \frac{\text{lbf}}{\text{ft}^2}\right)(10\ \text{ft}) \\ &= 1040\ \text{lbf/ft} \end{aligned}$$

Because load factors are not used in the ASD method, the beam's design load remains 1040 lbf/ft.

The answer is (C).

505. The columns should be designed as concentrically loaded columns at B2, C2, B3, C3, B4, and C4. Each of these columns supports two typical interior beams and two typical interior girders in addition to the load from the column above, if any. The members framing into the column are symmetrical, leading to a concentric configuration. (See *Illustration for Sol. 505.*)

506. The metal deck span symbol must be placed perpendicular to the secondary beam system. The secondary beam system is the system of beams that are spaced at 10 ft, spanning the 25 ft direction. (See *Illustration for Sol. 506.*)

Illustration for Sol. 505

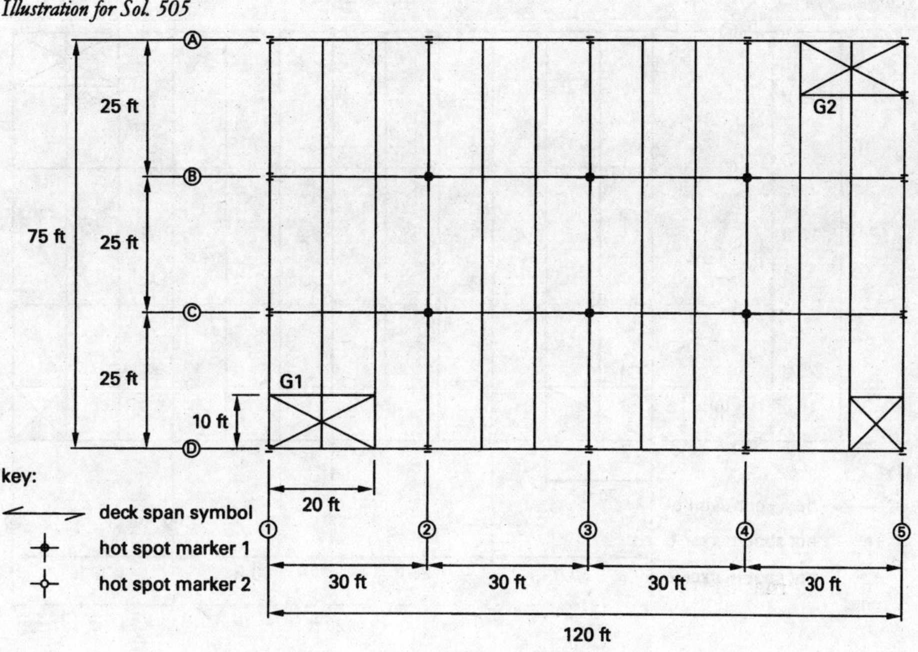

floor framing plan

Illustration for Sol. 506

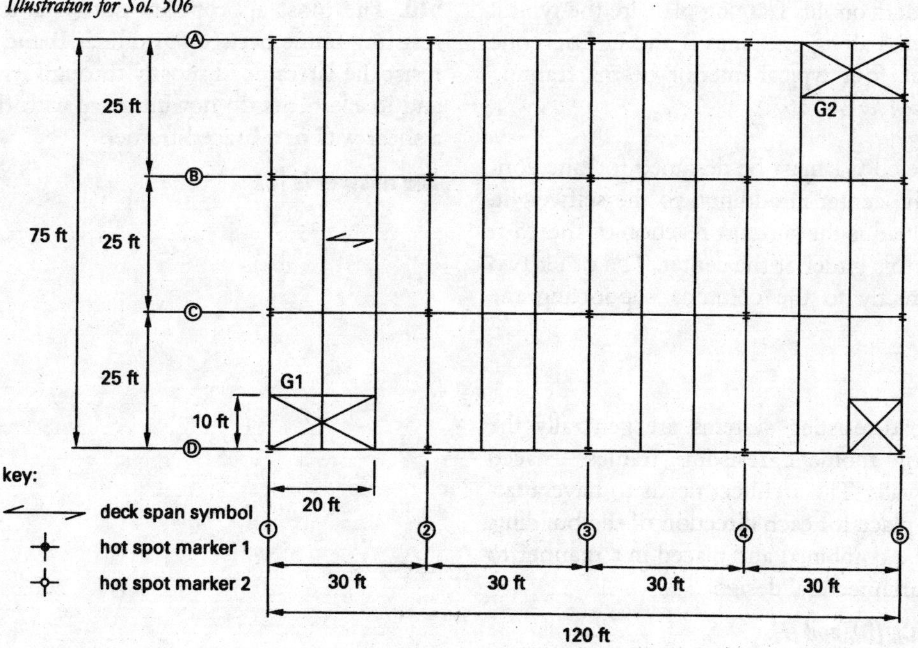

floor framing plan

Illustration for Sol. 507

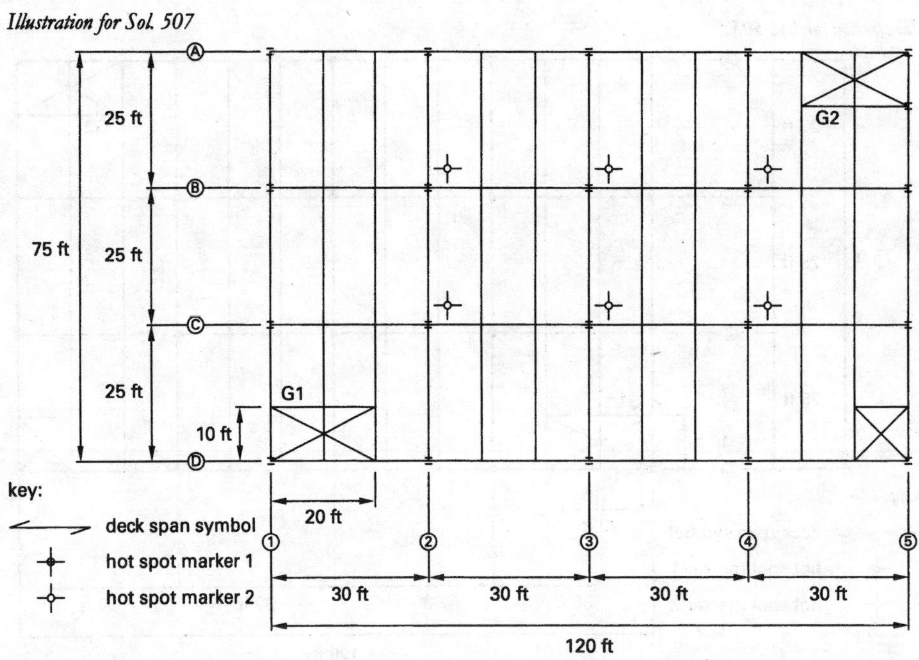

507. The largest girders on this framing plan are the typical interior girders aligned along grid lines B and C. Each one of these girders has four typical interior beams framing into it. (See *Illustration for Sol. 507.*)

508. The girder labeled G1 must be designed for one concentrated load at the center in addition to the selfweight. This concentrated load is the support reaction of the 15 ft beam framing into this girder at the center. The other two beams connect directly to the columns supporting the girder G1.

The answer is (A).

509. The lateral load-resisting systems are generally the three categories of moment resisting frames, braced frames, and shear walls. The architect needs to have a lateral load system in place for each direction of the building. The elements can be combined and placed in a manner to accommodate the architectural design.

The answer is (B), (C), (D), and (E).

510. The most appropriate option is to have a moment-resisting frame between grid lines B and C. This frame can resist the lateral load mostly through its rigid connections, and its elements do not interfere with the opening, unlike a shear wall or a braced frame.

The answer is (C).

4.630
1
0,000
166.420
770
13
12
10

DIVISION 6: CONSTRUCTION & EVALUATION

Multiple Choice

511. (A) (B) (C) (D)
512. (A) (B) (C) (D)
513. (A) (B) (C) (D)
514. (A) (B) (C) (D)
515. (A) (B) (C) (D) (E) (F)
516. (A) (B) (C) (D) (E) (F)
517. (A) (B) (C) (D) (E) (F)
518. (A) (B) (C) (D)
519. (A) (B) (C) (D)
520. (A) (B) (C) (D)
521. (A) (B) (C) (D)
522. (A) (B) (C) (D)
523. (A) (B) (C) (D) (E) (F)
524. (A) (B) (C) (D)
525. (A) (B) (C) (D)
526. (A) (B) (C) (D) (E) (F)
527. (A) (B) (C) (D)
528. (A) (B) (C) (D) (E) (F)
529. (A) (B) (C) (D)
530. (A) (B) (C) (D)
531. (A) (B) (C) (D)
532. (A) (B) (C) (D)
533. (A) (B) (C) (D)
534. ____________
535. (A) (B) (C) (D)
536. (A) (B) (C) (D)
537. (A) (B) (C) (D)
538. (A) (B) (C) (D) (E) (F)
539. (A) (B) (C) (D)
540. (A) (B) (C) (D) (E) (F)
541. (A) (B) (C) (D)
542. ____________
543. (A) (B) (C) (D)
544. (A) (B) (C) (D)
545. (A) (B) (C) (D)
546. (A) (B) (C) (D)
547. (A) (B) (C) (D) (E) (F)
548. (A) (B) (C) (D)
549. (A) (B) (C) (D) (E) (F)
550. (A) (B) (C) (D)
551. (A) (B) (C) (D) (E) (F)
552. (A) (B) (C) (D)
553. (A) (B) (C) (D)
554. (A) (B) (C) (D)
555. (A) (B) (C) (D)
556. (A) (B) (C) (D)
557. (A) (B) (C) (D)
558. (A) (B) (C) (D)
559. (A) (B) (C) (D)
560. (A) (B) (C) (D) (E) (F)
561. (A) (B) (C) (D) (E) (F)
562. (A) (B) (C) (D)
563. (A) (B) (C) (D)
564. (A) (B) (C) (D)
565. (A) (B) (C) (D)
566. (A) (B) (C) (D)
567. (A) (B) (C) (D)
568. (A) (B) (C) (D)
569. (A) (B) (C) (D)
570. (A) (B) (C) (D)
571. (A) (B) (C) (D)
572. (A) (B) (C) (D)
573. (A) (B) (C) (D)
574. (A) (B) (C) (D)
575. (A) (B) (C) (D)
576. (A) (B) (C) (D)
577. (A) (B) (C) (D) (E) (F)
578. (A) (B) (C) (D) (E) (F)
579. (A) (B) (C) (D)
580. (A) (B) (C) (D)
581. (A) (B) (C) (D)
582. (A) (B) (C) (D)
583. (A) (B) (C) (D) (E) (F)
584. (A) (B) (C) (D)
585. (A) (B) (C) (D)
586. (A) (B) (C) (D)
587. (A) (B) (C) (D)

Case Study 1

588. (A) (B) (C) (D)
589. (A) (B) (C) (D) (E) (F)
590. (A) (B) (C) (D) (E) (F)
591. (A) (B) (C) (D) (E) (F)
592. (A) (B) (C) (D)
593. (A) (B) (C) (D) (E) (F)
594. ____________
595. (A) (B) (C) (D)
596. (A) (B) (C) (D) (E) (F)
597. (A) (B) (C) (D) (E) (F)
598. (A) (B) (C) (D)
599. (A) (B) (C) (D)
600. (A) (B) (C) (D)

Case Study 2

601. (A) (B) (C) (D)
602. (A) (B) (C) (D)
603. (A) (B) (C) (D)
604. (A) (B) (C) (D)
605. (A) (B) (C) (D) (E) (F)

Construction & Evaluation

511. Which of the following is used to determine the workability of concrete?

(A) Steiner tunnel test

(B) cylinder test

(C) electrical impedance test

(D) Kelly ball test

512. During which period in the curing process does concrete gain the most compressive strength?

(A) 0–3 days

(B) 3–7 days

(C) 7–14 days

(D) 14–28 days

513. The limits of excavation and the building footprint are located by a surveyor and marked on the site using

(A) grade stakes

(B) batter boards

(C) corner pins

(D) a transit

514. Which of the following devices is used to depressurize a space to test for air infiltration?

(A) nanometer

(B) blower door

(C) flow hood

(D) duct blower

515. Which of the following are expected results of a properly designed and implemented building commissioning plan? (Choose the four that apply.)

(A) increased energy efficiency

(B) comprehensive training program for maintenance staff

(C) verification of 100% of the building systems by the commissioning agent (CxA)

(D) operation and maintenance manuals delivered to the owner in a useful and organized format

(E) record drawings for all heating, ventilation, and air conditioning (HVAC) and electrical components

(F) improved indoor air quality

516. Which of the following statements is correct regarding sick building syndrome? (Choose the three that apply.)

(A) Increasing the quantity of outdoor air in the heating, ventilating, and air conditioning (HVAC) system can help prevent or remedy sick building syndrome.

(B) Insufficient ventilation in areas with high concentrations of odor or chemicals can cause nausea and headaches.

(C) Radon and asbestos cause sick building syndrome.

(D) Sick building syndrome causes long-term symptoms that continue after the occupants leave the building.

(E) Legionnaires' disease is an example of a building-related illness.

(F) All sick building syndrome symptoms are the result of poor performance of the HVAC system.

517. Which of the following hazardous materials may be found in insulation products? (Choose the two that apply.)

(A) asbestos

(B) lead

(C) polychlorinated biphenyls (PCBs)

(D) radon

(E) crystalline silica

(F) glass fiber

518. An amount of money withheld from each application for payment is known as

(A) retainage

(B) deduction

(C) overhead

(D) liquidated damages

519. A cabinetry subcontractor drops off a box of countertop material and hardware samples at an architect's office with a transmittal requesting selections by the end of the week. What should the architect do with the materials?

(A) Review the options and call the subcontractor with the selections.

(B) Review the options, make selections, and inform the contractor in writing of the choices.

(C) Send the samples back to the subcontractor.

(D) Send the samples to the contractor.

520. The architect has the authority to

(A) stop work

(B) reject work that does not comply with the construction documents

(C) order changes to the work that deduct from the contract sum

(D) accept nonconforming work

521. Which of the following is most likely to be included in an informational submittal?

(A) shop drawings of a storefront window assembly

(B) Safety Data Sheets (SDS) for trowel-on block filler

(C) vinyl wall base samples

(D) cut sheets for a paper towel dispenser

522. A developer from New York owns a large piece of property along the James River in Virginia and plans to construct a retirement community and golf course. This is an area where there are many pockets of unstable shrink/swell soil, so the architect advises the owner to hire a geotechnical engineer to conduct testing and prepare a soils report for the property. The developer bids construction of the clubhouse and provides a copy of the soils report to each of the bidders along with the contract documents. The low bidder and the developer reach an agreement based upon American Institute of Architects (AIA) Document A201, *General Conditions of the Contract for Construction*. Three weeks into the site excavation, the contractor finds areas of shrink/swell soil in locations not indicated in the soils report. The cost of additional excavation and/or foundation design and reinforcement is the responsibility of the

(A) contractor

(B) geotechnical engineer

(C) owner

(D) architect

523. At the completion of a project, what is the architect required to provide to the owner? (Choose the three that apply.)

(A) final certificate of payment

(B) occupancy permit

(C) consent of surety to release retainage and lien and bond waivers

(D) warranty that the construction complies with all applicable codes

(E) insurance coverage transfer from the architect to the owner

(F) inspection

524. While removing floor tile in the lobby of an old theater, a contractor suspects that the mastic may contain asbestos. In accordance with American Institute of Architects (AIA) Document A201, *General Conditions of the Contract for Construction*, she stops work and reports her findings to the owner. The owner hires a testing laboratory to evaluate the samples, which confirms the contractor's suspicions. The project is at a standstill for three weeks while abatement takes place. When the area is clear, the contractor prepares a change order request for a time extension and compensation for expenses incurred as a result of the discovery. The owner refuses, stating that the contractor's proposal for four extra weeks and $10,000 to cover shutdown and startup costs is unreasonable. What is the next step?

(A) The architect should issue a construction change directive and order the work to proceed so that more time is not lost while the owner and contractor negotiate.

(B) The claim should proceed directly to mediation.

(C) The contract time should automatically be extended by three weeks because the project was shut down for three weeks.

(D) The initial decision maker (IDM) should review the claim and make a decision.

525. According to American Institute of Architects (AIA) Document A201, *General Conditions of the Contract for Construction*, the

(A) architect must approve the contractor's proposed construction schedule before work can begin

(B) architect must approve the contractor's proposed schedule of submittals

(C) contractor is responsible for preparing record drawings

(D) architect is responsible for reviewing all submittals provided by the contractor

526. For which of the following reasons should an architect withhold all or part of a certificate for payment? (Choose the four that apply.)

(A) There are mathematical errors on the contractor's application for payment.

(B) The architect has been notified by the owner that the plumbing subcontractor's attorney has informed him of the subcontractor's intent to place a lien on the project.

(C) The contractor has failed to correct a portion of the work that the architect has rejected.

(D) One month remains in the construction period on a project with $5000 liquidated damages per day, and the architect suspects that work will not be completed by the deadline; not enough unpaid funds remain to cover the liquidated damages for the expected delay.

(E) The contractor withheld the required retainage.

(F) The window supplier has notified the architect that it has not been paid for materials delivered to the contractor's storage facility.

527. During the construction of a church, the building committee decides to replace the porcelain tile floor specified for the chapel with a poured terrazzo flooring material. The architect requests a proposal from the contractor for the change. The contract states that the contractor may add 20% for overhead and profit and an additional 5% for coordination on change orders. The contractor's base price for labor and materials for the change is $22,250. What is the approximate total value of the change order?

(A) $26,700

(B) $27,800

(C) $28,000

(D) $28,400

528. Which of these should be included in an advertisement to bid? (Choose the four that apply.)

(A) the name and address of the architect

(B) the date, time, and location of the pre-bid conference

(C) the amount of the deposit required to obtain copies of the bidding documents

(D) the names of acceptable subcontractors

(E) bid forms

(F) the date, time, and location at which bids are due

529. A contractor submits the following bid form.

> Tussey Mountain Construction
> 6734 Raystown Road
> Saxton, Pennsylvania
>
> *BASE BID: The undersigned, having inspected the construction site and familiarized him/herself with all conditions likely to be encountered affecting the cost and schedule of work, and having examined all of the Contract Documents, hereby proposes to furnish all labor, materials, tools, equipment, and services required to perform all of the work in strict accordance with the Contract Documents for the Base Bid Sum of:*
>
> <u>Seven hundred fifty-six thousand, four hundred fifty-two dollars and 0/100</u> dollars
> <u>$765,452.00</u>
>
> *and if this proposal is accepted, will execute a formal contract to this effect.*

How should the architect interpret this bid?

(A) The bid is $765,452.

(B) The bid is $756,452.

(C) The bid is invalid and must be discarded.

(D) The architect should call the bidder and ask what amount was intended.

530. A contractor submits a list of proposed subcontractors to the owner and architect for construction of a small office building. The architect reviews it and notes that the proposed plumbing subcontractor is a company with a history of poor workmanship; one of the architect's clients on a previous project spent thousands of dollars to correct the plumber's errors. The architect expresses his concerns to the owner, who agrees that he prefers not to have this subcontractor as a part of the project. If the owner-contractor agreement references American Institute of Architects (AIA) Document A201, *General Conditions of*

Construction & Evaluation

the Contract for Construction, what can the owner and architect do?

(A) Do nothing, as the selection of subcontractors is entirely within the purview of the general contractor and the list of subcontractors is submitted to the architect and owner for information only.

(B) Submit to the contractor the name and contact information for a plumbing subcontractor the owner prefers to use for the project and require the contractor to hire that firm.

(C) Require the general contractor to use a different plumbing subcontractor with no adjustment to the contract sum.

(D) Require the general contractor to use a different plumbing subcontractor, with the understanding that the contract sum or contract time may be adjusted to reflect the new subcontractor's proposed price and/or schedule.

531. Five general contractors are invited to bid on a small office renovation project. The drawings are mailed to the bidders at the beginning of June, with bids due on July 2. The documents state that bidders are to list a unit price per square yard for providing and installing carpet. In the meantime, the owner decides to choose and order carpet through a local flooring distributor and provide it to the contractor to install. The architect issues an addendum to this effect on June 22, requesting that bidders delete the unit price and include installation of the carpet in their bids. Upon receipt of the addendum, one of the prospective bidders calls the architect and says that he has already delivered his bid to the owner's office. How should the architect respond?

(A) Ask the contractor the amount he wishes to add to or deduct from the price and adjust the bid after the bid opening.

(B) Tell the contractor to retrieve the bid from the owner, correct it to reflect receipt of the addendum and the revised price, and resubmit it to the owner.

(C) Require the contractor to submit another bid.

(D) Explain that the bid will not be considered valid without acknowledgment of receipt of the addendum.

532. Which of these statements regarding building officials is correct?

(A) If a building should collapse, the building official could be held personally liable for failing to properly inspect the structure whether or not the official acted in good faith.

(B) A building official must obtain a court order to enter a building if the official believes that the building is not in compliance with the code or is unsafe.

(C) The interpretation of the building official having jurisdiction becomes the final decision.

(D) A user may occupy a property before the building official has completed a final inspection and issued a certificate of occupancy.

533. Which of the following decisions may minimize the effect of inclement weather on construction time?

(A) the use of prefabricated elements

(B) the use of designs that contribute to improved sequencing

(C) the use of union labor

(D) beginning construction in the spring

534. The contractor must submit the application for payment to the architect ____ days in advance of the scheduled payment date. (Fill in the blank.)

535. Which of the following materials has the smallest dimensional tolerances?

(A) precast concrete tees

(B) 2 × 4 wood framing at a window opening

(C) steel beams

(D) wood paneling

536. During a hotel construction project in the Outer Banks of North Carolina, a hurricane slams into the coast, leveling a building that was framed one week prior. Which type of clause permits the contractor to request a change to the contract time or contract sum due to the damage?

(A) indemnification

(B) joinder

(C) force majeure

(D) named peril

537. Which of the following statements is true?

(A) "Clerk of the works" is another term for the architect's project representative.

(B) If a contractor discovers an error in the contract documents, the architect is required to absorb the cost of correcting the drawings and pay for the cost of construction related to the error.

(C) A construction change directive must be signed by the contractor to be valid.

(D) The contractor is responsible for notifying the surety of any change orders issued during a project.

538. A renovation project at a large classroom building on a college campus is scheduled to take place in two phases during the next summer and the winter break when classes are not in session. All windows in the building are to be replaced, and the window manufacturer's representative advises the college to purchase all the windows at one time to take advantage of considerable savings. The college facilities staff thinks this is a good idea but does not have room to store the windows on campus, so the college requests that the contractor purchase and store the windows until they are needed. The contractor submits the first pay application, which includes a request for payment for 60% of the windows line item on the schedule of values. What should the architect do prior to certifying the pay application? (Choose the four that apply.)

(A) Request copies of bills of sale and insurance for the windows.

(B) Visit the location where the windows are stored.

(C) Submit documentation to the owner's attorney for evaluation prior to certifying the pay application.

(D) Request written approval from the owner.

(E) Verify that the contractor has secured insurance coverage for the materials.

(F) Verify that the storage conditions comply with the specification requirements.

539. An architect suspects that blocking has been installed in the wrong location and asks that a portion of the work be uncovered. When the drywall is removed, the blocking is found to be properly installed. Who is responsible for paying for the removal and replacement of the portion of the wall?

(A) architect

(B) owner

(C) contractor

(D) architect and owner should split the cost

540. For a project using American Institute of Architects (AIA) Document A201, *General Conditions of the Contract for Construction*, claims concerning which of the following would be referred to the initial decision maker? (Choose the three that apply.)

(A) the discovery of hazardous materials on the project site

(B) a request for additional compensation due to a discrepancy in the contract documents

(C) a request for additional time due to poor weather conditions

(D) an emergency that endangers workers on the jobsite

(E) a loss covered by insurance

(F) the termination of the contract for cause

541. An architect's signature on a certificate for payment indicates that the architect has

(A) inspected and accepted the work performed

(B) reviewed the invoices submitted to the contractor by subcontractors

(C) verified that the contractor is entitled to payment for work performed to date

(D) received payment for work performed to date

542. During the bid period, a contractor wants to propose a substitution of a material specified in the contract documents. According to American Institute of Architects (AIA) Document A701, *Instructions to Bidders*, the request for substitution must be received by the architect ____ days prior to the receipt of bids. (Fill in the blank.)

Construction & Evaluation

543. Which of the following is used to formally incorporate a substitution into the work prior to award of the contract?

(A) change order

(B) addendum

(C) alternate listing

(D) construction change directive

544. At the scheduled time for a public bid opening, a contractor comes rushing into the room three minutes late, clutching his bid, and asks the architect to accept it because he was stuck in traffic. None of the bids has been opened yet. According to American Institute of Architects (AIA) Document A701, *Instructions to Bidders*, what should the architect do?

(A) Refuse to accept the bid, stating that the deadline has passed.

(B) Since none of the bids have been opened yet, ask the other bidders if they will object to accepting the late bid. If none object, accept the bid.

(C) Accept the bid with prejudice.

(D) Stop the bidding process and require that all bids be resubmitted at a later time.

545. Procedures a bidder must follow to propose a substitution will be found in the

(A) advertisement to bid

(B) "front-end" of the specifications (Division 01)

(C) instructions to bidders

(D) general conditions

546. When the owner wants to make sure some amount of money is included in the bid for a particular item before the exact specification for the item is known, the architect should use a(n)

(A) allowance

(B) add alternate

(C) material bond

(D) unit price

547. According to American Institute of Architects (AIA) Document A201, *General Conditions of the Contract for Construction*, which of the following methods may be used to make changes in the work once construction has started? (Choose the three that apply.)

(A) work modification form

(B) order for minor change in the work

(C) change order

(D) construction change directive

(E) addendum

(F) verbal directive

548. During a site visit, the architect notices that a worker has installed studs at 24 in on center, not 16 in on center as shown on the drawings. Under the provisions of American Institute of Architects (AIA) Document A201, *General Conditions of the Contract for Construction*, the authority to reject this work rests with the

(A) architect

(B) owner

(C) owner and architect

(D) general contractor

549. During construction, the contractor makes a claim to the initial decision maker (IDM) to extend the contract time because the owner failed to account for the lead time associated with certain equipment to be provided by the owner and installed by the contractor, and this delayed the project for four weeks. Under American Institute of Architects (AIA) Document A201, *General Conditions of the Contract for Construction*, which of the following actions by the IDM is permitted? (Choose the four that apply.)

(A) Tell the owner and contractor that a determination cannot be made due to a lack of information.

(B) Request additional information from the contractor.

(C) Refer the claim to the owner's attorney.

(D) The IDM is not permitted to resolve claims.

(E) Approve the claim.

(F) Reject the claim.

550. A pressure test on plumbing supply piping reveals a leak in the system. According to American Institute of Architects (AIA) Document A201, *General Conditions of the*

Contract for Construction, the responsibility for fixing the leak and paying for a follow-up test rests with the

(A) owner

(B) contractor

(C) plumbing subcontractor

(D) owner and contractor jointly

551. When reviewing applications for payment, which of the following must the architect do? (Choose the four that apply.)

(A) Verify that adequate safety precautions are being observed by the contractor.

(B) Determine if the completed work will be in accordance with the contract documents.

(C) Become generally familiar with the progress and quality of the work.

(D) Keep the owner informed about the progress of the work.

(E) Check if the quantities of the installed work are as required by the contract documents.

(F) Endeavor to guard the owner against defects in the work.

552. During a construction phase site visit, the architect notices that a finish subcontractor has not prepared the substrate for the vinyl tile in accordance with the standard referenced in the specifications. What should be the architect's first response?

(A) Inform the owner in writing of the situation.

(B) Withhold the appropriate amount on the contractor's application for payment.

(C) Notify the contractor the work is not in conformance with the contract documents.

(D) Notify the subcontractor that their work is not being properly installed.

553. After visiting the project site to review an application for payment, the architect decides to withhold the certificate for payment under the provisions of American Institute of Architects (AIA) Document A201, *General Conditions of the Contract for Construction.* Which of the following statements about this situation is true?

(A) The architect is required to withhold the entire amount.

(B) The architect must notify the owner, who then notifies the contractor.

(C) The architect and contractor must agree on a revised amount before the revised application can be approved for payment.

(D) The architect can nullify a previous certificate to protect the owner.

554. According to American Institute of Architects (AIA) Document A201, *General Conditions of the Contract for Construction*, the contractor must submit an affidavit that all bills have been paid by the contractor before the owner's final payment is made. This affidavit must be submitted to the

(A) architect

(B) owner

(C) owner's surety

(D) owner's attorney

555. Which of the following statements is correct?

(A) The architect may stop work if the contractor's performance is not satisfactory or is at variance with the contract documents.

(B) The owner may carry on the work and deduct costs normally due to the contractor for any corrections required because of unsatisfactory work.

(C) The architect may stop the work if the architect reports safety problems on the site.

(D) The owner is not required to refuse to give the contractor proof that he or she can meet the financial obligations of the project.

556. A project is about 60% complete when the owner begins receiving field reports from the architect stating that the contractor is failing to properly supervise the job, which is resulting in incorrect work. After receiving several unsatisfactory reports, the owner becomes concerned about the contractor's performance and progress and asks the architect for advice. What should be done if the work is being performed under the conditions of American

Institute of Architects (AIA) Document A201, *General Conditions of the Contract for Construction*?

(A) After receiving the architect's field reports, the owner should stop the work and arrange for a meeting between the owner, architect, and contractor to determine the cause of the problems and what the contractor intends to do. If the contractor does not correct the work, the owner may carry out the work with other contractors and deduct the cost of the repairs from the original contractor's construction cost by change order.

(B) The architect should recommend that the owner give the contractor written notice of nonconformance with the contract documents and if, after seven days, the contractor has not begun corrective measures, the owner should terminate the contract.

(C) The architect and owner should discuss the problem to see if the owner is willing to accept the nonconforming work in exchange for a reduction in the contract sum. If not, the owner should give seven days' written notice to terminate the contract. The owner has the option of finding another contractor to finish the job.

(D) The architect should, with the owner's knowledge, reject nonconforming work and notify the contractor that it must be corrected promptly. The architect should then remind the owner that the owner can have the work corrected after giving the contractor a seven-day written notice to correct the work and then an additional three days with a written notice.

557. Substantial completion indicates

(A) that the owner can make use of the work for its intended purpose, and the requirements of the contract documents have been fulfilled

(B) that the contractor has completed correction of all punch list items

(C) that the final certificate for payment has been issued by the architect, and all documentation has been delivered to the owner

(D) the date on which the contractor prepares the punch list

558. In what order should project closeout activities take place?

(A) contractor compiles punch list, architect issues certificate of substantial completion, consent of surety is received and final payment to contractor is released, architect receives notice from contractor that the project is ready for final inspection, architect prepares the final certificate for payment

(B) contractor compiles punch list, architect issues certificate of substantial completion, architect receives notice from contractor that the project is ready for final inspection, architect prepares the final certificate for payment, consent of surety is received and final payment to contractor is released

(C) architect receives notice from contractor that the project is ready for final inspection, contractor compiles punch list, consent of surety is received and final payment to contractor is released, architect prepares the final certificate for payment, architect issues certificate of substantial completion

(D) architect receives notice from contractor that the project is ready for final inspection, consent of surety is received and final payment to contractor is released, contractor compiles punch list, architect issues certificate of substantial completion, architect prepares the final certificate for payment

559. Which of the following requires on-site approval?

(A) mock-ups

(B) product data

(C) samples

(D) shop drawings

560. Which of the following sections of the *Americans with Disabilities Act (ADA) Accessibility Guidelines* apply primarily to the design and construction of public facilities? (Choose the two that apply.)

(A) Title I

(B) Title II

(C) Title III

(D) Title IV

(E) Title V

(F) Title VI

561. According to American Institute of Architects (AIA) Document B101, *Standard Form of Agreement Between Owner and Architect*, which of the following services is included in the architect's basic services for project close-out? (Choose the four that apply.)

(A) forwarding written warranties to the owner

(B) sending a consent of surety to the owner

(C) commissioning

(D) meeting with the owner to determine the need for facility operation services

(E) post-occupancy walk through within one year

(F) transfer project insurance from the contractor to the owner

562. Which of the following is a characteristic of a fast-track construction schedule?

(A) The contract for the work is awarded after contractors review the completed construction documents and submit their bids.

(B) The design and construction phases of the project occur simultaneously.

(C) The architect is responsible for scheduling and overseeing the construction process.

(D) The decision to fast-track a project may be postponed until after bids are received.

563. Which of the following is the most appropriate way to announce bid results?

(A) The architect should make a statement at the conclusion of the bid opening identifying the apparent low bidder.

(B) After evaluating all of the bids, the owner should make a decision of award, and the architect should notify the bidders.

(C) The owner should call all of the bidders and give them the results.

(D) The owner should publish the bid results in the local newspaper.

564. Bids are received for constructing an addition housing an early childhood education center and building a playground at an elementary school. The following bids are submitted.

bidder	base bid	bid alternate 1	bid alternate 2
ABC Construction	$244,150	$22,465	–$6725
Sunny Day, Inc.	$265,430	$15,846	–$5000
Grover and Sons	$270,000	$14,000	–$2000
B&E General Contractors	$246,765	$18,768	–$7500

The school district plans to accept both bid alternates. Which company has submitted the low bid?

(A) ABC Construction

(B) Sunny Day, Inc.

(C) Grover and Sons

(D) B&E General Contractors

565. When an architect makes an impartial interpretation of the contract documents during construction administration, in accordance with the general conditions, in what capacity is he considered to be acting?

(A) arbitratory

(B) quasi-judicial

(C) mediative

(D) professional

566. An architect is visiting a project site on a rainy afternoon to observe the progress of work and certify a pay application. While photographing the site, she witnesses a construction worker slip on a wet board and fall from the scaffolding. The worker is obviously injured and appears to be unconscious. After calling 911, what should the architect do?

(A) Notify the superintendent immediately and then fully document the accident with a written report and photographs.

(B) Report the incident to the superintendent immediately and then notify the owner before taking other action.

(C) Conduct an investigation.

(D) Do nothing more; construction safety is the responsibility of the contractor.

567. Which of the following statements is the most acceptable for an architect to certify?

(A) "The architect certifies to the owner that, in the architect's professional opinion, the contractor has spent the amount indicated and is entitled to payment in the amount certified."

(B) "The architect certifies to the owner that, to the best of the architect's knowledge, information, and belief, the work has progressed to the point indicated, the quality of the work is in accordance with the contract documents, and the contractor is entitled to payment in the amount certified."

(C) "The architect certifies that the contract documents comply with all applicable codes, standards, and regulations."

(D) "Based on the architect's observations and other information available to the architect, the contractor has complied with the *International Building Code* (IBC) throughout the course of construction."

568. According to American Institute of Architects (AIA) Document A701, *Instructions to Bidders*, bids must be submitted on

(A) standard AIA bid forms

(B) the contractor's standard bid form

(C) forms provided with the bidding documents

(D) forms provided on the owner's website

569. A local code official has the authority to enforce all but which of the following codes or acts?

(A) *Americans with Disabilities Act* (ADA)

(B) *Life Safety Code* (NFPA 101)

(C) *International Building Code* (IBC)

(D) ICC/ANSI A117.1

570. A contractor is installing a colonnade at the perimeter of a dining courtyard in an open-air shopping mall. The drawings show 12 in diameter columns spaced at 8 ft on center. However, the description in the millwork specification calls for 10 in diameter Roman Doric columns. The contractor should

(A) provide 12 in diameter columns

(B) provide 10 in diameter columns

(C) consult the owner

(D) consult the architect

571. In what order should the steps in the process of concrete construction occur?

(A) construct the formwork, place and tie the reinforcing steel, apply a release agent to the forms, perform slump testing, pour and vibrate the concrete

(B) construct the formwork, apply a release agent to the forms, place and tie the reinforcing steel, pour and vibrate the concrete, perform slump testing

(C) construct the formwork, apply a release agent to the forms, place and tie the reinforcing steel, perform slump testing, pour and vibrate the concrete

(D) perform slump testing, construct the formwork, apply a release agent to the forms, place and tie the reinforcing steel, pour and vibrate the concrete

572. Which of the following would require issuance of a change order?

(A) The owner and architect decide to delete undercabinet lighting from all of the kitchens in an apartment project.

(B) The architect changes the location of a few lighting fixtures in a suspended grid ceiling to better illuminate workstations shown on the interior designer's modular furniture plan.

(C) In the course of answering a question from the contractor, the architect notices a discrepancy between the plan and section and prepares a sketch to clarify the drawings.

(D) The architect revises the color schedule based on the manufacturers' products the contractor intends to install.

573. Four years ago, an architecture firm completed the design of a new high school. Construction was completed two years later. A year and a half after final completion, the district superintendent calls the architect and explains that there is a leak in the roof of the chemistry classroom. The architect informs the contractor and then schedules a meeting at the site to investigate the situation. It is found that the work is constructed in compliance with the requirements of the contract documents, but one of the roofing membranes is brittle due to sun exposure and has begun to crack. Who is responsible for correcting the problem?

(A) the roofing manufacturer

(B) the school district

(C) the contractor

(D) There is not enough information given to answer the question.

574. Who is responsible for preparing a punch list?

(A) architect

(B) contractor

(C) owner

(D) architect with the assistance of project consultants

575. Which of these statements about mechanic's liens is true?

(A) A mechanic's lien gives a contractor, subcontractor, or supplier clear title to an owner's property.

(B) Liens are permitted on publicly owned projects.

(C) A lien applies to all of the owner's assets.

(D) A contractor must provide evidence that a project is free of liens before receiving payment.

576. In order to defer specific design decisions until pricing information is available and to provide flexibility to adjust project scope and cost after bids are received, the architect may include

(A) allowances

(B) alternates

(C) unit prices

(D) value engineering

577. Which of the following statements about building commissioning services are correct? (Choose the three that apply.)

(A) Commissioning services can be provided by the same firm that designed the systems being evaluated.

(B) Commissioning services typically cost between 0.5% and 6% of the total construction cost.

(C) Commissioning services are required by American Institute of Architects (AIA) Document B101, *Standard Form of Agreement Between Owner and Architect.*

(D) Commissioning services should be contracted during the pre-design phase of project planning.

(E) The commissioning agent offers a warranty to the owner that the systems will perform as specified after commissioning is complete.

(F) The *International Building Code* (IBC) requires all buildings to be commissioned.

578. A 6000 ft^2 tenant space has been designed in an existing office building. The owner and contractor have signed a lump sum contract based on AIA Document A101, *Standard Form of Agreement Between Owner and Contractor where the basis of payment is a Stipulated Sum*, and AIA Document A201, *General Conditions of the Contract for Construction.* The scope of the project requires the contractor to remove the existing partitions and finishes as well as provide and install new construction, finishes, heating, ventilating, and air conditioning (HVAC) modifications, lighting and electrical work, and phone and data systems. The contract also requires the contractor to provide and install new cubicles and connect them to power and data service.

While the construction is taking place, the owner is approached by an independent contract furniture dealer who convinces the owner that the dealer can provide reconditioned cubicles at a much lower cost than the new products originally specified; however, the cubicle layout will need to be changed because the reconditioned modular furniture parts are not the same sizes as the products originally specified. The owner approaches the architect and explains that he or she wants to use the reconditioned cubicles to save money. Which of the following statements are correct? (Choose the three that apply.)

(A) If the owner deletes the specified cubicles from the original construction contract and signs a separate contract with the furniture dealer to provide and install the furniture, the contractor will be responsible for the coordination of the furniture dealer's work.

(B) Removing the specified cubicles from the original construction contract and replacing them with the reconditioned cubicles is accomplished through a change order.

(C) The potential material cost savings associated with the reconditioned furniture may be negated by the additional design costs necessary to revise the modular furniture layout and redesign the electrical and data connection points.

(D) The architect is obligated to provide additional design services at no cost when a change is made to save the owner money.

(E) When the construction contract and the furniture contracts are separate, the architect is responsible for preparing the installation schedule and coordinating the work.

(F) The architect should advise the owner to consider all associated costs of this change before proceeding with a change order.

579. The plumbing engineer's specifications for a new elementary school include a requirement that all toilets be wall-hung fixtures. The specifications list three manufacturers' acceptable models. The contractor sends the architect a submittal including cut sheets for all of the plumbing fixtures, but the submitted toilets sit on the floor rather than being wall-mounted. The contractor claims that the specified wall-mounted fixtures cannot be used in this building because the plumbing chase is too small to accommodate the carrier needed to support the fixture. What is the first course of action that the architect should take?

(A) Accept the fixtures as described in the submittal.

(B) Have the plumbing engineer review the space requirements for the fixture carriers.

(C) Redesign the chase between the restrooms to provide the needed space.

(D) Require the plumbing engineer to reject the submittal, and have the contractor resubmit with the specified toilet fixtures.

580. Which of these statements about substantial completion is correct?

(A) Substantial completion occurs when the project receives a certificate of occupancy.

(B) Substantial completion is the date upon which the warranty period begins.

(C) The date of substantial completion is determined at the beginning of the project in the general contractor's schedule.

(D) When the project is determined to be substantially complete, the owner must make final payment to the contractor.

581. Which of these project management tools or approaches requires developing a project schedule that associates time and budget allowances with each activity?

(A) use of a project monitoring chart

(B) critical path method

(C) integrated project management

(D) use of a schedule of values

582. Which of these statements about the architect's review of an application for payment is true?

(A) The architect's signature on the application for payment indicates that the architect has inspected and approved the work for which the contractor is requesting payment.

(B) The architect's certification of an application for payment is the same as providing a warranty to the owner that the work has been completed in accordance with the requirements of the construction documents.

(C) The architect is required to review the progress of the work summarized on the application for payment within two weeks of receipt from the contractor.

(D) If the architect refuses to certify the amounts listed on an application for payment and does not provide an explanation of the refusal or evidence that the quantities are inaccurate, the contractor can stop work.

583. Which of the following are benefits of constructing an on-site mockup of the exterior building envelope? (Choose the four that apply.)

(A) The owner and architect can use the assembly to confirm the colors and types of masonry and mortar to be used for an addition matching the existing construction.

(B) Construction of the mockup can provide a way for the contractor to determine the most efficient construction sequence.

(C) The fire resistance of individual materials specified for use on the project may be determined through testing of the on-site mockup in lieu of laboratory testing.

(D) The mockup wall assembly can be used to work out the connections between materials and to determine the water and air resistance properties of the assembly.

(E) A mockup allows manufacturers to determine the length of the warranty that will be available for their products when they are installed in this particular configuration.

(F) The mockup can be used to establish appearance criteria and may be used as a reference to evaluate the quality of future work.

584. The owner decides to relocate a door opening before a wall is framed. The contractor confirms that there will be no change to the project time or cost associated with this modification because work in this area has not yet begun. Which of these documents should the architect use to direct the contractor to make the change?

(A) construction change directive

(B) amendment to the construction contract

(C) change order

(D) architect's supplemental instructions

585. A museum lobby renovation includes the fabrication and installation of a custom grade reception desk. The drawings call for the vertical faces of the desk to be constructed of premium grade maple and cherry and for the countertops to be plastic laminate. The specification includes information on the required brand and color of laminate. The contractor submits shop drawings for the desk showing the countertops constructed as specified, but the plastic laminate color number and manufacturer listed do not match the color and brand noted in the specifications, and no samples have been provided. How should the architect respond to this shop drawing submittal?

(A) Mark the submittal "approved," and write in the color of plastic laminate that should be provided.

(B) Call the contractor, ask which plastic laminate product was intended, write in the response, and mark the submittal "approved as noted."

(C) Mark the submittal "revise and resubmit," and direct the contractor to provide one of the specified plastic laminate products for the countertops.

(D) Mark the submittal "rejected" and return it to the contractor.

586. After a two-week vacation, an architect returns to the office Monday morning and finds an application for payment waiting. The envelope is stamped with last Friday's date. How should the architect process this application?

(A) Call the contractor to discuss the project's progress over the past two weeks.

(B) Compare the quantities listed on the pay application to the approved schedule of values, and visit the job site.

(C) Confer with others in the office who have been working on the project to determine whether or not to approve the application.

(D) Undertake a detailed site inspection, and review subcontractor's invoices.

587. When is the contractor usually entitled to submit an application for payment that requests payment of the retainage?

(A) following the approval of the first application for payment

(B) after each subcontractor completes his or her portion of the work and the retainage associated with that line item can be released

(C) when the project has reached substantial completion

(D) after the final completion inspection

Case Study 1

Problem 588 through Prob. 600 refer to the following case study. Refer to Resource 6.1 through Resource 6.8 to assist in answering the problems.

The owner of the Vermilion Building, which was built in the 1930s, has been working with Diazo Architects to upgrade the building's west elevator. The facility is within a block of Community Hospital and houses a number of outpatient clinics. The building has not undergone a comprehensive renovation since the 1980s, at which time the elevator was not modified.

Diazo Architects uses American Institute of Architects (AIA) Document B101, *Standard Form of Agreement Between Owner and Architect,* to prepare its contracts with clients. Compass Engineering is Diazo Architects' mechanical, electrical, and plumbing engineering consultant. Diazo Architects has engaged Trace Systems, a consultant that specializes in elevator design. The architect-consultant agreements are based on AIA Document C141, *Standard Form of Agreement Between Architect and Consultant.*

The existing elevator shaft is constructed of 12 in thick concrete masonry units and has a 2-hour fire-resistance rating, which the architect has determined complies with the current building code requirements. The existing elevator cab is large enough to comply with *Americans with Disabilities Act (ADA) Accessibility Guidelines* and state accessibility code requirements but is showing its age, so the owner has decided to replace it with a new cab. In addition, the owner wants to modernize the elevator machinery to take advantage of significant improvements in energy-efficient motor technology. Upgrades to the elevator controls and in-cab communications system are also required.

The project scope includes the following items.

- Remove the existing elevator cab and construct a new cab within the existing shaft.
- Remove the existing geared elevator equipment and replace with a gearless machine.
- Enlarge the existing elevator machine room; this space must be separated from other areas of the building with 2-hour fire-rated construction.
- Install new heating, cooling, and ventilation equipment serving the elevator machine room. (The elevator machine room is currently an unconditioned space.)
- Provide new access stairs to the elevator machine room from the third floor.
- Install new finishes, controls, handrails, and lighting in the elevator cab.
- Replace the existing hall controls and indicator lights with models that comply with *ADA Accessibility Guidelines.*

The building has two underground levels and three stories above grade, as well as the penthouse that houses the elevator machine room and the mechanical penthouse. The elevator machine room can be accessed from inside the building, but the only access to the mechanical penthouse is from the roof via stairs on the east side of the building. The west elevator services the sub-basement (SB) level through to the third floor. The building has a second elevator on the east side of the building; this elevator will remain in operation while the west elevator is under construction.

The current elevator machine room has unrated, uninsulated walls. The insulation in all of the exterior walls of the penthouse will be increased to R-19. Diazo Architects has completed a code analysis for this project and has determined that the elevator machine room must be separated from the mechanical penthouse with 2-hour fire-rated construction; the stair and elevator enclosures also must be 2-hour fire-rated. The floor of the penthouse is poured-in-place reinforced concrete that provides a 2-hour fire rating for the top of the elevator shaft. The ceiling of the penthouse has nominal R-20 ceiling insulation that will remain unchanged.

The owner invited four general contractors to prepare proposals for the construction work, which was awarded to a local firm, Bluecurve Construction Services (BCS). Bluecurve's subcontractors are Green Triangle Vertical Transportation (GTVT) and Straightedge Mechanical (SM), which provides mechanical, electrical, and plumbing construction services. The owner-contractor agreements are AIA Document A101, *Standard Form of Agreement Between Owner and Contractor where the basis of payment is a Stipulated Sum,* and AIA Document A201, *General Conditions of the Contract for Construction.*

Construction of the project began in October and is scheduled to be complete in April. Assume that the project is not taking place in leap years, the contractor will work five days per week every week, and that activity durations are to be expressed in number of business days, rather than number of calendar days. The original contract amount was $490,000, but change orders throughout the project have increased the cost to $508,423.36.

Resource 6.1 Third Floor Plan

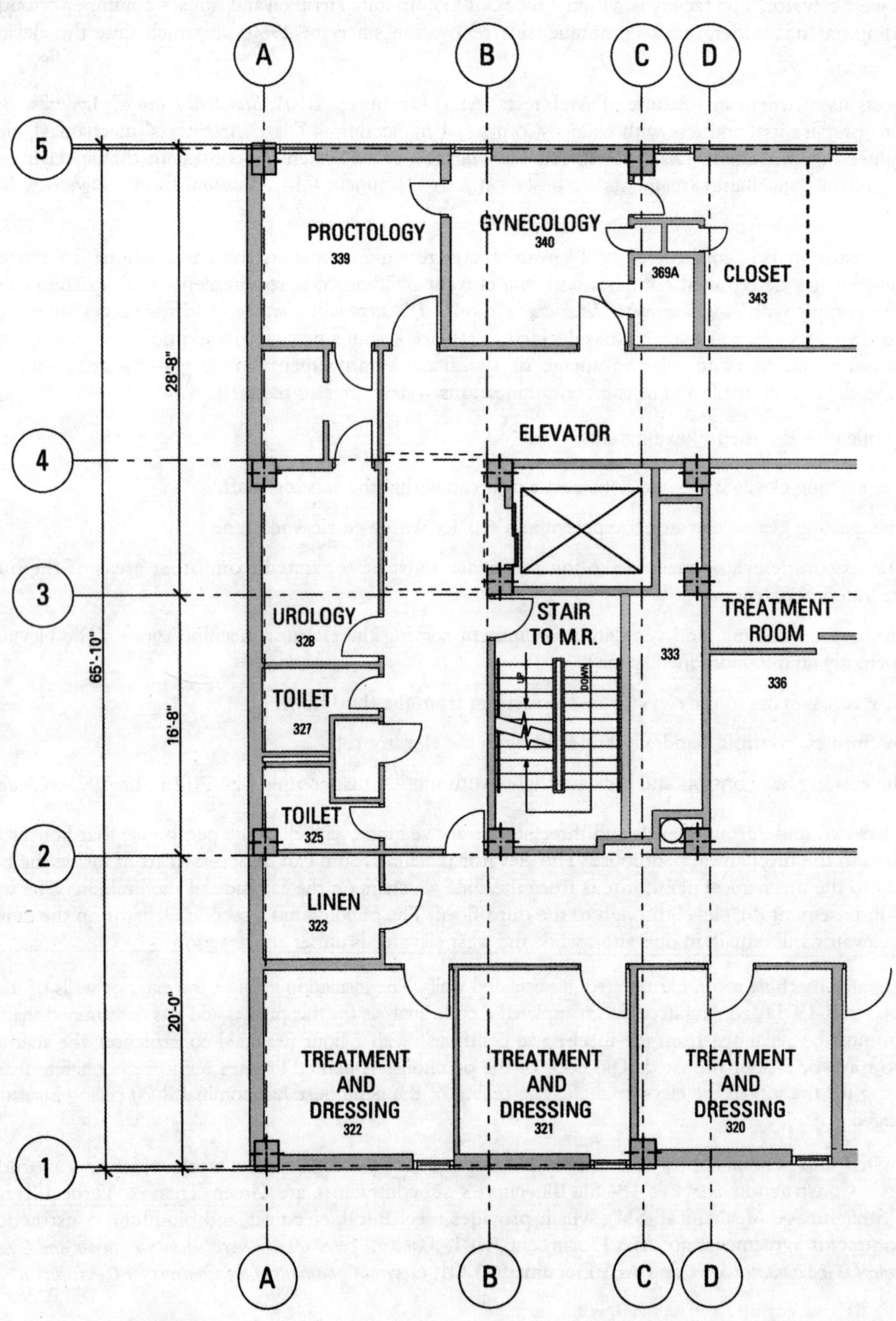

Resource 6.2 Elevator Machine Room Plan

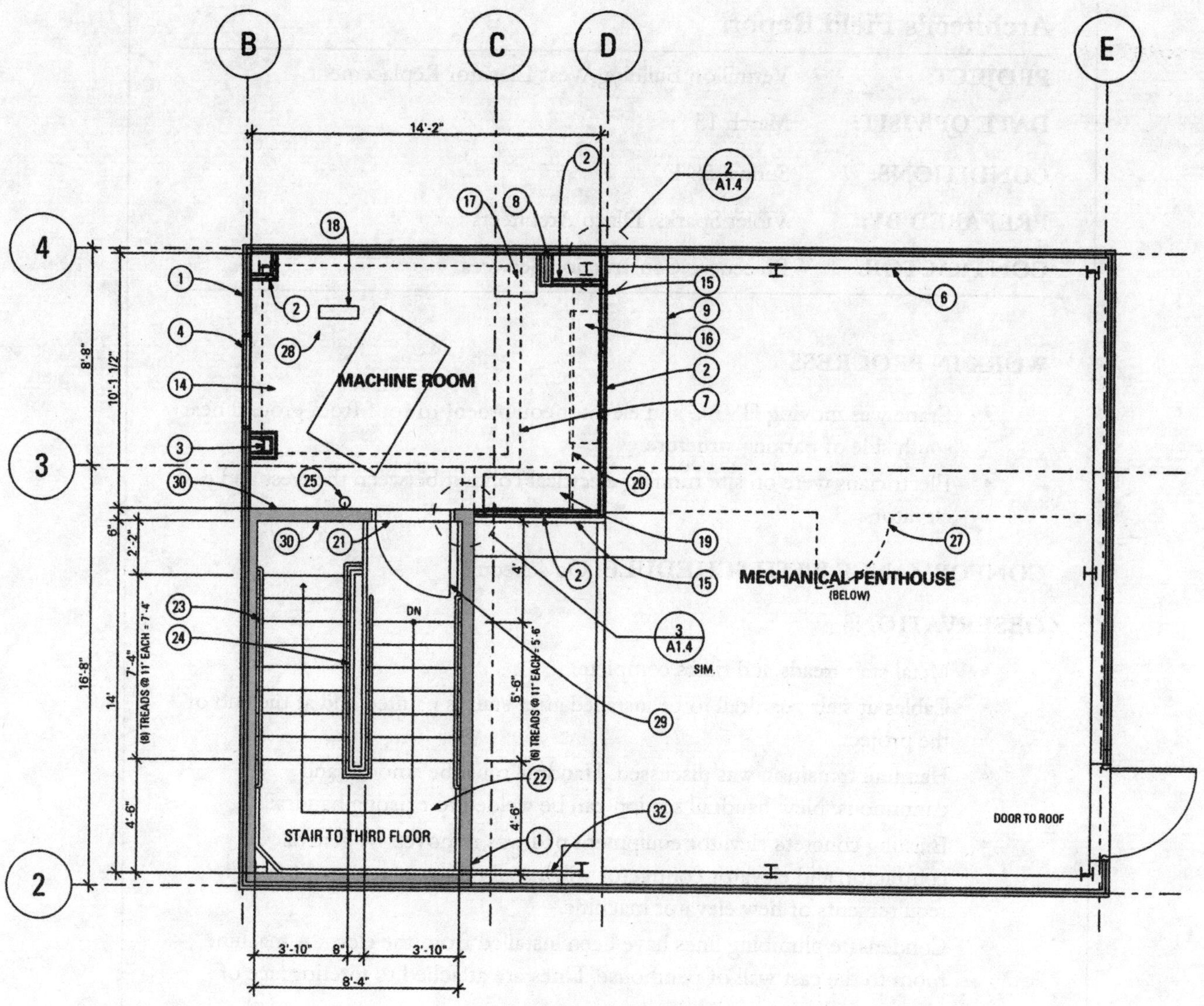

GENERAL NOTES:

1. FIELD VERIFY ALL CONDITIONS AND DIMENSIONS PRIOR TO CONSTRUCTION AND IMMEDIATELY NOTIFY THE ARCHITECT IF DISCREPANCIES ARE FOUND BETWEEN PLANS AND ACTUAL CONDITIONS.

2. ELEVATOR MACHINE ROOM, ELEVATOR SHAFT AND STAIRS ARE ENCLOSED BY A 2-HOUR FIRE RATED WALL.

3. THE MECHANICAL PENTHOUSE IS ONLY ACCESSED FROM THE ROOF.

FLOOR PLAN KEYNOTES ◯ →

1. EXISTING WALLS TO REMAIN SHOWN SHADED.
2. NEW WALLS SHOWN RENDERED.
3. EXISTING STEEL COLUMN TO REMAIN.
4. EXIST. WINDOW TO REMAIN.
5. EXISTING DOOR TO REMAIN.
6. LINE OF EXIST. CONCRETE BLOCK LEDGE.
7. DASHED LINES INDICATE EXIST. MASONRY SHAFT WALL BELOW.
8. EXIST. METAL STUD/GYP. BD FURRING AT EXISTING PIPE.
9. EXIST. EXPOSED STEEL DUCTWORK TO REMAIN. - SEE MECH.
10. EXIST. CONCRETE STAIR.
11. EXIST. STEEL HANDRAIL/GUARDRAIL TO REMAIN.
12. EXIST. ADHERED EPDM ROOF.
13. EXIST. CONCRETE EQUIP. BASE TO BE REMOVED.
14. EXISTING CONCRETE FLOOR SLAB - CLEAN AND REPAINT.
15. EDGE LINE OF EXIST. CANTILEVERED CONCRETE FLOOR.
16. NEW A/C SPLIT UNIT - SEE MECH. PROVIDE UNISTRUT FRAMING CHANNEL SYSTEM - TO SUPPORT UNIT @ +36" A.F.F. ANCHOR TO FLOOR AND ROOF FRAMING ABOVE
17. TRANSFORMER - SEE ELEC.
18. ELEV. GOVERNOR BY ELEV. SUPPLIER.
19. ELEV. CONTROLLER BY ELEV SUPPLIER.
20. LINE OF CEILING BREAK ABOVE.
21. METAL THRESHOLD. SEE DETAIL 4/ A2.0
22. LINES OF NEW CHECKERED STEEL PLATE STAIR AND STEEL TUBE STRINGERS.
23. LINES OF NEW 1-1/2" D. STEEL PIPE HANDRAIL.
24. LINES OF NEW STEEL TUBE/SS CABLE GUARDRAIL.
25. EXIST. FIRE-EXTINGUISHER TO BE REINSTALLED.
26. NEW CONDENSING UNIT - SEE MECH/ELEC.
27. EXISTING METAL WIRE PARTITION AND DOOR TO REMAIN.
28. PAINT ALL WALLS AND CEILING IN MACHINE ROOM.
29. 3'-0" X 6'-8" H.M. DOOR AND FRAME - PAINT
30. PATCH AND PAINT WALL.
31. PIPING SUPPORT - SEE DETAIL 3/A1.5.
32. STL. TUBE STRINGER EXTEND THRU WALL AND WELD TO EACH EXISTING COLUMN.

Construction & Evaluation

Resource 6.3 Architect's Field Report

Architect's Field Report

PROJECT:	Vermilion Building West Elevator Replacement
DATE OF VISIT:	March 15
CONDITIONS:	Sunny, 58°F
PREPARED BY:	Violet Sparks, Diazo Architects
CONTRACTOR:	Bluecurve Construction Services

WORK IN PROGRESS

- Crane was moving HVAC and elevator equipment to roof from ground near south side of parking structure.
- Electricians were on site running electrical conduit between the west and east elevators.

CONFORMANCE WITH SCHEDULE: On schedule.

OBSERVATIONS

- Metal stair treads and risers complete.
- Cables at stair guardrail to be installed after stair is painted and at the end of the project.
- Handrail transition was discussed. Handrail must be smooth and continuous. New handrail section can be welded to existing handrail.
- Existing concrete elevator equipment pad was removed by general contractor, and elevator contractor will install new concrete pad to meet requirements of new elevator machine.
- Condensate plumbing lines have been installed from the elevator machine room to the east wall of penthouse. Lines are attached to interior face of exterior wall.
- New electrical panel installed on interior face of north wall of penthouse as directed by Change Order.
- New A/C and condensing unit hoisted onto roof and ready for installation.
- Roof curb for new condensing unit has been installed.

ITEMS TO VERIFY

- Superintendent must coordinate with code official regarding geometry and installation of handrail transition.

Resource 6.4 Request for Proposal (RFP) Scoring Criteria Summary

	criteria	total value	general contractors A	B	C	D
1	project cost	25	25.0	19.5	22.3	24.5
2	targeted business and economic development	5	4.8	4.9	4.8	4.7
3	safety policies and record	5	4.9	3.0	4.0	3.9
4	project schedule	20	20.0	20.0	20.0	20.0
5	project approach and work plan	20	15.5	11.9	13.7	14.0
6	respondent's team qualifications	25	21.6	14.9	18.3	24.5
	final RFP score	100	91.8	74.2	83.1	91.6

Resource 6.5 West Elevator Construction Schedule

West Elevator Construction Schedule

Activity	Start	Finish
Notice to Proceed	Oct 17th	
PRECONSTRUCTION PHASE		
Engineer and submit shop drawings	Oct 6th	Oct 31st
Submit bonds and insurance	Oct 17th	Oct 27th
Secure Building Permit	Oct 17th	Nov 7th
Review and approval shop drawings	Nov 3rd	Nov 14th
Fabricate Elevator Equipment	Nov 17th	Jan 30th
Submit Staging Plan	Dec 31st	Dec 31st
CONSTRUCTION PHASE		
Mobilize site office	Jan 5th	Jan 5th
Penthouse/Machine Room Demo	Jan 6th	Jan 9th
Install electrical conduit	Jan 6th	Jan 12th
Install 2-hour shaft walls	Jan 12th	Jan 15th
Install 2-hour hollow metal door	Jan 14th	Jan 15th
Install new steel stairs	Jan 16th	Jan 20th
Demolition of existing elevator	Jan 21st	Jan 30th
Install condensing unit curbs	Jan 26th	Jan 27th
Install sump pump in elevator pit	Jan 29th	Feb 3rd
Install new elevator	Feb 2nd	Mar 27th
Set new condensing unit	Feb 4th	Feb 5th
Install shaft lighting	Feb 12th	Feb 13th
Patch and paint walls and doors	Mar 9th	Mar 13th
Install elevator flooring	Mar 23rd	Mar 24th
PROJECT CLOSEOUT		
Building/Mechanical Electrical Inspect	Mar 23rd	Mar 27th
Punch List/ Substantial Completion	Mar 24th	Mar 27th
Testing, Commissioning of elevator	Mar 30th	Apr 15th
Final Completion		Apr 10th

Timeline columns: Oct, Nov, Dec, Jan, Feb, Mar, Apr

Legend: Remaining Work; Critical Path; Substantial Completion; Permits, Inspections

Construction & Evaluation

Resource 6.6 Certificate of Substantial Completion

Certificate of Substantial Completion

PROJECT: Vermilion Building
West Elevator Replacement

PROJECT NUMBER: GC 1045
CONTRACT FOR: General Construction
CONTRACT DATE: October 17

TO OWNER: Vermilion Building Corporation, LLC

TO CONTRACTOR: Bluecurve Construction Services

PROJECT OR PORTION OF THE PROJECT DESIGNATED FOR PARTIAL OCCUPANCY OR USE SHALL INCLUDE:

Use of West Elevator, including full access to Elevator Machine Room Penthouse – W477.

The Work performed under this Contract has been reviewed and found, to the Architect's best knowledge, information, and belief, substantially complete. Substantial Completion is the stage in the progress of the Work when the Work or designated portion is sufficiently complete in accordance with the Contract Documents so that the Owner can occupy or utilize the Work for its intended use. The date of Substantial Completion of the Project or portion designated above is the date of issuance established by this Certificate, which is also the date of commencement of applicable warranties required by the Contract Documents, except as stated below:

Diazo Architects	*Violet Sparks, RA*	April 5
ARCHITECT	**BY**	**DATE OF ISSUANCE**

A list of items to be completed or corrected is attached hereto. The failure to include any items on such list does not alter the responsibility of the Contractor to complete all Work in accordance with the Contract Documents. Unless otherwise agreed to in writing, the date of commencement of warranties for items on the attached Punch List will be the date of issuance of the final Certificate of Payment or the date of final payment.

Cost estimate of Work that is incomplete or defective: $ 5000.00

The Contractor will complete or correct the Work on the list of items attached hereto within (10 calendar days) from the above date of Substantial Completion.

Bluecurve Construction Services	Rusty D. Walker, Jr.	April 10
CONTRACTOR	**BY**	**DATE**

The Owner accepts the Work or designated portion as substantially complete and will assume full possession at

12 NOON (*time*) on April 7 (*date*).

Vermilion Building Corporation, LLC	Sterling Atherton, President	April 14
OWNER	**BY**	**DATE**

The responsibilities of the Owner and Contractor for security, maintenance, heat, utilities, damage to the Work, and insurance shall be as follows:

Contractor shall maintain all required insurance coverages until the project reaches final completion. Contractor shall be responsible for damages to the Work in corridor areas caused by building occupants. Owner shall be responsible for security, heat, and utilities.

Resource 6.7 Punch List

Punch List – General Construction

PROJECT: Vermilion Building West Elevator Replacement
GENERAL CONTRACTOR: Bluecurve Construction Services (BCS)
PREPARED BY: Violet Sparks, Diazo Architects
DATE: April 3

This punch list should in no way be construed to alleviate the contractor of his obligation to complete any other items not listed but otherwise covered in the contract documents. The contractor shall make all corrections and additions to items that have been noted requiring additional attention.

The following general and specific construction items were noted during a walk-through on April 2. Please initial and date each item as it is completed and return a copy of this completed form to this office.

GENERAL COMMENTS:

1) Paint elevator entry sill – all floors
2) Clean all hard surfaces, including elevator machine room floor
3) Clean carpet and vacuum at elevator entries
4) See Elevator, Mechanical, and Electrical Punch Lists for additional items
5) Submit O&M Manuals and Warranties

SPECIFIC CONSTRUCTION ITEMS:

Item		Party	Date	Initials
1	Basement Elevator Entry Touch up wall paint next to door	BCS		
2	3rd Floor Elevator Entry Remove auxiliary key box and touch up wall paint	BCS		
3	3rd Floor Main Lobby Entrance Install metal cover plate on north wall Complete work on south wall	BCS		
4	Stair to Elevator Machine Room Paint metal treads and risers at stairway Paint exposed electrical conduit	BCS		
5	Sub-Basement Level, Room SB65 Paint exposed electrical conduit and cast-iron plumbing to match wall color	BCS		
6	Roof Level Paint exposed electrical conduit and condensing unit	BCS		
7	Elevator Cab Interior Install seamless rubber sheet flooring	BCS		

(continued)

Construction & Evaluation

Resource 6.7 Punch List (continued)

Punch List – General Construction – Elevator

PROJECT:	Vermilion Building West Elevator Replacement
GENERAL CONTRACTOR:	Bluecurve Construction Services (BCS)
SUBCONTRACTOR:	Green Triangle Vertical Transportation (GTVT)
PREPARED BY:	Violet Sparks, Diazo Architects
DATE:	April 3

This punch list should in no way be construed to alleviate the contractor of his obligation to complete any other items not listed but otherwise covered in the contract documents. The contractor shall make all corrections and additions to items that have been noted requiring additional attention.

The following general and specific construction items were noted during a walk-through on April 2. Please initial and date each item as it is completed and return a copy of this completed form to this office.

Item		Party	Date	Initials
1	Remove job-related materials from job site	GTVT		
2	Correct car speed to meet acceptable standards per recorded operating performance range (196–204 ft/min) – currently 217 ft/min	GTVT		
3	Install signage at elevator entrances per code	GTVT		
4	Complete wiring of overlay group controller and lobby panel	GTVT		
5	Install all trough covers in controller and tie-wrap unused wiring	GTVT		
6	Paint machine and related beams	GTVT		
7	Install elevator cab flooring	GTVT		
8	Final inspection for emergency power and fire service shall be completed as directed by the Elevator Inspection Division	GTVT		
9	Provide inspection certificate and mount inside cab	GTVT		

(continued)

Resource 6.7 Punch List (continued)

Punch List – Electrical Construction

PROJECT: Vermilion Building West Elevator Replacement

GENERAL CONTRACTOR: Bluecurve Construction Services (BCS)

SUBCONTRACTOR: Straightedge Mechanical (SM)

PREPARED BY: Violet Sparks, Diazo Architects
Jonathan Cerulean, Compass Engineering

DATE: April 3

This punch list should in no way be construed to alleviate the contractor of his obligation to complete any other items not listed but otherwise covered in the contract documents. The contractor shall make all corrections and additions to items that have been noted requiring additional attention.

The following general and specific construction items were noted during a walk-through on April 2. Please initial and date each item as it is completed and return a copy of this completed form to this office.

Item		Party	Date	Initials
1	Provide panel and circuit number on all receptacles	SM		
2	Provide stainless steel cover plate on old fire alarm annunciator backbox in vestibule	SM		
3	Clean light fixtures in elevator equipment room	SM		
4	Provide label on sump pump cord at receptacle	SM		
5	Provide testing and certification of fire alarm system with copy to owner	SM		
6	Provide contractor's marked-up as-built drawings	SM		
7	Provide operation and maintenance manuals per specifications	SM		

(continued)

Construction & Evaluation

Resource 6.7 Punch List (continued)

Punch List – Mechanical Construction

PROJECT: Vermilion Building West Elevator Replacement

GENERAL CONTRACTOR: Bluecurve Construction Services (BCS)

SUBCONTRACTOR: Straightedge Mechanical (SM)

PREPARED BY: Violet Sparks, Diazo Architects
Jonathan Cerulean, Compass Engineering

DATE: April 3

This punch list should in no way be construed to alleviate the contractor of his obligation to complete any other items not listed but otherwise covered in the contract documents. The contractor shall make all corrections and additions to items that have been noted requiring additional attention.

The following general and specific construction items were noted during a walk-through on April 2. Please initial and date each item as it is completed and return a copy of this completed form to this office.

Item		Party	Date	Initials
1	Seal wire penetration of the mechanical room floor	SM		
2	Label cords for sump pump	SM		
3	Test and verify that sump pump operates properly	SM		
4	Tighten hangers and secure discharge piping from the sump; pipes shall not sway or move	SM		
5	Provide copies of the inspector's sign-off sheets	SM		
6	Provide contractor's marked-up as-built drawings	SM		
7	Provide operation and maintenance manuals per specifications	SM		

Resource 6.8 Contractor's Application for Payment

Contractor's Application for Payment

Application is made for Payment, as shown below in connection with the Contract.

1. ORIGINAL CONTRACT SUM $490,000.00
2. Net change by Change Orders $18,423.36
3. CONTRACT SUM TO DATE: (line 1+/- 2) $508,423.36
4. TOTAL COMPLETED & STORED TO DATE $508,423.36
   (Column G on G703)
5. RETAINAGE
   a. 5.00% of Completed Work........ $0.00
      (Column D + E on AIA Document G703)
   b. 0.00% of Completed Work........ $0.00
      (Column F on AIA Document G703)
   Total Retainage (Line 5a + 5b or
   Total in Column 1 of AIA Document G703) $0.00
6. TOTAL EARNED LESS RETAINAGE........ $508,423.36
   (Line 4 less Line 5 Total)
7. LESS PREVIOUS CERTIFICATES FOR PAYMENT
   (Line 6 from prior Certificate) $381,763.98
8. CURRENT PAYMENT DUE $126,659.38
9. BALANCE TO FINISH, PLUS RETAINAGE
   (Line 3 less Line 6) $0.00

CHANGE ORDER SUMMARY	ADDITIONS	DEDUCTIONS
Total Change Orders approved in previous months by Owner	18,423.36	0.00
Total Approved this Month		
TOTALS	18,423.36	0.00
NET CHANGES by Change Order		

Construction & Evaluation

588. All four of the invited contractors submitted proposals and qualifications data. The scores from the review of their proposals are tabulated in the RFP Scoring Criteria Summary included in Resource 6.4.

All of the contractors received similar scores for their performance in the targeted business and economic development criteria category, and all four presented project schedules that showed that the work can be completed within the owner's time frame. As a result, the owner decided to discard those two categories and award the project based on the remaining criteria. Based on the spreadsheet, which contractor was awarded the contract?

(A) Contractor A

(B) Contractor B

(C) Contractor C

(D) Contractor D

589. Violet Sparks of Diazo Architects visited the site to review the project's progress. She prepared and distributed the Architect's Field Report dated March 15, which is included in Resource 6.3. Based on this report, which of the following statements are accurate? (Choose the three that apply.)

(A) The metal stair, including cables and handrails, is complete.

(B) The elevator contractor was on site fixing the control panel in the cab.

(C) A crane was on site to hoist the new heating, ventilating, and air conditioning (HVAC) and elevator equipment to the roof.

(D) The plumber was on site to install the condensate drain line.

(E) A meeting with the code official is needed to verify the condition of the handrail transition.

(F) Cables at the stair guardrail will be installed after the stair is painted.

590. While walking through the Vermilion Building on a construction field visit, the owner decides that he wants all of the areas depicted on the Third Floor Plan shown in Resource 6.1 to comply with *International Building Code* (IBC) accessibility requirements. He asks the architect to review the existing conditions and prepare a proposal request to add required modifications into the project. Which of the following modifications will be necessary to make accessible the third-floor spaces shown? (Choose the three that apply.)

(A) The door from the corridor to Gynecology 340 needs to be reversed or relocated because it does not have adequate floor clearance on the swing side of the door.

(B) The closet between Toilet 325 and Toilet 327 should be demolished so that these restrooms can be reconfigured to have appropriate clearances at doors and fixtures.

(C) The door from the corridor to Proctology 339 must be reversed so that it swings into the corridor.

(D) If room 369A (adjacent to Gynecology 340) is used as a dressing room, the door opening must be modified to meet minimum width requirements and the room must be made larger.

(E) The door to Linen 323 should be reversed so that it swings into the room rather than into the corridor.

(F) The door at the stair is 36 in wide, but must be reversed to swing into the corridor.

591. According to the West Elevator Construction Schedule included in Resource 6.5, which of the following statements are correct? (Choose the two that apply.)

(A) The project is scheduled to be substantially complete on April 10.

(B) Penthouse and machine room demolition is scheduled to begin January 6.

(C) Installation of the new elevator is the task with the longest duration.

(D) Painting of walls and doors is scheduled to be completed before installing elevator flooring.

(E) There are six critical path work items.

(F) The project duration is 175 days.

592. According to the West Elevator Construction Schedule included in Resource 6.5, how many days will it take to install the new elevator at the Vermilion Building?

(A) 10

(B) 37

(C) 51

(D) 122

Construction & Evaluation

593. During the period between substantial completion and final completion, which of the following items or tasks are the owner's responsibility? (Choose the two that apply.)

(A) insurance coverage for the work

(B) repair of damages to the work in corridor areas caused by building occupants

(C) verification of completion of the items on the punch list

(D) issue of final certificate for payment

(E) building security

(F) heat and utilities

594. According to the architect's code analysis described in Case Study 1, certain walls require a 2-hour fire rating. Place the hot spot marker where these walls should be on the Elevator Machine Room Plan shown in Resource 6.2.

595. During construction, the contractor has issued a request for information regarding how the existing handrail and the new stair handrail are to be joined together. The architect reviews the drawings and realizes that, although the drawings clearly show the geometry of both the new handrail and the existing handrail, they do not indicate the method of attachment. The architect should respond with which document?

(A) change order

(B) architect's supplemental instructions (ASI)

(C) construction change directive

(D) proposal request

596. Which of the following documents are included in the contract between Vermilion Building Corporation, LLC and Bluecurve Construction Services? (Choose the four that apply.)

(A) the owner-architect agreement that defines the architect's responsibilities to the project

(B) Bluecurve Construction Services' proposal

(C) change orders issued throughout the course of the project

(D) addenda issued during the bidding period

(E) drawings and specifications of the project

(F) supplementary conditions written by Vermilion Building Corporation's attorney

597. The project specifications normally require the contractor to submit shop drawings for which of the following items? (Choose the three that apply.)

(A) elevator cab

(B) air conditioner split system

(C) electrical conduit

(D) elevator cab flooring

(E) gypsum board

(F) elevator motors and controller

598. The contractor has submitted the application for payment provided asResource 6.8. At which point in the project should the architect expect to receive this document?

(A) This will be the contractor's first application for payment.

(B) This application for payment will be submitted with the contractor's notice that the project is ready for final inspection.

(C) This application for payment will be submitted with the contractor's punch list and request for a substantial completion inspection.

(D) This application for payment will be submitted when the elevator equipment installation is complete.

599. During the design development phase, the owner tried to save money by not requiring the contractor to paint the new metal stairs, including the steel handrail and guardrail. After the stairs were installed and the welding was completed, the owner decided to have them painted after all, to cover unsightly spots created by the welding process. How should the architect respond to this decision?

(A) Issue a change order and adjust the contract price with the estimated cost of the change.

(B) Prepare architect's supplemental instructions and send them to the contractor.

(C) Make the change on the contractor's next application for payment.

(D) Prepare a request for proposal and send it to the contractor.

600. Which system upgrade has the greatest potential to decrease the Vermilion Building's energy consumption?

(A) installing light emitting diode (LED) fixtures to replace the incandescent fixtures in the elevator and the elevator machine room

(B) improving the *R*-value of the wall and ceiling insulation in the penthouse

(C) installing a heating, ventilating, and air conditioning (HVAC) system to condition the elevator machine room

(D) replacing the geared elevator motor with a gearless machine

Case Study 2

Problem 601 through Prob. 605 refer to the following case study. Refer to Resource 6.9 and Resource 6.10 to assist in answering the problems.

Parallax Architects has been working with Archie Seren at Zenith Property Management for many years. Archie is the vice president of the company, which owns and operates One Constellation Place, a 20-story office building with approximately 15,000 ft^2 of gross floor area on each floor. A bank and a clothing store occupy the first floor, and various professional companies occupy the upper floors. The tenant spaces range from 2000 ft^2 office suites to a space for the largest tenant, which is an aerospace engineering company that occupies three floors.

Bob Vega, principal architect at Parallax Architects, has become a trusted advisor to Archie. When prospective tenants consider leasing space in the building, Zenith Property Management hires Parallax Architects to meet with the tenant, evaluate their proposed program (or help them develop a program, if they do not have one), and determine how that program may fit into one of the available vacant spaces. Archie relies on Bob's firm to respond quickly, turn around schematic plans within a few days, and design with his company's budget and building fit-out standards in mind. Zenith Property Management's leases usually include a tenant improvement allowance, determined based on the size of the space and the length of the lease, and the management company prefers to coordinate the construction on the tenant's behalf.

Solstice Corporation is an accounting firm, with several offices in the United States. The company is interested in leasing 5500 ft^2 of space on the third floor of Zenith Property Management's building. Bob and Archie met with the company's representatives and developed a preliminary layout for the suite, which Solstice Corporation approved. After the lease was negotiated, Parallax Architecture prepared construction documents for the project and assisted Solstice Corporation with selecting the finishes that will be used in the space.

Zenith Property Management sent the drawings and specifications to construction firms for pricing. Solstice Corporation needs to move into the space within five months because its lease in another office complex will end at that time. The contractor has 16 weeks upon receipt of the notice to proceed to complete the work. Archie has obtained proposals from four contractors, all of whom have worked at One Constellation Place in the past. Solstice Corporation will participate in the review of the contractors' qualifications, but Archie will make the final decision. Zenith Property Management is not required to accept the lowest price. Instead, Zenith Property Management's evaluation of the contractors will consider the proposed schedule; the qualifications, including recent project experience and past performance on the owner's projects; references, skills, and the experience of personnel assigned to the project; and overall project cost.

The contract between Zenith Property Management and the general contractor will be based on American Institute of Architects (AIA) Document A101, *Standard Form of Agreement Between Owner and Contractor where the basis of payment is a Stipulated Sum*, and AIA Document A201, *General Conditions of the Contract for Construction.*

Parallax Architects and Zenith Property Management have based their agreement on American Institute of Architects Document B121, *Standard Form of Master Agreement Between Owner and Architect for Services provided under multiple Service Orders*, and the contract is amended with a new service order for each project.

Resource 6.9 Acoustical Panel Ceilings

SECTION 09 51 10
ACOUSTICAL PANEL CEILINGS

PART 1 - GENERAL

1.1 STIPULATIONS
A. Drawings and General Conditions of the Contract for Construction apply to this Section.

1.2 SUMMARY
A. Section includes acoustical panels and exposed suspension systems for ceilings.
B. Products furnished, but not installed under this Section, include anchors, clips, and other ceiling attachment devices to be cast in concrete.

1.3 ACTION SUBMITTALS
A. Product Data: For each type of product.
B. Samples for Verification: For each component indicated and for each exposed finish required, prepared on Samples of size indicated below.
1. Acoustical Panel: Set of 6 6 in × 6 in Samples of each type, color, pattern, and texture.
2. Exposed Suspension-System Members, Moldings, and Trim: Set of 6 in long Samples of each type, finish, and color.

1.4 INFORMATIONAL SUBMITTALS
A. Coordination Drawings: Reflected ceiling plans, drawn to scale, on which the following items are shown and coordinated with each other, using input from installers of the items involved.
1. suspended ceiling components
2. structural members to which suspension systems will be attached
3. size and location of initial access modules for acoustical panels
4. location and configuration of movable partition systems
5. items penetrating finished ceiling including the following.
a. lighting fixtures
b. air outlets and inlets
c. speakers
d. sprinklers
6. perimeter moldings
B. Product Test Reports: For each acoustical panel ceiling, for tests performed by manufacturer and witnessed by a qualified testing agency.
C. Evaluation Reports: For each acoustical panel ceiling suspension system, from ICC-ES.

1.5 CLOSEOUT SUBMITTALS
A. Maintenance Data: For finishes to include in maintenance manuals.

PART 2 - PRODUCTS

2.1 METAL SUSPENSION SYSTEMS, GENERAL
A. Metal Suspension-System Standard: Provide manufacturer's standard direct-hung metal suspension systems of types, structural classifications, and finishes indicated that comply with applicable requirements in ASTM C 635/C 635M.
B. Attachment Devices: Size for five times the design load indicated in ASTM C 635/C 635M, Table 1, "Direct Hung," unless otherwise indicated. Comply with seismic design requirements for IBC Seismic Design Category B.
C. Wire Hangers, Braces, and Ties: Provide wires complying with the following requirements:
1. Zinc-Coated, Carbon-Steel Wire: ASTM A 641/A 641M, Class 1 zinc coating, soft temper.
2. Size: Select wire diameter so its stress at three times hanger design load (ASTM C 635/C 635M, Table 1, "Direct Hung") will be less than yield stress of wire, but provide not less than 0.106 in diameter wire.

2.2 METAL SUSPENSION SYSTEM
A. Manufacturers: Subject to compliance with requirements, available manufacturers offering products that may be incorporated into the Work include, but are not limited to, the following:
1. Armstrong World Industries, Inc.; Prelude® XL®.
2. Chicago Metallic Corporation; Seismic 1200.
3. USG Interiors, Inc. (Subsidiary of USG Corporation); Donn® DX®.
B. Wide-Face, Capped, Double-Web, Steel Suspension System: Main and cross runners roll formed from cold-rolled steel sheet; pre-painted, electrolytically zinc coated, or hot-dip galvanized according to ASTM A 653/A 653M, not less than G30 coating designation; with prefinished 02/11 in wide metal caps on flanges.
1. Structural Classification: Intermediate-duty system.
2. End Condition of Cross Runners: Override (stepped) type.
3. Face Design: Flat, flush.
4. Cap Material: Steel cold-rolled sheet.
5. Cap Finish: Painted white.
6. Fire Rating: See Drawings for required fire rating at each location.

2.3 METAL EDGE MOLDINGS AND TRIM
A. Manufacturers: Subject to compliance with requirements, available manufacturers offering products that may be incorporated into the Work include, but are not limited to, the following:
1. Armstrong World Industries, Inc.
2. Chicago Metallic Corporation.
3. USG Interiors, Inc.; Subsidiary of USG Corporation.
B. Roll-Formed, Sheet-Metal Edge Moldings and Trim: Type and profile indicated or, if not indicated, manufacturer's standard moldings for edges and penetrations that comply with seismic design requirements; formed from sheet metal of same material, finish, and color as that used for exposed flanges of suspension-system runners.
1. Provide manufacturer's standard edge moldings that fit acoustical panel edge details and suspension systems indicated and that match width and configuration of exposed runners unless otherwise indicated.
2. For lay-in panels with reveal edge details, provide stepped edge molding that forms reveal of same depth and width as that formed between edge of panel and flange at exposed suspension member.
3. For circular penetrations of ceiling, provide edge moldings fabricated to diameter required to fit penetration exactly.

Resource 6.10 Acoustical Suspension System Data Submittal Sheet

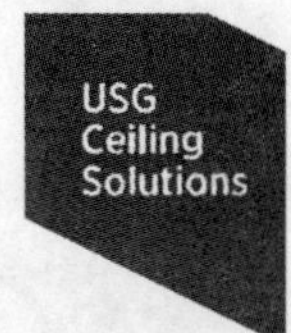

USG Ceiling Solutions

USG DONN® BRAND DX®/DXL™ ACOUSTICAL SUSPENSION SYSTEM

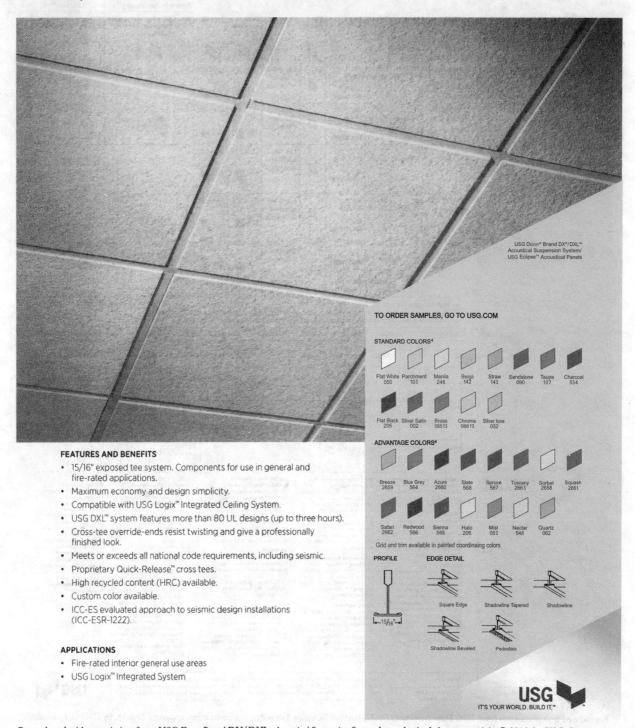

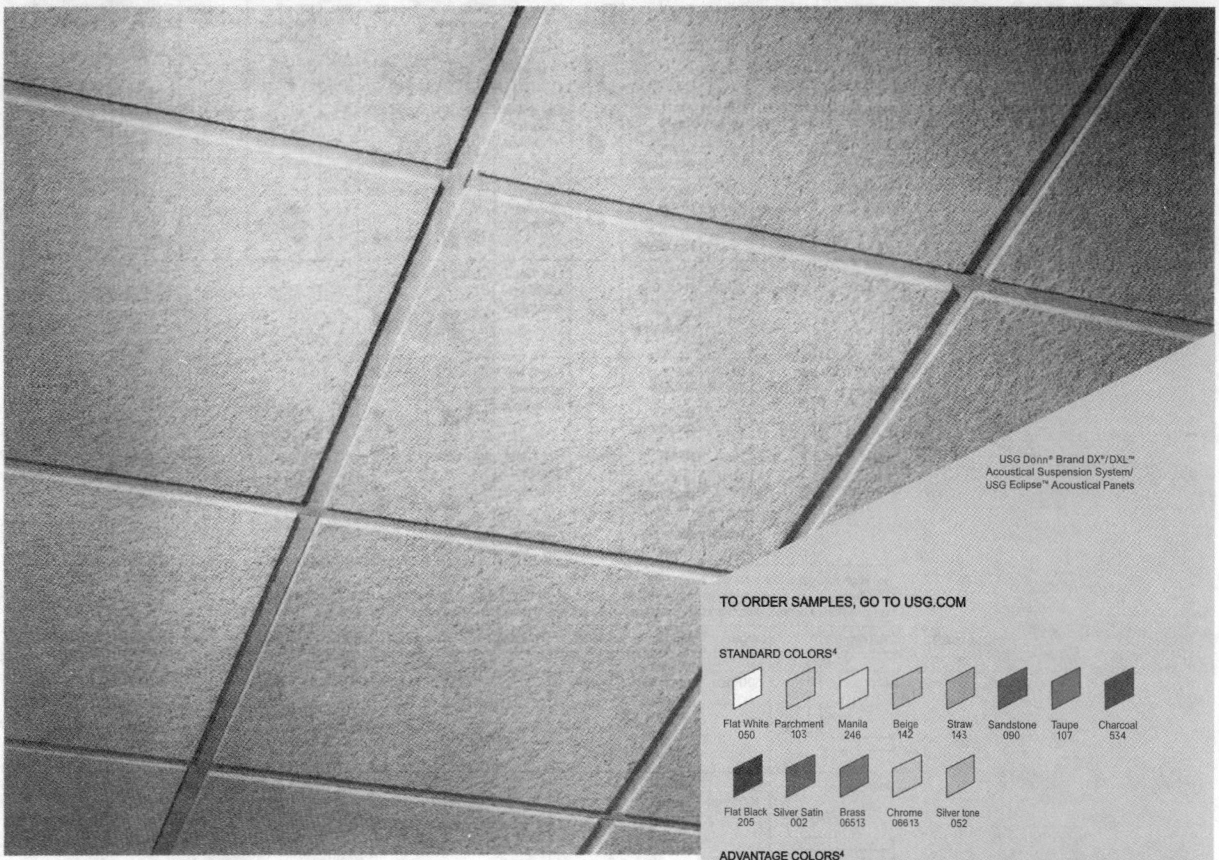

USG Donn® Brand DX®/DXL™ Acoustical Suspension System/ USG Eclipse™ Acoustical Panels

TO ORDER SAMPLES, GO TO USG.COM

STANDARD COLORS[4]

Flat White 050	Parchment 103	Manila 246	Beige 142	Straw 143	Sandstone 090	Taupe 107	Charcoal 534
Flat Black 205	Silver Satin 002	Brass 06513	Chrome 06613	Silver tone 052			

ADVANTAGE COLORS[4]

Breeze 2659	Blue Grey 564	Azure 2660	Slate 568	Spruce 567	Tuscany 2663	Sorbet 2658	Squash 2661
Safari 2662	Redwood 566	Sienna 565	Halo 206	Mist 053	Nectar 546	Quartz 062	

Grid and trim available in painted coordinaing colors

PROFILE

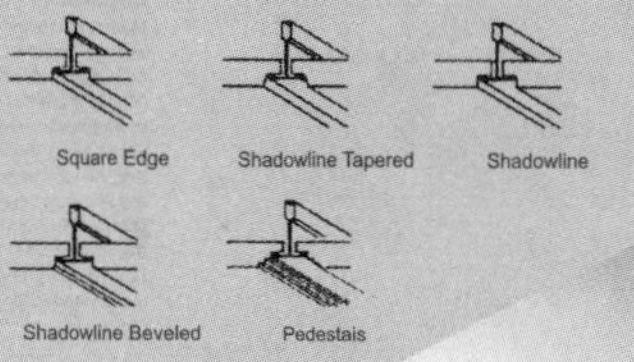

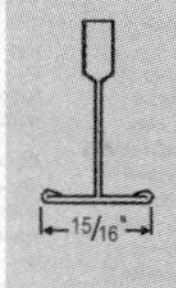

15/16"

EDGE DETAIL

Square Edge
Shadowline Tapered
Shadowline
Shadowline Beveled
Pedestals

FEATURES AND BENEFITS

- 15/16" exposed tee system. Components for use in general and fire-rated applications.
- Maximum economy and design simplicity.
- Compatible with USG Logix™ Integrated Ceiling System.
- USG DXL™ system features more than 80 UL designs (up to three hours).
- Cross-tee override-ends resist twisting and give a professionally finished look.
- Meets or exceeds all national code requirements, including seismic.
- Proprietary Quick-Release™ cross tees.
- High recycled content (HRC) available.
- Custom color available.
- ICC-ES evaluated approach to seismic design installations (ICC-ESR-1222).

APPLICATIONS

- Fire-rated interior general use areas
- USG Logix™ Integrated System

USG
IT'S YOUR WORLD. BUILD IT.™

Resource 6.10 Acoustical Suspension System Data Submitted Sheet (continued)

USG DONN® BRAND DX®/DXL™ ACOUSTICAL SUSPENSION SYSTEM

ORDER SAMPLES/LITERATURE
usg.com | samplit@usg.com
fax: 888 874-2348

TECHNICAL SERVICES
800 USG.4YOU (874-4968)

SEE LEED REPORT TOOL for detailed sustainability information, as well as the MOST UP-TO-DATE TECHNICAL INFORMATION, at usgdesignstudio.com

DONN: System meets or exceeds load compliance specifications per ASTM C635 · 10: YEAR AVAILABILITY · HRC: HIGH RECYCLED CONTENT

	ASTM Class	Length	Height	Item No.	Fire Rating	Color	Post-consumer RC	Total RC	Seismic Design Category[1] IBC	ICC-ES Evaluated Installation	4' Hanger Spacing	Rated Load[2] 5' Hanger Spacing	6' Hanger Spacing[6]
15/16" TEE SYSTEM Main Tee	Intermediate Duty	12' 3600mm	1.64" 42mm	DX/[3,4,7,12] DXL24		Flat White Standard Advantage	up to 39%	up to 47%	A-C	7/8" Molding ACM7 Clip	12 lbs./LF	6.1 lbs./LF	3.6 lbs./LF
				DX/[3,4,12] DXL24HRC			57% HRC	65% HRC					
	Heavy Duty	12' 3600mm	1.64" 42mm	DX/[3,4,7,12] DXL26		Flat White Standard Advantage	up to 39%	up to 47%	A-F	7/8" Molding ACM7 Clip	16 lbs./LF	7.3 lbs./LF	4.9 lbs./LF
				DX/[3,4,12] DXL26HRC			57% HRC	65% HRC					
Cross Tee 1"		2' 600mm	1" 25mm	DX/[3,4,7,12] DXL216		Flat White Standard Advantage	up to 25%	up to 33%					
				DX/[3,4,12] DXL216HRC			57% HRC	65% HRC					
Cross Tee 1-1/2"		4' 1200mm	1-1/2" 38mm	DX/[3,4,7,12] DXL424		Flat White Standard Advantage	up to 20%	up to 47%					
				DX/[3,4,12] DXL424HRC			57% HRC	65% HRC					
				DX422[5,7,9]	Class A	Flat White Standard Advantage	up to 25%	up to 33%					
				DX422HRC[5]			57% HRC	65% HRC					
		5' 1500mm	1-1/2" 38mm	DX/[3,4,7,12] DXL524		Flat White Standard	up to 39%	up to 46%					

High Recycled Content (HRC)
Classified as containing greater than 50% total recycled content. Total recycled content is based on product composition of postconsumer and preconsumer (postindustrial) recycled content per FTC guidelines.

Firecode®

MOLDING[10]

Wall Angle	Length	Item No.	Color	Wall Angle	Length	Item No	Color	Postconsumer RC	Total RC
2" × 2"	10' 3000mm	M20SM-2 (up to 65% recycled content) HRC	Flat White	7/8" × 7/8"	12' 3600mm	M7[8]	Flat White Standard Advantage	up to 65% HRC	
						M7HRC[8]		57% HRC	65% HRC
Shadowline[11] 7/8", 9/32", 1¼", ¾"	10' 3000mm	MS274[5] 2" shelf for seismic (Up to 65% recycled content) HRC	Flat White Custom	1" × 2"	10' 3000mm	M20[5]	Flat White Custom	up to 65% HRC	
						M20HD Heavy Duty		up to 58% HRC	
						M20SM Seismic		up to 65% HRC	

PHYSICAL DATA/ FOOTNOTES

Product literature and samples
Date sheet: AC3167.Sample flat white – seismic: 271370. Sample flat white: 215673. Sample main tee: 206563. Sample flat black :205100,

Material
Double-web G30 hot-dipped galvanized steel body and G30 hot-dipped galvanized steel cap.

Recycled content
For details, see LEED report tool at usgdesignstudio.com,

Installation
Must be installed in compliance with ASTM C636, ASTM E580, CISCA and standard industry practices, within all applicable code requirements. Altemative assemblies and installation methods may be utllized when approved by the Authority Having jurisdiction. USG recommends checking with the Authority Having Jurisdiction prior to designing and installing a suspended ceiling system.

ICC Evaluation Service, Inc., Report Compliance
Suspension systems manufactured by USG Interiors,LLC, have been reviewed and are approved by listing in ICC-ESR-1222. Evaluation Reports are subject to reexamination, revision and possible cancellation. Please refer to usgdesignstudio.com or 800USG.4YOU (874- 4968) for current reports,

L.A. Research Report Compliance
USG Donn® Brand suspension systems manufactured by USG Interiors, LLC, have been reviewed and are approved by listing in the following L.A. Research Report number: 25764.

Code compliance
The Information presented is correct to the best of our knowledge at the date of issuance. Because codes continue to eyolve, check with a local official prior to designing and installing a ceiling system, Other restrictions and exemptions may apply.

The City of New York BSA and MEA Report Compliance
USG Donn® Brand suspension systems have been approved by listing in one or more of the following City of New York Board of Standards and Appeals, and Department of Building, Material and Equipment Acceptance reports: BSA 618-60 -SM, BSA 184-77-SM, BSA 796-81-SM, MEA 366-93-M, MEA 133-95-M, MEA 3 2-99 -M, MEA 123-00-M.

ASTM C635 Standard for Load Compliance
System meets or exceeds load compliance specifications per ASTM C635. Main tees will not deflect more than 1/8" over 48" span (or L/360) in Light Duty. Intermediate Duty or Heavy Duty categories.

Notes

1. All USG DX®/DXL™ main-tee and cross-tee connections meet IBC requirements for tension and compression strength.
2. Load test data shows uniform load in lbs./LF based on simple span tests in accordance with ASTM C635 deflection limit of L/360.
3. UL fire-rated listing, labeling and follow-up applies only to fire-rated components.
4. Color program for imperial only. Consult Customer Service for custom color and metric-tee colors.
5. Non-fire-ratedonly.
6. Cross-tee hole punch spacings also available for 20" and 30" modules.
7. Available in metric.
8. USG DX® cross tees available in additional sizes and lengths.
9. Non-fire-rated applications may mix USG DX® and DXL™ parts.
10. For moldings information, see *Perimeter Interface* selector.
11. Panels must be specified to be field-cut and field-revealed and to provide widest possible lay-on edge.
12. For USG DXL™, channel moldings are also acceptable in some designs. Check *UL Fire Resistance Directory* for molding options.
13. Brass and chrome available on limited items.

Notice
We shall not be liable for incidental and consequential damages, directly or indirectly sustained, nor for any loss caused by application of these goods not in accordance with current printed instructions or for other than the intended use. Our liability is expressly limited to replacement of defective goods. Any claim shall be deemed waived unless made in writing to us within thirty (30) days from date it was or reasonably should have been discovered.

Manufactured by
USG Interiors, LLC
SSO West Adams Street
Chicago, Il, 60661

Safety First! Follow good safety/industrial hygiene practices during installation. Wear appropriate personal protective equipment. Read SDS and literature before specification and installation.

USG

Construction & Evaluation

Table for Prob. 601

	Polaris Construction Services	Kepler Brothers, LLC	Retrograde Corporation	Apogee Building & Construction
cost	$532,250	$525,000	$526,100	$585,825
schedule	16 wk	16 wk	18 wk	14 wk
owner's experience with this contractor on previous projects	work completed on time, one owner-requested change order	multiple contractor-initiated change orders	no change orders, inconsistent workday start-end times and number of workers on site	responsive, addressed issues quickly and professionally, project completion was two weeks behind schedule
recent work	5000 ft^2 tenant fit-out at Corona Corporate Center	emergency suite at Caldera Medical Center	single-family residence	Armstrong Elementary School gymnasium

601. Key information from the proposals submitted by the construction companies is given in the table.

Which firm presents the strongest qualifications and should be recommended to be awarded this project?

(A) Polaris Construction Services

(B) Kepler Brothers, LLC

(C) Retrograde Corporation

(D) Apogee Building & Construction

602. All the proposals received from the general contractors exceed the amount of the tenant improvement allowance agreed upon in Solstice Corporation's lease. The proposed construction schedule cannot be modified. Which change to the project scope should the architect suggest at this point to reduce the overall project cost?

(A) Require the general contractors to have their electrical subcontractors redesign the lighting system, on a design-build basis, to reduce the cost of the work.

(B) Reduce the size of the suite.

(C) Substitute a less expensive ceiling system and carpet tile for the products specified in the construction documents.

(D) Send the construction documents to other contractors and solicit additional bids.

603. While the contractors were reviewing the documents and preparing their proposals, Parallax Architects completed the design for a custom-built reception desk for Solstice Corporation's entrance. Because the desk's design was not complete when the documents were issued to the contractors for pricing, each contractor was instructed to include a $5000 allowance in his or her proposal for the desk. The owner specified that the desk is to be built by Meridian Millwork Company.

The invoice with itemized costs to the contractor from Meridian Millwork Company is given.

item	quantity	cost	extended
labor: finish carpenter	22 hr	$52.25/hr	$1149.50
labor: laborer	5 hr	$32.75/hr	$163.75
labor			$1313.25
4×8 sheets A2 plywood, plain-sliced	3 ea	$80/ea	$240.00
quartz countertop and facing, waterfall/riser, 1.18 in	22 ft^2	$125/ft^2	$2750.00
file/storage drawers (box, face, soft close slides)	6 ea	$300/ea	$1800.00
keyboard tray	1 ea	$300/ea	$300.00
hardware	1 ls	$350/ls	$350.00
grommet and power strip	2 ea	$100/ea	$200.00
materials			$5640.00
sales tax			$564.00
delivery			$250.00
total			$7767.25

The contractor received the desk at the site. Installing the desk and making the connections to power and data systems took two laborers three hours at $50 per hour. The contractor's overhead and profit rate is 15%.

What is the change to the contract sum that should be recorded on the change order?

(A) $2767.25

(B) $3067.25

(C) $3932.34

(D) $4277.34

604. Solstice Corporation decides to use vinyl composition tile (VCT) in the employee break room and server rooms, rather than install the ceramic tile flooring that was originally specified. The general contractor prepares a proposal for the change, as shown in the table.

ceramic tile: materials and installation	$5245.00
contractor's overhead and profit (15%)	$786.75
total cost for ceramic tile	$6031.75
vinyl composition tile: materials and installation	$3265.50
contractor's overhead and profit (15%)	$489.83
total cost for vinyl composition tile	$3,755.33

Which statement is correct?

(A) This change can be made with American Institute of Architects (AIA) Document G710, *Architect's Supplemental Instructions.*

(B) A credit change order should be issued in the amount of $1979.50.

(C) The contract amount should be reduced by $2276.42.

(D) The contractor has the right to delay performance of the work until receipt of a change order adjusting the contract sum.

605. Refer to Resource 6.9 and Resource 6.10. The contractor submits the attached cut sheet and notes on the cover sheet indicates that an intermediate duty, $^{15}/_{16}$ in tee system will be provided in white. Which specification criteria are documented in the submittal? (Choose the four that apply.)

(A) The suspension system complies with the load compliance standards stated in the specification.

(B) The size of the suspension wire that will be provided complies with the minimum thickness given in the specification.

(C) The galvanization on the system components complies with the standards required by the specification.

(D) The system is acceptable for use in the seismic design category specified for this project.

(E) This product can be used in a 1-hour fire-rated application.

(F) The recycled content of this product meets the minimum requirements of the specifications.

Construction & Evaluation

Solutions

Multiple Choice

511. (A) (B) (C) ●
512. ● (B) (C) (D)
513. (A) ● (C) (D)
514. (A) ● (C) (D)
515. ● ● (C) ● (E) ●
516. ● ● (C) (D) ● (F)
517. ● (B) (C) (D) (E) ●
518. ● (B) (C) (D)
519. (A) (B) ● (D)
520. (A) ● (C) (D)
521. (A) ● (C) (D)
522. (A) (B) ● (D)
523. ● (B) ● (D) (E) ●
524. (A) (B) (C) ●
525. (A) ● (C) (D)
526. (A) ● ● ● (E) ●
527. (A) (B) ● (D)
528. ● ● ● (D) (E) ●
529. (A) ● (C) (D)
530. (A) (B) (C) ●
531. (A) ● (C) (D)
532. (A) (B) ● (D)
533. ● (B) (C) (D)
534. 10 days
535. (A) (B) (C) ●
536. (A) (B) ● (D)
537. (A) (B) (C) ●
538. ● ● (C) (D) ● ●
539. (A) ● (C) (D)
540. (A) ● ● (D) (E) ●
541. (A) (B) ● (D)
542. 10 days
543. (A) ● (C) (D)
544. ● (B) (C) (D)
545. (A) (B) ● (D)
546. ● (B) (C) (D)
547. (A) ● ● ● (E) (F)
548. ● (B) (C) (D)
549. ● ● (C) (D) ● ●
550. (A) ● (C) (D)
551. (A) ● ● ● (E) ●
552. (A) (B) ● (D)
553. (A) (B) (C) ●
554. ● (B) (C) (D)
555. (A) ● (C) (D)
556. (A) (B) (C) ●
557. ● (B) (C) (D)
558. (A) ● (C) (D)
559. ● (B) (C) (D)
560. (A) ● ● (D) (E) (F)
561. ● ● (C) ● (E) ●
562. (A) ● (C) (D)
563. (A) ● (C) (D)
564. (A) (B) (C) ●
565. (A) ● (C) (D)
566. ● (B) (C) (D)
567. (A) ● (C) (D)
568. (A) (B) ● (D)
569. ● (B) (C) (D)
570. (A) (B) (C) ●
571. (A) (B) ● (D)
572. ● (B) (C) (D)
573. (A) (B) (C) ●
574. (A) ● (C) (D)
575. (A) (B) (C) ●
576. (A) ● (C) (D)
577. ● ● (C) ● (E) (F)
578. (A) ● ● (D) (E) ●
579. (A) ● (C) (D)
580. (A) ● (C) (D)
581. ● (B) (C) (D)
582. (A) (B) (C) ●
583. ● ● (C) ● (E) ●
584. (A) (B) (C) ●
585. (A) (B) ● (D)
586. (A) ● (C) (D)
587. (A) (B) (C) ●

Case Study 1

588. ● (B) (C) (D)
589. (A) (B) ● (D) ● ●
590. ● ● (C) ● (E) (F)
591. (A) ● (C) ● (E) (F)
592. (A) ● (C) (D)
593. (A) (B) (C) (D) ● ●
594. See Sol. 594.
595. (A) ● (C) (D)
596. (A) (B) ● ● ● ●
597. ● ● (C) (D) (E) ●
598. (A) ● (C) (D)
599. (A) (B) (C) ●
600. (A) (B) (C) ●

Case Study 2

601. ● (B) (C) (D)
602. (A) (B) ● (D)
603. ● (B) (C) (D)
604. (A) ● (C) (D)
605. ● (B) ● ● ● (F)

511. The Steiner tunnel test is not a concrete test. It is used to determine the surface burning characteristics of interior finish materials.

The cylinder, electrical impedance, and Kelly ball tests all quantify different characteristics of concrete. The cylinder test involves breaking a cylinder formed of concrete from a specific pour in order to test the concrete's compressive strength at prescribed intervals (usually 7, 14, 21, or 28 days) during the curing process. The electrical impedance test is used to assess the moisture level of a slab by measuring the amount of electricity conducted through the material. Slabs with a greater moisture content conduct more electricity. The Kelly ball test measures the workability of the uncured concrete. Workability is influenced by the proportions of cement, aggregate, water, and admixtures included in the mix and the shape and size of the aggregates. A metal ball is dropped into freshly poured concrete, and the depression formed by the ball is measured and compared to the slump test results.

The answer is (D).

512. Concrete gains the most compressive strength during the first few days of curing. This is the most critical time in the curing process, and it is important that the concrete be protected from freezing or evaporation during this time. If the concrete is unprotected and environmental conditions are unfavorable, the ultimate compressive strength of the concrete could be greatly reduced.

Theoretically, concrete continues to gain strength well after the 28th day. But for the purposes of design strengths and testing, the compressive strength of concrete is always referred to as its strength 28 days after it is placed.

The answer is (A).

513. Grade stakes are used to indicate how much cut or fill is required at a specific location to reach finish grade. They are set by a survey crew and reset periodically during excavation to monitor progress.

A transit is a surveying tool used to determine the elevations of points on a site. It is typically mounted on a tripod for stability. Transits can be as sophisticated as a laser level with a sight that "shoots" elevations using a prism, or as simple as a handheld scope.

Batter boards are temporary supports erected to hold wires or strings that indicate the excavation line for a building site. The corners of the building or limits of excavation are marked at the intersection of the lines using a plumb bob. Batter boards are set back from the excavation line and are preferred to corner stakes or pins placed at the corners of the structure because they will not be disturbed during construction operations.

The answer is (B).

514. Buildings that are well-sealed use energy more efficiently. All of the pieces of equipment listed are diagnostic tools used to quantify how much air is leaking in or out of the building envelope, and to identify the locations of leaks.

A nanometer measures differences in pressure between two spaces. A flow hood is placed over a register or diffuser to measure output. A duct blower is a fan attached directly to the ductwork to check for leaks. A blower door is a fan that can be mounted in a door frame. It is used to pressurize or depressurize a building to measure air infiltration or leakage.

The answer is (B).

515. Building commissioning can be expected to provide increased energy efficiency, improved indoor air quality, a comprehensive training program for maintenance staff (conducted either by the commissioning agent or the contractor), and organized operations and maintenance manuals (assembled by the contractor, design professional, or commissioning agent). Building commissioning does not ensure verification of 100% of building systems (that responsibility lies with the contractor) and does not include record drawings.

Building commissioning is a process that helps to assure that a building owner "gets what he paid for." Commissioning takes place in parallel to the traditional design process. The commissioning agent (sometimes abbreviated as CxA or CXA) is hired and reports directly to the owner. The commissioning agent's job is to verify that the owner's goals are being accomplished and to advocate for the owner. Sometimes the CxA is a member of the owner's staff, but often a third-party consultant is hired to fill this role.

The first step in commissioning is to document the owner's goals, which must be quantifiable. For example, perhaps the owner wishes to improve energy efficiency by 10%, as compared to a "study" building. The CxA can evaluate the performance of designed systems in comparison to the baseline building to determine whether the design will meet the owner's objectives.

The CxA should be a part of the project team from the beginning and should have input into the programming phase, review the construction documents and specifications for compliance with the owner's goals, and conduct site checks during construction. The CxA is responsible for testing a representative sample of the systems. The presence of a CxA on a project team does not relieve the design professionals of any of their responsibilities; the architect and engineer retain responsibility for the design of the building and its systems, and the contractor holds the responsibility for the installation and full testing of the systems. The commissioning process is a quality control check to ensure that the finished building operates in the way that the owner intended.

At the end of the project, the CxA should prepare a report summarizing the owner's goals, the results of the CxA's evaluations, and any outstanding issues or further testing needed (such as seasonal testing of an HVAC system). Building commissioning is a prerequisite for Leadership in Energy and Environmental Design (LEED) certification. More information on building commissioning can be found at the Building Commissioning Association's website, bcxa.org.

The answer is (A), (B), (D), and (F).

516. Sick building syndrome is a term used to describe conditions where a significant number of building occupants report some type of physical malaise within a specified period of time, usually about two weeks. Physical symptoms can include dizziness, skin irritation, headaches, nausea, sore throats, and other respiratory problems. Generally, these symptoms disappear or are significantly reduced when the occupants leave the building. Occupant complaints are usually the first indicator that there is a problem in the building, and further testing and inspection is warranted to determine the source of their discomfort.

Sick building syndrome can usually be traced to a few common causes. Insufficient or contaminated outdoor air entering the HVAC system is the most common reason for occupant complaints. This can be caused by improper balancing of the system, or by locating the air intakes too close to a source of contamination such as an exhaust, parking, or trash collection area. Insufficient ventilation of spaces where there is a high concentration of chemicals or contaminants—such as a janitor's closet, smoking area, or copy room—could be another reason. Occasionally, occupant complaints are linked to mold growth in hidden areas of the building or within the HVAC system. Designing the HVAC system to prevent the accumulation of stagnant water and cleaning the ductwork frequently helps prevent mold growth. Complaints can also arise when materials with high levels of volatile organic compounds (VOCs) are introduced, such as new carpeting or paint. Low-VOC materials should be specified when possible.

The answer is (A), (B), and (E).

517. Lead may be found in paint in older buildings (pre-1978) and in plumbing pipes, solder, and roof flashings. It is linked to neurological problems, particularly in young children.

Polychlorinated biphenyls (PCBs) were outlawed in the 1980s but still can be found in older electrical equipment. PCBs are thought to cause a variety of types of cancer.

Radon is a naturally occurring, colorless, odorless, and carcinogenic gas that can be detected in spaces where a building comes in contact with the earth, such as a basement or crawlspace.

Crystalline silica is a natural material found in sand or stone and may be present in masonry products. It becomes respirable when the masonry is cut or ground and dust is released and can irritate the respiratory membranes. It is a carcinogen. Crystalline silica is also an ingredient in many latex paints.

Asbestos and glass fiber have been common components of insulation products. Asbestos was banned from most construction products in the 1970s and 1980s when it was determined that exposure to disturbed material causes cancer and related respiratory diseases. It can still be found in old buildings in wall and pipe insulation, floor and ceiling tiles, and equipment. Glass fiber requires special handling procedures to comply with Occupational Safety and Health Administration (OSHA) standards, such as protective clothing, respirators, and eye protection to keep the fibers away from the body. Prolonged unprotected exposure to glass fiber can irritate the skin and respiratory tract; it is undetermined if the material can cause cancer.

The answer is (A) and (F).

518. Retainage is a percentage of the contract sum held back from applications for payment, usually around 10%. The money is paid to the contractor when the project has been completed satisfactorily; in the meantime, the retainage gives the owner leverage to ensure that the work is completed on time and in accordance with the construction documents. Retainage also helps to protect the owner against lien claims by ensuring that the owner has funds available to pay for materials or labor should the contractor fail to pay for them. Before retainage is released or decreased, the surety company that provided the contractor's performance bond should give written consent to the payment.

The answer is (A).

519. The architect should return the samples to the subcontractor without reviewing them. The subcontractor should first submit them to the contractor for review for compliance with the construction documents, in accordance with American Institute of Architects (AIA) Document A201, *General Conditions of the Contract for Construction*, Sec. 3.12.5 and Sec. 3.12.6. The contractor may then submit them to the architect for review and selections.

The answer is (C).

520. American Institute of Architects (AIA) Document B101, *Standard Form of Agreement Between Owner and Architect*, Sec. 3.6.2.2, gives the architect the authority to reject work that is not in compliance with the construction documents. To determine whether work is in compliance, the architect may require third-party testing or sampling. AIA Document A201, *General Conditions of the Contract for Construction*, Sec. 4.2.6, notifies the contractor of this authority.

Only the owner has the authority to stop work (AIA Document A201, Sec. 2.3), order changes that affect the cost or duration of the project through a change order or construction change directive (AIA Document A201, Sec. 7.2.1 and Sec. 7.3.1), or accept nonconforming work (AIA Document A201, Sec. 12.3).

The architect can order minor changes that do not affect the contract sum or time (AIA Document A201, Sec. 7.4, and AIA Document B101, Sec. 3.6.5.1), but it is generally advisable to inform the owner as soon as practicable and obtain written agreement with the change.

The answer is (B).

521. Shop drawings, samples, and cut sheets are examples of action submittals, which must be reviewed and approved by the architect before the work can proceed. Submittals are addressed in both American Institute of Architects (AIA) Document B101, *Standard Form of Agreement Between Owner and Architect*, Sec. 3.6.4, and AIA Document A201, *General Conditions of the Contract for Construction*, Sec. 3.12. Administrative procedures regarding submittals should be defined in Division 01 of the specifications.

Submittals are prepared by or on behalf of the contractor specifically for the project and are submitted to the architect to explain the products the contractor intends to install. The contractor is responsible for verifying materials and dimensional information and for coordinating the information in the submittal with the project as a whole. The architect reviews the information for the purpose of confirming that the products are in accordance with the requirements of the construction documents and the design intent. If the submittal deals with a system or materials specified by a consultant, the architect should forward it to the appropriate consultant for their review, and upon return, review and stamp it. After review of any submittal, the architect should stamp the submittal and mark it "approved," "approved as corrected (or indicated)," "revise and resubmit," or "not approved," and return it to the contractor.

Safety Data Sheets (SDS) are prepared by any supplier of hazardous materials and are examples of the type of data that is sometimes requested as an informational submittal as described in AIA Document A201, Sec. 3.12.4. The architect is not required to review or approve such submittals. This information is required by the Occupational Safety and Health Administration (OSHA) for any materials used in a workplace and must be kept current and accessible to employees during working hours. The documents include information on the physical properties of the chemicals, required protective equipment, appropriate responses to exposure, and health risks.

The answer is (B).

522. AIA Document A201, Sec. 3.7.4, addresses concealed or unknown conditions on the site, including subsurface characteristics.

The contractor's responsibility in this situation is to inform the architect and owner about the conditions observed within 21 days of discovery. The architect will investigate the conditions and report his or her findings to the owner. The owner will decide how to proceed. If adjustment to the contract sum or contract time is necessary because of the discovery, the scope of work may be adjusted through a change order addressing the unforeseen conditions.

The contractor may rely on the accuracy of the information provided by the owner according to AIA Document A201, Sec. 2.2.3. Unless it can be proven that the geotechnical report was in error, the geotechnical engineer will probably not be held financially responsible for the additional work because it is nearly impossible to define all of the subsurface conditions on a site with absolute accuracy. The architect fulfilled his obligation to the owner by making the owner aware of the prevalence of this condition locally and requesting that the owner arrange appropriate tests. It is also important to note that the soils report was not incorporated into the contract documents because the geotechnical engineer was hired by the owner, not the architect, and the engineer was not acting as a consultant to the architect. Since the contractor, geotechnical engineer, and the architect fulfilled their contractual responsibilities, the owner is responsible for the additional costs.

The answer is (C).

523. Architects do not issue occupancy permits; these permits are authorized by the code official in the project jurisdiction. The architect is not responsible for property insurance on the project. Therefore, the architect cannot be responsible to transferring this insurance to another party.

American Institute of Architects (AIA) Document B101, *Standard Form of Agreement Between Owner and Architect*, Sec. 3.6.6, deals with project completion. The architect must perform an inspection to determine the date of substantial completion and final completion. The architect must also obtain from the contractor and forward to the owner any written warranties required by the contract documents, consent of the surety to release retainage and make the final payment, and releases or waivers of liens or bonds indemnifying the owner against liens. The architect must also prepare a final certificate for payment.

The answer is (A), (C), and (F).

524. AIA Document A201, Sec. 10.3, addresses the discovery of hazardous materials. The contractor was correct to stop work and immediately notify the owner of her suspicions, and the owner was correct to engage a testing agency to confirm that asbestos was present. The contractor has the right to an appropriate extension of the contract time and fair compensation for costs related to stopping and restarting the work. This change is negotiated between the owner and contractor, and the contract is modified by change order.

If the owner and contractor cannot agree, the contractor may assert a claim, and the issue is referred to the initial decision maker as discussed in AIA Document A201, Sec. 15.2.

The answer is (D).

525. Although the contractor must submit a construction schedule for the architect's review, the architect need not approve it. The contractor bears responsibility for coordinating and scheduling the work. AIA Document A201, Sec. 3.10.1, states that the schedule must show that the work will be completed within the time frame allotted and requires the contractor to revise the schedule as necessary to keep the architect and owner apprised of expected changes.

AIA Document A201, Sec. 3.11, requires the contractor to maintain on site a copy of drawings, specifications, addenda, and other official project-related correspondence, including shop drawings and change orders. The contractor is responsible for annotating these documents as the project progresses to maintain a record of the work as constructed. These are submitted to the architect for delivery to the owner at the end of the project.

Record drawings may be required of the contractor by the specifications, but AIA Document A201 does not include this requirement. (Record drawings are also often prepared by the architect as an additional service to the owner.)

The architect is responsible for reviewing only the submittals that are required by the contract documents according to AIA Document A201, Sec. 3.12.4. If additional submittals are forwarded to the architect, the architect may return them to the contractor without action.

According to AIA Document A201, Sec. 3.10.2, the architect must approve the contractor's proposed schedule of submittals at the start of the project. This is to ensure that there will be a reasonable amount of time allowed for the architect to review the submittal, for the contractor to make corrections or revisions as necessary based upon the architect's review, and for the architect to approve the submittal without delaying the progress of the work.

The answer is (B).

526. American Institute of Architects (AIA) Document A201, *General Conditions of the Contract for Construction*, Sec. 9.5, addresses reasons that an architect may withhold a certificate for payment. The reasons include defective work not remedied, claims or probable claims against the project, failure of the contractor to pay subcontractors, damage to the owner or another contractor, evidence that the work will not be completed within the contract time, and repeated failure to carry out the work in accordance with the contract documents. The purpose of the architect's certification is to endeavor to protect the owner's interests in the project by not releasing payments until the contractor has properly completed the work.

Architects should always check over the math before certifying pay applications as this is a common source of error. Contractors often submit a rough draft, or pencil copy, for the architect's review before submitting the final pay application. This gives the architect a chance to point out errors or to raise questions with the contractor about work completed before the pay application is processed, which helps minimize delays.

The answer is (B), (C), (D), and (F).

527. The cost of labor and materials is \$22,250. The addition for overhead and profit is 20%, for a total of 1.20 × \$22,250, or \$26,700.

The addition for coordination is 5%, and this is applied after the addition for overhead and profit, for a total of 1.05 × \$26,700 = \$28,035.

The owner should also receive proper credit for the deleted porcelain tile, including labor, materials, and overhead and profit. This is not part of the calculation in this problem, however.

The answer is (C).

528. An advertisement to bid is a notice published in a local newspaper or posted with a plan room to notify contractors of a project and give them the basic information necessary for them to obtain a set of bid documents for review. Publicly funded work is usually required to be advertised a specified number of times in approved publications.

A plan room is a place (physical or online) where contractors can obtain information about projects currently out for bid.

An advertisement to bid includes the following information.

- a name, location, and description of the project
- the name and address of the owner and architect
- instructions for obtaining a set of bidding documents and/or locations where bid documents may be viewed (such as plan rooms, the architect's office, etc.)
- the date, time, and location of the pre-bid conference, if scheduled
- the date, time, and location the bids are due
- the type and amount of bid bond required
- the date and time of the bid opening and whether or not the bids will be read publicly
- any other information that the owner or the owner's attorney feels should be included

Bid forms are generally included in the bid package provided to interested contractors. Selection of subcontractors is the general contractor's responsibility and is not a part of an advertisement to bid.

The answer is (A), (B), (C), and (F).

529. Bid amounts must be expressed on the bid form both in words and in numerical form. If there is a discrepancy between the two, the words prevail. The bid is valid and should be interpreted as $756,452.

The answer is (B).

530. AIA Document A201, Sec. 5.2, addresses subcontractors. The contractor is required to submit a list of proposed subcontractors to the architect and owner for review. If the architect and/or owner have objections to any of the proposed subcontractors, they must notify the contractor in writing within 14 days. The contractor is responsible for proposing an alternate subcontractor. Assuming that the original proposed subcontractor was "reasonably capable" of performing the work, the contractor will be entitled to an adjustment of the contract sum or time to reflect the new subcontractor's price or schedule, which will be documented in a change order. After the list of subcontractors has been approved, the contractor may not make changes unless he obtains the permission of the owner and architect.

The answer is (D).

531. The contractor should retrieve his bid from the owner, correct it, and resubmit it prior to the deadline for receipt of bids. This is the best way to modify the price. The architect should not interfere with the bidding process by modifying the bid in any way.

The answer is (B).

532. The *International Building Code* (IBC) Sec. 104 outlines the duties and powers of the building official. This person is responsible for interpreting the code and inspecting projects for compliance with its policies and procedures. The final decision on matters of interpretation of code requirements is the building official's. IBC Sec. 104.6 states that a building code representative may enter any structure or premises at any reasonable time if he believes that the building is noncompliant or presents a danger. In IBC Sec. 104.8, the building official is absolved of personal liability for decisions made in a professional capacity provided that those decisions are made "in good faith and without malice in the discharge of duties required by this code or other pertinent law or ordinance." IBC Sec. 110.1 states that no building may be occupied until the building official has issued a certificate of occupancy.

The answer is (C).

533. Inclement weather can have a significant impact on the amount of time it takes to erect a building. One way to minimize this effect is to construct portions of the building off-site and bring them to the site for installation. This allows work to continue indoors even when weather conditions on site prohibit progress.

Designs that facilitate sequencing can also help to reduce the amount of time necessary for construction. While the contractor is responsible for coordinating the project schedule, architects can help make the project more efficient by developing details that allow certain trades to come on to the job site, complete their work, and leave before the next trade arrives. This simplifies scheduling for the general contractor and can result in cost savings for the owner and better construction details.

Use of union labor tends to lengthen the construction period. It is impossible to choose a "best" time to begin construction, such as the spring, because inclement weather is unpredictable.

The answer is (A).

534. Applications for payment must be submitted at least 10 days in advance of the scheduled payment date according to American Institute of Architects (AIA) Document A201, *General Conditions of the Contract for Construction*, Sec. 9.3.1. The date of payment is established in AIA Document A101, *Standard Form of Agreement Between Owner and Contractor.*

AIA Document A201, Sec. 9.4.1, states that the architect then has seven days to review the application and either certify it and send it to the owner for payment, or reject it and provide the reasons for the rejection to the contractor in writing.

The answer is 10 days.

535. Tolerance is the amount that an element of a building is permitted to be "off" from the specified dimension. Acceptable tolerances for building materials are dependent on their level of quality, their physical properties, the stage in the construction process during which they are to be installed, and the way the materials will be used. Two adjacent, different materials can both be within their acceptable tolerances and not align exactly. For these reasons, it is important the architect's drawings allow for some "play," or dimensional adjustment, and that tolerances specified by the architect agree with cited industry standards for that specific material. Architects should be aware that requiring exceptionally high levels of precision and low tolerances can cause construction costs to escalate; however, if such accuracy is critical to the project, these requirements must be specified.

Wood paneling has the most restrictive tolerances, as even small deviations from the prescribed dimensions are noticeable.

The answer is (D).

536. Force majeure means "greater force" and is used to describe situations where damages or delays are caused by forces beyond the control of either party to a contract. American Institute of Architects (AIA) Document A201, *General Conditions of the Contract for Construction*, Sec. 8.3, allows the contractor to request an extension of the contract time due to "unavoidable casualties or other causes beyond the Contractor's control." The contractor must initiate any claims within 21 days of the event per AIA Document A201, Sec. 15.1.2. The contract may then be modified by a change order or construction change directive issued by the architect.

Examples of acts that may excuse performance under a force majeure clause are natural disasters, acts of war, terrorist attacks, and labor disputes such as union strikes.

The answer is (C).

537. It is the contractor's responsibility to notify the surety of any change orders issued during a project so that the amount of insurance coverage may be increased or decreased as necessary.

A clerk of the works is a representative hired by the owner to monitor progress on site and keep project records. The architect's project representative is an employee of the architect who is on site whenever construction is under way. This full-time representation is an additional service and is contracted separately using American Institute of Architects (AIA) Document B352, *Duties, Responsibilities and Limitations of Authority of the Architect's Project Representative.*

If a contractor discovers an error on the drawings or in the specifications, it is the architect's responsibility to correct the error in the documents at no cost; however, the architect is not responsible for the cost of construction to correct the error unless it can be proven that the architect was negligent.

According to AIA Document A201, *General Conditions of the Contract for Construction*, Sec. 7.3, Construction Change Directives, only the owner and architect's signatures are required on a construction change directive for it to be valid.

The answer is (D).

538. In certifying applications for payment, it is the architect's responsibility to protect the interests of the owner. The architect should do whatever is necessary to determine that the materials are in the possession of the contractor and are being stored properly before consenting to payment for the windows. In most cases, requesting a copy of the bill of sale and verifying that the items are indeed in the contractor's possession and are being stored appropriately will be adequate documentation to certify the pay application.

When an owner is willing to pay for materials stored off site, the situation should be addressed in the supplementary conditions, which should define where the materials are to be stored, what type of insurance is required, and how the materials will be transported to the site. Each time the contractor submits a pay application that includes a request for payment for stored materials, he or she should also submit supporting documentation, such as a bill of sale and evidence of insurance coverage. If the supporting documents are not submitted with the application for payment, the architect may request them from the contractor. The architect should also visit the site where the materials are being stored to verify that they are at the specified location; that the contractor is adhering to the security precautions defined in the supplementary conditions; and that the materials are being stored in an environment that complies with the specification requirements for weather protection, temperature, the surface on which they are stored, and other factors that preserve the integrity of the product until it is delivered to the job site.

If there is any question or concern about the appropriateness of the documents or the provisions for protecting the owner's interest in the materials, those concerns should be referred to the owner's attorney for evaluation. In a situation such as this, the architect may also wish to obtain written approval from the owner prior to certifying the application for payment.

The answer is (A), (B), (E), and (F).

539. The owner is responsible for paying for uncovering and rebuilding the wall. Presumably, the architect requested that the drywall be removed because there was a

Construction & Evaluation

reason to suspect that the construction was in error and the architect was protecting the owner's interests.

If the blocking had been in the wrong location, the contractor would be responsible for the cost of uncovering and repairing the work.

The answer is (B).

540. The 2007 revisions to AIA Document A201, introduced the role of the initial decision maker (IDM). The IDM is a third party, named in the agreement, who will serve as the first reviewer in the event of a project dispute. The agreement requires that the opinion of the IDM be solicited before proceeding with mediation or arbitration. If a third-party IDM is not named in the agreement, then by default the architect will fulfill the responsibilities of this role.

There are a few exceptional circumstances which do not require a decision by the IDM.

- *hazardous materials.* If hazardous materials (other than those addressed in the contract documents) are discovered on a job site, the contractor has the authority to stop work without consulting the IDM. The owner must pay for testing to verify the presence of these materials, and the contract time or amount must be adjusted to account for the project shutdown as outlined in AIA Document 201, Sec. 10.3.
- *emergencies.* If a situation arises that puts personnel or property in danger, the contractor may take whatever action is necessary to prevent damage, without prior authorization. This situation is discussed in Sec. 10.4.
- *losses covered by insurance.* Section 11.3.9 and Sec. 11.3.10 explain the procedures to be followed in the case of insured losses. Claims related to insured losses do not require preliminary review by the IDM. Claims for additional compensation due to a conflict in the construction documents, requests for additional time due to adverse weather conditions, and termination of the contract for cause are all issues that would be referred to the IDM.

The answer is (B), (C), and (F).

541. The architect is responsible for reviewing and certifying certificates for payment as defined in Sec. 9.4 of American Institute of Architects (AIA) Document A201, *General Conditions of the Contract for Construction.* On receiving an application for payment from the contractor, the architect has seven days to review the work performed and determine whether progress is as stated by the contractor and whether the level of quality of the work matches that defined by the contract documents. If both attributes are present, the architect will issue a certificate for payment to the owner for the amount requested by the contractor. If either is not present, the architect has the option of rejecting the application or certifying a lesser amount.

The answer is (C).

542. According to AIA Document A701, no substitutions can be considered unless a written request for such approval has been received by the architect at least 10 days prior to the date for receipt of bids.

If the substitutions are approved, the architect must issue an addendum providing this information to all bidders no later than four days prior to the date for receipt of bids.

The answer is 10 days.

543. Change orders and construction change directives modify the original contract documents after the contract is awarded. An alternate listing is simply the list of alternates that the contractor must include in the bid. Addenda are used to make changes to the contract documents after they are issued for bidding but before the contract is awarded.

The answer is (B).

544. AIA Document A701 requires that bids be deposited at the designated location prior to the time and date indicated for receipt. Bids submitted after the deadline are ineligible for consideration and should be returned to the bidder unopened.

The answer is (A).

545. The procedure a contractor must follow to propose a substitution during bidding is defined in the instructions to bidders. After the contract is awarded, if the contractor wishes to propose a substitution, he or she must consult the instructions in the general requirements of the specifications. (These instructions, in Division 01, are sometimes referred to as front-end documents.) The advertisement to bid simply states that bidding is being accepted for a particular project and gives information about how to view the project documents and submit a bid.

The answer is (C).

546. When the owner wants to make sure some amount of money is included in the bid before the exact amount of the item is known, the architect should use an allowance. For example, the contractor may be asked to include a $10,000 allowance on a residential project for kitchen appliances. This gives the architect and owner the opportunity to choose the appliances at a later date. If the cost of the selected appliances exceeds the allowance, the contractor is owed the difference.

Alternates are used to require the contractor to provide a price for a defined scope of work that varies from the base bid scope of work. Alternates can be either "add" or "deduct," depending on the change to the contract amount.

The owner may require the contractor to present a material bond. This bond ensures that subcontractors or suppliers will be paid by the surety if the contractor fails to compensate them, and it helps protect the owner from liens.

A unit price is a way to obtain a price commitment from a contractor on a portion of work before the total quantity of the work is known.

The answer is (A).

547. A work modification form or verbal instructions given by the architect are not acceptable ways to change the scope of the work. An addendum is used to make changes to the contract documents during the bidding period. According to AIA Document A201, Article 7, changes in the work can be made by change order, construction change directive, or order for a minor change in the work without invalidating the contract, subject to limitations in the article and elsewhere in the contract documents.

The answer is (B), (C), and (D).

548. According to AIA Document A201, Sec. 4.2.6, the architect has the authority to reject work that does not conform to the contract documents.

The answer is (A).

549. Under the provisions of Sec. 15.2 of AIA Document A201, when reviewing a claim, the IDM must take one or more of the following actions: 1) approve the claim, 2) reject the claim, 3) suggest a compromise, 4) request additional supporting data from the claimant or a response with supporting data from the other party, or 5) advise the parties that the IDM is unable to resolve the claim due to a lack of sufficient information to evaluate the merits of the claim or because the IDM concludes that it will be inappropriate for the IDM to resolve the claim.

The role of the IDM is new to the 2007 AIA documents. However, if the agreement does not specify otherwise, these responsibilities are the architect's by default.

The answer is (A), (B), (E), and (F).

550. AIA Document A201, Sec. 13.5.3, requires the contractor to be responsible for all costs made necessary by failures, including costs of repeated tests.

The answer is (B).

551. The architect is not responsible for safety at the site; for the means, methods, or techniques of construction; or for verifying quantities of materials. American Institute of Architects (AIA) Document B101, *Standard Form of Agreement Between Owner and Architect*, and Document A201, *General Conditions of the Contract for Construction*, state the reasons the architect visits the site and his or her responsibilities regarding applications for payment. When reviewing pay applications, the architect is responsible for determining whether work completed complies with the requirements of the contract documents. He or she should be generally familiar with the progress of the work and communicate this to the owner. The goal of the architect's involvement and review should be to endeavor to guard the owner against defects in the work.

The answer is (B), (C), (D), and (F).

552. According to American Institute of Architects (AIA) Document A201, *General Conditions of the Contract for Construction*, the architect's communications by and with subcontractors and materials suppliers shall be through the contractor. The architect should inform the contractor of the improper installation, and the contractor is responsible for coordinating the repair with the subcontractor.

The answer is (C).

553. The architect can nullify a previous certificate to protect the owner.

AIA Document A201, Sec. 9.5.1, allows the architect to withhold the whole amount or a partial amount. If payment is to be withheld, the architect must notify the owner and contractor. The architect and contractor do not necessarily have to agree on the amount, although they should attempt to arrive at a mutually agreeable sum that accurately represents the amount of work completed.

The answer is (D).

554. AIA Document A201, Sec. 9.10.2, requires various documents be submitted to the architect prior to the final payment. The architect then forwards these documents to the owner while keeping a copy for the project records.

The answer is (A).

555. American Institute of Architects (AIA) Document A201, *General Conditions of the Contract for Construction*, Sec. 2.2.1, states that the owner is obligated to furnish the contractor with reasonable evidence that financial arrangements have been made to fulfill his or her obligations under the contract.

AIA Document A201, Sec. 2.3 and Sec. 2.4, authorizes the owner to stop work for deficiencies in performance or safety violations or carry on the work with the owner's own forces to correct portions of the project where the contractor's performance is unsatisfactory and deduct the costs of the corrections from the contract sum. The architect is not given the authority to stop the work, but the architect should report situations warranting such action to the owner.

The answer is (B).

556. The first step is to officially notify the contractor that the work is incorrect. The architect must do this in writing. The incorrect work should be rejected, and the contractor should be told to promptly correct it in accordance with the contract. If the contractor does not correct the work, the owner may correct the work with his or her own forces or terminate the original construction contract.

Stopping the work always has a detrimental effect on the entire project, and it does not provide for the normal notice to the contractor of nonconforming work. Quick termination of the contract without trying other remedies is not in accordance with the contract.

The contractor should always be notified in writing of any problems with the work and asked to correct the situation. The owner does have the option of accepting nonconforming work, but this is often not the best course of action because it can lead to disagreement about what amount should be deducted from the contract sum for acceptance of the nonconforming work.

The answer is (D).

557. Substantial completion is the point at which the owner can make use of the work for its intended purpose, and the requirements of the contract documents have been fulfilled. This is a critical point in construction because it marks the date that the building owner assumes the warranty on equipment. It is possible for a project to be deemed substantially complete even if punch list items remain incomplete.

The answer is (A).

558. When the contractor considers the work to be substantially complete, he or she is responsible for compiling the "punch list," the list of work to be completed or corrected. The contractor must notify the architect when the project is ready for the punch list inspection. During this inspection, the architect verifies that the project has been completed according to the contract documents and makes note of any items that still must be corrected. The architect then prepares the certificate of substantial completion, which sets the deadline for correction of the punch list items and governs the transfer of responsibility from the contractor to the owner for items such as utilities, maintenance, and security, among others.

The contractor notifies the architect when the project is ready for a second, final inspection. If this inspection is acceptable, the architect prepares and issues the final certificate for payment.

The final payment and retainage is not due to the contractor until he or she fulfills the obligations of American Institute of Architects (AIA) Document A201, *General Conditions of the Contract for Construction*, Sec. 9.10.2, which include receipt of the consent of surety. When this and the other necessary documents have been received, the contractor can receive the final payment due.

The answer is (B).

559. Product data, samples, and shop drawings may all be provided by the contractor for the architect's review. This documentation is known as a submittal and can be reviewed at the architect's office. The architect then distributes copies of the paperwork to the project participants.

A mock-up is a full-sized sample of a portion of the construction, commonly built on the job site. It can be either separate from the building or, if approved, can be integrated into the building. A mock-up is called for in individual sections of the specifications for items that will be repeated throughout the project, innovative construction techniques, and other instances where it is useful to see the "finished product" before it is truly finished. Mock-ups can be very expensive, so they should only be specified where necessary. They become more cost effective if the approved mock-up can then be integrated into the building.

The answer is (A).

560. The *ADA Accessibility Guidelines* is a federal law passed in 1990 that prohibits discrimination against individuals with disabilities. The law is divided into five sections, or titles.

- Title I—Employment
- Title II—Public Services, including public transportation and state and local government activities and facilities
- Title III—Public Accommodations, including all public facilities such as restaurants, retail stores, hotels, commercial facilities, privately owned transportation systems, and some places that offer examinations or courses (private clubs and places of worship are excluded)
- Title IV—Telecommunications
- Title V—Miscellaneous

Title II and Title III require that all new construction and modifications to existing buildings be accessible to people with disabilities. Public entities may choose to use either the Uniform Federal Accessibility Standards (UFAS) or the *ADA/ABA Guidelines* to achieve this goal.

The answer is (B) and (C).

561. AIA Document B101, Article 4, addresses additional services that the architect will provide only if specifically designated or approved in advance by the owner. Commissioning is one of these services, among others, such as programming, geotechnical services, existing facilities surveys, site analysis, landscape design, interior design, detailed cost estimating, on-site project representation, record drawings, and post-contract evaluation beyond one meeting with the owner to review the facility's performance, within one year of substantial completion.

The answer is (A), (B), (D), and (E).

562. In the traditional design-bid-build process, the architect completes a set of documents to define the scope of the work, and these documents are released to contractors for competitive bidding. In a fast-tracked project, the design documents are developed as construction proceeds and are not final until the project is completed.

Construction sequencing and management of the work are the responsibility of the construction manager or a representative of the general contracting firm. Fast-tracking requires cooperation and coordination among all parties from the start. For this reason, the decision to fast-track must be made at the beginning of the project.

In a "fast-tracked" project, the owner, construction manager, contractor, and designer collaborate so that portions of the design and construction phases can occur at the same time. A fast-tracked schedule can reduce the time of a project from 10% to 30% because it eliminates the bid phase and allows materials with long lead times to be purchased before the building design is completed.

The answer is (B).

563. During a bid opening, the architect or a designated representative will open the bids, read them aloud, and record in a bid log the base bid amounts, bids for proposed alternates, confirmation of receipt of addenda, and whether required supporting documentation (such as a bid bond) is included with the bid. The architect should not announce the apparent low bidder at the bid opening.

The owner should evaluate the bids and make a decision about the award within a reasonable amount of time. The architect may then notify all of the bidders of the owner's decision. The delay allows time for the owner to complete evaluation of the bids and also provides an opportunity for a contractor to retract a bid in the event that a mathematical error is discovered after submission.

The answer is (B).

564. The low bidder is determined by the base bid plus any accepted bid alternates.

For ABC Construction,

$$\$244{,}150 + \$22{,}465 - \$6725 = \$259{,}890$$

For Sunny Day, Inc.,

$$\$265{,}430 + \$15{,}846 - \$5000 = \$276{,}276$$

For Grover and Sons,

$$\$270{,}000 + \$14{,}000 - \$2000 = \$282{,}000$$

For B&E General Contractors,

$$\$246{,}765 + \$18{,}768 - \$7500 = \$258{,}033$$

B&E General Contractors is the low bidder.

The answer is (D).

565. An architect's interpretations of the contract documents are performed in a *quasi-judicial* capacity. American Institute of Architects (AIA) Document A201, *General Conditions of the Contract for Construction*, Sec. 4.2.12, states,

> Interpretations and decisions of the Architect will be consistent with the intent of, and reasonably inferable from, the Contract Documents... When making such interpretations and decisions, the Architect will endeavor to secure faithful performance by both Owner and Contractor, will not show partiality to either, and will not be liable for results of interpretations or decisions rendered in good faith.

The answer is (B).

566. American Institute of Architects (AIA) Document A201, *General Conditions of the Contract for Construction*, Sec. 10.2, charges the contractor with responsibility for safety precautions and programs. Though the architect should bring obviously unsafe conditions to the contractor's attention, it is the contractor's responsibility to resolve those conditions.

Despite the best preventative measures, however, accidents can occur on construction sites, and it is important to obtain assistance for injured persons as quickly as possible. The architect should first activate the emergency medical services system by calling 911 and reporting the accident, or by asking another witness to do so. In the event of an emergency, the architect should do whatever is possible to safeguard human life.

The superintendent should be notified as soon as possible of the accident. AIA Document A201, Sec. 10.4, gives the contractor the authority to act to prevent threatened damage, injury, or loss of life.

When the emergency situation has been resolved, the architect should fully document the incident, noting the name of the worker and any available information about his or her condition, the names of any other witnesses, the time and location of the incident, conditions observed at the site, and any other pertinent information. If a camera is available, the architect should also take pictures. This is not an investigation; it is simply documenting what the architect witnessed.

The answer is (A).

567. "The architect certifies to the owner that, to the best of the architect's knowledge, information, and belief, the work has progressed to the point indicated, the quality of the work is in accordance with the contract documents, and the contractor is entitled to payment in the amount certified" is excerpted from American Institute of Architects (AIA) Document G702, *Application and Certification for Payment.* The architect is stating to the owner that, in the architect's professional opinion and based upon the information available, the contractor has completed the percentage of work listed on the pay application and is due a payment in the amount specified.

An architect cannot and should not certify anything that is outside of his or her direct knowledge or control. For example, the architect does not know how much the contractor has spent and cannot assure that the contract documents or contractor's work are in full compliance with the codes because the codes are constantly changing and are sometimes at variance with each other. By signing such a statement, the architect is making an express warranty or guarantee (which are the same thing in the eyes of the law). An action such as this raises the standard of reasonable care required of the architect. The standard of care means that an architect is required to do what a reasonably prudent architect would do in the same community in the same time frame, given the same or similar facts and circumstances. While the law protects professionals who act reasonably and prudently and who use their best professional judgment, when a professional makes a guarantee or oversteps his boundaries, he may be held liable or negligent for his actions.

Clauses in the certification such as "to the best of the architect's knowledge, information, and belief," "based on the architect's observations and other information available to the architect," or "in the architect's professional opinion" help to qualify the statements and present them as accurate representations of the architect's perception of the situation, rather than a representation of the facts. Still, the architect should not certify information of which the architect does not have direct knowledge, for it puts the burden of responsibility for the accuracy of that information on the architect.

The answer is (B).

568. AIA Document A701 states that bids shall be submitted on the forms included with the bidding documents. These may be tailored to the project by including a listing of alternates and unit prices, and by asking for acknowledgment of any addenda issued during the bid phase.

The answer is (C).

569. A local code official would be authorized to enforce all of the codes or standards listed except the *Americans with Disabilities Act* (ADA). The ADA is civil rights legislation that gives building users the right to sue the owner of a building if they are denied access to a facility because the building is not accessible. The other three options are model codes or standards that, when adopted by a community government, become the building code. Depending on the jurisdiction, the code official could enforce ICC/ANSI A117.1 or the *ADA/ABA Guidelines,* either of which can be adopted to define the standards for accessibility.

The answer is (A).

570. Although it is commonly believed that the specifications take precedence when there is a conflict between drawings and specs, American Institute of Architects (AIA) Document A201, *General Conditions of the Contract for Construction,* clearly states that this is not the case. No order of precedence governs the interpretation of the contract documents; rather, they "are complementary, and what is required by one shall be as binding as if required by all." AIA Document A201 Sec. 1.2.1 goes on to state that the contractor is required to provide what is "reasonably inferable" from the contract documents.

If a conflict arises between two parts of the contract documents, the contractor should bring it to the architect's attention and ask for an interpretation. AIA Document A201, Sec. 4.2.11, gives the architect the responsibility to "interpret and decide matters concerning performance under, and requirements of, the Contract Documents on written request of either the Owner or Contractor." An interpretation of the contract documents that does not change the contract sum or contract time would be considered a minor modification to the work and would be within the architect's authority.

The answer is (D).

571. Formwork should be constructed first, and then a release agent such as oil is applied to make it easier to remove the forms from the cured concrete. It is important to apply the release agent before placing the reinforcing steel, because if oil is on the surface of the rebar it could prevent the concrete from adhering properly to the steel. Next, the reinforcing bars are placed and tied. When the concrete arrives on site, slump testing is performed to ensure that the mix complies with specified limits for workability and water content. If the results of the slump test are within acceptable limits, the concrete may be poured and vibrated to fill the forms.

The answer is (C).

572. Architect's supplemental instructions (ASIs) allow the architect to clarify information in the construction documents or make minor changes to the work, provided that those changes do not affect the contract sum or time. This authority is provided by American Institute of Architects (AIA) Document A201, *General Conditions of the Contract for Construction*, Sec. 7.4. Change orders modify the contract between the owner and the contractor and are used in situations where a change to the project time or cost is necessary.

The answer is (A).

573. There are two different issues related to the contractor's post-final-completion responsibilities to the owner addressed in American Institute of Architects (AIA) Document A201, *General Conditions of the Contract for Construction*. The first is the warranty period established in AIA Document A201, Sec. 3.5. This section of the general conditions requires the contractor to warrant that the "work will conform to the requirements of the contract documents and will be free from defects, except for those inherent in the quality of the work the contract documents require or permit." This warranty begins on the substantial completion date and continues through the period of the applicable statute of limitations or repose, whichever is shorter. The length of this period varies from state to state and can be anywhere from 2 to 12 years.

The second obligation the contractor has to the owner is the one-year correction period outlined in AIA Document A201, Sec. 12.2.2. The correction period and the warranty period run concurrently. Within the first year after substantial completion, the contractor must correct any work found not to be in accordance with the contract documents at no cost to the owner.

In this situation, the work is in compliance with the contract documents. The first question that should be investigated is whether a separate warranty was required for the roofing materials. Warranty requirements for individual materials or assemblies should be outlined in the product specifications. If the material failed within its warranty period, the roofing manufacturer may be responsible for the repair. However, if it is found that the architect incorrectly specified a product not suited for the environmental conditions at the site or for this particular application, the architect may be held responsible for the cost of the repair.

The answer is (D).

574. The contractor is required by American Institute of Architects (AIA) Document A201, *General Conditions of the Contract for Construction*, Sec. 9.8.2, to prepare a punch list when the contractor believes that the work is substantially complete. A punch list is a written summary of items that need to be repaired or corrected before final payment. Substantial completion is the point at which the project is complete enough for the owner to use it for its intended purpose. This is a critical point in the course of construction because it marks the date upon which the owner takes responsibility for insurance and utilities, and warranty periods for equipment begin.

The punch list is submitted to the architect, who is then responsible for completing an inspection of the project to determine whether the contractor's assessment is correct and the project is substantially complete. This is a more in-depth look at the project than the architect's earlier observations. The architect must verify that the contractor has complied with the requirements of the contract documents, and to do this, the architect may request assistance from consultants to verify the portions of the work that they designed.

If the architect agrees that substantial completion has been attained, a certificate of substantial completion is issued, which allows the owner to occupy and use the project and assume the responsibilities mentioned previously. The contractor then has a specified period of time to remedy items on the punch list before the architect returns for a final completion inspection.

The answer is (B).

575. A mechanic's lien gives a contractor, subcontractor, or material supplier the right to place a claim against an owner's property if proper payment for materials or services has not been provided. (In some states, an architect can also file a lien if the firm has not been paid for professional services rendered.) A lien encumbers the title to a property and can force an owner to sell it to pay the company providing materials or services. The claim is relevant only to the project, not the owner's other assets.

Liens are not permitted on publicly owned projects; bonds are used instead. A contractor is required to submit evidence that the work is free of liens before receiving payments per American Institute of Architects (AIA) Document A201, *General Conditions of the Contract for Construction*, Sec. 9.3.3, and Sec. 9.10.2. The contractor may also be required to submit AIA Document G706, *Contractor's Affidavit of Payment of Debts and Claims*, and/or AIA Document G706A, *Contractor's Affidavit of Release of Liens*, to ensure that the owner will have clear title to the property upon final payment.

The answer is (D).

576. An allowance is the amount that an architect estimates an item will cost when the cost of the material cannot be precisely determined at the time of bidding. This estimated cost is stated in the specifications, and each contractor bidding on the project is required to include the same amount for this line item. The allowance allows some choices about specific elements of the project to be deferred until the construction phase. The allowance also provides a set amount of money that is included in the contract amount that is available to pay for that item.

A unit price is a set cost per unit of work that is established in the bid. Unit prices are most often used when the exact quantity of work is undetermined, but the work itself can be clearly defined through drawings and specifications. For example, the bid form may request a price per linear foot for concrete piles. If the actual subsurface conditions vary from those anticipated and the piles have to be shorter or longer, the unit price amount can be used to adjust the contract sum appropriately. The anticipated quantity is included in the base bid; if the actual quantity is greater than or less than the anticipated amount, the contract price can be adjusted based on the unit cost proposed in the bid. This helps protect the owner from an artificially inflated change order proposal after the contract has been awarded, and it protects the contractor from underbidding based on unanticipated increases in unit quantities.

Value engineering is a process used to analyze the project's goals, proposed solutions, and budget to determine whether changes to the design might result in more value—or return on investment—to the project while complying with the original budget. Value engineering may be undertaken at any stage of design or construction but the earlier in the project that value engineering analysis is conducted, the greater the potential savings.

Alternates are requests in the bidding documents for the contractor to supply a price for some variation to an element in the base bid. Alternates usually modify the quality of a material or the amount of work to be provided. For example, the base bid may include a type of specialty brick, whereas the bid alternate may include a standard brick that is less expensive but still acceptable. Alternates can also be used to delete or add elements. When the bids are evaluated, the owner can review the costs of the alternates and adjust the scope of the work as necessary to fit the budget by accepting or declining the proposed changes. Alternates are classified as additive (or "add") or deductive (or "deduct"), depending on the anticipated impact on the item's price.

The answer is (B).

577. Building commissioning is the process of verifying that building systems and equipment are designed, installed, tested, and capable of being operated and maintained according to the owner's operational needs. Commissioning services can be provided by the same firm that originally designed the building systems being evaluated, provided that this fact is disclosed to the owner. (If commissioning services are being contracted in order to meet requirements for Leadership in Energy and Environmental Design (LEED) certification, the size of the project determines whether the commissioning agent may be a member of the design team.) The *Architect's Handbook of Professional Practice* estimates that professional fees for these services can vary from 0.5–6% of total construction costs, with fees increasing proportionately to the complexity of the systems within the building and the extent of the commissioning activities. AIA Document B101, Article 4, categorizes and addresses commissioning as an additional service (i.e., it is not required).

Building commissioning is a key part of designing and constructing high-performance buildings because it offers the owner reassurance that the additional time and money spent on controls, sensors, and equipment will be paid back over time through energy-efficient building operation.

Commissioning plans should be established during the pre-design phase, and commissioning activities will continue throughout the design, construction, and operations phases. Commissioning is required for buildings seeking LEED certification, and this program sets its own requirements for these services.

The answer is (A), (B), and (D).

578. The owner may choose to delete the furniture work from the construction contract and hire the furniture vendor independently; however, if this happens, the owner will take on the responsibility for coordinating the furniture dealer's work with the general contractor's work, including connections to power and data services and the installation of ceilings, floor finishes, and other building elements.

The owner may make changes to the work according to the terms of AIA Document A201, Sec. 7. The owner has the right to adjust the contractor's contract through change orders. In this case, it will be possible to delete the new cubicles from the contract and replace them with the reconditioned items. The savings of reconditioned versus new furniture, however, may not be as great as promised by the dealer if making this change requires the redesign of the electrical system or additional architectural design efforts to make the new furniture system functional. The architect should consider whether or not this change necessitates an adjustment to the architect-owner agreement as well, since the architect is entitled to compensation for the additional design efforts associated with the owner's change. All costs should be considered by the owner before committing to the change.

The answer is (B), (C), and (F).

579. Before rejecting the submittal, accepting the features as described, or redesigning the chase, it is prudent to research the claim made by the contractor. The toilets are specified in documents prepared by the plumbing engineer, so it is appropriate for the architect to request that this consultant evaluate the space needed for the carrier and determine whether or not the contractor's claim is accurate. The other options should be considered only after this research is completed.

The answer is (B).

580. The certificate of occupancy is provided by a code official, and its issuance is not related to the determination of substantial completion.

The certificate of substantial completion includes the establishment of a prescribed schedule for closeout activities, which determines the timing for the completion of the work. The contractor must complete all of the work required by the contract and participate in the closeout activities, which include the architect's inspection of the work, the contractor's completion of the items on the punch list, submission of documents as required in the contract, and the determination of final completion.

At final completion, the owner makes the final payment to the contractor, including the withheld retainage.

Substantial completion is the date upon which the work has reached a level of completion that allows the owner to occupy the building or a portion of the building and use it for its intended purpose. The substantial completion date is also the date on which the warranty period begins, and it marks the end of the contractor's schedule for the project.

The answer is (B).

581. A project monitoring chart is an architectural project management tool that is used to predict both the time and the amount of money (or percentage of the overall project budget) needed to complete certain tasks. The actual time and money expended during the project can be compared periodically to the budgeted numbers in order to determine whether or not the project is on track.

A similar approach is earned value management, which may be used by a contractor to determine the percentage of project completion of each line item on the schedule of values. This information is then transferred to the contractor's periodic applications for payment.

The answer is (A).

582. The architect's signature on the certificate is not a warranty and does not represent that the architect has inspected the work. According to AIA Document A201, *General Conditions of the Contract for Construction*, once an application for payment has been submitted for review, the architect must visit the site and review the progress of the work within seven days.

AIA Document B101, *Standard Form of Agreement Between Owner and Architect*, defines a certificate for payment as a representation to the owner that "to the best of the architect's knowledge, information, and belief" the work has progressed to the point indicated and is in accordance with the contract requirements. Therefore, the corresponding funds may be released to the contractor.

It is important that the amount that the architect certifies on applications for payment accurately represents the progress of work completed to date. The difference between the percentages of completion indicated on the current application for payment and the percentages shown for each item on the previous submission indicate the work that has been accomplished during the payment period.

If the architect certifies percentages of completion greater than what is evidenced on site, the owner may be at risk because construction funds may be released too soon, and the contractor will be receiving payment for work and materials that have not been provided. If the architect certifies percentages of completion that are less than that completed on site, the contractor will not receive adequate compensation in a timely manner and may not be able to pay bills for materials and labor.

If the contractor is not provided appropriate and timely payment, the contractor may stop the work in accordance with the provisions in AIA Document A201, Sec. 9.7.

The answer is (D).

583. Fire resistance ratings for individual materials are determined through stringent and controlled laboratory testing. Interior and exterior wall assemblies are also tested in the lab to determine their fire resistance ratings. The conditions under which these tests must be performed are not easily replicated at a job site, so it is not practical or acceptable to determine fire resistance ratings through on-site testing of a mockup.

The terms of a product warranty are determined by the manufacturer based on the properties of the material; they are not dependent upon site conditions.

Construction of a mockup can be costly, but it may allow the owner to realize savings in the long term through early confirmation of the design. One of the most common reasons to construct a mockup is to allow the owner to see the individual components in one assembly and to establish appearance criteria. The sample can then be used as a reference throughout the construction process to gauge the quality of the work. On-site mockups are also useful for simulating proposed details, evaluating the connections between materials, and determining the appropriate sequencing of construction activities. The mockup can be used for a variety of tests, including determining the water and air resistance properties of the assembly. Some of the tests that may be conducted on a mockup are destructive, so the sequence in which tests are run must be carefully planned.

The answer is (A), (B), (D), and (F).

584. Construction change directives and change orders are used when a change to the project will modify the project time or cost. A construction change directive is issued when the owner and contractor cannot agree on the terms of the change, but the work must proceed to keep the project on schedule. When the owner and contractor come to an agreement on the terms, the construction change directive is replaced with a change order that modifies the contract.

This proposed change will not affect the project time or cost, so the architect should use AIA Document G710, *Architect's Supplemental Instructions*, to instruct the contractor to move the door opening.

The answer is (D).

585. Because each plastic laminate manufacturer offers a different selection of colors and patterns and because there often is no "equal" provided by another manufacturer, it is important that the contractor submit the specified product. The specified product should be provided unless the contractor has received approval to substitute a different product. The correct response is to mark the submittal "revise and resubmit" and request that the contractor provide additional information about the products that will be incorporated into the desk.

The answer is (C).

586. After a two-week absence from the office, the architect should check in with the contractor to find out how the job is progressing, but this conversation cannot be the only evaluation of the project's status.

The architect is legally and ethically required to see in person whether or not work has progressed sufficiently, even if others in the office may offer their observations.

AIA Document B101, *Standard Form of Agreement Between Owner and Architect*, specifies that the architect's review of the application for payment is not an inspection of the completed work or means and methods of construction, the architect is not required to review receipts or invoices from suppliers or subcontractors, and the architect is not required to determine how funds received by the contractor are being distributed to others.

According to AIA Document B101, Sec. 3.6.3, reviewing the schedule of values is a key part of the process of approving an application for payment. The schedule of values is a list of all of the elements of the project, prepared by the contractor at the beginning of construction. Each element is assigned a monetary value or cost. The sum of all of these values is the total cost of the work, which is due to the contractor upon completion of the contract requirements. The architect's responsibility is to evaluate the percentage of completion of each line item on the schedule of values that the contractor claims on each application for payment in comparison to the progress observed on site. The goal of this evaluation is to keep payments to the contractor on pace with the work completed so that the contractor is compensated in a fair and timely manner and so that the owner is protected from paying too much too quickly or paying for work that is unacceptable or incomplete. Before certifying an application for payment, the architect must be confident that work has progressed to the point indicated by the contractor and that the quality of the work is in accordance with the contract documents. Since the application for payment was received on the Friday before the architect returned to the office, the architect is obligated to make this site visit and complete the review and processing of the application for payment within seven days of receipt, or before Friday of that week.

The answer is (B).

587. Retainage is the percentage of the contract sum that is withheld from each payment throughout the course of the project to create a fund that protects the owner from a situation in which the contractor does not have sufficient funds to compensate creditors or subcontractors and cannot complete the work. The time at which it is released to the contractor depends on the arrangements agreed upon in the owner-contractor agreement, but it is usually held by the owner until the end of the project. The contractor may then request release of the retainage through the final application for payment.

The terms of retainage, however, are subject to negotiation as part of the contract discussions, and the contractor may negotiate an arrangement in which the percentage of retainage decreases as the project moves forward. Retainage affects the first subcontractors more than those who come to the site near the end of the project because they may not receive full compensation for their work until the project comes to an end, which could be months or even years after their responsibilities are complete.

The answer is (D).

588.

evaluation criteria	maximum score	general contractors A	B	C	D
1 project cost	25	25.0	19.5	22.3	24.5
2 targeted business and economic development	0	CATEGORY DISCARDED			
3 safety policies and record	5	4.9	3.0	4.0	3.9
4 project schedule	0	CATEGORY DISCARDED			
5 project approach and work plan	20	15.5	11.9	13.7	14.0
6 respondent's team qualifications	25	21.6	14.9	18.3	24.5
final RFP score	75	67.0	49.3	58.3	66.9

A best-value procurement approach is used when the final award is not based on the lowest possible bid. According to the spreadsheet, Contractor A has the highest score, at 67 out of 75, and would be awarded the project.

The answer is (A).

589. In the Observations section of the Architect's Field Report, the architect has noted that the stair treads and riser work are complete, but the handrails and cables have not yet been installed. The field report mentions the elevator contractor in relation to planned work, but it does not state that the contractor was on site fixing the control panel at the time of the visit. The condensate drain lines had already been installed at the time of the visit.

The field report states that the crane was on site moving HVAC and elevator equipment to the roof from the ground near the south side of the structure at the time of the visit); that the superintendent must coordinate with the code official regarding the geometry and installation of the handrail transition; and that the cables at the stair guardrail are to be installed after the stair is painted and at the end of the project).

The answer is (C), (E) and (F).

590. The door from the corridor to Proctology 339 and the door to Linen 323 both have adequate clearance on both sides and can remain as they are. The door at the stair complies with the minimum width requirements and correctly swings in the direction of egress travel.

There is not enough clearance on the swing side of the door to Gynecology 340. The bathroom doors appear to be too small, there is not enough clearance on the swing side of the doors. Adequate clearances are likely not provided at the fixtures, assuming that the fixtures are installed so that water and sewer service is provided from the plumbing chase between the rooms. If room 369A is used as a dressing room, a 5 ft turning radius must be provided inside the room and a 36 in wide door is required.

The answer is (A), (B), and (D).

591. The project is scheduled to be substantially complete on March 27 according to the Project Closeout section of the schedule. The task with the longest duration is fabrication of the elevator equipment. Seven critical path items are indicated. The Notice to Proceed is scheduled for October 17. Final Completion is scheduled for April 10. The project description states that the project does not take place in leap years, and the contractor will work five days per week. Although there are 175 days between these dates, the project description states that activity durations are to be expressed in the number of business days, rather than the number of calendar days. The total project duration is 125 days based on these constraints.

Demolition of the penthouse and machine room is scheduled to begin January 6. The painting of the walls and doors is scheduled to be complete before the elevator flooring is installed.

The answer is (B) and (D).

592. The elevator installation is scheduled to start February 2 and finish March 27. The case study narrative states that the project does not take place in leap years, and the contractor will work five days per week. Activity durations are to be expressed in the number of business days, rather than the number of calendar days. The duration of the task is 37 business days.

The answer is (B).

593. The certificate of substantial completion establishes the responsibilities of each of the parties during the period between substantial completion and final completion. The table shown summarizes each party's responsibilities.

task or item	responsibility owner	contractor	architect
insurance coverage for the work		X	
repair of damages to the work in corridor areas caused by building occupants		X	
verification of completion of the items on the punch list			X
issue of final certificate for payment			X
building security	X		
heat and utilities	X		

The certificate for this project, included in Resource 6.6, assigns responsibility for insurance coverage and the repair of damages in the corridor areas caused by building occupants to the contractor. A list of items that must be completed by the contractor during this period is attached to the certificate. The punch list is prepared by the contractor and verified by the architect, and one of the items included on the list for this project is the submission of the operations and maintenance manuals.

American Institute of Architects (AIA) Document A201, *General Conditions of the Contract for Construction*, requires the architect to perform a final inspection to verify that all work has been performed in accordance with the contract requirements. Per AIA Document A201, Sec. 9.10.1, the architect must issue the final certificate for payment.

The owner is responsible for providing building security, heat, and utilities according to the certificate of substantial completion. In addition, the owner must release withheld retainage on completed work to the contractor according to the AIA Document A201, Sec. 9.8.5. The retainage amount can be adjusted for incomplete items.

The answer is (E) and (F).

594. According to the architect's code analysis described in the Case Study 1 project narrative, the walls that require a 2-hour fire rating are those that form the enclosure for the stairs and/or the elevator machine room.

595. A proposal request is solicited from the contractor if the information provided by the architect to clarify the issue results in a change to the contract time or cost. In this case, the architect must generate the drawings and specifications necessary to describe the work and then prepare a proposal request. A construction change directive is issued when the owner and contractor cannot agree on a price for the work, but it must proceed in order to keep the project on schedule. The terms of the agreement will be settled after the work has begun and a change order will be executed when there is an agreement. A change order will be issued only after the contractor's proposal for additional work or significant modifications to the work defined in the original contract has been accepted. Architect's supplemental instructions are the appropriate way for the architect to provide clarification to the contractor. If the contractor believes that the instructions received from the architect will result in a change to the project time or cost, a modification to the contract may be pursued through the change order process.

The answer is (B).

596. The contract is prepared using American Institute of Architects (AIA) Document A101, *Standard Form of Agreement Between Owner and Contractor.* Sec. 1.1.2, which states that the documents listed in the agreement, in aggregate, represent the entire agreement between the parties. The terms of any previous negotiation or agreements between the owner and contractor that are not specifically incorporated into the final contract are not part of the contract documents, so the original proposal prepared by Bluecurve Construction Services is not part of the contract. Option (B) is incorrect.

The owner-architect agreement is separate from the agreement between the owner and contractor. The architect and contractor have no contractual relationship.

AIA Document A201, *General Conditions of the Contract for Construction*, Sec. 1.1.1, defines the contract documents as the agreement itself (in this case, AIA Document A101); AIA Document A201; supplementary conditions; drawings; specifications; addenda issued during the bidding period; and modifications to the contract issued throughout the project, including change orders, construction change directives, or minor changes to the work documented in the architect's supplemental instructions.

The answer is (C), (D), (E), and (F).

Construction & Evaluation

Illustration for Sol. 594

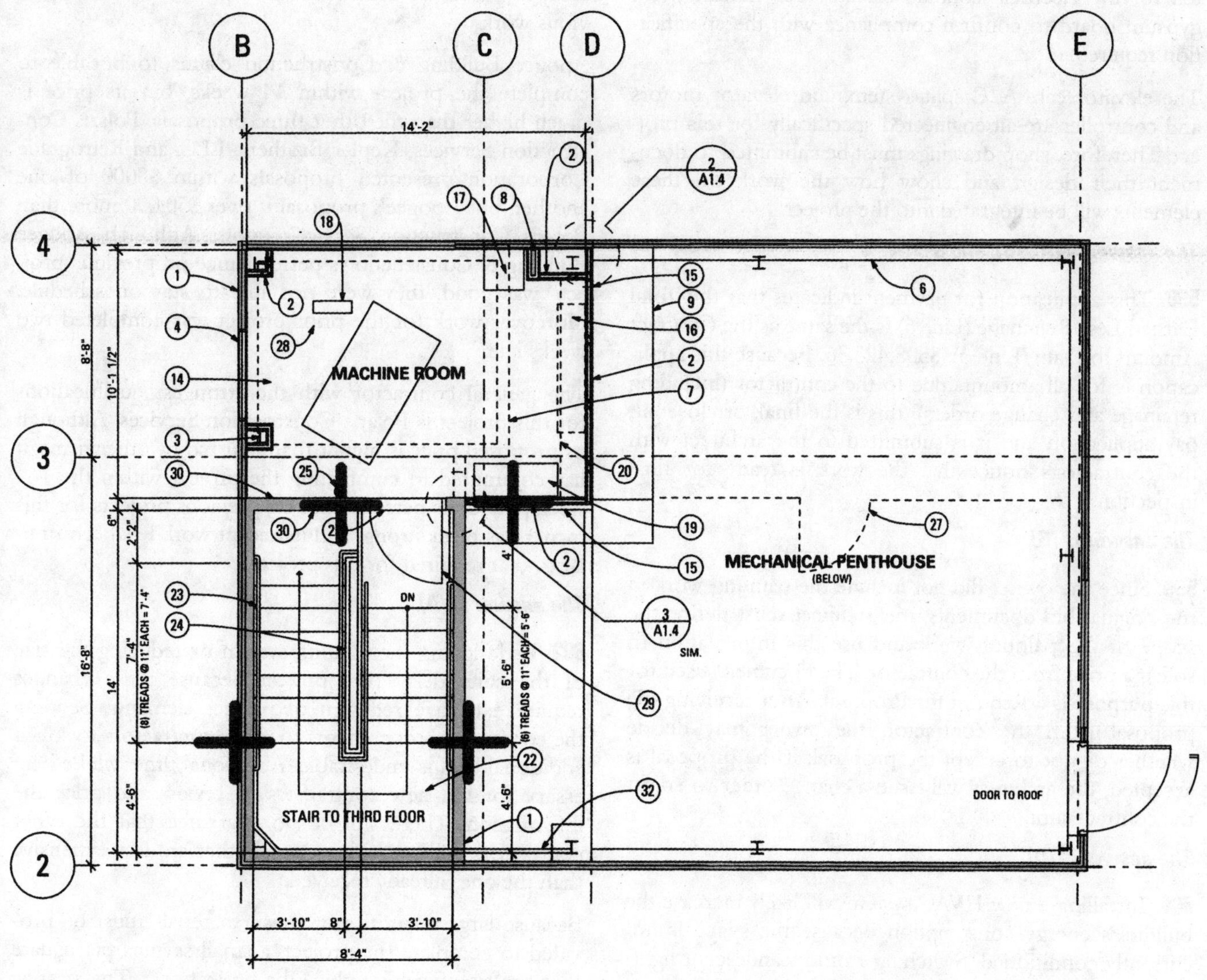

GENERAL NOTES:

1. FIELD VERIFY ALL CONDITIONS AND DIMENSIONS PRIOR TO CONSTRUCTION AND IMMEDIATELY NOTIFY THE ARCHITECT IF DISCREPANCIES ARE FOUND BETWEEN PLANS AND ACTUAL CONDITIONS.

2. ELEVATOR MACHINE ROOM, ELEVATOR SHAFT AND STAIRS ARE ENCLOSED BY A 2 HOUR FIRE RATED WALL.

3. THE MECHANICAL PENTHOUSE IS ONLY ACCESSED FROM THE ROOF.

FLOOR PLAN KEYNOTES

1. EXISTING WALLS TO REMAIN SHOWN SHADED.
2. NEW WALLS SHOWN RENDERED.
3. EXISTING STEEL COLUMN TO REMAIN.
4. EXIST. WINDOW TO REMAIN.
5. EXISTING DOOR TO REMAIN.
6. LINE OF EXIST. CONCRETE BLOCK LEDGE.
7. DASHED LINES INDICATE EXIST. MASONRY SHAFT WALL BELOW.
8. EXIST. METAL STUD/GYP. BD FURRING AT EXISTING PIPE.
9. EXIST. EXPOSED STEEL DUCTWORK TO REMAIN. - SEE MECH.
10. EXIST. CONCRETE STAIR.
11. EXIST. STEEL HANDRAIL/GUARDRAIL TO REMAIN.
12. EXIST. ADHERED EPDM ROOF.
13. EXIST. CONCRETE EQUIP. BASE TO BE REMOVED.
14. EXISTING CONCRETE FLOOR SLAB - CLEAN AND REPAINT.
15. EDGE LINE OF EXIST. CANTILEVERED CONCRETE FLOOR.
16. NEW A/C SPLIT UNIT - SEE MECH. PROVIDE UNISTRUT FRAMING CHANNEL SYSTEM - TO SUPPORT UNIT @ +36" A.F.F. ANCHOR TO FLOOR AND ROOF FRAMING ABOVE
17. TRANSFORMER - SEE ELEC.
18. ELEV. GOVERNOR BY ELEV. SUPPLIER.
19. ELEV. CONTROLLER BY ELEV SUPPLIER.
20. LINE OF CEILING BREAK ABOVE.
21. METAL THRESHOLD. SEE DETAIL 4/ A2.0
22. LINES OF NEW CHECKERED STEEL PLATE STAIR AND STEEL TUBE STRINGERS.
23. LINES OF NEW 1-1/2" D. STEEL PIPE HANDRAIL.
24. LINES OF NEW STEEL TUBE/SS CABLE GUARDRAIL.
25. EXIST. FIRE-EXTINGUISHER TO BE REINSTALLED.
26. NEW CONDENSING UNIT - SEE MECH/ELEC.
27. EXISTING METAL WIRE PARTITION AND DOOR TO REMAIN.
28. PAINT ALL WALLS AND CEILING IN MACHINE ROOM.
29. 3'-0" X 6'-8" H.M. DOOR AND FRAME - PAINT
30. PATCH AND PAINT WALL.
31. PIPING SUPPORT - SEE DETAIL 3/A1.5.
32. STL. TUBE STRINGER EXTEND THRU WALL AND WELD TO EACH EXISTING COLUMN.

597. Material cut sheets and product data must be submitted for the electrical conduit, elevator cab flooring, and gypsum board to confirm compliance with the specification requirements.

The elevator cab, A/C split system, and elevator motors and controller are all engineered specifically for this project. Therefore, shop drawings must be submitted to document their design and show how the work on these elements will be integrated into the project.

The answer is (A), (B), and (F).

598. This application for payment indicates that the Total Earned Less Retainage (Line 6) is the same as the Contract Amount to Date (Line 3): $508,423.36. Because this application is for all amounts due to the contractor (including retainage and change orders), this is the final, or closeout, pay application and it is submitted to the architect with the contractor's notice that the work is ready for final inspection.

The answer is (B).

599. Since the owner did not include the painting work in the original bid documents, the architect must define the scope of the painting work and use this information to solicit a price from the contractor. The document used for this purpose is a Request for Proposal. After receiving the proposal from the contractor, the owner may decide whether or not to accept the proposal; if the proposal is accepted, the architect will issue a change order to adjust the contract sum.

The answer is (D).

600. Installing a new HVAC system will likely increase the building's energy consumption because the space is not currently conditioned. Switching from incandescent lighting to LED fixtures will decrease the amount of energy consumed, as will improving the R-value of the penthouse enclosure. The elevator equipment, however, has not been upgraded for many years and is likely far less efficient than a new, gearless replacement. Replacing the elevator motor has the greatest potential to decrease this building's overall energy consumption.

The answer is (D).

601. Kepler Brothers, LLC proposed the lowest cost, but their previous project for this owner was beset by change orders. This may be an indication that the firm bids low to get the job but then uses change orders to increase the construction price.

Retrograde Corporation proposed the second lowest cost, but it cannot complete the project within 16 weeks. Given the tenant's schedule, this extended construction period is not acceptable. The owner may also have questions about the company's commitment to the project and scheduling abilities based on attendance and performance on previous work.

Apogee Building & Construction claims to be able to complete the project within 14 weeks, but its price is much higher than the other three proposals. Polaris Construction Services, Kepler Brothers, LLC, and Retrograde Corporation presented proposals within $8000 of one another, but Apogee's proposal is over $50,000 more than Polaris Construction Service's quote. Although Apogee Building & Construction's performance on previous projects was good, they were not able to stay on schedule. Moreover work for the prior project was completed two weeks late.

The general contractor with the strongest qualifications for this project is Polaris Construction Services. Although its proposed price is higher than that bid by other firms, it has committed to completing the project within the 16–week period, its performance on previous projects for this owner has been strong, and its recent work has been similar to that required for this project.

The answer is (A).

602. Redesigning the lighting system or reducing the size of the suite delays the project because these changes require extensive redesign of project elements. Sending the construction documents to other contractors to solicit additional bids is undesirable. Additional time will be necessary for the new contractors to review and price the information. There will be no guarantee that the other contractors will present proposals that are less expensive than the ones already received.

Because large quantities of finish materials must be provided to complete the project, a small savings per square foot can significantly reduce the project cost. This change can usually be made with little to no redesign of connection details or building systems, although additional effort may be required to find products available at a lower cost that still comply with performance or aesthetic requirements.

The answer is (C).

603. American Institute of Architects (AIA) Document A201, *General Conditions of the Contract for Construction*, Sec. 3.8, allows the owner the opportunity to request that contractors include an allowance in their proposals to pay for materials that are undefined at the time that the proposals are presented. The owner may choose the company or supplier that provides materials covered by allowances. In this case, the owner chose to have the desk fabricated by Meridian Millwork Company.

The invoice from Meridian Millwork Company to Polaris Construction Services states that the final cost of the desk

Construction & Evaluation

to the contractor is \$7767.25. AIA Document A201, Sec. 3.8.2, states that allowances cover the costs of materials only. The cost to the contractor to receive and install the item, as well as overhead and profit costs associated with the item, are to be included in the contract sum (contractor's proposal) but are not included in the allowance. These costs can be estimated based on the amount of the allowance given in the request for bids and the scope of the work described.

In this case, the desk cost, C, is more than the allowance amount, A, so the contract sum, S, is adjusted by a debit change order.

$$\begin{aligned} S &= C - A \\ &= \$7767.25 - 5000.00 \\ &= \$2767.25 \end{aligned}$$

Therefore, the change order amount should be \$2767.25.

If the cost of the desk is less than the allowance amount, the owner will be due a credit in the amount of the difference.

The answer is (A).

604. Cost changes to a project must be recorded on a change order document. AIA Document G710 is used to record clarifications to the design intent or minor changes that do not result in a price change.

If the contractor and owner do not agree on the amount of the change, the owner can issue a construction change directive, and the contractor is required to proceed with the work while negotiations regarding the cost continue. When resolved, a change order is issued to formalize the change.

When a lower-cost product is substituted for a more expensive one, the amount of the change order is the difference in the cost of the product. The amount of overhead and profit earned by the contractor is not affected per AIA Document A201, *General Conditions of the Contract for Construction*, Sec. 7.3.8.

Calculate the material cost difference, C_M, between the ceramic tile flooring, T_M, and VCT flooring, V_M.

$$\begin{aligned} C_M &= T_M - V_M \\ &= \$6031.75 - \$3755.33 \\ &= \$2276.42 \end{aligned}$$

However, \$2276.42 is not the total amount to be reduced. According to AIA Document A201, Sec. 7.3.8, a change that results in a net decrease in the contract sum must be the actual net cost as confirmed by the architect.

Calculate the contractor's overhead and profit cost difference, C_O.

$$\begin{aligned} C_O &= T_O - V_O \\ &= \$786.75 - \$489.83 \\ &= \$296.92 \end{aligned}$$

Calculate the cost difference, C.

$$\begin{aligned} C &= C_M - C_O \\ &= \$2276.42 - \$296.92 \\ &= \$1979.50 \end{aligned}$$

The answer is (B).

605. The size of the suspension wire is not stated on the cut sheet, so there is no evidence that it complies with the requirement that its stress at three times the hanger design load be less than the yield strength of the wire, nor that it complies with the minimum size of 0.106 in. The specification does not include a minimum requirement for recycled content.

The cut sheet provides evidence of compliance with four of the criteria defined in the specification: load compliance per ASTM C 635, G30 galvanization, acceptability for use in Seismic Design Category B (the cut sheet indicates that this product may be used in Category A through Category C), and that the product is available with a 1-hour fire rating.

The answer is (A), (C), (D), and (E).